REPORT

OF THE

JOINT COMMITTEE

ON

THE CONDUCT OF THE WAR,

AT THE

SECOND SESSION THIRTY-EIGHTH CONGRESS.

SHERMAN—JOHNSTON.
LIGHT-DRAUGHT MONITORS.
MASSACRE OF THE CHEYENNE INDIANS.
ICE CONTRACTS.
ROSECRANS'S CAMPAIGNS.
MISCELLANEOUS.

WASHINGTON:
GOVERNMENT PRINTING OFFICE.
1865.

IN THE SENATE OF THE UNITED STATES, *February* 20, 1865.

Resolved by the Senate of the United States, (the House of Representatives concurring,) That in order to enable the Joint Committee on the Conduct of the War to complete their investigations of certain important matters now before them, and which they have not been able to complete, by reason of inability to obtain important witnesses, they be authorized to continue their sessions for thirty days after the close of the present Congress, and to place their testimony and reports in the hands of the Secretary of the Senate.

Resolved further, That the Secretary of the Senate is hereby directed to cause to be printed of the reports and accompanying testimony of the Committee on the Conduct of the War five thousand copies for the use of the Senate and ten thousand copies for the use of the House of Representatives.

Attest:

J. W. FORNEY, *Secretary.*

HOUSE OF REPRESENTATIVES OF THE UNITED STATES, *March* 1, 1865.

Resolved, That this House do concur in the foregoing resolution with the following amendment:

Strike out the words "thirty days" and insert the words *ninety days* in lieu thereof.

Attest:

EDWARD McPHERSON, *Clerk.*
By CLINTON LLOYD, *Chief Clerk.*

SENATE OF THE UNITED STATES, *March* 2, 1865.

Resolved, That the Senate agree to the foregoing amendment of the House of Representatives.

Attest:

J. W. FORNEY, *Secretary.*

I certify the foregoing to be a true copy of the original resolution and the amendment of the House thereto and the concurrence of the Senate therein.

J. W. FORNEY,
Secretary of the Senate of the United States.

SHERMAN—JOHNSTON.

Testimony of Major General William T. Sherman.

WASHINGTON, *May* 22, 1865.

Major General W. T. SHERMAN sworn and examined.

By the chairman:

Question. What is your rank in the army?

Answer. I am a major general in the regular army.

Question. As your negotiation with the rebel general Johnston, in relation to his surrender, has been the subject of much public comment, the committee desire you to state all the facts and circumstances in regard to it that you deem of public interest, or which you wish the public to know.

Answer. On the 15th day of April last I was at Raleigh, in command of an army composed of three armies—the army of the Ohio, the army of the Cumberland, and the army of the Tennessee. My enemy was General Joseph E. Johnston, of the confederate army, who commanded about 50,000 men retreating along the railroad from Raleigh, by Hillsborough, Greensborough, Salisbury, and Charlotte. I commenced pursuit by crossing the curve of that road in the direction of Ashborough and Charlotte. After the head of my column had crossed the Cape Fear river at Aven's ferry, I received a communication from General Johnston and answered it; copies of which I sent promptly to the War Department, with a letter addressed to the Secretary of War, as follows:

"HEADQUARTERS MILITARY DIVISION OF THE MISSISSIPPI,
"*In the Field, Raleigh, North Carolina, April* 15, 1865.

"I send copies of a correspondence begun with General Johnston, which, I think, will be followed by terms of capitulation. I will grant the same terms as General Grant gave General Lee, and be careful not to complicate any points of civil policy.

"If any cavalry has started towards me, caution them that they must be prepared to find our work done. It is now raining in torrents, and I shall await General Johnston's reply here, and will prepare to meet him in person at Chapel Hill.

"I have invited Governor Vance to return to Raleigh with the civil officers of his State. I have met ex-Governor Graham, Mr. Badger, Moore, Holden, and others, all of whom agree that the war is over, and that the States of the south must resume their allegiance subject to the Constitution and laws of Congress, and must submit to the national arms. This great fact once admitted, all the details are easy of arrangement.

"W. T. SHERMAN, *Major General.*

"General U. S. GRANT and Secretary of War."

I met General Johnston, in person, at a house five miles from Durham Station, under a flag of truce. After a few preliminary remarks, he said to me that, since Lee had surrendered his army at Appomattox Court House, of which he had just been advised, he looked upon further opposition by him as the greatest possible of crimes; that he wanted to know whether I could make him any general concessions—anything by which he could maintain his hold and control of his army, and prevent its scattering; anything to satisfy the great yearning of their people; if so, he thought we could arrange terms satisfactory to both parties. He wanted to embrace the condition and fate of all the armies of the southern confederacy to the Rio Grande; to make one job of it, as he termed it. I asked him where his powers were; whether he could command and control the fate of all the armies to the Rio Grande? He answered that he thought he could obtain the power, but he did not possess it at that moment. He did not know where Mr. Davis was, but he thought if I could give him time he could find Mr. Breckinridge, whose orders would be obeyed everywhere, and he could pledge to me his personal faith that whatever he undertook to do would be done.

I had had frequent correspondence with the late President of the United States, with the Secretary of War, with General Halleck, and with General Grant; and the general impression left upon my mind was that if a settlement could be made consistent with the Constitution of the United States, the laws of Congress, and the proclamation of the President, they would be not only willing but pleased thus to terminate the war by one single stroke of the pen.

I needed time to finish the railroad from the Neuse bridge up to Raleigh, and thought I could put in four or five days' good time in making repairs to my road, even if I had to send the propositions to Washington. I therefore consented to delay twenty-four hours to enable General Johnston to procure what would satisfy me as to his authority and ability, as a military man, to do what he undertook to do. I therefore consented to meet him the next day, the 17th, at 12, noon, at the same place.

We did meet again. After a general interchange of courtesies he remarked that he was then prepared to satisfy me that he could fulfil the terms of our conversation of the day before. He then asked me what I was willing to do. I told him, in the first place, that I could not deal with anybody except men recognized by us as "belligerents," because no military man could go beyond that fact. The Attorney General has since so decided, and every man of common sense so understood it before; there was no difference of opinion on that point. As to the men and officers composing the confederate armies, I told him that the President of the United States, by a published proclamation, had enabled every man in the southern confederate army of the rank of colonel and under to procure and obtain amnesty by simply taking the oath of allegiance to the United States, and agreeing to go to his home and live in peace. The terms of General Grant to General Lee extended the same principles to officers of the rank of brigadier general and upwards, including the highest officer in the confederate army, viz., General Lee, the commander-in-chief. I was, therefore, willing to proceed with him upon the same principles.

Then a conversation arose as to what form of government they were to have in the south. Were the States there to be dissevered; and were the people to be denied representation in Congress? Were the people there to be, in the common language of the people of the south, slaves to the people of the north? Of course I said "No; we desire that you shall regain your position as citizens of the United States, free and equal to us in all respects, and with representation, upon the condition of submission to the lawful authority of the United States as defined by the Constitution, the United States courts, and the authorities of the United States supported by those courts."

He then remarked to me that General Breckinridge, a major general in the confederate army, was near by, and if I had no objection he would like to have him present. I recalled his attention to the fact that I had on the day before explained to him that any negotiations between us must be confined to belligerents. He replied that he understood that perfectly. "But," said he, "Breckinridge, whom you do not know, save by public rumor, as the Secretary of War, is, in fact, a major general; I give you my word for that. Have you any objection to his being present as a major general?" I replied, "I have no objection to any military officer you desire being present as a part of your personal staff." I, myself, had my own officers near me at call.

Breckinridge came, a stranger to me, whom I had never spoken to in my life, and he joined in the conversation. Whilst that conversation was being carried on, a courier arrived and handed General Johnston a package of papers. He and Breckinridge sat down and looked over them for some time, and put them away in their pockets. What they were I know not; but one was a slip of paper, written, as General Johnston told me, by Mr. Reagan, postmaster general of the southern confederacy. They seemed to talk about it *sotto voce*, and finally handed it to me; I glanced over it. It was preceded by a preamble, and closed with a few general terms. I rejected it at once.

We then discussed matters—talked about slavery—talked about everything. There was a universal assent that slavery was as dead as anything could be; that it was one of the issues of the war, long since determined; and even General Johnston laughed at the folly of the confederate government in raising negro soldiers, whereby they gave us all the points of the case. I told them that slavery had been treated by us as a dead institution; first by one class of men from the initiation of the war, and then from the date of the emancipation proclamation of President Lincoln, and finally by the assent of all the parties.

As to reconstruction, I told them I did not know what the views of the administration were. Mr. Lincoln up to that time had, in letters and by telegrams to me, encouraged me, by all the words that could be used in general terms, to believe in not only his willingness but his desire that I should make terms with civil authorities, governors, and legislatures, even as far back as 1863. It then occurred to me that I might write off some general propositions, meaning little or meaning much, according to the construction of parties, what I would term "glittering generalities," and send them to Washington, which I could do in four days. That would enable the new President to give me a clue to his policy in the important juncture which was then upon us; for the war was over—the highest military authorities of the southern confederacy so confessed to me openly, unconcealedly, and repeatedly.

I therefore drew up that memorandum (which has been published to the world) for the purpose of referring it to the proper executive authority of the United States, and enabling him to define to me what I might promise, simply to cover the pride of the southern men, who thereby became subordinate to the laws of the United States, civil and military. I made no concessions to General Johnston's army, or the troops under his direction and immediate control. And if any concessions were made in those general terms, they were made because I then believed, and I now believe, they would have delivered into the hands of the United States the absolute control of every confederate officer and soldier, all their muster-rolls, and all their arms. It would save us all the incidental expenses resulting from the military occupation of that country by provost marshals, provost guards, military governors, and all the machinery by which alone military power can reach the people of a civilized country. It would have surrendered to us the armies of Dick Taylor and Kirby Smith, both of them capable of doing infinite mischief to us by exhausting the resources of the whole country upon which we were to depend for the future extinguishment of our debt, forced upon us by their wrongful and rebellious conduct.

I never designed to shelter a human being from any liability incurred in consequence of past acts to the civil tribunals of our country. And I do not believe a fair and manly interpretation of my terms can so construe them, for the words "United States courts," "United States authorities," "limitations of executive power" occur in every paragraph.

And if they seemingly yield terms better than the public would desire to be given to the southern people, if studied clearly and well it will be found that there is an absolute submission on their part to the government of the United States, either through its executive, legislative, or judicial authorities.

Every step in the progress of those negotiations was reported punctually, clearly, and fully by the most rapid means of communication that I had. And yet I neglected not one single precaution necessary to reap the full benefits of my position in case the government amended, altered, or absolutely annulled those terms.

As these matters are necessarily mingled with the military history of the period, I would like, at this point, to submit to the committee my official report, which has been in the hands of the proper officer, viz: General Rawlings, chief of staff of the army of the United States, since about the 12th instant. It was made by me at Manchester, Virginia, after I had returned from Savannah, whither I went to open up the Savannah river and reap the fruits of my negotiations with General Johnston, and to give General Wilson, far in the interior, a safe and sure base from which he could draw the necessary supply of clothing and food for his command.

It was only after I had fulfilled all this that I learned, for the first time, through the public press, that my conduct had been animadverted upon, not only by the Secretary of War, but by General Halleck and the press of the country at large. I did feel hurt and wronged that Mr. Stanton coupled with the terms of my memorandum, confided to him, a copy of a telegram to General Grant, which he had never sent to me. He knew, on the contrary, that when he was at Savannah that I had negotiations with civil parties there, for he was present in my room when those parties were conferring with me; and I wrote him a letter setting forth many points of it, in which I said I aimed to make a split in Jeff. Davis's dominions by segregating Georgia from their cause. Those were civil negotiations; and far from being discouraged from making them, I was encouraged by Secretary Stanton himself to make them.

By coupling the note to General Grant with my memorandum he gave the world fairly and clearly to infer that I was in possession of it; now, I was not in possession of it; and I have reason to know that Mr. Stanton knew I was not in possession of it.

Next met me General Halleck's telegram, indorsed by Mr. Stanton, in which they publicly avowed an act of perfidy, namely, the violation of my truce, which I had a right to make, and which by the laws of war and by the laws of Congress is punishable by death, and no other punishment.

Next they ordered an army to pursue my enemy, who was known to be surrendering to me, in the presence of General Grant himself, their superior officer; and, finally, they sent orders to General Wilson and to General Thomas, my subordinates, acting under me on a plan of the most magnificent scale, admirably executed, to defeat my orders and to thwart the interests of the government of the United States.

I did feel indignant—I do feel indignant. As to my own honor, I can protect it. In my letter of the 15th of April I used this language: "I have invited Governor Vance to return to Raleigh with the civil officers of his State." I did so because President Lincoln had himself encouraged me to a similar course with the governor of Georgia when I was in Atlanta. And here was the opportunity which the Secretary of War should have taken to put me on my guard against making terms with civil authorities, if such were the settled policy of our government. Had President Lincoln lived, I know he would have sustained me.

The following is my report, which I desire to have incorporated into and made part of my testimony:

"HEADQUARTERS MILITARY DIVISION OF THE MISSISSIPPI,
"*In the Field, City Point, Va., May* 9, 1865.

"GENERAL: My last official report brought the history of events, as connected with the armies in the field subject to my immediate command, down to the first of April, when the army of the Ohio, Major General J. M. Schofield commanding, lay at Goldsborough, with detachments distributed so as to secure and cover our routes of communication and supply back to the sea at Wilmington and Morehead city; Major General A. H. Terry, with the 10th corps, being at Faison's depot. The army of the Tennessee, Major General O. O. Howard commanding, was encamped to the front and right of Goldsborough; and the army of Georgia, Major General H. W. Slocum commanding, to its left and front; the cavalry, Brevet Major General J. Kilpatrick commanding, at Mount Olive. All were busy in repairing the wear and tear of our then recent hard march from Savannah, and in replenishing clothing and stores necessary for a further progress.

"I had previously, by letter and in person, notified the lieutenant general commanding the armies of the United States, that the 10th of April would be the earliest possible moment at which I could hope to have all things in readiness, and we were compelled to use our railroads to the very highest possible limit in order to fulfil that promise. Owing to a mistake in the railroad department, in sending locomotives and cars of the five-foot gauge, we were limited to the use of the few locomotives and cars of the four-foot eight and a half inch gauge, already in North Carolina, with such of the old stock as was captured by Major General Terry at Wilmington and on his way up to Goldsborough; yet such judicious use was made of them, and such industry displayed in the railroad management by Generals Easton and Beckwith, and Colonel Wright and Mr. Van Dyne, that by the 10th of April our men were all re-clad, the wagons reloaded, and a fair amount of forage accumulated ahead.

"In the mean time Major General George Stoneman, in command of a division of cavalry, operating from East Tennessee, in connexion with Major General George H. Thomas, in pursuance of my orders of ——— ———, had reached the railroad about Greensborough, N. C., and had made sad havoc with it; and had pushed along it to Salisbury, destroying *en route* bridges, culverts, depots, and all kinds of rebel supplies, and had extended the breach in the railroad down to the Catawba bridge. This was fatal to the hostile armies of Lee and Johnston, who depended on that road for supplies and as their ultimate line of retreat. Brevet Major General Wilson, also in command of the cavalry corps organized by himself under Special Field Orders No. ——, of ——— ———, 1864, at Gaylesville, Alabama, had started from the neighborhood of Decatur and Florence, Alabama, and moved straight into the heart of Alabama, on a route prescribed for General Thomas after he had defeated General Hood at Nashville, Tennessee; but the roads being too heavy for infantry, General Thomas had devolved the duty on that most energetic young cavalry officer General Wilson, who, imbued with the proper spirit, has struck one of the best blows of the war at the waning strength of the confederacy. His route was one never before touched by our troops, and afforded him abundant supplies as long as he was in motion, viz., by Tuscaloosa, Selma, Montgomery, Columbus, and Macon. Though in communication with him, I have not been able to receive as yet his full and detailed reports, which will in due time be published and appreciated.

"Lieutenant General Grant also, in immediate command of the armies about Richmond, had taken the initiative in that magnificent campaign, which, in less than ten days, completed the evacuation of Richmond, and resulted in the destruction and surrender of the entire rebel army of Virginia, under the command of General Lee. The news of the battles about Petersburg reached me at Goldsborough on the 6th of April. Up to that time my purpose was to move rapidly northward, feigning on Raleigh, and striking straight for Burkesville, thereby interposing between Johnston and Lee. But the auspicious events in Virginia had changed the whole military problem, and, in the expressive language of Lieutenant General Grant, the "confederate armies of Lee and Johnston became the strategic points." General Grant was fully able to take care of the former, and my task was to destroy or capture the latter.

"Johnston at the time, April 6, had his army well in hand about Smithfield, interposing between me and Raleigh. I estimated his infantry and artillery at thirty-five thousand, (35,000,) and his cavalry from six to ten thousand, (6,000 to 10,000.) He was superior to me in cavalry, so that I held General Kilpatrick in reserve at Mount Olive, with orders to recruit his horses and be ready to make a sudden and rapid march on the 10th of April.

"At daybreak on the day appointed, all the heads of columns were in motion straight against the enemy; Major General H. W. Slocum taking the two direct roads for Smithfield; Major General O. O. Howard making a circuit by the right, and feigning up the Weldon road to disconcert the enemy's cavalry; Generals Terry and Kilpatrick moving on the west side of the Neuse river, and to reach the rear of the enemy between Smithfield and Raleigh. General Schofield followed General Slocum in support. All the columns met, within six (6) miles of Goldsborough, more or less cavalry, with the usual rail barricades, which were swept before us as chaff; and by 10 a. m. of the 11th, the 14th corps entered Smithfield, the 20th corps close at hand. Johnston had rapidly retreated across the Neuse river, and, having his railroad to lighten up his trains, could retreat faster than we could pursue. The rains had also set in, making the resort to corduroy absolutely necessary to pass even ambulances. The enemy had burned the bridge at Smithfield, and as soon as possible Major General Slocum got up his pontoons and crossed over a division of the 14th corps.

"We then heard of the surrender of Lee's army at Appomattox C. H., Virginia, which was announced to the armies in Orders, and created universal joy. Not an officer or soldier of my armies but expressed a pride and satisfaction that it fell to the lot of the armies of the Potomac and James so gloriously to overwhelm and capture the entire army that had held them in check so long; and their success gave new impulse to finish up our task.

"Without a moment's hesitation we dropped our trains, and marched rapidly in pursuit to and through Raleigh, reaching that place at 7.30 a. m. on the 13th, in a heavy rain. The next day the cavalry pushed on through the rain to Durham's Station, the 15th corps following as far as Morrisville Station, and the 17th corps to Jones's Station. On the supposition that Johnston was tied to his railroad, as a line of retreat by Hillsborough, Greensborough, Salisbury, and Charlotte, &c., I had turned the other columns across the bend of that road towards Ashborough.—(See General Field Orders No. 55.) The cavalry, Brevet Major General J. Kilpatrick commanding, was ordered to keep up a show of pursuit towards the 'Company's Shops', in Alamance county. Major General O. O. Howard to turn to the left by Hackney's Crossroads, Pittsborough, St. Lawrence, and Ashborough; Major General H. W. Slocum to cross Cape Fear river at Aven's ferry, and move rapidly by Carthage, Caledonia, and Cox's Mills. Major General J. M. Schofield was to hold Raleigh and the road back, and with his spare force to follow an intermediate route.

"By the 15th, though the rains were incessant and roads almost impracticable, Major General Slocum had the 14th corps, Brevet Major General Davis commanding, near Martha's Vineyard, with a pontoon bridge laid across Cape Fear river at Aven's ferry, with the 20th corps, Major General Mower commanding, in support; and Major General Howard had the 15th and 17th corps stretched out on the roads towards Pittsborough, while General Kilpatrick held Durham Station and Chapel Hill University. Johnston's army was retreating rapidly on the roads from Hillsborough to Greensborough, he himself at Greensborough.

"Although out of place as to time, I here invite all military critics who study the problems of war to take their maps and compare the position of my army on the 15th and 16th of April, with that of General Halleck about Burkesville and Petersburg, Virginia, on the 26th of April, when, according to his telegram to Secretary Stanton, he offered to relieve me of the task of cutting off Johnston's retreat. Major General Stoneman at the time was at Statesville, and Johnston's only line of retreat was by Salisbury and Charlotte. It may be that General Halleck's troops can outmarch mine, but there is nothing in their past history to show it. Or it may be that General Halleck can inspire his troops with more energy of action. I doubt that also, save and except in this single instance, when he knew the enemy was ready to surrender or 'disperse,' as advised by letter of April 18, addressed to him when chief of staff at Washington city, and delivered at Washington by Major Hitchcock, of my army.

"Thus matters stood at the time I received General Johnston's first letter and made my answer of April 14, copies of which were sent with all expedition to Lieutenant General Grant and the Secretary of War, with my letter of April 15. I agreed to meet General Johnston, in person, at a point intermediate between our pickets, on the 17th at noon, provided the position of the troops remained *statu quo.* I was both willing and anxious thus to consume a few days, as it would enable Colonel Wright to finish our railroad to Raleigh. Two bridges had to be built and twelve miles of new road made. We had no iron except by taking up that on the branch from Goldsborough to Weldon. Instead of losing by time, I gained in every way, for every hour of delay possible was required to reconstruct the railroad to our rear, and improve the condition of our wagon roads to the front, so desirable in case the negotiations failed, and we be forced to make the race of near two hundred miles to head off or catch Johnston, then retreating towards Charlotte.

"At noon of the day appointed I met General Johnston for the first time in my life, although we had been exchanging shots constantly since May, 1863. Our interview was frank and soldierlike, and he gave me to understand that further war on the part of the confederate troops was folly; that 'the cause' was lost, and that every life sacrificed after the surrender of Lee's army was the highest possible crime. He admitted that the terms conceded to General Lee were magnanimous and all he could ask; but he did want some general concessions that would enable him to allay the natural fears and anxieties of his followers, and enable him to maintain his control over them until they could be got back to the neighborhood of their homes, thereby saving the State of North Carolina the devastation inevitably to result from turning his men loose and unprovided on the spot, and our pursuit across the State. He also wanted to embrace in the same general proposition the fate of all the confederate armies that remained in existence. I never made any concession as to his own army, or assumed to deal finally and authoritatively in regard to any other. But it did occur to me that there was presented a chance for peace that might be deemed valuable to the government of the United States, and was at least worthy the few days that would be consumed in reference. To push an army whose commander had so frankly and honestly confessed his inability to cope with me were cowardly and unworthy the brave men I led. Inasmuch as General Johnston did not feel authorized to pledge his power over the armies in Texas, we adjourned to meet the next day at noon.

"I returned to Raleigh and conferred freely with all my general officers, *every one* of whom urged me to conclude terms that might accomplish so complete and desirable an end. All dreaded the weary and laborious march after a fugitive and dissolving army back towards Georgia, over the very country where we had toiled so long. There was but one opinion expressed, and if contrary ones were entertained, they were withheld or indulged in only by that class who shun the fight and the march, but are loudest, bravest and fiercest when danger is past.

"I again met General Johnston on the 18th, and we renewed the conversation. He satisfied me then of his *power* to disband the rebel armies in Alabama, Mississippi, Louisiana, and Texas, as well as those in his immediate command, viz., North Carolina, South Carolina, Georgia and Florida. The points on which he expressed especial solicitude were lest their States were to be dismembered, and denied representation in Congress, or any separate political existence whatever; and the absolute disarming his men would leave the south powerless and exposed to depredations by wicked bands of assassins and robbers.

"The President's (Lincoln's) message of 1864; his amnesty proclamation; General Grant's terms to General Lee, substantially extending the benefit of that proclamation to all officers above the rank of colonel; the invitation to the Virginia legislature to reassemble in Richmond by General Weitzel, with the supposed approval of Mr. Lincoln and General Grant, then on the spot; a firm belief that I had been fighting to re-establish the Constitution of the United States; and last, but not least, the general and universal desire to close a war any longer without organized resistance, were the leading facts that induced me to pen the 'memorandum' of April 15, signed by myself and General Johnston. It was designed to be, and so expressed on its face, as a mere 'basis' for reference to the President of the United States and constitutional commander-in-chief, to enable him, if he chose, at one blow to dissipate the military power of the confederacy, which had threatened the national safety for years. It admitted of modification, alteration and change. It had no appearance of an ultimatum, and by no false reasoning can it be construed into a usurpation of power on my part. I have my opinion on the questions involved, 'and will stand by the memorandum;' but this forms no part of a military report.

"Immediately on my return to Raleigh, I despatched one of my staff, Major Hitchcock, to Washington, enjoining him to be most prudent and careful to avoid the spies and informers that would be sure to infest him by the way, and to say nothing to anybody until the President could make known to me his feelings and wishes in the matter.

"The news of President Lincoln's assassination, on the 14th of April, (wrongly reported to me by telegraph as having occurred on the 11th,) reached me on the 17th, and was announced to my command on the same day, in Field Orders No. 56. I was duly impressed with its horrible atrocity and probable effect on the country. But when the property and interests of millions still living were involved, I saw no good reason why to change my course, but thought rather to manifest real respect for his memory by following, after his death, that policy which, if living, I felt certain he would have approved, or at least not rejected with disdain.

"Up to that hour I had never received one word of instruction, advice or counsel as to the plan or policy of government looking to a restoration of peace on the part of the rebel States of the south. Whenever asked for an opinion on the points involved, I had always evaded the subject. My letter to the mayor of Atlanta has been published to the world, and I was not rebuked by the War Department for it. My letter to Mr. ——, of Savannah, was shown by me to Mr. Stanton before its publication, and all that my memory retains of his answer is, that he said, like my letters generally, it was sufficiently "emphatic and could not be misunderstood." Both these letters asserted my belief that, according to Mr. Lincoln's proclamations and messages, when the people of the south had laid down their arms and submitted to the lawful power of the United States, *ipso facto*, the war was over as to them; and furthermore, that if any State in rebellion would conform to the Constitution of the United States, 'cease war,' elect senators and representatives to Congress, if admitted, (of which each house of Congress alone is the judge,) that State becomes instanter as much in the Union as New York or Ohio. Nor was I rebuked for these expressions, though it was universally known and commented on at the time. And again, Mr. Stanton in person at Savannah, speaking of the terrific expense of the war, and difficulty of realizing the money necessary for the daily wants of government, impressed me most forcibly with the necessity of bringing the war to a close as soon as possible for *financial reasons*.

"On the evening of April 23 Major Hitchcock reported his return to Morehead city with despatches, of which fact General Johnston, at Hillsborough, was notified, so as to be ready in the morning for an answer. At 6 o'clock a. m. on the 24th Major Hitchcock arrived, accompanied by General Grant and members of his staff, who had not telegraphed the fact of his coming over our exposed roads for prudential reasons. I soon learned that the memorandum was disapproved without reasons assigned, and I was ordered to give the forty-eight hours' notice and resume hostilities at the close of that time; governing myself by the substance of a despatch then enclosed, dated March 3, 12 m., at Washington, D. C., from Secretary Stanton to General Grant, at City Point, but not accompanied by any part of the voluminous matter so liberally lavished on the public in the New York journals of the 24th of April. That was the first and only time I ever saw that telegram, or had one word of instructions on the important matters involved in it. And it does seem strange to me that every bar-room loafer in New York can read in the morning journals 'official' matter that is withheld from a general whose command extends from Kentucky to North Carolina.

"Within an hour a courier was riding from Durham's Station towards Hillsborough with notice to General Johnston of the suspension of the truce, and renewing my demand for the surrender of the armies under his immediate command, (see two despatches of April 24, 6 a. m.,) and at 12 m. I had the receipt of his picket officer. I therefore published my Orders No. 62 to the troops terminating the truce at 12 m. on the 26th, and ordered all to be in readiness to march at that hour, on the routes prescribed in Special Field Orders No. 55 of

April 14, from the positions held April 18. General Grant had orders from the President to direct military movements, and I explained to him the exact position of the troops, and he approved of it most emphatically; but he did not relieve me, or express a wish to assume command.

"All things were in readiness, when, on the evening of the 25th, I received another letter from General Johnston asking another interview to renew negotiations. General Grant not only approved, but urged me to accept; and I appointed a meeting at our former place at noon of the 26th, the very hour fixed for the renewal of hostilities. General Johnston was delayed by an accident to his train, but at 2 p. m. arrived.

"We then consulted, concluded, and signed the final terms of capitulation. These were taken by me back to Raleigh, submitted to General Grant, and met his immediate approval and signature. General Johnston was not even aware of the presence of General Grant at Raleigh at the time. There was surrendered to us the second great army of the so-called confederacy; and though undue importance has been given to the so-called negotiations which preceded it, and a rebuke and public disfavor cast on me wholly unwarranted by the facts, I rejoice in saying that it was accomplished without further ruin and devastation to the country, without the loss of a single life to those gallant men who had followed me from the Mississippi to the Atlantic, and without subjecting brave men to the ungracious task of pursuing a fleeing foe that did not want to fight. As for myself, I know my motives, and challenge the instance, during the past four years, when an armed and defiant foe stood before me, that I did not go in for a fight, and I would blush for shame if I had ever insulted or struck a fallen foe.

"The instant the terms of surrender were approved by General Grant, I made my orders, No. 65, assigning to each of my subordinate commanders his share of the work, and, with General Grant's approval, made Special Field Orders No. 66, putting in motion my old army, no longer required in Carolina, northward for Richmond. General Grant left Raleigh at 9 a. m. of the 27th; and I glory in the fact that during his three days' stay with me I did not detect in his language or manner one particle of abatement in the confidence, respect, and affection that have existed between us throughout all the various events of the past war; and though we have honestly differed in other cases as well as this, still we respect each other's honest convictions. I still adhere to my then opinions, that by a few general concessions, 'glittering generalities,' all of which in the end *must* and will be conceded to the organized States of the south, this day there would not be an armed battalion opposed to us within the broad area of the dominions of the United States. Robbers and assassins must in any event result from the disbandment of large armies; but even these should be and can be taken care of by the local civil authorities without being made a charge on the national treasury.

"On the evening of the 28th, having concluded all business requiring my personal attention at Raleigh, and having conferred with every army commander, and delegated to him the authority necessary for his future action, I despatched my headquarters wagons by land along with the 17th corps, the office in charge of General Webster, to Alexandria, Va., and in person, accompanied only by my personal staff, hastened to Savannah to direct matters in the interior of South Carolina and Georgia.

"I had received across the rebel telegraph wires cipher despatches from General Wilson, to the effect that he was in receipt of my orders No. 65, and would send General Upton's division to Augusta, and General McCook's division to Tallahassee, to receive the surrender of those garrisons, take charge of the public property, and execute the paroles required by the terms of surrender. He reported a sufficiency of forage for his horses in southwest Georgia, but asked me to send him a supply of clothing, sugar, coffee, &c., by way of Augusta, Georgia, when he could get it by rail. I therefore went rapidly to Goldsborough and Wilmington, reaching the latter city at 10 a. m. of the 29th, and the same day embarked for Hilton Head, in the blockade runner Russia, Captain A. M. Smith.

"I found General Q. A. Gillmore, commanding department of the south, at Hilton Head, on the evening of April 30, and ordered him to send to Augusta at once what clothing and small stores he could spare for General Wilson, and to open up a line of certain communication and supply with him at Macon. Within an hour the captured steamboats Jeff. Davis and Amazon, both adapted to the shallow and crooked navigation of the Savannah river, were being loaded, the one at Savannah, and the other at Hilton Head. The former started up the river on the 1st of May, in charge of a very intelligent officer, (whose name I cannot recall,) and forty-eight men, (all the boat could carry,) with orders to occupy temporarily the United States arsenal at Augusta, and open up communication with General Wilson, at Macon, in the event that General Upton's division of cavalry was not already there. The Amazon followed next day; and General Gillmore had made the necessary orders for a brigade of infantry, to be commanded by General Molyneux, to follow by a land march to Augusta, as its permanent garrison. Another brigade of infantry was ordered to occupy Orangeburg, South Carolina, the point furthest in the interior that can at present be reached by rail from the sea-coast, (Charleston.)

"On the 1st of May I went to Savannah, where General Gillmore also joined me, and the arrangements ordered for the occupation of Augusta were consummated. At Savannah I found the city under the most admirable police, under direction of Brevet Major General

Grover, and the citizens manifested the most unqualified joy to hear that, so far as they were concerned, the war was over. All classes, Union men as well as former rebels, did not conceal, however, the apprehensions naturally arising from a total ignorance of the political conditions to be attached to their future state. Anything at all would be preferable to this dread uncertainty.

"On the evening of the 2d of May I returned to Hilton Head, and there, for the first time, received the New York papers of April 28, containing Secretary Stanton's despatch of 9 a. m. of the 27th of April to General Dix, including General Halleck's from Richmond of 9 p. m. the night before, which seems to have been rushed with extreme haste before an excited public, viz., morning of the 28th. You will observe from the dates that those despatches were running back and forth from Richmond and Washington to New York, and there published, whilst General Grant and I were together in Raleigh, N. C., adjusting, to the best of our ability, the terms of surrender of the only remaining formidable rebel army in existence at the time east of the Mississippi river. Not one word of intimation had been sent to me of the displeasure of the government with my official conduct, but only the naked disapproval of a skeleton memorandum sent properly for the action of the President of the United States. The most objectionable features of my memorandum had already (April 24) been published to the world in violation of official usage; and the contents of my accompanying letters to General Halleck, General Grant, and Secretary Stanton, of even date, though at hand, were suppressed. In all these letters I had stated clearly and distinctly that Johnston's army would *not* fight, but if pushed would 'disband' and scatter into small and dangerous guerilla parties, as injurious to the interests of the United States as to the people themselves; that all parties admitted that the rebel cause of the south was abandoned, that the negroes were free, and that the temper of all was most favorable to a lasting peace. I say all these opinions of mine were withheld from the public with a seeming purpose; and I do contend that my official experience and former services, as well as my past life and familiarity with the people and geography of the south, entitled my opinions to at least a decent respect.

"Although this despatch (Mr. Stanton's of April 27) was printed 'official,' it had come to me only in the questionable shape of a newspaper paragraph headed 'Sherman's truce disregarded.' I had already done what General Wilson wanted me to do, viz., had sent him supplies of clothing and food, with clear and distinct orders and instructions how to carry out in western Georgia the terms for the surrender of arms and parolling the prisoners made by General Johnston's capitulation of April 26; and had properly and most opportunely ordered General Gillmore to occupy Orangeburg and Augusta, strategic points of great value at all times, in peace and war. But as the Secretary had taken upon himself to order my subordinate generals to disobey my 'orders,' I explained to General Gillmore that I would no longer confuse him or General Wilson with 'orders' that might conflict with those of the Secretary, which, as reported, were sent, not through me, but in open disregard of me and of my lawful authority.

"It now becomes my duty to paint in justly severe character the still more offensive and dangerous matter of General Halleck's despatch of April 26 to the Secretary of War, embodied in his to General Dix of April 27. General Halleck had been chief of staff of the army at Washington, in which capacity he must have received my official letter of April 18, wherein I wrote clearly that if Johnston's army about Greensborough was pushed, it would 'disperse;' an event I wished to prevent. About that time he seems to have been sent from Washington to Richmond, to command the new military division of the James, in assuming charge of which, on the 22d, he defines the limits of his authority to be the 'department of Virginia, the army of the Potomac, and such part of North Carolina as may not be occupied by the command of Major General Sherman, (see his General Order No. 1.) Four days later, April 26, he reports to the Secretary that he had ordered Generals Meade, Sheridan, and Wright to invade that part of North Carolina which *was* occupied by my command, and pay no regard to any truce or orders of mine. They were ordered to '*push* forward regardless of any orders save those of Lieutenant General Grant, and cut off Johnston's retreat.' He knew at the time he penned that despatch, and made those orders, that Johnston was not retreating, but was halted under a 48 hours' truce with me, and was laboring to surrender his command and prevent its dispersion into guerilla bands; and that I had on the spot a magnificent army at my command, amply sufficient for all purposes required by the occasion. The plan of cutting off a retreat from the direction of Burksville and Danville is hardly worthy one of his military education and genius.

"When he contemplated an act so questionable as the violation of a truce made by competent authority, he should have gone himself and not have sent subordinates, for he knew I was bound in *honor* to *defend and maintain* my *own* truce and pledge of faith, even at the cost of many lives. When an officer pledges the faith of his government, he is bound to defend it, and he is no soldier who would violate it knowingly.

"As to Davis and his stolen treasure, did General Halleck, as chief of staff, or commanding officer of the neighboring military division, notify me of the facts contained in his despatch to the Secretary? No, he did not. If the Secretary of War wanted Davis caught, why not order it, instead of, by publishing in the newspapers, putting him on his guard to hide away and escape? No orders or intimation to arrest Davis or his stolen treasure ever came to me; but, on the contrary, I was led to believe that the Secretary of War rather preferred he should escape from the country, if it were made unknown to him.

"But even on this point I enclose a copy of my letter to Admiral Dahlgren, at Charleston, sent him by a fleet steamer from Wilmington on the 25th of April, two days before the bankers of Richmond had imparted to General Halleck the important secret of Davis's movements, designed, doubtless, to stimulate his troops to march their legs off to catch *their* treasure for *their* own use. I know now that Admiral Dahlgren did receive my letter on the 26th, and had acted on it *before* General Halleck had even thought of the matter. But I don't believe a word of the treasure story; it is absurd on its face, and General Halleck or anybody has my full permission to chase Jeff. Davis and cabinet, with their stolen treasure, through any part of the country occupied by my command.

"The last and most obnoxious feature of General Halleck's despatch is where he goes out of his way and advises that my subordinates—Generals Thomas, Stoneman, and Wilson—should be instructed 'not to obey Sherman's commands.' This is too much, and I turn from the subject with feelings too strong for words, and merely record my belief that so much mischief was never before embraced in so small a space as the newspaper paragraph headed 'Sherman's truce disregarded,' authenticated as 'official' by Mr. Secretary Stanton, and published in the newspapers of April 28.

"During the night of May 2, at Hilton Head, having concluded my business in the department of the south, I began my return to meet my troops, then marching towards Richmond from Raleigh. On the morning of May 3 we ran into Charleston harbor, where I had the pleasure to meet Admiral Dahlgren, who had, in all my previous operations from Savannah northward, aided me with a courtesy and manliness that commanded my entire respect and deep affection. Also General Hatch, who, from our first interview at his Tullifenny camp, had caught the spirit of the move from Pocotaligo northward, and had largely contributed to our joint success in taking Charleston and the Carolina coast. Any one who is not *satisfied* with war should go and see Charleston, and he will pray louder and deeper than ever that the country may in the long future be spared any more war. Charleston and secession being synonymous terms, the city should be left as a sample, so that centuries will pass away before that false doctrine is preached again in our Union.

"We left Charleston the evening of the 3d of May, and hastened with all possible speed back to Morehead city, which we reached at night of the 4th. I immediately communicated by telegraph to General Schofield, at Raleigh, and learned from him the pleasing fact that the lieutenant general commanding the armies of the United States had reached the Chesapeake in time to countermand General Halleck's order and prevent his violating my truce, invading the area of my command, and driving Johnston's surrendering army into fragments. General Johnston had fulfilled his agreement to the very best of his ability, and the officers charged with issuing the paroles at Greensborough reported about 30,000 already made, and that the greater part of the North Carolina troops had gone home without waiting for their papers; but that all of them would doubtless come in to some of the military posts, the commanders of which are authorized to grant them. About 800 of the rebel cavalry had gone south, refusing to abide the terms of the surrender, and it was supposed they would make for Mexico. I would sincerely advise that they be urged to go and stay. They would be a nuisance to any civilized government, whether loose or in prison. With the exception of some plundering on the part of Lee's and Johnston's disbanded men, all else was quiet. When to the number of men surrendered at Greensborough are added those at Tallahassee, Augusta, and Macon, with the scattered squads who will come in at other military posts, I have no doubt full fifty thousand armed men will be disarmed and restored to civil pursuits by the capitulation made near Durham's Station, North Carolina, on the 26th of April, 1865, and that, too, without the loss of a single life to us.

"On the 5th of May I received and here subjoin a further despatch from General Schofield, which contains inquiries I have been unable to satisfy, similar to those made by nearly every officer in my command whose duty brings him in contact with citizens. I leave you to do what is expedient to provide the military remedy.

["'By telegraph from Raleigh, N. C., May 5, 1865.]

"'Major General W. T. SHERMAN, *Morehead City:*

"'When General Grant was here, as you doubtless recollect, he said the lines had been extended to embrace this and other States south. The order, it seems, has been modified so as to include only Virginia and Tennessee. I think it would be an act of wisdom to open this State to trade at once. I hope the government will make known its policy as to the organs of State government without delay. Affairs must necessarily be in a very unsettled state until that is done. The people now are in a mood to accept almost anything which promises a definite settlement. What is to be done with the freedmen is the question of all, and it is the all-important question. It requires prompt and wise action to prevent the negro from becoming a huge elephant on our hands. If I am to govern this State, it is important for me to know it at once. If another is to be sent here, it cannot be done too soon, for he will probably undo the most that I shall have done. I shall be glad to hear from you fully when you have time to write. I will send your message to General Wilson at once.

"'J. M. SCHOFIELD, *Major General.*'

'I give this despatch entire to demonstrate how intermingled have become civil matters with the military, and how almost impossible it has become for an officer in authority to act a pure military part. There are no longer armed enemies in North Carolina, and a soldier can deal with no other sort. The marshal and sheriff, with their possés, (of which the military may become a part,) are the only proper officers to deal with civil criminals and marauders. But I will not be drawn out into a discussion of this subject, but instance the case to show how difficult is the task become to military officers, when men of rank, education, experience, nerve, and good sense of General Schofield feel embarrassed by them.

"General Schofield, at Raleigh, has a well-appointed and well-disciplined command; is in telegraphic communication with the controlling parts of his department, and remote ones in the direction of Georgia, as well as with Washington, and has military possession of all strategic points. In like manner, General Gillmore is well situated in all respects, except as to communication with the seat of the general government. I leave him, also, with every man he ever asked for, and in full and quiet possession of every strategic point in his department. And General Wilson has, in the very heart of Georgia, the strongest, best appointed, and best equipped cavalry corps that ever fell under my command; and he has now, by my recent action, opened to him a source and route of supply by way of the Savannah river, that simplifies his military problem. So that I think I may, with a clear conscience, leave them and turn my attention once more to my special command—the army with which I have been associated through some of the most eventful scenes of this or any war.

"I hope and believe none of these commanders will ever have reason to reproach me for any 'orders' they may have received from me. And the President of the United States may be assured that all of them are now in position, ready and willing to execute to the letter and in spirit any orders he may give. I shall henceforth cease to give them any orders at all, for the occasion that made them subordinate to me is past; and I shall confine my attention to the army, composed of the 15th and 17th, the 14th and 20th corps, unless the commanding general of the armies of the United States orders otherwise.

"At 4 p. m. of May 9 I reached Manchester, on James river, opposite Richmond, and found all the four corps had arrived from Raleigh, and were engaged in replenishing their wagons for the resumption of the march towards Alexandria.

"I have the honor to be, your obedient servant,

"W. T. SHERMAN,
"*Major General, Commanding.*

"General JOHN A. RAWLINGS,
"*Chief of Staff, Washington, D. C.*"

Question. Did you have, near Fortress Monroe, a conference with President Lincoln; and if so, about what time?

Answer. I met General Grant and Mr. Lincoln on board a steamboat, lying at the wharf at City Point, during the evening of the 27th of March. I renewed my visit to the President on board the same steamer, anchored in the stream, on the following day, General Grant being present on both occasions.

Question. In those conferences was any arrangement made with you and General Grant, or either of you, in regard to the manner of arranging business with the confederacy, or in regard to terms of peace?

Answer. Nothing definite; it was simply a matter of general conversation; nothing specific and definite.

Question. At what time did you learn that President Lincoln had assented to the assembling of the Virginia rebel legislature?

Answer. I knew of it on the 18th of April, I think; but I procured a paper with the specific order of General Weitzel, also a copy of the amnesty proclamation, on the 20th of April.

Question. You did not know, at that time, that that arrangement had been rescinded by the President?

Answer. No, sir; I did not know of that until afterwards. The moment I heard of that, I notified General Johnston of it.

Question. Then at the time you entered into this arrangement with General Johnston you knew that General Weitzel had approved of the calling together of the rebel legislature of Virginia, by assent of the President?

Answer. I knew of it by some source unofficially, and succeeded in getting a copy of the paper containing General Weitzel's order on the 20th or 21st of April.

Question. But at the time of your arrangement you did not know that that order had been rescinded?

Answer. No, sir; I learned that several days afterwards, and at once sent word to General Johnston.

Question. At the time of your arrangement you also knew of the surrender of Lee's army, and the terms of that surrender?

Answer. I had that officially from General Grant; I got that at Smithfield, on the 12th April.

Question. I have here what purports to be a letter from you to Johnston, which seems to imply that you intended to make the arrangement on the terms of Lee's surrender. The letter is as follows:

"HEADQUARTERS MILITARY DIVISION OF THE MISSISSIPPI,
"*In the Field, Raleigh, N. C., April* 14, 1865.

"GENERAL: I have this moment received your communication of this date. I am fully empowered to arrange with you any terms for the suspension of further hostilities as between the armies commanded by you and those commanded by myself, and will be willing to confer with you to that end. I will limit the advance of my main column to-morrow to Morrisville, and the cavalry to the University, and expect that you will also maintain the present position of your forces until each has notice of a failure to agree.

"That a basis of action may be had, I undertake to abide by the same terms and conditions as were made by Generals Grant and Lee at Appomattox Court House, on the 9th instant, relative to our two armies; and, furthermore, to obtain from General Grant an order to suspend the movements of any troops from the direction of Virginia. General Stoneman is under my command, and my order will suspend any devastation or destruction contemplated by him. I will add that I really desire to save the people of North Carolina the damage they would sustain by the march of this army through the central or western parts of the State.

"I am, with respect, your obedient servant,

"W. T. SHERMAN, *Major General.*

"General J. E. JOHNSTON, *Commanding Confederate Army.*"

Answer. Those were the terms as to his own army; but the concessions I made him were for the purpose of embracing other armies.

Question. And the writing you signed was to include other armies?

Answer. The armies of Kirby Smith and Dick Taylor, so that afterwards no man within the limits of the southern confederacy could claim to belong to any confederate army in existence.

Question. The President addressed a note to General Grant, perhaps, not to you, to the effect of forbidding officers of the army from entering into anything but strictly military arrangements, leaving civil matters entirely to him.

Answer. I never saw such a note signed by President Lincoln. Mr. Stanton made such a note or telegram, and says it was by President Lincoln's dictation. He made it to General Grant, but never to me. On the contrary, while I was in Georgia, Mr. Lincoln telegraphed to me, encouraging me to discuss matters with Governor Brown and Mr. Stephens.

Question. Then you had no notice of that order to General Grant?

Answer. I had no knowledge of it, official or otherwise.

Question. In the published report of your agreement there is nothing said about slavery, I believe?

Answer. There was nothing said about slavery, because it did not fall within the category of military questions, and we could not make it so. It was a legal question which the President had disposed of, overriding all our action. We had to treat the slave as *free*, because the President, our commander-in-chief, said he was free. For me to have renewed the question when that decision was made would have involved the absurdity of an inferior undertaking to qualify the work of his superior.

Question. That was the reason why it was not mentioned?

Answer. Yes, sir. Subsequently I wrote a note to Johnston stating that I thought it would be well to mention it for political effect when we came to draw up the final terms with precision. That note was written pending the time my memorandum was going to Washington, and before an answer had been returned.

Question. At the time you entered into those negotiations was Johnston in a condition to offer any effectual resistance to your army?

Answer. He could not have resisted my army an hour if I could have got hold of him; but he could have escaped from me by breaking up into small parties, or by taking the country roads, travelling faster than any army with trains could have pursued.

Question. Then your object in negotiating was to keep his army from scattering into guerilla bands?

Answer. That was my chief object. I officially notified the War Department.

Question. And not because there was any doubt about the result of a battle?

Answer. There was no question as to the result of a battle, and I knew it; every soldier knew it; every man in North Carolina knew it .Johnston said in the first five minutes of our conversation that any further resistance on his part would be an act of folly, and all he wanted was to keep his army from dispersing.

By Mr. Loan:

Question. In your examination by the chairman you stated that you were acting in pursuance of instructions from Mr. Lincoln, derived from his letters and telegrams at various times.

Answer. Yes, sir.

Question. Have you any of those letters and telegrams which you can furnish to the committee?

Answer. I can furnish you a copy of a despatch to General Halleck, from Atlanta, in which I stated that I had invited Governor Brown and Vice-President Stephens to meet me; and I can give you a copy of Mr. Lincoln's answer, for my despatch was referred to him, in which he said he felt much interested in my despatch, and encouraged me to allow their visit. But the letter to which I refer specifically was a longer letter, which I wrote to General Halleck from my camp on Big Black, Mississippi, at General Halleck's instigation, in September, 1863, which was received in Washington, and submitted to Mr. Lincoln, who desired to have it published, to which I would not consent. In that letter I gave my opinions fully and frankly, not only upon the military situation, but also the civil policy necessary. Mr. Lincoln expressed himself highly pleased with my views, and desired to make them public, but I preferred not to do so.

Question. And by subsequent acts he induced you to believe he approved of those views.

Answer. I know he approved of them, and always encouraged me to carry out those views.

By the chairman:

Question. The following is a letter published in the newspapers, purporting to have been addressed by you to Mr. Johnston, dated April 21, 1865:

"HEADQUARTERS MILITARY DIVISION OF THE MISSISSIPPI,
"*In the Field, Raleigh, N. C., April* 21, 1865.

"GENERAL: I send you a letter for General Wilson, which, if sent by telegraph and courier, will check his career. He may mistrust the telegraph, therefore better send the original, for he cannot mistake my handwriting, with which he is familiar. He seems to have his blood up, and will be hard to hold. If he can buy corn, fodder, and rations down about Fort Valley, it will obviate the necessity of his going up to Rome or Dalton.

"It is reported to me from Cairo that Mobile is in our possession, but it is not minute or official.

"General Baker sent in to me, wanting to surrender his command, on the theory that the whole confederate army was surrendered. I explained to him or his staff officer the exact truth, and left him to act as he thought proper. He seems to have disbanded his men, deposited a few arms about twenty miles from here, and himself awaits your action. I will not hold him, his men, or arms, subject to any condition other than the final one we may agree on.

"I shall look for Major Hitchcock back from Washington on Wednesday, and shall promptly notify you of the result. By the action of General Weitzel in relation to the Virginia legislature, I feel certain we will have no trouble on the score of recognizing existing State governments. It may be the lawyers will want us to define more minutely what is meant by the guarantee of rights of person and property. It may be construed into a compact for us to undo the past as to the rights of slaves and 'leases of plantations' on the Mississippi, of 'vacant and abandoned' plantations. I wish you would talk to the best men you have on these points; and, if possible, let us in our final convention make these points so clear as to leave no room for angry controversy.

"I believe if the south would simply and publicly declare what we all feel, that slavery is dead, that you would inaugurate an era of peace and prosperity that would soon efface the ravages of the past four years of war. Negroes would remain in the south, and afford you abundance of cheap labor, which otherwise will be driven away; and it will save the country the senseless discussions which have kept us all in hot water for fifty years.

"Although, strictly speaking, this is no subject of a military convention, yet I am honestly convinced that our simple declaration of a result will be accepted as good law everywhere. Of course I have not a single word from Washington on this or any other point of our agreements, but I know the effect of such a step by us will be universally accepted.

"I am, with great respect, your obedient servant,

"W. T. SHERMAN,

"*Major General United States Army.*

"General J. E. JOHNSTON,

"*Commanding Confederate Army.*"

That is the letter in which you say that it would be well to declare publicly that slavery is dead?

Answer. Yes, sir, that is the letter.

By Mr. Loan:

Question. Will you furnish the committee a copy of the letters written by you to Mr. Stanton, in January last, from Savannah?

Answer. I will do so.

The CHAIRMAN. And when the manuscript of your testimony is prepared it will be submitted to you for revision, and you can add to it any statement or papers that you may desire or consider necessary.

The WITNESS, (subsequently.) I have revised the above, and now subjoin copies of letters from my letter-book in the order of their bearing on the questions raised by this inquiry.

"HEADQUARTERS MILITARY DIVISION OF THE MISSISSIPPI,

"*In the Field, Raleigh, N. C., April* 18, 1865.

"GENERAL: I enclose herewith a copy of an agreement made this day between General Joseph E. Johnston and myself, which, if approved by the President of the United States. will produce peace from the Potomac to the Rio Grande. Mr. Breckinridge was present at our conference in the capacity of major general, and satisfied me of the ability of General Johnston to carry out to the full extent the terms of this agreement; and, if you will get the President to simply indorse the copy and commission me to carry out the terms, I will follow them to the conclusion.

"You will observe that it is an absolute submission of the enemy to the lawful authority of the United States, and disperses his armies absolutely; and the point to which I attach most importance is, that the dispersion and disbandment of these armies is done in such a manner as to prevent their breaking up into guerilla bands. On the other hand, we can retain just as much of an army as we please. I agreed to the mode and manner of the surrender of arms set forth, as it gives the States the means of repressing guerillas, which we could not expect them to do if we stripped them of all arms.

"Both Generals Johnston and Breckinridge admitted that slavery was dead, and I could not insist on embracing it in such a paper, because it can be made with the States in detail. I know that all the men of substance south sincerely want peace, and I do not believe they will resort to war again during this century. I have no doubt but that they will in the future be perfectly subordinate to the laws of the United States. The moment my action in this matter is approved, I can spare five (5) corps, and will ask for orders to leave General Schofield here with the 10th corps, and to march myself with the 14th, 15th, 17th, 20th, and 23d corps, *via* Burkesville and Gordonsville, to Frederick or Hagerstown, there to be paid and mustered out.

"The question of finance is now the chief one, and every soldier and officer not needed should be got home at work. I would like to be able to begin the march north by May 1.

"I urge, on the part of the President, speedy action, as it is important to get the confederate armies to their homes as well as our own.

"I am, with great respect, your obedient servant,

"W. T. SHERMAN,
"*Major General, Commanding.*

"Lieutenant General U. S. GRANT, or Major General HALLECK,
"*Washington, D. C.*"

"HEADQUARTERS MILITARY DIVISION OF THE MISSISSIPPI,
"*In the Field, Raleigh, N. C., April* 18, 1865.

"GENERAL: I received your despatch describing the man Clark detailed to assassinate me. He had better be in a hurry, or he will be too late.

"The news of Mr. Lincoln's death produced a most intense effect on our troops. At first I feared it would lead to excesses; but now it has softened down and can easily be guided. None evinced more feeling than General Johnston, who admitted that the act was calculated to stain his cause with a dark hue; and he contended that the loss was most serious to the south, who had begun to realize that Mr. Lincoln was the best friend the south had.

"I cannot believe that even Mr. Davis was privy to the diabolical plot, but think it the emanation of a set of young men of the south, who are very devils. I want to throw upon the south the care of this class of men, who will soon be as obnoxious to their industrial classes as to us.

"Had I pushed Johnston's army to an extremity, it would have dispersed and done infinite mischief. Johnston informed me that General Stoneman had been at Salisbury, and was now about Statesville. I have sent him orders to come to me.

"General Johnston also informed me that General Wilson was at Columbus, Ga., and he wanted me to arrest his progress. I leave that to you.

"Indeed, if the President sanctions my agreement with Johnston our interest is to cease all destruction.

"Please give all orders necessary according to the views the Executive may take, and influence him, if possible, not to vary the terms at all, for I have considered everything, and believe that the confederate armies once dispersed we can adjust all else fairly and well.

"I am yours, &c.,

"W. T. SHERMAN,
"*Major General, Commanding.*

"General H. W. HALLECK, *Chief of Staff, Washington, D. C.*"

Lest confusion should result to the mind of the committee by the latter part of the above letter, I will state it was addressed to General Halleck as chief of staff, when he was the proper "maker of orders" to the commander-in-chief. The whole case was changed when, on the 22d of April, he became the commander of the separate division of the James.

As stated in my testimony, General Grant reached Raleigh on the 24th. On the 25th, on the supposition that I would start next day to chase Johnston's army, I wrote him the following letter, delivered in person:

"HEADQUARTERS DIVISION OF THE MISSISSIPPI,
"*In the Field,, Raleigh, N. C., April* 25, 1865.

"GENERAL: I had the honor to receive your letter of April 21, with enclosures, yesterday, and was well pleased that you came along, as you must have observed that I held the military control so as to adapt it to any phase the case might assume.

"It is but just I should record the fact that I made my terms with General Johnston under the influence of the liberal terms you extended to the army of General Lee at Appomattox Court House on the 9th, and the seeming policy of our government as evinced by the call of the Virginia legislature and governor back to Richmond under yours and President Lincoln's very eyes. It now appears this last act was done without any consultation with you or any knowledge of Mr. Lincoln, but rather in opposition to a previous policy well considered.

"I have not the least desire to interfere in the civil policy of our government, but would shun it as something not to my liking; but occasions do arise when a prompt seizure of results is forced on military commanders not in immediate communication with the proper authority. It is probable that the terms signed by General Johnston and myself were not clear enough on the point, well understood between us, that our negotiations did not apply to any parties outside the officers and men of the confederate armies, which could easily have been remedied.

"No surrender of any army, not actually at the mercy of an antagonist, was ever made without "terms," and these always define the military status of the surrendered. Thus, you stipulated that the officers and men of Lee's army should not be molested at their homes so long as they obeyed the laws at the place of their residence.

"I do not wish to discuss these points involved in our recognition of the State governments in actual existence, but will merely state my conclusions to await the solution of the future.

"Such action on our part in no manner recognizes for a moment the so-called confederate government, or makes us liable for its debts or acts.

"The laws and acts done by the several States during the period of rebellion are *void*, because done without the oath prescribed by our Constitution of the United States, which is a 'condition precedent.'

"We have a right to use any sort of machinery to produce military results; and it is the commonest thing for military commanders to use the civil governments *in actual existence* as a means to an end. I do believe we could and can use the present State governments lawfully, constitutionally, and as the very best possible means to produce the object desired, viz: entire and complete submission to the lawful authority of the United States.

"As to punishment for past crimes, that is for the judiciary, and can in no manner of way be disturbed by our acts; and so far as I can I will use my influence that rebels shall suffer all the personal punishment prescribed by law; as also the civil liabilities arising from their past acts.

"What we now want is the new forms of law by which common men may regain the positions of industry so long disturbed by the war.

"I now apprehend that the rebel armies will disperse, and, instead of dealing with six or seven States, we will have to deal with numberless bands of desperadoes, headed by such men as Mosby, Forrest, Red Jackson, and others, who know not and care not for danger and its consequences.

"I am, with great respect, your obedient servant,

"W. T. SHERMAN, *Major General.*

"Lieutenant General U. S. GRANT, *Present.*"

On the same day I wrote and mailed to the Secretary of War the following:

"HEADQUARTERS MILITARY DIVISION OF THE MISSISSIPPI,
"*In the Field, Raleigh, N. C., April* 25, 1865.

"DEAR SIR: I have been furnished a copy of your letter of April 21 to General Grant, signifying your disapproval of the terms on which General Johnston proposed to disarm and disperse the insurgents, on condition of amnesty, &c. I admit my folly in embracing in a military convention any civil matters; but, unfortunately, such is the nature of our situation that they seem inextricably united; and I understood from you at Savannah that the financial state of the country demanded military success, and would warrant a little bending to policy.

"When I had my conference with General Johnston, I had the public examples before me of General Grant's terms to Lee's army and General Weitzel's invitation to the Virginia legislature to assemble.

"I still believe the general government of the United States has made a mistake; but that is none of my business—mine is a different task; and I had flattered myself that, by four years of patient, unremitting, and successful labor I deserved no reminder such as is contained in the last paragraph of your letter to General Grant. You may assure the President that I heed his suggestion.

"I am truly, &c.,

"W. T. SHERMAN, *Major General, Commanding.*

"Hon. E. M. STANTON, *Secretary of War, Washington.*"

The last sentence refers to the fact that General Grant had been sent to Raleigh to direct military movements. That was the first time in my life I had ever had a word of reproof from the government of the United States, and I was naturally sensitive. But all I said to any one was to General Meigs, who came with General Grant, that it was not kind on the part of Mr. Secretary Stanton. The fact, however, did not qualify my military conduct. The final interview with General Johnston followed, and the terms of capitulation were agreed on and signed, and General Grant started for Washington, bearing the news; when on the 28th of April I received in the New York Times the most extraordinary budget of Mr. Stanton, which for the first time startled me, and I wrote to General Grant this letter:

"HEADQUARTERS MILITARY DIVISION OF THE MISSISSIPPI,
"*In the Field, April* 28, 1865.

"GENERAL: Since you left me yesterday I have seen the New York Times of the 24th instant, containing a budget of military news, authenticated by the signature of the Secretary of War, which is grouped in such a way as to give very erroneous impressions. It embraces a copy of the basis of agreement between myself and General Johnston, of April 18, with commentaries which it will be time enough to discuss two or three years hence—after the government has experimented a little more in the machinery by which power reaches the scattered people of the vast country known as the south; but, in the mean time, I do think that my rank (if not past services) entitled me at least to the respect of keeping secret what was known to none but the cabinet until further inquiry could be made, instead of giving publicity to documents I never saw, and drawing inferences wide of the tru th.

"I never saw or had furnished me a copy of Mr. Stanton's despatch to you of the 3d of March, nor did Mr. Stanton, or any human being, ever convey to me its substance, or anything like it; but, on the contrary, I had seen General Weitzel's invitation to the Virginia legislature, made in Mr. Lincoln's very presence, and had failed to discern any other official hint of a plan of reconstruction, or any ideas calculated to allay the fears of the people of the south, after the destruction of their armies and civil authorities would leave them without any government at all. We should not drive a people into anarchy, and it is simply impossible for our military power to reach all the masses of their unhappy country.

"I confess I did not want to drive General Johnston's army into bands of armed men, going about without purpose, and capable only of infinite mischief. But you saw, on your arrival at Raleigh, that I had my armies so disposed that his escape was only possible in a disorganized shape, and as you did not choose to direct military operations in this quarter, I infer that you were satisfied with the military situation. At all events, the moment I learned (what was proper enough) the disapproval of the President, I acted in such a manner as to compel the surrender of General Johnston's whole army on the same terms as you had prescribed to General Lee's army when you had it surrounded and in your absolute power.

"Mr. Stanton, in stating that my orders to General Stoneman were likely to result in the escape of 'Mr. Davis to Mexico or Europe,' is in deep error. General Stoneman was not at Salisbury then, but had gone back to Statesville. Davis was supposed to be between us, and Stoneman was beyond him. By turning towards me he was approaching Davis, and had he joined me, as ordered, I then would have had a mounted force needed for that and other purposes. But even now I don't know that Mr. Stanton wants Davis caught, and as my official papers, deemed sacred, are hastily published to the world, it will be imprudent for me to state what has been done in that respect.

"As the editor of the Times has (it may be) logically and fairly drawn the inference from this singular document that I am insubordinate, I can only deny the intention. I have never in my life questioned or disobeyed an order, though many and many a time have I risked my life, my health, and reputation in obeying orders, or even hints to execute plans and purposes not to my liking. It is not fair to withhold from me plans and policy (if any there be) and expect me to guess at them, for facts and events appear quite different from different stand-points. For four years I have been in camp dealing with soldiers, and I can assure you that the conclusions at which the cabinet arrived with such singular unanimity differ from mine. I conferred freely with the best officers in this army as to the points involved in this controversy, and, strange to say, they were singularly unanimous in the other conclusion, and they will learn with pain and sorrow that I am deemed insubordinate, and wanting in common sense; that I, who have labored day and night, winter and summer, for four years, and have brought an army of 70,000 men, in magnificent condition, across a country deemed impassable, and placed it just where it was wanted almost on the day appointed, have brought discredit on the government. I do not wish to boast of this, but I do say that it entitled me to the courtesy of being consulted before publishing to the world a proposition rightfully submitted to higher authority for adjudication, and then accompanied by statements which invited the press to be let loose on me.

"It is true that non-combatants, men who sleep in comfort and security whilst we watch on the distant lines, are better able to judge than we poor soldiers, who rarely see a newspaper, hardly can hear from our families, or stop long enough to get our pay. I envy not the task of reconstruction, and am delighted that the Secretary has relieved me of it.

"As you did not undertake to assume the management of the affairs of this army, I infer that on personal inspection your mind arrived at a different conclusion from that of Mr. Secretary Stanton. I will therefore go on and execute your orders to the conclusion, and when done will, with intense satisfaction, leave to the civil authorities the execution of the task of which they seem to me so jealous; but as an honest man and soldier I invite them to follow my path, for they may see some things and hear some things that may disturb their philosophy.

"With sincere respect,

"W. T. SHERMAN,
"*Major General, Commanding.*

"Lieutenant General U. S. GRANT,
"*General-in-Chief, Washington, D. C.*

"P. S.—As Mr. Stanton's singular paper has been published, I demand that this also be made public, though I am in no manner responsible to the press, but to the law and my proper superiors.

"W. T. SHERMAN,
"*Major General, Commanding.*"

Since my arrival at Washington I have learned from General Grant that this letter was received, but he preferred to withhold it until my arrival, as he knew I was marching towards Washington with my army. Upon my arrival I did not insist on its publication till it was drawn out by this inquiry. I also append here the copy of a letter from Colonel T. S. Bowers, Assistant Adjutant General, asking me to modify my report as to the point of violating my truce, with my answer.

"HEADQUARTERS ARMIES OF THE UNITED STATES,
"*Washington, May* 25, 1865.

"Major General W. T. SHERMAN, *Commanding Military Division of the Mississippi:*

"General Grant directs me to call your attention to the part of your report in which the necessity of maintaining your truce at the expense of many lives is spoken of. The general thinks that in making a truce the commander of an army can control only his own army, and that the hostile general must make his own arrangements with other armies acting against him.

"Whilst independent generals acting against a common foe would naturally act in concert, the general deems that each must be the judge of his own duty, and responsible for its execution.

"If you should wish, the report will be returned for any change you deem best.

"Very respectfully, your obedient servant,

"T. S. BOWERS, *Assistant Adjutant General.*"

"HEADQUARTERS MILITARY DIVISION OF THE MISSISSIPPI,
"*Washington, D. C., May* 26, 1865.

"COLONEL: I had the honor to receive your letter of May 25 last evening, and I hasten to answer. I wish to precede it by renewing the assurance of my entire confidence and respect for the President and Lieutenant General Grant, and that in all matters I will be most willing to shape my official and private conduct to suit their wishes. The past is beyond my control, and the matters embraced in the official report to which you refer are finished. It is but just the reasons that actuated me, right or wrong, should stand of record; but in all future cases, should any arise, I will respect the decision of General Grant, though I think it wrong.

"Supposing a guard has prisoners in charge, and officers of another command should aim to rescue or kill them, is it not clear the guard must defend the prisoners? Same of a safe-guard. So jealous is the military law to protect and maintain *good faith* when pledged that the law adjudges death and no alternative punishment to one who violates a safe-guard in foreign parts. (See Article of War No. 55.) For murder, arson, treason, and the highest military crimes, the punishment prescribed by law is death, or some minor punishment; but for the violation of a 'safe-guard' death, and death alone, is the prescribed penalty. I instance this to illustrate how in military stipulations to an enemy our government commands and enforces 'good faith.' In discussing this matter I would like to refer to many writers on military law, but am willing to take Halleck as the text. (See his chapter No. 27.) In the very first article he states that *good faith* should always be observed between enemies in war, because when our faith has been pledged to him, so far as the promise extends he ceases to be an enemy. He then defines the meaning of *compacts* and *conventions*, and says they are made sometimes for a general or a partial suspension of hostilities for the 'surrender of an army,' &c. They may be *special*, limited to particular places or particular forces, but of course can only bind the armies subject to the general who makes the truce and co-extensive only with the extent of his command. This is all I ever claimed, and clearly covers the whole case. All of North Carolina was in my immediate command, with General Schofield, its department commander, and his army, present with me. I never asked the truce to have effect beyond my own *territorial* command. General Halleck himself, in his Orders No. 1, defines his own limits clearly enough, viz., "such part of North Carolina as was not occupied by command of Major General Sherman." He could not pursue and cut off Johnston's retreat towards Salisbury and Charlotte without invading my command, and so patent was his purpose to *defy* and *violate* my truce that Mr. Stanton's publication of the fact, not even yet recalled, modified, or explained, was headed, '*Sherman's truce disregarded*,' that the whole world drew but one inference. It admits of no other. I never claimed that that truce bound Generals Halleck or Canby within the sphere of *their* respective commands as defined by themselves.

"It was a *partial truce* of very short duration, clearly within my limits and right, justified by events, and as in the case of prisoners in my custody, or the violation of a safe-guard given by me in my own territorial limits, I was bound to maintain *good faith.*

"I prefer not to change my report, but again repeat that in all future cases I am willing to be governed by the interpretation of General Grant, although I again invite his attention to the limits of my command and those of General Halleck at the time, and the pointed phraseology of General Halleck's despatch to Mr. Stanton, wherein he reports that he had ordered his generals to pay no heed to my orders within the clearly defined area of my command.

"I am, &c.,

"W. T. SHERMAN,

"*Major General U. S. A., Commanding*,

"Colonel T. S. BOWERS,

"*Assistant Adjutant General, Washington, D. C.*"

I now add the two letters written to Mr. Stanton at Savannah, and the despatch from Atlanta, mentioned in the body of my testimony, and Mr. Lincoln's answer.

"HEADQUARTERS MILITARY DIVISION OF THE MISSISSIPPI,

"*In the Field, Savannah, January* 2, 1865.

"SIR: I have just received from Lieutenant General Grant a copy of that part of your telegram to him of December 26, relating to cotton, a copy of which has been immediately furnished to General Easton, my chief quartermaster, who will be strictly governed by it.

"I had already been approached by all the consuls and half the people of Savannah on this cotton question, and my invariable answer has been, that all the cotton in Savannah was prize of war and belonged to the United States, and nobody should recover a bale of it with my consent, and that as cotton had been one of the chief causes of this war it should help pay its expenses; that all cotton became tainted with treason from the hour the first act of hostility was committed against the United States some time in December, 1860; and that no bill of sale subsequent to that date could convey title.

"My orders were that an officer of the quartermaster's department, United States army, might furnish the holder, agent, or attorney a mere certificate of the fact of seizure, with description of the bales marked, &c., the cotton then to be turned over to the agent of the Treasury Department to be shipped to New York for sale. But since the receipt of your despatch I have ordered General Easton to make the shipment himself to the quartermaster at New York, where you can dispose of it at pleasure. I do not think the Treasury Department ought to bother itself with the prizes or captures of war.

"Mr. Barclay, former consul at New York, representing Mr. Molyneux, former consul here, but absent since a long time, called on me in person with reference to cotton claimed by English subjects. He seemed amazed when I told him I should pay no respect to consular certificates, and that in no event would I treat an English subject with more favor than one of our own deluded citizens, and that for my part I was unwilling to fight for cotton for the benefit of Englishmen openly engaged in smuggling arms and instruments of war to kill us; that, on the contrary, it would afford me great satisfaction to conduct my army to Nassau and wipe out that nest of pirates. I explained to him, however, that I was not a diplomatic agent of the general government of the United States, but that my opinion, so frankly expressed, was that of a soldier, which it would be well for him to heed. It appeared also that he owned a plantation on the line of investment of Savannah, which, of course, is destroyed, and for which he expected me to give him some certificate entitling him to idemnification, which I declined emphatically.

"I have adopted in Savannah rules concerning property, severe, but just, founded upon the laws of nations and the practice of civilized governments, and am clearly of the opinion that we should claim all the belligerent rights over conquered countries, that the people may realize the truth that war is no child's play.

"I embrace in this a copy of a letter dated December 31, 1864, in answer to one from Solomon Cohen, a rich lawyer, to General Blair, his personal friend, as follows:

"'GENERAL: Your note enclosing Mr. Cohen's of this date is received, and I answer frankly through you his inquiries.

"'*First*. No one can practice law as an attorney in the United States without acknowledging the supremacy of our government. If I am not in error, an attorney is as much an officer of the court as the clerk, and it would be a novel thing in a government to have a court to administer law that denied the supremacy of the government itself.

"'*Second*. No one will be allowed the privileges of a merchant; or, rather, to trade is a privilege which no one should seek of the government without in like manner acknowledging its supremacy.

"'*Third*. If Mr. Cohen remains in Savannah as a denizen, his property, real and personal, will not be disturbed unless its temporary use be necessary for the military authorities of the city. The title to property will not be disturbed in any event, until adjudicated by the courts of the United States.

"'*Fourth*. If Mr. Cohen leaves Savannah under my Special Order No. 143, it is a public acknowledgment that he 'adheres to the enemies of the United States,' and all his property becomes forfeited to the United States. But as a matter of favor he will be allowed to carry with him clothing and furniture for the use of himself, his family, and servants, and will be transported within the enemy's lines, but not by way of Port Royal.

"'These rules will apply to all parties, and from them no exception will be made.

"'I have the honor to be, general, your obedient servant,

"'W. T. SHERMAN, *Major General.*

"'Major General F. P. BLAIR,
"'*Commanding 17th Army Corps.*'

"This letter was in answer to specific inquiries; it is clear and specific, and covers all the points, and should I leave before my orders are executed, I will endeavor to impress upon my successor, General Foster, their wisdom and propriety.

"I hope the course I have taken in these matters will meet your approbation, and that the President will not refund to parties claiming cotton or other property, without the strongest evidence of loyalty and friendship on the part of the claimant, or unless some other positive end is to be gained.

"I am, with great respect, your obedient servant,

"W. T. SHERMAN,
"*Major General, Commanding.*

"Hon. EDWIN M. STANTON,
"*Secretary of War, Washington, D. C.*"

"HEADQUARTERS MILITARY DIVISISON OF THE MISSISSIPPI,
"*In the Field, Savannah, January* 19, 1865.

"SIR: When you left Savannah a few days ago you forgot the map which General Geary had prepared for you, showing the route by which his division entered the city of Savannah—being the first troops to occupy that city. I now send it to you.

"I avail myself of the opportunity also to enclose you copies of all my official orders touching trade and intercourse with the people of Georgia, as well as for the establishment of the negro settlements.

"Delegations of the people of Georgia continue to come, and I am satisfied that a little judicious handling and by a little respect being paid to their prejudices, we can create a schism in Jefferson Davis's dominions. All that I have conversed with realize the truth that slavery as an institution is defunct, and the only questions that remain are what disposition shall be made of the negroes themselves. I confess myself unable to offer a complete solution for these questions, and prefer to leave it to the slower operations of time. We have given the initiative, and can afford to await the working of the experiment.

"As to trade matters I also think it is to our interest to keep the people somewhat dependent on the articles of commerce to which they have been hitherto accustomed. General Grover is now here, and will, I think, be able to manage this matter judiciously, and may gradually relax and invite cotton to come in in large quantities. But at first we should manifest no undue anxiety on that score, for the rebels would at once make use of it as a power against us. We should assume a tone of perfect contempt for cotton and everything else in comparison with the great object of the war—*the restoration of the Union with all its rights and power.* If the rebels burn cotton as a war measure, they simply play into our hands by taking away the only product of value they now have to exchange in foreign ports for war ships and munitions. By such a course also they alienate the feelings of the large class of small farmers that look to their little parcels of cotton to exchange for food and clothing for their families. I hope the government will not manifest too much anxiety to obtain cotton in large quantities, and especially that the President will not indorse the contracts for the purchase of large quantities of cotton. Several contracts, involving from six to ten thousand bales, indorsed by Mr. Lincoln, have been shown me, but were not in such a form as to amount to an order for me to facilitate their execution.

"As to treasury trade agents and agents to take charge of confiscated and abandoned property, whose salaries depend on their fees, I can only say that as a general rule they are mischievous and disturbing elements to a military government, and it is almost impossible for us to study the law and regulations so as to understand fully their powers and duties. I rather think the quartermaster's department of the army could better fulfil all their duties and accomplish all that is aimed at by the law. Yet on this subject I will leave Generals Foster and Grover to do the best they can.

"I am, with great respect, your obedient servant,

"W. T. SHERMAN,
"*Major General, Commanding.*

"Hon. EDWIN M. STANTON,
"*Secretary of War, Washington, D. C.*"

"HEADQUARTERS MILITARY DIVISION OF THE MISSISSIPPI,
"*In the Field, Atlanta, Georgia, September* 15, 1864.

"My report is done, and will be forwarded as soon as I get a few more of the subordinate reports. I am awaiting a courier from General Grant. All well, and troops in fine, healthy camps, and supplies coming forward finely.

"Governor Brown has disbanded his militia to gather the corn and sorghum of the State. I have reason to believe that he and Stephens want to visit me, and I have sent them a hearty invitation.

"I will exchange 2,000 prisoners with Hood, but no more.

"W. T. SHERMAN,
"*Major General, Commanding.*

"General HALLECK, *Washington, D. C.*"

"WASHINGTON, D. C.,
"*September* 17, 1864—10 a. m.

"Major General SHERMAN: I feel great interest in the subjects of your despatch mentioning corn and sorghum, and contemplated visit to you.

"A. LINCOLN,
"*President of the United States.*"

I have not possession here of all my official records, most of which are our west. I have selected the above from my more recent letter books, and offet them to show how prompt and full have been my official reports, and how unnecessary was all the clamor made touching my actions and opinions at the time the basis of agreement of April 18 was submitted to the President. All of which is most respectfully submitted.

W. T. SHERMAN,
Major General U. S. A.

LIGHT-DRAUGHT MONITORS.

IN THE SENATE OF THE UNITED STATES, *June* 29, 1864.

Resolved, That the Committee on the Conduct of the War be instructed to inquire what progress has been made in the construction of the iron-clad steam gunboats contracted for in the year 1862, by whom the contract was made on the part of the government, who planned the models of the same, and who is responsible therefor; have any of them been finished; if so, what was the condition of the vessel after she was launched; are the other vessels contracted for to be built on a plan or model similar to the Chimo, lately launched at Boston; and all information which may be had touching said gunboats.

Attest:

J. W. FORNEY, *Secretary*.

The Joint Committee on the Conduct of the War submit the following report:

During the year 1862 the necessity for some light-draught armored vessels for operations on our western rivers and the shallow bays and sounds upon the Atlantic and Gulf coasts became so urgent that the Navy Department determined to provide some for that purpose if possible. Application was made to Mr. John Ericsson, the inventor of the original Monitor, for a plan of a light-draught monitor, to carry one turret, and to have a draught of from six to six and a half feet. On the 9th of October Mr. Ericsson submitted to the department a plan, which, to use his own words, "was not intended as a working plan, yet it defined with clearness and precision the general principle, and the mode of building the vessel, engines, boilers, and propellers."

Mr. Ericsson not having time to make all the calculations and detailed working plans, that work was confided to Chief Engineer Alban C. Stimers, of the United States navy. Mr. Stimers had been engaged with Mr. Ericsson in the construction of the first monitor, had gone in that vessel, in the capacity of engineer, from New York to Hampton roads, had there assisted in the contest between the Monitor and the rebel iron-clad, the Merrimac, and since that time had been engaged more or less, by order of the Navy Department, in superintending the construction of the other monitors contracted for by the department. The detailed plan having been prepared by Mr. Stimers, the department advertised for proposals as follows:

[Advertisement.]

LIGHT-DRAUGHT VESSELS FOR RIVERS AND BAYS.

NAVY DEPARTMENT, *February* 10, 1863.

The Navy Department will receive proposals for the construction and completion, in every respect, (except guns, ordnance stores, fuel, provisions, and nautical instruments,) of armored steamers, of about seven hundred tons, of wood and iron combined, having a single revolving turret.

On personal application at the Navy Department in Washington, or to Rear-Admiral Gregory, No. 413 Broadway, New York, parties intending to offer can examine the plans and specifications, which will be furnished to the contractors by the department.

No offer will be considered unless from parties who are prepared to execute work of this kind, having suitable shops and tools, of which, if not known to the department, they must present evidence with their bid.

The act of Congress approved July 17, 1862, prohibits the transfer of any contract or order, or interest therein.

The bidders will state the price, and the time within which they will agree to complete the vessel or vessels, and the bid must be accompanied by the guarantee required by law, that if awarded to them they will promptly execute the contract.

Propositions will be received until the 24th day of February, and they must be indorsed "Proposals for vessels for river defence," to distinguish them from other business letters.

From the bids thus received a general average price was established, of a little less than $400,000 each, and during the months of March, April, and May, 1863, contracts were made for the building of twenty light-draught monitors upon the same plan. Mr. Stimers was placed in charge of their construction, and the contractors were directed to look to him for instructions. He was ordered to consult with Mr. Ericsson in preparing his plans and drawings for contractors, and, at his own request, was authorized to establish an office and employ assistants in New York city, where he could have facilities for frequent and easy consultation with Mr. Ericsson.

In May, 1864, the first of these vessels, the Chimo, built by Mr. Aquila Adams, was launched at Boston. She was found to be a failure, so far as the original design was concerned, of a light-draught river monitor. All these vessels having been designed upon the same plan, further work was at once suspended upon them. A commission was appointed on the 11th of June, 1864, to examine them, and to recommend what should be done with them to remedy their defects. The commission reported on the 9th of July, 1864, recommending that five of the vessels should be changed into torpedo boats, by removing the turrets, &c., in order to lighten their draught, and that the other fifteen should be changed by building up their sides twenty-two inches, increasing their draught, but rendering them more serviceable as monitors. That recommendation was adopted by the department, and the proposed changes have been carried out.

These vessels were found to be defective in draught and in speed. Instead of being some fifteen inches out of the water when fully completed and equipped, as was the original design, it was found that they would barely float, their decks being awash with the water. Their speed, instead of being from seven to nine knots an hour, was found upon trial to be only from three and a half to four knots an hour. The increased draught was caused, first, by reason of a miscalculation of the weights of the materials and the amount of displacement; and, secondly, in consequence of the additions and alterations made in the plans after the contracts were entered into. Many of these alterations were considered necessary from the experience gained by the navy in the attack made by the monitors and other vessels upon the rebel forts in the harbor of Charleston, and were adopted to obviate defects which that engagement showed to exist in the monitors. The addition of a water-tank around the vessel was made upon the suggestion of Admiral Smith, chief of the Bureau of Yards and Docks, for the purpose of enabling these light-draught vessels, when navigating unknown waters, to sink themselves, so that when they should run aground they could be floated off by pumping the water out of the tanks.

The errors in the calculations of weights and amount of displacement would appear from the testimony to be in a great part attributable to Mr. Stimers and those in his employ. He had almost the entire control of the matter ; to him was intrusted the making the calculations, drawing the plans, and superintending the work of construction. He had the calculations made by a young man in his office, who Mr. Stimers says was a man of ability, but too young and inexperienced to make all the calculations upon which were to be built twenty vessels, at a cost of several millions of dollars. Mr. Stimers says that although he had great confidence in the ability of this young man, yet he deemed it necessary that his work should be reviewed by others of more experience ; for that purpose he says that he submitted the calculations to Mr. Lenthall, chief of the Bureau of Construction and Repairs, stating that they were the work of a young man, and it was important that they should be verified, and requested that it should be done, which was refused. This statement of Mr. Stimers is flatly denied by Mr. Lenthall.

Mr. Stimers also states, that according to orders, he consulted with Mr. Ericsson in regard to the plans and alterations and additions to the original plan, and also consulted, or endeavored to do so, with the Chief of the Bureau of Steam Engineering, Mr. Isherwood, and the chief of the Bureau of Construction and Repairs, Mr. Lenthall. Mr. Ericsson, while admitting that he was shown many of the plans and drawings prepared under the directions of Mr. Stimers, denies that he was consulted at all, even in regard to those matters which were shown to him. And Mr. Lenthall and Mr. Isherwood deny that they were ever consulted by Mr. Stimers in regard to these light-draught monitors.

The defect in the speed was caused mainly by the increased draught of those vessels ; the principal difficulty being caused by the immersion of the overhang protecting the rudder, which prevented the screw from properly operating, in consequence of its being partially enclosed in a box under the water. Some of the witnesses attribute some of the lack of speed to the engines not being such as should have been put in those vessels.

The fact having been fully established that those vessels, as originally planned and constructed, failed to accomplish the purpose for which they were designed, your committee have not deemed it necessary to take testimony in regard to all the details, nor in their report to refer to all the details which appear in the testimony.

It is due to Engineer Stimers to state that his duties as general inspector and superintendent of the construction of monitors and iron-clads were very arduous. He says:

"I had to visit Boston, Philadelphia, Chester, Pennsylvania, and Wilmington, Delaware, besides a great many places about New York. There were new vessels also being built in Cincinnati and Pittsburg, although I did not visit there until some time after that; but there was a great deal of correspondence growing up, making out all these new contracts, teaching civilian inspectors what their duties were, and learning what were the views of the Navy Department, and of Captain Ericsson. I was consequently occupied pretty closely."

He does not appear to have been influenced by any desire other than to make as serviceable vessels as possible. A misunderstanding arose between him and Mr. Ericsson, which led Mr. Ericsson to deny any responsibility in the matter, and for some reason there was an unfriendly feeling towards Mr. Stimers upon the part of the chief of the Bureau of Steam Engineering and the chief of the Bureau of Construction and Repairs. Mr. Stimers states that he always regarded those officers as inimical to the construction of iron-clad vessels. He says:

"I always felt that it was a regular fight—that we had to conquer them before we could get them to do anything. On the one side it was a fight with the bureaus, and on the other side it was a fight with the contractors, to make them do anything right. It was a very unpleasant position which I held."

On the other hand those officers deny that they either had or have now any unfriendly feelings towards monitor or iron-clad vessels, but express a very poor opinion of Mr. Stimers.

When it was found that these vessels were failures as originally designed and constructed, Mr. Stimers was removed from the position he had held in relation to them, and they were placed in charge of other officers, and altered as recommended by the commission appointed to examine them. The five changed into torpedo boats were altered at a cost of from $50,000 to $60,000 each; the other fifteen were altered at a cost of from $80,000 to $100,000 each. With these alterations they would appear to be a very serviceable class of vessels, though not so serviceable as they should be, considering the expenditure of time and money upon their construction, except those fitted up as torpedo boats, which are of but little utility.

Your committee cannot refrain from the expression of the opinion that it was unwise to order the construction of so many vessels upon precisely the same plan, without first testing the questions involved, by the construction of one or two, or at least carrying them so far forward towards completion as to enable the department to understand and remedy the defects which have been shown to exist in those light-draught monitors.

Respectfully submitted.

B. F. WADE,
Chairman.

LIGHT-DRAUGHT MONITORS

NAVY DEPARTMENT, *December* 15, 1864.

SIR: In conformity with your verbal request of yesterday, I have the honor to submit, for the use of the Committee on the Conduct of the War, a few hasty notes on the light-draught monitors. As the war progressed and assumed greater proportions, and our armies penetrated into the interior of the rebel territory, the navy occupied and patrolled the great rivers and the numerous estuaries, but the class of vessels that of necessity performed this work and protected the army communications were found to be insufficient or unsuitable for the duty. They were wooden boats of light draught, purchased from the merchant service; their machinery, boilers and magazines were above the water-line, and their crews had no protection whatever against sharpshooters hiding behind trees upon the river bank. This necessitated the building up of light iron bulwarks (the vessels were too frail to carry anything heavier) as a protection against musketry. The enemy, however, found many high points upon their inland waters where they could plant batteries of artillery, which looked down upon the gunboats, and were consequently out of reach of their heavy guns. Gallant attempts to attack such batteries, to pass them, and to keep open the army lines of communication, were attended with many fatal disasters and a loss somewhat of the prestige of the gunboats. From every squadron and flotilla the department was called upon for a light-draught iron-clad vessel that should be able to resist the ordnance used by the rebels. The urgency of the demand, and the painful accidents and disasters constantly occurring, could not be treated with indifference. An invulnerable vessel of light-draught not only had never been attempted, but an extended inquiry seemed to forbid the consideration of the subject. Nevertheless, the inventor of the Monitor, at the request of the department, and after several weeks' consideration of the subject, proposed a general plan of a monitor, to draw about six feet and four inches of water, to have a single iron turret eight inches thick, with two eleven-inch guns, and to be otherwise well protected against the projectiles used by the rebels. The department would have been glad to have been spared from further experiments in the unexplored fields which the necessities of this war forced it to tread, but it did not shrink from the responsibility which attaches to radical measures, although neither the past nor the present afforded any light to guide it. The rebel government furnishes an example of perseverance and faith in the construction of iron-clad vessels, which is probably due to the fact that opposition and investigation are silenced in that section of our country. Wherever their iron-clads have appeared, they have been defeated or destroyed: the Merrimack by the Monitor; the Atlanta by the Weehawken; the Tennessee by Rear-Admiral Farragut's fleet; the Louisiana and Mississippi, with six or seven semi-iron-clads, when Rear-Admiral Farragut captured New Orleans; one up the Yazoo, and two up the Red river, to prevent their falling into Rear-Admiral Porter's hands; the Arkansas by the Essex; several half iron-clads by the flotilla of Acting Rear-Admiral Davis at Memphis; the Chattahooche blown up in the Appalachicola river, and the Albemarle sunk by Lieutenant Cushing. Notwithstanding the invariable and fatal disasters attending these vessels, which are of the same type, the rebels are known to have quite a number now under construction on the rivers and at the few ports remaining in their possession.

The department accepted the general plan of Captain Ericsson, but his offer to build was declined. The law requires that advertisements shall be issued, and contracts given to the lowest bidder. The elaboration of the plan of Captain Ericsson and the preparation of the drawings and specifications were confided to Chief Engineer Stimers, who was instructed to consult with and follow the directions of that gentleman. Chief Engineer Stimers had been associated with Captain Ericsson in the construction of the original Monitor, and took passage in that vessel to Hampton roads as a volunteer, at a time when many of our engineers and constructors predicted that she would never be heard of again. It was owing to his zeal and skill and faith that all the engines of that vessel performed their functions during that memorable contest with the Merrimack, and from that field he was transferred to New York as general superintendent of iron-clads under construction. Chief Engineer Stimers is responsible for the detailed drawings of the light-draught monitors, and for the calculations as to their displacement. It was expected that they would not draw over six and a half feet of water, and be out of water amidships about fifteen inches. The contracts were made generally in the spring of 1863, and the vessels were to have been finished in the fall of that year. The last contracts made for vessels of this class were in June, 1863. The Chimo, at Boston, was the first one finished. She was under the entire direction of Chief Engineer Stimers. Instead of being fifteen inches out of water, she was only three on an average, showing a miscalculation of twelve inches. The department immediately removed Mr. Stimers from the position of general superintendent, and placed the question as to what should be done to remedy the difficulties occasioned by his error in the hands of Rear-Admiral Gregory, Chief Engineer Wood, and Captain Ericsson. As Rear-Admiral Dahlgren and Acting Rear-Admiral Lee had asked for several monitors to be fitted with torpedo arrangements, without turrets, the gentlemen to whom the matter had been submitted determined that the five most advanced of the light-draught monitors should be fitted to meet the wants of Rear-Admiral Dahlgren and Acting Rear-Admiral Lee, and that all the others, fifteen in number, should have their sides built up fifteen inches higher, in the same manner that the roof of a house is raised, and an additional half story put on. This will give those fifteen vessels 130 tons each more capacity, and a draught of a little less than eight feet. Of course the cost is increased, but not much out of proportion to the increased capacity. Vessels that are built from ten to fifteen feet out of water are insensible to an error of a foot in the draught, though it is not unusual with engine builders to find themselves under the necessity of raising their shafting to remedy such errors; but in steamers calculated to be only fifteen inches above the water, a foot of error is fatal. A simpler and cheaper craft would have been a casemated vessel like the rebel iron-clads; but such a vessel on shore in the inland waters is helpless, whereas a turreted vessel discharges her guns towards every point of the compass, whether aground or not. This was exemplified when the Osage, a light-draught turreted steamer, got aground in Red river in April last. She was attacked, while in this position, by a large force under the rebel General Greene, whose command was entirely cut to pieces, with the loss of their general, in the insane attempt to capture a monitor, although hard and fast aground.

The foregoing is a brief summary of what I should testify to before your committee. The whole subject has given the Secretary much anxiety, but the department cannot be justly held responsible for anything more than correct ideas. Mechanical details belong to those permanent officers whose specialty it is to put into practical operation such vessels as the exigency of the war forces the department to adopt.

I am, very respectfully, &c.,

G. V. FOX,
Assistant Secretary of the Navy

Hon. B. F. WADE,
Chairman Committee on the Conduct of the War, U. S. Senate.

TESTIMONY TAKEN AT BOSTON, MASSACHUSETTS.

BOSTON, MASS., *Tuesday, December* 20, 1864.

W. L. HANSCOM, sworn and examined.

By Mr. Gooch:

Question. Please state your place of residence and present occupation.

Answer. I reside in Boston. I am naval constructor at the Charlestown yard, and have been there a little over five years.

Question. Where were you stationed before that?

Answer. At the Kittery navy yard.

Question. For how long a time?

Answer. I was there about six years as naval constructor.

Question. Have you ever constructed any ships that you modelled yourself?

Answer. Yes, sir.

Question. How many, and what were their names?

Answer. The Mohican and Kearsarge, (which are both of the same model,) the Canandaigua, the Genesee, the Tioga, the Maratanza, the Monadnoc, an iron-clad, and others.

Question. Will you state to the committee what you know in relation to the light-draught iron-clad monitors, or gunboats, as they are called.

Answer. My attention was first directed to these vessels upon the trial trip of the Chimo. A few days previous to that time the opinion had been circulated that that one, at any rate, was to be a failure, and that there were 19 others precisely like the Chimo. Two or three days after she made her trial trip I went and examined her. She was afloat then, and minus her powder, shot and shell. I took the height of the top of the plating at the side of the vessel above the water at that time. On the starboard side it was out 1 inch; on the port side, $3\frac{3}{4}$ inches—making a mean height above the water of $2\frac{3}{8}$ inches. The stern was under water 1 inch, and the stem was out of water 7 inches.

By Mr. Wade:

Question. Had she a turret on then?

Answer. Yes, sir; her turret was on, the guns were in the turret, the pilot-house was on—in fact, she was very nearly completed—but had not her powder, shot, or shell on board, and probably some 15 or 20 tons of coal less than her regular amount.

By Mr. Gooch:

Question. What effect would the addition of her full amount of coal, shell, &c., have had upon her?

Answer. It would have carried her down about five inches, in my opinion and that would have brought the top of the plating at the side about three inches below the water. The tortoise back would have been just above the water. Rather a small margin for a man to go to sea with.

Question. Could the boat have been used for any purpose, as she was?

Answer. I don't think she could—that is to say, out of the harbor. While she was riding at the wharf the guns could have been fired on board of her, without any danger of her going down.

Question. Could she have been used even for harbor defence?

Answer. She was scarcely fitted for that, being so far under water as to be unsafe.

By Mr. Wade:

Question. What was her speed?

Answer. I was informed that it was a little less than four knots at that time.

By Mr. Gooch:

Question. Do you know how much it was intended that those boats should be out of water when finished, with their full armament and all their equipments on board?

Answer. My impression is, that it was intended to have the top of the plating at the side above the water 15 inches. I saw, on one of their drawings, a line drawn to represent the water, and I measured that, and found it to be 15 inches below the top of the plating.

Question. These vessels were built with water compartments?

Answer. Yes, sir.

Question. What was the object of that?

Answer. The object was to sink the vessel down and protect the sides in case of an engagement.

Question. Would it have been a useful arrangement in the event that the vessel had been as high out of the water as it was intended?

Answer. I think it would.

Question. But in these vessels it was entirely unnecessary?

Answer. It was entirely unnecessary.

By Mr. Wade:

Question. I will ask you, as a naval constructor, is there any difficulty in ascertaining how much a vessel of given dimensions will be out of water when it is completed, supposing you build it with a view to have it of a certain height above the water? Are there any rules by which vessels can be constructed so as to be a certain height above the water?

Answer. Yes, sir; there are rules by which we can determine very closely the draught of water of the vessel if we know at the commencement the weight that is to be taken on board.

Question. In ordinary ship-building is there any rule as to what proportion of the ship, when loaded, should be out of water?

Answer. We lay it down as a fixed principle, that one-third part of the entire capacity must be above the load line for safety in a sea-going vessel.

Question. Suppose that the rule is not observed, or that there is any considerable variation from it, one way or the other, what will be the effect?

Answer. In proportion to the deviation from that rule, we risk the safety of the vessel, whether it be more or less above the water.

Question. Well, when the contractor knows precisely what his loading is to consist of, or how much burden the vessel is to carry, would it be gross negligence for him to deviate, say a foot, from the design?

Answer. It would.

Question. Do you know what pains were taken to ascertain as to the construction of these vessels?

Answer. I do not, sir.

Question. I will ask you whether there would have been much difficulty in ascertaining how much this vessel would be out of water, the parties knowing what they were to build and what they were to carry?

Answer. No, sir. There was less obstruction, so to speak, in the way of ascertaining accurately the weight of the ship than there is with wooden vessels, for the weight of different kinds of iron does not vary so much as that of different kinds of wood. In their specific gravity they are almost invariably the same.

Question. You say, Mr. Hanscom, that these vessels were faulty. Can you describe in what the difficulty consists?

Answer. It may be summed up in want of capacity to sustain the great weight. The fault was in not ascertaining the weight of the vessel and the capacity of the displacement. It might have been one of these only. They might have ascertained the exact weight of the vessel, and failed to discover the exact displacement; or they might have made an error in both particulars.

Question. Is it practicable, in boats built on this principle, to make them so that they will have the ordinary speed?

Answer. I think it might be done.

Question. How should that be done—by the engines or by the build of the vessels?

Answer. By the proper engines and the proper form of the vessel, both.

Question. Was the plan of this description of vessel unknown to naval constructors?

Answer. It was a new thing to naval constructors. The form of the bottom was not new to naval constructors. All of them must have seen vessels of a similar form.

Question. Could they be improved for any warlike purpose by divesting them of their turrets?

Answer. That would bring them out of the water, and it would be possible to move them with greater safety from one port to another.

Question. But could they be worked in action without exposing the men to being picked off by sharpshooters?

Answer. No, sir, they could not. The men are exposed without the turret, and the vessels are hardly fit for war purposes without the turrets.

Question. What would be the effect of building the sides up fifteen inches?

Answer. That would raise them some above the water, and it would increase the draught.

Question. How much, in your judgment, would it increase the draught?

Answer. The additional weight would not increase the draught over two inches.

Question. Then they would be able to bear the turrets, and work with them?

Answer. Yes, sir, but the draught would be increased beyond what was seemingly first intended.

Question. Can they, in your judgment, be made useful vessels by building up in this way?

Answer. Something may be done with them if they are raised up. In their present condition nothing can be done with them in the way of fighting. There may be some rivers or harbors where these vessels may be very useful.

Question. Would they ever be sea-going boats?

Answer. No, sir; they would be dangerous at sea.

Question. What would be the effect of a storm on such a vessel at sea; would it swamp her?

Answer. The tendency would be to break her in pieces amidships. The great strain upon the rivets in the thin iron would be apt to break them, or tear the iron out. The reason of that is, that they have not the strength sufficient to sustain them when the support is changed from the middle to the end. The iron-clad that I am building is tied up by bands of iron running from top to bottom, to sustain her when the support is changed from end to end. That may be illustrated by putting a board into the water; while it is on its edge it won't break. In other words, the relative strength is as the distance from the circumference to the centre.

Question. If I have understood you, Mr. Hanscom, you consider these vessels, as originally draughted and built, a failure?

Answer. I do.

Question. And that in that condition they would be utterly useless as war vessels?

Answer. Yes, sir.

Question. And you say you think they might be made of some use by altering them as it is now proposed to alter them?

Answer. Yes, sir, that is so. I think that by raising them up 22 inches, as I understand it is proposed to do, they may be serviceable in some particular cases.

Question. I will inquire of you now whether contracts have been made with the government for the alteration of them all?

Answer. I have understood that to be the case.

Question. Are you informed of the progress that has been made in the construction of these vessels?

Answer. I am not. I think there is one—the Squando—which is very nearly completed.

Question. Do you know with whom the contracts were originally made?

Answer. I do not.

Question. Who planned the models of these light-draught monitors?

Answer. I can only tell that from hearsay.

Question. What is your understanding about it?

Answer. I have heard it stated that Mr. Stimers and Captain Ericsson got them up; then some alterations were suggested which Captain Ericsson would not agree to.

Question. By whom were those suggestions made?

Answer. I have heard that they were made by Mr. Stimers.

Question. Did you understand that they were built according to their suggestions?

Answer. Yes, sir.

Question. Do you understand that all the vessels constructed are to be of a model similar to that of the Chimo?

Answer. I understand that to be so.

Question. As a prudent naval constructor, would you advise the altering of all these monitors in the way the Squando is being altered, or would it be better to try the experiment on some few of them first, to see what purpose they would answer?

Answer. I should recommend that one be tried before the others are completed.

Question. Is there any doubt in your mind as to the entire success of this altered one?

Answer. Well, I don't know what would be called success. They would not be very good; they would not have much speed; they would not be very light draught; they would not be very well protected from the enemy's shot, because the sides are too thin, and the deck too rounding, offering a surface at right angles with the line of fire. If we are to consider all these things, I should say that they would be imperfect vessels, after they were completed, even by raising the deck 22 inches.

Question. And you would not have sufficient confidence to go on and finish them all until you had tried some?

Answer. No, sir.

By Mr. Odell:

Question. What is the character of the alterations now being made on the Chimo?

Answer. The turret has been removed, and a gun has been placed on a platform laid upon the deck, to be used without any protection to the men. Some other alterations have been made, but I do not know the extent of them.

Question. What is your opinion of the value of the boat, with the intended alterations, when completed?

Answer. As a fighting vessel, she will possess very little value. It is proposed to make a torpedo boat of the Chimo, but with the little speed she has, she will be very unsuitable for that, and her value is very little.

By Mr. Wade:

Question. And to put her to this use would be an entire change from her original design, would it not?

Answer. Yes, sir.

By Mr. Odell:

Question, Is there a distinct class of vessels known as torpedo boats?

Answer. Yes, sir.

Question. What are their peculiarities?

Answer. They are much smaller than these light-draught monitors, and possess considerable speed. I think I can give you very nearly the size. The length is about 75 feet, beam about 15 feet, and depth about 7 feet. That forms a distinct class of boats.

By Mr. Wade?

Question. What is the speed of such boats generally?

Answer. I understand that they go eight knots an hour. I have heard that the one that went from Mystic, Connecticut, made eight knots, and believe it to be so.

By Mr. Odell:

Question. What would be the proportionate cost of the two boats?

Answer. A regular torpedo boat, such a boat as is known by that name now, might cost about one-tenth the price of one of these monitors.

Question. How many of these vessels are being altered to torpedo boats?

Answer. I have understood, six. The Secretary's report tells the exact number.

Question. You have already stated that, in your judgment, a torpedo boat would cost about one-tenth what these boats cost: would a regular torpedo boat be equally efficient for the purpose?

Answer. I should think it would be more efficient, being much more easily handled, and having greater speed; and, furthermore, it would not be so easily seen in the night time.

By Mr. Gooch:

Question. Are not these boats altogether too large to be used successfully as topedo boats?

Answer. They are much larger than I would build for that purpose if I was directed to build a torpedo boat?

Question. Will you state what would be considered an unreasonable deviation from the estimate in relation to the draught of these vessels?

Answer. Anything more than three inches would, if it was fully known at the commencement of the design what was the weight to go on board.

Question. Then, if the vessel varied more than three inches in her draught of water, you would say that there had been a gross error in the calculations?

Answer. Yes, sir, if it was the intention to obtain a specified draught of water; and in this case it was absolutely necessary for the success of the boats to meet that expectation of a certain draught.

Question. These boats, when now completed, will draw nearly two feet more than it was contemplated they should draw, will they not?

Answer. They will draw at least twenty inches more than was contemplated at the commencement of the work.

Question. If these boats had been so constructed as to have drawn any more water than it was originally designed they should draw, could they have been used for any other purpose except for harbor and river defence, or on smooth water?

Answer. No, sir, I think not; they are not sea-going vessels by any means.

Question. How much is the speed of a boat diminished in consequence of her being fifteen inches lower in the water than was contemplated?

Answer. That is very difficult to tell. My impression is that these vessels fall nearly one-half short of the expected speed. Comparing the Chimo with the Casco, finished with the turret off, I find that the speed of the Chimo is diminished about one-fifth.

Question. How much is the Casco out of water, or what is her draught?

Answer. I have not measured that. I judge that she is out now about twenty inches.

Question. Then she is out of water as much as it was contemplated she should be?

Answer. A little more; but she has no gun, or powder, shot, or shell on board.

Question. Then, with the same engines, even if these vessels had been out of the water as much as was contemplated, their speed would not have exceeded five knots an hour?

Answer. I don't think it could. The speed of all these vessels will not be the same, because much will depend on the friction of the machinery.

Question. Judging from the tests that have been made of these boats, you think their speed could not exceed five knots an hour, even if they had been so constructed as to comply with the original conditions?

Answer. Yes, sir. I don't think it could have gone over five knots in any case?

By Mr. Odell:

Question. You consider that one of the failures of these boats consists in lack of speed?

Answer. Yes, sir

Question. Could that have been regulated by different propelling power?

Answer. I think it could.

Question. That is one of the mistakes in the boats?

Answer. Yes, sir; that helps to complete the failure.

By Mr. Gooch:

Question. Won't you state what you deem to be the defects of these boats, so far as you have discovered them?

Answer. Among the different points that constitute the failure are, want of speed, want of a proper construction of the bottom of the vessel, the thickness of the side armor, and the roundness of deck.

Question. The model of the boat remaining the same, can the weight be reduced so as to make this, in your judgment, a serviceable boat?

Answer. No, sir.

By Mr. Wade :

Question. I will inquire whether, in your judgment, a skilful constructor could have built these boats originally, so as to have complied with the designs of the Navy Department?

Answer. I think he could.

Question. State whether you constructed the Monadnock, so called?

Answer. I did.

Question. What are her tonnage and speed?

Answer. The tonnage is 1,564; the speed is variously estimated from nine to eleven knots.

Question. Is she a turreted boat?

Answer. She has two turrets and four 15-inch guns, with two pilot-houses on top of the turrets.

Question. When was she finished?

Answer She was reported ready for sea on the 1st of October, but did not get off until about the 8th.

Question. Do you recollect her draught of water, with all her loading on board, equipped for the voyage?

Answer. It was about twelve feet.

Question. By nautical men is she deemed a success or not?

Answer. I believe she is deemed a success in every way, for that class of vessels. I will state a few facts in regard to her. I received an order to build a vessel of wood, to be plated with iron, to carry four 15-inch guns, with a certain number of men, 300 tons of coal, provisions for a certain length of time, and machinery to weigh so much, the draught of water not to exceed twelve feet, and the vessel to be from eighteen inches to two feet out of water when ready for sea. The plating was to be five inches on the side, and an inch and a half on deck. The turrets were to be ten inches thick, twenty-one feet inside diameter, with pilot-houses on the tops of the turrets. After the vessel was commenced I was notified that parties in Philadelphia were to construct the engines and machinery, and that they were referred to me for any information in regard to the location of the machinery, length of shaft, and form of the vessel. I received a letter from these parties, however, requesting me to meet them in New York to determine upon the position of the turrets and the machinery, and the general arrangement. It was impossible for me at that time to leave the yard on account of the multiplicity of business, but my brother, who was stationed at the Kittery navy yard, and had the building of another of these vessels, met this party in New York, representing himself and me. They came to some conclusion in regard to the location of the turrets and the machinery, and the general arrangement. But while they were doing that, I drew a plan of the position of the turrets and the machinery, and the general arrangements of the ship; and when he returned I received from these parties in Philadelphia a sketch showing the conclusions they had come to, which did not meet my views at all; and in reply I sent them a sketch of my plan, with instructions to follow it, as the whole thing at that time seemed to rest upon me. They replied to that, stating that they regretted that I had come to such conclusions; that they were very objectionable, and that, inasmuch as they had no authority in the case, they would have no responsibilty; and, in conclusion, they regretted that their machinery would not have a fair test by being so arranged.

Question. Is the speed of the Monadnock in consequence of the superiority of the engines over the iron-clad you have heretofore described, or is it owing to the construction of the boat?

Answer. I think it is in part due to both. I think the engines are very excellent, very well contrived, and work free from friction; and that the form of the boat offers less resistance, in proportion to the displacement, than these little light-draught monitors.

Question. What do you say of the engines of this light-draught monitor that made only five miles an hour?

Answer. I have not examined them closely, but there seems to be a fault in those engines. The size of those engines would seem to allow us to hope for more speed than they have attained.

Question. May not this account for the slowness of the vessel, instead of it being attributable to the build of the vessel?

Answer. I think a large proportion of the hindrance to speed is to be attributed to that. The position of the propeller is not the very best to give speed. A certain portion of the arm of the propeller is in a box, and of course that adds nothing towards propelling the boat.

AQUILA ADAMS sworn and examined.

By Mr. Wade:

Question. Are you acquainted with any of the light-draught monitors that have been built in this vicinity?

Answer. I am not acquainted with any except the one I built myself.

Question. What is the name of that?

Answer. The Chimo.

Question. Please to state what time the contract for that was made.

Answer. Either in March or April; I think March, 1863.

Question. What were to be her dimensions and draught of water?

Answer. I do not recollect precisely, but I will state as near as I recollect, if that will answer your purpose. She was to be 225 feet in length, have 45 feet beam, and to draw 6 feet 6 inches.

Question. Was she to be an iron-clad monitor, with a turret?

Answer. Yes, sir.

Question. State whether you built her on that plan.

Answer. I built her for that purpose; that is, for the purpose of a light-draught monitor.

Question. Did you build her according to any plan furnished by any body?

Answer. Yes, sir; I built her according to plans and specifications furnished by the general inspector, Mr. Stimers.

Question. Did he see her from time to time, as you were at work on her?

Answer. Yes, sir.

Question. Did she correspond, as you were at work on her, with his views?

Answer. Yes, sir, as near as a thing of that nature could.

Question. When you had finished and launched her, what were her appearance and condition?

Answer. Well, immediately after she was launched, that is, previous to her having her turret on, or her pilot-house, and with some of her deck-plating not yet on, it was thought that she drew more water than was anticipated, but they had not sufficient data at that time to tell positively whether that was the case or not.

Question. Without these things on board, how much of her was out of water?

Answer. When she was launched, I think she was thirty-seven inches out forward and nineteen aft.

Question. How much was she out after you got on her turret and when she was fitted for sea?

Answer. I think that when we went on our trial trip her stern was from three to four inches under water; that is to say, the water came up on the crown. Her bow was in the neighborhood of eight inches out of water; that is to say, she was a little by the stern, owing to having her coal on board—that is, aft amidships, and putting that on board sent one end down a little and the other up a little; but as her ammunition is to be stored forward, she could have been trimmed with that, and would probably have been on an even keel if that had been on board.

Question. Where would that have brought her?

Answer. I should think that might have brought her pretty well down even with the water with that amount of coal on board.

Question. Was her turret on at this time?

Answer. Yes, sir; everything complete ready for sea, with the exception of her ammunition. I won't say everything; for instance, her boats were not lashed up in place; they might weigh a ton or two tons; but she was reported ready for sea.

Question. What would a proper supply of ammunition for that vessel weigh?

Answer. Somewhere about forty or fifty tons. That is something that the Navy Department decides. Of course that is optional with the party going with the boat. When she was completed, the captain reported the fact, and that he was ready to go to sea in her.

Question. Was the trial trip a successful one?

Answer. Well, that would depend upon what you might call success. She did not come up to the anticipated speed, and she drew more water than they had calculated upon.

Question. How much water did she draw at that time?

Answer. I should think she drew ten inches more than was calculated. This is from memory, you know, and I cannot speak accurately, having no data; and it is all so close, that a very little variation would sink her.

Question. Well, sir, was she in a condition to go from one harbor to another safely, with all her load on board?

Answer. I expressed a willingness at that time to go on from Boston to New York in her, and so did the captain and all my officers and men.

Question. Do you consider that she would have been seaworthy when thus loaded?

Answer. I should not consider that she would have been seaworthy in very rough weather. In rough weather we should have made a port, provided we had undertaken to go round that way. That was the intention.

Question. She was not in a condition, then, to stand ordinary rough weather?

Answer. No, sir.

Question. If she was really a vessel that could go round and do business, why did they want to alter her?

Answer. That I don't know. That was not a matter within our control or province to ask any questions about it.

Question. Are you a naval constructor?

Answer. No, sir.

Question. What is your business in relation to ships?

Answer. Well, before I built this one, I built marine engines and stationary engines. Before the war broke out my business was confined almost exclusively to Cuba.

Question. Then you are not a naval architect?

Answer. No, sir.

Question. If I understand you, you differ from Mr. Hanscom in his idea that the vessel was really of no use before she was built up?

Answer. As I understand him, he does not believe she is of use as a torpedo boat.

Question. He didn't believe she could be of use as a monitor, did he?

Answer. No; I think he had an idea that she could not be used as a monitor as she was when completed.

Question. Well, your opinion is, if I understand you, that she could be?

Answer. I think she could have been used as such for harbor and river defence; that is, I think she could have been used here in this harbor.

Question. Your opinion is, that they are making a great mistake in changing them?

Answer. No, sir; I don't think so.

Question. Well, do you believe the Chimo will answer the purpose that it was designed these monitors should answer, without any change or alteration?

Answer. I think she would answer in the harbor where she was constructed, but I don't think her suitable to go from harbor to harbor, or from river to river.

Question. But why did you and your whole crew agree to go on her so willingly, if you don't think she is a proper vessel for that purpose?

Answer. I don't think she is a proper sea vessel, but I think she could have made the voyage, and was willing to take that risk on account of the occasion. They seemed to want her, and had made great efforts to get her done.

Question. Have they used her since she was finished?

Answer. No, sir; she is not completed. You understand that she was completed as a monitor first.

Question. You say they wanted her very much. Why, then, didn't they use her?

Answer. I imagine that they didn't consider her seaworthy, and didn't consider it safe to risk that property in going between harbor and harbor. I think it was a wise precaution; but, at the same time, I felt willing to risk myself on her.

Question. What speed did she make?

Answer. On the trial trip, I think she made $3\frac{3}{4}$ knots.

Question. Was that as much as was expected of her when she was constructed?

Answer. No, sir. All I know in regard to what was expected of her is what I have heard, from time to time, among engineers.

Question. What did they think she would make?

Answer. It was variously estimated from five to seven knots. Some have gone as high as eight knots; but very few.

Question. What are you doing with her now?

Answer. Well, we are making a torpedo boat of her.

Question. Is it not necessary that a torpedo boat should have considerable speed, and be so far seagoing as to be safe in going from harbor to harbor?

Answer. She is safe now. The removal of the turret and pilot-house raises her perhaps twenty inches out of the water. The Casco, which has been changed in the same way, has succeeded in going from here to New York, making a speed, as I have understood, of five knots an hour. I consider the Chimo safe now.

Question. Do you consider her any better for the purpose of a torpedo boat than the ordinary boats built for that purpose?

Answer. I don't think she is so good for that purpose.

Question. How much does it cost to build a good and efficient torpedo boat?

Answer. Well, such a boat as I have heard Mr. Wood has designed and is getting up I should say would cost somewhere from seventy thousand to eighty thousand dollars.

Question. What is the cost of this monitor?

Answer. Well, the original contract price was, I think, three hundred and ninety-five thousand dollars. But they have made changes in her since they first started, as we have gone along, and it is a question yet to be decided how much they are to allow for the changes they have made; that is, for the deviations from the understanding of what she was to be.

Question. How have they changed the vessel from the original contract?

Answer. They have added a number of things. There is quite a list of them. I could better give you that list at some other time. If I gave you one now, it would be only a partial one.

Question. About how much should you think the cost of these deviations from the original plan would be?

Answer. I should think it would be one hundred thousand dollars.

Question. And still, with all her alterations, she is good for nothing, as I understand you, for the original purpose designed?

Answer. She is good for nothing for the original purpose designed. That I understand to be the decision of the head ones at Washington, and therefore they say, "Change her."

Question. And, in your judgment, she is not equal, as a torpedo boat, to a boat that would cost seventy thousand or eighty thousand dollars?

Answer. No, sir. I would state, however, that this boat will carry a gun on her deck, which a torpedo boat would not.

Question. Would it be of much use to have a gun on deck, the gunners being entirely exposed to sharpshooters, and every danger of that kind?

Answer. Well, it has always appeared to me a very singular idea to have an iron-clad boat with a gun exposed.

Question. That would be the case with this, however.

Answer. Yes, sir; that is the case with this. But what they design to use the boat for I don't know. I don't even know the design they intend to use for firing the torpedo, or anything of that kind. They give me my ideas of what I am to do from time to time.

Question. You are the mere builder of the ship, according to the plans and directions of some other person?

Answer. Yes, sir.

Question. And that person was Mr. Stimers?

Answer. Yes, sir. It was to him that I looked for instructions.

Question. So you do not profess skill in the construction of ships?

Answer. No, sir.

Question. Only in building them according to plans furnished?

Answer. Yes, sir.

Question. To what do you attribute the slowness of the Chimo?

Answer. Well, I attribute her slowness to her increased draught.

Question. And your opinion is that, had she been built according to the design of the department, she might have performed better?

Answer. My opinion is that had she been built according to the original intentions in regard to her—that is, the first ideas—she would have made more speed.

Question. If you can recapitulate now some of the alterations or deviations from the original contract or design, I would like to have some of the most essential ones, to see what it was that they altered her for from time to time.

Answer. Well, one pretty important change was putting in additional cross-floors, as they are called; in other words, strengthening the bottom of the ship by adding cross-floors and kelsons.

Question. What would be the expense of that, and how far would it increase the weight?

Answer. That I don't recollect; it was a year and a half ago, and I don't recollect much about that, only I know the fact that the change was made. Then another important change was the addition of a large and heavy wrought-iron ring to the bottom of the turret—a ring something like fifteen inches wide and five inches thick, and, I should think, from a rough estimate, it might weigh fifteen or eighteen tons. That one item would sink her an inch, if I am right in the weight, and I think I am. Then they added two inches to the thickness of the pilot-house, and added to the height of those two thicknesses; that is to say, those two thicknesses were carried up higher than the original pilot-house. That added to her weight considerably. Then it was originally intended that the engines should have cast-iron frames. Instead of having cast-iron frames they were ordered to be made of wrought-iron.

Question. That was an additional expense, I suppose?

Answer. An additional expense, but not much addition to the weight, as near as I can recollect. Then there was an addition of about twenty per cent., I think, to her condensing surface. Then it was originally designed to put in the Worthington pumps, as they are called, but it was finally decided not to put them in, and they gave us a design for a pump. That added very much to the cost and to the weight. There were one or two iron bulkheads added, which are the partitions that go across the vessel. Iron was substituted for wood, I think.

Question. What was the object of that—to give her additional strength?

Answer. Yes, sir; to give her additional strength. A wooden one, of the same strength, would have been heavier, I think.

Question. But an iron one would cost the most, would it not?

Answer. Yes, sir.

Question. It is said that Captain Ericsson and Mr. Stimers disagreed about something in regard to the construction of this vessel. Do you know how that was?

Answer. No, sir, I do not. The only thing I know about it is this: in completing the ship I asked if I should say built by so-and-so, and designed by Mr. Stimers? No, Mr. Stimers said, I should not say that, because they were not designed by him, but that I might write Captain Ericsson for instructions about it. I had never corresponded with Captain Ericsson, and knew no more about him than I did about the man in the moon; but at that time Mr. Stimers disowned the design, as he had once or twice before.

Question. Did your contract include the engines?

Answer. Yes, sir, everything; I built the ship complete, machinery and all.

Question. Do you know of any defect in the engines of this boat?

Answer. No, sir; I do not know of any defect in the design.

Question. Had the engines sufficient power to work well?

Answer. Yes, sir; I think less boiler would have answered, and that would have lightened the ship.

Question. Would it not have weakened the power of the engines?

Answer. It would have weakened the power of the engines, provided the boiler could not have supplied all the steam necessary. But the fact is that there were thirteen engines on board of her—that is, what we should call thirteen engines; they were not all independent. In other words, two engines drove a pump; two other engines drove a pump; another engine drove a pump another engine drove another pump; another engine drove another pump; and we used two engines for turning the turret, and two engines for turning the blowers.

Question. Is that so on all these turreted iron-clads?

Answer. Yes, sir; there is an immense amount of machinery on board of them. Now, then, there might be a case when we should want to run all these engines at the same time. Such a contingency might occur, and then we should want all the steam the boiler could supply; but it is not a contingency that would be very likely to occur. If the ship sprung a leak, for instance, it might be necessary to run all the engines possible, but it is very doubtful. At any rate the vessel had two pumps, each of them capable of taking out three thousand gallons a minute.

Question. Had she more of these engines than are ordinarily used in such a ship?

Answer. About the same number, sir, as in vessels of the monitor class.

Question. Was her boiler larger than is usual in the same kind of ships?

Answer. I have no data to make that assertion upon, but that is my impression.

By Mr. Gooch:

Question. You say the monitor was completed and made a trial trip. Since then you have been directed by the government to make alterations. Are you making those alterations for a sum agreed upon, or are you to be paid what they cost?

Answer. I am to be paid what they cost.

Question. Can you tell us what they will cost?

Answer. I cannot, sir.

Question. Can you approximate it?

Answer. Yes, sir, I can approximate it; I should think they might cost in the neighborhood of $50,000; I should think more.

Question. How long is it since you first commenced making these alterations?

Answer. I think I commenced about June.

Question. Could you in that time, if the government needed a torpedo boat, have constructed one and finished it?

Answer. Just about.

Question. So that the government, if it had desired a torpedo boat, could have had it in less time than it could have these alterations made?

Answer. Provided this boat was done, I think I could have built a new torpedo boat, having had this experience, in the time that I have been making this change.

Question. How much longer will it take you to complete the change, so that your boat will be ready for service?

Answer. Ten days, or a fortnight, perhaps.

Question. In your judgment will not this boat be totally worthless as a torpedo boat?

Answer. Well, as I understand, or as I form an opinion of what a torpedo boat should be, I think she is entirely useless.

Question. And being useless for a torpedo boat, can you conceive any purpose for which she can possibly be used?

Answer. No, sir; I am not much acquainted with the torpedo arrangements any way, but so far as my ideas are concerned, and so far as I have heard others express their ideas, they want something small; something that they can manœuvre readily; something with speed—with such speed as it can have in proportion to its size.

By Mr. Odell:

Question. You made your contract, Mr. Adams, with the Navy Department?

Answer. Yes, sir.

Question. Do you give the government credit for the material you take out of the vessel?

Answer. Everything we take out belongs to the government. Some portions of it have been sold to parties who had not got their boats done. The turret still remains on my place.

Question. Do you understand that your contract price was about the same that was given for the other nineteen?

Answer. Yes, sir; I understand it to be so.

Question. Were the contracts made by bids?

Answer. My impression is that the government called for bids, and then, after studying the matter over, and seeing the variation of the bids, established a price.

Question. Did you make a bid?

Answer. I don't think I did. I have forgotton whether I did or not. I think I took it at their own price.

Question. If you had made a bid, wouldn't you be likely to remember it?

Answer. I made a bid for different machinery at that time, but I don't think I bid for these boats. I think I solicited one of them at their own price.

Question. Do you know who did bid for them?

Answer. No, sir; I don't. I think Mr. Archibald bid, and Merrick & Sons.

Question. As far as you know, have the parties to whom these contracts were originally awarded built these vessels?

Answer. Yes, sir; they have now. There was a boat given out, I think, to a Portland man by the name of Leonard, and he made some arrangement with parties here to build the hull, and he would build the wood-work. The parties here started to build the hull, but the Portland folks thought it was not right, but that, if the department had decided to give one of the boats to Portland, the boat should be built there for the benefit of the place. So the department stopped the work here, and ordered it to be built in Portland; and it was taken down there, and is being built there.

Question. When were you to have this vessel finished?

Answer. I think it was to be done in eight or nine months after the date of the contract. She was done about May, I think.

Question. You contracted to build this vessel, according to the plans and specifications furnished you by Mr. Stimers, for $395,000?

Answer. Yes, sir.

Question. And from those plans you have deviated, from time to time, as he has directed you?

Answer. Yes, sir.

Question. Now I will ask you whether those deviations were made with any stipulation as to cost, or whether you had any agreement with Mr. Stimers as to what they should cost?

Answer. Well, perhaps I had better explain a little. We were furnished with drawings to work by. Now, when we came to make any deviation from what we conceived to be the original idea, we corresponded concerning it, but did not stop work; we kept on at our own risk, following his directions. There were some changes made that we did not know to be changes, and, of course, kept on; but those who had built boats before, similar to them, and understood that these were to be in such and such respects like those they had built before, knew the changes, and perhaps corresponded in relation to them, and perhaps not. At any rate we have tried, from time to time, to get a settlement; to have a full understanding in relation to these extras; but up to the present time have not succeeded in so doing. The matter has been before the board—that is to say, the constructors say, "We consider that such and such things are extra." The board says, "We do not consider such things extra, but we consider such and such things extra, and we will allow you an equitable price for those things." That thing remains to be fully acted upon.

Question. You say some of these things are changes, but you did not know it. How could that be, with the specifications before you?

Answer. The specifications did not go into details; they were changes from the usual manner of building such vessels.

By Mr. Wade:

Question. Then there was no stipulation as to the price of these extras?

Answer. No, sir.

Question. You have received compensation for this vessel, in harmony with the first contract, at the rate of $395,000?

Answer. We have received the original contract price, and $25,000 on the extras upon the original contract.

Question. You refer in your testimony to $100,000 as being about the sum claimed by you for extras. Does that refer to the completion of the boat as a monitor, according to the original design?

Answer. Yes, sir.

By Mr. Gooch:

Question. Were you delayed in time in consequence of these alterations?

Answer. Yes, sir; very much.

By Mr. Odell:

Question. Was there any forfeiture in case the vessel was not completed within the time specified?

Answer. I think it was not put in that form. I think the price was to be so many thousand dollars if it was done at such a time; so many thousand dollars if it was done at such a time; and so many thousand dollars if it was done at such a time. The amounts and dates I do not recollect now.

By Mr. Gooch:

Question. Was Mr. Stimers present when the Chimo was launched?

Answer. Yes, sir.

Question. Do you know what his opinion was as to her draught of water when she was launched?

Answer. His assistant, I think, first mentioned to him that his opinion was that she drew more water than had been anticipated. Then Mr. Stimers took the data that he had at hand, and made a calculation, as near as he could, how much she would be out of water when all was aboard, and I think he left it in the neighborhood of four inches out of water; and that came very near to what was actually the case.

Question. Do you know whether or not he reported that fact to the department?

Answer. I do not; but I think he did. I think there was a correspondence in regard to it.

Question. Do you know why he went on and completed her, putting the turrets and everything on, when he knew that, when completed, she would be only four inches out of water?

Answer. No, sir; I do not.

WEDNESDAY, *December* 21.

GEORGE SEWELL sworn and examined.

By Mr. Wade:

Question. Will you please to state what relation you have to the navy, ship-building, &c.?

Answer. I am chief engineer in the navy.

Question. Are you in government employ?

Answer. Yes, sir; I am chief engineer of the navy yard at Charlestown.

Question. Are you an architect or draughtsman in ship-building?

Answer. Ship-building is not exactly in the line of steam-engineering, but it is part of our profession to acquaint ourselves with everything of the kind that is going on, and I have a good knowledge of the art.

Question. How long have you been engaged in the navy, and how long have you been an engineer?

Answer. I have followed the profession for over twenty-five years, and have been in the navy since 1847.

Question. What do you know in relation to the light-draught monitors that are building in the vicinity of Boston?

Answer. I have never been officially connected with them. The only knowledge I have of them is derived from observation now and then.

Question. How many are building in this vicinity that you know of, of that class?

Answer. There are three or four over to East Boston, now on the stocks.

Question. Can you state what progress has been made upon those?

Answer. I cannot, as I have not been over there to look at them for some time. One that was built there—the Casco—has gone to New York.

Question. How is it with the one called the Chimo?

Answer. She was built at South Boston. She is now at the navy yard, fitting for sea.

Question. Did you see her after she was launched, or about the time of her being launched?

Answer. Yes, sir.

Question. Describe her condition then, if you please.

Answer. I should think she was about thirty inches out of water at the bow, and at the stern about fifteen inches, as near as I recollect. I never measured it, but judging by my eye I should say that was about the distance. Amidships, she would be a mean between 30 and 15—or, 22½. She is nearly straight, I think.

Question. What had she on board at that time?

Answer. There was nothing above deck. She had her boilers and machinery in.

Question. Her turret on?

Answer. Her turret was not on; her pilot-house was not on.

Question. Her furniture, coal, &c.?

Answer. No, sir; no chains, anchors, furniture, coal, or anything of the kind; no water.

Question. Did you see her afterwards, when these things had been put on board?

Answer. I did.

Question. What was her condition then?

Answer. On her return from the trial trip I went over to South Boston and went on board of her. I should think that the top of the armor-plating on the stern was about one or two inches under water; I should think her bow was probably out eight or nine inches.

Question. How were the sides?

Answer. The sides appeared to be some four or five inches out of water. The surface of the water was quite rough, and I could not tell exactly. I did not measure these distances, but judged by my eye.

Question. Had she all the ammunition on board necessary for a voyage at that time?

Answer. That I can't say, but I think not. She would have to go to the navy yard to get her ammunition, and she had not been there.

Question. How much water did she draw at the time?

Answer. That I don't know.

Question. Had you the means of knowing anything of her speed at the trial trip?

Answer. None whatever, except hearsay. I was absent from the city at the time, on duty.

Question. Did you examine her engines and propelling power?

Answer. I merely went below and took a cursory glance at the engine-room; that is all.

Question. Did you discover anything that you supposed to be a defect in that apparatus for propelling her?

Answer. I did not, so far as the efficiency of the engines was concerned.

Question. From your knowledge of ships, what do you say of her sailing qualities, when you saw her, equipped as she was; was she fit to go to sea?

Answer. In my opinion, she was not.

Question. What use could the government have put her to, as a vessel designed to be serviceable in time of war?

Answer. She would have been useful for harbor defence here. In the condition she was in she could never have been taken to another harbor, where she would have been obliged to encounter rough weather to get her there.

Question. In your judgment, would it have been perilous to have undertaken to take her round to New York?

Answer. I think it would.

Question. Well, the government, convinced of that, have undertaken her alteration, have they not?

Answer. Yes, sir.

Question. What have they done?

Answer. They have taken off the turret, and the guns that were in the turret; they have taken out all the pipes and valves which were intended to fill the compartments to sink the vessel lower in the water when fighting; they have taken out of her the heavy condenser for the main engines, and substituted something lighter; they have taken out the turret engines, and all the gearing and machinery connected with them.

Question. Have they built up her sides?

Answer. They have not.

Question. Well, with all these out, to what warlike purpose could she be put that would be useful, in your judgment?

Answer. I am not aware of any useful purpose to which she can be applied in the present war, but I think the Navy Department have some duty which she can perform.

Question. Could she be useful for harbor defence in her present condition, without a turret?

Answer. She might be of some service in repelling the entrance of a hostile vessel into this port, or any port where she might be located. She is to have one gun mounted on deck.

Question. How much better would she be than any wooden vessel, for that purpose?

Answer. Not any. She will not be as good, owing to her lack of speed, which a wooden vessel would have carrying the same armament.

Question. State whether her men, in managing that gun, would not be totally exposed to the enemy?

Answer. Not more so than on the double-enders, and vessels of that kind, where the bulwarks are thrown down so as to fight the guns.

Question. But the men would have no protection in managing the gun, from the enemy's shot, would they?

Answer. Not the slightest.

Question. Do you know what speed she can make in her altered condition?

Answer. I do not. I do not think she has been tried under steam since she has been altered. The Casco, however, that has been altered precisely as the Chimo is to be, and has gone to New York, makes, I am told, five knots. They altered her in a way which gave the propeller a better chance to work. They cut away some of the box behind, and put on new screws of less pitch.

Question. Do you know whether she draws more water than the original contract contemplated?

Answer. I can't say as to that. I don't recollect what their draught of water was to be. I have heard it was either six or six and a half feet. I never had anything official about it.

Question. The government, if I understand it, have raised up the sides of some of these vessels?

Answer. They have contracted, I believe, to raise the sides of all that were not launched, twenty-two inches.

Question. Do you know how many of them had been launched at that time?

Answer. I only know of two—the Casco and the Chimo. The Naubuck was ready to be launched, and I believe has since been launched, without any raising. She was built at Brooklyn, by Mr. Perine.

Question. Do you know of any alterations that were made by Mr. Stimers, or directed by him to be made, from time to time, while these vessels were in progress?

Answer. I have no knowledge of anything of the kind.

Question. They are raising up one of them in this harbor, or about here, are they not?

Answer. I think they are raising up three of them, making them twenty-two inches deeper in the hold.

Question. What will be the effect of this alteration on the boats with regard to their efficiency?

Answer. It will improve their efficiency very much. It will lift the overhang clear out of the water, or nearly so, I think, and, as the overhang goes up, it will leave twenty-two more inches of the screw available for propulsion. It will lift it nearly out of the box. That will be a very great improvement. They will also be much stronger.

Question. You speak of the screws being partly in a box. What necessity was there for that?

Answer. None that I am aware of.

Question. Did it not impair the efficiency of the screw, and decrease its propelling power very much?

Answer. Certainly it did, to a very serious extent.

Question. What useful purpose was it made for?

Answer. That I can't say; I don't know of any useful purpose.

Question. Is it useful for the screws of vessels to be boxed in this way?

Answer. Not so thoroughly boxed as in this case. In some of the monitors the upper edge of the blade will be something like a foot inside of the overhang.

Question. Did you see the first monitor that was built—the one that had the engagement with the Merrimack?

Answer. I did. I have been on board of her.

Question. How does this craft differ from her in its build and construction?

Answer. The original monitor had no tanks all round the vessel for the purpose of sinking her at will; it had not the immense raft of timber round it which appears in these iron-clads, and the original monitor's deck was flat, this is crowning. That deck was built in the ordinary way, and this deck is made up of an immense number of beams, put close together and caulked, making a very heavy deck.

Question. How about the shape of it?

Answer. I can't say so much about the shape of it. I don't think the screw of the original monitor entered at all into the overhang, but I will not be certain on that point; I can't say as to that. These monitors have an ordinary inclined engine for propelling them, but the original monitor had two of Ericsson's patent lever engines in.

Question. Will you give us your opinion as to the additional draught of water that will be caused by building up the sides of these monitors twenty-two inches?

Answer. Well, the displacement of these vessels per inch is about sixteen tons. I shouldn't think that raising the sides (the iron is about five-eighths of an inch thick) would add to the weight of the vessel more than forty or fifty tons. It may sink her two or three inches; I should not think it would exceed four.

Question. What do you know about the torpedo boats?

Answer. We have only one real torpedo boat, and that is the Stromboli. She is about seventy-five feet in length, fifteen or seventeen feet beam, and draws, I think, six feet water. In the Stromboli there are two water-tight doors. In the inner door there is what we call a ball-joint, or spherical joint, and through that sphere runs what is called an out-rigger, which can be extended out between twenty-five and thirty feet. The operation is this: to start with, the outer door is shut and the water pumped out of the compartment between the two doors; then the inner door is opened, and you go in and attach a torpedo to the end of this bar; you then close the inner door, open the outer door, and, with some machinery inside, you advance this bar with the torpedo on it. After you explode it you bring the bar in again, shut the outer door, and then pump the water out between the two doors, open the inner door, and go in and put on another torpedo, close the inner door, open the outer door, run out the torpedo-bar and explode the torpedo, and so continue as long as necessary.

Question. What is the speed of such a vessel?

Answer. The Stromboli runs from six to seven knots, and cost, I believe, about $75,000.

Question. In your judgment, as acquainted with ships, would it be as efficient as one of these monitors for use as a torpedo boat?

Answer. Oh, she is worth a dozen of them, being so much smaller, and more manageable, and having the power of exploding her torpedoes one after the other without exposing the men on deck. Now, in this vessel, (the Chimo,) unless they alter her from her present condition, after you have exploded one torpedo you have got to expose yourself to the attacks of the enemy on the beach or in the bushes, in order to attach another, while in this other vessel nobody is exposed.

Question. Would it be more economical for the government to convert these monitors into torpedo boats than to build new ones?

Answer. I should advocate building new ones. They are small vessels, and can be built rapidly, and are really what you want; and these are mere makeshifts.

By Mr. Gooch:

Question. Do you consider these boats of any value whatever as torpedo boats?

Answer. I can't see where they can be of any real value; but the Navy Department, no doubt, can make them serviceable.

Question. Do you know for what purpose these boats were originally intended?

Answer. I do not. I was at sea when they were commenced. They must have been intended, however, for some very shallow streams, as they wanted a very light draught.

Question. Do you know what it was designed the speed of these boats should be?

Answer. Well, I can only speak from hearsay, that they were to go nine knots.

Question. Can you point out the reason why they fall so far short in speed?

Answer. Well, they draw more water than it was intended they should, which, of course, makes the resistance greater. I consider this overhang and the boxing of the screw as the main causes of their falling off in speed; but a vessel drawing more water of course requires more power to attain the same speed.

Question. Is there any necessity for that overhang on the monitor?

Answer. I am opposed to it, and have always been. I can see no good in it; on the contrary, it is a positive detriment, and endangers the safety of the vessel at sea. One great objection to this overhang is the drag in the water, which is very detrimental to the speed; and another is, the great opportunity which it gives a heavy sea to destroy the vessel. It presents such an immense flat surface for the sea to strike against, that it is difficult to make them sufficiently strong. The overhang evidently sunk the first monitor, by tearing what they called in her the upper hull from the lower hull.

Question. What are the reasons given for that overhang by the inventor, Mr. Ericsson?

Answer. It is, as I understand it, to prevent the stern from being run into by an enemy's vessel, and the destruction of the rudder and probably the screw. The Monadnock has very little overhang indeed.

Question. The Casco is now about as much out of water as it was designed these vessels should be, is she not?

Answer. I can't say as to that.

Question. How much is she out of water?

Answer. I have not heard, and I have not had a chance to see for myself. Pretty much everything that was done on her was done over to East Boston, where she was built, and as I never had any official connexion with these vessels whatever, what I know about them is from my own private observation.

Question. With how much accuracy ought the draught of water of such a vessel to be estimated?

Answer. Within two or three inches at the most. It is a simple mathematical calculation. You make your drawings; you see what weight you are going to put in; you see by the formation of the hull what the displacement is to be; we all know what a cubic foot of water weighs; a vessel always displaces her own weight exactly, and it is very easy to ascertain what the draught is to be.

Question. Then, if this vessel draws over three inches more water than was originally estimated, it is an inexcusable error or mistake on the part of the constructor?

Answer. Yes, sir; that is, if there was on more put on her in the shape of weight than was intended when she was originally designed. If more weight has been put in than was intended when the vessel was designed, she will necessarily draw more water. Just as much as the weight is increased, of course, she goes down—an inch to about every sixteen tons.

Question. Do you know who determined the amount of weight on these vessels?

Answer. I do not.

Question. But they were found to be so deep in the water, even before the armament was taken on board, that they were not fit for service, were they not?

Answer. That was the common talk among those who were building them, and among professional men who noticed these things. That was the talk, long before the Chimo was launched, of the builder, Mr. Adams; he often said she would not float; meaning by that, not that she would sink, but that she would float so deep that she would not be serviceable.

Question. Will these monitors that are now being built up ever be fit for sea service?

Answer. They will not be fit for sea steamers at all; can be taken from port to port in fine weather.

Question. They will only be fit for harbors and rivers?

Answer. Harbors and rivers.

Question. They will draw 22 more inches than it was originally intended they should, in order to bring them as far out of water as was designed?

Answer. I don't know what the original intention was, and I don't know what their present draught is; but they will draw, I should think, about four inches more water than they do at present, with the additional raising of the sides and deck.

Question. Do you know who is superintending the construction of those that have been built here?

Answer. Mr. Wilmarth, superintendent of the Chimo. I think Chief Engineer Moore is now superintending those at East Boston that are being raised in the hold. Mr. Robinson superintended the Naubuck at Brooklyn, and the late Chief Engineer Long superintended, a part of the time, the one built at Chester.

Question. Suppose that these vessels were originally designed to navigate rivers where only vessels with a draught not exceeding six and a half feet could go, will these vessels be of any use for that purpose when they are built up?

Answer. They will not, unless the depth of water will allow for the increased weight that has been put on them.

By Mr. Wade:

Question. Are you acquainted with the currents of our western streams?

Answer. No, sir; I have never been out there.

Question. Suppose the current is four miles an hour, would the Chimo be able to stem that current and go up stream?

Answer. It would depend on what speed she can make.

By Mr. Gooch:

Question. What is the thickness of the armor-plate of these vessels?

Answer. Three inches at the surface of the water.

Question. Would not the thickness of the plate and the fact that the men who work the guns must all be exposed on deck, without protection, render them of very little, if any, value for harbor defence?

Answer. They would be as valuable as other vessels of the navy whose guns are exposed.

Question. Do you know how many men it will take to man the Chimo in her present condition?

Answer. I think the admiral said yesterday that forty-four was her complement.

Question. How many are usually required on a torpedo boat?

Answer. I think the crew of the Stromboli amounts to either nine or eleven persons, all told.

Question. Is a gun exposed on deck of any value to a torpedo boat?

Answer. It would not be to a vessel like the Stromboli. In this case it would. It could be used to clear the banks of any enemy while the men were exposed in attaching the torpedoes.

Question. And, with the speed of these boats, could they ever catch anything?

Answer. Never.

THURSDAY, *December* 22.

NATHANIEL MCKAY sworn and examined.

By Mr. Wade:

Question. Where do you reside?

Answer. In East Boston.

Question. What business or profession do you follow?

Answer. I follow ship building, steam-engines and boilers.

Question. How long have you been engaged in that business?

Answer. Ever since 1848. I was foreman for my brother from 1851 to 1857, and have been in business for myself since 1857.

Question. Have you done any work for the government?

Answer. Yes, sir.

Question. Please state what work you have done for the government.

Answer. On the 4th day of May, 1863, I received a contract for a light-draught monitor called the Squando, and in about 20 days after that I received the plans and specifications.

Question. From whom did you receive the plans?

Answer. Mr. Stimers.

Question. With whom did you make the contract for building her?

Answer. With the Navy Department. I wrote a letter to the department on the 20th of April stating that I would like to build a vessel such as were being built at East Boston, and they sent on a board to examine my premises, and then gave me a contract.

Question. What was the contract price for building it?

Answer. $395,000, for six months.

Question. What were the dimensions of the craft to be?

Answer. She was to be 225 feet long, 45 feet wide, and 9 feet and one inch deep.

Question. What depth of water was she to draw; was anything said about it in the contract?

Answer. No, sir; she was supposed to draw 6½ feet of water. We had nothing to do with the draught. We had nothing to do but build the vessel as the plans came.

Question. Is Mr. Stimers a ship-builder?

Answer. I don't know his experience; he is an engineer in the navy, and has been for some years.

Question. Do you know whether he has ever attended to ship-building as a profession?

Answer. No, sir; I never knew anything about him except that his first start was on the original Monitor at Hampton Roads. He took her down there, and he has been to sea a good deal.

Question. You have built the vessel according to his directions?

Answer. Yes, sir; every blow that has been struck, every rivet that has been driven, has been according to his directions.

Question. Did not the contract specify how she was to be built?

Answer. She was to be a light-draught monitor, according to plans and specifications furnished by the department.

Question. How could you contract for the prices without specifications as to how she was to be built? She might be finished in one way much cheaper than in another, might she not?

Answer. Oh, they were all to be built alike as I understand it; there were to be twenty in all, and there were twelve out when I took mine.

Question. Did you know what the specifications were to be?

Answer. I had looked at the one at the Atlantic works and at others.

Question. As you progressed with the work, were there any alterations from the original design?

Answer. Alterations as fast as they could come by Adams express.

Question. Can you specify some of the principal alterations?

Answer. Some of them were cross-floors on the bottom; a ring round the turret and pilot-house, making the turret and pilot-house thicker, vacuum engines and the condenser lengthened.

Question. Was there any change in the bulkheads?

Answer. Yes, sir; there were several new bulkheads added. It was necessary that that should be done, but they didn't think of it before there were hundreds of alterations.

Question. Were these alterations or deviations from the original plan attended with more expense than that plan?

Answer. Yes, sir.

Question. How much more do you suppose?

Answer. Well, over a hundred thousand dollars.

Question. Was there any price agreed upon between you and Mr. Stimers for these alterations?

Answer. Sometimes he would make a bargain when he sent on the alterations; finally, the department found that he was giving so many orders that they cut him off from making alterations unless they were notified and knew what the changes were to be, so we would have to wait a week or so to see whether the changes would be made or not. He said he had to write to Washington and submit them to the department.

Question. Then all the material changes were submitted to the department?

Answer. No, sir; very few of them. When they found that Mr. Stimers was going so far in these alterations, and there was so much fault by other people, they stopped him.

Question. Did the department know that he was making alterations to the extent of $100,000?

Answer. I don't think he said a word to them about it, but went right along and did just as he pleased. He did not care for the department or anybody else.

Question. Do you know whether he received any directions from Mr. Ericsson in regard to these alterations?

Answer. I never heard Ericsson's name mentioned in the matter until recently.

Question. Did the $100,000 include the raising at the sides of the vessel?

Answer. No, sir. Those were made while Mr. Stimers was there.

Question. Before it was decided to raise them up?

Answer. Yes, sir.

Question. How much will raising them cost?

Answer. We have a special contract for that at $90,000.

Question. Then the boat, when completed, will cost $190,000 more than was supposed at first.

Answer. Yes, sir.

Question. What condition is your vessel in now?

Answer. My vessel will be ready to launch the last day of this month.

Question. Will you state the reasons that induced the department to have the sides of the vessel raised up?

Answer. Because they thought she would not be seaworthy.

Question. Had you seen any of these monitors after they had been launched?

Answer. Yes, sir; I had been on board the Chimo.

Question. What was her condition when she was launched, and how did she appear in the water?

Answer. She was very low in the water. I was on board the Casco also after she was launched.

Question. Did these vessels have all their munitions of war, fuel, and the like, on board when you saw them?

Answer. The Casco did not have any fuel on board of her; she was not completed.

Question. How was it with the Chimo?

Answer. The Chimo had her turret off when I was on board of her.

Question. Did you see her with the turret on after she was launched?

Answer. No, sir; I did not go on board of her.

Question. Why was the turret taken off?

Answer. I understood she drew too much water and could not carry it.

Question. In your judgment, would she be a seaworthy boat according to the original plan?

Answer. Some people say they would go to sea in her, and some say they would not. I should not want to go to sea in her.

Question. That depends upon a man's hardihood and courage; but we want to know whether she could traverse the ocean, from port to port, with safety?

Answer. There is not an iron-clad in the world that could traverse the ocean. I have never seen one that could.

Question. Could she do so as well as any of them?

Answer. Well, yes, sir.

Question. How many inches was she out of water?

Answer. At the centre of the stern she was two and a half inches out of water; forward she was some fifteen inches out.

Question. Do you know anything of her speed?

Answer. I do not.

Question. What useful purpose could she be put to, as a ship-of-war, with her turret off?

Answer. Well, I suppose she is just as good as any of those double-enders, or any of those gunboats that fight with batteries on shore. There is nothing to affect the men any more than on a wooden vessel, and no splinters to hurt them. I think she would be better in a battle than any wooden vessel, because the men would not be so liable to be hurt.

Question. Do you know how much water the Chimo drew?

Answer. About eight feet, I should think.

Question. Do you recollect what the double-enders draw?

Answer. I think they draw about the same.

Question. Do you consider the Chimo of any value at all as a ship-of-war?

Answer. She was not intended for a ship-of-war.

Question. What was she intended for?

Answer. For a torpedo boat, as I understand.

Question. I mean, for what was she originally designed?

Answer. To go up rivers and into shallow places, and encounter the enemy wherever they should be met. I think these vessels are better than a gunboat would be; they are iron, and they can resist shot and shell better.

Question. What is the thickness of the armor of this vessel?

Answer. Three inches.

Question. How was it on the deck?

Answer. Two half-inch plates, making one inch.

Question. You have built one of these vessels and nearly finished raising up the sides, how far?

Answer. Twenty-two inches.

Question. With her full complement of men and munitions of war on board, what will her draught of water be?

Answer. I don't think it will be any more than it was before, or not more than six inches more.

Question. That would give her a draught of about ten feet and a half?

Answer. I think she will not draw that.

Question. Is so long and shallow a vessel as she is strong enough to go to sea?

Answer. Well, I shouldn't think she would go to sea; there is no iron vessel of that class that will. It is impossible, as I said before, for a vessel of that class to go to sea, with the power they have in them; they were never intended to go to sea; they would probably go round Cape Cod, like many of our sound steamers, that were never meant to go to sea. These monitors were intended for rivers and harbors. No vessel was ever built any stronger in the sides or deck than they are; they are as strong as they could be made.

Question. As strong as they could be made of these given dimensions; but if you had built them higher they could have been made stronger?

Answer. Oh, yes. There could be no trouble except in the bottom of the vessel; the sides are amply strong, they would never give out at all except from shot or shell.

By Mr. Odell:

Question. You stated that you wrote to the department for the privilege of building one of these vessels?

Answer. Yes, sir.

Question. How came you to do that?

Answer. I wanted something to do.

Question. I understand that; but were there no bids made for the building of these twenty vessels?

Answer. There were, but I did not bid. I think they got a great many bids, and then gave what they thought it was worth.

Question. You mean to say that the department fixed a price which they would give for building these twenty vessels?

Answer. Yes, sir. I suppose they received a great many bids, und averaged them the same as they do in a great many other cases.

Question. You understand that the same price was paid for them all?

Answer. Yes, sir.

Question. How much have you received upon your first contract?

Answer. There are about $75,000 due on the original contract.

Question. Now, what arrangement did you make with the government or any of its agents in regard to compensation for the changes that were made from the original plan? Was any price agreed upon?

Answer. Sometimes they would put down the amount that was to be paid; for instance, Mr. Stimers said that other parties had agreed to lengthen the pilot-house for $1,000, and he would give us that; I think the price to be paid for the bulkheads was $1,400 or $1,500.

Question. What proportion of these alterations, amounting to $100,000, did you have any agreement with the government in reference to the compensation that was to be paid?

Answer. But a very small proportion of them; sometimes we would write them that such a thing was extra, and sometimes we would not, they came so thick We expect the Navy Department will pay us every cent for the deviations from the original plans.

Question. By what arrangement do you expect this to be done?

Answer. We expect they will look over the different plans and give us just what a private individual would for the extra work. We know they will.

Question. Who is to be the judge of it?

Answer. The engineers. That is all the way we expect to be used. We received a great many plans, and we have endeavored to follow them as far as we possibly could.

Question. These alterations that you are now making, under contract, for $90,000, you understand to have been ordered in consequence of the failure of the vessels to realize the expectations of the Navy Department?

Answer. Yes, sir, or of Mr. Stimers; he furnished us the plans.

Question. At whose instigation was this change made?

Answer. Well, Mr. Wood and Admiral Gregory directed the change. I have done my business through them entirely. I suppose they found the vessels were not efficient, and they had to make the change. Mr. Stimers was dismissed and Mr. Wood put in his place.

By Mr. Wade:

Question. Who agreed to pay $90,000 for raising the sides of the vessel?

Answer. Admiral Gregory, at the Parker House, after we had fought him there, with some of the other builders, for four or five hours, to get more.

By Mr. Odell:

Question. Is the same price to be paid for these alterations on each of the vessels?

Answer. No, sir; the price to be paid depends upon the stage the work is in. My vessel was further advanced than some of the others, and I get $90,000. None get over that, some less. I think these vessels will be very efficient when they are done.

Question. Efficient for what purpose?

Answer. For river and harbor defence; that is what they were originally intended for.

Question. As a practical man, would you say that their armor was sufficient to resist the force of such armaments as they would naturally come in conflict with?

Answer. Well, they would not stand some fortifications that have a much heavier armor.

Question. How much force would they stand?

Answer. Field artillery. There are a great many places up the James, the York, and all the southern rivers, for instance, where you could not go with a gunboat, that you could reach with these iron-clads.

Question. Is the strength of their armor the same as that of the double-enders?

Answer. The double-enders have no armor at all; they were merely low wooden vessels; they have nothing but little thin bulwarks of iron. I think these vessels, when completed, will be very good vessels. There is plenty of work in them, and everything is done in the best possible manner.

Question. What speed do you expect to get out of this vessel?

Answer. I think she will go five or six knots.

Question. You said your contract was to finish this vessel in six months.

Answer. Yes, sir. In four months at $395,000, in six months at $386,000. One reason we did not finish her in four months was, because there were not men enough in the country to do it; and another reason was, the plans never came to hand until a year after the contract was made.

Question. Didn't you know the number of men in the country when you made your contract?

Answer. Well, sir, you might get them all on the vessel, but you could not get them all on one sheet.

Question. Do you feel yourself under any obligation in consequence of not completing the vessel at the time specified in the contract?

Answer. Not at all, sir.

Question. Has the work been done as rapidly as it could be done under the circumstances in which you were placed by the government.

Answer. Yes, sir. We worked as rapidly as we could. We have worked night and day on it; but there have been so many alterations and so much delay that we have got almost discouraged. We hope, however, to live through it.

By Mr. Wade:

Question. If the speed of your boat is five knots and the current is four, how rapidly will she go up?

Answer. Well, if the current is very strong, it would be like trying to make water run up hill. You can't make water run up the roof of this house.

On a subsequent day Mr. McKay submitted the following statement, requesting that it might be appended to his deposition:

The draught of water of the Squando, when ready for sea, will be 7 feet 9 inches; dimensions as she now is: length, 225 feet 4½ inches; breadth, 45 feet 1⅞ inch; depth amidships, 11 feet ⅝ inch.

In regard to any orders I received in reference to the alteration or construction, they all came from the office of Chief Engineer Stimers. The first drawing came to us on the 27th day of May, 1863—the last received from him was at the time of his removal from office. We received one general plan as late as April 26, 1864, eleven months after the date of contract. We have received in all from Mr. Stimers 120 letters. Most of these are in relation to alterations and deviations from the first plans we received from him. We have received also 83 sheets, containing plans and drawings enough in number and size to contain the drawings for the machinery of our entire navy, with all the plans complete. We received also a bound book, 4 by 6, of 92 pages, printed in small type. Each mechanic in charge had to have one of these books in his pocket, so that he would not make any deviation from the plans or specifications. It was called the "Specification Book," and termed by our mechanics "the monitor prayer book." If there had been any deviations from this book the work would have been condemned. It came from Mr. Stimers's office. He made some additions to it, after the issue of the first volume, which were pasted in the back of the book. I am aware that there has been a mistake in those vessels in all their weights. In the first place, had Mr. Stimers remained in power, he would have sunk every one of them by his additional alterations on alterations. He was not satisfied to finish the vessels as they were intended, nor do I think he would ever have finished them, for they would have sunk at the wharf with the immense quantity of iron he put in them, which was of no value, and only for experiments. There seemed to be no end to the work, as long as he had a draughtsman. The engines are finished in the most elaborate style, all polished. Parts that should have been made of cast-iron were made of wrought, at a cost, when finished, of two dollars per pound. A great many parts which should have been made of cast-iron were made of brass, and finished in the most elaborate style, got up regardless of expense. This looked well on paper, and Mr. Stimers did not care how long it took a man to finish it. Had those engines been got up as simple and plain as the engines on the Monadnock, and the engines for the naval vessels generally, by Mr. B. F. Isherwood, they would have been completed in three or four months, where it took six months to make them. I can confidently say that there is more copper pipe in one of those boats than there is in one of our large frigates. They were as thick again as were required. Those were Mr. Stimers's instructions. All of the orders were in this way. There is more machinery and parts of machinery in the Squando than there is in the iron-clad Monadnock. If the plans furnished from first to last were spread out they would cover the entire deck of the vessel, and there would not be room enough left for Mr. Stimers to add another.

I cannot see that the Navy Department are at fault for this mistake. The country was in want of vessels-of-war, and the department are in duty bound to furnish them as ordered. They have done their duty, as far as I can see. They are merely agents for the people; and I am confident they have been very efficient in the discharge of all their duties. Mr. Fox had great confidence in Mr. Stimers's abilities to construct those vessels and superintend the directions of the plans and their entire arrangements. Mr. Fox did all in his power to make those vessels efficient. He placed an agent with full power, and that agent did all that he knew to make them seaworthy and fit for harbor defence, and failed to accomplish his design; and he was removed immediately, as I am aware any business man would remove an agent when he did not perform his duty in accordance with his instructions. I am confident that no detail of the instructions of the light-draught monitors was ever executed in any of the departments at Washington. I never received a letter nor a word from Mr. Lenthall on them, except for our approved bills, when they had been passed by Mr. Stimers, with his signature as approved. I called on Mr. Isherwood once for some information; he told me that he knew nothing about them. This was a short time after I received the contract. A mistake has been made, and the country must bear it. This country is only in its infancy in naval warfare. I am aware that the navy has done a great deal, and is now doing daily, and getting a great deal of valuable experience; and they will produce, in a short time, some of the most efficient vessels-of-war that ever floated. The navy commenced the war with three steam vessels, and have now over six hundred. I think that great credit is due to the Navy Department for their efficiency in keeping such a fleet at sea, to guard all the rivers, inlets, and coast of the south. Where is there a country as large as this, or a Navy Department in the world, that has done so much as ours in so short a time, and made so few mistakes? Look at France and England, that have been building armed vessels for hundreds of years, and have not succeeded yet; and we have been at war but two or three years, and have now afloat some of the most efficient iron-clads in the world.

I am confident that I never should take another government contract with such a field of plans as I have had the last eighteen months. The following is an extract from one of the one hundred and twenty letters received from Mr. Stimers: "You will readily understand, therefore, why I would prefer you to follow strictly the plans sent. Being myself an engineer, I don't require the opinion of a board to enable me to decide upon the excellence of the plans of something of which I have had a special experience."

N. McKAY.

EBEN HOYT sworn and examined.

By Mr. Wade:

Question. What is your position in the navy?

Answer. Chief engineer.

Question. Where are you located?

Answer. In East Boston and Chelsea. I am now inspecting the light-draught monitors Squando and Nanset, also an iron double-ender, iron propeller boats, turrets, &c., for the government.

Question. You have inspected them from time to time, of course, as they have progressed?

Answer. Yes, sir, day by day. I was first ordered to this duty in May, 1863, as the inspector of the Chimo, at South Boston; and in September was detached from the Chimo, and ordered to East Boston, to inspect the monitors Squando and Nanset, also other work.

Question. Are these light-draught monitors all of the same dimensions, build, &c.?

Answer. They were intended to be, and they were all built from the same drawings and specifications.

Question. When was the Chimo commenced?

Answer. The keel was laid about the middle of May, 1863.

Question. What draught was she intended to have?

Answer. The only evidence I have as to that is what appears in the specifications. The specifications state that the loaded draught of water was to be six feet six inches.

Question. Was she to be a turreted vessel?

Answer. With a single turret, mounting two guns—one 150-pounder Parrott rifle, and one 11-inch gun.

Question. The drawings and specifications were made by whom?

Answer. The drawings and specifications were issued from Mr. Stimers's office. I have been present at his office on several occasions, and have seen him (Mr. Stimers) supervising the detail drawings, but I have no knowledge from whence the general drawing originally came. The practice of the office was, to send the drawings to the government inspecting engineers, to be by them furnished to the contractors. All the drawings, specifications, and directions that I received came from Chief Engineer Stimers, and, at the latter part of the work, were approved by Admiral Gregory.

Question. Are you acquainted with Mr. Stimers as an engineer?

Answer. I have been acquainted with him very nearly eight years.

Question. Was he ever a ship-builder and draughtsman?

Answer. Mr. Stimers is a practical engineer and draughtsman, and has been for many years interested in matters connected with iron and wooden ship-building. I have had quite an intimate acquaintance with Mr. Stimers professionally. I made my first cruise in the frigate Merrimac, in 1857, on the Pacific station, and Mr. Stimers was chief engineer of the vessel.

Question. He has been more an engineer than a builder of ships, has he not?

Answer. Well, the term "mechanical engineer" includes designer and builder. For instance, our present duty, in connexion with these iron-clads, is to superintend and inspect all the machinery and workmanship that enter into the construction of the hull, the armature, the turret, and every part of the vessel; and the same, also, with the iron double-enders. There is a difference between an engineer and an engine-driver. To be a driver involves simply a very elementary knowledge of steam, and the manipulation of certain machinery; but to be a mechanical engineer involves, of course, a knowledge of the details of publication and construction, and of all matters appertaining to the profession.

Question. It amounts to this, then, that you consider Mr. Stimers a mechanical engineer?

Answer. I consider Mr. Stimers a thorough mechanical engineer.

Question. Did Mr. Stimers, in the construction of these vessels, change the original design at any time?

Answer. I have no evidence that the original specifications and drawings were of Mr. Stimers's design. Mr. Stimers, as general inspector, did make quite a number of changes in the vesssls. For instance, in the first drawing received by Mr. Adams (builder of the Chimo) there were no cross-floors to stiffen the bottom of the hull, and it was evident that without these cross-floors there would not be sufficient strength. We will say that the draught of water is seven feet. There would be, then, an upward pressure of three pounds per inch upon every square inch, which would tend to break the vessel up. That pressure is now resisted by stanchions and cross-floors. On the first drawing there were no cross-floors shown. Afterwards, another general drawing came, showing cross-floors and transverse bars of reverse iron under the boilers; also a heavy base ring, fitted to base of turret; two inches of armor plating were added to the pilot-house, and two inches to the smoke-pipe. These last changes were shown to be necessary by the experience gained at Charleston.

Question. Were these changes made before the craft was launched?

Answer. Yes, sir; long before. There was a time, in the construction of the Chimo, when the drawings did not keep pace with the work, but I cannot remember any time when the drawings were not in advance of the work on the Nanset and the Squando. I wish to call particular attention to this statement, because the assertion was made here, a moment ago, that such was not the case, but that parties were delayed on account of not receiving the drawings. So far as my experience is concerned, I am satisfied that the drawings, with the exception I have named, have been in advance of the work. We must not, however, confound the alterations from the original plans with the alterations in raising the boats.

Question. When this craft was launched, and her turret put on, and her coal and munitions of war put on board, did she sink lower in the water than she was expected to?

Answer. I was not present when all the coal, munitions and appurtenances were placed on board, but I will make this statement: that with water in the boilers, and some coal on board, (the exact quantity I cannot now state,) the vessel did draw more water than the draught proposed by the specifications.

Question. How much more?

Answer. At the time I allude to the Chimo was drawing, to the best of my recollection, six, or, at most, seven inches more water than the draught specified. The draught of water specified is six feet six inches. She then drew a little over seven feet—seven feet and one inch.

Question. Is it difficult for a draughtsman to ascertain beforehand how deep his vessel will be in the water, if he knows the weight she will carry?

Answer. It is mathematically and practically impossible. Statements are made and presented to the public that certain iron-clad vessels have approached to within one-fourth of an inch of their intended draught. Take, for instance, the Dictator for an illustration. Now, as I understand the displacement per inch of that vessel, one-fourth of an inch of the intended draught would be perhaps nine tons in a fabric weighing some thousands of tons. I will give you one illustration to show how material varies. The tops of these light-draught monitor cross-floors are fitted with angle iron, toppings $2\frac{1}{2}$ inches by $\frac{5}{16}$ iron. Messrs. Morris & Tasker, of Philadelphia, a firm that manufactures large quantities of this angle iron, have tables showing the various forms, and usually the weights per lineal foot of each sized bar. The weight of this iron is given as five pounds per lineal foot; the actual weight was six pounds and five one-hundredths per lineal foot. It would be utterly impossible, therefore, in building an iron structure, to do more than approximate to the weight of that structure. To ascertain the draught of water it is necessary to ascertain the exact form of the hull and the weight of the vessel, and what she is to take on board. But in practice we deal with uneven plates and angle iron; also with woods of various density.

Question. I know, but I put the question hypothetically. If you know the shape of the vessel and the weight of the cargo, or whatever is to be on board, are there not rules to ascertain how much she will draw?

Answer. The difficulty is not in the mathematical calculation, but in the fact that the weight of the material will vary. You may assume, for instance, that a plate of iron one foot square and one inch in thickness weighs forty pounds. A plate exactly one foot square and one inch in thickness will weigh forty pounds; that is, that would be the average weight in a number of plates; but there will be a variation in the thickness and density of all plates used in practice. Mr. Stimers insisted that all of the light-draught monitor armor plates be fully one inch in thickness, and many of the plates weighed forty-three pounds per square foot, and were but slightly over the required thickness.

Question. How near can you approximate, practically, to it?

Answer. I have had experience inspecting ten iron vessels, and from my observation I should judge that it would be proper to add full ten per cent. in weight over the calculations to the iron structure. You have, for instance, plates that are intended to be one quarter of an inch in thickness, but the rolls in rolling the iron will spring, and you will find the plate thicker in the centre.

Question. Of course, then, if you were constructing a craft that was to draw only six and a half feet of water, you would make that allowance to start upon?

Answer. I should say, decidedly, that an allowance of that kind should be made. The iron we get now is somewhat different from the material furnished before the war. The mills have been hard pressed, and they are not careful to give exact thicknesses called for. For instance, we get angle-iron that comes from certain rollers that have turned out thousands of tons. In rolling the angle iron through these rollers it enlarges the spaces which form the outline of the angle-iron; consequently we have increased weight per lineal foot. This evil would be corrected by requiring certain weights per foot or per plate.

Question. Why was the turret taken off the Chimo, when it was originally designed that it should have a turret?

Answer. I do not know, sir. If the intention was to lighten the vessel, my opinion is that other things could have been taken from the vessel that would have secured sufficient lightness for all practical purposes—without taking the turret off—say for harbor defence.

Question. Don't you know that it was because, after the vessel was launched, it was found that she could not carry her turret efficiently?

Answer. It is very evident, sir, that the boat had a greater draught of water than was intended. It is now a question only of engineering and opinion as to what should have been removed from that vessel to have lightened her. You will see, by looking at the plan, that there are a great many heavy weights besides the turret, and a great many small pieces, the aggregate of which would make quite a number of tons.

Question. Do you believe that, as originally constructed, she would have answered the purpose for which she was designed?

Answer. If that purpose was harbor defence, I believe the Chimo would have been an efficient vessel.

Question. What do you mean by that?—to lie still in the harbor and use her turret?

Answer. No, sir. I assume that the Chimo had a speed of five knots an hour, which I deem sufficient speed for harbor purposes; and also the fact, (and the calculation has been made. by reliable parties,) knowing the then condition of the vessel, that it would have required 270 tons weight to have brought the crown of her deck level with the water.

Question. Then you think the commissioners who directed the raising up of the sides of these vessels were mistaken?

Answer. No, sir, I do not say that is the case.

Question. Suppose they were designed to sail up rivers and into shoal water, and defend themselves against an enemy, were they efficient for that purpose?

Answer. No, sir, they were not. They could not successfully contend with a very strong current.

Question. What was the difficulty?

Answer. The difficulty was excessive draught of water and too little speed.

Question. So far as these two elements are concerned, they will not be changed for the better by raising the sides, will they?

Answer. It will not lighten the draught of water, nor increase the speed. They were called "light-draught iron-clad monitors," with a draught of 6 feet 6 inches. It is very evident now that they are no longer light-draught monitors—at least comparatively.

Question. You say that, as originally constructed, they drew too much water, and had not speed enough to be useful on rivers; now the government propose to raise them up on the sides 22 inches: will that decrease the draught or increase the speed?

Answer. It certainly will not decrease the draught; and that addition alone, provided no other alterations were made, certainly would not increase the speed.

Question. Then they will be no better in their altered condition for the purpose originally designed than they were before they were altered?

Answer. If you please, I will make an explanation. There is one other alteration that has been made—the raising of the stern overhang. The overhang of the Chimo was much submerged, and perhaps fully one-third of the effective propelling power was destroyed by that overhang. In raising the sides of these other vessels the overhang has also been raised 22 inches; also its shape has been altered; and if these boats make more speed than the Chimo did, it will be entirely due to the fact that the overhang and the propellers have been altered and improved. The pitch of the old propellers was twelve feet; these are nine feet. The overhang, also, has been so altered that the water is projected directly aft by the propellers, and they will be far more effective than before. If there is an increase of speed, therefore, it will be due to this alteration.

Question. Do you think there will be an increase of speed from the same propelling power?

Answer. No, sir, I do not, as the hull will offer more resistance.

Question. What is the use of that overhang?

Answer. The overhang is placed there to protect the rudder and propellers. My opinion, as an engineer, is that one-third of that overhang would accomplish all that it is necessary to accomplish, and furnish sufficient protection. If the rudder was entirely unprotected except the post, a shot striking the thin plates would hardly produce greater damage than to make a hole through the rudder, which would not materially affect the strength or usefulness of the same. I have seen side-wheel steamers used in front of Vicksburg with many of their paddle-boards knocked out by shot, and the only apparent effect was that the engine moved a little faster, but the boats were not much disabled.

Question. Then, if I understand you now, you say that if the original purpose of these light-draught monitors was to ascend rivers and to navigate shoal waters, that design has not been accomplished, either by the vessels as originally constructed or by their alteration.

Answer. No, sir, certainly not. There is one other point to be considered. The Chimo was floating in salt water. If she had been used as a river boat, and on the Mississippi, or any of our fresh-water rivers, it is very evident the draught of water would have been increased. Then there is another fact. These vessels in construction amount to this: an iron scow, containing machinery, boilers, coal, &c., supported by a pine raft. It receives support from that raft as long as the raft has buoyancy. Assuming the weight of pine to be 47 pounds per foot, and the weight of salt water 64 pounds per foot, there will be that relative proportion of buoyancy. But it will be impossible to prevent the water from percolating through this raft, and ultimately it will become saturated, and in that case the buoyancy is decreased, and the draught of water increased. It is increased in proportion as you add pounds of water to each cubic foot of pine.

Question. What is the thickness of the armor of the Chimo?

Answer. Three inches.

Question. Her turret was to be more than that, was it not?

Answer. The turret is eight inches in thickness.

Question. Is armor three inches thick sufficient to resist rifled ordnance?—say a Parrott 32-pounder?

Answer. Three inches of armor, arranged as it is on that vessel, with that large amount of oak armor backing, is sufficient to resist shell from either rifled or smooth-bore ordnance, but entirely inadequate to resist solid shot. Of course I am speaking of the heaviest description of ordnance.

Question. What thickness of armor is used on a large monitor, like the Dictator?

Answer. I understand the armor of the Dictator to be ten inches in thickness, and the turret fifteen inches.

Question. You don't suppose that the light armor of these vessels was designed to encounter fortifications on land?

Answer. I presume they were intended to encounter the enemy wherever found. If they were intended for picket-boats, to accompany army operations, and contend with sharpshooters and field artillery, the armor is amply sufficient, and the thickness of the turret is amply sufficient; but of course it must be evident to you that such a vessel would be very unfit to encounter another monitor like the Dictator or the Monadnock.

Question. You say she would be sufficient for harbor defence. Would she be sufficient to resist the armaments she would be likely to encounter?

Answer. I speak of harbor defence as opposed to the aggressive powers of a foreign foe. I am not aware of any vessel built by the British or French government, that carries armor sufficient to resist our projectiles, that would be able to enter our harbor. Their heavy vessels have a draught of from 27 to 34 feet. We assume that these monitors will have a draught of seven or eight feet, and such vessels would be very efficient to defend Boston, Newburyport, Gloucester, and others of our coast towns.

Question. Suppose the enemy should encounter her with craft like the Monadnock or Dictator, or any of that class of vessels?

Answer. The Monadnock or Dictator, or any of that class, would speedily overpower a vessel of this class. They have greater powers of offence and greater powers of resistance.

Question. Then she would not be first rate for harbor defence?

Answer. I say these vessels would be well adapted for harbor defence against a foreign foe, with the means that European powers have to assail us. For instance, the Alabama, the Georgia, and other confederate vessels have been in the vicinity of our coast, and we have anticipated raids from them. Now, it is very evident that a light-draught monitor would be very ample protection for almost all our harbors against that class of vessels; and their value will be evident, when we consider the fact that many of our harbors and some valuable seaports are without any means of defence, not even land fortifications.

Question. You would not recommend the building of such vessels for harbor defence?

Answer. No, sir. With the experience we have had with that class of vessels I should not deem it advisable to build any more like them for any purpose whatsoever.

Question. Another question is, are they well adapted for torpedo boats?

Answer. They are very poorly adapted to be used as torpedo boats against ships or steamers. They may be valuable boats to be used in blowing out obstructions, or any purpose of that kind, where speed is not an important consideration. A torpedo boat to encounter an enemy at sea, or to encounter a floating structure, like a steamer, must have speed. If its speed is not superior to that of the enemy, it is very certain that the torpedo will fail to do damage.

Question. How much would it cost to build an efficient torpedo boat?

Answer. Well, it would depend entirely upon the purpose for which it has to be used.

Question. Such as we do build?

Answer. I do not know what they have cost.

Question. Would it be over $100,000, in your judgment?

Answer. There is no doubt that a torpedo boat could be built that would be a valuable torpedo boat, after the design of Chief Engineer Wood, which we believe to be the best, for $100,000. I of course refer to a small craft.

By Mr. Gooch:

Question. You suggested that this boat might have been lightened, so as to have answered the purpose for which she was already designed, without taking off the turret?

Answer. Yes, sir; that is decidedly my opinion.

Question. Will you inform us how you would have lightened her, and still have left the turret?

Answer. Well, sir, I should have removed one boiler, the water compartments, pipes, and all the attendant valves and appurtenances for same; I should have removed the vacuum engine and its condenser, substituting a simple pump, and a jet condenser; I should have docked the vessel, and removed two-thirds of the overhang, leaving simply a sufficient amount to protect the propellers and rudder post; also reduced thickness of armature at stern; removed Andrews's pumps, engines and pipes, and made many other minor changes. I don't say that that would have made the Chimo a thoroughly efficient boat, but I believe that, for the purposes of harbor defence, and in smooth water, she would have been a better boat than she is now.

Question. And do you think you could in that way have lightened her so that she would not have drawn more than six and a half feet?

Answer. No, sir.

Question. How much would have been her draught of water after you had lightened her all you could?

Answer. Well, her draught would have been, we will say, six feet eleven inches. It would not have made a difference of more than a few inches; still it would have been an improvement. Then there would have been the difficulty which I have mentioned, and which all these boats will have to contend with, and that is, that they are now in salt water, and will have to pass into fresh water to be available on many of our rivers. Then there is this other fact, which is a very important fact, but one that has not been discussed, that this pine raft will very soon become saturated; constantly increasing the draught of water.

Question. Assuming that these boats draw seven feet in salt water, how much more will they draw in fresh water?

Answer. It is a matter of calculation. I will approximate it by saying that it will make a difference of one inch and a half.

Question. And how much will the draught be increased when the pine raft becomes thoroughly saturated with water, as it will?

Answer. Well, I should say five inches and a half. The timbers of these vessels are not "fayed," as we say, close together; it would be impracticable to do that; consequently the water circulates around and among the timbers; but, as I said before, in time the water will saturate them. I should judge that if one of these vessels, that is now being altered by raising the sides twenty-two inches, was placed in fresh water, and considering that the pine raft becomes nearly saturated, the draught of water would be increased at least seven inches.

Question. Then would the Chimo have floated, in that condition of things, in fresh water?

Answer. Yes, sir.

Question. Would she have floated and could people have lived on board of her in fresh water?

Answer. I think so. The total depth from the crown of the deck to the bottom of the keel in the Chimo was nine feet and one inch; consequently we may add weight by saturating the pine raft, and virtually add weight by passing from salt water to fresh water, until we approach a draught of nine feet and one inch, and you see the vessel is still floating. I suppose that with a draught of eight feet and ten inches the vessel would sink; the water would pass into crevices and places not water-tight. You see that if the calculation that has been made is correct, with the Chimo's deepest draught, she was still 272 tons above water.

Question. Do you know whether the commission appointed to decide what alterations should be made in these vessels, considered the suggestions you have made in regard to retaining the turret?

Answer. I have never had any conversation with the parties, but presume they did. It was a matter that was considered by Mr. Stimers.

Question. You say it was a matter considered by Mr. Stimers. Did he propose to make these alterations?

Answer. No, sir; I am not aware that he did. Mr. Stimers was aware of one fact, that the material was weighing more than was anticipated in his calculations, and he was also aware of the fact that the pine and oak being used were not seasoned. Now, properly seasoned oak will weigh 53 pounds per cubic foot; but the oak that was used on these vessels in some cases weighed 64 pounds per cubic foot.

Question. Why were these builders permitted to use oak not seasoned?

Answer. There was no other suitable timber in the country. These contracts called for an immense amount of timber. Some of these deck timbers were 45 and 50 feet in length before being moulded and sided. I do not believe it would be possible to procure an equal amount of oak timber like that used in these twenty monitors in any reasonable time. I think, in that respect, the country was almost exhausted.

Question. You say that Mr. Stimers was aware that the material was heavier than had been estimated?

Answer. Yes, sir; he was aware of the fact, because an order was issued from his office that this oak timber should be kiln-dried; but he was informed by the contractors that it was utterly impossible. I don't say that it would have been impossible to arrange some apparatus to have done that, but it seemed to be, at the time, practically impossible.

Question. When Mr. Stimers became aware that the weight of the material was greater than had been estimated, in vessels where it was so necessary as in these, that the exact displacement should be known, was it not his duty at once to make the calculation as to the effect of that increased weight?

Answer. It would certainly appear so, sir.

Question. You have stated that the weight of the material would exceed the estimate some ten per cent.?

Answer. Yes, sir. For instance, in the specification (for the light-draught monitors) we are told that the total displacement of a draught of six feet and six inches is 1,175 tons. And, on the other hand, the displacement per inch is given in the specification at $17\frac{2}{10}$ tons. Now, this displacement of 1,175 tons includes the weight of coal, men, and provisions, and all, at this draught of six feet six inches, and at least 120 tons should have been added to the 1,175 tons estimated displacement—this 120 tons would add about seven inches to the calculated draught of water.

Question. The fact being known that the material was ten per cent. heavier than was estimated, would not a calculation at once have shown that the displacement would be so much greater as to sink these vessels so low as to impair their efficiency, if not to destroy it altogether?

Answer. No, sir, I think not. When I made the statement that Mr. Stimers was aware of the fact that the material weighed more than had been calculated, I estimated the difference, from personal experience, at ten per cent. I don't know what his opinion was with regard to this increase. He may not have considered the increase to be nearly so large as that.

Question. Knowing that it was in excess of the estimate, was it not his duty, where it was so indispensable that the exact displacement should be known, in order to determine how much these vessels would be out of water, at once to have made a calculation to determine accurately what the excess of weight was, and the effect of it?

Answer. Yes, sir, it was his duty to have taken that matter into consideration, and to have ascertained what the draught of water would be, considering that excess.

Question. That would be particularly the case where twenty vessels were being built according to the same plans and specifications, would it not?

Answer. Yes, sir.

By Mr. Wade:

Question. When did you become aware that these vessels would sink lower in the water than was contemplated by the original design?

Answer. Well, it was always my opinion that they would do that, but the practical evidence of the fact was after the launch of the Chimo.

Question. When was the department informed that these vessels could not be built according to the original design, to draw six feet and a half of water?

Answer. I don't know that the department ever received any information. I presume that the department were immediately informed of the draught of the Chimo, after launching, and also from time to time as those additional weights were placed on board. At least, Mr. Stimers was in Boston and personally supervised the completion of that work, and I think Admiral Gregory was present when she was about completed and ready for trial.

By Mr. Gooch:

Question. As soon as you began to put in the timbers you knew that the weight of the material was greater than the estimate?

Answer. Yes, sir. I would also say that these vessels are very strong. They have great longitudinal strength. They have also great transverse strength. The floors are not, perhaps, quite as strong as might be desired, but excepting the overhang, so far as strength is concerned, they will be abundantly capable of steaming about in our bays, harbors, and rivers, and perhaps at sea.

Question. Have you made any estimates, so that you can tell us what will be the expense of the alterations that were made on these vessels, under the original contracts?

Answer. No, sir. In all cases where any additions were proposed, Mr. Stimers sent the contractors a letter informing them that these alterations were proposed to be made, and usually sending drawings, and asking the contractors to estimate the probable cost of these additions. In some cases the contractors and Mr. Stimers did not agree as to cost, some of the contractors insisting that the drawings that were sent represented parts that were not included in the original contract. But I think the contracts and specifications amply covered them. The boats were to be fitted complete with all their appurtenances; and it would be impossible in a general drawing, or in any specifications, to describe all the parts. For that reason, in all the government contracts there is a provision that whatever omissions may have been made in the specifications or drawings shall not relieve the contractor from his responsibility to fit them complete for sea.

By Mr. Odell:

Question. Do you consider the engine a success?

Answer. I consider the engine a decided success. It is well arranged, strong, simple, and compact, and I think will be perfectly reliable; in fact it is so very simple that there are but few parts liable to get out of order.

Question. Is it in harmony with the vessel—with her size, proportions, &c.?

Answer. I consider the engine entirely in relation to the amount of steam the boilers can furnish. I think the engine will work off all the steam that the boilers will make. If that is the case, then the boilers and the engine are in harmony. But, of course, to obtain greater speed it would have been necessary to have had more heating and grate surface, and a proportionate area of piston.

Question. I will put the question in this form: Is the failure in speed to be attributed to a defect in the hull, or in the propelling power?

Answer. I think it is to be attributed entirely to a defect in the hull—to that overhang to which I have referred. There was an immense mass of oak in the Chimo that was submerged, and in addition to the legitimate resistance which the hull meets with, that had to be towed astern. And, aside from that, it obstructed the full and free action of the propellers. The alterations remove that difficulty very thoroughly. There is a very great improvement in that respect.

DONALD McKAY sworn and examined.

By Mr. Gooch:

Question. Where do you reside, Mr. McKay?

Answer. I reside in Boston.

Question. How long have you been engaged in ship-building?

Answer. It is somewhat over thirty years.

Question. Have you built any vessels for the government? and if so, state what.

Answer. The iron-clad monitor Nanset is the first vessel I have built for the government. I am now building an iron double-ender gunboat.

Question. Will you give to the committee all the information you have in relation to the iron-clad monitors, such as you are now building?

Answer. My contract was made with the Bureau of Construction and Repair, acting in the name of the Secretary of the Navy, dated the 10th day of June, 1863, with instructions that the plans and specifications would be furnished me by Admiral Gregory, of New York. I have no knowledge who planned the model of the same, or who is responsible therefor, further than the statement of Chief Engineer Stimers to me, to the effect that he designed her in all her details, both of hull and machinery; and from the commencement to the time of Mr. Stimers's removal as general inspector of iron-clads I received all plans and instructions in relation to her construction directly from him. Hence I have reason to believe that he is responsible.

It was found on launching the Chimo and Casco that they had too much weight for their displacement. (These are of the same class as the Nanset.) This discrepancy in weight may be accounted for, first, by excess of weight of the material used, both iron and wood, the actual weights being much over those made by calculations based on the rules laid down, and the tables of weights as furnished by the manufacturers of iron. In all my tests of the weight of iron I have found it to overrun the standard. It was intended to use seasoned timber, but such as was required could not be found in the country; hence it was necessary to use unseasoned, producing a heavy excess of weight in this particular.

Furthermore, experiments with the monitors at Charleston suggested a number of improvements necessary to be made to make them more efficient, necessitating an addition of considerable weight of material, which, in my judgment, the boats would have borne, and not materially exceeded the contemplated draught of water, but for the excess of material as above stated, as by a calculation which I made I found that after they were equipped for sea it would have required 400 tons to have entirely immersed them.

When it was discovered that more displacement was required to make them as efficient as possible, it was decided to raise the decks, and build up the hulls twenty-two inches of those not too far advanced. This I have done with the Nanset, with all possible despatch. This alteration, I believe, will make the boats more efficient and comfortable, and add materially to the strength, and, in my judgment, the money spent in this alteration is well spent.

The material and workmanshp of the Nanset and the other boats, so far as I have seen them, are of the very best; and instead of the department's paying too high for them, I would say that I would not to-day contract to duplicate the Nanset for less than $200,000 more than the price agreed to be paid for her.

A good deal has been said in opposition to this class of vessels by some of the builders, and others who have had no experience in ship-building, and know nothing of its science, and, furthermore, are unfriendly to the government, and say and do what they can in opposition to the administration.

The committee should, I think, take into consideration the prejudice and jealousy of various parties, who are not disposed to look with favor upon anything not designed by themselves. I consider this class of boats, if properly built according to this general plan and specification, with an increase of speed, say eight knots, the best yet designed for our coast and harbor defences.

Question. What alterations have been made from the original plans and specifications, as furnished by Admiral Gregory?

Answer. From time to time changes were made. Plans were always sent forward at the time the changes were ordered.

Question. Can you describe more particularly the alterations which have been made?

Answer. No alterations were made in the dimensions of the hull. The changes consisted in adding more material; for instance, strengthening the pilot-house, adding a base ring to the turret, and vacuum engines, and some other things that were deemed essential by the inspector, after the experience at Charleston and other places where the monitors were in action.

Question. You account for the increased displacement above the estimate from the fact that the weight of the material used in the construction was greater than had been estimated?

Answer. Yes, sir, and in the extra weight of material added for improvements.

Question. Ought they not to have taken that into account in making their original estimate?

Answer. Yes, sir, I think they should.

Question. Has not the displacement been increased considerably in consequence of the alterations?

Answer. It has. More material has been added to the vessel, which would require more displacement to carry the weights.

Question. Ought not the calculations, where so much exactness was required as in estimating the displacement of these vessels, to have been made on the actual facts, instead of relying upon any rules?

Answer. Ship-builders generally rely upon the rules and tables of weights, both of iron and wood, as laid down, in making their calculations for displacement. It would have been impossible to have made these calculations on actual weights, except all the material of hull and machinery were first got out ready for use, and weighed before the model was made and displacement calculated; this, as you know, would be entirely impracticable. As near as I can calculate, if the vessel had been constructed of seasoned timber, and iron at standard weight, and no alteration made increasing the weights, she would not have exceeded the intended draught of water of 6 feet 6 inches.

Question. Was it not a well-known fact to everybody who had paid any attention to the subject, that it was not possible to obtain seasoned timber, such as these vessels called for, at the time the contracts were made?

Answer. Yes, sir; it was not in the country. Individuals could not obtain it, and the government could not obtain it. There was not a ton of seasoned oak in the market suitable for these boats.

Question. Then to call for the use of that material in four or six months was to call for an impossibility?

Answer. Well, oak cannot be seasoned in less than three years.

Question. Then the contracts called for an impossibility in that particular?

Answer. Yes, sir.

Question. Within what time was it possible for you to have finished this vessel, provided there had been no alteration in the original plans?

Answer. Well, I think it would take a year to complete these vessels. They were much more difficult than any one had any idea of when they commenced them.

Question. In what time did you think it was possible to complete the Nanset when you commenced her?

Answer. I thought I could complete her within the time specified in the contract.

Question. What was the time mentioned in your contract?

Answer. It was eight months.

Question. The Nanset is being built up twenty-two inches, is she not?

Answer. Yes, sir.

Question. Will you tell us for what purpose that vessel will be efficient when she is completed?

Answer. Well, I think she will be as efficient a vessel as any of the monitors that have been built before. I think she will have more strength. Her longitudinal strength will be far superior to that of the first monitors.

Question. Would this vessel be an efficient vessel if an attack was to be made upon the ports in Charleston harbor?

Answer. I think a vessel of that class would be a very efficient vessel. There is so little surface above the water that I think the invention is a very valuable one. They are difficult to hit, and they might fire and do great execution, and receive very little damage. They might get an unlucky shot, and sink; but I think the chances are very much in their favor.

Question. Would such a monitor be efficient in an attack upon Wilmington?

Answer. Yes, sir; I think she is just the vessel they want. I think she would be of great value to the government, and as many more like her as they could get there.

Question. Was any price agreed upon for the alterations that were made in this vessel as she progressed from time to time, until the proposed alteration, whereby you are to raise her up twenty-two inches?

Answer. No, sir; except that in some cases Mr. Stimers requested me to make an estimate of the cost, which I did, and he signified his acceptance.

Question. What was the original contract price?

Answer. $386,000. They were all on the same scale, the whole twenty.

Question. Did you have any communication with any of the department, except Mr. Stimers, in relation to the alterations that were made?

Answer. No, sir; I have never had any communication with the department, or the Bureaus of Construction and Repair and Steam Engineering, at Washington, on the subject.

Question. Since making the contract, which you say was made with the department, or somebody representing the department, have you made any contract or agreement with anybody, except Mr. Stimers, in relation to the Nanset?

Answer. No, sir; not until I commenced the alteration of raising her twenty-two inches; when I made agreements with and received orders from Admiral Gregory and Chief Engineer Wood.

Question. What is the amount of the alterations, exclusive of the last one proposed—the building up of the sides?

Answer. I have never made any calculation.

By Mr. Odell:

Question. You feel you have a claim against the government?

Answer. Oh, yes; I have got several thousand dollars, which have already been granted by Mr. Stimers from time to time.

By Mr. Gooch:

Question. You have seen the Chimo?

Answer. Yes, sir.

Question. Would she have been of any service without the alterations?

Answer. No; I think she drew too much water—that is, with all her equipments on board.

Question. In your judgment, could these vessels have been so altered as to have retained their turrets, and yet been so lightened as to have made them serviceable?

Answer. That I have not calculated. It would involve questions for engineers to decide, and engineers differ in respect to it.

Question. Will you state to the committee just how far these boats will be trustworthy at sea after they have been built up twenty-two inches?

Answer. Well, I think they will be full as trustworthy as any monitor that has been built (except the Monadnock and Dictator class) since the commencement of the war. I have seen almost all of them, and I think these will be full as good and safe boats in every respect.

Question. How far do you consider that the monitors are trustworthy?

Answer. I think they were never intended for sea-going vessels. A sea-going vessel is a vessel that can visit a foreign coast; that can, as Englishmen say, "coast round Cape Horn;" but I don't think any of these vessels are fit to go to sea. They are fit to go up and down our American coast, in the care of good pilots, and go from port to port, as they have done. I think that is the design of this class of monitors; and the usefulness they will be to the country will be in defending our harbors and coast. I think that, after these vessels are built up, they will be fully as good as those down at Charleston, and stronger.

By Mr. Wade:

Question. You speak of their strength—you mean of the wood-work, not of the armor?

Answer. Yes, sir; I mean altogether.

Question. What was the thickness of the armor of the original monitor?

Answer. I have understood that it was five one-inch plates.

Question. Will you state the difference between this class of monitors and those now in use?

Answer. Well, the other monitors have not near the amount of wood backing that these have. I consider these vessels more efficient in every respect than the first class of monitors—better sea-boats, better for war purposes, heavier built, better constructed, and more costly vessels.

Question. And yet they were to be of lighter draught?

Answer. They were to be, in the first place, of lighter draught.

Question. If you had been called upon to design an iron-clad monitor, which was to draw as much water as these will when completed, should you have built her on the same model that these are being built?

Answer. Well, similar to that. I might have made them a little shorter and a little wider, but I should have had to make them about the same shape. To get that draught, you have got to make something very nearly resembling a box. It is very difficult to get a vessel of that draught to carry that armament. There are over five hundred tons of iron in one of these vessels.

Question. What do you estimate the speed of the Nanset will be when she is completed?

Answer. I consider that it will be six knots in smooth water.

Question. What alteration have you made in the overhang?

Answer. We have reduced its weight, and have raised the whole work, allowing the water to have free course to pass from the propeller. We have made a great improvement upon the overhang.

Question. What has been the effect of that alteration?

Answer. It has never been tried.

Question. What do you estimate will be the advantage from the alteration of the overhang?

Answer. I think it will increase the speed a knot and a half.

Question. Is the overhang now as small as it can be, and still protect the rudder?

Answer. Yes, sir. Men of experience consider that the rudder must be protected. I consider it as very essential to protect the rudder; but there are a good many who think that the rudder may be entirely bare. I am not of that opinion.

Question. In your opinion, is it a practicable thing to build an iron-clad sea-going monitor if no limitation is made as to draught?

Answer. Yes, sir; I can build one that will be sea-going. They have built them in England, and we can build them here. They have built them for Russia, for the Spanish government, and for the Germans, to be used in the Danish war.

Question. How far have they been tested?

Answer. Very satisfactorily.

Question. Are they similar to ours?

Answer. I think they are copies, *fac similes,* of Ericsson's first monitors in the turret arrangement, and very nearly so in the hull, and they have been very efficient.

Question. Do you know the size of those English monitors?

Answer. They are vessels of some 1,500 or 1,600 tons, some of them carrying two turrets. These vessels could be constructed so that there would be no danger in going across the Atlantic. I should have no hesitation in crossing the Atlantic in the Monadnock. She could go across as safely as an English steamer. I consider these vessels of the Monadnock class the finest ever built for sea-going and war purposes. I think they could not possibly be better for that class of vessels.

Question. For what purpose could these light-draught monitors be used that the Monadnock could not be?

Answer. The Monadnock draws about twelve feet of water. It is a very important thing to get a vessel drawing only seven and a half or eight feet. You can choose your point, and if you find the enemy are getting too much for you, you can run into shoal water and get out of the way.

By Mr. Odell:

Question. What do you estimate the cost of the Nanset will be, after she shall have been completed under the plans you are now at work upon?

Answer. The cost will be somewhere between five and six hundred thousand dollars, when completed for sea—much less than I would build one for now.

Question. You state that your original contract was for $386,000, and that, by a subsequent contract, you are to have $86,000 for raising the sides twenty-two inches, and that you have a claim in addition to these two amounts?

Answer. Yes, sir; we have a claim for alterations made from time to time.

Questions. And for these alterations no specified price was agreed upon?

Answer. No, sir; they were ordered without stipulation in regard to cost, except in a few instances

Question. How are you going to adjust these accounts?

Answer. We send in our bills for a certain piece of work; for instance, adding the ring to the turret; setting forth that we have done so and so, giving the weight of the iron, and our opinion that it is worth so much. In almost all cases they have cut it down. We have not settled yet; but I have been told that every man who has settled has settled without a dollar of profit.

By Mr. Wade:

Question. The original plan of these monitors contemplated the introduction of water compartments, for the purpose of sinking the vessel down when necessary?

Answer. Yes, sir.

Question. That apparatus has been abandoned in the improved monitors?

Answer. Yes, sir, the pipes have been taken out. I consider that these vessels, if built according to the present plans and orders, will be good vessels, and valuable to the country. At least, mine will be. I cannot vouch for the others further than that I have seen a good many, and have observed that the work was well and substantially done.

B. F. LEONARD sworn and examined.

By Mr. Gooch:

Question. Will you state your place of residence and occupation?

Answer. My place of residence is Carver, Massachusetts; my occupation has been that of machinist and engine-builder previous to inspecting. I commenced my inspecting duties in iron-clads the 1st of June, 1863.

Question. By whom were you employed for that purpose?

Answer. Mr. Stimers employed me.

Question. Had you known Mr. Stimers prior to that time?

Answer. I had not.

Question. How happened you to be employed for that purpose?

Answer. I was recommended to Mr. Stimers by an acquaintance of mine, Mr. Murdock, formerly employed in the Bureau of Engineering at Washington.

Question. What vessels have you inspected?

Answer. None but the Suncook, one of the light-draught iron-clad monitors, now being built by the Globe works at South Boston.

Question. Will you give us all the information you have in relation to these iron-clad monitors?

Answer. My instructions have been received from Mr. Stimers until this last alteration was ordered, and since then from Chief Engineer Wood. The keel of the Suncook was partly laid when I commenced inspection, and I found some iron which was not as thick as required by the specifications, and had that removed and other iron put in its place; and from that time I believe the work has been done according to the contract and specifications. As regards the efficiency of the vessel when finished, I am of opinion that it will not answer the purpose it was intended for on account of drawing too much water.

Question. How far is the Suncook advanced?

Answer. Well, the deck is very nearly on, and her sides plated, with the exception of riveting up inside the hull, and a little of the vertical cross-floors. The contract proposes launching the 15th of next month.

Question. Can you describe the alterations which were made from the original plans and specifications, as she has progressed from stage to stage?

Answer. I cannot. The alterations are such as Mr. Hoyt described. We have had three general plans. The last is the one where the vertical cross-floors are described, the ring round the turret, the increased thickness of the pilot-house, and also the addition of the vacuum engine and the condenser.

Question. Do you know what it is estimated the Suncook will draw after the alterations are made?

Answer. No, sir; I have never seen any estimates.

Question. Do you know what it is estimated her speed will be?

Answer. I never have seen any estimates of her speed.

Question. Had you ever had any connexion with, or knowledge of, wooden or iron-clad vessels before you were appointed inspector?

Answer. No, sir; I had never been employed in the construction of any.

Question. Had you any knowledge of, or had you ever been employed in connexion with marine engines?

Answer. No, sir. I had been engaged a number of years in building stationary engines, and I also had a knowledge of the materials used in ship-building, such as iron. I have built rolling-mills, and the machinery for rolling-mills, and I consider that I am a judge of iron and of the materials of which ships are constructed.

Question. But you had no particular knowledge of ship-building or of marine engines until since your appointment to your present office?

Answer. No, sir.

Question. Has there been any other inspection of the Suncook except that made by you since your appointment?

Answer. No, sir, except an inspection of the boilers by a committee chosen for that purpose.

FRIDAY, *December* 23.

Rear-Admiral SILAS H. STRINGHAM sworn and examined.

By Mr. Wade:

Question. What is your position in the navy of the United States?

Answer. I am rear-admiral on the retired list of the navy of the United States.

Question. And stationed where?

Answer. In command of the station and navy yard at Boston.

Question. How long have you followed the seas?

Answer. Fifty-four years last June.

Question. What knowledge have you of the light-draught monitors, twenty of which were ordered to be built by the government?

Answer. I have very little knowledge except as they have been turned over to me to assist in fitting them out at the navy yard.

Question. Have you seen any of them after they were launched?

Answer. I have seen the Casco and the Chimo at the navy yard.

Question. Did you examine them enough to form an opinion as to their usefulness as vessels-of-war?

Answer. Well, I must say I did not give them a critical examination. They were not under my charge at all, except to assist in fitting them out; and an older officer being responsible for them, I did not give them a critical examination.

Question. Was the turret on either of these vessels when you saw it?

Answer. No, sir.

Question. It had been taken off?

Answer. Yes, sir.

Question. What useful purpose could such a thing be applied to with the turret taken off?

Answer. I must say that I don't know exactly to what use they could be applied to be serviceable. With a big gun on deck they might lay off at a distance and bombard an enemy; but I should think a small wooden vessel, a bomb-boat, or a schooner, would be equally serviceable.

Question. What do you think of their seaworthiness in that condition?

Answer. They might make the passage from one port to another in that condition; but if they were to undertake to go to sea without another vessel to take care of them, it would be very dangerous. They would not be seagoing vessels.

Question. Did you hear what their speed was?

Answer. I heard that the speed of the Chimo, before the turret was taken off, was three or four knots.

Question. Would that be sufficient power to enable them to ascend our rivers?

Answer. In some cases it would, and in others it would not. Some of our rivers average three and a half knots an hour. With a strong breeze against them, although they would not hold much wind, they would not make any speed against it; they might just hold their way.

Question. Would they be useful, in your judgment, rigged up as torpedo boats?

Answer. From what I have heard I think they might be so. Showing but very little surface on the water, they might, in the night, go into places where they would not be discovered.

Question. Would they answer that purpose as well as smaller wooden craft built for the purpose?

Answer. I think the wooden craft would have more speed, and be better adapted to that purpose.

Question. What would be the effect on their usefulness in shoal water and in our rivers if the sides were built up 22 inches, and the draught increased a foot?

Answer. If the deck was raised as well as the sides, I don't think it would be much of an improvement, except that it would give better accommodations to the men.

Question. Would it add much to their usefulness?

Answer. I think not. My opinion, however, cannot be considered a very strong opinion, because I have not, as I said before, examined them critically.

Question. Would vessels that draw more than six and a half feet of water be very useful about the shoals of southern ports and in southern rivers?

Answer. Not in North Carolina ports and those waters, and I have no doubt these were intended for that purpose. You cannot build an iron-clad to have only that draught; their weight must take them down.

SATURDAY, *December* 24, 1864.

ISAAC NEWTON sworn and examined.

By Mr. Wade:

Question. What position do you hold in the navy?

Answer. First assistant engineer.

Question. Where are you stationed?

Answer. I have been here in Boston for four or five months superintending the alterations on the Casco and the Chimo.

Question. How long have you acted as an engineer?

Answer. Well, I should say about ten years. I entered the navy June 14, 1861, as first assistant engineer.

Question. What information have you in regard to the light-draught monitors so called, twenty of which were ordered by the government?

Answer. My acquaintance with the monitors commenced with the first vessel of that class; I assisted in superintending her construction, and was chief engineer of her for about five months.

Question. Were you with her when she had her encounter with the Merrimac?

Answer. Yes, I was connected with her shortly after her keel was laid; was with her on the James river during McClellan's campaign, and after that I was detached and ordered to report to Rear-Admiral Gregory at New York.

Question. What do you know about the construction of the light-draught monitor called the Chimo?

Answer. She is one of the twenty ordered by the government in 1863.

Question. Who modelled and designed her?

Answer. Mr. Simers.

Question. Did Mr. Ericsson have anything to do with it?

Answer. I should say not. Of course the turret, and the machinery that appertains to the turret, are his.

Question. Yes; but I will ask you who is responsible for the draught and build of that vessel?

Answer. Mr. Striners.

Question. Did you have a knowledge of the progress of the work as it went on?

Answer. As much as I could, being at headquarters, where all the correspondence with the contractors was carried on, and where all the drawings were made. I had general charge of the drawings at the office in New York.

Question. Was the plan altered from time to time as the work progressed?

Answer. I do not think the model was altered; the details, that did not affect the total weight very much, were.

Question. But they did affect the expense?

Answer. There were several things found to be necessary during the fights in Charleston harbor, which were ordered to be put on these vessels in common with all other monitors; for instance, a base ring was found necessary at the bottom of the turret, and some additions of weight were made in that way.

Question. Can you give any idea of the expense of these deviations from the original plan?

Answer. No, I cannot tell you that exactly; I could ascertain it by reference to papers; but it would be a mere guess if I undertook to give it now.

Question. What do you say, as an engineer and a gentleman skilled in ship-building, to the draught and build of these monitors for the purpose designed—that is, for shallow water?

Answer. If there had been no mistake made in the draught of water they would have been efficient for that—in still water.

Question. What mistake was made in the draught, in your judgment?

Answer. I think there was a mistake of about ten inches.

Question. Please explain that.

Answer. They were too deep in the water. A great trouble was that they trim about one foot by the stern. This latter is not a very unusual mistake in ship-building. In an engineering point of view this error in the trim is no greater than, if as great as, was made in balancing the weights with the displacement on the two-turreted wooden monitor Monadnock. In this case, as the constructor had the free disposal of the principal weights, there was no difficulty in adjusting them equally with the displacement. In single-turreted vessels, the steam machinery being in one end, and the quarters for officers and men in the other, it is a very difficult matter to trim them without the use of ballast in the forward part. There is no objection, however, in this, if provision is made for it in the design.

Question. How happened that?

Answer. Because there was more weight aft of the centre of gravity of the displacement than before it, and from an under-estimate of weights.

Question. Was it difficult for a competent draughtsman to construct her so that she would not draw more than six and a half feet of water?

Answer. It is not difficult for a competent draughtsman to ascertain displacement; but to arrive at the weight he should not take the results of his calculations, but leave a margin, unless he is going to build her himself, and can have her under his own eyes, and weigh everything.

Question. I speak of cases where it is essential to have the vessel of a particular draught. Would it not be necessary that some particular pains should be taken to ascertain the weight?

Answer. The draughtsman should calculate the weights, and then add a margin to that. I should say that would be the only safe way.

Question. What margin should you say it would be proper to add?

Answer. That is a very difficult question to answer. I should say ten per cent. at least.

Question. Did I understand you to say that a mistake of ten inches was made in the draught?

Answer. I think about ten inches. One of the great troubles was that they trimmed badly; they were by the stern. If they had been on an even keel it would not have been so bad, but I think they would have been too far down even then.

Question. Was this same mistake made in regard to the whole twenty?

Answer. They were all supposed to be identical. They were all built from tracings taken from the same drawings and from the same specifications.

Question. Did you see the Chimo after she was launched?

Answer. Yes; I saw her after she was completed.

Question. Well, what was her appearance when she was launched?

Answer. I did not see her when she was launched. When I saw her and took charge of her she was finished—had her turret, guns, and everything on.

Question. What induced them to take the turret off?

Answer. She could not carry it. However, that was an after consideration, I think. The immediate cause was that some high officer in the navy required some of them for special service without turrets.

Question. You say she could not have carried her turret?

Answer. I do not think she could have carried her turret. It would have been an evenly balanced thing whether or no she could. It would have been necessary to take one of her boilers out, and make radical changes to dispense with weight.

Question. In your judgment was she good for anything as a war vessel when she was finished?

Answer. She was too deep; she would not have been a very efficient war vessel.

Question. What could she do?

Answer. Well, if another vessel came up close to her, she could fire at her; she could not go after her, without her opponent's speed was very slow.

Question. You say she could not carry her turret?

Answer. In smooth water I think she could have carried it.

Question. Would it have been safe to take her from harbor to harbor?

Answer. I should say no—decidedly not.

Question. Without her turret she would be no better than a wooden vessel, would she?

Answer. If they wanted her for a torpedo boat or a reconnoitring vessel she would be better, because she could go up and let the enemy shoot while the reconnoissance was being made.

Question. What was the speed of the Chimo on her trial trip?

Answer. I understood it was from three and a half to four knots.

Question. Would that give her sufficient power to ascend our rivers?

Answer. Of course, if there was no great current in the river, she could go up.

Question. Against tide-water in our harbors would she make any speed?

Answer. She would just about hold her own in that respect.

Question. Is there any rule by which ship-builders ascertain the amount of water a vessel will displace?

Answer. Certainly; that is necessary in building any ship. That is ascertained by calculating the capacity of the immersed portions of the vessel.

Question. Is it difficult to ascertain, within two or three inches, what a ship will draw if she is to be built for a certain service?

Answer. I should say it was, decidedly, unless you weigh the materials that go into the vessel.

Question. Provided it is essential to have a particular draught, should not that pains be taken?

Answer. If you allow a sufficient margin, I should say not. If you add a certain margin to the specific gravity of the materials, as laid down in the tables, your vessel will draw less rather than more.

Question. Do you know whether or not any alteration was made in the build of these vessels?

Answer. I should think not.

Question. Some of these vessels have been built up on the sides twenty-two inches, have they not?

Answer. Yes; fifteen of them.

Question. What will be the effect of that on them?

Answer. It will make them much better boats.

Question. What will they be good for when they are built up in that way?

Answer. They will be good for operations on rivers and in other waters—Albrmarle sound, for instance; they will be better boats than before.

Question. They will draw quite as much water, if not more?

Answer. Of course they will draw more, because more weight has been added; but they will still be very light-draught iron-clads.

Question. Well, if their object was to ascend rivers, would they be useful boats as a general thing; wouldn't they draw too much water?

Answer. That is a very light draught, considering the impregnability and battery of the ships and their strength.

Question. You mean for sea-going boats?

Answer. They are not what I call sea-going boats. I think they can be taken down our coast with safety, watching times. You perceive a great deal has been added to their strength by raising the sides, and they are more comfortable.

Question. But for the purpose for which they were originally designed—that is, to draw not more than six and a half feet of water, and for service on rivers and shoals—they would not be useful?

Answer. Their usefulness would only be impaired as much as the additional one foot adds to their draught.

Question. What is the thickness of the armor on these vessels?

Answer. On the sides three inches, and the backing, I think, is very thick—it must be four feet thick. They are very hard things to shoot through, even with their three-inch armor on.

Question. What was the thickness of the original monitor?

Answer. Five inches, with a backing of three feet of white oak.

Question. Would this armor, the light draught, be heavy enough to withstand the heaviest artillery?

Answer. I should say not the heaviest, but such as, at the time they were planned, they would be likely to meet in rivers, and such calibre as they would be likely to meet now. They would not stand 15-inch guns, nor, probably, 11-inch, at close quarters, with a heavy charge; but they would stand temporary batteries thrown up on rivers, &c.

Question. As an engineer, would it be difficult for you to construct a vessel, with the armament and impregnability contemplated in these light-draught monitors, that would not draw more than six and a half feet of water?

Answer. I should say, with my present experience, I could readily do so, but at the time these were proposed I could not, because I knew nothing about them. It was a problem never before attempted.

By Mr. Gooch:

Question. Describe particularly the service which the fifteen light-draught monitors, now being built up, will be able to perform.

Answer. They will be able to hold and defend a great part of our inland waters.

Question. What, in your opinion, will be the maximum and service speed?

Answer. The speed will depend upon the depth of water which they navigate. The speed will be eight miles; the maximum a little more.

Question. Did Engineer Stimers accompany the original Monitor on her trip to Hampton roads, and was he on board during the fight with the Merrimac; and if so, what part did he perform during the engagement?

Answer. He did accompany the original Monitor; he was on board during the engagement; he operated the turret in a very efficient manner, and at the same time encouraged the gunners, and thereby, no doubt, promoted the energetic and effective service of the guns.

Question. How many different classes of monitors have been constructed by the government since the original Monitor, and what is the difference and function of each class?

Answer. The Passaic class, the Canonicus class, the Monadnock and Miantonomah class, the Dictator and Puritan class, the Kalamazoo class, now in process of construction, and the light-draughts, besides some river monitors built out west, like the Chickasaw and Winnebago, which proved so efficient at the battle of Mobile bay.

The Passaic and Canonicus classes have iron hulls and single turrets; the midship section of these is nearly the same, except that the latter have less wooden backing and much thicker armor; they also have thicker deck plating; they have finer models and much more steam power; they are also provided with a different anchor arrangement. The Monadnock and Miantonomah classes are for all practical purposes identical; they have two turrets, wooden hulls, two propellers; the iron armor is the same as the Passaic class, but the deck plating is heavier. These classes are of moderate draught of water, are very manageable, have proved themselves to be capable of enduring heavy weather, and are peculiarly adapted for harbor defence, and operations against the rebels.

The efficient service of the Passaic class in the South Atlantic squadron is now a matter of history.

The Dictator and Puritan class are relatively large vessels; have very fine models, immense steam power, by far the heaviest armor ever put afloat; they will have very high speed, and can handle their guns where probably no English iron-clad could fire a gun, at least with any accuracy. From their greater speed they are fitted for marine offensive operations against the iron-clads of a naval enemy; they can stand any weather without discomfort. The Kalamazoo class are adapted for the same work as that just mentioned; they have two turrets, and armor even thicker; their hulls are of wood, built in the strongest manner.

Question. Who planned these different classes of monitors?

Answer. The original Monitor, Passaic, Dictator, and Puritan classes were planned by Ericsson's own hand, and built accordingly. The Canonicus class and light-draughts Ericsson furnished a general plan, which was modified and, in the case of light-draughts, radically changed by Chief Engineer Stimers. The hulls of the wooden monitors were planned by the naval constructors; those for the Kalamazoo class by Mr. Delano. The turrets and all appurtenances to them, the pilot-house, steering gear, wrought-iron gun-carriages, and friction gear-port stoppers, &c., were made from Ericsson's drawings.

Question. Who was the general inspector of each of these classes of monitors?

Answer. Of the iron vessels and the turrets of the wooden ones Mr. Stimers, until he was detached from that duty.

Question. What duty have you performed since you left the Monitor?

Answer. Superintended a great part of the planning, examined the execution of the work to a considerable extent, instructed contractors, carried on correspondence, examined bills and accounts and similar office work, besides, on several occasions, accompanying the monitors down the coast.

Question. Are you sure Captain Ericsson had no part in planning the light-draught monitors?

Answer. With the exception of the turrets, nothing has been made to his drawings.

Question. Do you know if Mr. Stimers had consultations with Captain Ericsson in relation to the light-draught monitors?

Answer. I know he called at his office several times.

Question. Do you know whether there was a rupture between Captain Ericsson and Mr. Stimers; and if so, what was its cause, and at what time did it occur?

Answer. There was a rupture, and it was occasioned by the manner in which Mr. Stimers tested the friction gear of the Canonicus, and it occurred last winter.

Question. Do you know what instructions Mr. Stimers received from the Navy Department in relation to the light-draught monitors?

Answer. I do not know what instructions he received.

Question. When was Mr. Stimers removed from his position as general inspector, and why was he removed?

Answer. Last June; the order which removed him did not give the reason; therefore I cannot state why.

Question. You were chief engineer of the original Monitor during her engagement with the Merrimac; will you state your opinion why that battle, decisive as it was, was not more so?

Answer. It was due to the fact that the power and endurance of the 11-inch Dahlgren guns, with which she was armed, were not known at the time of the battle; hence the commander would scarcely have been justified in increasing the charge of powder above that authorized in the Ordnance Manual.

Subsequent experiments developed the important fact that these guns could be fired with thirty pounds of cannon powder with solid shot. If this had been known at the time of the action, I am clearly of opinion that, from the close quarters at which Lieutenant Worden fought his vessel, the enemy would have been forced to surrender.

Furthermore, I think that if our gallant commander had not been severely injured by a shot or shell, fired but a very few yards off, and which struck the sight aperture in the pilot-house through which he was looking, we would have stood a very good chance of "badgering" her to a surrender, as our shots, striking near the water-line, had already made her leak seriously. The leaking—so it has been stated in rebel sources—was aggravated by her futile attempt at ramming the Monitor.

It will, of course, be admitted by every one that if but a single 15-inch gun could possibly have been mounted within the Monitor's turret (it was planned to carry the heaviest ordnance) the action would have been as short and decisive as the combat between the monitor Weehawken, Captain John Rodgers, and the rebel iron-clad Atlanta, which, in several respects, was superior to the Merrimac. I think, also, that this very decisive result would have been obtained if the 12-inch wrought-iron gun at the New York navy yard had been in the Monitor's turret and fired with respectable charges. This gun has been fired with two 224-pound shot with forty-five pounds of powder.

Question. Have you watched the career of the iron-clads during the present war?

Answer. I have done so, attentively.

Question. With what result?

Answer. It has firmly riveted my conviction from the beginning that the monitor system of iron-clads is a complete and positive solution of the great naval question of the day.

Question. What do you consider the special function of iron-clad vessels?

Answer. To protect our harbors from the attack of foreign fleets, to fight foreign iron-clads, and for such operations against the rebels as the exigencies of the war require. It has been admitted by the British defence commission, and other high authorities, that no forts, of any description, can prevent the passage of a fleet of steamships through an unobstructed channel. I think General Barnard expresses the same opinion in his Dangers and Defences of New York. The experience of the present war certainly corroborates this view of the case. The enemy's iron-clads must be met by iron-clads.

A further consideration of this question also suggests that we should have three classes of iron-clads: 1st, Dictators and Kalamazoos, to catch swift foreign iron-clads; 2d, Passaics and Canonicuses, as heavily armed as the former, but only fast enough to navigate the coast; 3d, light-draughts, to hold and defend our rivers, &c. Of course the 3d class cannot be as impregnable as the other two. The 2d class we *must* have, to defend our harbors.

Question. Are you familiar with the experiments which have been carried on at Shoeburyness, England, with guns against armor?

Answer. Yes, as much as one on this side of the Atlantic can be. These experiments have been very extensive, but at the same time of quite a desultory character, as may be instanced by the fact that Whitworth, a long time since, penetrated a Warrior target with a *flat*-headed *steel* shot, but it was a very long time before the ordnance authorities found out that the efficiency of the projectile itself was not in the *flat* front, but in the material of which it was made.

Question. As an engineer, what bearing, in your mind, have these experiments on the iron-clad question?

Answer. To condemn broadside iron-clads for general naval purposes.

Question. Why?

Answer. Without going into any of their other deficiencies, I will simply state that, from the nature of the case, it is impossible to build them of any practicable and manageable size which can sustain armor of the thickness required to keep out shot from modern ordnance now in service. The English iron-plate committee have, I believe, virtually reported this.

Question. Are you familiar with what has been done in England in constructing powerful ordnance for iron-clad warfare?

Answer. Yes; it has been chiefly in fabricating wrought-iron guns on what is termed the Armstrong coil system, which consists in shrinking successive cylinders, made of long bars of iron coiled spirally and welded over each other.

Question. How will our ordnance designed for the same service compare with theirs?

Answer. English ordnance for this duty is still in the experimental stage; no guns which will compare with ours have been introduced into service. We have plenty of 15-inch guns, mounted and used in turrets in battle, which are permitted by the Ordnance Manual to be fired with sixty pounds of powder and solid shot against iron-clads; no broadside iron-clad yet designed can resist this gun. The only gun in England proposed for service, which will compare with it for this purpose, is the experimental 13½-inch Armstrong, which is not yet, I believe, regarded as a success. Mr. Fox, I believe, insisted on the introduction of the 15-inch; without it our turrets would be toothless. My present standard of perfection for a gun for iron-clad warfare is a piece of 15-inch calibre, with strength sufficient to stand with safety one hundred pounds of cannon powder and a solid spherical shot of steel. I consider an impregnable vessel, with the speed of about fourteen knots, mounting one or two such guns, capable of being trained to any point of the horizon—in other words, mounted on a swift monitor—to be a match for the whole iron-clad fleet of England, for they must either get out of the way or be sunk *seriatim.*

Question. You have stated that the monitor system solves the problem, &c. Will you state your reasons for this opinion?

Answer. It is the system which permits of the *maximum* thickness with the *minimum* capacity of vessel; not only are the guns protected, but the hull from one end to the other is covered with armor, and the propeller and rudder are also completely protected. It permits of the use and perfect control of the heaviest ordnance which can be fabricated. It is the only system which is alike applicable to light-draught vessels for service in shoal water, as well as the very largest class with very heavy armor and armament.

Question. Are you familiar with the construction, impregnability, and ordnance power of the heavy turret iron-clads built and building by the government?

Answer. I am.

Question. In your opinion, as engines of war, how do they compare with the iron-clads built and building in England?

Answer. With the exception of two or three badly designed turret ships the English have simply rung the changes on broadside iron-clads. They are now convinced that the plan at first adopted of merely protecting the central portion of the vessel and the water-line is erroneous. The Warrior, according to the London Mechanics' Magazine, is now to be lengthened in three places, so that she can carry armor over the entire length. I should think this was a virtual condemnation of the new semi-protected iron-clads of Mr. Reed, the chief constructor of the navy, from which so much was expected. They cannot carry armor of the whole length. *Cæteris paribus*, the area to be covered with armor varies as the square, while the displacement or the capacity to carry it varies as the cube of the lineal dimensions; hence the necessity for very large iron-clads built on the English plans.

The following is a list of the iron-clads built and building for the English navy:

Names of vessels.	ALL VESSELS BUILT AND BUILDING.									SIDE ARMOR AND CASEMATE.				CUPOLA.								
	Tonnage.*	Length.	Beam.	Height out of water.	Draught.	No. of rifle guns.	Kind and size of rifle guns.	No. of smooth-bores.	Kind of smooth-bores.	Length of casemated part.	Thickness of armor plates.	Thick. of backing.	Thick. of skin.	No. of cupolas.	Thick. of armor.	Backing.	Skin.	Diam. of cylinder.	Length of stroke.	Indicated H. P.	Speed in knots.‡	Mean draught.
		ft. in.	ft. in.				lbs.		lbs.	ft. in.	in.	in.	in.					in.	ft. in.			ft. in.
Warrior	6,109	380 0	58 4	20 0	26 3½	10 4	110 40	26	68	213 0	4½	18	9–16	....	....	....	....	†104	4 0	5,471	14.4	§25 11½
Black Prince	6,109	380 0	58 4	20 0	26 9	11 4	110 40	26	68	213 0	4½	18	9–16	....	....	....	....	†104	4 0	5,774	13.6	§26 9½
Resistance	3,710	280 0	54 1	18 2	24 10	6	110	10 2	68 32	143 0	4½	18	9–16	....	....	....	....	†70¾	3 6	2,424	11.8	24 10½
Defence	3,720	280 0	54 2	18 2	24 11	6	110	10 2	68 32	143 0	4½	18	9–16	....	....	....	....	†70¾	3 6	2,533	11.6	24 10
Hector	4,089	280 0	56 5	18 7	24 8	10	110	24	68	216 0	4½	18	9–16	....	....	....	....	82	4 0	......	......	......
Valiant	4,063	280 0	......	18 7	24 8	10	110	24	68	216 0	4½	18	9–16	....	....	....	....	82	4 0	......	......	......
Royal Oak	4,056	273 0	58 6	18 10	24 7½	11	110	24	68	All......	4½	....	......	....	....	....	....	82	4 0	3,703	12.5	24 8
Prince Consort	4,045	273 0	58 5	18 7	25 10½	11	110	24	68	All......	4½	....	......	....	....	....	....	92	4 0	4,234	13.1	24 8½
Caledonia	4,125	273 0	59 2	18 7	25 10½	11	110	24	68	All......	4½	....	......	....	....	....	....	92	4 0	......	......	......
Ocean	4,047	273 0	58 5	18 7	25 10½	11	110	24	68	All......	4½	....	......	....	....	....	....	92	4 0	......	......	......
Royal Alfred	4,045	273 0	58 5	18 10	25 7½	11	110	24	68	All......	4½	....	......	....	....	....	....	82	4 0	......	......	......
Zealous	3,716	252 0	58 7	18 0	25 3	12	110	8	68	103 0	4½	....	......	....	....	....	....	82	4 0	......	......	......
Achilles	6,079	380 0	58 3½	20 2	26 3½	12	110	20	68	213 0	4¼	18	9–16	....	....	....	....	†104	4 0	......	......	......
Minotaur	6,621	400 0	59 3½	20 2	25 8	12	110	26	68	...(‖)...	5½	9	9–16	....	....	....	....	†104	4 4	......	......	......
Northumberland	6,621	400 0	59 3½	20 2	25 8	12	110	26	68	...(‖)...	5½	9	9–16	....	....	....	....	†104	4 4	......	......	......
Agincourt	6,621	400 0	59 3½	20 2	25 8	12	110	26	68	...(‖)...	5½	9	9–16	....	....	....	....	101	4 6	......	......	......
Favorite	2,186	225 0	46 9	14 1	20 5	10	110	.....	.....	66 3	4½	....	......	....	....	....	....	64	2 8	......	......	......
Research	1,253	195 0	38 6	12 0	14 0	2	110	2	68	34 9	4½	....	......	....	....	....	....	50	2 0	......	......	......
Enterprise	990	180 0	36 0	12 5	14 4	4	110	.....	.....	34 0	4½	....	......	....	....	....	....	45	1 6	......	......	......
Royal Sovereign	3,963	240 7	62 0½	9 7	22 11	5	.(¶).	.....	.....	All......	5½	....	......	4	5½	17	1½	82	4 0	......	......	......
Prince Albert	2,529	240 0	48 0	8 6	20 0	.(**).	.....	.....	.....	All......	4½	18	½	4	5½	17	1½	72	3 0	......	......	......
Lord Warden	4,067	280 0	58 9	18 9	25 3	36	.(††).	.....	.....	All......	4½	....	......	....	....	....	....					
Lord Clyde	4,067	280 0	58 9	18 9	25 3	36	.(††).	.....	.....	All......	4½	....	......	....	....	....	....					
Bellerophon	4,246	300 0	56 0	15 6	23 6	10 4	300 110	.....	.....	90 3	6	10	1½	....	....	....	....	No engines ordered.				
Pallas	2,372	225 0	50 0	15 0	21 0	.....	.....	.....	.....	39 2	4½	....	......	....	....	....	....					

*Not the tons displacement. †Effective. ‡Speed attained at the measured mile, in smooth water, with boilers new and free from scale, bottom of vessel clean, and with picked coal and stokers, conditions which cannot obtain in service. §The draught of these vessels exceeded this at the trial. ‖ All except 24 feet at the bow partially protected. ¶ 12 ton guns. ** Armament not yet decided on. †† 110 or 63 pound rifle guns, probably; 5½-inch thickness armor plate.

N. B. The "length" given is in every case the length between perpendiculars. The "draught" is the mean low draught, taking the *actual* draught of ships completed and equipped, and the estimated draught for the others. The "length of the casemated part" is the length of protected battery. The height out of water is measured at the top of the plank-sheer, and does not include the hammock berthing. In the Royal Sovereign and Prince Albert it is measured to the top of the deck only, as the bulwarks will be made to turn down.

Without stating anything further than that they are penetrable from one end to the other, and carry no ordnance which can penetrate our heavy monitors, while the monitors have guns which can easily penetrate them, I think the inference is safe that they are no match for our vessels.

Question. Will you state the function of the overhangs, so-called, of the monitors; whether you consider it an element of weakness, and whether any of the vessels have exhibited signs of weakness in this part; whether it has been improved since the original Monitor, and whether it can be still further improved?

Answer. The overhang is a projection of the hull, both at the bow and stern. At the bow it permits of taking in the anchor under fire; at the stern it completely protects those important parts, the propeller and rudder. The armor also forms a projection on the sides, which prevents the vessels from rolling, and adds immensely to the longitudinal strength from the peculiar manner it is attached to the hull proper. As the models have been made somewhat finer, the stern overhangs have been made smaller since the first Monitor. I do not believe the overhang of the first Monitor was ruptured. None of the Monitors which have succeeded her have exhibited any signs of weakness in this part. I think that no further improvement is essential. The Dictator, Canonicus, Monadnock, and Kalamazoo classes have only the aft overhang; the armor projection at the sides was partially abandoned in the Canonicus class, and wholly so in the Monadnock class. I think this to be a mistake; one of the most experienced officers in iron-clads has informed me that the increased rolling is a serious objection.

Question. Could the Navy Department, on any other than the monitor system, have constructed an efficient iron-clad fleet?

Answer. They could not. If broadside iron-clads had been adopted, in order to compete with those which foreign powers were producing, they must at least have been their equals in size, &c., for it is easily demonstrable they, the conditions, could not be met with smaller proportions. It would have cost us more money and three times as much time to have built a Warrior and Black Prince than it did to construct both the Passaic and Canonicus classes, and they would have been to us worse than useless vessels. The rapid fire of broadside vessels is, of course, in many cases, necessary in silencing forts, and, I believe, they have always been on hand when required during the present war.

Question. What rate of speed have you seen one of the Passaic and Canonicus classes of monitors attain?

Answer. I have seen the Montauk, one of the Passaic class, steam but a trifle short of 8½ knots; this was on a trip from New York to Hampton roads. She was in good trim, her bottom clean, and the steam machinery in good order. I have seen the Canonicus steam nearly nine knots, but, from the great steam power of this class, I am clearly of opinion that, with a few not very expensive or extensive alterations to the motive machinery, about ten knots could be readily attained.

Question. What is your opinion of the part the monitors performed in the naval battle in Mobile bay?

Answer. They certainly performed a very important part at that battle; the result, without their presence, to say the least, would have been very doubtful. The iron-clads consisted of the Manhattan and Tecumseh, of the Canonicus class, armed with 15-inch guns, and the Chickasaw and Winnebago, light Mississippi monitors. The Tecumseh was sunk by a torpedo, and, therefore, did not participate in the fight. The iron-clads took a position between the wooden ships and Fort Morgan, for the purpose of keeping down its fire, as well, I suppose, as to partially protect the wooden vessels by being placed between them and the fort. When the Tennessee started from under the guns of Fort Morgan, for the fleet, she paid no attention to the monitors, but to keep out of their way if anything, but made for the wooden ships. She was severely rammed by the heavy wooden vessels striking at high speed, and received their fire with but trifling injury, while, in return, she inflicted severe injury with her guns. If the ram had been equipped with large smooth-bores, throwing spherical shells with time fuzes, instead of the unreliable rifle shells from the comparatively small-bore rifles with which she was armed, the damage to the wooden vessels would have been still greater. If Lieutenant Commander Perkins, of the monitor Chickasaw, who hammered away at the Tennessee's stern at *close quarters*, had been possessed of the Manhattan's turret, with the 15-inch guns, the Tennessee could scarcely have held out ten minutes after he came within iron-clad range. The loss in killed and wounded in this battle was, I think, 219, exclusive of those lost on the Tecumseh; no one was injured on the monitors. I understand that the rebel officers taken prisoners said that if it had not been for the d—d monitors they would have sunk every wooden ship in the bay.

ASTOR HOUSE, NEW YORK, *December* 28, 1864.

GEORGE W. HOLLOWAY sworn and examined.

By the chairman:

Question. Please state your position in the navy of the United States.

Answer. I am acting first assistant engineer in the United States navy. I am stationed on board the United States steamer Casco, now lying at the navy yard in Brooklyn.

Question. How long have you been connected with that steamer?

Answer. Ever since the 21st of October, 1864.

Question. This Casco is what is called a light-draught steamer, one of the twenty that were ordered to be built?

Answer. Yes, sir.

Question. By whom was she built?

Answer. By the Atlantic Works.

Question. What is her draught?

Answer. I think it is seven feet five inches.

Question. That is when she has her complement on board?

Answer. No, sir, that was her draught when leaving Boston; we had but fifty tons of coal on board and nearly all our ordnance.

Question. Were you on board of her from Boston here, acting as engineer?

Answer. Yes, sir.

Question. How far was she above the water-line, or out of water, when she was running?

Answer. She appeared, when she was under headway, to draw more water at the stern than she did when her engines were started, or when lying at anchor.

Question. Describe how she worked on the passage, and what were her sea-going qualities, as you discovered on that voyage.

Answer. She worked very well all the way. We worked the engines moderately, they being new; we worked them up so as not to allow the crank-pin to heat too much, because we had a steamer in tow, and thought there was no need of running any risk. We run her as fast as we could without heating the crank-pin.

Question. Was she towed from Boston?

Answer. She was towed by the steamer Pierson.

Question. What speed does she make by herself?

Answer. I am not able to say what speed she can make. I have never been on a trial trip when the log has been held, to know what speed she would make.

I went down the river, and had a trial trip previous to that, but I never ascertained her speed.

Question. You say her engine worked well; how was it about the power of the engine? Did you put on pretty much all the power without straining the bottom of the boat?

Answer. At the trial trip previous to leaving Boston she worked very well at sixty turns. As soon as we came to run a speed of about sixty-five or seventy turns there appeared to be a very great deal of vibration in the bottom.

Question. What did you infer from that? that the bottom was not stout enough to bear the power of the engine at high speed?

Answer. I did not consider that the bottom was stiff enough to run the engine faster than sixty-five turns unless necessity required it.

Question. What speed do you suppose she would make by such an effort from the engine as would be safe?

Answer. I suppose there can be got five knots out of her safely without doing any injury.

Question. Would she make as much head if she was loaded down, or when she had more load on, with the same power?

Answer. I think it would retard the speed. The overhang at the stern appears to form a very strong eddy by being down. She appears to haul a great deal of tide-water when she is down.

Question. What is that occasioned by?

Answer. It is occasioned by not having clearance in the overhang—hanging in the water so much.

Question. Cannot that be remedied?

Answer. It could be remedied by the vessel being higher out of the water.

Question. Do you consider her a safe boat to navigate from harbor to harbor along the coast?

Answer. By herself? No, sir. I should not think she was, by my experience.

Question. How is it about leaking on the voyage? Did you discover?

Answer. The leakage appeared to be in the iron work on top. It appears that there has been no cement put between the layers of the sheets, and the water runs right through and finds its way down into the hold below.

Question. Was she under water so as to occasion that when she came along?

Answer. Yes, sir, several times.

Question. How was it when you came around Point Judith, where there was anything of a sea? Did it make over her?

Answer. We had no sea that you could call a sea; but what there was appeared to wash right over her, and that is the time she would leak—when she would be buried in the water.

Question. When she had a full complement of naval stores, fit for sea, she would lie still deeper in the water, would she not?

Answer. Yes, sir, certainly.

Question. What would she do on our rivers, or against a strong tide? Would she make much headway?

Answer. You could not get a great deal of speed out of her against a very heavy current.

Question. I suppose you had nothing to do with her construction?

Answer. No, sir.

Question. Nor the alterations of the plans in the course of construction?

Answer. No, sir.

By Mr. Odell:

Question. You were assigned to her, after she was completed, as working engineer?

Answer. Yes, sir.

Question. Have you anything further to state on this subject?

Answer. There is one other statement. I should consider that she would be safe to be towed from one harbor to another, provided she was braced properly in her bottom; she appears to have no strength at all in her bottom.

Question. Can she go with her own engine without being towed?

Answer. You could not get speed enough to stem a heavy gale of wind.

CHARLES A. CROOKER sworn and examined.

By the chairman:

Question. Please state the relation you hold to the navy of the United States.

Answer. I am acting master, in command of the steamer Casco. I have been connected with that steamer since November 22, 1864.

Question. Was she fully completed when you had connexion with her first?

Answer. She was, as far as the contractors were concerned; the men at the yard were doing some work on her.

Question. Have you any knowledge of the contract by which she was built?

Answer. None at all.

Question. You came around with her from Boston to New York?

Answer. Yes, sir.

Question. Describe what you observed with regard to her seaworthiness, and all you noticed about her.

Answer. In our passage from Boston to New York we had a very smooth sea nearly the whole of the way, and she was quite buoyant for a vessel of her kind. In coming around Point Judith, where there was something of a chopper—not a heavy sea, a short sea—the water came over her so as to go down her hatchways, consequently she leaked through the deck considerably; and in coming into the sound, past little Gull island, it was rugged, and she took seas over in the same manner and made considerable water. Her hawse-pipes forward are very bad, very leaky, and the leak is there now.

Question. What load did she have on board when you came around?

Answer. She had when leaving Boston probably 125 tons, including all.

Question. How much more would be on her when fitted for a cruise or voyage, with a full complement of men, munitions of war on board, provisions, &c.?

Answer. About fifty tons more.

Question. What amount of water did she draw on her way around as she was then loaded?

Answer. Seven feet five inches.

Question. How much more would it have sunk her to have had a full complement on board, as you have just stated?

Answer. Very little. I have not calculated the displacement of water—say one and a half or two inches.

Question. How much was she out of water when she was loaded in the way you brought her around?

Answer. She was above the water seven inches aft—one foot three and a half inches midships, and one foot five and a half forward.

Question. She had a turret?

Answer. No, sir.

Question. That had been taken off?

Answer. It had either been taken off or was never put on. There was no indication of its having been put on.

Question. She was intended for a turret?

Answer. She was.

Question. You understood her to be one of the twenty light-draught monitors of the same model?

Answer. Yes, sir.

Question. So far as you know, were they all alike?

Answer. So far as I know, they are. There is another one at the yard in Charlestown—the Chimo.

Question. Did you have any trial by which you could satisfy yourself what speed she would make?

Answer. Yes, sir. We put into Newport harbor on account of the fog, and when it cleared away I got under way without the steamer in tow, and going out on the smooth water with some sixty revolutions, she made, as near as I could judge, about five or five and a half knots. I did not heave a log, because we were going only a short distance.

Question. Could she have made her way through the rough water without the aid of the steamer?

Answer. I presume she could have made her way through. I do not think there was any current to interfere with her.

Question. What effect did the little sea that you observed have upon her?

Answer. But very little. In coming around Point Judith I could perceive that she rolled some, and there was a little rise and fall to her bows.

Question. What inference did you draw from that—that she was weak?

Answer. No, sir; it was not rough enough to try her.

Question. If she will not make over five miles an hour, would she be useful on any of our rivers?

Answer. Well, I should think not, if there is much current. She would make about five knots at the present time; in the course of a few months she will not be able to make that.

By Mr. Odell:

Question. Why not?

Answer. On account of her bottom fouling. I am unacquainted with iron vessels, and don't know how soon they foul.

By the chairman:

Question. Do you understand that they foul quicker than wooden bottoms?

Answer. Very much quicker.

Question. If she would not be able to navigate our rivers, for what useful war purpose could she be put to without the turret?

Answer. I do not know, except for some harbor defence. She is very long—225 feet—and in a narrow river it would be difficult to turn her around, or to work her, except to go right ahead. If there were short turns a vessel of that kind would be difficult to manage.

Question. Her men, of course, would have no protection from attacks from the banks of the river, seeing she carries no turret?

Answer. Not the slightest; not in working her gun.

Question. If she would be of no use for this purpose, would she be good for a torpedo vessel?

Answer. That would depend upon whether it was a narrow river. If there was plenty of sea room for her to work in, I do not know but she would. I am unacquainted with the torpedo business, and hardly know what kind of vessel would be required. She works very slowly. I suppose for a torpedo vessel you would require one to work fast. She is heavy and moves slowly.

Question. You say she might possibly be used for harbor defence; how could you use her to defend a harbor?

Answer. When you are not near enough for sharpshooters to operate. A dozen sharpshooters, in coming up one of those rivers, would pick off every one of the gunners. She might do on our wide rivers, where there is little current.

Question. For what is called light-draught steamers, do they not draw too much water?

Answer. I should think they did—seven feet five inches.

Question. Do you know how they came to draw more than six and a half feet of water?

Answer. No, sir; except it is the weight of iron that is put on.

Question. Are you acquainted with ship-building?

Answer. No, sir.

Question. How far is she seaworthy?

Answer. I hardly like to give an opinion in regard to her seaworthiness. I do not feel confident.

Question. It is an opinion, of course?

Answer. This is the first one I have ever been in.

Question. You have been in her further than anybody else, and you are an old seaman?

Answer. I find that all my old seamanship was nearly thrown away on one of these vessels.

Question. Would she be safe to go without being towed, coastwise, from harbor to harbor, in your judgment?

Answer. I should think not. I should think if her engines should be disabled there would be no chance to save her. She has no other propelling power, and there is no opportunity for rigging any.

By Mr. Odell:

Question. Did you have your water on board?

Answer. We condensed our water.

Question. Do you know of anything important that we have not inquired about?

Answer. I do not know anything more than what they are doing now, or trying to do, here at the yard with her—putting a screen around the pilot-house and fitting her iron pipes. I presume it will be a hard matter to make her decks tight without taking up the iron plating.

Mr. W. W. W. Wood sworn and examined.

By Mr. Odell:

Question. What is your connexion with the navy?

Answer. I am a chief engineer in the navy, and have been for the last twenty years, and am now general inspector of all machinery being constructed for the navy under Rear-Admiral Gregory, general superintendent.

Question. State what you know of the facts connected with the building of these twenty vessels, and whether they have met the intention in their construction.

Answer. It was the intention of the department to construct these light-draught vessels to draw about six feet for the purpose of placing turrets on board of them, making them, in fact, turreted, light-draught monitors, after the plan of Captain Ericsson; they were designed to carry one turret with two guns, and to be propelled by two screws, and were intended for service on our coast, bays, and rivers. The design, I think, included a water compartment around them for the purpose of admitting water and sinking them down several inches; and in view of relieving them, in the event of their getting aground, very rapidly, having an immense pumping power for the purpose of discharging the water from these reservoirs. That plan was rather novel, and had not been adopted in case of other vessels of the monitor type.

Mr. Stimers made the designs of the vessels and had the superintendence of them up to the time of the completion of the Chimo. That vessel was ready for service and was found to draw rather more water than was intended; the department then relieved him from that duty and placed the whole thing under the supervision of Captain Ericsson, Rear-Admiral Gregory, and myself. In the mean time the different commanders of the squadron south were very desirous of getting some vessels around with torpedoes for the purpose of protecting the wooden fleets from the attacks of the rebel iron-clads. And it was then determined to convert six of these vessels, almost completed, into torpedo vessels, retaining the impregnable pilot-house, placing one 11-inch gun forward, making some modifications and changes in relation to the screws, cutting out the overhang at the stern underneath, giving greater clearance for the exit of the water abaft the screws, by which greater speed would be obtained, lightening them as much as possible by removing the heavy condensing apparatus at the stern, and sending them south for the use of the commanders, and for the service of the department by them. The others it was decided to raise twenty-two inches, to retain the turrets and strengthen the bottoms by placing in additional cross-flooring, cutting away the raft at the stern and the overhang, so as to give them easier angles of clearance; to adopt screws of nine feet instead of twelve feet, as originally intended, so as to secure greater speed and strength, and at the same time retain all the impregnability of the structure first contemplated. The change in raising them would probably produce some five or six inches greater draught, with the additional height of twenty-two inches. So far as the machinery is concerned they have immense boiler power, and the object was to obtain greater speed by working up the engine at higher velocity with screws of diminished pitch—which changes have been very nearly completed in nearly the whole of them at this time. One of them will be launched on Saturday next (December 31,) as I understood this morning, and these will be very soon completed. Others will follow in rapid succession.

Question. Do you mean to say that Mr. Stimers had the designing of the whole of these twenty steamers?

Answer. The details of the design were made by him, so far as I know, (for the whole of them,) from a plan first submitted by Captain Ericsson, but very materially changed by him in the final execution of the work.

Question. You spoke of his being relieved; you mean from the superintendence of the whole of them?

Answer. Yes, sir; the department removed him.

Question. Are you aware of the reasons of his being removed?

Answer. No, sir. I never heard any reasons assigned for it; I was simply ordered to assume the duties incident to the general inspection of the whole work under contract for the department.

Question. As a practical engineer, and one acquainted with the intentions and designs of the government in the use of these vessels, were they what the government intended?

Answer. I think that they drew more water than the government originally intended; in other respects, I do not know sufficient of the designs of the department to give an opinion.

Question. As they were launched on the original design, were they fit for the use intended and designed by the government?

Answer. They drew too much water to be as useful as the government probably intended.

Question. How much water did they draw with the turret on?

Answer. It varied in the different vessels; I will be able to give you that to-morrow.

Question. We want only a general idea.

Answer. Only one of them was thoroughly equipped for sea, and I think that the top of her armor was probably some three inches under the water at the extremity, aft.

Question. You mean to say that, with the turret on, a part of the vessel was submerged?

Answer. Yes, sir; the extremity, aft.

Question. Do you know about the cost of the vessels—the original contract?

Answer. I should prefer to bring the exact figures to-morrow; I believe it was $395,000.

Question. What do you know about the cost of the alterations, say, on the six which are now intended for torpedo boats?

Answer. We are receiving the bills for them now; the exact amount has not yet been determined. Inspectors were placed at the different establishments to keep a record of the time of the mechanics employed, and the material, that an account might be rendered when completed. These bills have not yet come in to such an extent as to enable me to know the cost of the changes. It will vary in the different vessels in proportion to the work required. Some of them were further advanced than others, and of course the cost of changing, in consequence, will be greater. The cost of raising up the vessels varied from about $55,000 to $80,000 each, dependent upon the state of progress of the work at the time the changes were decided to be made. The work was immediately stopped, as soon as this error in the draught was known, on all the vessels.

Question. Will you state what, in your judgment, was the fault in the construction of these vessels?

Answer. It was an error in the calculation of the displacement; the vessels had not sufficient displacement to sustain the weight at six feet draught.

Question. Is that an error that is necessary among scientific men?

Answer. It is an error that is very frequently made. I have always found it in vessels of this kind; it is not admissible because these monitors are so constructed as to show but very little surface above the water as a target to fire at; and if they go down any deeper, of course it becomes a very serious matter. One of the difficulties was, that the material furnished in a great many cases was thicker, and of course weighed more than Mr. Stimers estimated. He probably did not make a proper allowance for this variation in the practical execution of the work, and he had very little margin to work on.

Question. Having but little margin, was it not important that it should be watched with great care for the interest of the government?

Answer. It was decidedly very important.

Question. It was a matter that could have been corrected at the time, could it not?

Answer. It could have been corrected at the time.

Question. It was within the control of the constructors?

Answer. It was within the control of the constructor.

Question. Do you know anything in relation to the delay in the completion of those contracts?

Answer. At the time these vessels were first designed, this class of vessels had never been very thoroughly tested under fire, or at least not sufficiently so as to develop all the faults of design in this type of vessels. As the work progressed and the faults were discovered, it was necessary to change, in very many cases, the plans from the original designs, in order to make them more perfect and more impregnable, and that they might answer more fully the purposes for which they were constructed. Some delay took place on this account, and from the great difficulty in obtaining materials at that time. I have heard these reasons stated by some contractors.

Question. So far as you know, was the delay from reasons such as contractors could overcome?

Answer. I do not think that they could be overcome; the iron mills had already as many contracts as they could fill.

Question. Are you acquainted with the condition or terms of the contract in reference to the time of completion?

Answer. I have read the contract; I do not now remember exactly the time specified; it varied.

Question. Do you consider that it was possible for these vessels to be built within the time prescribed by the Navy Department to the contractors, taking the circumstances into consideration?

Answer. Under certain conditions they might have been executed in that time, I think; that is, if they could have obtained all the materials and all the men, and thrown aside everything else.

Question. Were those conditions within the control of the contractors?

Answer. I should think not.

Question. You have referred to the alteration of these boats for torpedo boats. Are you familiar with the kind of torpedo boat the department are constructing?

Answer. Yes, sir; I have constructed all that they have had constructed.

Question. What kind of boat have they constructed for that purpose?

Answer. We constructed six small picket boats, about 40 feet long, 11 feet bottom, to carry a howitzer, a crew of eleven men, with a rifle screen to protect them, to make no noise, to return the water of condensation to the boilers, to carry about eight days' fuel, to make a speed of about ten miles an hour, and carry a torpedo. The first one of these boats constructed was the one with which Lieutenant Cushing destroyed the Albemarle. I gave the designs for the construction of the boat, the torpedo, and everything about it. They are very remarkable little boats, I can assure you, and they do not cost over $5,500 each. The torpedoes are entirely new in their construction, very powerful and certain in action, and are capable of destroying any number of vessels in a very short time.

By the chairman:

Question. How long have they been known or invented?

Answer. I have had this matter under consideration for about a year and a half, since the advent of iron-clad vessels, and no failure has ever been made in any of the experiments.

Question. You have given us a description of the torpedo boat and its success; now please state how these monitors can be used for the same purpose, and what the prospect of the usefulness of these six boats is.

Answer. My opinion is that if these vessels were in Hampton roads, or in the sounds at the mouth of the Roanoke river, or at the entrance of Savannah river, or in Mobile bay, or in the harbor of Charleston, they would be able very probably to destroy the rebel iron-clads, if they should come out to make an attack on our wooden fleet. Greater speed would make them very much more desirable, but in case of an attack upon any of our vessels they would be able to reach and to destroy the enemy's vessels without doubt.

Question. Would they be as serviceable as the torpedo boats you have just described for that purpose?

Answer. These small picket steamers to which these torpedoes have been attached are very valuable vessels. The iron-clads are fortified with armor, and the probability is that they would stand a very much better chance of not being sunk by the enemy's shot than what the smaller vessels would. But a torpedo vessel proper has been constructed, and is now in the James river—the Spuyten Devil, formerly the Stromboli. Her crew are not exposed at all; they work by a steam engine beneath the water-line, and it is so arranged that the torpedoes can be discharged every four minutes probably. She is also armed with shell, and worked by some apparatus to remove obstructions, and to be fired at any practicable depth of water. The vessel is now lying at Dutch gap, in advance of the fleet.

By Mr. Odell:

Question. Did you state the cost?

Answer. No, sir; I suppose her cost will not vary far from $110,000; she is armor-plated to a considerable extent.

Question. The first cost of the monitors was $395,000, as estimated, and the change from their original intention to torpedo boats will add very materially to that sum. How much?

Answer. I should judge it would vary from $50,000 to $60,000 each; probably not so much. I have not examined the accounts.

Question. Is there any advantage in these boats for torpedo purposes, to compensate for the great disparity between these torpedo boats proper you have described and the cost of these boats after the pattern we are examining into?

Answer. My own impression has been that time was the object, and to place these vessels in service so that the country might receive the benefit of them—that this was the most advantageous thing that could be done at the time. These vessels could be converted in very much shorter time than other vessels of that class could be built, costing less money.

Question. Could not you have built boats after the pattern of the Spuyten Devil quicker than these alterations have been made?

Answer. No, sir.

Question. In regard to the class of light-draught torpedo boats, are they provided with any armament?

Answer. Yes, sir; they are designed to carry one 11-inch gun forward.

Question. What protection will the men have, the turret being removed, in working the gun?

Answer. The same protection that all our wooden vessels have. The wooden bulwark don't amount to anything; in fact I consider that the men are safer on these iron-clads alongside a 11-inch gun, than with a light wooden bulwark such as they have on the wooden vessels. In one case you have the danger from splinters, and in the other you have not, and the probability is that the torpedo vessel, in going into action, would shell all the banks of the river and drive away all the sharpshooters at a great distance, so that they could not approach at all. I presume no prudent commander, in going up a river or approaching an ambush, would fail to do so. That matter was all considered in making the alteration.

Question. You have referred to the alteration of the other fourteen monitors by raising them twenty-two inches; please give us the intention and probable effect of that alteration.

Answer. The alteration involved in raising up these vessels is simply to make them serviceable vessels; to increase their strength and retain the turrets. They would then be very serviceable as monitors, drawing about 7½ feet of water. That is the only change that could be made under the circumstances to remedy the fault of construction.

Question. The change is a necessity growing out of the failure in the original construction?

Answer. Yes, sir; in consequence of the error of displacement.

Question. To what use can these vessels be put?

Answer. I think they will be serviceable vessels for harbor defence in our bays and sounds.

Question. What speed will you be able to get out of them?

Answer. I think we shall get from 6 to 7 knots an hour out of them. In the torpedo vessels the raft was not cut away at the stern, as will be the case with all the others. The overhang was cut out underneath, in order to get a freer exit of the water passing from the screw. The Chimo was reported to have made 5 knots with 60 revolutions, as well as I remember; these engines will be worked up to 90 or 100 revolutions; they have boiler power sufficient to produce that speed. The bottoms of them are reported to spring, but that is the case, more or less, with all iron structures. The stanchions which are placed on the floors underneath the deck will counteract that vibration to a very considerable extent.

By the chairman:

Question. State how far these monitors have progressed towards completion.

Answer. Some of them will be completed in probably six or eight weeks from this time.

Question. What expense could we save in abandoning any portion of them? Are they all very forward?

Answer. Oh, yes, sir; they are too far advanced; there are no changes you could make in them to save expense if you determine to complete the vessels. Captain Ericsson, Admiral Gregory, and myself have had this matter under consideration for some time past, and we have determined to complete them and make them as efficient as possible with the least amount of expenditure.

Question. You would not consider them of any value in their original state, before being raised for any war purpose, would you?

Answer. They might lie in our harbors and use their turrets, with their draught of water; but for all the purposes of navigation and moving about I should consider that they would have been inefficient.

Question. Where is Mr. Stimers now?

Answer. On board the Wabash, as chief engineer, now off Wilmington, North Carolina.

By Mr. Odell:

Question. Please state about the disproportion of the boiler to the cylinder.

Answer. The boilers are very largely in excess of the power required for cylinders of that capacity; that adds to the weight.

Question. Is the propelling power of these vessels a failure, or is the failure in the construction of the hulls?

Answer. They are a failure so far as the dimensions of the steam cylinder is concerned, in proportion to the amount of boiler power. The boilers are capable of supplying a greater amount of power than can be transmitted by engines of the dimensions placed on board.

Question. Why did they make that disproportion between the boiler and the engines to be propelled?

Answer. In the first place there were a number of engines placed on board for various purposes, that were to be supplied with steam, which would render a large boiler power absolutely necessary; but the cylinders constituted the motive power of the vessels, and they were, I consider, inadequate. I presume the constructing engineer thought they were entirely sufficient for the purpose. They were not so, however, in my judgment.

Question. Have you seen the original plan submitted of the light-draught monitors designed by Mr. Ericsson?

Answer. I have.

Question. In your judgment as an engineer, which plan was preferable, or most likely to accomplish the object?

Answer. My opinion is, that the plan submitted by Captain Ericsson was decidedly preferable to the one ultimately adopted. They could have been built in much less time and at much less expense, and therefore would have fulfilled all the essential objects of the department in the construction of those vessels.

Question. You say that the boiler in this engine was in excess of the cylinder and stroke of the engine; about how much larger should the cylinder and how much longer should the stroke have been, to have been in harmony with the power of the boiler?

Answer. I should have placed in them at least from 40 to 50 per cent. more power.

Question. How much would that have added to the propelling power of the engine?

Answer. It would have been in the same ratio.

JOHN ERICSSON sworn and examined.

By the chairman:

Question. In what relation do you stand towards the twenty monitors ordered to be built by the Navy Department, and afterwards built under the superintendence of Mr. Stimers?

Answer. I have nothing whatever to do with those twenty monitors, directly or indirectly.

Question. What do you know about those monitors—whether they are effective or otherwise, and whether or not they are in accordance with your first plans? State all that you think material upon the subject.

Answer. It will be necessary for me to commence where the department desired me to plan a light-draught vessel for the Mississippi and its tributaries. In the latter part of August, 1862, Mr. Fox called at my office in this city and told me it was very desirable to have vessels of a very light draught for the Mississippi and the other rivers, and he desired me to make some plan, but his condition was four feet draught of water. I told him that could not be done; that it was necessary to have six feet draught to make a boat impregnable. He left me. I commenced reflecting upon the subject. Let me state that this was an unofficial, private conversation, and perhaps it is proper for me to say now that the whole of my services in connexion with the government have been voluntary, and the communications with me have nearly all been unofficial. I have received no compensation for my labors; never asked any. My professional emoluments make me independent of that, and what I have done has been from motives of patriotism, and with very great pleasure. Having reflected upon the subject, I found there were so many difficulties in it that I must give it up, and for three weeks I did not act. Mr. Stimers then informed me that Mr. Fox had written to him a letter saying that he must not give up the light-draught vessels, and that I was the only man that could plan them. I then took up the subject again, and by the 9th day of October, 1862, I had my plans and specifications ready, and sent them on that day to the Secretary of the Navy. He did not acknowledge the receipt of them, but I heard through Mr. Stimers, informally, that they were received.

The plan of light-draught monitor which I forwarded to the Navy Department was not intended as a working plan, yet it defined with clearness and precision the general principle and the mode of building the vessel, engines, boiler, and propellers. It was understood by the Navy Department that I had not time to attend to the detail of calculations and planning. Accordingly the work was confided to Chief Engineer Stimers.

Several months elapsed. I heard nothing on the subject. I expected in the mean time that an advertisement would appear in the papers for building vessels according to the plans I had sent in. Nothing having been done, Mr. Stimers called on me one day in December and said that he had returned from Washington, where he had received instructions to make out plans of these light-draught vessels founded upon my original plan that I had sent in; but, much to my surprise, he did not come for advice or instruction, but only to tell me what he was going to do, thereby giving me to understand that he had received full authority to act. I had been, and I am now, under the impression that the department intended that he should do nothing without consulting me. Mr. Fox said, at that first conversation, he was desirous of having the vessels built in three months. My mind, therefore, was directed to great simplicity in the construction of these vessels. We had no iron and no rolling mills; they were all occupied; it was therefore a necessary point to dispense with the use of iron as much as possible. On the Mississippi we had no workmen that could do this; for, let me state emphatically, I planned these vessels for the Mississippi and its tributaries. I conceived the idea of building a plain, oval tank with a flat bottom and upright sides, that could be done in an ordinary establishment in forty days. Around this I attached a raft made of timber, the idea being to give stability and impregnability to this wooden raft. Wood is plenty out west; iron and workmen they have none. I saw no difficulty, and would have entered into a contract to furnish such a vessel in ninety days, if built upon this simple plan. The engine itself I proposed to be on the simplest high-pressure principle, employing patterns and casting such as they were in the habit of using out west, so as not to lose time by planning and making patterns.

Having stated this, I will now proceed to tell you of my interview with Mr. Stimers. You see that the leading feature of my plan, in order to meet the difficulties of the day, was simplicity as well as impregnability. Here is a copy of the plan I sent to the Secretary of the Navy. (Exhibits a plan.) For this I never got any acknowledgment, excepting indirectly. Mr. Stimers told me that Chief Engineer Isherwood objected to my boiler because it was of low evaporating power, and he had devised two boilers that would extend across the entire vessel, built in a very different manner from the simple boilers that I had planned. I objected strongly to that at once, and told him if they made such boilers, standing side-by-side, it would be impossible to brace the vessel so as to make it sufficiently strong. I argued this point at considerable length with him, but he did not yield the point; he thought the kind of boiler that Mr. Isherwood had devised was the best. He next informed me that he was going to put in engines of only twenty-two inches diameter, and thirty inches stroke. I told him that that was utterly insufficient—that that power would not be enough to propel so big a vessel. He further stated to me that he was going to place these engines fore and aft in the vessel, using bevel gear to drive the propellers. I remonstrated against it, and told him it would not answer. When he left me he did not say that he would not use such engines, nor did he say that he would. He further stated to me that the propellers, as I had arranged them, were objected to; that they should be placed side-by-side, instead of one after the other. Then he left my office and, I believe, went to work to plan a vessel on this general principle, (showing the drawing,) but with the modifications that I have stated. I heard nothing further, though I knew he was planning the vessels, and had several engineers assisting him. His office was next door to mine. I was never invited to enter that office; nor would I have entered it, as far as that goes, because my plan was deviated from. The planning went on for a very long time. I was consulted only as to certain arrangements about the turrets, not in relation to the vessels, the hulls, the engines, or the boilers. At last his plans were ready, and I am informed that he went to Washington with them. A few days after he returned to New York again. He called on me and told me that he was going to introduce a series of water tanks, or water compartments, all round the vessel. That involved an entire change of the whole system, which I objected to, stating that the difference in the draught of water that could be obtained by these tanks was not worth having—it would be only a few inches. He proceeded with a new set of plans upon this new system, and at last got his plans ready and went to Washington with them, without ever exhibiting them to me, or consulting or advising with me. The plans were shown to the contractors, I am informed, and they regulated their prices according to the work specified, which plans I had disapproved and utterly repudiated.

But let me state here that I have reason to believe that the department was then under the impression that Mr. Stimers had consulted with me. I had several private letters from Mr. Fox that indicated that he supposed that Mr. Stimers had consulted me in relation to the details. It was a delicate subject for me to meddle with. I could not object to it, because no direct information had been asked; I had simply advised the engineer strongly against what he was doing.

Now, when these plans were ultimately sent in and presented to the contractors, I received a letter that brought out the fact that Mr. Stimers had not acted according to my advice. So I supposed at that time that the department were aware that he had deviated from my plans, or, rather, that he had not taken my advice in what he was doing. The contractors were then in Washington. Mr. Stimers was looked upon by the department as a very efficient, skilful engineer. I myself believed him to be so, and I did something to impress that idea on the department. It was not till he had made all these plans that I discovered that he was not a planner. Though he is an engineer of good general knowledge, and very efficient in many things, he is not a man who has the ability to plan.

I believe now that I have stated everything that relates to the original conception of these vessels—what I did propose to build—and I will now show you the plan of that which has been built, but which I again repudiate as not being at all in accordance with my original plan.

Question. What do you suppose the cost of a vessel constructed on your plan would have been?

Answer. The question was put to me whether I would build a vessel on my original plan, and at what price. I said I would construct vessels on my own plan, and I gave the department the price, $375,000 each. The department thought that, in view of the simplicity of my mode of building, it was too high. So my offer was rejected, and offers were accepted to build the vessels on Mr. Stimers's plans—for I call them his plans. In the mean time prices had advanced and iron was difficult to be had; the rolling mills had nearly doubled their prices. This (exhibiting the plan of the present monitors) is the second plan that Mr. Stimers produced and carried to Washington, and which was carried into execution.

Question. How does it differ from your plan, and wherein do you regard this as defective?

Answer. The great difference is this: that instead of having a simple tank, surrounded or bedded in a wooden raft, this is a double vessel, very complicated to build, heavy, expensive, and full of braces. It is very difficult to exhaust the water out of these tanks. A system of piping had to be carried around the entire vessel. Powerful pumps had to be applied to these pipes in order to exhaust the tanks of water after they had been filled. The change involved great additional weight, great expense, and took three if not four times the length of time to build as the simple plan which I proposed. I have stated that the tanks were useless because they contained so little water, that when you pumped them out, if the vessel could have carried the weight which they expected, it would not have changed the draught of water more than six inches. Let me state in this connexion that in my original plan of a wooden raft, which makes the ship so strong, I attached it directly to the vessel's sides, whereas in this new plan there is a tank intervening between the two, so that the wooden raft had to be attached to the tank itself. I have before stated that I objected to the boiler that Mr. Stimers put in, and that the engines were too small to do the work, but Mr. Stimers said that Mr. Isherwood insisted on having engines of only eighteen inches in diameter, and Mr. Stimers says he got them up to twenty-two inches. The turret was arranged very nearly in accordance with my principle and my instructions. The draughtsman came and took my instructions in relation to many parts about the turret. I have stated that the propellers were differently placed from my original plan, and that I objected to the change. Here let me say that these arguments and these objections I made to Mr. Stimers, and that I never had occasion to make the statements to the department. In consequence of introducing the tanks the raft was diminished; it was not so impregnable as on the original plan. I place these deviations at the door of Mr. Stimers, for he had power to do anything, the department supposing he was working upon the general plan which I had submitted.

Question. For what purpose were these tanks of water provided in the vessels designed by Mr. Stimers?

Answer. I do not know of any that I can find any reason for.

Question. Were they anything but an incumbrance to the ship? Could they have been of any use?

Answer. Yes, if the ship had been sufficiently buoyant, and they could have contained water enough. It is certainly a good feature that when you do not know the depth of the river, and you go along cautiously, and yet find yourself on a bar, by pumping out the tanks you are relieved and go ahead. But I prefer to get a sounding apparatus on board and to take the depth as you go along. Practical officers of the navy, however, applauded the idea. Admiral Smith, I know, was very much in favor of it.

Question. Were not these water-tanks entirely abandoned by the commissioners who were consulted as to what could be done with these vessels afterwards, when it was determined to raise them?

Answer. Decidedly; they not only abandoned the tanks, but took out the pipes, pumps, and everything that added to the weight of the vessel, as the only means of raising her up.

Question. You advised a more powerful engine than Mr. Stimers insisted upon having. What kind of engine did you advise?

Answer. Two small inclined engines of thirty inches diameter, operating directly upon the screw shaft.

Question. How much more powerful would your engines have been than Mr. Stimers's?

Answer. About ninety per centum—nearly twice as powerful. The boilers put in were disproportioned to the size of the cylinders—nearly twice as powerful as they ought to have been. That loads the vessel down, and that is what we are laboring under now.

Question. Could you have constructed these vessels on your original plan at the price you stated to the department?

Answer. Yes, unquestionably. I named a price that yielded a profit, or I would not have advised my friends to enter into it.

Question. What will be the cost of raising up these monitors twenty-two inches, in your judgment?

Answer. I made a rough estimate under the present high prices, and told the department I thought it would cost about $100,000 each vessel; but it appears that they have got it done for less.

Question. Will that cure the original defects in the construction of the vessel of which you spoke?

Answer. It will not. It is the best that can be done. The vessels are all too far advanced to admit of any radical change.

Question. You understood these vessels to have been designed originally for the navigation of the Mississippi and its tributaries. Will these monitors, when they are improved by building them up, be useful for that purpose?

Answer. Yes; they should be efficient river vessels.

Question. Will they not draw too much water?

Answer. A great many of our western rivers will admit them. It will enable us to hold all the principal places if we have these turreted vessels going. I would say here that I look upon them as a great improvement upon the western iron-clads.

Question. You think they can be made efficient vessels for the navigation of our rivers?

Answer. Decidedly.

Question. Would they be seagoing vessels in their improved state?

Answer. By no means; they might go from inlet to inlet; they were never intended for anything more.

Question. With their present weak engines can they stem the current of the Mississippi—say four miles an hour?

Answer. Easily; very readily.

Question. Do you know anything about the speed of the one they have constructed, that was brought around from Boston—the Casco?

Answer. She ought to go six sea miles easily. With the propellers as now changed there is less pitch given to them, so that if they run the engines up to a higher speed, I will undertake to navigate that vessel six knots at any time. By removing the turrets we have brought the vessels very nearly to the original draught.

Question. What speed would your engine give to your vessel?

Answer. In rivers I calculated eight knots, or a little more than nine statute miles. That I look upon as being sufficient speed for such vessels.

Question. Do you consider that the monitors that you do not raise up can be converted into torpedo boats, so as to be of any essential service?

Answer. I think the torpedoes can be operated from them, but as gunboats I deem them to be more important.

Question. As originally built, without the sides being built up—just as Stimers built them, and as the Casco was finished—are they of any use for war purposes?

Answer. Not till the turret was removed, because they were under water instead of above. When the turret is removed it is then a very good gunboat. There are no such gunboats in any country as they would be; no impregnable gunboats, as these will be.

Question. There is no protection for the men?

Answer. They will be shot down, as on other boats. That is a small objection. If the gun is shot away we put on another gun. There being no bulwarks the men are less exposed, because there are no splinters.

Question. But sharpshooters can take aim better than when the men are behind bulwarks?

Answer. The guns they carry are very powerful 11-inch shell guns, and they will be able to clear the shores.

Question. In your judgment, can the Casco go from harbor to harbor without being towed by some other craft?

Answer. Yes, in fine weather; but with strong head winds it is better to have her towed. But all the monitors will do better by themselves than it is supposed.

Question. Do you know any reason why the department did not adopt your plan?

Answer. I believe the reason is that the water-tank system was looked upon as a very essential improvement for river boats. Some of our ablest men were of that opinion. But for that feature, I am of opinion, from what I heard at the time, that they would not have been built upon Mr. Stimers's plan. That was looked upon as a considerable improvement on my system.

Question. If there is anything material that you think is essential for us to know, besides what you have stated, please state it.

Answer. By raising the vessel twenty-two inches we have greater strength of sides, and they are better able to resist the longitudinal strain than before; and, barring the increased draught of water, they would be good and efficient vessels in every way.

Question. Have you made any material improvements upon the plan of the monitors since your first conception of them?

Answer. None whatever; but the form of the hull has more of a sea-going character; instead of a floating battery, the hull now looks like any of the ordinary ships. That is the only change of any account.

Question. Are the large monitors, as we call them, of the Dictator class, built on the same plan as the original monitors?

Answer. The plan is essentially the same; there is less overhang at the bow; with that exception, it is essentially the same. But the Dictator is a fine sea-going monitor, exceedingly sharp, lively as a duck, and steers in the most perfect manner. Two men can steer her like a pilot-boat. She turns around in twice her own length.

Rear-Admiral FRANCIS H. GREGORY sworn and examined.

By the chairman:

Question. In what position do you stand in regard to the navy?

Answer. At the breaking out of these troubles they promoted me (I do not call it so) on the retired list. I was an applicant for sea service; I wanted it very much. The government thought proper to set me to work superintending the building of vessels soon after 1861. They built twenty-three gunboats very soon, and then came an order giving me the general superintendence of all vessels of wood and iron, and all the machinery building by contract outside of the navy yard on the Atlantic seaboard. I have been at that since.

Question. Are you acquainted with the class of light-draught steamers ordered by the department, twenty in number, of which the Chimo was one?

Answer. Yes, sir.

Question. What do you know in regard to the contract for their building?

Answer. I did not know anything of the plan of the vessels or the contracts until they were made. When a portion of them were contracted for, I received an order stating that the contracts were given out and they would be under my general superintendence.

Question. Who is responsible for the draught and plan of these monitors?

Answer. I should suppose that the Bureau of Construction would be. It has been usual in the service ever since I was in it, for fifty-six years, to make use of all the talent they have about them. In old times the board of commissioners, where they had naval constructors at the different stations, used to consult them to build a frigate or sloop-of-war. They would call upon all those people to send in plans, and have the advantage of the experience and talent of the whole body.

Question. To whom did they ultimately intrust the superintendence of them—the draught and specification?

Answer. In all previous instances they always came from the Bureau of Construction or from the naval commissioners.

Question. What agency had Mr. Stimers in the construction of these vessels?

Answer. He had almost everything to do with it, I believe; because not many days after I had received the orders stating to me that they were under my general superintendence, there came an order stating, very laconically, that Mr. Stimers would have charge of those vessels building on the Ericsson plan, and he took the charge. I understood at the time that Mr. Ericsson was to be consulted on all occasions. I believe that was the view and intention of the government at the time. Mr. Stimers is an ambitious man, pretty talented, but he had not experience, and was led away by his ambition, I suppose. He wanted to control the whole thing, and he drew up the plans, so far as I know anything about it; because under him was established a large office, with many of the finest draughtsmen in the country, and they made drawings which were passed around to the different contractors. But after some time a letter was written to me from the Secretary of the Navy saying that Mr. Stimers was not authorized to make any deviation from any plans, contracts, or instructions that had been given, without the sanction of the department, or the proper bureau.

Question. What time was that?

Answer. I have got all the dates at the office; it was some few months after they commenced. Another order came from the Secretary of the Navy at that time saying that he was to make no communications to the contractors, or to the bureaus, or the department, excepting through me.

Question. Did he go on to do anything without consulting you?

Answer. Yes, sir.

Question. What did he do without your knowledge or consent?

Answer. He went to work making expensive alterations in the vessels from the original plans. They had plans and specifications drawn up; then he would figure it over, perhaps, and think he could make some improvement; so he would issue his order to change. After a while a number of contractors came to me to know how they could get along—increasing the expense, work partly completed, new plan ordered, to tear it all down: who is going to pay for this? In that way there was a very heavy bill of extra charges made.

Question. Did you agree that the government should be responsible for these alterations?

Answer. No, sir; I did not know anything about it.

Question. Do you know whether the Bureau of Construction knew what alterations he was making?

Answer. No, sir; I do not believe they knew any more than I did.

Question. Have you any idea of the expense of these alterations and deviations from the original plan?

Answer. Oh yes, sir; that is a matter of warfare between myself and the contractors now settling up; some of them bring in bills of $50,000 and $80,000, but we don't give it to them. But this was done: When Mr. Stimers was checked, then if he wanted to make any alterations or suggestions he addressed his letter to me, and I would refer it to the bureau, and invariably they would write back, "You will consult Mr. Ericsson, and if he agrees to it, and you approve of it, it will be done." In that way a good many alterations were made by authority, supposed to be an advantage to the vessels.

Question. Was Mr. Ericsson, in fact, consulted about these alterations, and did he assent to them?

Answer. Many of them he did not at all. We had a rule that when any contractor made an authorized alteration that increased the expense, to pay them that bill right off outside of the contract. As soon as they were done they were entitled to receive the pay, and I gave them always the certificates to get it. But in some instances bills were brought to me, and I did not know that the alterations had been made.

Question. Have you the means of forming any estimate of the amount that will have to be paid for these alterations of plan?

Answer. It will amount to somewhere between $40,000 and $50,000 for each one.

Question. That is exclusive of the expense of building up the twenty-two inches?

Answer. Yes, sir; that is an appendix to the original contract. I was aware a long while before any action was taken upon it that these vessels were a failure entirely; that they were not going to float; they had not displacement enough to float all that was put into them.

Question. Did you make that known to Mr. Stimers?

Answer. Certainly I did; and he showed me their calculations gone over and over again, and assured me that Mr. Ericsson knew all about it, and it had his approbation, and that the bureau at Washington understood it. I knew better than that.

Question. Did you ever communicate your suspicions that these vessels were total failures to the department?

Answer. I did to the Bureau of Construction.

Question. Who was at the head of it?

Answer. Mr. Lenthall; I advised him once by letter to have an investigation.

Question. About what stage of the building was that?

Answer. When they were pretty well done.

Question. You have seen some of these after they were launched?

Answer. I have seen them in every stage they have been in. I have them under my charge now.

Question. What do you say of them? What are they good for in the condition in which Mr. Stimers had them finished?

Answer. Nothing at all—could not float. The first one we got afloat was the Chimo. Mr. Stimers proposed to go to Boston and take that vessel entirely under his own charge, pledging himself to put her to sea in one month completely equipped, armed and ready for service. I was asked my opinion about that. I said I did not know whether it could be done; if anybody could do it I supposed he could. I was asked if I recommended it. "Yes," said I, "I recommend it," and I signed the paper. I was to have nothing to do with it. So he went on to Boston and called about him all the engineers, anybody and everything, anyhow and in every way, worked there night and day, and got her to go on a trial trip. I went there; her stern was four inches under water then; he wanted to go to sea. But they could do nothing with her, and they all came to a stand. As soon as the Secretary of the Navy found this out he tripped Stimers right up. I think the Secretary of the Navy and Mr. Fox believed all that while that Mr. Ericsson was the counsellor throughout; but Mr. Ericsson did not know anything about it, because when they found that these vessels were complete failures, and the department was astounded, I was telegraphed to and went with two of the first engineers in the service, with Mr. Ericsson, and there we got at the regular building plan, and Mr. Ericsson told me that was the first time he ever saw it. He spread it out, and said he did not think a man could be capable of so much folly. Then we were ordered to consider what could be done with them, and we went into that consideration with Ericsson, Wood, and King, and we came to the conclusion that the only remedy was to raise the decks. Some were nearly completed; others were on the stocks. Then it fell to me to bring all this about. With Mr. Ericsson's advice I called together the contractors. They wanted this, that, and the other. We pinned them down, looked into the thing closely, and, according to the condition that each vessel was in, I made an agreement with them for from $50,000 to $90,000. Some had the decks on, and it was an immense work to take them off. Now we have one ready to be launched to-morrow. That will be a fine vessel—just what they intended at first.

Question. Will she be able to ascend our rivers?

Answer. Oh, yes, sir.

Question. How much water will she draw?

Answer. They will draw about 7 feet—not more.

Question. What speed?

Answer. I suppose about 7 knots.

Question. Do you expect that with the engines they have got?

Answer. Yes, sir; we have been altering the form of the stern. Mr. Stimers had got the propeller into a box; the water could not get to it nor from it. Now we have altered the form of the vessel to advantage and put in different propellers.

Question. Do you think they will be sea-boats?

Answer. They never will be very good sea-boats; they will be as good as any of these monitors; they will be a foot out of water.

Question. Will you be able to get them from place to place without towing?

Answer. Oh, yes, sir, I should think so; they have always had tow wherever they have been, lest their machinery might give out.

Question. How about their being finished in the time the contracts called for?

Answer. The contract called for their completion at a specified time, but they were not finished, and could not have been.

Question. What was the reason?

Answer. There was more work than they calculated; it was a new business, and nobody made any right calculation at all. I have seen so much of that iron work, and there was never an instance in which it was done. The Dictator was to be done in twelve months, and it is not done yet. They would have forfeited their contracts; they could not have helped it.

Question. They are built of green timber instead of seasoned?

Answer. No, sir. We had a regular timber inspector, the best we could get. In some instances it was represented that they could not get the timber that the contract called for—that it was not to be had—and the bureau in some instances would permit them to use that nearest to it, because they wanted to get the vessels out. I do not know that there was any damage done to the public on that score; if there was, I did it, because they trusted that business to me.

Question. How long will it take now to complete the remainder of the vessels?

Answer. I think we will have them all out by May.

Question. How much do you suppose it will cost to complete them?

Answer. They are to cost $55,000, $60,000, $70,000, $80,000, and $90,000, according to the state they were in. That is going to finish them, fit them out, and do everything to make them complete, as the contract originally called for. We only give them this money for pulling to pieces and reconstructing. One of them is to cost more than $90,000—the Tunxis. She was the second vessel; she was fitted out right after the Chimo, and we attempted to get her out, but we found it would not do—she was too deep in the water. So we brought her back and made another effort to finish her up; mounted her guns and everything; but it was found she would not answer any purpose at all. One considerable expense attending all this is that the bottom frames were so weak that we had to put in additional floors. One of the vessels was found so weak on her bottom that we had to take her to pieces. She is now hauled up in Philadelphia, not by the contractor, but by another party, under a special agreement to be taken to pieces, her turret taken off, and to be reconstructed and delivered to the government, as she ought to have been originally, with all the alterations, for $115,000. Then there are five of them that are to be made into torpedo boats. That suggestion came from Mr. Ericsson. I was against it. The boats are sluggish in their movements, 225 feet long, and you cannot get them into narrow waters. It is like setting a trap for certain game; if the game comes to it, very well. I was ordered to make five of them. After a while I thought Mr. Ericsson's genius was going to fix torpedoes; I had not enough of it, and did not pretend to have. Come to find out, *he* had not. I had fixed torpedoes on the picket-boats, and we put them on. There are three of them here now.

Question. Is not that torpedo boat much more efficacious than these can be made?

Answer. Certainly.

Question. Do you or not believe that it is a useless expense to undertake to turn any of these into torpedo boats?

Answer. It will not be much expense with these we have got now, because it is all done pretty much.

Question. Can you use them to any advantage at all for that purpose?

Answer. I do not think they can be, and I have already represented that to the department. I said to Mr. Ericsson, "Why not make gunboats of them?" So he mounted an 11-inch gun right on the deck. I would sooner stand my chance on open decks than behind wooden bulwarks. I have recommended to the department to make these five stationary vessels, where they want to guard some passage. They do not want half the crew that they would otherwise.

Question. But they are totally inefficient vessels for the purposes they were designed for; you could not do anything with them?

Answer. I do not think you could put them to any better use than we have put them. The more I looked into the torpedo business the less I liked it. At last I proposed to Mr. Ericsson to mount a pivot-gun, and take the turret off, and put a pilot-house on. I believe the Secretary of the Navy, Mr. Fox, and Mr. Lenthall thought everything was going on very nicely, and that Mr. Ericsson was the adviser all along; I thought so till some time before they came to the conclusion to the contrary.

By Mr. Odell:

Question. How could you be deceived about Mr. Ericsson's not having advised, when you were right here and saw him every day?

Answer. All that business was done between him and Mr. Stimers. Mr. Stimers would bring plans to me. I would say, "Has that been submitted to Mr. Ericsson?" He would say, "Yes." Then come to find out, Mr. Stimers had probably gone and talked with Mr. Ericsson on the subject, and Mr. Ericsson did not understand it, perhaps, or know anything about it. And Mr. Ericsson soon got out with Mr. Stimers, and did not pay much attention to him. But many times when Mr. Stimers would make propositions to me he did it unwillingly, because he wanted to be supreme and go right to head-quarters, or dictate himself. When he was compelled by the orders of the government to submit everything to me, I would ask him, "Have you seen Mr. Ericsson about that?" and he would say, "Yes, and he understands it," or "Mr. Fox understands it." I would send his letters addressed to me to the bureau, and the answer invariably was, "You will advise with Mr. Ericsson; if he concurs, and you approve of it, it may be done."

Question. Is there anything else that is important in connexion with this matter that you wish to state?

Answer. Not that I know of.

NAVY DEPARTMENT, *January* 16, 1865.

SIR: I have the honor to acknowledge the receipt of your letter of the 14th ultimo, enclosing a copy of a resolution of the Senate in the following words:

"*Resolved*, That the Committee on the Conduct of the War be instructed to inquire what progress has been made in the construction of the iron-clad gunboats contracted for in the year 1862, by whom the contract was made on the part of the government, who planned the models of the same, and who is responsible therefor; have any of them been finished? if so, what was the condition of the vessel after she was launched? are the other vessels contracted for to be built on a plan or model similar to the Chimo, lately launched at Boston? and all information which may be had touching said gunboats."

I am requested in the letter transmitting a copy of the resolution to "furnish the committee, as soon as convenient, with such information upon the subject-matter of the resolution as may be in possession of the Navy Department."

I presume that a mistake has been made by the committee or by the Senate in their inquiry relative to the "iron-clad gunboats contracted for in the year 1862." In the spring and summer of 1863 contracts were made for twenty turreted vessels of the monitor class. Not doubting that the resolution of the Senate and the investigations and inquiries of the committee have reference to those contracts and those vessels, my response will be made as if the resolution read 1863 instead of 1862. The mistake of a year in regard to the execution of these contracts—provided they are, as I suppose, those referred to—is important to the contractors as well as to the department, and should therefore be corrected.

In answer to that part of the resolution which inquires "by whom the contract was made on the part of the government," I have to state it was by the chief of the Bureau of Construction, under advertisement issued by this department on the 10th of February, 1863. A reference to the message of the President and accompanying documents of the 1st session of the present Congress may be had for a list of bidders and award of contracts under direction of this department.

It is asked "Who planned the models of the same, and who is responsible therefor?"

The general idea of a light-draught iron-clad inside of a raft of wood was furnished by Captain John Ericsson, of New York, the distinguished inventor, at the request of this department. The details of the plan, and the preparation of the working drawings, were intrusted to Chief Engineer A. C. Stimers, who was instructed by the Bureau of Construction to consult with Captain Ericsson and take directions from him. To that extent Chief Engineer Stimers is responsible.

"Have any of them been finished? if so, what was the condition of the vessel after she was launched?"

None of the light-draught turreted vessels are quite finished. The Casco, converted into a boat for reconnoitring and torpedo purposes, has recently made a passage from Boston to New York. Complaints were made by the officers of discomforts, as complaints were formerly made of the brigs and schooners of the navy, so many of which, like the Grampus, Somers, Porpoise, and Bainbridge, have gone to sea and never been heard of. The Chimo was the first of her class which was got into the water, and led to the discovery that due allowance had not been made for all the weights. She floated on an even keel only about three inches above the water, instead of fifteen as was intended and expected. Several of the same class which have been since launched have varied considerably from this, all of them being high out of the water, notwithstanding all were made from the same drawings, showing that there have been variations in model or in the weight of materials used in construction.

Before any of this class of vessels had been launched Rear-Admiral Dahlgren and Acting Rear-Admiral Lee had strenuously urged the department to send them some monitor-hulls without turrets, to be used for the purpose of reconnoissance and as torpedo boats. Five of the light-draughts most advanced were therefore ordered to be finished without the turret. When relieved of this weight the necessity and expense of raising their sides, and thereby increasing their capacity, was obviated. The other fifteen were recommended to be enlarged by building them higher, thus increasing their capacity about one hundred and thirty tons, and rendering them consequently more efficient. Previously the same plan was adopted in constructing and completing the second batch of monitor vessels which have just passed through the baptism of fire at Fort Fisher, and have remained at anchor on that coast—exposed as it is in the winter season—ninety miles from a harbor, during the most terrific gale of wind ever experienced, according to the Wilmington papers, and performing, as Rear-Admiral Porter reports, to the admiration of everybody.

"Are the other vessels contracted for to be built on a plan or model similar to the Chimo, lately launched at Boston?"

I have already stated that twenty light-draught monitors were contracted for in the spring and summer of 1863. All were designed upon the monitor plan, which has been so serviceable, but modifications and alterations were made of five, omitting the turrets for specific purposes by special request of naval officers.

The resolution, in conclusion, calls for "all information which may be had touching said gunboats."

The necessity of light-draught iron-clads to operate in the bays, sounds and rivers, as well as for defensive purposes, was forced upon the department at an early period of the present struggle. Not only was the contest in which we were engaged peculiar, but the means and measures to meet and suppress it, particularly those of the navy, were novel and without precedent. Most of the lines of army communication were by water, and the navy was expected to protect them and render them secure. A brief experience and a few engagements made it evident that light-draught, unprotected, wooden boats, with magazines, machinery and boilers exposed, could be driven off by field artillery behind earth works. Light-draught iron-clads became, therefore, an imperious necessity, and the convictions of the department, and of all indeed who gave the subject intelligent consideration, were irresistibly in favor of such vessels; but we were without models, and the wants of the country were pressing. Neither of the maritime powers of Europe had built or attempted to build a light-draught iron-clad. The Navy Department, in this emergency, was compelled to feel its way, without experience or precedent in any quarter to guide it. Appeals had been made in vain to Congress to provide a proper establishment for the construction of iron and armored vessels, where plans and models might have been developed and matured with studied deliberation and skill. When the contracts for these vessels were entered into, delays were inadmissible. Difficulties with foreign powers seemed imminent, and, in the absence of any national establishment, immediate contracts for the construction of armored vessels were called for on every hand. The authorities of the States and cities on the seaboard were appealing to the department and the government for iron-clad vessels to defend their harbors from the two or three rovers that were then already abroad, and great apprehensions were entertained that certain formidable ships in the process of construction in France and England for the rebels would soon visit our coast. Many who may now be forward to criticise and censure the enlarged and energetic action that was taken were at that time profuse in censure of the department for delays in not more promptly providing whatever vessels were necessary for the service.

Congress having omitted to provide an establishment for the construction of an iron navy where this class of armored vessels of light-draught could be constructed, the department has been compelled to rely on contractors and outside parties in different sections of the country for the work. The parties contracting have generally exerted themselves to meet in good faith the requirements of the government, and it is a subject of just congratulation that, in this great emergency, when the department was compelled to act without precedent to guide it, and when the government had omitted to furnish a suitable establishment, private enterprise and our skilled mechanics have so well met the difficulties presented.

Mr. J. B. Eades, of St. Louis, furnished the light-draught river boats which have been so successful on the Mississippi and also in the bay of Mobile. Captain Ericsson, the inventor of the Monitor class of vessels, furnished the idea which is now near practical consummation. Although as yet untried, these vessels differ so little from the original Monitor that there is every reason to anticipate their success. To predict otherwise would be presumption, yet it has been the misfortune of the department to encounter hostility and forebodings of failure with every improvement which has been made during the war, and often from those of whom encouragement and support might reasonably have been expected. Some of the best engineers and constructors in the service of the government, as well as others, expressed their want of confidence in the first Monitor, and declared it would prove a failure; it was represented that she could not float—that she would plunge to the bottom when launched, and that to send her to Hampton roads would be recklessness amounting to crime. A constant succession of struggles against prejudice, ignorance, and fixed habits and opinions, has been the fate of the department at every step which the extraordinary exigencies of this war has compelled it to take. While it is not difficult to criticise and point out mistakes in a new description of vessel, which the change in naval warfare has suddenly called into existence, and to suggest alterations and improvements on what has already transpired, it is a satisfaction to the department, which was compelled to encounter this opposition, to know that this class of vessels, subjected at the beginning to ridicule, and subsequently to obloquy and denunciation, has been successfully tried in battle and in storm—that these vessels have equalled the expectations of the country in periods of peril, and are being extensively copied abroad. Other governments are adopting them, while many of the discontented of our own country still question the wisdom of building vessels of the class which has at a critical moment rendered unequalled service to the Union and saved the capital of the nation.

In encouraging contrast with the illiberal and prejudiced opinions which have opposed all improvements, denounced them in advance as failures, and been dissatisfied even with successful results, are the observations and reflections of the sagacious and sensible author of the recent valuable work on "English and French Neutrality," who, appreciating the difficulties of the department, remarks, at page 458 of his instructive volume:

"It is no small proof of ability in the management of the navy that there was skill enough to provide, and independence enough to use, a form of warship and a kind of cannon before untried, but which time and experience have shown were alone, of all ships and weapons then known, capable of meeting the emergency."

At the present time the call for light-draught iron-clads comes from every squadron engaged in this struggle. Acting Rear-Admiral Lee says that within the limits of his command there must be a large increase of light-draught iron-clads. Vice-Admiral Farragut, before he left the scene of his great exploits, asked for additional iron-clads, especially those of light-draught, and declared that the coast could not be held unless he had them. In each of the blockading and river squadrons they are required.

Nearly two years have elapsed since any contracts have been entered into for this class of vessels, and it is hoped the present war is so near its close that no further expenditures for additional ones will be necessary; but should the war continue a year longer, more will be wanted.

My acknowledgments are due to the committee for this opportunity to express my views. I shall feel under obligations to them or others, as will the whole country, for any improvements or suggestions which they may propose in consequence of their investigations, or for any undetected errors or mistakes which they may discover, in order that their conclusions and recommendations in this great emergency may be brought to the aid of the department on this most interesting and important subject.

I am, very respectfully, your obedient servant,

GIDEON WELLES,
Secretary of the Navy.

Hon. B. F. WADE,
Chairman of the Committee on the Conduct of the War.

WASHINGTON, *January* 21, 1865.

Captain G. V. FOX, Assistant Secretary of the Navy, sworn and examined.

By the chairman :

Question. What is your official position?

Answer. I am Assistant Secretary of the Navy.

Question. The committee have been instructed to inquire into the matter of the construction, &c., of the light-draught monitors, so called. Will you state to the committee the objects and purposes for which those monitors were constructed?

Answer. They were intended for in-shore work in rivers, creeks, inlets, and bays where our vessels were obliged to go in the operations of the war; such as defending the lines and communications of the army, and for offensive operations on the part of the navy; the whole southern country being filled with creeks, very differently from our northern country. We cannot keep possession of such places with wooden boats. Light-draught wooden boats have their magazines, machinery, and boilers above the water, and they can be prevented entering into these creeks by musketry; or if not by musketry, by artillery. We lost a great many vessels, men, and valuable officers in attempting it, and they finally demanded, as it were, some iron vessels, which would penetrate those rivers and creeks, and hold them against the lighter works which the enemy used.

Question. Were those monitors constructed upon any new plan?

Answer. They were a copy of the original Monitor, with the addition of what is called a raft of wood around them of three feet thick, for the purpose of preventing them from being rammed, penetrated, and sunk, as many of our vessels had been.

Question. What draught were they intended to have?

Answer. From six feet eight inches to seven feet.

Question. Were they all constructed upon the same plan?

Answer. Precisely, with this difference, that when we had contracted for thirteen of them the fight at Charleston took place, which demonstrated the necessity of additions to all the monitors to strengthen them. The contract for the additional number, involving the changes demonstrated to be necessary by that fight, did not involve any extra expense.

Question. With whom did you consult first with reference to the construction of those monitors?

Answer. We consulted with the people in our department. Mr. Lenthall is our chief of construction, and he declared it would be impossible to make an iron-clad vessel for seven feet of water.

Question. What draught of water were they designed to have, according to contract?

Answer. From six and a half to seven feet—I think not to exceed seven feet. I then wrote to Captain Ericsson, inquiring if it was possible to construct such a vessel. At first he thought it was impossible. It never had been done anywhere in the world. He finally presented this plan of a monitor with a wooden raft.

Question. Did he make a proposition to the Navy Department as to how he would build them?

Answer. Yes, sir, at the request of the department.

Question. Who superintended the construction?

Answer. We advertised for proposals on the general plan of Captain Ericsson, modified and changed by Mr. Stimers.

Question. Do you recollect the difference between the plan proposed by Captain Ericsson and the plan as modified by Mr. Stimers?

Answer. There was considerable difference in the engines and machinery. Captain Ericsson's was only a general idea, without a plan. He is a peculiar man, and he works out his plan as he goes along. He tried that with the original Monitor and the Dictator. At the commencement he gives a general idea of a vessel, and as he goes on he works out the details. Stimers's plan is an elaboration of Ericsson's.

Question. After the plan of these monitors was first designed, was the plan not changed?

Answer. Some additions and extras were added.

Question. Was the department consulted from time to time in reference to these alterations and changes?

Answer. It seems that they were not, though it should have been done. I ought to state here, as you want to know why we took Stimers's plan instead of Ericsson's, that Ericsson gave a general idea only, and Mr. Stimers, who was working in Captain Ericsson's office, under his directions, and on perfectly amicable terms, elaborated his plan, and Mr. Lenthall and Mr. Isherwood preferred Stimers's plan to Ericsson's. When we advertised for proposals there was only the matter of ten thousand dollars difference between Captain Ericsson's offer and Mr. Stimers's. Stimers's plan was elaborate and full, and, in the opinion of Lenthall and Isherwood, was better than Captain Ericsson's.

Question. Did not one important difference consist in this: that one contemplated water-tanks, to be filled with water, which could be pumped out, and the vessels thereby lightened if they run aground?

Answer. That arrangement was added by Admiral Smith. Stimers did not propose it. They were put in on Admiral Smith's suggestion. That was a very important variation from the original plan, and has involved a great deal of expense and trouble.

Question. Did not that add very much to the weight of the craft?

Answer. Yes, sir, it complicated the question very much.

Question. Was the department consulted about that variation before it was carried into effect?

Answer. Yes, sir. It was approved or consented to by Mr. Lenthall, who was our chief constructor. He did not think very favorably of it, or very unfavorably of it; but Admiral Smith thought well of it, and the change was made at his suggestion.

Question. Did it not involve a great deal of machinery, such as pipes, pumps, &c.

Answer. Yes, sir.

Question. Do you know what the additional expense has been of the various changes which have been made from time to time from the original draught or proposition?

Answer. I should not like to say from recollection, as that is a matter of exact record, and can be obtained at the department. I don't think the matter is entirely closed yet between the department and the contractors.

Question. Did these monitors, according to their original plan, with turrets, answer the purposes for which they were designed?

Answer. They would not float; that is, they floated so near the surface of the water that it was not safe to send them where they were wanted. The building of light-draught vessels on the western waters involved no complication, because they were not to go to sea. The building them on the coast of the United States involved other questions, because of the fact that they would have to be taken by sea around to the ports where they were needed, and that sea on the Atlantic coast is the worst in the world. It is bad enough in summer; and in winter no coast is so bad. Therefore these boats had to be constructed entirely different from the western boats. Here we have to take them to sea to get them where we want them, and that constitutes the complication of building them on the seaboard.

Question. After they failed to answer the purpose according to their origina construction, did you undertake to change them?

Answer. We put them into the hands of Admiral Gregory, Captain Ericsson, Chief Engineer Wood, and associated Chief Engineer King with them, and called upon them to propose to the department what had better be done to render them useful. They recommended that they should be lifted up in precisely the same manner as were the second class of monitors which were found to be too low. We built them up twenty-two inches, with the exception of five. As Admirals Dahlgren and Lee wanted some monitors sent to them without turrets, it was determined that five of them should be floated by taking the turrets out, instead of by lifting them up.

Question. Have any of them been finished so as to be submitted to a test to determine their usefulness?

Answer. No, sir. I think I should say in regard to these vessels that they were an experiment, as everything else connected with naval matters has been during this war. We had no tools when the war commenced. When the President declared the coast of the United States, which was greater than that of all Europe, under blockade, there were no vessels, no men, no sailors, and but very few officers to make the blockade effectual. That clique of traitors, of which Barron and Maury were the chief, had run the government for twenty-five or thirty years, and when they went off they took away many of the archives of the department, and when we went in there, there was nothing but a great war upon hand. All those old ships of ours seemed to have been built with the idea that they never should enter southern ports. The gun department, under Admiral Dahlgren's charge, had been kept in a high state of efficiency. Our guns were the best shell guns in existence, and are now. They have never been surpassed. In the matter of constructing vessels we had very little experience, and we were called upon to take charge of this whole southern coast. In building our monitors we had no aid from former experience; men differed as to the practicability of the plan; Lenthall said the monitors would go to the bottom, and Isherwood had no confidence. And yet we went ahead and built them; and when we were called upon to assist in the attack on Charleston, every captain of the monitors declared they could not remain there in a storm of wind. Our own people, as loyal as you and I are, had no faith; but we had to go ahead or fail, and go ahead we did. We won with the original Monitor, and we thought that the best type of a vessel for shore work. Abroad no vessel for war purposes had been built of a light draught. They had never built anything of a lighter draught than from twenty to twenty-seven feet. Those vessels could not be used on the coast of the United States except in one or two ports. They are built for European warfare. When a vessel is built of 8,000 tons the question is a simple one. Suppose you have to carry, as did the knights of old, eighty pounds of arms; if you were ten times as strong and large as you are, you could carry them easily, and even more. So in England, they met this question of carrying heavy arms by building vessels so big that they could carry the arms with no difficulty. But the question with us was to construct the smallest vessel and yet have it carry an armor that should resist shot. At the west that question was a very simple one, where the vessel was not exposed to a gale of wind and high seas. But on the Atlantic coast the question was a very different one. We lost one monitor in a gale.

Now, in reference to these light-draught monitors, so called, we took the Monitor as a type of a shore vessel, because it had been successful. These vessels have failed inasmuch as they were overloaded. It was a miscalculation from want of skill and care in the engineer who worked out the weights. There should have been more allowance made for them. If that had been done, and the vessels had been built without those water tanks, with engines of very simple construction, without the surface condensers, and without any unnecessary jimcracks, they would have been finished a year ago, and we should have had them to assist in the attack on Wilmington, which was one object in having them constructed. As it was, we had to make the attack without them.

By Mr. Gooch:

Question. Are you sufficiently acquainted with the plan of Captain Ericsson to be able to say he could have built those monitors as he designed, and not have had them draw over six or six and a half feet of water?

Answer. It is a matter of calculation as to what a vessel will draw, and Ericsson has more ability to make that calculation truly than any man living. I will add that his vessel would have been more simple, more cheaply made, with less machinery, and would have been done in less time. But the price he proposed was only, I think, $10,000 less than the enlarged and elaborate plan of Mr. Stimers, which, in the opinion of Lenthall and Isherwood, would make a much superior vessel.

Question. Were not instructions given to Stimers to confer with Captain Ericsson?

Answer. Mr. Lenthall has that order. I have seen it. I hunted it up, because I carried that order from the Secretary to Lenthall. It was, not to permit any change or alteration without consulting with Captain Ericsson; and we never imagined it was otherwise.

Question. When was it first discovered that such was not the case?

Answer. I cannot say when; but it was after the work was very well advanced.

Question. Then, among the changes you made, you proposed to build the sides of the monitors up twenty-two inches?

Answer. Yes, sir; to lift them up as you would lift up the roof of a house, and put in half a story of walls.

Question. How much will that increase the draught beyond that originally contemplated?

Answer. About a foot.

Question. Then for what purpose will those monitors be useful?

Answer. A vessel of eight feet draught will be able to enter any of the southern creeks and ports which we have been in. They will go into all the southern ports, where we have been operating, and in case of a war with a maritime power, with England for instance, she will have to attack us with wooden vessels, because her iron-clads are of too great draught to operate on our coast with the exception of two or three harbors; and one light-draught monitor, in my opinion, is more than a match for any wooden vessel in the English navy, not excepting the Victoria, a three-decker, and 130 guns; for this reason she can keep in shoal water and choose her distance, while the other vessel cannot reach her. At such a distance as she chooses she would be invulnerable, and could set the other vessel on fire with shell without difficulty.

Question. When these vessels are built up as now proposed, how will their ability to go from port to port compare with those originally designed?

Answer. These vessels are not built for sea-going vessels, but they will be very much improved for this reason: the strength of a vessel is in a great degree dependent on her depth. The higher the sides of a vessel, the stronger she is, because it is like taking a plank and attempting to break it edgewise; if it is two inches you will snap it; if it is six inches you cannot. The stronger they are, the better able they are to get along the coast.

Question. If these vessels had been far enough out of water as to have rendered it desirable, in case of a fight, that they should be sunk lower, would not the tanks suggested by Admiral Smith have been an improvement?

Answer. Unquestionably; and not only that, but if in running with the tanks full she should get aground, the pumping out of the water would lift her four inches, and that four inches might allow her to get off in one hour, or on one tide, when otherwise she might remain for days. But the objection to the tanks was, that it complicated the problem, which was already a complicated one, of getting a light-draught vessel with a heavy armor; and it also added to the expense, and delayed their construction, so that we have been obliged to operate without them, when they were designed to be of great use in the war.

Question. What was intended or expected to be the speed of these monitors?

Answer. My impression is that the speed was to be about seven and a half knots.

Question. Do you know what the speed of those which have been tried has proved to be?

Answer. The only one that has been tried is the one which came around from Boston without a turret, and fitted out as a torpedo vessel. She ran five knots.

Question. Do you know whether or not there has been any fault or imperfection in the engines of those vessels, which has prevented their attaining the speed originally contemplated?

Answer. There has been some dispute about the engines. Captain Ericsson thinks there is a great deal too much boiler for the size of the engine. Isherwood thinks there is not. It is a difference of opinion among experts about these engines, and they are investigating it in the House of Representatives. The engines were unnecessarily expensive in their design, I think It is the tendency of an engineer, and of a naval engineer especially, to elaborate; and that, in time of war, adds not only to the expense, but creates enormous delay, for the reason that establishments that make engines are accustomed to make plain and cheap ones; and if they are called upon to make any others there is likely to be great delay.

Question. Will it not probably be possible to increase the speed of those vessels, and will not their efficiency depend very much upon their rate of speed?

Answer. A vessel which is built for the purpose of operating in the creeks and shoal waters of our southern coast, and in our harbors, as these were, can never operate anywhere else. Speed is not an important object. In a vessel which goes to sea, speed is almost the highest consideration; but in a harbor, these vessels must operate on the defensive, and not on the offensive; and on the defensive you are to be attacked, and if you are to be attacked in port your speed is not important. One of the elements of speed, and a very important element, is size; and size you cannot get with a light-draught, shoal-water vessel, cased with iron. The Monadnock is the fastest iron-cased vessel we have got of the monitor class.

Question. What is her speed?

Answer. She will go ten knots, which is eleven and a half statute miles.

Question. Is she considered a great success?

Answer. Yes, sir; everybody is perfectly delighted with her. She has two screws, two turrets, and she can fire directly ahead, or behind, or on either side, and Captain Parrott says he would just as soon be in her as in any other vessel. I saw a letter this morning from Captain Thatcher, commanding the Colorado, and he, who has heretofore had all the prejudices of his class against iron-clads, says "I am a convert from this day forth to iron-clads; they have done better than anything else." While they were all very anxious, during the storm at Beaufort, about their big frigates, these iron-clads were safely riding at anchor with the sea rolling over them.

WASHINGTON, *January* 23, 1865.

Mr. JOHN LENTHALL sworn and examined.

By the chairman:

Question. What connexion have you with the Navy Department?

Answer. I am chief of the Bureau of Construction and Repairs.

Question. What do you know about the building of twenty light-draught monitors, under the act of Congress appropriating ten millions of dollars for that purpose?

Answer. The design for those vessels, which I saw, was a sketch submitted by Captain Ericsson. The next was a more perfect plan, proposed by Engineer Stimers. That was shortly before the advertisement was made for contracts.

Question. Did Mr. Ericsson ever submit any proposition to construct any of these vessels?

Answer. I think he did; but it did not come to me. I think it was made directly to the Navy Department.

Question. Can you state wherever, and in what particulars, the plan of Mr. Stimers differed from that of Mr. Ericsson?

Answer. I should think the external forms of the vessels were almost identical. I never compared them, the one with the other, but my impression at the time was that they were of the same external form. The plan that Mr. Stimers finally determined on embraced a water chamber, which was not embraced in the plan of Mr. Ericsson. That, I think, was the main feature of difference between them.

Question. Do you know what led the department to prefer the plan of Mr. Stimers to that of Mr. Ericsson?

Answer. I cannot say. I will state that I recollect there were some minor differences as to some of the outlines of the vessels, but nothing of any moment. I made no particular examination of them however.

Question. What agency had the Bureau of Construction and Repairs in making the contracts for the building of these monitors and seeing that those contracts were executed?

Answer. When the plans had been prepared an advertisement was issued by the Navy Department, and all the bids were received by it. The department opened the bids and awarded the contracts. When that was done, I was directed, as in all other cases, to prepare the contracts. The contracts were executed by me merely as the agent of the department for executing such papers.

Question. You had no power to judge and determine concerning the merits of the different plans, &c.?

Answer. No, sir; there was, at that time, not sufficient data upon which any one could do that but the person who devised the plan. It was merely an outline plan.

Question. Were these light-draught monitors with turrets an experiment at that time?

Answer. No, sir, I think not; they were of the same general class and type of vessel as the other monitors. These were designed more particularly for rivers, while the others were for bays and harbors.

Question. These were designed to be of lighter draught and for shoaler water than any you had before?

Answer. Yes, sir; these were to be of six or seven feet draught. The others were ten or eleven feet.

Question. Was Mr. Stimers, in constructing those vessels, directed to take the advice and counsel of Mr. Ericsson?

Answer. Yes, sir; I remember that, after the contract had been made—probably six weeks after—one of the contractors suggested a change or modification, and he was directed to consult with Captain Ericsson upon the subject. That letter was addressed to Admiral Gregory. There was no direct communication with Mr. Stimers.

Question. Had the department frequent correspondence with Mr. Stimers while those vessels were being built?

Answer. No, sir, not a great deal; I think none directly with Mr. Stimers.

Question. Was the department consulted from time to time in regard to the alterations that were made?

Answer. I think not; or very seldom.

Question. Had he any communication or correspondence with your bureau, or with the department?

Answer. He had none direct with me.

Question. Do you know whether he had with the Navy Department?

Answer. I cannot tell.

Question. Do you know whether he did make alterations without consulting with your bureau or with the department?

Answer. I think there were some alterations made by him; I do not know what they were; I cannot call them to mind now.

Question. Can you tell what the expense of those alterations was?

Answer. We have paid some extra bills. Some of the alterations were suggested as modifications rendered necessary by the experience before Charleston. Some of those were paid for; I do not know but all of them have been paid for.

Question. Do you know whether Mr. Stimers did consult Mr. Ericsson, as he was directed to do, as to the propriety of any of these alterations?

Answer. I do not know; after giving the order for him to do so, I took it for granted that the order was carried out. I had no means of knowing whether he carried it out or not.

Question. Have you any evidence that he did so consult with him?

Answer. No, sir; I have no evidence one way or the other.

Question. I think you have already stated that you do not know why the department preferred the plan of Mr. Stimers to that of Mr. Ericsson?

Answer. No, sir; I do not know. Externally they were substantially the same. I did not measure them, or put the one drawing upon the other. But to the eye they appeared to be substantially the same thing.

Question. Was not Ericsson's the simplest and the easiest and quickest to get up?

Answer. The water chamber was the principal addition made to Mr. Stimers's vessel.

Question. What useful purpose was that water chamber supposed to subserve?

Answer. It was, I presume, to increase the draught of the vessel upon occasion to lower it in the water, when under fire in time of action.

Question. That addition was afterwards abandoned, was it not?

Answer. When they had to reduce the weight of the vessel, they had to abandon it.

Question. Were these light-draught monitors as constructed by Mr. Stimers of any consequence? would they answer the purpose for which they were originally designed?

Answer. They were more deeply immersed than it was supposed they would be. Their decks were down on awash with the water.

Question. And they could not carry their turrets?

Answer. They could not carry their turrets with all that it was intended to put on them. They were intended to be fifteen inches out of the water, or about that much.

Question. Was it not a great fault in the construction of a vessel to make such a difference in the amount of displacement?

Answer. It appears now that all the alterations increased the weight of the vessel, which, I suppose, was not at first intended or calculated. There was a constant addition of weight.

Question. Should not a naval constructor know how he was increasing the weight, and calculate so as not to sink his vessel down too far in the water?

Answer. I had supposed that was done; I do not know whether it was done or not.

Question. They certainly could not have done so if the vessel would not carry all the weight it was contemplated it should carry. However, I will ask what was the condition of these monitors at the time it was ascertained they would not answer their original design? How many were completed?

Answer. I think only one, when it was ascertained that they would not carry the weight that it was designed to place on them.

Question. At how early a period was it ascertained that they were defective in that respect?

Answer. I have not the dates with me, but I think it was some time in the spring, or early in the summer of last year.

Question. I would like to ascertain about that.

Answer. I think it was ascertained from a vessel in Boston, the Chimo.

Question. Can you tell in what condition each of these twenty light-draught monitors were at that time?

Answer. I do not remember now. I think I can ascertain from the records of the bureau.

Question. As soon as it was ascertained that those monitors were defective in that respect, did the department stop all further work on them?

Answer. I think it did; but the work on these monitors was under the control of Admiral Gregory. He communicated with me or the department as he seemed to think necessary.

Question. As I understand it, after it was ascertained that those monitors would not answer the purpose for which they were originally designed, a commission was appointed to examine them, and devise what remedy could be applied?

Answer. That was ordered by the department; I do not now remember when it was.

Question. They proposed that the sides of the vessels should be built up twenty-two inches.

Answer. Yes, sir; they made that suggestion.

Question. What will be the expense of that?

Answer. Admiral Gregory received proposals from all the contractors, varying from $70,000 to $90,000. Some of the vessels were in a greater state of forwardness than others.

Question. And the expense of building up the sides was greater according to the greater state of forwardness of the vessel?

Answer. Yes, sir.

Question. Are you a nautical man enough to be able to say whether these vessels in their improved state will be useful vessels?

Answer. I think they will be useful for river service—not for sea service.

Question. What speed have they now, according to the best information which the department has?

Answer. I think they have made four knots.

Question. That would hardly enable them to stem the current of the Mississippi, would it?

Answer. I do not know what the current of the Mississippi is, and therefore I cannot tell. Of course their greater immersion has reduced their speed from what it would otherwise have been.

Question. Do you recollect the speed of the one without a turret which was brought around from Boston to New York?

Answer. I do not remember exactly. I think it was something over four knots, as near as I can now recollect. But I hardly think a trial on the ocean is a fair trial for these vessels.

Question. Was it really prudent in the department to direct the construction upon the same model of so many vessels, when it was rather an experiment?

Answer. So far as being monitor vessels was concerned, they were not an experiment.

Question. But we had not made any light-draught monitors to ascend rivers, &c., at that time?

Answer. No, sir. I am not competent to judge as to the policy of building so large a number, for that would not come within the sphere of my judgment. When they commenced I did not know how many they intended to make, and at the time the advertisement was issued I do not think the department itself had determined how many it would make. But I cannot state as to that.

Question. These were all to be built upon the same model?

Answer. Yes, sir; that is often the case. When the first authority was given to build steam frigates, six were built at once. They told me to design and build five of them; and they were all upon the same model.

Question. But they were a kind of vessel which was old-fashioned and well understood?

Answer. Yes, sir.

Question. Will you furnish the committee, from the records of your bureau, whatever information you have concerning the time when it was discovered these monitors were defective, when the commission was appointed, and when and what they reported; the condition in which each vessel was at that time, and the expense of raising or modifying each vessel as proposed?

Answer. I will do so, as far as I can.

NAVY DEPARTMENT, BUREAU OF CONSTRUCTION AND REPAIR,
January 26, 1865.

SIR: In reply to the inquiries in the memorandum handed me by the committee, I would respectfully state—

1. The department was informed by Admiral Gregory, on the 31st May, 1864, that the Chimo had proved defective.

2. The work that might interfere with modifications to these vessels was then suspended.

3. Some of the vessels were nearly completed; others from two-thirds to three-fourths finished.

4. The committee to examine the vessels was appointed by the department on the 11th June, and their report was dated the 9th July, 1864.

5. Accompanying is the cost, as agreed on by Admiral Gregory, for making these vessels twenty-two inches deeper, which increased their tonnage one hundred and thirty tons. Five of these vessels have been converted for torpedo purposes.

Respectfully, your obedient servant,

JOHN LENTHALL,
Chief of Bureau.

Hon. BENJAMIN F. WADE,
Chairman of the Committee on the Conduct of the War, United States Senate, Washington.

STATEMENT.

Name.	Cost of raising vessel 22 inches.	Name.	Cost of raising vessel 22 inches.
Nauset	$86,000 00	Etlah	$82,500 00
Cohoes	89,000 00	Klamath	89,000 00
Waxsaw	89,140 25	Yuma	89,000 00
Squando	90,000 00	Koka	58,665 86
Shawnee	90,000 00	Shiloh	82,500 00
Suncook	87,500 00	Tunxis	115,500 00
Wassuc	55,275 60	Yazoo	68,000 00
Umpqua	85,000 00		

WASHINGTON, *February* 11, 1865.

ALBAN C. STIMERS sworn and examined.

By the chairman:

Question. What is your position in the navy of the United States?

Answer. I am a chief engineer of the navy.

Question. We have been directed by a resolution of the Senate to inquire into the building of certain light-draught iron-clads, twenty in number, with which we understand you had something to do.

Answer. Yes, sir.

Question. Please tell us, in your own way, all that you know about their construction, and whatever of importance you may think it necessary to state in that connexion.

Answer. These vessels of course have a history, and I propose to give you a full understanding of that history, as far as I know it, in order that you may know something about them. We were building monitors designed by Captain Ericsson. Admiral Gregory was the general superintendent of their construction. I served under him in the capacity of general inspector. The duty of general inspector was only to see that the materials were good, and that the work was well done. In performing that duty, I had to visit the various points where the vessels were building, to examine them. There were serving under me local inspectors, who during the time I was absent followed my instructions in regard to these examinations. Besides the duty of general inspector proper, I had other duties to perform.

The first monitor was about to be built, it having been proposed by Captain Ericsson, and accepted by the government, after the advice of a board of our highest naval officers, among whom was Rear-Admiral Joseph Smith; who being a bureau officer, it was placed under his direction to be built. I was ordered to superintend that building. At the time I received those orders I was engaged in the blockading fleet off Charleston, and I came here to receive instructions. They were the usual instructions, to see that the materials were good and that the work was well done, and to use all vigilance. But in charging me verbally in regard to it, the Secretary said: "You have been chosen for this duty because we understand you to be an engineer who looks at new things without prejudice, either for or against; and we want such a man for this thing. Now I wish you to go to New York and work with Captain Ericsson, as well as you can. This being a new thing, it is probable that he will find a great many details which he will want to modify. Whatever you and he can agree upon between you, as being better for the vessel or for the government, you can do it. Do not trouble us with letters about matters which we certainly cannot understand here. This is so different from things which we have had to do with before, that you must judge about these things yourself. We believe that Captain Ericsson is devoted to what he projects, and will think more of his reputation than he will of a dollar or two; and you will look out for the interests of the government."

It was provided in the contract that the vessel should have masts and sails sufficient to drive it six knots an hour, in a fair breeze of wind. That was put in in Washington—not by Captain Ericsson.

Question. By whose order was that put in?

Answer. I suppose it was upon the recommendation of the Board of Admiralty that examined the plans, but I do not know. The contract was given to me in that way. Captain Ericsson laid it before me, and pointed out many things of that kind that he thought it would be better to change. I took the advice of such naval officers as I could meet with, whom I thought good authority, in regard to the masts and sails. I consulted with Admiral Stringham, and he agreed with me that it would be very bad to put them on; and under the authority which had been given to me, I assumed to leave them out. And it was understood that, in regard to many matters, questions of cost, &c., they should be left until the final payment. There was a reserve of twenty-five per cent., to be paid after it was found that everything was satisfactory. I state these things to show you that in building this very new class of vessels, there had to be a great deal of consultation between the designer and the inspector, besides the duty which was imposed upon me of looking to the excellence of the materials and workmanship. When the Monitor was completed, we went down with it to Hampton roads and fought with the Merrimac. Its success was so marked that it was decided by the government that they would not experiment any more, as we were in the midst of a great war, but would adopt immediately something which had proved itself so successful. They accordingly went on to build more of the same class right away after that; we commenced ten vessels that were to be like the original Monitor, with the exception of having such improvements as our experience in going from New York to Hampton roads, and in the battle there, had pointed out as proper. As I had been the superintendent of the first vessel, had gone in her to sea, and had been with her during the fight, I was looked to by the government to point out those things which would be improvements; and it was stipulated in the new contracts that the working drawings should be submitted to me. I do not remember the exact expression in the contract, but it was discussed in the Navy Department, and it was decided to put that clause in—that is, that Captain Ericsson should show me his plans before they were issued to the workmen. That, however, did not work well in operation, as Captain Ericsson was a proud man, and I did not think it good policy to do anything to hurt his feelings. He therefore was not in the habit of showing me his drawings. He was an older man than I was, and I had respect for his age and experience; and I found the drawings as I could. Still we had to consult together a great deal about these new vessels.

We had only that one trip at sea, and that one battle of the first vessel, for experience. While this was going on, and these vessels were being built, the government looked forward to building more. They found that the war assumed greater proportions, and they wanted a greater number of these vessels. Besides, they had always felt that it was necessary to prepare for foreign wars.

When I was going to New York to assume the new duties of constructing more vessels, the Secretary of the Navy said to me: "I wish you to keep in your mind always that these vessels may not be used in this war, but may be required to protect our harbors against the iron-clad vessels of foreign nations. Always keep in view, during their construction, that that is the most important point to consider. Those things which occur in battle between heavy ships and iron vessels are the things for which you must provide."

I was showing you that they were going on to build more vessels. But there was no one to design them, and that created a difficulty at once. Of course I was familiar with that to a certain extent, but I was busy as general inspector, and had no time to design vessels. It was proposed in the first place that I should design some vessels, for they did not like all of Captain Ericsson's plans; and it was proposed that I should design some vessels in New York, and leave out some of the things which they considered imperfections in his plans. But after I got there I told them I should have my hands full to act as general inspector. And I found, too, that Captain Ericsson had some feeling upon the subject. He did not like that any other than himself should design monitors. I told them that I thought we could get all his genius for our benefit better by looking to him as the head of the whole matter, leaving him to design everything, while I would act as general inspector, and would employ all my time to see those plans carried out. That plan was accordingly adopted.

Now when we came to build some more than these ten monitors, we did not like some of their peculiarities. We wanted more speed, and some other qualities which they did not possess. Captain Ericsson was himself too busy to design others; I was too busy to make them, and we had no one else to go to. I then suggested to Captain Fox, the Assistant Secretary of the Navy, that if he would permit me to establish an office in New York near Captain Ericsson's office, and hire some draughtsmen, and put an assistant engineer there, an officer of the government, to see that they performed their work properly, we could get Captain Ericsson to draw a general plan which would embody these changes, and then he could let me have the drawings which he had, and these draughtsmen could modify them. It would only require a few directions to make the modifications. If he would do that, I would promise him that no drawing should go out of my office until it had been submitted to Captain Ericsson for his approval; so that we could retain Captain Ericsson as designer, without putting upon him the labor of making the designs. That was thought the best way of getting out of the difficulty, and it was done. About this time of getting up a new class, of which we built nine, of the river and harbor monitors, Captain Ericsson drew a general plan and submitted a general description of the river and harbor monitors of the Tippecanoe class. Those plans and descriptions were submitted here, advertised for, and contractors took contracts to build them. The specifications were made out in my office, constantly consulting with Captain Ericsson and Mr. Fox about the changes upon which we all agreed. The general plan was made by Captain Ericsson and transferred to me; and from that we made out the working plans.

Just about this time we talked also about a light-draught vessel. We were getting possession of the western rivers, on which we needed some of them, as well as in a great many of our harbors, where we found that we wanted vessels of a light draught to go under heavy batteries and come out again. Mr. Fox was very solicitous that we should get up something of that kind. Captain Ericsson said he would get up a general plan, in the same way as before; he did so, and it was sent on to Washington. There was considerable delay about it, however; and they were in a great hurry for the vessels, for they wanted them very much indeed. Every letter from Mr. Fox contained something about hurrying up Captain Ericsson about the light-draught monitors. I had occasion to come on to Washington at times, and the first time after the plans were sent on here—perhaps a month after—I inquired at the department what they were going to do about the light-draught monitors, or whether they had given up the project altogether. Mr. Fox said, "No, not at all." But he said they had been going on here, acting independently of the bureaus of construction and engineering. The first monitors were built under the direction of Admiral Joseph Smith, who was chief of the Bureau of Yards and Docks, not of Construction. The contracts for the Passaic class were given out by him, but were afterwards transferred to the chief of the Bureau of Construction. I think there was some delay about the confirmations of the chiefs of the bureaus of construction and engineering by the Senate, which caused some delay in this matter. But it was partly because those two officers did not believe in iron-clads, and especially in the monitors, in Ericsson, and all that; they were opposed to the whole thing, and lent no assistance to it. The Secretary and Assistant Secretary, advised by Admiral Smith, brought these things out independently of the bureau. Mr. Fox said: "Now that our heads of bureaus are confirmed in their places, they must do their work. We have taken all the responsibility thus far, but now these men must take their responsibility. I have therefore sent the plans down to the Bureau of Construction. Mr. Lenthall says that he does not see anything in his part of the ship which is at all out of the way, and he does not advise any changes. I have also sent the plans to the Bureau of Engineering, to see if the chief of that bureau has any objection to the arrangement of the machinery. He says he thinks there ought to be some modifications; but he is out of town, and you must wait until to-morrow to see him, and then you will find out his views. You have Captain Ericsson's views about the machinery; if you find that the chief of the Bureau of Engineering has views to which Captain Ericsson will not agree, try to get the two together, so that we can get a plan on which both will agree, because we want these vessels to meet Captain Ericsson's views, and the views of our bureau. If you cannot bring them together so that they will be reconciled, then we will build one on Ericsson's plan, and one on the plan of the bureau; and if you have a plan, we will build one on your plan also." Said I, "No, sir, I have no plan; I have more to do than ever."

The next day I saw Mr. Isherwood, the chief of the Bureau of Steam Engineering, and I found that he wanted the coal-bunkers arranged in a different way—he wanted entirely different boilers—he wanted different engines. Instead of their being athwart engines, connected directly with the screw-shaft, he wanted them connected with bevel gearing. Not to go through the whole matter, he had changed everything—coal-bunkers, boilers, engines, and propellers. I discussed these matters with him, and brought him to consent to some modifications, which I thought perhaps Captain Ericsson would agree to. He gave me some sketches, plans, &c., and it was decided that as I had draughtsmen, I should take them to New York, and if Captain Ericsson agreed to them, I should embody them in a new plan and send it on again to Washington. I went to Captain Ericsson, and he did not like any of the proposed changes at all. He thought each one injurious to the vessel—that it made the plan less excellent than his was. "But," said he, "if they will not build more than one of these vessels unless I give way, of course I think the government ought to have them; they will be very useful indeed, and I think they ought to build more than one right away. The chief of the Bureau of Steam Engineering knows how to work engines, and drive the vessel along, of course; so I think we better consent"—with the exception, however, that he would not listen to gear-engines at all. He said they would certainly fail if placed in such limber vessels as these would be. As the chief of the bureau had given me these plans, and these directions to work them into a general plan if I found I could do it, with the understanding that I was to retain the original type if the bevel-gear arrangement would not work so well, I withdrew that part, and Captain Ericsson assented to all the rest. I afterwards reported to the chief of the Bureau of Steam Engineering that I found I could not work in the bevel-gear plans. I do not remember that I told him why I could not work them in, but I told him that I could not, and he gave his approval to the plans which I did work in. The diameter of the cylinders, however, was reduced from the design of Captain Ericsson, who had fixed upon thirty-six inches. The chief of the bureau thought eighteen inches large enough, but consented to my making them twenty-two inches. I took the plans to my office, and placed them in charge of a second assistant engineer who had been an apprentice in the Novelty Iron Works for several years, and was acquainted with drawing, calculating, &c.

Question. What was his name?

Answer. Theodore Allen. He was quite a young man, but the ablest engineer that I had under my control, except the local inspectors, whom I could not employ for that purpose. I placed these plans in his charge, and detailed certain draughtsmen to work for him. I had in this office a superintendent of the draughtsmen, whom I took upon the recommendation of Captain Ericsson; in fact who came out of his house. I chose him because he could always have the *entrée* of Ericsson's house; could take the drawings to him, and talk to him about them, &c. He was an old engineer, and was an apprentice at the same time and place with our oldest engineers in the navy. His name was Crabbs. I gave this in charge to this young engineer, with directions to superintend the draughtsmen who were to assist him; and I gave them the directions which I had agreed upon with the chief of the bureau, and also such other directions about the matter as I could present. I ought perhaps to state that when I found I had to re-draw the plans, I consulted Mr. Harlan, of the firm of Harlan, Hollingsworth & Co., of Wilmington, Delaware, who may be termed with propriety light-draught iron ship-builders, upon some of the details of iron hulls. When I informed Captain Ericsson of this, I told him that I had done it because they were the most experienced and most successful builders of light iron sea-going vessels in the world. He did not appear to like this appeal from himself to others on my part, and asked if I really thought they deserved that I should claim for them such distinction. I challenged him to name another, either in this country or in Europe, who could rival them in that peculiar branch. After reflecting a moment, he acknowledged that I was probably correct.

You will observe that although I have never looked upon myself as the designer of any of these vessels, I was the general inspector of them all. All the plans, both generally and in detail, as well as the materials and the workmanship, had to be approved by me. When, therefore, plans were drawn in my office, instead of by Captain Ericsson himself, I took advantage of the opportunity to improve them, and to throw upon him the *onus* of proving that my amendments were not good. This he sometimes did, both with this and the Saugus class of vessels. In all such cases the drawings were modified to meet his approval. After the vessels were commenced, and we were all committed to their construction, the contracts having been given out, Captain Ericsson became angry about something in connexion with them, and wrote a letter to the Secretary of the Navy, in which he declared he would have nothing further to do with them—that his plans had been modified so extensively that he did not any longer recognize them as his own, &c., &c. Up to this time, however, he had accepted each of the proposed modifications as it was made; and he even continued afterwards to examine, and approve or condemn the drawings taken to him by my superintendent of draughtsmen, whose orders from me were, from first to last, to go himself with every drawing which was not an exact copy of some drawing of Captain Ericsson, and ascertain whether he accepted it as his design, and if not, to learn the modifications required. In such cases I examined the modifications demanded; if I approved of them they were made, and the drawings issued to the builders; otherwise, I would go personally and confer with Captain Ericsson, and we would agree upon the plans to be used. Captain Ericsson made three sets of plans in all their details, as follows: First, the original Monitor; second, the Passaic class of monitors, of which ten were built; third, the Dictator and Puritan, ocean monitors, of which only those two were built. In my office there were made four sets of plans in the manner which I have already described: First, the Saugus class of harbor and river monitors, of which nine were built; second, the light-draught monitors, of which there were twenty; third, turrets, pilot-houses, and impregnable smoke-pipes for wooden monitors of the Monadnock class, of which there were four built, with two turrets on each; fourth, the same for wooden monitors of the Kalamazoo class, of which there were also four built, with two turrets each—the turrets being larger and thicker, and with different detailed arrangements from the others. Of all this work it was held that Captain Ericsson was the designer, and I the general inspector, until the light-draught monitors were accounted failures, when it was published throughout the country that I was the designer of them. I corrected the statement to that effect in the New York Times soon after the monitors were commenced, and when it was considered by every one that such a statement was highly complimentary to me. Since they have been considered failures as they were first built, I have not before this made any public denial of the charge of being their designer, as I believed that the truth would finally come to light, and that my abilities and my arduous industry would eventually be fully appreciated as effectually as if I entered upon a newspaper controversy with those who are determined, if possible, to make me the scapegoat for their shortcomings. I had to visit Boston, Philadelphia, Chester, Pennsylvania, and Wilmington, Delaware, besides a great many places about New York. There were new vessels also being built in Cincinnati and Pittsburg, although I did not visit there until some time after that; but there was a great deal of correspondence growing up, making out all these new contracts, teaching civilian inspectors what their duties were, and learning what were the views of the Navy Department, and of Captain Ericsson. I was consequently occupied pretty closely.

When we came to arrange this machinery in the new way they came to me and said that they did not know whether the ships would balance in that way. It will be understood that these vessels were designed to draw the same amount of water at one end as the other. Now, if you move the weights in the ship you of course affect the draught of water, and it is necessary to make calculations about the displacement of the vessel in all its length, and then regulate the weights in such a way that she would lie nearly level on the water. They made their calculations, and reported to me that the vessel was not large enough to hold the weights to be put upon it—that it did not displace water enough. I said, "How do you mean—does it draw more than six feet of water?" They replied, "It draws not only six feet of water, but all the vessel above the water will not sustain the weight to be put upon it." In the ordinary course of things I would go and consult with Captain Ericsson upon such a matter. I do not remember whether I did or not; if not, it was because I did not have time. The remedy was obvious, which was to make the vessel larger. I directed that to be done, and the vessel was increased in size. They then came to me and said, "Now we have it all right." In getting such a thing they make it by trial in error, taking the dimensions and making the calculations afterwards. They say, "We have a vessel which will draw six feet and four inches; the side armor will be fifteen inches out of the water, and it will carry all the weight." I said, "Have you calculated for contingencies?" "Yes, sir," was the reply, "we have figured it all out." Then I said, "If you are certain, we better go at it."

Before this, I had employed on this very class of vessels, which had to be changed in their dimensions to get them to float properly, a naval architect of considerable ability, to make the calculations, and I put them beside the calculations of this young engineer. This other man, whom I had employed on the recommendation of Captain Ericsson, had been taken away, and I could get no other in his place. Mr. Allen was the only one to whom I could trust anything of this kind. I had no time to make the calculations myself; therefore, so far as I was concerned, I had to trust to him, and then send the plans on to Washington. I took a schedule of his calculations of the weights because I knew that such a thing should not be trusted to any one man, and particularly to one so young. I carried this to Mr. Fox, and he sent me down to Mr. Lenthall, chief of the Bureau of Construction. I said to Mr. Lenthall, "Here is the calculation of the weights; in the first column is the quantity in cubic feet of iron and wood; here is the description, and the first item is the coal placed under the engines; next comes the thickness of the iron, next the wood, the number of cubic feet, which we use in arriving at the weights; next comes the weight of the iron, and the final column gives the total." After going through the detail in that way, describing each part, then came the calculations for the draught. I then said, "Mr. Lenthall, here are these weights; you know better than I how such things are done, and how much such materials weigh, and you have people in your employ who understand it. I have not calculated these matters myself at all, and it has only been done by a young second assistant engineer in my office—a very competent young man. There they are, any way." When I did that I considered that I had transferred my responsibility for these weights to Mr. Lenthall, he being the chief of the Bureau of Construction for the navy.

Question. Did that schedule of weights that you furnished correspond to the usual way of making these naval estimates?

Answer. So far as I know, it did; but there is one item which I will mention to show one of the errors, of which I have since learned. While this was going on, during another visit to Washington, I asked Mr. Lenthall, "How many pounds per cubic foot would you allow in such calculations for white oak, such as would probably be used in such vessels?" The answer which he gave me was characteristic of the man. "Ah! well," said he, "you see now, live oak, for instance, will not float in water; we have to put pine with it to make a raft to float; then white oak is not so heavy as live oak; pine floats." I said, "Now, how many pounds to the cubic foot would you allow?" "Well," said he, "some is heavier than others; and, if you take the same stick, one end will be heavier than the other." The amount of it is, if I had not known the man for a great many years I should have supposed that he did not know.

Question. Was that all the answer you got in regard to the allowance you should make for weight?

Answer. Yes, sir. Then I went to Boston. We were building there a wooden monitor, and the constructor took me on board of her. She was then well in train. He showed her to me, and I said to him, "I see that your timber here is about as green as we probably will use in the light-draught vessels, where there is to be a great deal of oak." He said, "Yes; you cannot get seasoned timber sufficient for the purpose." I said to him, "How many pounds per cubic foot do you allow in calculating for your displacement?" He gave me the number of pounds and the decimals; I think it was 52.6, or something of that kind. Whatever it was, it was one or two pounds less than fifty-five pounds. I told this young man to allow fifty-five pounds per cubic foot, thus allowing a little margin. I find by these calculations that there were 470,000 pounds allowed for the weight of the live oak. Since these vessels were built I have taken pains to have some of the oak weighed, and I find that it weighs seventy pounds to the cubic foot. That would make a difference in the draught of the vessel of three inches just for the white oak alone.

By Mr. Gooch:

Question. Depending entirely upon the condition of the oak as to seasoning?

Answer. Yes, sir. I do not doubt but that Mr. Hanscom, the constructor in Boston, answered me correctly. He had probably been weighing his timber. He was building his own vessel in the navy yard, where he had all the facilities, and could arrive at this thing. I suppose he gave me what his timber did weigh, but I had no such facilities myself. I then brought these plans back to Washington, as I have said, and they were again submitted to the bureau, who approved of the plans and thought they were all satisfactory. Admiral Smith also saw them; he had always felt an interest in these vessels. He said, "Why do you have so much wood on the outside of them? That is more than you want for armor backing." I replied that it was a part of the plan of Captain Ericsson. He said, "There is such a fine opportunity to put a water tank right around there, so that when you are navigating new waters of unknown depth, or new channels, when you get aground you can pump out the water and raise your vessel off; and then, when you are free, you can let the water in again and go on again." I said, "Admiral, that is a point that was first suggested by Mr. Stevens, of Hoboken, in his battery. It has been discussed a great deal by our naval officers, and they all appear to think it to be a good plan. I am asked on every hand in the navy why we do not have these tanks in the monitors." The reason why we did not have it was because Captain Ericsson did not put it in. Here was a case where we were permitting the bureaus of the Navy Department to interfere with his plans. I said to the admiral, "Now that an officer of your rank and abilities—a man that has looked into these matters as much as you have—suggests this thing, and recommends it, if you will say that you are in earnest in your recommendation I will speak of it." He said, "Certainly I am." I told Mr. Fox what the admiral had said, and he said, "Take it down to Mr. Lenthall and find out from him whether there is any objection on his part to the introduction of such an arrangement in the vessel." I went down and saw him; but, instead of answering the question whether there was any objection to the construction of it, he objected to it, but applied his objection to having any such arrangement in the vessel any way; that is, he said it was not necessary. I finally wormed out of him his views as to whether it was objectionable as a piece of construction. He said, "No; you can build that in without any difficulty at all. So far as the construction goes, there is no objection whatever." I went back and told Mr. Fox what Mr. Lenthall had said. I said to Mr. Fox, "You yourself are a naval officer; you are an expert in these things, and you ought to be a good judge of whether a thing is useful or not to an officer commanding a ship." He said, "I think it would be." I said, "Then there are you and Admiral Smith who think it would be a good thing." He replied, "In that case I think you better have it. You better take your plans back to New York and have them so far modified as to introduce this." I did so, and came back again. Just about this time the Navy Department, or at least the government, expected to make an attack on Charleston; and as several monitors were to be employed down there, it was thought advisable that I should go down and report to the admiral commanding the fleet for duty in connexion with it. It was expected that I would explain them to him, and to the officers and crew, and that I would assist in making any repairs if they should receive injury, and lend a hand generally in regard to them. That took me away from the north for some two months. While I was away, these had all been advertised and bid upon, and a great many contracts given out, so that when I came back

I found everything in a great deal of confusion, because all my general inspection had been going on as it best could. When the head one is away you can understand that things will get into confusion. I was not the head of the whole system, because Admiral Gregory was the head; but I was the head of inspection. I came back and found that when the engines came to be drawn out in detail they were not approved by Captain Ericsson. He had not only disapproved the engines, but he did not like the man, and I had to turn him away and hire another man to design the engines. He was a man who had had a great deal of experience in such work. Captain Ericsson liked the man, and told me to send him in to him; he talked with him, and said he would do. "He has a good head on him," said he. I gave thought to the matter when I had an opportunity. I still retained the same young man in general charge of these matters as long as I remained there.

In this Charleston fight, when they went in and made their attack, we found a great many points there which needed improvement. That was the next experience which we had after the fight between the Monitor and the Merrimack. That afforded us a great fund of new experience. When I came back, it was decided that that information should be all used in improving the monitors that were then being built, so that when we did get the vessels they should be good ones. It was decided to add these improvements to these light-draught monitors, and we improved them in such a way that it added to the draught of the vessels six inches. The deck of these vessels was very peculiar; it rounded up in the middle with a crown of twenty-three inches, so that when the side was nine inches out of water, the middle would be thirty-two inches. They had much more displacement above water than the other vessels, so that we considered it rather a good thing than otherwise to have this side armor down in the water out of the reach of shot. When we came to finish the first vessel, I went on to Boston and attended to it personally. I put everything in—p.led on everything according to the original intention—although I saw she was going down pretty well; but I wanted to ascertain just where we did stand in regard to these matters. I therefore put on everything that was to be put on the vessel. I found that the side of the vessel would be, on an average, two inches out of water, It would float very even. The disposition of the weights was very good—a little up by the stern, as every naval officer likes to have it. At this point Captain Ericsson was very much afraid that these vessels would break in two; he had expressed such fears before, because of the arrangement of the boilers. He said that in his arrangement of the boilers he had diagonal stays going down over the boilers, whereas in the new arrangement you could not get in the stays at all, and the vessel's back would break when she got into a sea. I did not concur in that opinion, but thought these vessels would pass from one port to another in perfect safety, and I expected to go from Boston to New York in that vessel. But Mr. Fox, as I understood, went on to the north to see Captain Ericsson, who impressed upon him the danger of sending that vessel to sea, stating that it might founder in passing from Boston to New York, and advised him not to build the other vessels in that way. Captain Ericsson is one of those strong men who will influence people very much by his manner and his abilities. I think he impressed the Navy Department fully with the idea that it was dangerous to send these vessels to sea. I was then removed from the position of general inspector, and the department decided to raise several of these vessels up, and to make them torpedo boats, not requiring turrets. In regard to some fifteen of them they decided to raise up the sides twenty-two inches; that would add some six inches to the draught of water, but would leave the vessel eighteen inches out of water; and I think they are going on now and building the vessels with these changes. I do not know what other detail changes they are making, for I have been at sea. I have every reason to think that they are very good vessels, and they will certainly be an advantage to the service in many respects, which have impressed themselves upon me more than ever before since I have been out in this fleet of Admiral Porter's. I have been in the frigate Wabash, down in the fleet which has been attacking Fort Fisher, where we had several monitors.

Question. Describe the classes of monitors you had down there.

Answer. We had three of the river and harbor monitors that were built from drawings which were issued from my office, made in the same way and upon the same general plan as the light-draught monitors. We then had the Monadnock, a vessel built in the Boston navy yard by Mr. Hanscom. All these vessels there drew more water than was at first intended. For instance, it was intended that the Monadnock should be three feet out of water at the side; she was two feet six inches. These other vessels were expected to be eighteen inches full; they are twelve inches. And all except the first monitor draw more water than was at first intended. We always find, in approaching completion, that we gain new experience during the progress of construction; and we have added and added weight here and there. I had, from my position on the Wabash, a better opportunity to watch these vessels in gales of wind, and to observe the difference between a vessel two feet and a half out of water, and one which was only one foot. I would say now that I would not build a vessel of that class. I would make very sure, indeed, that she would be at least two feet out of water, and I would make my design for three feet. I found that every naval officer felt much more secure in a vessel high out of water—felt that he had much more leeway when the vessel was leaking badly, before the vessel would sink. In calculating upon the matter, we find that we can build a vessel with the sides three feet out of water, and still retain all the good qualities.

By the chairman:

Question. The vessel is more exposed to the enemy's fire?

Answer. Yes, sir; and it requires much more weight and more machinery, &c.; but it is worth that much more when you get it, because of the additional safety of the vessel. It is more roomy inside. It is easier to ventilate such a vessel.

Question. Were you in the fleet at the time of the bombardment of Fort Fisher?

Answer. Yes, sir; during both attacks; I was in a wooden frigate, the Wabash.

Question. Do you consider these light-draught monitors of any use as they were first built, before the sides were built up. Could they be put to any use as war vessels?

Answer. The Chimo, which was finished and tried, had one serious fault, aside from the great draught of water; that was the want of speed. This want of speed was due to the very fact of the increased draught of water. In order to protect the propellers from shot, they were covered over in the monitor vessels by an overhang aft. To build a vessel to draw only six feet of water, and then have an overhang go down into the water, and almost be closed in over the propeller, you require the propeller to be of a larger diameter than six feet, or you would not get any speed at all. This propeller was made nine feet in diameter. It was not expected in the original design that there would be water confined in there, but it turned out to be so, in consequence of the increased draught. If you consider the action of a screw propeller, you will observe that in the revolution the angular blade, as the vessel is advancing, presses the water backwards. Engineers say that such a propeller slips twenty per cent., for instance. The water comes between a solid and a vacuum in this action of the screw. If the water in this box, made by the overhang, had been a solid, you could not have revolved the propeller at all; and with the vessel having that increased draught the water is carried along in the vessel, and the propeller, in its action, does nothing but churn the water, with one hundred per cent. slip; and to that extent you retard the velocity of the vessel, for if you do not make revolutions, you can make no speed.

Question. The overhang kept the screw from having any foothold, as you might say?

Answer. It was just like a dead weight hanging on it—a great friction; and the boilers were limited to a pressure of fifty pounds to the square inch. I considered at that time that if we should cut away this overhang, in such a way as to provide for the increased draught of water—and it was a small affair to do that—free these propellers and permit them to revolve properly, we should have a very fair speed, such as was expected in the first place, with the exception that it requires more power to drive a vessel deep in the water than one that is light.

Question. What was the expected speed of these vessels?

Answer. The chief of the Bureau of Engineering made calculations upon the subject, and said they would go nine knots an hour. I never calculated the speed.

Question. What do you suppose they would do as finally made, with overhang and all?

Answer. We tried this vessel, and it went three knots and a half. The people were walking about the decks, taking observations. The pilot, taking his points from the light-house here and something there, declared that the vessel was going six knots; but I borrowed a chip log of a Russian frigate which was in the harbor, and hove it. They reported at one time four knots, and at another time three knots and a half. My belief was that the speed was three knots and a half, and I so reported. It is a common thing, upon such vessels and upon such occasions, to report the highest that any one will name.

Question. Would she be able to go up a river, or stem a strong tide?

Answer. No, sir; three and a half knots is not fast enough; but I still consider that if we cut away the overhang so as to clear the propellers, we might get seven knots, which is about what the others would do.

Question. Were the engines and boilers correct?

Answer. They worked admirably. I was very much surprised to find the machinery work so well in that particular vessel as it did. I went to Boston on the 1st of May with the intention of completing that vessel in one month. I did do it in six weeks, very much to the astonishment of all people who understand these matters; but the government gave me unlimited power to do things as I wished—allowed me to spend some extra money, because we wanted the vessel in the waters of North Carolina for a special purpose.

Question. Do you or not believe that iron-clads for light-draught purposes, such as are built on the plan of the ironsides, are better than those of the monitor form?

Answer. No, sir, I do not, for a reason which I have partially explained; you have to carry so much more weight above the water. If you take a given draught and dimensions of vessel you can certainly carry only a given weight of iron for armor above water. The study should then be to put on the armor in such a form that it will have as great thickness as possible. If you have large area, then you have small thickness, and the shot goes through. In the monitor arrangement of vessel the hull is low, and the turret which surrounds the guns is the smallest armature you can put around a gun and have it operate.

Question. That is, you can make it equally strong with less weight of iron than in any other form?

Answer. Yes, sir.

Question. Because you do not have so large a surface to cover?

Answer. Yes, sir; and then, again, you can handle your heavy guns with a ess number of men, because a large portion of the work is done by steam

The turning around of the turret, and the taking aim of the gun, is all done by steam.

Question. Do you believe these large 15-inch guns are more destructive of the enemy's works or ships, than the same amount of metal distributed through more guns?

Answer. I think they are more destructive against iron-clads, or almost anywhere that you wish to destroy a very strong structure. There might be cases where a greater number of guns would have more effect than the large 15-inch guns; for instance, where there are a great number of people, and you wish to keep up a very rapid fire in order to keep them away from their guns. That might be better done with a larger number of smaller guns; but I think for naval fighting, for sea fighting, or rather for fighting ships, the 15-inch gun is far preferable to any other which has been made.

Question. How many of these guns failed in the fight at Fort Fisher?

Answer. I understood there were three.

Question. Were they on these monitors?

Answer. Yes, sir.

Question. Did these monitors have a 9-inch gun with the 15-inch gun?

Answer. In the Passaic class we put in an 11-inch gun with the 15-inch gun, because we did not have enough of the 15-inch guns made.

Question. Did any of the 11-inch guns fail?

Answer. No, sir; I never heard of an 11-inch gun failing.

Question. How many of the 15-inch guns do you suppose you had in that fight?

Answer. I think there were ten. One of them failed because a shell exploded in it, which, I believe, it is understood will burst any ordinary gun we have; and that might have been the cause of the other failures; I do not know. The officers of the vessel on which that gun failed told me that they had the same confidence in the gun as before. The engineer of the ship, who had no occasion to go into the turret, says he will go there now as readily as before.

Question. What do you know of the Parrott gun failing?

Answer. I know that several of the 100-pounders failed. I visited one ship to see a big shot that came into the boiler, and one of these guns had failed on that ship. I examined the gun, and found that it failed in a very peculiar way, one that I never heard of before. This Parrott gun was made with a wrought-iron band shrunk on the breech. This band extends forward partly over the hollow part of the gun. This gun had broken transversely, immediately at the base of the cylindrical part of the bore, and the breech had then blown out. I saw the fracture of that gun, and it was as true and correct as anything could be made, except it was absolutely cut with a knife. I saw it a day or two after it occurred, before it got rusted, and I came to the conclusion that the band which had been shrunk on was too tight. There was a tension of the band and compression of the iron. If the gun had never been fired it never would have broken; but every time you fired it this tension of the outer band affected the cast-iron within it as if it had been struck with the blow of a sledge. The part which was hollow would be affected in a way that the part which was solid would not. This band, with its compression, acted as a shear to cut off the cast-iron from the circumference to the centre all around. When you had fired it a sufficient number of times to loosen the metal, it would blow out. That was merely my view of the matter.

Question. How much additional expense did the extra work upon these vessels, from time to time, amount to—that is, expense that was not contemplated in the original contract before you commenced to alter them?

Answer. When you come to speak of expense in such matters, of dollars and cents, I would refer to a certain time in August or September, 1863, when I made estimates of how much it would be for this extra expense. My estimates then amounted to some thirty-two or thirty-three thousand dollars. There were afterwards more things put on, which would make it cost two or three thousand dollars more. Many of these things had to be paid for by the contractors afterwards, when prices had risen. I do not think these things have been paid for by the government yet, and I think they will cost the government more than I estimated.

Question. You finally abandoned this tank arrangement on the sides?

Answer. That was in operation in the Chimo.

Question. Has it been retained there?

Answer. I do not know. I have heard people say they were going to abolish it, but I do not know whether they have or not.

By Mr. Gooch:

Question. If I understand you correctly, so far as the estimates of weights are concerned, they were never, to your knowledge, reviewed by anybody?

Answer. I do not know whether they were or not.

Question. And these twenty vessels were built upon the estimates of this young and inexperienced engineer, Allen, of whom you have spoken?

Answer. Yes, sir. I do not like the term "inexperienced," as applied to him, except relatively, for he had done, to my knowledge, a great deal of the estimating of weights for the Novelty Works while he was an apprentice there. While I was assistant engineer, I was waiting orders for more than a year, and, with the consent of the Secretary of the Navy, I went to the Novelty Iron Works, and was employed as a draughtsman there. The Secretary thought it would be of great advantage to me as an engineer, and that the government would some day get the benefit of it. During the time I was there this young man was there. He was the nephew of the president of the works; and his uncle told me that if I could advance the young man in any way he would be obliged to me. I therefore employed him as assistant in the work I was doing. And I know that after that he had to do a great deal of calculating and estimating of weights. And I will say that in these first vessels that he calculated—those of the Saugus class—when we came to launch them, they corresponded very nearly with his calculations; the draught of water did not vary half an inch from his estimate.

Question. What was his age?

Answer. About twenty-four years old, I should think. He went to the Novelty Works when he was sixteen. I never did consider him an old experienced engineer, but then he had had a peculiar experience beyond what men generally get at his age.

By the chairman:

Question. Did you expect Mr. Lenthall to review this work, so as to correct it if he found anything wrong?

Answer. I thought that if I had been chief of a bureau, giving out contracts for which I was responsible, I should have done it.

By Mr. Gooch:

Question. In your judgment, was it the duty of the chief of the bureau to have verified these estimates?

Answer. Decidedly so.

Question. Was it not possible—was it not a practicable thing—to have determined exactly the amount of displacement by the application of well-known rules, or the weighing of portions of the material of which the weight was not exactly known?

Answer. I do not think you could have arrived at the weight in a case of this kind with the accuracy that you could in ordinary vessels. The constructor in a navy yard knows his timber; he knows what house he is going to take it out of. The merchant builder knows his timber, and can weigh it; but here were twenty vessels being built all over the country, from Maine to Missouri. You did not know where the timber which you got grew, you did not know where you were to get it, or anything about it. You could, therefore, only make a general estimate.

Question. As the draught of water in these vessels could vary so little without destroying their efficiency, was it not of the very greatest importance that every test should be applied to determine exactly the weight of the materials?

Answer. Yes, sir; I think we all committed errors in that respect. But these two bureaus were always inimical to these vessels. I always had the feeling that they would naturally oppose anything which I proposed, because I was connected with them. For instance, when I asked the chief of the Bureau of Steam Engineering for engineers to inspect the work, he said, "I have nothing to do with them. These vessels are not being built under the bureau, and you cannot have naval engineers for that purpose." I answered, "These are naval vessels; they are built for the Navy Department, and the navy will be injured or benefited as they are bad or good; therefore, I think we ought to have a system of inspection which will insure their excellence." He said, "I am not going to order good inspectors to watch the riveting of a lot of old boiler iron, and that is the end of it." I went to him again; I tried to come over his feelings by calling to mind our old friendships and old associations. I said to him, "My dear fellow, I will be able some of these days to do you as much of a favor as this will be for you to do me"—putting it upon the ground of a personal favor. He said, "I intend that you shall do everything for me that I ask of you, and that I shall do nothing for you that you ask of me." Of course there was nothing more to be said.

Question. Then there was not that co-operation which there should have been upon the part of the Bureaus of Engineering and of Construction in relation to these monitors?

Answer. No, sir; I always felt that it was a regular fight—that we had to conquer them before we could get them to do anything On the one side it was a fight with the bureaus, and on the other side it was a fight with the contractors, to make them do anything right. It was a very unpleasant position which I held.

By the chairman:

Question. Had the Navy Department any knowledge of this want of co-operation on the part of the bureaus?

Answer. It never appeared to me that the Navy Department appreciated the *animus* of these men. It always seemed to me, when I complained to Mr. Fox, that he did not quite believe I gave the right tone to it—he thought perhaps that I was partly at fault. But I think—in fact, I know—that the Navy Department knew they were not giving much assistance. I consider that the Secretary and the Assistant Secretary and Admiral Smith deserve the greatest credit for the production of the monitors, assuming that the monitors are creditable.

By Mr. Gooch:

Question. Was there a good understanding between you and Captain Ericsson during the progress of the construction of these monitors?

Answer. Yes, sir, until after all the plans were out and had been issued. About a year ago we had a difference, which still remains, and I have felt that it was in part his personal feeling towards me that has governed his action in regard to these light-draught vessels. First, he represented that I was the designer, and therefore entirely responsible for everything connected with them.

Then he represented that the plans were very poor indeed; he denied some things that he was the author of.

Question. What was the exact condition of the work when this rupture between yourself and Captain Ericsson took place?

Answer. The plans were nearly all issued to the contractors for building. The rupture took place in reference to this harbor and river class of monitors. I think that perhaps there were a few drawings sent out afterwards, because, although there was a rupture between us, and I did not visit him personally, there was constant communication between my office and his, and I thought that one of my assistants was very officious in making this breach as wide as possible; however, that did not prevent my sending the drawings to Captain Ericsson for his approval. I remember now particularly, that the drawing for the gun-carriages for the light-draught monitors went down to him for his approval after we had our difficulty—that is, the modifications of the gun-carriages which were necessary.

Question. Who do you say is the author or designer of the light-draught iron-clad monitors?

Answer. Captain Ericsson first designed the vessel; the Bureau of Engineering modified the machinery, and then the water tank was added, as I have explained. I was obliged to have these drawings made in my office, and I had to decide a great many points about the details. Captain Ericsson, therefore, says that I was the designer of the vessel. I might as well turn around and say that such a man who drew it had designed it, because he did a great deal.

By the chairman:

Question. Did not Captain Ericsson furnish a plan of these light-draught monitors for the department?

Answer. Yes, sir.

Question. Did you also exhibit one?

Answer. Not then.

Question. Did you at any time?

Answer. No, sir; only the modifications directed by the bureau.

Question. Then you did not furnish the department with any draught of a monitor on your own plan?

Answer. No, sir; I put in modifications according to the direction of the heads of the bureaus here.

By Mr. Gooch:

Question. Did Captain Ericsson submit full plans and specifications in relation to the monitors which he proposed to build?

Answer. He presented similar plans to these, with rather fuller specifications.

Question. Were those plans and specifications accompanied by full estimates made in relation to weights and displacements?

Answer. I do not know.

Question. Then you do not know whether a monitor built precisely as he proposed would have drawn more water than was contemplated or not?

Answer. No, sir; except that this young engineer calculated this vessel with Captain Ericsson, and said that with that arrangement it would sink.

Question. Without any weights other than those contemplated by Captain Ericsson?

Answer. Yes, sir.

By the hcairman:

Question. Do you profess to be a designer yourself?

Answer. I have designed works. I feel myself competent to design an iron-clad vessel, including hull, armature, and machinery. It has been my special study, ever since I commenced to learn the profession of engineering, to become a constructing engineer. I regard my services in the navy as a sea-going engineer as tributary to my profession as a constructing engineer. My main studies have been to ascertain how ships and machinery should be constructed. In regard to ships, I have confined myself to the construction of iron ships. Preparatory to that, it is necessary to study naval architecture, which I commenced to do as early as 1852. I do not profess to know how to build a wooden ship, but I do profess to know how an iron ship should be built, in all of its details.

WASHINGTON, *February* 17, 1865.

Mr. B. F. ISHERWOOD sworn and examined.

By the chairman:

Question. What is your official connexion with the Navy Department?

Answer. I am the chief of the Bureau of Steam Engineering.

Question. What knowledge of, and what connexion with, the construction of the twenty light-draught monitors lately constructed by the order of the government, did you have at any time?

Answer. I have never had any connexion with them in any way or manner.

Question. Have you ever been brought into such relations to them in any way as to know anything about their construction? And if there have been any faults or errors about their construction, do you know what they are?

Answer. As I never saw either the drawings or the specifications of those vessels, I have really no knowledge upon the subject except from mere rumor and hearsay.

Question. Did you ever have any conversation with Engineer Stimers with regard to their construction?

Answer. None at all, with the exception, I think, that he once spoke to me about the boilers to be put in them. I made some suggestions with regard to the boilers, which were not followed, however. That is the only conversation or communication I ever had with him on the subject.

Question. Do you know anything about their engines?

Answer. No, sir; I never saw either the drawings or specifications of those vessels; and consequently, of my own knowledge, I could say really nothing about it. Since they have been completed I have been on board one of them.

Question. Which one was that?

Answer. The Chimo, at Boston; I happened accidentally to be in Boston near where she was lying at the dock, and, as a matter of curiosity, I went on board and looked at it.

Question. Did you inspect her engines?

Answer. No, sir; I gave merely a cursory glance at the vessel.

By Mr. Gooch:

Question. Did Mr. Stimers ever seek to obtain from you any information in relation to the engines or boilers of these monitors?

Answer. No, sir, except what I have stated. I made a little sketch of a boiler—suggested an idea of a boiler, which was not followed.

Question. No application was ever made to you by Mr. Stimers, or anybody else, for any instruction or information in relation to the boilers or engines of these monitors?

Answer. Nothing but what I have just stated. Some time after all the plans had been adopted, I believe, I was asked for an estimate of how fast a certain quantity of boiler ought to drive a certain amid-ship section, and I made the estimate; that was all. I had no plans, or anything of the kind, before me; I had merely so many square feet of amid-ship section, to tell how a certain amount of boiler could drive that.

Question. Do you know whether those boilers and engines were built after the plans of any boilers or engines of yours used in other monitors?

Answer. At that time I had never made any drawings for boilers for other monitors. Since then I have made drawings for machinery for the wooden monitors we built, and in those I used what is known as the modern boiler, an entirely different boiler from what is in these light monitors.

Question. Have you given such examination or attention to these monitors that you have formed any opinion as to the causes of their failure?

Answer. I have certainly formed an opinion with regard to the causes of their failure. I think the failure is entirely due to the errors of detail; not to the general design of the vessel, but to errors of detail made by the engineer who had the designing of the work.

Question. Whom do you mean?

Answer. Chief Engineer Stimers. The work was put entirely into his hands.

By the chairman:

Question. Did you make such an inspection of the Chimo that you can give a confident opinion upon that subject?

Answer. Merely such a general inspection that an expert would make in looking over a thing of that kind; that is all. I do not see anything in the general design of those vessels which would prevent their being very good vessels.

Question. Of course you would not know from a general inspection but what they would float with their turrets on?

Answer. I could not tell that from a general inspection. It would require considerable time and labor to go into the whole matter.

By Mr. Gooch:

Question. It is represented that the speed of these light-draught monitors is only about one-half what it was contemplated or designed it would be. Did you form any opinion as to the causes of this defect in speed?

Answer. In the first place the draught of water is very much greater than it was intended to have been. It was intended to have been six feet, but it is very much greater than that. In the second place, as I observed the position and arrangement of the screw on board the Chimo, it seemed to me to be so extremely faulty that I did not see how a screw arranged as that was could properly apply the power. To the two causes I think is due the deficiency in speed.

Question. What was the fault in the arrangement of the screw?

Answer. A large portion of it was boxed up in the overhang, a thing which struck my attention instantly upon looking at the vessel from the dock. It was impossible for the screw to properly transmit the power to the water; an immense amount of power was wasted. I think, according to the quantity of boiler put in those vessels, recollecting the amount of amid-ship section given to me, there was power enough in those vessels, if properly applied, to have made the required speed.

WASHINGTON, *March* 14, 1865.

Mr. JOHN LENTHALL recalled and examined.

By Mr. Gooch:

Question. I understand that you wish to add something to your testimony in relation to the light-draught monitors. I suppose it is in connexion with the testimony of Engineer Stimers.

Answer. Yes, sir. The chairman permitted me to look at that portion of it which referred to me.

Question. You have examined that portion of it?

Answer. Yes, sir.

Question. You can go on and make such additional statement as you desire.

Answer. Having seen portions of the testimony of Chief Engineer Stimers, taken under oath by the Committee on the Conduct of the War, in which he refers particularly to me in the case of the light-draught monitors, I would ask that my statement on the same subject may accompany his. I would repeat, that the first I knew of these vessels was from the outline plan shown me by the Assistant Secretary of the Navy, in which Mr. Ericsson proposed a "monitor vessel to have a draught of water of six feet."

I saw no details or specifications, but my recollection is that there was an offer from him to contract to build such vessels at a specified price. This plan, executed with the experience acquired by Mr. Ericsson in vessels of that class, it was fair to presume would answer the purpose proposed, but from the want of details it was impossible for me or any other person to test that presumption by figures.

The next I saw or knew of the plan was that it, or one closely resembling it, was in the hands of Chief Engineer Stimers, who stated that it had been confided to him for execution.

Chief Engineer Stimers, selected by the department for this particular service, had been engaged on all the monitor vessels from their commencement, and they were under his exclusive control and superintendence; he had an independent office in New York, with numerous engineers, clerks and draughtsmen under his orders; he had been associated with Mr. Ericsson, and had had opportunities of instruction by him, and, it seemed fair to presume, was quite familiar with all his views in the construction of monitor vessels, and well acquainted with the nature and qualities of the materials used in them.

In the interview with Chief Engineer Stimers, he informed me that he proposed to add a water chamber to Mr. Ericsson's plan, which he said had been recommended by Admiral Smith, and, though I did not understand him as seeking information from me, this addition struck me as so obviously unnecessary and very injudicious, that I expressed that opinion strongly to him.

The reason for this opinion is very apparent, for' as Mr. Ericsson's intention was to have a vessel of the monitor class of the smallest practicable draught of water, there could be no advantage, but a certain detriment, in adding any unnecessary thing to the weight of the vessel, which could only act to increase its draught of water. Mr. Ericsson, as I afterwards learned, protested against it.

The interviews with Chief Engineer Stimers were but of a few minutes' duration, and the remarks were purely conversational, nothing being referred to me for an opinion, nor anything being said from which I could infer one was desired, and I had no further communication with him on the subject.

At a subsequent period, Chief Engineer Stimers brought to the bureau, by order of the department, as he stated, an outline trace plan of the light-draught monitors, with some general specifications and a detailed estimate of all the weights, showing the load draught of water to be six feet five and one-half inches (6 ft. 5½) in fresh water. The originals of all these, he stated, were in his office in New York.

This drawing or outline of the hull showed the water-chambers which he said he had been authorized to add. He stated that the calculation of the weights had been carefully made, and that in the previous contracts for monitor vessels the bidders had not been furnished with this information, which they should have had.

In looking down this list of materials I perceived that the weight of the timber per cubic foot was fully what we find in the books and tables which all engineers possess, and is known to every man who either is, or pretends to be, a mechanie, and that the whole of the white oak was much less than the one-fifth part of the total weight of the vessel complete. Besides this, in all the monitor vessels built and building under Chief Engineer Stimers's immediate control, a very large quantity of timber of the same kind was used in their construction, and no person had better opportunities of knowing their weights.

With regard to the weight of the iron of the hull, the water-chambers and pipes, the steam machinery, the turret and gear, and the equipments, embracing nearly the whole of the remaining weight, there were no plans or details from which I, or any one else, could verify an estimate, and to this day I have not seen any of the details.

When Chief Engineer Stimers handed me the specifications and estimate of weights, for the information of bidders, he seemed to do it with a great deal of self-satisfaction—took the entire credit of it to himself, and did not name any other person as having made them, or say a single word to throw the shadow of a doubt on their accuracy. He made no statement that he had not made them, and was not responsible for them, but, on the contrary, seemed much inflated with his having shown how such things ought to be done.

If the Assistant Secretary of the Navy knew that Chief Engineer Stimers did not make these calculations, he did not name it to me; and such a confession from him would inevitably have impaired the confidence reposed in him.

Chief Engineer Stimers also furnished to the department an estimate of what he considered should be the contract price, which could only be based on an estimate of the materials and the labor.

As the department was only waiting for Chief Engineer Stimers's plans, as soon as they were handed in I was instructed to draw up an advertisement for bidders, which was published forthwith, and a copy is herewith handed in.

During the four weeks the advertisement was running, several persons examined the plans, &c., deposited by Chief Engineer Stimers in the bureau, and made copies of his estimates of weights, on which to base their bids; but all stated that it would be necessary for them to visit Chief Engineer Stimers at his New York office to obtain proper and necessary explanations before they could make an offer. In fact, the plans and specifications deposited in the bureau were too meagre to base a bid on, unless supplemented verbally by the designer of the work.

The statement of the offers and of the awards will be found on pages 967 and 969 of the message of the President and accompanying documents of the 1st session of the 38th Congress.

I was not asked to examine or approve these plans, nor had I reason to suppose any such action was expected of me in this case any more than in those of the preceding nine monitor vessels, or of the Dictator and Puritan, for which I had been directed to execute the contracts.

I was never requested by Chief Engineer Stimers, or any one else, to examine his specifications or estimates in any stage of their progress, for there were no detailed drawings from which it could be done, and it could only be the originator of them, who had predetermined how they were to be filled up, who could make an estimate at all.

Thesep lans, it was understood, were to be submitted to Mr. Ericsson, and the details carried out according to his idea. His knowledge of vessels of the monitor class required no approval from any one, and the insertion of the water-chamber, in opposition to my expressed judgment, shows how little I had to do with the design.

Had the weights estimated by Chief Engineer Stimers been correct, or had they been even approximately adhered to, it would not have been found necessary after the completion to have deepened the vessels, and that necessity was caused by his errors of calculation, and by his subsequent additions and alterations after the contracts were made, and among other things this water-chamber did much to load the vessels to such an extent as to bring their decks awash.

With the most careful estimate of timber there may be a variation of 3 to 4 per cent. in the weight, making for the white oak about one inch difference in the draught of water; but I have never known white oak to reach 70 pounds per cubic foot, as Chief Engineer Stimers stated with regard to the timber used in these vessels. Lve oak has that weight; none of that was used.

The execution of these contracts by the Bureau of Construction was purely a ministerial duty, in the same way that it made those of the nine vessels of the Tecumseh class of monitors, and the Dictator and Puritan, so that the contract should be in the same bureau through which the bills of payment were to pass.

Within about a month after the first contracts were made, I was directed by the department to give an order that any changes and modifications in those vessels that might be thought necessary or advantageous should be submitted to Mr. Ericsson, and have his sanction, before being carried out. This, it appears, was not done; but Chief Engineer Stimers, on his own responsibility, without the knowledge of the bureau or sanction of Mr. Ericsson, made changes involving large expenditures of money and much delay in the completion of the work. This fact was first learned from the contractors, who also complained that after they had completed part of the work from one set of drawings, another set was substituted, and the work already completed had to be pulled down and rebuilt. So far was Mr. Ericsson from approving these alterations, that as soon as he learned them unofficially, he disavowed, in writing, any responsibility for them.

When this was ascertained, and the large sums required to meet the extra bills of the contractors thus incurred by the not only unauthorized action of Chief Engineer Stimers, but by his action in direct disregard of the instructions of the department, the latter directed the bureau to give an unqualified order to make no more changes or modifications, and Chief Engineer Stimers was finally only restrained when each of the contractors was notified not to make any alterations or additions without authority of the bureau, and on a determined price.

Had Chief Engineer Stimers, to whom the department had solely confided the execution of the work, carried out the original programme of Mr. Ericsson with ordinary ability, according to the intent of the department, these vessels would have required no enlargement.

In preparing the detailed plans of the machinery Chief Engineer Stimers permitted his subordinates to insert their patents, and the contractors have been called on by them to pay patent fees, and to which they have demurred.

It has been stated that a reason why this work was placed in Chief Engineer Stimers's hands, and he provided with a separate office in New York, with numerous clerks, draughtsmen, &c., was owing to my opposition to iron and iron-clad vessels, particularly to those of the monitor type. This is so far from being the fact that the very reverse is the truth, for in October and November of 1861, in conjunction with the present chief of the Bureau of Steam Engineering, B. F. Isherwood, I prepared drawings and specifications for vessels to be built of wood, armored with thick ironplates, propelled by two screws, and to have two revolving towers of thick ironplates, differing from the usual monitor vessels as regards hull in not having wings or overhangs at the sides, in being propelled by two screws instead of one, and as regards the towers, in having two instead of one, and of being supported and revolving them on their circumference instead of on a central spindle. The drawings of the hull were completed; those of the machinery were made in detail and photographed, and the specifications for it, for the armor, towers, hull, &c., were printed and ready to be placed in the contractors' hands so that the work could have gone forward without interruption or delay.

The directions for building these vessels were countermanded; but lately there have been constructed, and are in progress of construction, at the navy yards, eight vessels of this type, with the exception that the turrets are according to Mr. Ericsson's system, with a central spindle, and that they were made larger to carry heavier armor and thicker turrets. Of these vessels the Monadnock has been for a sufficient length of time in service of varied description, and is acknowledged a successful iron-clad vessel.

We also, in March, 1862, made a report to the department on the subject of iron-clad sea-going vessels, and to the opinions of which we still adhere, and a copy of it is submitted. We prepared, with great labor, complete specifications and drawings of the largest class of sea going iron-armored vessels, as it was understood at the time the department contemplated to build such vessels, and for which, indeed, advertisements were issued for offers, and bids received; but the policy of Congress not being to construct a navy of this class, further action was suspended on them.

NAVY DEPARTMENT,
Bureau of Construction, March 17, 1862.

SIR: The subject of the design and construction of naval vessels-of-war under the new conditions which recent progress has imposed having for some time occupied our attention, we take the liberty of briefly submitting the following considerations in relation thereto:

After the preparation of drawings and specifications for iron-plated steam-batteries we were brought into communication, during the last few months, in consequence of submitting them for proposals to construct, with the principal establishments engaged in the manufacture of iron. We found there was but little reason to suppose that such plates as it was desirable to have could be obtained in the quantity and time required. There were but few forges prepared to undertake them, and the rolling-mills would need new and expensive machinery before they could produce a plate, as such masses of rolled iron are not used in private business. Indeed, although we found both forges and mills willing to undertake portions of the work, and hopeful of success, yet doubtless great disappointment and delay would have resulted. No means of bending were in existence, and many of the details of manufacture have still to be contrived. Some forged plates could have been commenced at once, but, after the rolling-mills were once prepared, would obviously require more time and money for their production than the rolled ones; and it appears, judging from our own and foreign experience, that rolled plates, in consequence of their greater cheapness and rapidity of production, must be mainly relied on for such constructions.

The propositions of the principal rolling-mills embodied the conditions of a large order a long time, and the advance of a very considerable sum of money. These terms, in effect, were, that the government should be at all the expense of the necessary machinery, but have no right to the final ownership; thus assuming the risk of a large loan, and establishing a monopoly for the benefit of individuals. Nor could the mills, with safety, accept a less objectionable arrangement; for the appliances and machinery sufficient for the manufacture of the plates used in the construction of ordinary iron vessels are wholly inadequate to the production of those necessary for iron-plated ships-of-war, and no private establishment can be expected to provide them unless assured of constant employment by the government.

Considering these facts in connexion with the state of transition in which the methods of naval war now are, and with the inevitable tendency to the substitution of iron in place of wood for the hulls of armed vessels, and the certainty that iron plating must be used on all such vessels, whether of wood or iron, we are led to respectfully suggest the advantage, if not the absolute necessity, of the government at once preparing a factory to make for itself the most important and costly parts, both for the iron hulls and for the armature.

Having an efficient establishment of its own of this kind, it can, in an emergency, receive much aid in those parts which are similar to what are used in merchant iron steamers from private parties, without diverting them from their usual course of manufacture, and thus moderate prices only will be charged.

The establishment that we suggest ought to contain all the tools, facilities, and machinery for the complete preparation of the materials for iron ships of the largest size, and for their construction; also for the rolling and bending of their armor plates, and for the building of the steam machinery for their propulsion. It should be altogether a storehouse and workshop, and not a military establishment. It should be situated upon deep water, and have a large water front; and the location should be convenient for coal and iron, and secure from the possibility of attack by foreign foes.

We do not consider any of the navy yards suitable for this purpose, and the whole of their resources will be required for some years to come for the current wants of the present navy. The necessity and importance of an establishment that is to provide a future navy sufficient for securing a country like ours from foreign aggression—for, owing to our trans-oceanic position to the great powers of the world, our security must be sought in a navy—is, we respectfully submit, a national question, second to none, and as such we strongly urge it for consideration. No time could be more favorable than the present for the creation of such an establishment. The recent change in the construction of naval vessels has rendered nearly useless the formidable wooden ships composing the navies of Europe, and the few we possess will soon be worn out.

Under such circumstances we shall, with an establishment in operation of the magnitude and efficiency we propose, start equal with the first powers of the world in a new race for the supremacy of the ocean.

We shall start with the advantage of no loss of old stock and workshops; with matured plans, embodying all the improvements and appliances of modern science, gained at the expense of the dear-bought experience of our competitors. Every dollar will be fruitfully spent, and a few years will, and at the least practicable cost, put the nation in possession of a fleet of first-class, invincible ocean ships, which will prove not only the efficient protector of its honor and interests, but the best prevention against their being assailed.

There seems no doubt that this country must hereafter maintain not only a larger navy than it has heretofore done, but of an essentially different character, and we are of opinion that the cruising vessels on which alone reliance must be placed for offensive war, and the preservation of our ports from the losses and inconveniences of blockades, should be frigate-built iron steamships of sufficient strength to be used as rams, clad with invulnerable armor plates, furnished with maximum steam-power, and of a size larger than any vessel we now possess.

Such a vessel could be adapted to, and carry, any armament deemed the most efficient. Subordinate to these should be a class of corvettes, of the same character, but having a less draught of water.

The first maritime nations of Europe have for some years past been gradually initiating this system, and if their experience is to profit us, now is the time to introduce it. It is obviously cheaper, more effective, and more sustaining of the national honor to preserve our coasts from the presence of an enemy's naval force by keeping the command of the open sea, with all the power it gives of aggression upon his own shores and commerce, than to rely on any system of harbor defence which requires every point to be protected that may be assailed by any enemy, having, in that case, the choice of time and place, and the advantage of perfect security for his own ports and commerce. In addition to these considerations a clear coast is manifestly essential to any effective system of privateering. Though harbor defences might prevent the enemy's entrance to a port, they could not drive him from its gates ; and if blockaded by his large iron-plated steamships, no privateer could either get out himself, or send in a prize.

The harbor defences are indeed valuable adjuncts, and should not be neglected, but they cannot constitute a navy, or perform its proper functions.

Wealth, victory, and empire are to those who command the ocean, the toll-gate as well as the highway of nations, and if ever assailed by a powerful maritime foe, we shall find to our prosperity, if ready, how much better it is to fight at the threshold than upon the hearthstone.

With great respect, we have the honor to be, sir, your obedient servants,

JOHN LENTHALL,
B. F. ISHERWOOD.

Hon. GIDEON WELLES,
Secretary of the Navy.

[Advertisement.]

LIGHT-DRAUGHT VESSELS FOR RIVERS AND BAYS.

NAVY DEPARTMENT, *February* 10, 1863.

The Navy Department will receive proposals for the construction and completion in every respect, (except guns, ordnance stores, fuel, provisions, and nautical instruments,) for Armored Steamers, of about seven hundred tons, of wood and iron combined, having a single revolving turret.

On personal application at the Navy Department in Washington or to Rear-Admiral Gregory, No. 413 Broadway, New York, parties intending to offer can examine the plans and specifications, which will be furnished to the contractors by the department.

No offer will be considered unless from parties who are prepared to execut work of this kind, having suitable shops and tools, of which, if not known to the department, they must present evidence with their bid.

The act of Congress approved July 17, 1862, prohibits the transfer of any contract, or order, or interest therein.

The bidders will state the price and the time within which they will agree to complete the vessel or vessels, and the bid must be accompanied by the guarantee required by law, that if awarded to them they will promptly execute the contract.

Propositions will be received until the 24th day of February, and they must be indorsed "Proposals for vessels for river defence," to distinguish them from other business letters.

Testimony of Mr. B. F. Isherwood.

WASHINGTON, *April* 25, 1865.

Mr. B. F. ISHERWOOD, chief of the Bureau of Steam Engineering, appeared before the committee and submitted the following statement:

Having understood that Chief Engineer Stimers, in his evidence before the Committee on the Conduct of the War, made statements referring to me in connexion with the designing and constructing of the vessels popularly known as light-draught monitors, I addressed the committee a note asking for a copy of those parts of his evidence, and received from it the following extracts, which I presume contain all in which reference is made to me:

"Mr. Fox said: Now that our heads of bureaus are confirmed in their places, they must do their work. We have taken all the responsibility thus far, but now these men must take their responsibility. I have, therefore, sent the plans down to the Bureau of Construction. Mr. Lenthall says that he does not see anything in his part of the ship which is at all out of the way, and he does not advise any changes. I have also sent the plans to the Bureau of Engineering, to see if the chief of that bureau has any objection to the arrangement of the machinery. He says he thinks there ought to be some modifications; but he is out of town, and you must wait until to-morrow to see him, and then you will find out his views. You have Captain Ericsson's views about the machinery; if you find that the chief of the Bureau of Engineering has views to which Captain Ericsson will not agree, try to get the two together, so that we can get a plan on which both will agree, because we want these vessels to meet Captain Ericsson's views and the views of our bureau. If you cannot bring them together so that they will be reconciled, then we will build one on Ericsson's plan, and one on the plan of the bureau; and if you have a plan, we will build one on your plan also. Said I, 'No, sir, I have no plan; I have more to do than ever.'

"The next day I saw Mr. Isherwood, the chief of the Bureau of Steam Engineering, and I found that he wanted the coal-bunkers arranged in a different way—he wanted entirely different boilers—he wanted different engines. Instead of their being athwart engines, connected directly with the screw-shaft, he wanted them connected with bevel gearing. Not to go through the whole matter, he had changed everything—coal-bunkers, boilers, engines, and propellers. I discussed these matters with him, and brought him to consent to some modifications which I thought perhaps Captain Ericsson would agree to. He gave me some sketches, plans, &c., and it was decided that as I had draughtsmen I should take them to New York, and if Captain Ericsson agreed to them, I should embody them in a new plan and send it on again to Washington. I went to Captain Ericsson, and he did not like any of the proposed changes at all. He thought each one injurious to the vessel—that it made the plan less excellent than his was. 'But,' said he, 'if they will not build more than one of these vessels unless I give way, of course I think the government ought to have them; they will be very useful indeed, and I think they ought to build more than one right away. The chief of the Bureau of Steam Engineering knows how to work engines and drive the vessel along, of course; so I think we better consent,' with the exception, however, that he would not listen to gear engines at all. He said they would certainly fail if placed in such limber vessels as these would be. As the chief of the bureau had given me these plans and these directions to work them into a general plan if I found I could do it, with the understanding that I was to retain the original type if the bevel-gear arrangement would not work so well, I withdrew that part, and Captain Ericsson assented to all the rest. I afterwards reported to the chief of the

Bureau of Steam Engineering that I found I could not work in the bevel-gear plans. I do not remember that I told him why I could not work them in, but I told him that I could not, and he gave his approval to the plans which I did work in." * * * * * *

"Question. As the draught of water in these vessels could vary so little without destroying their efficiency, was it not of the very greatest importance that every test should be applied to determine exactly the weight of the materials?

"Answer. Yes, sir; I think we all committed errors in that respect. But these two bureaus were always inimical to these vessels. I always had the feeling that they would naturally oppose anything which I proposed, because I was connected with them. For instance, when I asked the chief of the Bureau of Steam Engineering for engineers to inspect the work, he said, 'I have nothing to do with them. These vessels are not being built under the bureau, and you cannot have naval engineers for that purpose.' I answered, 'these are naval vessels; they are built for the Navy Department, and the navy will be injured or benefited as they are bad or good; therefore, I think we ought to have a system of inspection which will insure their excellence.' He said, 'I am not going to order good inspectors to watch the riveting of a lot of old boiler iron, and that is the end of it.' I went to him again; I tried to come over his feelings by calling to mind our old friendships and old associations. I said to him, 'My dear fellow, I will be able some of these days to do you as much of a favor as this will be for you to do me,' putting it upon the ground of a personal favor. He said, 'I intend that you shall do everything for me that I ask of you, and that I shall do nothing for you that you ask of me.' Of course there was nothing more to be said.

"Question. Then there was not that co-operation which there should have been upon the part of the Bureaus of Engineering and of Construction in relation to these monitors?

"Answer. No, sir; I always felt that it was a regular fight—that we had to conquer them before we could get them to do anything. On the one side it was a fight with the bureaus, and on the other side it was a fight with the contractors to make them do anything right. It was a very unpleasant position which I held.

* * * * * * *

"Question. Who do you say is the author or designer of the light-draught iron-clad monitors?

"Answer. Captain Ericsson first designed the vessel; the Bureau of Engineering modified the machinery, and then the water-tank was added, as I have explained. I was obliged to have these drawings made in my office, and I had to decide a great many points about the details. Captain Ericsson, therefore, says that I was the designer of the vessel. I might as well turn around and say that such a man who drew it had designed it, because he did a great deal.

"By the chairman:

"Question. Did not Captain Ericsson furnish a plan of these light-draught monitors for the department?

"Answer. Yes sir.

"Question. Did you also exhibit one?

"Answer. Not then.

"Question. Did you at any time?

"Answer. No, sir; only the modifications directed by the bureau.

"Question. Then you did not furnish the department with any draught of monitor on your own plan?

"Answer. No, sir; I put in modifications according to the direction of the heads of the bureaus here."

The statements in the above extracts, so far as I have knowledge, are falsehoods, and the whole tenor of the evidence is of the same nature. The true facts are as follow:

In the construction of the large number of monitors previously to these light-draughts, all of which were under the control of Chief Engineer Stimers, I had never been called on for an opinion; nor had any reference to me ever been made of the smallest detail in connexion with them, nor is it pretended to the contrary by any one. They had been wholly confided to Mr. Ericsson and Chief Engineer Stimers; the latter was detailed for that duty by the department itself, and not on my recommendation, as he falsely asserts in a letter of the 15th March, 1865, published in the Army and Navy Journal of March 18. I had the opinion then, which after experience has confirmed, that he was utterly incompetent to the duties assigned him. All the recommendations for detail made by this bureau are made in writing, so there can be no question as to this fact. The matter is not important further than as evidence of that reckless want of veracity which vitiates all the statements of Chief Engineer Stimers. He was furnished with a suite of offices in New York, and had under him some forty draughtsmen and clerks—all employed by himself—besides a number of naval engineers. His employés were nearly as numerous as all in all the Bureaus of the Navy Department, and to all intents and purposes he was at the head of an independent bureau of the largest magnitude located in New York for the construction of monitor vessels. He had no correspondence with the Bureau of Steam Engineering, either direct or indirect; referred nothing to it, and received no instructions or orders from it. In fact, that bureau had no knowledge even of the number of monitor vessels he was building, and he was not even nominally under its authority. I presumed his communications to the department were made direct, the same as from any bureau.

With the designing and construction of the light-draught monitors I had as little to do as with the previous monitors, or with the Dictator, and presumed, as I had every reason to, that they were to be controlled by the same agency, and that no interference was expected from me any more than with them. The department never referred them, or anything connected with them, to me—such reference is always made in writing—nor had I any knowledge that such vessels were to be built, or were in contemplation, until Chief Engineer Stimers entered my office with a sketch which had been made for them by Mr. Ericsson, as he then informed me. He did not state the department had sent him to me, nor did I understand from him that he came to submit it to me for approval. On the contrary, the impression he gave me was that his visit was simply a formal call, the possession of the sketch an accidental occurrence, and its exhibition made merely to show me what he was then engaged in. Our very brief conversation—certainly less than half an hour—was confined to the machinery alone, the hull and remainder of the vessel not coming within my province. In the course of this conversation, which was the only one I ever had with him or any other person on the subject, I suggested that a better arrangement of boiler could be made, and a better type employed, giving him a sketch of one which I had formerly used in some gunboats of my own design. I further suggested that the two screws by which the vessel was to be propelled had better be separated far enough to prevent their actions from interfering, as Mr. Ericsson's sketch showed them considerably overlapping. I might also have said it would be found difficult to manage the single screw engines promptly enough in starting and backing, but that this objection could be avoided by connecting them with a particular arrangement of bevel gear, (not to multiply the speed,) as had been very successfully practiced on some light-draught iron-clads built for the Mississippi river and its tributaries. As before stated, the interview was very brief, and certainly a stranger witnessing it would have inferred from the manner and language of Chief Engineer Stimers that he was a superior condescending to explain his plans to an inferior, in order that he might receive his admiration. Nothing was said in it about Mr. Fox or Mr. Ericsson, nor about the detailing of naval engineers for the inspection of these vessels while being constructed. The whole of Chief Engineer Stimers's account of his appeal to "my feelings" and asking "as a personal favor" that such details might be made, is a pure invention, which will be easily believed when you are informed that at that very time he was endeavoring, by the basest arts, the vilest calumnies, and the most dishonest practices, to supplant me as chief of the Bureau of Steam Engineering, which facts he knew at the time I was well aware of. Further, at the very moment when he says he was asking for "engineers to inspect the work," he already had a large number detailed to him and under his exclusive orders, and could have had as many more by simply asking the department, which never, so far as I know, refused any request of his. He selected whichever engineers he wished, and they were ordered direct by the department, without going through even the formality of a detail by the Bureau of Steam Engineering; and the first knowledge I had of who were detailed was after the orders were issued. Many engineers whose services were really of great value at sea on board their respective vessels were thus transferred to a duty which could have been as well done by others without their rare sea experience.

A long time after the interview referred to, and the work had been contracted for and commenced, the department required me to give an estimate of the probable speed of these light-draught monitors, furnishing me for data a memorandum in Chief Engineer Stimers's handwriting, of which the following is a copy:

"Midship section, 250 square feet. Grate surface, 150 square feet. Diameter of cylinders, 22 inches. Stroke, 30 inches. 2 cylinders. Screws, (two,) 9 feet diameter, 12 feet pitch, 4 blades; dip of screws, 5 feet 9 inches. Maximum steam pressure, 60 pounds; cut off, $\frac{7}{10}$. Height of openings in dry pipe above top of water, 18 inches."

These figures were the whole data given. I replied in writing—and I will take occasion here to state that all transactions of such nature between the department and bureau have been in writing—stating I had made the calculation on the assumptions that the resistance of the vessel per square foot of greatest immersed transverse section was the same as that of ordinarily modelled naval vessels, and that the machinery was properly designed in its details. Thus it will still be seen that the department asked no approval or disapproval from me of the plans. All it ever required, and that after the plans were adopted and the work commenced, was an estimate of the speed from the section of the vessel and the quantity of machinery to be used, and this, it will be observed, was required in writing. Had an opinion of the vessel or its machinery ever been asked, it would have been required, in like manner, in writing.

I never knew, until I read it in Chief Engineer Stimers's evidence, that he had repeated my suggestions to Mr. Ericsson, who had dissented from them; be that as it may, however, the fact is that but one of mine was followed, namely, the mere spreading apart of the screws until they did not overlap, which did not require the slightest change of hull or machinery. Neither the boiler I suggested, nor the mode of connecting the single engines by bevel-gear, were accepted; but instead of this boiler, Chief Engineer Stimers put in the vessel one afterwards patented by himself, and which, as he must have sworn when he took out the patent, he believed to be original with himself, he could not possibly intend, without the most shocking moral obliquity, to attribute to me. I knew, however, nothing of these things at the time, nor for a long while afterwards. I believe it is not pretended by any one that any portions of the vessel other than its motive machinery was ever the subject of even a casual conversation with me. The only plan I ever saw, namely, the sketch by Mr. Ericsson, was so meagre, being merely an outline of the hull with the position of the machinery indicated, but no details given, that neither I nor any other person could have formed an opinion on it; the data necessary for that was wholly wanting.

I believe the truth is, that, after the vessels were commenced, most of the features and detail, both of hull and machinery, were changed by Chief Engineer Stimers, without the authority or knowledge of any one, from the original plan devised by Mr. Ericsson, which was the only one I ever saw or heard of. These changes were so far from being submitted to me, that I never even knew of them. I never saw, and to this day have never seen, any of the drawings from which the work was executed, all of which were furnished directly by him to the contractors, and signed with his name. They were not examined by any other person, and the whole responsibility of their errors rests on him alone. So far was Mr. Ericsson from approving them, that I have since learned he addressed a protest in writing against them as soon as he became aware of the facts. The entire designing and superintending of this work was left in the hands of Chief Engineer Stimers alone, the department, with the greatest liberality, furnishing him with everything he asked, either in material or personnel. So little was the Bureau of Steam Engineering concerned in the matter, that not even a copy of the specifications written and printed by Chief Engineer Stimers, and distributed largely over the country to promote his fame, was ever sent to it, any more than the expensive engravings made and distributed for the same purpose.

If any such conversation occurred between Mr. Fox and Chief Engineer Stimers as the latter relates, in regard to anticipated disagreement of views between Mr. Ericsson and myself on the subject of those light-draught monitors, I can only say I never had any knowledge of it, nor any intimation of the kind from Mr. Fox.

In relation to Chief Engineer Stimers's statement that he did not furnish the department with any draught of a monitor on his own plan, and that he only "put in modifications to Mr. Ericsson's plan according to the directions of the heads of the bureaus here," I can only say that I do not know whether or not he presented a plan of his own, but most certainly none of the modifications he made to Mr. Ericsson's were either suggested, or approved, or known to the bureaus referred to.

The most astonishing part of the whole is that, with the facts above stated, so well known to scores of people, and capable of being supported both by documentary proof, and not less so by its absence, Chief Engineer Stimers should have the matchless effrontery to attempt throwing the responsibility of the parentage of his wretched abortions upon the two mechanical bureaus of the navy. He has said these bureaus were inimical to these vessels; if this was true they could not have approved them or assisted in designing them; but this allegation has as little truth as all the others made by him. They simply had nothing to do with them whatever, and were neither friendly nor unfriendly. Their construction had been confided to other persons and a separate organization; the result is before the world. Chief Engineer Stimers had no occasion "to fight these bureaus and to conquer them," as he says. The department gave him direct all he asked, and there was nothing to fight them about.

Further corroborations of these views will be found in the following letters, published over the names of the chiefs of these bureaus, and written in the first moments of surprise when they found themselves accused of things of which they only derived knowledge from the accusation itself.

"WASHINGTON, *March* 1, 1865.

"*To the Editors of the Boston Daily Advertiser:*

"In your issue of the 20th ultmo, I find a letter from Chief Engineer A. C. Stimers, United States Navy, in relation to what are popularly known as the "light-draught monitors," which contains statements so utterly at variance with the truth, and so calculated to convey erroneous impressions, that I must ask a small portion of your space to correct them.

"The original design of these vessels was made by Mr. Ericsson, who furnished, so far as I am aware, merely an outline plan, no details and no specifications; and had this sketch been filled up with ordinary ability, the vessels would probably have had the contemplated draught of water.

"But Chief Engineer Stimers, to whom the immediate supervision of their construction was committed by the department, not content with carrying out Mr. Ericsson's ideas and furnishing working drawings upon his plan, undertook many and expensive alterations. Neither the working drawings containing these departures from the original plan, nor any other working plan, were ever submitted to either of the mechanical bureaus of the Navy Department, and they first learned of the alterations through the contractors, who complained that after they had completed portions of their work, the plans had been withdrawn and others widely different substituted.

"On the discovery of this system, or rather want of system, Chief Engineer Stimers was informed that these alterations, involving large expense, must not be made; but he still persisted in them, and it was only when a letter was written to each of the builders directing them not to make further alterations without the consent of the bureaus and an agreement beforehand as to the cost, that the department was enabled in the least degree to control the construction of the vessels. It is these unauthorized, and at the time unknown, changes and additions, more than anything else, that necessitated the enlargement of the vessels.

"So far was this carried, that patented inventions were inserted in the drawings, with the knowledge of Chief Engineer Stimers, by persons employed in his office, and claims were afterwards made for patent fees upon the contractors.

"When the advertisement was issued, in order to place the work under contract, Chief Engineer Stimers deposited in the Bureau of Construction an outline plan and some general specifications, accompanied by his estimate of the weights of the vessel and machinery, which weights, he stated in it, corresponded to a draught of water 6 feet 5½ inches. Most, if not all of the contractors, have a copy of his paper containing these weights, and on them they based their bids. Had these weights been adhered to by him, the vessel would not have required enlargement.

"I was never asked to make any calculations of the weight or draught of water of the light-draught, or any other of the monitor vessels. I never approved plans, as Chief Engineer Stimers states, in relation to them, and was never asked to do so; and the statements in my letter to the Hon. Mr. Grimes, read by him in the Senate, are strictly true in every respect, both in the spirit and the letter.

"There were never any plans submitted to me of which I, or any other person, could give an opinion or make a calculation, and Chief Engineer Stimers's assertion that 'when the plans were finally completed, they were examined and approved by the two Bureaus of Construction and Engineering,' is without the slightest color of truth.

"Chief Engineer Stimers further states that 'his superintendent of draughtsmen, Mr. Crabb, had orders from him, from first to last, to take all drawings to Captain Ericsson for approval'—conveying the impression that Captain Ericsson did approve them; whereas it appears he protested against them in writing.

"During the progress of the construction of the light-draught monitors, Chief Engineer Stimers assumed the entire credit of them, and it is a ludicrous surprise to the hundreds of persons who recollected his pretensions then, that he is now endeavoring to shift the responsibility of his errors to others. He seems to shrink as abjectly from accepting the results of his own acts when failures, as he was eager and bold to assume credit for labors not his own when he thought they would render him famous.

"So far from submitting to be instructed by Mr. Ericsson, he assumed to be his rival, and in the endeavor to imitate him underwent the fate of the frog who attempted to expand himself to the bulk of the ox.

"All the facts herein stated, and much more, are well known to hundreds, and, in the endeavor to avoid the responsibility which belongs to him, and him alone, he forfeits the charity which might be extended to his ignorance as an engineer.

"JOHN LENTHALL."

"NAVY DEPARTMENT,
"*Bureau of Steam Engineering, March* 2, 1865.

"*To the Editors of the Boston Daily Advertiser:*

"My attention has been called to a letter in your issue, of the 20th ultimo, on the subject of the 'light-draught monitors,' signed by Chief Engineer A. C. Stimers, United States navy, and containing assertions in relation to my connexion with the same, so opposed to the truth as to require a flat denial, with such statements as will enable the public to justly judge between us.

"My letter to the Hon. Mr. Grimes, chairman of the Committee on Naval Affairs of the Senate, read to that body and referred to by Chief Engineer Stimers, is strictly correct in every particular; and the tenor of its statements, as quoted by Chief Engineer Stimers, 'that I have had nothing to with the construction of the iron-clads in question,' is known to be true by every one of the hundreds of persons having connexion with them, and by none so well as by Chief Engineer Stimers himself. The real facts are as follows:

"The first knowledge I had of any intent to build such vessels was from Chief Engineer Stimers, who entered my office with a sketch—and it was hardly complete enough to deserve that name—by Mr. Ericsson for a monitor vessel of six feet draught of water. His purpose was to show me the machinery alone for the hull, turrets, &c., and the making of the contracts did not lie within my province. On this sketch no detail of machinery was given, its position only was indicated, and a few general dimensions expressed, together with the type of boiler. I was not asked to approve anything in relation to it, nor was I consulted about it; and the only suggestions I offered were, first, that the two screws by which the vessel was to be propelled ought to be separated so as to prevent their actions interfering—the sketch showed them overlapping greatly; second, that if the boilers were arranged with a fore-and-aft fire-room, as almost universally adopted in steamers, it would be a better distribution of them for space and convenience than the one shown on the sketch, which had two athwartship fire-rooms, one at each end of the boilers; and I further suggested the use of vertical water-tubes by the sides of the furnaces. In place of this, however, another arrangement of tubes, as I since learned, was used, devised by Chief Engineer Stimers, for which he applied for a patent, and on which one contractor informed me in presence of a third person he had paid a fee. A long time after the interview referred to, which was the only one that ever took place on the subject, I was required to give an estimate of the probable speed, the data submitted to me being the number of square feet of grate and heating surface in the boiler, the capacity of the cylinders, and the immersed amidship section in square feet of the vessel at six feet draught of water. These figures were the whole data; and I replied, stating I had made the calculation on the assumptions that the resistance of the vessel per square foot of section was the same as that of ordinarily modelled naval vessels, and that the machinery was properly proportioned.

"The whole designing and superintending of this work was placed in the hands of Chief Engineer Stimers. I had no further communication with him on the subject, gave no directions in regard to it either directly or indirectly, and had not the slightest knowledge concerning it. I never saw, and to this day have never seen, any of the drawings from which the work was executed, all of which were furnished by him directly to the contractors, and signed with his name, nor have I ever seen a copy of the specifications, which were made by him after the contracts were executed, though they were, as I have since learned, printed and distributed all over the country; but not a copy was sent to me. During the progress of the work, Chief Engineer Stimers claimed all the merit of it, and its whole responsibility, asserting in the presence of dozens that he and he alone was the author of every part and parcel of it, a claim which no thorough engineer would have dreamed of disputing with him, after examining its character. It now appears, indeed, that the plans of machinery and of vessel designed by Chief Engineer Stimers, including his water-chamber, which contributed so much to overload her, were so completely the opposite of those intended by Mr. Ericsson, and indicated in his original sketch, that he protested in writing against them. Chief Engineer Stimers's statement, therefore, that 'when the plans were finally completed they were examined and approved by the two Bureaus of Construction and Steam Engineering,' is not only an untruth, but made the more contemptible by its intent to throw on others the responsibility of his own utter incompetency. That a person should not have ability equal to the performance of a task which his self-conceit makes him undertake, is not uncommon; but it is very uncommon to find so little manhood as not only to shrink from the responsibility of the failure when it comes, but the baseness to attempt screening himself by falsely charging it upon the well-won reputation of others.

"B. F. ISHERWOOD."

MASSACRE OF CHEYENNE INDIANS.

THIRTY-EIGHTH CONGRESS, SECOND SESSION.

CONGRESS OF THE UNITED STATES.

IN THE HOUSE OF REPRESENTATIVES, *January* 10, 1865.

On motion of Mr. Orth,

Resolved, That the Committee on the Conduct of the War be required to inquire into and report all the facts connected with the late attack of the third regiment of Colorado volunteers, under Colonel Chivington, on a village of the Cheyenne tribe of Indians, near Fort Lyon.

Attest: ——— ———, *Clerk*.

The Joint Committee on the Conduct of the War submit the following report:

In the summer of 1864 Governor Evans, of Colorado Territory, as acting superintendent of Indian affairs, sent notice to the various bands and tribes of Indians within his jurisdiction that such as desired to be considered friendly to the whites should at once repair to the nearest military post in order to be protected from the soldiers who were to take the field against the hostile Indians.

About the close of the summer, some Cheyenne Indians, in the neighborhood of the Smoke Hills, sent word to Major Wynkoop, the commandant of the post of Fort Lyon, that they had in their possession, and were willing to deliver up, some white captives they had purchased of other Indians. Major Wynkoop, with a force of over 100 men, visited those Indians and received the white captives. On his return he was accompanied by a number of the chiefs and leading men of the Indians, whom he had invited to visit Denver for the purpose of conferring with the authorities there in regard to keeping peace. Among them were Black Kettle and White Antelope of the Cheyennes, and some chiefs of the Arapahoes. The council was held, and these chiefs stated that they were friendly to the whites, and always had been, and that they desired peace. Governor Evans and Colonel Chivington, the commander of that military district, advised them to repair to Fort Lyon and submit to whatever terms the military commander there should impose. This was done by the Indians, who were treated somewhat as prisoners of war, receiving rations, and being obliged to remain within certain bounds.

All the testimony goes to show that the Indians, under the immediate control of Black Kettle and White Antelope of the Cheyennes, and Left Hand of the Arapahoes, were and had been friendly to the whites, and had not been guilty of any acts of hostility or depredation. The Indian agents, the Indian interpreter and others examined by your committee, all testify to the good character of those Indians. Even Governor Evans and Major Anthony, though evidently willing to convey to your committee a false impression of the character of those Indians, were forced, in spite of their prevarication, to admit that they knew of nothing they had done which rendered them deserving of punishment.

A northern band of the Cheyennes, known as the Dog Soldiers, had been guilty of acts of hostility; but all the testimony goes to prove that they had no connexion with Black Kettle's band, but acted in despite of his authority and influence. Black Kettle and his band denied all connexion with or responsibility for the Dog Soldiers, and Left Hand and his band of Arapahoes were equally friendly.

These Indians, at the suggestion of Governor Evans and Colonel Chivington, repaired to Fort Lyon and placed themselves under the protection of Major Wynkoop. They were led to believe that they were regarded in the light of friendly Indians, and would be treated as such so long as they conducted themselves quietly.

The treatment extended to those Indians by Major Wynkoop does not seem to have satisfied those in authority there, and for some cause, which does not appear, he was removed, and Major Scott J. Anthony was assigned to the command of Fort Lyon; but even Major Anthony seems to have found it difficult at first to pursue any different course towards the Indians he found there. They were entirely within the power of the military. Major Anthony having demanded their arms, which they surrendered to him, they conducted themselves quietly, and in every way manifested a disposition to remain at peace with the whites. For a time even he continued issuing rations to them as Major Wynkoop had done; but it was determined by Major Anthony (whether upon his own motion or at the suggestion of others does not appear) to pursue a different course towards these friendly Indians. They were called together and told that rations could no longer be issued to them, and they had better go where they could obtain subsistence by hunting. At the suggestion of Major Anthony (and from one in his position a suggestion was equivalent to a command) these Indians went to a place on Sand creek, about thirty-five miles from Fort Lyon, and there established their camp, their arms being restored to them. He told them that he then had no authority to make peace with them; but in case he received such authority he would inform them of it. In his testimony he says:

"I told them they might go back on Sand creek, or between there and the headwaters of the Smoky Hill, and remain there until I received instructions from the department headquarters, from General Curtis: and that in case I did receive any authority to make peace with them I would go right over and let them know it. *I did not state to them that I would give them notice in case we intended to attack them.* They went away with that understanding, that in case I received instructions from department headquarters I was to let them know it.''

And in order, as it were, to render these Indians less apprehensive of any danger, One Eye, a Cheyenne chief, was allowed to remain with them to obtain information for the use of the military authorities. He was employed at $125 a month, and several times brought to Major Anthony, at Fort Lyon, information of proposed movements of other and hostile bands. Jack Smith, a half-breed son of John S. Smith, an Indian interpreter, employed by the government, was also there for the same purpose. A United States soldier was allowed to remain there, and two days before the massacre Mr. Smith, the interpreter, was permitted to go there with goods to trade with the Indians. Everything seems to have been done to remove from the minds of these Indians any fear of approaching danger; and when Colonel Chivington commenced his movement he took all the precautions in his power to prevent these Indians learning of his approach. For some days all travel on that route was forcibly stopped by him, not even the mail being allowed to pass. On the morning of the 28th of November he appeared at Fort Lyon with over 700 mounted men and two pieces of artillery. One of his first acts was to throw a guard around the post to prevent any one leaving it. At this place Major Anthony joined him with 125 men and two pieces of artillery.

On the night of the 28th the entire party started from Fort Lyon, and, by a forced march, arrived at the Indian camp, on Sand creek, shortly after daybreak. This Indian camp consisted of about 100 lodges of Cheyennes, under Black Kettle, and from 8 to 10 lodges of Arapahoes under Left Hand. It is estimated that each lodge contained five or more persons, and that more than one-half were women and children.

Upon observing the approach of the soldiers, Black-Kettle, the head chief, ran up to the top of his lodge an American flag, which had been presented to him some years before by Commissioner Greenwood, with a small white flag under it, as he had been advised to do in case he met with any troops on the prairies. Mr. Smith, the interpreter, supposing they might be strange troops, unaware of the character of the Indians encamped there, advanced from his lodge to meet them, but was fired upon, and returned to his lodge.

And then the scene of murder and barbarity began—men, women, and children were indiscriminately slaughtered. In a few minutes all the Indians were flying over the plain in terror and confusion. A few who endeavored to hide themselves under the bank of the creek were surrounded and shot down in cold blood, offering but feeble resistance. From the sucking babe to the old warrior, all who were overtaken were deliberately murdered. Not content with killing women and children, who were incapable of offering any resistance, the soldiers indulged in acts of barbarity of the most revolting character; such, it is to be hoped, as never before disgraced the acts of men claiming to be civilized. No attempt was made by the officers to restrain the savage cruelty of the men under their command, but they stood by and witnessed these acts without one word of reproof, if they did not incite their commission. For more than two hours the work of murder and barbarity was continued, until more than one hundred dead bodies, three-fourths of them of women and children, lay on the plain as evidences of the fiendish malignity and cruelty of the officers who had so sedulously and carefully plotted the massacre, and of the soldiers who had so faithfully acted out the spirit of their officers.

It is difficult to believe that beings in the form of men, and disgracing the uniform of United States soldiers and officers, could commit or countenance the commission of such acts of cruelty and barbarity as are detailed in the testimony, but which your committee will not specify in their report. It is true that there seems to have existed among the people inhabiting that region of country a hostile feeling towards the Indians. Some of the Indians had committed acts of hostility towards the whites ; but no effort seems to have been made by the authorities there to prevent these hostilities, other than by the commission of even worse acts. The hatred of the whites to the Indians would seem to have been inflamed and excited to the utmost; the bodies of persons killed at a great distance—whether by Indians or not, is not certain—were brought to the capital of the Territory and exposed to the public gaze for the purpose of inflaming still more the already excited feeling of the people. Their cupidity was appealed to, for the governor in a proclamation calls upon all, "either individually or in such parties as they may organize," "to kill and destroy as enemies of the country, wherever they may be found, all such hostile Indians," authorizing them to "hold to their own private use and benefit all the property of said hostile Indians that they may capture." What Indians he would ever term friendly it is impossible to tell. His testimony before your committee was characterized by such prevarication and shuffling as has been shown by no witness they have examined during the four years they have been engaged in their investigations; and for the evident purpose of avoiding the admission that he was fully aware that the Indians massacred so brutally at Sand creek, were then, and had been, actuated by the most friendly feelings towards the whites, and had done all in their power to restrain those less friendly disposed.

The testimony of Major Anthony, who succeeded an officer disposed to treat these Indians with justice and humanity, is sufficient of itself to show how unprovoked and unwarranted was this massacre. He testifies that he found these Indians in the neighborhood of Fort Lyon when he assumed command of that post; that they professed their friendliness to the whites, and their willingness to do whatever he demanded of them; that they delivered their arms up to him; that they went to and encamped upon the place designated by him; that they gave him information from time to time of acts of hostility which were meditated by other and hostile bands, and in every way conducted themselves properly and peaceably, and yet he says it was fear and not principle which prevented his killing them while they were completely in his power. And when Colonel Chivington appeared at Fort Lyon, on his mission of murder and barbarity, Major Anthony made haste to accompany him with men and artillery, although Colonel Chivington had no authority whatever over him.

As to Colonel Chivington, your committee can hardly find fitting terms to describe his conduct. Wearing the uniform of the United States, which should be the emblem of justice and humanity; holding the important position of commander of a military district, and therefore having the honor of the government to that extent in his keeping, he deliberately planned and executed a foul and dastardly massacre which would have disgraced the veriest savage among those who were the victims of his cruelty. Having full knowledge of their friendly character, having himself been instrumental to some extent in placing them in their position of fancied security, he took advantage of their inapprehension and defenceless condition to gratify the worst passions that ever cursed the heart of man. It is thought by some that desire for political preferment prompted him to this cowardly act; that he supposed that by pandering to the inflamed passions of an excited population he could recommend himself to their regard and consideration. Others think it was to avoid the being sent where there was more of danger and hard service to be performed; that he was willing to get up a show of hostility on the part of the Indians by committing himself acts which savages themselves would never premeditate. Whatever may have been his motive, it is to be hoped that the authority of this government will never again be disgraced by acts such as he and those acting with him have been guilty of committing.

There were *hostile* Indians not far distant, against which Colonel Chivington could have led the force under his command. Major Anthony testifies that but three or four days' march from his post were several hundreds of Indians, generally believed to be engaged in acts of hostility towards the whites. And he deliberately testifies that only the fear of them prevented him from killing those who were friendly and entirely within his reach and control. It is true that to reach them required some days of hard marching. It was not to be expected that they could be surprised as easily as those on Sand creek; and the warriors among them were almost, if not quite, as numerous as the soldiers under the control of Colonel Chivington. Whatever influence this may have had upon Colonel Chivington, the truth is that he surprised and murdered, in cold blood, the unsuspecting men, women, and children on Sand creek, who had every reason to believe they were under the protection of the United States authorities, and then returned to Denver and boasted of the brave deeds he and the men under his command had performed.

The Congress of the United States, at its last session, authorized the appointment of a commission to investigate all matters relating to the administration of Indian affairs within the limits of the United States. Your committee most sincerely trust that the result of their inquiry will be the adoption of measures which will render impossible the employment of officers, civil and military, such as have heretofore made the administration of Indian affairs in this country a byword and reproach.

In conclusion, your committee are of the opinion that for the purpose of vindicating the cause of justice and upholding the honor of the nation, prompt and energetic measures should be at once taken to remove from office those who have thus disgraced the government by whom they are employed, and to punish, as their crimes deserve, those who have been guilty of these brutal and cowardly acts.

Respectfully submitted.

B. F. WADE, *Chairman.*

NOTE.—See journal of committee, May 4, 1865.

MASSACRE OF CHEYENNE INDIANS.

Testimony of Mr. Jesse H. Leavenworth.

WASHINGTON, *March* 13, 1865.

Mr. JESSE H. LEAVENWORTH sworn and examined.

By the chairman:

Question. Where do you reside?

Answer. My home is in the city of Milwaukee, Wisconsin; but I am the Indian agent of the Kiowas, Camanches, and Apache Indians, who roam over the plains between Fort Larned, on the Sante Fé road, and the borders of Mexico, through the western part of Texas.

Question. What do you know about the band of Indians said to have been massacred by a force of troops under Colonel Chivington, of Colorado?

Answer. I am perfectly acquainted with them. I have known them intimately since 1862. Being in command of that southwestern frontier, I have constantly had occasion to come in contact with them.

Question. What is that band called?

Answer. That band is called the Cheyennes; but there were also ten lodges of Arapahoes with them. Their reservation is on the Arkansas river, commencing at the Big Timbers and extending up the river ninety miles, and bounded on the north by the Big Sandy. Fort Lyon is situated upon their reservation.

Question. Is this in the Territory of Colorado?

Answer. Yes, sir. Fort Lyon was my headquarters for nearly two years, and I had occasion to meet these Indians almost daily. The chiefs Black Kettle, White Antelope, and Big Jake have travelled with me hundreds and hundreds of miles. Left Hand, the second chief of the Arapahoes, and Little Raven, the first chief of the Arapahoes, have been with me on scouts and in my camps for months together. Left Hand was killed by Chivington; so I am told by the agent and by others. His lodge happened to be one of the ten. A year ago Little Raven requested me to try and get the military removed from his reservation, which I did, through Mr. H. P. Bennet. You will see the correspondence in the report of the Commissioner of Indian Affairs for 1864. I can say that they were always friendly. They have often stated to me that they would not fight the whites under any circumstances. Left Hand particularly has said that the whites might murder their men and do anything they pleased to them, but they would never fight the whites.

Question. What caused our troops to make this attack upon them?

Answer. I do not know the immediate cause of Colonel Chivington attacking this village. I know that a year ago this spring Major Waller, of the regular army, crossed the plains and passed the reservation of the Cheyennes and Arapahoes; and he communicated to the Indian department that if Colonel Chivington was not stopped in his course of hunting down these Indians it would get us into a war that would cost us millions of dollars. I also saw from the reports in the papers that Lieutenant Ayres was hunting these Indians from camp to camp. Knowing their disposition, and knowing Lieutenant Ayres, having appointed him myself as a lieutenant, I stated to the Indian department that if Colonel Chivington was not stopped in his course of sending Lieutenant Ayres after these Indians we should get into a general Indian war on the frontier.

Question. What was their object in hunting these Indians? what cause was there for it?

Answer. I could tell you the ostensible cause, but the real cause is beyond my knowledge. Colonel Chivington was ordered by General Curtis to rendezvous his forces last spring in the southeast part of Colorado for the ostensible purpose of making a raid into Texas. But, as they claimed, the Indian difficulties prevented him from doing so, and he kept his troops there hunting these Indians.

Question. You say that these Indians were of a remarkably friendly disposition?

Answer. Yes, sir.

Question. And inoffensive towards our people?

Answer. There never were two bands of Indians more friendly to the whites than Black Kettle's band and White Antelope's band, and One Eye, who was also killed in this massacre.

Question. Where were you when this massacre took place?

Answer. I was between Fort Leavenworth and the Camanche country, trying to meet the wild tribes of which I was appointed the agent. I found it very difficult to get to them. Little Raven had escaped from the massacre and got into the Camanche country. He was half a Camanche himself, speaking their language well, and is now with the Camanches with his band, and is one of the best men there. I am begging protection for him, if I can get to him.

Question. Can you state anything more in regard to this massacre?

Answer. I do not know anything positively, because I was not there; but I have my information from persons who were present. One of them, Captain Smith, is in this city now. He was there trading under the authority of Major Anthony; and I think Major Anthony is also in this city. He was second in command in that expedition. From them you can get more reliable information than I can give you, for mine is hearsay. I only know that these Indians were of a most friendly disposition. Mr. D. D. Colley is also here; he has been a trader in their camp for two years. His father, Major Colley, is their agent, and knows them intimately; better, if anything, than I do.

Question. Do you know whether these Indians had ever committed any depredations upon the whites?

Answer. I was not aware that they had; not this particular band.

Testimony of Mr. John S. Smith.

WASHINGTON, *March* 14, 1865.

Mr. JOHN S. SMITH sworn and examined.

By Mr. Gooch:

Question. Where is your place of residence?

Answer. Fort Lyon, Colorado.

Question. What is your occupation?

Answer. United States Indian interpreter and special Indian agent.

Question. Will you state to the committee all that you know in relation to the attack of Colonel Chivington upon the Cheyenne and Arapahoe Indians in November last?

Answer. Major Anthony was in command at Fort Lyon at the time. Those Indians had been induced to remain in the vicinity of Fort Lyon, and were promised protection by the commanding officer at Fort Lyon. The commanding officer saw proper to keep them some thirty or forty miles distant from the fort, for fear of some conflict between them and the soldiers or the travelling population, for Fort Lyon is on a great thoroughfare. He advised them to go out on what is called Sand creek, about forty miles, a little east of north from Fort Lyon. Some days after they had left Fort Lyon, when I had just recovered from a long spell of sickness, I was called on by Major S. G. Colley, who asked me if I was able and willing to go out and pay a visit to these Indians, ascertain their numbers, their general disposition toward the whites, and the points where other bands might be located in the interior.

Question. What was the necessity for obtaining that information?

Answer. Because there were different bands which were supposed to be at war; in fact, we knew at the time that they were at war with the white population in that country; but this band had been in and left the post perfectly satisfied. I left to go to this village of Indians on the 26th of November last. I arrived there on the 27th and remained there the 28th. On the morning of the 29th, between daylight and sunrise—nearer sunrise than daybreak—a large number of troops were discovered from three-quarters of a mile to a mile below the village. The Indians, who discovered them, ran to my camp, called me out, and wanted me to go and see what troops they were, and what they wanted. The head chief of the nation, Black Kettle, and head chief of the Cheyennes, was encamped there with us. Some years previous he had been presented with a fine American flag by Colonel Greenwood, a commissioner, who had been sent out there. Black Kettle ran this American flag up to the top of his lodge, with a small white flag tied right under it, as he had been advised to do in case he should meet with any troops out on the prairies. I then left my own camp and started for that portion of the troops that was nearest the village, supposing I could go up to them. I did not know but they might be strange troops, and thought my presence and explanations could reconcile matters. Lieutenant Wilson was in command of the detachment to which I tried to make my approach; but they fired several volleys at me, and I returned back to my camp and entered my lodge.

Question. Did these troops know you to be a white man?

Answer. Yes, sir; and the troops that went there knew I was in the village.

Question. Did you see Lieutenant Wilson, or were you seen by him?

Answer. I cannot say I was seen by him; but his troops were the first to fire at me.

Question. Did they know you to be a white man?

Answer. They could not help knowing it. I had on pants, a soldier's overcoat, and a hat such as I am wearing now. I was dressed differently from any Indian in the country. On my return I entered my lodge, not expecting to get out of it alive. I had two other men there with me: one was David Louderbach, a soldier, belonging to company G, 1st Colorado cavalry; the other, a man by the name of Watson, who was a hired hand of Mr. D. D. Colley, the son of Major Colley, the agent.

After I had left my lodge to go out and see what was going on, Colonel Chivington rode up to within fifty or sixty yards of where I was camped; he recognized me at once. They all call me Uncle John in that country. He said, "Run here, Uncle John; you are all right." I went to him as fast as I could. He told me to get in between him and his troops, who were then coming up very fast; I did so; directly another officer who knew me—Lieutenant Baldwin, in command of a battery—tried to assist me to get a horse; but there was no loose horse there at the time. He said, "Catch hold of the caisson, and keep up with us."

By this time the Indians had fled; had scattered in every direction. The troops were some on one side of the river and some on the other, following up the Indians. We had been encamped on the north side of the river; I followed along, holding on the caisson, sometimes running, sometimes walking. Finally, about a mile above the village, the troops had got a parcel of the Indians hemmed in under the bank of the river; as soon as the troops overtook them, they commenced firing on them; some troops had got above them, so that they were completely surrounded. There were probably a hundred Indians hemmed in there, men, women, and children; the most of the men in the village escaped.

By the time I got up with the battery to the place where these Indians were surrounded there had been some considerable firing. Four or five soldiers had been killed, some with arrows and some with bullets. The soldiers continued firing on these Indians, who numbered about a hundred, until they had almost completely destroyed them. I think I saw altogether some seventy dead bodies lying there; the greater portion women and children. There may have been thirty warriors, old and young; the rest were women and small children of different ages and sizes.

The troops at that time were very much scattered. There were not over two hundred troops in the main fight, engaged in killing this body of Indians under the bank. The balance of the troops were scattered in different directions, running after small parties of Indians who were trying to make their escape. I did not go to see how many they might have killed outside of this party under the bank of the river. Being still quite weak from my last sickness, I returned with the first body of troops that went back to the camp.

The Indians had left their lodges and property; everything they owned. I do not think more than one-half of the Indians left their lodges with their arms. I think there were between 800 and 1,000 men in this command of United States troops. There was a part of three companies of the 1st Colorado, and the balance were what were called 100-days men of the 3d regiment. I am not able to say which party did the most execution on the Indians, because it was very much mixed up at the time.

We remained there that day after the fight. By 11 o'clock, I think, the entire number of soldiers had returned back to the camp where Colonel Chivington had returned. On their return he ordered the soldiers to destroy all the Indian property there, which they did, with the exception of what plunder they took away with them, which was considerable.

Question. How many Indians were there there?

Answer. There were 100 families of Cheyennes, and some six or eight lodges of Arapahoes.

Question. How many persons in all, should you say?

Answer. About 500; we estimate them at five to a lodge.

Question. 500 men, women, and children?

Answer. Yes, sir.

Question. Do you know the reason for that attack on the Indians?

Answer. I do not know any exact reason. I have heard a great many reasons given. I have heard that that whole Indian war had been brought on for selfish purposes. Colonel Chivington was running for Congress in Colorado, and there were other things of that kind; and last spring a year ago he was looking for an order to go to the front, and I understand he had this Indian war in view to retain himself and his troops in that country, to carry out his electioneering purposes.

Question. In what way did this attack on the Indians further the purpose of Colonel Chivington?

Answer. It was said—I did not hear him say it myself, but it was said that he would do something; he had this regiment of three-months men, and did not want them to go out without doing some service. Now he had been told repeatedly by different persons—by myself, as well as others—where he could find the hostile bands.

The same chiefs who were killed in this village of Cheyennes had been up to see Colonel Chivington in Denver but a short time previous to this attack. He himself told them that he had no power to treat with them; that he had received telegrams from General Curtis directing him to fight all Indians he met with in that country. Still he would advise them, if they wanted any assistance from the whites, to go to their nearest military post in their country, give up their arms and the stolen property, if they had any, and then they would receive directions in what way to act. This was told them by Colonel Chivington and by Governor Evans, of Colorado. I myself interpreted for them and for the Indians.

Question. Did Colonel Chivington hold any communication with these Indians, or any of them, before making the attack upon them?

Answer. No, sir, not then. He had some time previously held a council with them at Denver city. When we first recovered the white prisoners from the Indians, we invited some of the chiefs to go to Denver, inasmuch as they had sued for peace, and were willing to give up these white prisoners. We promised to take the chiefs to Denver, where they had an interview with men who had more power than Major Wynkoop had, who was the officer in command of the detachment that went out to recover these white prisoners. Governor Evans and Colonel Chivington were in Denver, and were present at this council. They told the Indians to return with Major Wynkoop, and whatever he agreed on doing with them would be recognized by them.

I returned with the Indians to Fort Lyon. There we let them go out to their villages to bring in their families, as they had been invited through the proclamation or circular of the governor during the month of June, I think. They were gone some twelve or fifteen days from Fort Lyon, and then they returned with their families. Major Wynkoop had made them one or two issues of provisions previous to the arrival of Major Anthony there to assume command. Then Major Wynkoop, who is now in command at Fort Lyon, was ordered to Fort Leavenworth on some business with General Curtis, I think.

Then Major Anthony, through me, told the Indians that he did not have it in his power to issue rations to them, as Major Wynkoop had done. He said that he had assumed command at Fort Lyon, and his orders were positive from headquarters to fight the Indians in the vicinity of Fort Lyon, or at any other point in the Territory where they could find them. He said that he had understood that they had been behaving very badly. But on seeing Major Wynkoop and others there at Fort Lyon, he was happy to say that things were not as had been represented, and he could not pursue any other course than that of Major Wynkoop, except the issuing rations to them. He then advised them to go out to some near point, where there was buffalo, not too far from Fort Lyon, or they might meet with troops from the Platte, who would not know them from the hostile bands. This was the southern band of Cheyennes; there is another band called the northern band. They had no apprehensions in the world of any trouble with the whites at the time this attack was made.

Question. Had there been, to your knowledge, any hostile act or demonstration on the part of these Indians, or any of them?

Answer. Not in this band. But the northern band, the band known by the name of Dog soldiers of Cheyennes, had committed many depredations on the Platte.

Question. Do you know whether or not Colonel Chivington knew the friendly character of these Indians before he made the attack upon them?

Answer. It is my opinion that he did.

Question. On what is that opinion based?

Answer. On this fact, that he stopped all persons from going on ahead of him.

He stopped the mail, and would not allow any person to go on ahead of him at the time he was on his way from Denver city to Fort Lyon. He placed a guard around old Colonel Bent, the former agent there; he stopped a Mr. Hagues and many men who were on their way to Fort Lyon. He took the fort by surprise, and as soon as he got there he posted pickets all around the fort, and then left at 8 o'clock that night for this Indian camp.

Question. Was that anything more than the exercise of ordinary precaution in following Indians?

Answer. Well, sir, he was told that there were no Indians in the vicinity of Fort Lyon, except Black Kettle's band of Cheyennes and Left Hand's band of Arapahoes.

Question. How do you know that?

Answer. I was told so.

By Mr. Buckalew:

Question. Do you know it of your own knowledge?

Answer. I cannot say I do.

Question. You did not talk with him about it before the attack?

Answer. No, sir.

By Mr. Gooch:

Question. When you went out to him, you had no opportunity to hold intercourse with him?

Answer. None whatever; he had just commenced his fire against the Indians.

Question. Did you have any communication with him at any time while there?

Answer. Yes, sir.

Question. What was it?

Answer. He asked me many questions about a son of mine, who was killed there afterwards. He asked me what Indians were there, what chiefs; and I told him as fully as I knew.

By Mr. Buckalew:

Question. When did you talk with him?

Answer. On the day of the attack. He asked me many questions about the chiefs who were there, and if I could recognize them if I saw them. I told him it was possible I might recollect the principal chiefs. They were terribly mutilated, lying there in the water and sand; most of them in the bed of the creek, dead and dying, making many struggles. They were so badly mutilated and covered with sand and water that it was very hard for me to tell one from another. However, I recognized some of them—among them the chief One Eye, who was employed by our government at $125 a month and rations to remain in the village as a spy. There was another called War Bonnet, who was here two years ago with me. There was another by the name of Standing-in-the-Water, and I supposed Black Kettle was among them, but it was not Black Kettle. There was one there of his size and dimensions in every way, but so tremendously mutilated that I was mistaken in him. I went out with Lieutenant Colonel Bowen, to see how many I could recognize.

By Mr. Gooch:

Question. Did you tell Colonel Chivington the character and disposition of these Indians at any time during your interviews on this day?

Answer. Yes, sir.

Question. What did he say in reply?

Answer. He said he could not help it; that his orders were positive to attack the Indians.

Question. From whom did he receive these orders?

Answer. I do not know; I presume from General Curtis.

Question. Did he tell you?

Answer. Not to my recollection.

Question. Were the women and children slaughtered indiscriminately, or only so far as they were with the warriors?

Answer. Indiscriminately.

Question. Were there any acts of barbarity perpetrated there that came under your own observation?

Answer. Yes, sir; I saw the bodies of those lying there cut all to pieces, worse mutilated than any I ever saw before; the women cut all to pieces.

By Mr. Buckalew:

Question. How cut?

Answer. With knives; scalped; their brains knocked out; children two or three months old; all ages lying there, from sucking infants up to warriors.

By Mr. Gooch:

Question. Did you see it done?

Answer. Yes, sir; I saw them fall.

Question. Fall when they were killed?

Answer. Yes, sir.

Question. Did you see them when they were mutilated?

Answer. Yes, sir.

Question. By whom were they mutilated?

Answer. By the United States troops.

Question. Do you know whether or not it was done by the direction or consent of any of the officers?

Answer. I do not; I hardly think it was.

By Mr. Buckalew:

Question. What was the date of that massacre?

Answer. On the 29th of November last.

Question. Did you speak of these barbarities to Colonel Chivington?

Answer. No, sir; I had nothing at all to say about it, because at that time they were hostile towards me, from the fact of my being there. They probably supposed that I might be compromised with them in some way or other.

Question. Who called on you to designate the bodies of those who were killed?

Answer. Colonel Chivington himself asked me if I would ride out with Lieutenant Colonel Bowen, and see how many chiefs or principal men I could recognize.

Question. Can you state how many Indians were killed—how many women and how many children?

Answer. Perhaps one-half were men, and the balance were women and children. I do not think that I saw more than 70 lying dead then, as far as I went. But I saw parties of men scattered in every direction, pursuing little bands of Indians.

Question. What time of day or night was this attack made?

Answer. The attack commenced about sunrise, and lasted until between 10 and 11 o'clock.

Question. How large a body of troops?

Answer. From 800 to 1,000 men.

By Mr. Gooch:

Question. What amount of resistance did the Indians make?

Answer. I think that probably there may have been about 60 or 70 warriors who were armed and stood their ground and fought. Those that were unarmed got out of the way as they best could.

Question. How many of our troops were killed, and how many wounded?

Answer. There were ten killed on the ground, and thirty-eight wounded; four of the wounded died at Fort Lyon before I came on east.

Question. Were there any other barbarities or atrocities committed there other than those you have mentioned, that you saw?

Answer. Yes, sir; I had a half-breed son there, who gave himself up. He started at the time the Indians fled; being a half-breed he had but little hope of being spared, and seeing them fire at me, he ran away with the Indians for the distance of about a mile. During the fight up there he walked back to my camp and went into the lodge. It was surrounded by soldiers at the time. He came in quietly and sat down; he remained there that day, that night, and the next day in the afternoon; about four o'clock in the evening, as I was sitting inside the camp, a soldier came up outside of the lodge and called me by name. I got up and went out; he took me by the arm and walked towards Colonel Chivington's camp, which was about sixty yards from my camp. Said he, "I am sorry to tell you, but they are going to kill your son Jack." I knew the feeling towards the whole camp of Indians, and that there was no use to make any resistance. I said, "I can't help it." I then walked on towards where Colonel Chivington was standing by his camp-fire; when I had got within a few feet of him I heard a gun fired, and saw a crowd run to my lodge, and they told me that Jack was dead.

Question. What action did Colonel Chivington take in regard to that matter?

Answer. Major Anthony, who was present, told Colonel Chivington that he had heard some remarks made, indicating that they were desirous of killing Jack; and that he (Colonel Chivington) had it in his power to save him, and that by saving him he might make him a very useful man, as he was well acquainted with all the Cheyenne and Arapahoe country, and he could be used as a guide or interpreter. Colonel Chivington replied to Major Anthony, as the Major himself told me, that he had no orders to receive and no advice to give. Major Anthony is now in this city.

By Mr. Buckalew:

Question. Did Chivington say anything to you, or you to him, about the firing?

Answer. Nothing directly; there were a number of officers sitting around the fire, with the most of whom I was acquainted.

Question. Was there any business to transact at Chivington's camp when you were brought there?

Answer. None with me; except that I was invited to go there and remain in that camp, as I might be considered in danger of losing my life if I was away from there.

By Mr. Gooch:

Question. Were there any other Indians or half-breeds there at that time?

Answer. Yes, sir; Mr. Bent had three sons there; one employed as a guide for these troops at the time, and two others living there in the village with the Indians; and a Mr. Gerry had a son there.

Question. Were there any other murders after the first day's massacre?

Answer. There was none, except of my son.

Question. Were there any other atrocities which you have not mentioned?

Answer. None that I saw myself. There were two women that white men had families by; they were saved from the fact of being in my lodge at the time. One ran to my lodge; the other was taken prisoner by a soldier who knew her and brought her to my lodge for safety. They both had children. There were some small children, six or seven years old, who were taken prisoners near the camp. I think there were three of them taken to Denver with these troops.

Question. Were the women and children that were killed, killed during the fight with the Indians?

Answer. During the fight, or during the time of the attack.

Question. Did you see any women or children killed after the fight was over?

Answer. None.

Question. Did you see any Indians killed after the fight was over?

Answer. No, sir.

By Mr. Buckalew:

Question. Were the warriors and women and children all huddled together when they were attacked?

Answer. They started and left the village altogether, in a body, trying to escape.

By Mr. Gooch:

Question. Do you know anything as to the amount of property that those Indians had there?

Answer. Nothing more than their horses. They were supposed to own ten horses and mules to a lodge; that would make about a thousand head of horses and mules in that camp. The soldiers drove off about six hundred head.

Question. Had they any money?

Answer. I understood that some of the soldiers found some money, but I did not see it. Mr. D. D. Colley had some provisions and goods in the village at the time, and Mr. Louderback and Mr. Watson were employed by him to trade there. I was to interpret for them, direct them, and see that they were cared for in the village. They had traded for one hundred and four buffalo robes, one fine mule, and two horses. This was all taken away from them. Colonel Chivington came to me and told me I might rest assured that he would see the goods paid for. He had confiscated these buffalo robes for the dead and wounded; and there was also some sugar and coffee and tea taken for the same purpose. I would state that in his report Colonel Chivington states that after this raid on Sand creek against the Cheyenne and Arapahoe Indians he travelled northeast some eighty miles in the direction of some hostile bands of Sioux Indians. Now that is very incorrect, according to my knowledge of matters; I remained with Colonel Chivington's camp, and returned on his trail towards Fort Lyon from the camp where he made this raid. I went down with him to what is called the forks of the Sandy. He then took a due south course for the Arkansas river, and I went to Fort Lyon with the killed and wounded, and an escort to take us in. Colonel Chivington proceeded down the Arkansas river, and got within eleven miles of another band of Arapahoe Indians, but did not succeed in overtaking them. He then returned to Fort Lyon, re-equipped, and started immediately for Denver.

Question. Have you spent any considerable portion of your life with the Indians?

Answer. The most of it.

Question. How many years have you been with the Indians?

Answer. I have been twenty seven successive years with the Cheyennes and Arapahoes. Before that I was in the country as a trapper and hunter in the Rocky mountains.

Question. For how long time have you acted as Indian interpreter?

Answer. For some fifteen or eighteen years.

Question. By whom have you been so employed?

Answer. By Major Fitzpatrick, Colonel Bent, Major Colley, Colonel J. W. Whitfield, and a great deal of the time for the military as guide and interpreter?

By Mr. Buckalew:

Question. How many warriors were estimated in Colonel Chivington's report as having been in this Indian camp?

Answer. About nine hundred.

Question. How many were there?
Answer. About two hundred warriors; they average about two warriors to a lodge, and there were about one hundred lodges.

Testimony of Captain S. M. Robbins.

WASHINGTON, *March* 14, 1865.

Captain S. M. ROBBINS sworn and examined.

By Mr. Gooch:

Question. What is your position in the army?
Answer. I am a captain of the 1st Colorado cavalry.
Question. Were you with Colonel Chivington at the time of the attack on the Cheyenne Indians, in November last?
Answer. I was not.
Question. Have you any knowledge relating to that attack?
Answer. I have no personal knowlege of anything that transpired at Sand creek.
Question. Have you any knowledge in relation to matters connected with that massacre?
Answer. I know about the Indian difficulties in that country, but nothing with regard to that particular difficulty.
Question. What do you know about that campaign?
Answer. I only know that a campaign was organized against the Indians.

By Mr. Loan:

Question. What Indians?
Answer. The Cheyennes and Arapahoes, and all others that were hostile, or were supposed to be hostile.

By Mr. Gooch:

Question. Do you know under what orders Colonel Chivington was acting?
Answer. No, sir. I never saw any orders. I suppose that he acted under the authority of the department commander, General Curtis; but I know nothing positively about that.
Question. Where were you at the time of this attack?
Answer. In the city of Denver, Colorado.

By Mr. Loan:

Question. Who was the district commander at Denver?
Answer. Colonel Chivington was.
Question. You were on his staff?
Answer. Yes, sir.
Question. In what capacity?
Answer. Chief of cavalry.
Question. What was the character of these Cheyenne Indians on Sand creek?
Answer. I do not know.
Question. Do you know whether they were hostile or friendly?
Answer. I saw a portion of their chiefs in the city of Denver, some two months before this action, or massacre, or assault took place. They came there under an escort furnished by Major Wynkoop. They came for the purpose of holding a consultation with the governor, who I believe is acting superintendent of Indian affairs there. They were all the tribe I ever saw.

Question. What bands were killed there?

Answer. The Cheyennes and Arapahoes?

Question. What particular bands of these Indians?

Answer. I merely know from hearsay the names of those chiefs.

Question. As chief of cavalry, on Colonel Chivington's staff, do you know anything of the orders General Curtis sent him in regard to this matter?

Answer. No, sir.

Question. Do you know anything about the organization of the force that went out under Colonel Chivington?

Answer. I do.

Question. State it.

Answer. It was organized by direction of the Secretary of War, for the purpose of operating in that country against the Indians. It was a hundred-days regiment.

Question. Was Colonel Chivington the colonel of it?

Answer. No, sir; Colonel George H. Shoup was the colonel of it. There was great difficulty in furnishing the horses and ordnance stores necessary to mount and equip the regiment. Two months of their time had expired before they were ready to move. They moved from that point about the first of November. And on the 29th of November, I think, this action was fought, or this massacre was made, at Sand creek.

Question. At what time did Colonel Chivington join this command, and what other troops had he with him?

Answer. He joined the command in person, I should think about the 15th of November, and had with him part of six companies of the 1st regiment of Colorado volunteers.

Question. What was his whole force?

Answer. I should judge about 700 men.

Question. The regiment of hundred-days men, and the battalion of 1st Colorado volunteers?

Answer. The whole of the hundred-days regiment were not there. They were not all mounted.

Question. Will you state a little further about the Indians that came into Denver with Major Wynkoop? What was the object of their coming in?

Answer. For some time previous there had been massacres of whites, in the vicinity of Denver, by Indians, as we supposed, and prisoners were taken. Some time in August or September Major Wynkoop, commanding at Fort Lyon, received information from the Indians in the vicinity of Smoky Hill that they had some white prisoners whom they were anxious to give up, or exchange for two Indians that were with one of our companies as scouts. At all events, this communication from the Indians induced Major Wynkoop to take 150 men and two or three pieces of artillery and go out there. He went out there, and, as I understood, when he came back he brought the white prisoners the Indians had held, and a number of their principal chiefs came with him to Denver—out of the district in which Major Wynkoop was serving into the district of Colorado. There they had a consultation with Governor Evans, of Colorado, Colonel Chivington, and other prominent and leading men. The Indians made statements, which I heard interpreted by Mr. Smith, in regard to their friendly feelings towards the whites. Whether their acts justified them or not was rather an open question. They stated their desire for peace. My recollection is that the governor told them they had levied war against the United States, or what amounts to that, and that soon the white soldiers would cover the plains. He said that if they were friendly, as they had said, they must seek the protection of the military posts, for the whites could not discriminate between Indians on the plains. That their going on the military reservations would afford the best evidence of their friendly feelings towards the whites; and my understanding is that a portion of those Indians, if not all of them, sought the military reservation at Fort Lyon with that understanding.

By Mr. Gooch:

Question. Were they on that military reservation when this attack was made on them?

Answer. No, sir. I suppose it was found inconvenient to have so many of them in the vicinity of the post, on account of their natural thieving propensities, and they were ordered off on this Sand creek, about thirty-five miles from the fort, on their own reservation, where they could hunt.

Question. They were where they had been directed, by the military authorities, to go?

Answer. So I understand. Major Anthony, who is here, was a portion of the time in command at Fort Lyon, and he could tell about that.

For the information of the committee, I should like to say a friendly word, under the circumstances, in the Chivington interest. For a year and a half past there has been a state of war existing between the Indians and the whites, as far as the opinion of the Indians was concerned; whether by the authority of the head chiefs or not we cannot tell. At all events, the interruption of communication on the Arkansas route and on the Platte route raised the price of everything consumed by the people out here. And the people emphatically demanded that something should be done. The point I wish to make is, that perhaps Colonel Chivington might have been forced into this by the sentiment of the people.

Question. Would the sentiment of the people lead a man to attack Indians who were known to be friendly, and who were known to be trying to avert hostilities?

Answer. I should say it would. They wanted some Indians killed; whether friendly or not they did not stop long to inquire.

Testimony of Mr. D. D. Colley.

WASHINGTON, *March* 14, 1865.

Mr. D. D. COLLEY sworn and examined.

By Mr. Gooch:

Question. Where is your place of residence?

Answer. At Fort Lyon.

Question. What is your occupation?

Answer. I have been trading with the Indians more or less for the last three years.

Question. Will you state what you know in relation to the attack on the Cheyenne Indians by Colonel Chivington, on the 29th of November last?

Answer. I was in St. Louis at that time. But I was at Fort Lyon when two Indians came in and told Major Wynkoop that they had some white prisoners. They rode in and rode up to the major's headquarters. The major, as well as the balance of us, felt like using them a little rough, for we were all feeling a little hard towards the Indians. I went out and saw they were two Indians with whom I was well acquainted, and who I knew had been trying to keep peace between the Indians and the whites. Just as I went up to them the major came up and spoke very harsh to them, and told them to get down off their horses. I told the major that I knew them, and that they were both friendly. They then got down off their horses and went into the major's room, and told him that they had some white prisoners, and that he could get them by going after them.

The major took his command of 125 or 150 men, and was gone about two weeks, and brought the white prisoners. Some Indians, I do not know how many, 20 or 30 of them, came back with him, and went to Denver with him. I went there also. There they had a council with Colonel Chivington and Governor Evans, and promises were made to them. There was also a council held with them by Major Wynkoop. Major Anthony, after he took command at Fort Lyon, also held a council with them. It was thought best to have them come in at Fort Lyon. Major Wynkoop promised them protection if they would come in, and they came in on the strength of those promises. I talked with them several times after they had brought their families in. The major promised them protection until he could hear from General Curtis. Then if they proposed to make a treaty, all right; if not, he would let them go in time to get out of the country.

Shortly after that, Major Anthony took command of Fort Lyon by order of General Curtis. He said he was ordered to kill these Indians and drive them away. I told him what promises had been made them. They were called together, and they told him that they considered themselves prisoners of war, and that they would not fight under any circumstances. I know that a number of the chiefs present there had been laboring over a year to keep peace between the Indians and whites. They told Major Anthony that he could take them out and kill them if he saw fit. He told them he was sent there to fight Indians. But he would ask them to give up their arms, and some stock they had which belonged to the government; and if they did so he would issue to them prisoners' rations until such time as he had other orders. And they were living there and getting these rations until I left Fort Lyon to come to St. Louis.

Question. Did they comply with the terms proposed by Major Anthony?

Answer. Yes, sir.

Question. Do you know whether Colonel Chivington was informed of this arrangement?

Answer. I know that he was.

Question. How do you know that?

Answer. Because the Indian agent told me he had informed him.

Question. Informed him before he made his attack?

Answer. Yes, sir. When he came down there to make the attack he was told that the Indians were out there under promise of protection. They had been at the post until a short time before, when they had moved out on the Big Sandy at the request of Major Anthony. The Sioux, and a party of Cheyennes called the Dog soldiers, were at war with the whites. And these Indians on the Big Sandy would come in occasionally and report what the other Indians were doing.

Question. Do you know what induced Colonel Chivington to attack these Indians?

Answer. I do not know; I have my opinion.

Question. Can you think of any reason which induced him to make the attack?

Answer. I have thought for more than a year that he was determined to have a war with these Indians. That has been the general belief of men in our part of the country. I was acquainted with all the chiefs who were there, and I [illegible] they had all tried hard to keep peace between the Indians and whites. I was with a portion of this same village a year ago last winter, when the first talk of an outbreak commenced. All the chiefs who were killed by Colonel Chivington have labored as hard as men could to keep peace between the whites and Indians. They could not control the band called Dog soldiers, who had undoubtedly committed depredations.

Question. Do you know anything else in connexion with this matter that is important, which you have not stated?

Answer. I do not know that I do.

By Mr. Loan:

Question. What is the distinguishing name of this band of Indians upon which the attack was made?

Answer. They were known as Black Kettle's band. Black Kettle was the chief of the whole Cheyenne nation; but this was the band that was always with him. The other chiefs that were there were also with him.

Question. There must have been a chief to have led the hostile Indians?

Answer. Yes, sir. But this band was the one always with Black Kettle.

Question. About what number do you suppose were killed on Sand creek?

Answer. I should judge there were between 100 and 150. What I judge from is this: the inspector of the district went with me to Fort Lyon, and he went out to the battle-field. The bodies were lying there then. They spent half a day on the battle-field, and found 69 bodies.

Question. Were there any women and children killed?

Answer. The inspector told me that about three-fourths of them were women and children.

Testimony of Major Scott J. Anthony.

WASHINGTON, *March* 14, 1865.

Major SCOTT J. ANTHONY sworn and examined.

By Mr. Loan:

Question. What is your place of residence?

Answer. Fort Lyon, Colorado Territory.

Question. Do you hold any position in the military or civil service of the government?

Answer. None at present.

Question. Have you held any at any time?

Answer. I was major of the 1st Colorado cavalry from the 1st of November, 1862, until the 21st of January, 1865.

Question. Were you present at the killing of the Cheyenne Indians, on their reserve, not far from Fort Lyon, on Sand creek?

Answer. It was not an Indian reserve. I was present at the time.

Question. State what force was organized, under what orders it acted, under whose command it was, and what was done.

Answer. The command reached Fort Lyon on the morning of the 28th of November last, under command of Colonel Chivington. It consisted of a portion of the 1st regiment of Colorado cavalry, and about 600 men of the 3d regiment of Colorado cavalry; numbering in all in the neighborhood of 700 men, with two pieces of artillery. I joined them there with 125 men and two pieces of artillery. We left on the night of the 28th, for Sand creek, and reached there on the morning of the 29th at daybreak. We found an Indian camp of about 130 lodges, consisting mostly of Cheyennes; there were a small band of Arapahoe Indians with them. The Indians were attacked by us, under command of Colonel Chivington, about sunrise in the morning. Detachments from the command took position on two sides of their camp. There had been a little firing before that. When I first came up with my command, the Indians, men, women, and children, were in a group together, and there was firing from our command upon them. The Indians attempted to escape, the women and children, and our artillery opened on them while they were running. Quite a party of Indians took position under the bank, in the bed of the creek, and returned fire upon us. We fought them about seven hours, I should think, there being firing on both sides. The loss on our side was 49 men killed and wounded; on theirs I suppose it was about 125.

Question. Under what chief was that band of Indians?

Answer. Black Kettle, I think, was the principal chief. There were several chiefs in the camp, but Black Kettle, I think, was the head chief.

Question. Were there any warriors in that camp?

Answer. There were.

Question. What number, do you suppose?

Answer. I would not be able to tell very accurately. There were a great many men who fought us; I should think there were in the neighborhood of a hundred men who were fighting us while we were there. Perhaps there were not quite so many as that, but as near as I could judge there were from 75 to 100 Indians returning our fire. I was in command at Fort Lyon, and had held a council with these Indians before; had talked with them, and had recognized Black Kettle as their head chief.

Question. What was the result of the conference you had with them?

Answer. The circumstances were about these: I was in command at Fort Larned, 240 miles east of Fort Lyon, which place the Indians had attacked in the spring, stealing all the stock at the post, burning the bridges, and damaging the post considerably. Major Wynkoop, who had been in command at Fort Lyon, had had some difficulty with the Indians at that point. He had proposed terms of peace with the Indians, which action was not approved at the headquarters of the department or district.

Question. Were there any military orders issued disapproving his arrangements?

Answer. There were.

Question. Can you give the numbers of these orders, and by whom issued?

Answer. I have copies of them, I think. One was Special Order No. 4, paragraph No. 7, from headquarters of the district of Upper Kansas. There were several orders in regard to the same matter.

Question. What I want is the order of department headquarters disapproving of what Major Wynkoop had done, and also the order of district headquarters.

Answer. I do not think I have those orders in the city.

Question. Do you know who has them?

Answer. I do not. General Curtis was the commander of the department at the time this difficulty took place between Major Wynkoop and the Indians at Smoky Hill, and Major General Blunt was in command of the district. I was out with Major General Blunt in a campaign against the Indians.

Question. Did you ever see those orders from the department headquarters disapproving of Major Wynkoop's action in regard to that matter?

Answer. Only so far as it related to his unmilitary conduct.

Question. I mean his attempt to pacify the Indians?

Answer. I have never seen those orders; I have heard of them.

Question. Now, to return to the point when you were in command at Fort Lyon.

Answer. I took command there on the second day of November.

Question. You say you held a conference with the Indians? State what occurred.

Answer. At the time I took command at the post there was a band of Arapahoe Indians encamped about a mile from the post, numbering, in men, women, and children, 652. They were visiting the post almost every day. I met them and had a talk with them. Among them was Left Hand, who was a chief among the Arapahoes. He with his band was with the party at that time. I talked with them, and they proposed to do whatever I said; whatever

I said for them to do they would do. I told them that I could not feed them; that I could not give them anything to eat; that there were positive orders forbidding that; and that I could not permit them to come within the limits of the post. At the same time they might remain where they were, and I would treat them as prisoners of war if they remained; that they would have to surrender to me all their arms and turn over to me all stolen property they had taken from the government or citizens. These terms they accepted. They turned over to me some twenty head of stock, mules, and horses, and a few arms, but not a quarter of the arms that report stated they had in their possession. The arms they turned over to me were almost useless. I fed them for some ten days. At the end of that time I told them I could not feed them any more; that they better go out to the buffalo country where they could kill game to subsist upon. I returned their arms to them, and they left the post. But before leaving they sent word out to the Cheyennes that I was not very friendly towards them.

Question. How do you know that?

Answer. Through several of their chiefs; Neva, an Arapahoe chief; Left Hand, of the Arapahoes; then Black Kettle and War Bonnet, of the Cheyennes. A delegation of the Cheyennes, numbering, I suppose, fifty or sixty men, came in just before the Arapahoes left the post. I met them outside of the post and talked with them. They said they wanted to make peace; that they had no desire to fight against us any longer; that there had been difficulty between the whites and Indians there, and they had no desire to fight any longer. I told them I had no authority from department headquarters to make peace with them; that I could not permit them to visit the post and come within the lines; that when they had been permitted to do so at Fort Larned, while the squaws and children of the different tribes that visited that post were dancing in front of the officers' quarters and on the parade ground, the Indians had made an attack on the post, fired on the guard, and run off the stock, and I was afraid the same thing might occur at Fort Lyon. I would not permit them to visit the post at all. I told them I could make no offers of peace to them until I heard from district headquarters. I told them, however, that they might go out and camp on Sand creek, and remain there if they chose to do so; but they should not camp in the vicinity of the post; and if I had authority to make peace with them I would go out and let them know of it.

In the mean time I was writing to district headquarters constantly, stating to them that there was a band of Indians within forty miles of the post—a small band—while a very large band was about 100 miles from the post. That I was strong enough with the force I had with me to fight the Indians on Sand creek, but not strong enough to fight the main band. That I should try to keep the Indians quiet until such time as I received re-enforcements; and that as soon as re-enforcements did arrive we should go further and find the main party.

But before the re-enforcements came from district headquarters, Colonel Chivington came to Fort Lyon with his command, and I joined him and went out on that expedition to Sand creek. I never made any offer to the Indians. It was the understanding that I was not in favor of peace with them. They so understood me, I suppose; at least I intended they should. In fact, I often heard of it through their interpreters that they did not suppose we were friendly towards them.

Question. What number of men did you have at Fort Lyon?

Answer. I had about 280 men.

Question. What was the number of Indians around Fort Lyon at any one time when you were talking to them?

Answer. I do not think there were over 725 Indians—men, women and children—within the vicinity of the post.

Question. At the time you held the conference with the Arapahoes, Left Hand, and others, how many men were present above the age of eighteen?

Answer. I should suppose from 80 to 100.

Question. Why did you not capture those Indians at that time?

Answer. I might say I did. I did not take them because I had instructions from district headquarters, as I construed them, to go and fight them wherever I met them. While they were there at the post I did intend to open fire upon them, in accordance with my instructions.

Question. Why did you not do it?

Answer. They were willing to accede to any request I might make. They turned over to me their arms and the property they had stolen from the government and citizens.

Question. What property did they turn over?

Answer. Fourteen head of mules and six head of horses.

Question. Was it property purporting to have been stolen by them?

Answer. Yes, sir.

Question. From whom?

Answer. They did not say. Yet some of it was recognized; some of it was branded "U. S." Some was recognized as being stock that belonged to citizens. It was generally understood afterwards—I did not know it at that time—that the son of the head chief of the Arapahoes, Little Raven,and I think another, had attacked a small government train and killed one man.

Question. What had Little Raven to do with Black Kettle's band?

Answer. He was not with them at the time; Left Hand was.

Question. These Indians surrendered to you, and you took their arms from them?

Answer. Yes, sir.

Question. Did you issue rations to them?

Answer. I did.

Question. What authority had you for returning their arms to them and ordering them off?

Answer. I had no orders in the matter. My instructions were to act upon my own judgment. At the same time there were orders issued that they should not be fed or clothed at the post.

Question. Who issued those orders?

Answer. General Curtis.

Question. Were those orders issued after you had received the arms of the Indians?

Answer. Before that.

Question. Then why did you receive those arms, and feed those Indians in violation of General Curtis's orders?

Answer. I received the arms and told the Indians I could only issue them rations as prisoners. I fed them while there as prisoners, but afterwards released them.

Question. That is what I want to get at. Where did you get authority for releasing the prisoners that were captured?

Answer. I had no written authority for it.

Question. You did it upon your own judgment.

Answer. Yes, sir. That was my instructions, to act upon my own judgment in the matter. I thought we could not afford to feed them at the post; and they were in the buffalo country where they could subsist themselves.

Question. If they were dangerous to the government, why did you release them?

Answer. I did not so consider them then. They were most all women and children, this Arapahoe band.

Question. Who was the chief of that band?

Answer. Little Raven was the chief of those I held as prisoners.

Question. Was Black Kettle with his band at the fort at any time you were in command?

Answer. No, sir, not at the fort; they passed by it.

Question. Did you ever hold any conference with them?

Answer. I did.

Question. At what place?

Answer. At the commissary building, about a half a mile from the fort.

Question. What number of men were with Black Kettle at that time?

Answer. I should think not far from sixty.

Question. State what passed at that conference, so far as you can remember.

Answer. They came in and inquired of me whether I had any authority to make peace with them. They said that they had heard through the Arapahoes that "things looked dark"—that was the term they used—that we were at war with them; that they had come in to ascertain whether these bad reports they had received were correct or not. I stated to them that I had no authority to make peace with them. That their young men were then out in the field fighting against us, and that I had no authority and no instructions to make any peace with them. I told them they might go back on Sand creek, or between there and the headquarters of the Smoky Hills, and remain there until I received instructions from the department headquarters, from General Curtis; and that in case I did receive any authority to make peace with them I would go right over and let them know it. I did not state to them that I would give them notice in case we intended to attack them. They went away with that understanding, thatin case I received instructions from department headquarters I was to let them know it. But before I did receive any such instructions Colonel Chivington arrived there, and this affair on Sand creek took place.

Question. Why did you not arrest Black Kettle and his band there, or attack them when you had them at your mercy?

Answer. I did not do it, because I did not consider it a matter of policy to do it.

Question. Why not?

Answer. Because within 100 miles of us was a party of 2,500 or 3,000 Indians. Black Kettle's band belonged to the same tribe of Indians, and I believed that so soon as I made any attack upon Black Kettle's party, this whole tribe of Indians would rise and cut off our communication on both routes.

Question. How did you know that that party of 3,000 Indians were within 100 miles?

Answer. Black Kettle told me so himself. Jack Smith, the son of the Indian interpreter there, a half-breed, told me the same. One Eye, a Cheyenne chief, told me the same. On two different occasions One Eye told me when small raiding parties were going to start out from the main Sioux and Cheyenne camp to commit depredations on the road, and depredations were committed just about the time they said they would be, yet too soon for us to prevent it. I was satisfied in my own mind that if I had attacked Black Kettle there, although I might have taken his entire camp at any time, it would be the cause of opening up a general Indian war, and I was not strong enough to defend the settlements in case they commenced again.

Question. I understood you to say that the Indians were already at war with the whites.

Answer. Yes, sir. That is, they were sending out their raiding parties. Their men came there on Smoke Hill, and every little while a raiding party would make an attack on some train or some ranch, yet there was no large party at that particular time.

Question. Were there any other Indians at Sand creek, except Black Kettle's band and the Arapahoes of whom you have spoken?

Answer. There were none but Black Kettle's band, and, as I have since ascertained, a few lodges of Arapahoes, under Left Hand.

Question. Little Raven's band was not there?

Answer. No, sir. There was but a small portion of Black Kettle's band there. He was the chief of all the Cheyennes.

Question. There was a particular band that went with him, of which he was the immediate chief, notwithstanding he was also the chief of the whole nation?

Answer. Yes, sir.

Question. And it was the subordinate chiefs who were at war with the whites.

Answer. Yes, sir.

Question. Black Kettle had a band which were always with him?

Answer. Yes, sir.

Question. Now, what I want to know is, what other Indians were at Sand creek when you advised Black Kettle and his band to go over there?

Answer. I think there were only a very few Arapahoes under Left Hand.

Question. Did they have their women and children with them?

Answer. Yes, sir.

Question. How long were they at Sand creek before Colonel Chivington came along with his force?

Answer. I should think about twelve days.

Question. Did you receive any communication from those Indians on Sand creek during those twelve days? Did they furnish you with information of any kind?

Answer. I received some information; I do not know that it came from that band. I had employed at that time, on a salary of $125 a month and a ration, One Eye, who was a chief of the Cheyennes. He was to remain in this Cheyenne camp as a spy, and give me information from time to time of the movements of this particular band, and also to go over to the head of the Smoke Hill to the Sioux and Cheyenne camp there, and notify me whenever any movement was made by those Indians; but he had gone only as far as Sand creek when Colonel Chivington made this attack on the Indians at Sand creek, and he was killed there.

Question. Then you cannot tell whether you had any communications during those twelve days from the Indians on Sand creek?

Answer. They would send in to the post frequently. General Curtis had issued an order that no Indian should be permitted to visit the post. I had ordered them away, and the guard had fired upon them when they refused to obey that order—fired upon them several times. I told them they could not come in, and that if they had any communication to make with me I would meet them outside of the post and talk with them. They sent to me several times, but they were always begging parties.

Question. Did they give you any information whatever of the movements of any of the hostile Indians?

Answer. Yes, sir; One Eye did, and I think Jack Smith did. He came in at one time and stated that a party of Indians were going to make an attack on the settlements down in the vicinity of the mouth of Walnut creek. I reported the matter to the district headquarters, stating that there would be an attack made about such a day. The attack was made at about that time, so that the information he gave was correct.

Question. Were the women and children of this band of Black Kettle in camp with him?

Answer. Yes, sir.

Question. About what number of souls were in that camp when you attacked it?

Answer. I thought at the time there were a thousand or more; but, from information I have received since, I am satisfied that there were not so many as that; probably in the neighborhood of 700 men, women, and children.

Question. Did you send any word to Black Kettle that you intended to attack him or his band at any time?

Answer. None, whatever. It was a surprise, made without any notice whatever to them.

Question. What number of women and children were killed there?

Answer. I do not know. I made a report to Colonel Chivington the next day. I made it partly upon information I had received through the men who were with me, and partly from observation. I stated to him that there were 300 Indians killed, including women and children. I have ascertained since that there were not so many killed; at least I am satisfied that there were not over 125 killed. At one time I sent out a scouting party and told them to look over the ground. They came back and reported to me that they had counted 69 dead bodies there. About two-thirds of those were women and children.

Question. Was your command a mounted command?

Answer. Yes, sir.

Question. How did the remainder of the Indians escape?

Answer. On foot.

Question. What kind of country was it?

Answer. Prairie country, slightly rolling; grass very short.

Question. Do you say that Colonel Chivington's command of 700 mounted men allowed 500 of these Indians to escape?

Answer. Yes, sir; and we ourselves lost 49 in killed and wounded.

Question. Why did you not pursue the flying Indians and kill them?

Answer. I do not know; that was the fault I found with Colonel Chivington at the time.

Question. Did he call off the troops?

Answer. No, sir. The Indians took a position in the bed of the creek, which was from 200 to 500 yards wide. The banks upon the side of the creek were two or three feet high, in some places as high as ten feet; the bed of the creek was of sand, and perfectly level. The Indian warriors took their position right along the bank, dug holes in the sand in which to secrete themselves, and fired upon our men in that way. We fought them there. While the women and children were escaping, the men stood under the bank and fought us all day.

Question. How many pieces of artillery did you have?

Answer. We had four pieces.

Question. And the Indians held you in check there for seven hours?

Answer. I think fully seven hours. I was ordered back eighteen miles on the road before the firing ceased.

Question. Did you capture any prisoners?

Answer. Before I left I saw two prisoners in the Indian lodges, in their camp, where our men were quartered.

Question. Did you ever see those prisoners after Colonel Chivington returned?

Answer. Only one of them, Charles Bent.

Question. What became of the other?

Answer. I only ascertained from common report. I went to Colonel Chivington and told him that Jack Smith was a man he might make very useful to him; that he could be made a good guide or scout for us; "but," said I to him, "unless you give your men to understand that you want the man saved, he is going to be killed. He will be killed before to-morrow morning, unless you give your men to understand that you don't want him killed." Colonel Chivington replied, "I have given my instructions; have told my men not to take any prisoners. I have no further instructions to give." I replied to him that he could make that man very useful, and I thought that perhaps he had better give the men to understand that he did not want him killed. The colonel replied again, "I said at the start that I did not want any prisoners taken, and I have no further instructions to give." I then left him. I learned afterwards that Jack Smith was killed in the camp, in an Indian lodge.

Question. Jack Smith was a half-breed?

Answer. Yes, sir.

Question. And an interpreter?

Answer. I had never met him but once. He spoke English and Indian.

Question. Where was Jack Smith's father at that time?

Answer. He was in the Indian camp, trading with the Indians by my permission; and at the same time I had sent him there partly as a spy upon the camp. I wanted to know what movements they were going to make. When I was about to send him out there he said he wanted to take some goods out there to trade with the Indians, and I gave my permission.

Question. What property was captured there?

Answer. About 700 horses, I should think; quite a large number of buffalo robes. I do not know how many, though I think I saw 150 buffalo robes. There were a great many lodges, which were all burned. There were a great many blankets; some few bows and arrows, and I saw some few guns. However, outside of horses, the value to the white man of the whole would be very little.

By Mr. Buckalew:

Question. Were there any mules?

Answer. Yes, sir, there were some mules; I saw a few mules branded "U. S.," that were being driven away.

By Mr. Loan:

Question. What was done with that property?

Answer. I have never learned since.

Question. Did you have possession or control of any of that property?

Answer. Colonel Chivington instructed me to order my quartermaster to receive the stock, and feed them full rations of corn and hay while they remained at Fort Lyon. But there were only 407 head received at Fort Lyon, as I afterwards ascertained. As to the balance, I received information that led me to believe that 225 head of the stock was run off into New Mexico by a portion of Colonel Chivington's command; 60 more driven up the river nearly 100 miles, were there met by an officer who was coming down, and he brought them back to Fort Lyon. When Colonel Chivington's command left Fort Lyon he took away all of this stock that was there, and I have never heard of it since.

Question. Who issued the order to your quartermaster directing him to deliver this property over to Colonel Chivington?

Answer. There was no written order. A verbal order was given me by Colonel Chivington, which I turned over to the quartermaster.

Question. To whom was that stock delivered?

Answer. To Colonel Shoup.

Question. What position did he hold as an accounting officer?

Answer. There was no quartermaster, I think, that ever had it in charge, with the exception of the acting assistant quartermaster at Fort Lyon, who took it in charge for a few days, by verbal order from Colonel Chivington, and turned it over again in the same manner.

Question. Do you know of any acts of hostility committed by Black Kettle or any of his band that were encamped on Sand creek?

Answer. I do not, except this: I was out with Major General Blunt in an engagement with the Indians on Pawnee fork. There was one man there at that time whom I afterwards recognized as being of Black Kettle's party, and who fought us at Pawnee fork; that was War Bonnet. He was at Pawnee fork, and was very active there. He apparently had charge of a small band of Indians. It was on the 26th of August that we fought them there.

Question. How long had you been acquainted with War Bonnet?

Answer. I had met him but twice, with the exception of that fight I had with him on Pawnee fork.

Question. You had met him twice previous to that?

Answer. Since that.

Question. Where did you first meet him after that?

Answer. At Fort Lyon.

Question. Why did you not then arrest him and punish him for fighting at Pawnee fork?

Answer. I thought if I did so it would enrage the balance of the Indians, who were then encamped at Smoke Hill, and I was trying to keep them quiet, until such time as a sufficient number of troops had arrived to enable us to go out and fight the whole party.

Question. If you had reason to think that Black Kettle, or any of his party, intended to fight against the United States, or the whites, state what that reason was.

Answer. I had no reason to suppose it further than my general knowledge of the Indian character. I have been there for upwards of two years, and during that time it has been the constant complaint of travellers upon the road that the Indians were annoying their trains, even when they did not profess to be at war at all. It had always been a source of constant annoyance to us there. Trains came into the post and complained that the Indians were taking their property from them.

Question. How far from Fort Lyon were Black Kettle and his people encamped when you made the attack?

Answer. Between 30 and 40 miles.

Question. Why was not Mr. Smith, the trader, also killed?

Answer. As I came up with my command, my men formed in line very close to the Indian camp; among the first persons I saw was John Smith. I had not given any instructions to my men to fire. Firing was going on on both sides of me, a portion of Colonel Chivington's command on the right and another portion on the left were firing. I did not give any instructions to my men to fire. I saw John Smith, who appeared to be frightened, and I rode out in front of my men and called out to him to come to me. I held up my hands, called him by name, and swung my hat at him. He started towards me, and as he started, I supposed he imagined some one was firing at him. Whether they were or not I do not know; I did not see any shots fired at him. I am sure no man of mine fired. At that time all the command, with the exception of my men, were firing. As I was calling out to him to come to me, he turned and started to run the other way. Just at that time one of my men rode out and said, "Major, let me bring him out." The man rode past me, and as he rode around Smith, to take hold of him and lead him out of the Indian camp, he was shot; at least I thought so from his motions in the saddle. He passed on by again, and his horse was shot down. After his horse was shot down he attempted to get up, and some Indian ran up to him, snatched his gun from him, and beat him over the head and killed him. That was the first man of our command I saw killed. The Indians at that time commenced firing upon me, and then my men commenced firing.

By Mr. Buckalew:

Question. What became of Smith?

Answer. I did not know what became of him; I did not see him for three or four hours afterwards. The next I saw of him he was coming down the bank of the river, with some of our soldiers.

By Mr. Loan:

Question. What became of the buffalo robes that were taken there?

Answer. I do not know. I had some buffalo robes, my own bedding, which went at the same time, and we have never been able to ascertain what became of them. I went to Colonel Chivington and reported to him that John Smith had lost all his buffalo robes; I wanted them recovered. He said to me, "You go to John Smith and tell him that he need have no fear at all about the matter; I will give an order confiscating that property for the use of the hospital." I afterwards ascertained that I had lost all my own bedding and buffalo robes, and also provision for ten men for thirty days, that I had taken out there. The colonel said, "Well, we will give you an order confiscating that for the use of the hospital, and you can be reimbursed; you shall not lose a cent." However, the order never was issued, confiscating the property.

Question. Do you know by what authority the 225 head of stock were taken off to New Mexico?

Answer. I do not. Captain Cook told me he knew how many men there were, and he knew who had them in charge; but he never gave me the names.

This is the way in which we have been situated out there. I have been in command of a body of troops at Fort Larned or Fort Lyon for upwards of two years. About two years ago in September the Indians were professing to be perfectly friendly. These were the Cheyennes, the Camanches, the Apaches, the Arapahoes, the Kiowas, encamped at different points on the Arkansas river between Fort Larned and Fort Lyon. Trains were going up to Fort Lyon frequently. and scarcely a train came in but had some complaint to make about the Indians. I recollect that one particular day three trains came in to the post and reported to me that the Indians had robbed them of their provisions. We at the post had to issue provisions to them constantly. Trains that were carrying government freight to New Mexico would stop there and get their supplies replenished on account of the Indians having taken theirs on the road.

At one time I took two pieces of artillery and 125 men, and went down to meet the Indians. As soon as I got there they were apparently friendly. A Kiowa chief perhaps would say to me that his men were perfectly friendly, and felt all right towards the whites, but the Arapahoes were very bad Indians. Go to the Arapahoe camp, they would perhaps charge everything upon the Camanches, while the Camanches would charge it upon the Cheyennes; yet each band there was professing friendship towards us.

These troubles have been going on for some time, until the settlers in that part of the country, and all through western Kansas and Colorado do not think they can bear it. When these troubles commenced upwards of a year ago I received information that led me to believe that the Indians were going to make a general war this last spring. I supposed so at the time. They were endeavoring by every means to purchase arms and ammunition. They would offer the best horse they had for a revolver, or a musket, or a little ammunition.

This last spring it seemed to have commenced; I do not know how. I know, however, that at the different posts they were professing friendship. They were encamped in pretty large numbers in the vicinity of the posts, and while their women and children were dancing right alongside the officers' quarters, the Indians secreted themselves in a ravine in the neighborhood of the post, and at a signal jumped out and run off the stock, firing at the guards; at the same time the women and children jumped on their ponies, and away they went. They burned down the bridges, and almost held the post under their control for three or four days. About the same time they commenced depredations on the road. The mails could not pass without a pretty large escort. At least, whenever we sent them without an escort the Indians attacked them, and the people considered it very unsafe to travel the roads.

When the Indians took their prisoners (in fact, however, they generally took no prisoners) near Simmering spring, they killed ten men. I was told by Captain Davis, of the California volunteers, that the Indians cut off the heads of the men after they had scalped them, and piled them in a pile on the ground, and danced around them, and kicked their bodies around over the ground, &c. It is the general impression among the people of that country that the only way to fight Indians is to fight them as they fight us; if they scalp and mutilate the bodies we must do the same.

I recollect one occasion, when I had a fight on Pawnee fork with the Indians there, I had fifty-nine men with me, and the Indians numbered several hundred. I was retreating, and they had followed me then about five miles. I had eleven men of my party shot at that time. I had with my party then a few Delaware Indians, and one Captain Fall-Leaf, of the Delaware tribe, had his horse shot; we had to stop every few minutes, dismount and fire upon the Indians to keep them off. They formed a circle right around us. Finally we shot down one Indian very close to us. I saw Fall-Leaf make a movement as though he wanted to scalp the Indian. I asked him if he wanted that Indian's scalp, and he said he did. We kept up a fire to keep the Indians off, while he went down and took off his scalp, and gave his Delaware war-whoop. That seemed to strike more terror into those Indians than anything else we had done that day. And I do think, that if it had not been for that one thing, we should have lost a great many more of my men. I think it struck a terror to them, so that they kept away from us.

It is the general impression of the people of that country that the only way to fight them is to fight as they fight; kill their women and children and kill them. At the same time, of course, we consider it a barbarous practice.

Question. Did the troops mutilate the Indians killed at Sand creek?

Answer. They did in some instances that I know of; but I saw nothing to the extent I have since heard stated.

Question. State what you saw.

Answer. I saw one man dismount from his horse; he was standing by the side of Colonel Chivington. There was a dead squaw there who had apparently been killed some little time before. The man got down off his horse, took hold of the squaw, took out his knife and tried to cut off her scalp. I thought the squaw had been scalped before; a spot on the side of the head had evidently been cut off before with a knife; it might possibly have been done by a grape-shot, or something of that kind. I saw a great many Indians and squaws that had been scalped; I do not know how many, but several. There have been different reports about these matters. I heard a report some twenty days after the fight—I saw a notice in Colonel Chivington's report—that a scalp three days old, a white woman's scalp, was found in the Cheyenne camp. I did not hear anything about that until after Colonel Chivington had reached Denver. I was with him for ten days after the fight, and never heard a word about a white woman's scalp being found in the camp until afterwards.

On the other hand, on the day I left Fort Lyon to come east, on the 30th of January, I saw an official report from Major Wynkoop, together with affidavits from different men; among them was one man who was my adjutant at that time; he speaks in his affidavit about the bodies of the Indians having been so badly mutilated, their privates cut off, and all that kind of thing. I never saw anything of that; and I never heard it until I saw it in those affidavits at Fort Lyon, two months after the fight. Yet it was a matter of daily conversation between us at the posts. I, however, did myself see some bodies on the ground that were mutilated.

Question. Anything further than you have stated?

Answer. No, sir. I saw what convinced me that, in attempting to escape with two children, one squaw had been mortally wounded, and had drawn her e, gathered her two children near her, and cut both of their throats. That not done by our men. I did not see any one mutilating any Indian, with the exception of the one man I have spoken of, while Colonel Chivington was standing by the side of him.

I saw one instance, however. There was one little child, probably three years old, just big enough to walk through the sand. The Indians had gone ahead, and this little child was behind following after them. The little fellow was perfectly naked, travelling on the sand. I saw one man get off his horse, at a distance of about seventy-five yards, and draw up his rifle and fire—he missed the child. Another man came up and said, "Let me try the son of a bitch; I can hit him." He got down off his horse, kneeled down and fired at the little child, but he missed him. A third man came up and made a similar remark, and fired, and the little fellow dropped.

By Mr. Buckalew:

Question. Those were men of your command?

Answer. Of Colonel Chivington's command.

By Mr. Loan:

Question. Had the officers control of their men at that time?

Answer. There did not seem to be any control.

Question. Could the officers have controlled their men, or were the men acting in defiance of the orders of their officers?

Answer. I did not hear any orders given but what were obeyed. As a general thing the officers and men were doing just what they saw fit to do.

By Mr. Gooch:

Question. Did you communicate to Colonel Chivington, when he came to Fort Lyon, the relations you had had with those Indians?

Answer. Yes, sir.

Question. Did you, under the circumstances, approve of this attack upon those Indians?

Answer. I did not.

Question. Did you not feel that you were bound in good faith not to attack those Indians after they had surrendered to you, and after they had taken up a position which you yourself had indicated?

Answer. I did not consider that they had surrendered to me; I never would consent that they should surrender to me. My instructions were such that I felt in duty bound to fight them wherever I found them; provided I considered it good policy to do so. I did not consider it good policy to attack this party of Indians on Sand creek unless I was strong enough to go on and fight the main band at the Smoke Hills, some seventy miles further. If I had had that force I should have gone out and fought this band on Sand creek.

Question. The Arapahoes had surrendered to you?

Answer. I considered them differently from the Cheyennes.

Question. They were with the Cheyennes, or a part of them were?

Answer. I understood afterwards that some six or eight or ten lodges of the Arapahoes were there.

Question. Did you not know at the time you made this attack that those Arapahoes were there with the Cheyennes?

Answer. I did not. A part of the Cheyennes had left; a part of them said they did not believe we at the post felt friendly towards them; and I have since learned that a part of them had left.

Question. These very Indians had come in and held communication with you, and had taken up the position you had directed them to take?

Answer. No, sir; I told them they should not remain on the road, but they might go back on Sand creek, or some place where they could kill game.

Question. You advised them to go there?

Answer. Yes, sir.

Question. Did you not suppose that they understood from you that if they went there and behaved themselves they would not be attacked by you?

Answer. I do not think they thought so. I think they were afraid I was going to attack them. I judge so from words that came to me like this: "That they did not like that red-eyed chief; that they believed he wanted to fight them."

Question. You say you did not approve of the attack upon them by Colonel Chivington. Did you remonstrate with Colonel Chivington against making that attack?

Answer. I did.

Question. You felt that you ought not to make the attack under the circumstances?

Answer. I did. I made a great many harsh remarks in regard to it. At the same time I did not so much object to the killing of the Indians, as a matter of principle—merely as a matter of policy. I considered it a very bad policy, as it would open up the war in that whole country again, which was quiet for the time. I am very well satisfied the Indians intended a general outbreak as soon as the weather would permit.

Question. You think the attack made upon those Indians there, in addition to the other characteristics which it possesses, was impolitic?

Answer. I do, very much so. I think it was the occasion of what has occurred on the Platte since that time. I have so stated in my report to the headquarters of the district and of the department. I stated before Colonel Chivington arrived there that the Indians were encamped at this point; that I had a force with me sufficiently strong to go out and fight them; but I did not think it policy to do so, for I was not strong enough to fight the main band. If I fought this band, the main band would immediately strike the settlements. But so soon as the party should be strong enough to fight the main band, I should be in favor of making the war general against the Indians. I stated to them also that I did not believe we could fight one band without fighting them all; that in case we fought one party of Indians and whipped them, those that escaped would go into another band that was apparently friendly, and that band would secrete those who had been committing depredations before. As it was with Little Raven's band; his own sons attacked a train a short distance above Fort Lyon, killed one soldier, took a government wagon and mules, some horses, and took some women prisoners. One woman they afterwards outraged, and she hung herself; the other one, I think, they still hold. Some of the Indians have married her, as they call it, and she is still held in their camp, as I have understood; not now in the camp of those who took her prisoner, but she has been sold to the Sioux and Cheyennes. The instructions we constantly received from the headquarters, both of the district and the department, were that we should show as little mercy to the Indians as possible.

By Mr. Loan:

Question. Could you furnish us copies of those instructions?

Answer. I have in the city some private letters, and I think I have also some confidential communications, that go to show something of that nature.

Question. I should be glad to have copies of some of them.

Answer. I think I have some of them. I have copies of some letters I wrote to department and district headquarters. My reports were always approved; they sent back word every time that my reports were approved. I stated that I would hold on to those Indians; let them remain dormant until such time as troops enough arrived to fight the main band. They always approved my action in the matter. When Colonel Chivington arrived there with his command, I immediately reported to headquarters that he had arrived.

Question. Who was the district commander?
Answer. Major Henning.
Question. How did a major command a colonel?
Answer. Colonel Chivington was in entirely another district. The district I was in was in upper Arkansas, and was commanded by Major Henning. Colonel Chivington commanded the district of Colorado.
Question. Then Fort Lyon was not in Colonel Chivington's district?
Answer. No, sir.
Question. By what authority did you act in concert with Colonel Chivington?
Answer. By the authority of the instructions I had received from my own district commander, that I should fight the Indians wherever I met them. When Colonel Chivington came down I talked with him; he told me where he was going, and asked me if I wanted to go with him. I told him if he was going to make a general war with the Indians I did. He gave me to understand that he was going to make it general.
Question. Can you furnish us a copy of those instructions that authorized you to go under Colonel Chivington when he was out of his district?
Answer. I had no instructions to go under him at all. I have, however, some papers to show the feeling in regard to the district. I told Colonel Chivington, several times on that march to Sand creek, that One Eye was there, employed by me; that Black Kettle was there, and that I considered Black Kettle friendly towards us; that Left Hand was there; that, probably, John Smith was there by my permission; that there was a soldier there with Smith whom I had sent off as a sort of spy, too; and that I wanted, if he did fight those Indians, by all means to save those parties; that if he did fight them he should give notice beforehand in order to get them out. I advised him to surround the camp, and not let one escape, and then push right forward and fight the main band; that he was strong enough for them. I believed at the time that if we should attack the main band, it would put an end to all our Indian troubles there. And I supposed he was going to do it; that was the understanding at the time we left Fort Lyon. I took twenty-three days' rations for my men, with the understanding that we were to be gone at least that length of time.

Testimony of Major S. G. Colley.

WASHINGTON, *March* 14, 1865.

Major S. G. COLLEY sworn and examined.

By Mr. Loan:

Question. Where do you reside?
Answer. At Fort Lyon.
Question. Do you hold any official position, civil or military?
Answer. I am an Indian agent.
Question. Will you state what you know of the Indians out there, their disposition towards the whites, &c., and what you know about the massacre at Sand creek?
Answer. I was not present at that fight.
Question. How long have you been agent for those Indians?
Answer. My appointment was in July, 1861.
Question. Were you intimately acquainted with the character and conduct of Black Kettle and his band of Indians?
Answer. I think I was.
Question. What do you know about Left Hand's band of the Arapahoes?

Answer. I know nothing bad about them. I have been with them hundreds of times.

Question. What has been their general character for peace and good conduct towards the whites? Have they been guilty of any acts of hostility, theft, or anything of the kind?

Answer. Nearly a year ago I heard of some troubles on the Platte with some Cheyenne Indians. When the treaty was made with those Indians in 1860, before I went out there, there was claimed to be two bands of Cheyennes and Arapahoes; the one of the North Platte, and the one of the South Platte. This North Platte band was not a party to that treaty, and were dissatisfied with it. There was an effort made to get those Indians to join the southern band, as it was called, but the effort was never successful. The governor, myself, and another man met the northern Indians to see if we could not get them to unite with the southern Indians, and all go on a reservation. But we failed in that. Early in the spring of last year I understood from Denver, perhaps from Governor Evans himself, that there had been a collision between the soldiers and Indians. I did not know what effect it would have upon our Indians below. I immediately went out and found all the Indians I could, and communicated with them, and told them there had been trouble on the Platte, and asked them if they knew anything about it. They said they had heard of it, but supposed it was some of the Dog Soldiers over there, as this northern band is called. They said they themselves did not want to have any trouble, but if the soldiers followed them up they supposed they would have to fight. I told them I wished they would come in on the Arkansas as close as they could and stay there, and be out of trouble. Previous to this, for two years, we have been satisfied that there was an effort being made by the Sioux Indians to induce these Indians to join them and make war upon the whites. We have labored for two years to keep it down. The Sioux Indians, many of them from Minnesota, are there in that country, and have been endeavoring to unite these Indians for the purpose of making a general war upon the whites. These Indians said the Sioux had been there with the war-pipe, but they did not mean to go to war with the whites.

There were a great many depredations committed below our place, at Larned, by some Indians. It was sometimes reported that all the bands were engaged in them; then it was reported that they were committed by the Sioux. It was impossible to ascertain what Indians were engaged. But so far as I met the Cheyennes and the Arapahoes on the Arkansas, they disclaimed it, and pretended to be friendly.

In June last I received a circular from Governor Evans, requesting me to invite any of the Indians that had not been at war with the whites to Fort Lyon; the Cheyennes and Arapahoes of the North Platte to Fort Collins; the Cheyennes and Arapahoes of the Arkansas at Fort Lyon; the Kiowas and Camanches at Larned, and tell them if they would come in and behave themselves, they should be fed and cared for. I immediately sent Mr. Smith, Jack Smith, who was killed, and Colonel Bent, to all these Indians to carry them this information. During this time occurred this trouble at Fort Larned, by the Kiowas running off the stock. Orders were then issued that no Indians should come to that post, as I understood it. After One Eye had come back and said he had seen Black Kettle, who said he would bring in his Indians, I sent him out again to see what was going on.

During this time orders were issued, I understood from General Curtis, that no Indians should visit a military post; but it was a long while before One Eye got in; he did not get in until the 4th day of September, and he got in then by accident. If he had been met by a soldier he would have been shot; but he happened to meet some other soldiers, who took him prisoner and brought him in then. Major Wynkoop took him and kept him in the guard-house that day.

He told us that there were some white prisoners with the Cheyennes whom they had brought, and whom they were willing to deliver up, if we would go out for them. Major Wynkoop went out with one hundred men, had a conversation with the Indians, and brought in four prisoners, one girl and three children.

Black Kettle and his principal men, some twenty or thirty of them, came in with Major Wynkoop, and went to Denver and had a conference with Governor Evans. The governor declined to make any peace with them, but turned them over to the military. Black Kettle went out and brought in quite a number of lodges, and the young men came in to the post.

Before this time, General Curtis, through representations from some quarter, was apparently led to believe that the Indians were behaving very badly at Fort Lyon; and Major Wynkoop was relieved of his command by Major Anthony. At that time the Arapahoes were there, being fed by Major Wynkoop. When Major Anthony came, he said he was ordered to fight those Indians; but he found things different from what he expected, and he did not think it policy then to fight them; that there was no danger from those Indians; they could be kept there, and killed at any time it was necessary. He told them that he did not feel authorized to give them any rations, and that they better go out a piece where they could kill buffalo.

After Major Wynkoop had brought those Indians in, and until after this fight, I do not know of any depredations having been committed in our country. There may have been some committed below in the vicinity of Fort Larned; but during that time, two months or over, the Indians in our country did not commit any depredations.

Question. Have you any means of knowing the number of Indians in that camp on Sand creek?

Answer. I have no personal knowledge of the number of lodges there. But there were about one hundred lodges of the Arapahoes at the post at the time Major Anthony took the command there. Left Hand's band had gone out to Sand creek, and Black Kettle's band of the Cheyennes.

Question. How many were in Left Hand's band?

Answer. About eight lodges.

Question. How many to a lodge?

Answer. About five.

Question. About how strong was Black Kettle's band?

Answer. I do not know of my own knowledge. I only know from what men told me who had counted them. At one time when One Eye was out, we did suppose, from what we had heard, that the Indians were all going to unite against us.

Question. Judging from all your information as Indian agent, have you any reason to believe that Black Kettle or Left Hand had been guilty of or intended any hostility towards us?

Answer. I have no reason to believe that of either of them.

Question. Have you any reason to know that they desired to remain at peace, and were opposed to fighting the people of the United States?

Answer. Left Hand, who speaks English, told me that he never would fight the whites. He said that some of his boys got mad after he was fired at at Fort Larned. Left Hand had come in there and offered to assist in the recovery of some stock that had been stampeded there. He was fired on by the soldiers at Fort Larned. He said, "I was not much mad; but my boys were mad, and I could not control them. But as for me, I will not fight the whites, and you cannot make me do it. You may imprison me or kill me; but I will not fight the whites."

Question. What was the feeling of Black Kettle?

Answer. He himself always appeared to be friendly.

Question. Did you ever know of his committing any act of hostility towards the whites, or sanctioning it in others.?

Answer. I never did.

Question. What relation did he bear to the Cheyenne tribe of Indians?

Answer. He was acknowledged as the head chief of the southern bands of Cheyennes. There were subordinate chiefs who were heads of bands.

By Mr. Buckalew:

Question. What has become of Black Kettle?

Answer. I have seen a half-breed who was there with Mr. Smith, and could not get back to the soldiers, and ran off with the Indians, and was with them for fourteen days after they got over to the Sioux Indians. From what he told me—and I could rely upon it—Black Kettle was not killed, but Left Hand was wounded, and died after he got over there.

Question. Of the fight itself you know nothing?

Answer. No, sir; I was not there; I was at Fort Lyon at the time.

Question. The Jack Smith who was killed there was the son of a white man?

Answer. Yes, sir; of John Smith.

Question. He was an interpreter?

Answer. He interpreted for me; he spoke both English and Indian.

Question. Had you any reason to think that Mr. Smith or his son entertained any hostility to the whites?

Answer. The old gentleman was always our main man there, communicating with the Indians, for he had lived with them so long. Nobody doubted his fidelity to the government.

Question. Was there any reason to doubt that of the son?

Answer. Captain Hardee informed me, when he went out there on the stage, that he thought Jack Smith was one of the party that attacked the stage. When Jack came I told him what I had heard. He said he had rode up to the stage and wanted to know if his father was in the coach; and he wanted to know what the trouble was that he had heard of in the east; that they then fired upon them, and then the Indians returned the fire.

Question. Was there any other act of Jack denoting hostility?

Answer. I never heard of any. He was at Fort Lyon at work haying there for some men. In July last, I think, Colonel Chivington was at Fort Lyon. This One Eye was near about the fort, and wanted to go out and see the Indians, but was afraid of the soldiers. Colonel Chivington wrote out a certificate of his good character, stating that he was a friendly Indian, and then told him if he came across any soldiers to show that to them; if they shot before he got to them to show a white flag, and that would protect him. He was an Indian we relied upon a great deal for information. He was killed at Sand creek. I asked Colonel Chivington if there was any way these Indians, Black Kettle, Left Hand, and some others, could be treated with. He said his orders from General Curtis were that it could be done on these conditions: that they must give up their stolen property, make restitution for any damage they had done, &c., and I supposed he was going to do that.

Testimony of Governor John Evans.

WASHINGTON, *March* 15, 1865.

Governor JOHN EVANS sworn and examined.

By Mr. Loan:

Question. What is your present official position?

Answer. Governor of Colorado Territory, and superintendent of Indian affairs.

Question. Do you know anything of a band of Indians under the lead of a chief of the name of Black Kettle?

Answer. There is a band of Cheyenne Indians under a chief of that name, roaming over the plains.

Question. In what part of the country were they located, relative to the other bands of Indians?

Answer. The Indians that were with Black Kettle—I do not know that he was the leader of them entirely, but the Indians he went with, and was the chief among, were mainly roaming in the neighborhood of the Smoke Hill and Republican fork, and down on the south Arkansas. Sometimes they went up as far as the Platte.

Question. How many other bands were there?

Answer. There is a band up in the neighborhood of Fort Laramie, some of whose chiefs, the Shield and Spotted Horse, were with them.

Question. Was there any other band of the tribe of Cheyenne Indians than those on the Platte and those on the Arkansas?

Answer. Yes, sir; I think so. How far they were divided into bands it is rather difficult to say; and where each band is located is very difficult to say, because they range from away below the Arkansas to above Fort Laramie, or to Powder river. For years they have been in the habit of roaming back and forth over the plains.

Question. Will you give us the names of the head chiefs of the Cheyennes that you, as superintendent of Indian affairs, recognized?

Answer. There was Black Kettle, White Antelope, and Bull Bear among them.

Question. Having the supreme control of the Cheyenne nation?

Answer. No, sir; I do not think there was any such chief recognized. They had a party of about forty young men, called the Dog soldiers, who several years ago took the control of the tribe mainly out of the hands of the chiefs. They were clubbed together as a band of braves, and the chiefs could not control them.

Question. What part of the country did Black Kettle and the Indians with him occupy during last summer?

Answer. From information which I have received I think they were mainly on the head of the Smoke Hill.

Question. How far from Fort Lyon?

Answer. Sometimes nearer, sometimes farther off. As I stated before, they are entirely nomadic, and they pass from one part of the country to another. The most precise information I have of their precise locality, at any particular time, is the report of Major Wynkoop, who went out and saw their camp, in the latter part of August, or in the early part of September last.

Question. Where were they then?

Answer. At what is called Big Timbers, on the head of Smoke Hill.

Question. Have you any knowledge that they were north of Denver at any time during last summer? If so, state at what places they were.

Answer. I have the information from the chiefs that during the summer they were on the Platte, in the neighborhood of Plum creek, a little west of Fort Kearney; and on the Blue, east of Fort Kearney. They ranged away down into Kansas and Nebraska there during the summer.

Question. From whom did you derive this information?

Answer. It was either Black Kettle or White Antelope who told me so.

Question. At what time?

Answer. At the time of the depredations on the trains that were perpetrated in August last.

Question. I mean at what time did they tell you this?

Answer. They told me so on the 28th of September.

Question. You say they were down on Plum creek at the time these depredations were committed?

Answer. They said the Cheyennes committed them.

Question. What I want to know is whether you have information that Black Kettle, or any of the band that travel with him, had been north of Denver last summer. Did Black Kettle tell you that either he himself, or any of the band under his immediate control, had been there?

Answer. I inferred they had from his saying that the Cheyennes had committed those depredations. As a matter of course I told him they had committed them, because they had some white prisoners who had been captured there, and whom they claimed as theirs. He did not answer to that proposition. He said the Cheyennes committed the depredations east of Kearney. He did not say directly that they had been on the Blue. They gave up to Major Wynkoop the prisoners that were captured on the Little Blue, and then he said that the Cheyennes committed the depredations.

Question. Did Black Kettle say that his band had done it?

Answer. He did not say which band of Cheyennes. I inferred that they were his band because they did not speak of any other bands. These Cheyennes that range on the head of the Smoke Hill and Republican seem all to band together.

Question. What is the distance from their location about Fort Lyon to Fort Kearney, and from there to Little Blue?

Answer. I should have to guess at the distance.

Question. You have travelled that country frequently, have you not?

Answer. Not across in that direction.

Question. You have a general knowledge of that country and the bearing of it, and can estimate it from the route you have travelled?

Answer. From the Big Timbers on the head of the Smoke Hill.

Question. Or about Fort Lyon?

Answer. It is at least from ninety to one hundred miles from Fort Lyon, and from Big Timbers to Fort Kearney would probably be 150 miles. I may be mistaken as to that.

Question. How far east of Denver is Fort Lyon?

Answer. It is southeast.

Question. How far east?

Answer. Something like 100 miles.

Question. What distance is Fort Lyon from Denver by a right line?

Answer. I suppose about 200 miles. It is about 250 miles the way they travel. It must be quite 200 miles on an air line.

Question. Where was it that Black Kettle was telling you about this?

Answer. At Denver.

Question. State the circumstances under which that conversation arose.

Answer. He with other chiefs and headmen——

Question. Please name them.

Answer. I cannot give all their names.

Question. State as many as you can remember.

Answer. Black Kettle, White Antelope, and Bull Bear, of the Cheyennes; Nevy and two or three others of the Arapahoes. They were brought to Denver for the purpose of council by Major Wynkoop, after he had been out to their camp, brought there for the purpose of making a treaty of peace.

Question. You were acting as superintendent of Indian affairs?

Answer. Yes, sir.

Question. What propositions did you make to them, and what was the conclusion of that conference?

Answer. Major Wynkoop's report is published in my report to the Commissioner of Indian Affairs.

Question. That may be; but you can state it?

Answer. In brief, he reported that he had been out to their camp, and found them drawn up in line of battle. He sent in an Indian he had with him to get them to council instead of to fight; and he held a council in the presence of their warriors with their bows and arrows drawn. They agreed to allow these men to come to see me in reference to making peace, with the assurance that he would see them safe back again to their camp, as he states in his report or letter to me in regard to it.

Question. When you saw the Indians, what occurred?

Answer. The Indians made their statement, that they had come in through great fear and tribulation to see me, and proposed that I should make peace with them; or they said to me that they desired me to make peace. To which I replied that I was not the proper authority, as they were at war and had been fighting, and had made an alliance with the Sioux, Kiowas, and Comanches to go to war; that they should make their terms of peace with the military authorities. I also told them that they should make such arrangements, or I advised them to make such arrangements as they could, and submit to whatever terms were imposed by the military authorities as their best course.

Question. What reply did they make to that?

Answer. They proposed that that would be satisfactory, and that they would make terms of peace. The next day I got a despatch from Major General Curtis, commanding the department, approving my course, although he did not know what it was. But the despatch contained an order that no peace should be made with the Indians without his assent and authority; dictating some terms for them to be governed by in making the peace.

Question. Have you a copy of that despatch with you?

Answer. It is published in my annual report.

Question. Did you communicate that fact to the Indians?

Answer. It was after the Indians had left that I received a despatch. The despatch came to the commander of the district; and a copy was sent to me for the purpose of giving me notice.

Question. Was anything further said in that conference with the Indians?

Answer. I took occasion to gather as much information as I could in regard to the extent of hostile feelings among the Indians, and especially in regard to what bands had been committing the depredations along the line and through the settlements, which had been very extensive.

Question. What did Black Kettle say in regard to his band; and what did the other Indians say in regard to their bands?

Answer. Black Kettle said he and White Antelope had been opposed all the time to going to war, but they could not control their young men—these Dog soldiers; they have been very bad.

Question. These Dog soldiers were on the Blue?

Answer. They were in his camp; they were his young men; Black Kettle was an old man.

Question. Where was his camp?

Answer. At the Big Timbers.

Question. Where Major Wynkoop found them?

Answer. Yes, sir.

Question. How do you know that fact?

Answer. By the statement that their warriors were there.

Question. Did Major Wynkoop make that statement to you?

Answer. Yes, sir; in his letter to me giving the circumstances under which he brought these Indians to me.

Question. Did Major Wynkoop report to you that the Dog soldiers, of the Cheyennes, were in Black Kettle's camp?

Answer. He did not mention the Dog soldiers; but the Dog soldiers are warriors of the Cheyenne tribe.

Question. I understand that; but you say there is no head chief that you recognized as such. I wanted to know if these Dog soldiers belonged to the band under the lead of Black Kettle?

Answer. The Dog soldiers belonged to the bands commanded by Black Kettle, White Antelope, and Bull Bear, which all run together. There is no known separation among them.

Question. Do I understand you, then, to say that the Indians indiscriminately occupy that country from below the Arkansas to the North Platte?

Answer. The Cheyenne Indians, the Sioux Indians, the Arapahoe Indians, roam indiscriminately through there.

Question. Then there was no particular band that made their homes about the head of the Smoky fork?

Answer. There were a number of bands and tribes that hunted through there indiscriminately.

Question. What I want to know is the usual locality of Black Kettle's band?

Answer. It was like all the rest. He goes where he thinks there is the best hunting; he ranges from one part of the country to the other.

Question. Do you know that the Indians known as Dog soldiers ever were in Black Kettle's camp; and if so, at what time, and how do you know the fact?

Answer. I will not name them as Dog soldiers.

Question. I mean the warriors known as the Dog soldiers of the Cheyennes Indians. Have they ever been in his camp at any time that you know of?

Answer. Bull Bear, who was to see me, was the head of the Dog soldiers himself, the head one of that band, a sub-chief. They said they left nearly all their warriors at this bunch of timbers.

Question. Where Black Kettle's camp was?

Answer. Black Kettle was in the camp. You have the idea that Black Kettle had some particular camp. The distinction between White Antelope and Black Kettle, as an authority among the tribes, has varied at different times. The government has never recognized either of them as head chief that I know of.

Question. You have omitted to answer the question whether you know of these Dog soldiers, at any time or at any place, being in Black Kettle's camp or under his control?

Answer. I know the answer that Bull Bear gave when he came to Denver. He was recognized as the leader of the Dog soldiers. He, with Black Kettle and White Antelope, said that they left their warriors down at the bunch of timbers; and Major Wynkoop reports the same thing.

Question. You inferred that the warriors referred to were the Dog soldiers?

Answer. I did.

Question. At this conference, when Bull Bear told you this, what did he say in regard to war and peace?

Answer. He said he was ready to make peace. They spoke of some of their warriors being out. Their war is a guerilla warfare. They go off in little bands of twenty or thirty together and commit these depredations, so that there is scarcely ever more than that many seen in any of these attacks. They reported that some of their young men were out upon the war-path, or had been out, and they did not know whether they were in at the time. That, I think, was stated at that time, or in a communication that came from them a short time before this. I got a letter from Black Kettle through Bent; it was sent up to me. Upon which Major Wynkoop went out to their camp, and either that or their statement at the conference gave me the information that a portion of their warriors were still out.

Question. How did Major Wynkoop know in regard to this letter or its contents?

Answer. It was brought in to Major Colley, at Fort Lyon, where Major Wynkoop was in command, by two or three Indians; and immediately upon their coming in Major Wynkoop took these Indians, and went with them, as guides.

Question. That was before you saw the letter?

Answer. Yes, sir; and they immediately sent me a copy of the letter.

Question. Did these Indians propose to do anything that you, as their superintendent, directed them to do in this matter, for the purpose of keeping peace?

Answer. They did not suggest about keeping peace; they proposed to make peace. They acknowledged that they were at war, and had been at war during the spring. They expressed themselves as satisfied with the references I gave them to the military authorities; and they went back, as I understood, with the expectation of making peace with "the soldiers," as they termed them—with the military authorities.

Question. Why did you permit those Indians to go back, under the circumstances, when you knew they were at war with the whites?

Answer. Because they were under the control and authority of the military, over which I, as superintendent of Indian affairs, had no control.

Question. Did you make application to the district commander there to detain those Indians?

Answer. No, sir.

Question. Why did you not do it?

Answer. Because the military commander was at the council.

Question. What was his name?

Answer. Colonel Chivington. I told the Indians he was present and could speak in reference to those matters we had been speaking about.

Question. Were any orders given to Major Wynkoop, either by yourself or by Colonel Chivington, in regard to his action towards those Indians?

Answer. I gave no orders, because I had no authority to give any.

Question. Did Colonel Chivington give any?

Answer. He made these remarks in the presence of the council: that he was commander of the district; that his rule of fighting white men and Indians was to fight them until they laid down their arms; if they were ready to do that, then Major Wynkoop was nearer to them than he was, and they could go to him.

Question. Do you know whether he issued any orders to Major Wynkoop to govern his conduct in the matter?

Answer. I do not. Major Wynkoop was not under his command, however. I understood that Fort Lyon was not in the command that Colonel Chivington was exercising at the time. It was a separate command, under General Blunt, of the military district of the Arkansas, as I understood it.

Question. Were the Indian chiefs sent back to their homes in pursuance of any orders given to Major Wynkoop, that you know of?

Answer. No, sir. I will say further, in regard to my course, that it was reported to the Indian bureau, and approved by the Indian bureau as proper, not to interfere with the military, which will appear in my annual report. I have no official knowledge of what transpired after this council, so far as these Indians are concerned, except that I notified the agent that they were under the military authority, and I supposed they would be treated as prisoners.

Question. How long have you been superintendent of Indian affairs there?

Answer. Since the spring of 1862.

Question. Have you any knowledge of any acts committed by either of those chiefs, or by the bands immediately under their control—any personal knowledge?

Answer. In 1862, a party of these Dog soldiers——

Question. I am not asking about the Dog soldiers, but about Black Kettle's band.

Answer. They are the same Indians. The Dog soldiers were a sort of vigilance committee under those old chiefs.

Question. I understood you to say, a few minutes ago, that the Dog soldiers threw off the authority of the old chiefs, and were independent of them?

Answer. That they managed the tribe instead of the chiefs.

Question. What act of hostility was committed by the Dog soldiers, in pursuance of the authority of any of the chiefs of the nation?

Answer. That I could not say, for I have no way of ascertaining what authority they have—only what I gather from the agent, who was intimate with them.

Question. What is the name of that agent?

Answer. Colley. He is familiar with those Indians, and said that the Dog soldiers were to blame for their ugly conduct.

Question. That is what I understand; and I wanted you, as superintendent of Indian affairs, to tell us if these Dog soldiers were under the command of any chief that had control of them, and the name of that chief, if you know it.

Answer. The identification of the chief that commands them is what I am not able to do, because they have in that band, or tribe, the chiefs that I have mentioned. Which of them is superior in authority I am not advised.

Question. What was the general reputation of Black Kettle, as a hostile or a friendly Indian, during your control there as superintendent of Indian affairs?

Answer. Black Kettle has had the reputation of being himself a good Indian.

Question. Peaceably inclined, and well disposed towards the whites?

Answer. Yes, sir; and White Antelope more particularly. But I was going on to state in regard to their conduct. In the summer of 1862 a party of warriors of the Cheyennes came to Denver and called on me, and wanted something to eat.

Question. Can you designate what particular band they belonged to?

Answer. They were of the same band we are fighting about the Blue—Black Kettle, White Antelope, and Bull Bear's Indians, that range mainly down in the neighborhood of Smoke Hill. They came to Denver on a war expedition against the Utes. I advised them to cease their hostilities. When I went there I had an idea of trying to get everybody to live without fighting, the Indians among the rest. The Indians on the mountains and on the plains spent their time in chasing one another. I was in this delicate position: the Utes, who are a very warlike and dangerous tribe, had got a jealousy of the Indians on the plains, and the whites who live on the plains also. The whites were constantly giving presents to the begging portion of the plains Indians. The superintendency and the agency were constantly giving goods to them; and the Utes complained that the whites were fitting out the plains Indians in their war parties against the Utes, which was true to some extent. The Utes said that when they chased the Cheyennes and Arapahoes, which run together almost constantly, and the Sioux—there are parties of Sioux with the Arapahoes and Cheyennes in nearly all their war parties—when the Utes would chase them down into the plains, they had to stop because the whites interfered, and they did not dare to go down into the plains. They were of the opinion that the whites were taking the side of the Indians of the plains; and they were on the point of going to war with us.

I suggested to these Indians that it was better for them to make peace. I went with Colonel Leavenworth down to the camp of the Sioux, Arapahoes, and Cheyennes, at a subsequent period, and tried to arrange with them. I had a Ute agent with me to make the arrangement to quit fighting. When this party came, in 1862, I mentioned these things, showing the advantages, and they promised me they would go back; I gave them some bacon and flour, and other things, for subsistence. They started under a promise that they would go back, and not go up to the Utes, and jeopard our safety with them. Instead of that, they started for the South Park, the Ute battle-ground, where they usually fight, and the next day or two afterwards messengers came in from the settlers on the road, saying that the Indians were committing depredations; that they had cleaned out and outraged one landlord; had insulted a woman; had gone in and taken possession of several of these sparsely settled places; had made one woman cook for the whole party, and I think they had sent in for protection. Some six soldiers went up to protect the neighborhood; but when they got there, these Indians had gone back on the plains by another route.

Question. What was the name of the chief in command of that party?

Answer. I do not know; that was their first visit.

Question. Was it Black Kettle, or White Antelope, or Bull Bear?

Answer. I could not say it was not them, nor that it was. It was a party of warriors from the same party that Black Kettle, White Antelope and Bull Bear ranged with.

Question. Although you had a conversation with them, and furnished them with supplies, and induced them to return, you do not know the name of the chief?

Answer. There were several chiefs.

Question. Can you name any one of them?

Answer. I cannot give the name; I might get it if I were in my office.

Question. As governor of Colorado Territory, did you have any troops organized there last summer?

Answer. Yes, sir; I organized a regiment.

Question. For what term of service?

Answer. For one hundred days.

Question. Who was the colonel of that regiment?

Answer. George L. Shoup.

Question. Did you ever issue any orders to that regiment, or to any part of it?

Answer. No, sir.

Question. Were they organized as United States troops?

Answer. Yes, sir.

Question. Were they placed under the control of the district commander as soon as organized?

Answer. Before they were organized, for this reason: while the regiment was being raised, there was information come in of a camp of about 800 of these Indians; a report of which will be found in my annual report to the Commissioner of Indian Affairs. It came in in this way: Little Geary, a grandson of the signer of the Declaration of Independence, lives on the Platte, sixty miles south of Denver. In the night two Cheyenne chiefs came to him.

Question. What were their names?

Answer. It seems to me one of them was Crooked Neck. The statement I was going to make was this: these Indians came in and notified Geary to get out of the way. He was living on ranch with a large amount of stock, and with a Cheyenne wife. He had Spotted Horse there with him under protection. Spotted Horse, a Cheyenne Indian of Fort Laramie, had been friendly all the time, and was there under protection. These Indians made these statements to him, as you will see in the printed copy of my report to the Commissioner of Indian Affairs.

I think about 800 Indians were camped at the head of Beaver, at the Point of Rocks on the Beaver, which is about 120 miles east of Denver, composed of Arapahoes, Cheyennes, Sioux, Kiowas, Camanches and Apaches. They said that their plan was, in two or three nights, to divide into small parties of about 200, going in the neighborhood of ———, which was about 40 miles below Geary's; 100 going just above Geary's to Fort Lumpton; about 250 to the head of Cherry creek, which is 25 or 30 miles south of Denver; and the remainder of them to go to the Arkansas, at Fountaine que Bonille. That these parties were to be divided into little bands, and each take a farm-house, clean it out and steal the stock, and in this way commit the most wholesale and extensive massacre that has ever been known. I have no doubt it would have been so, but for the vigilance that was taken to prevent it.

Geary, who is an educated and sensible man, immediately took Spotted Horse, who heard these Indians give their account; it was done confidentially by them. Geary, who has been in my employ as a spy over the Indians, who has been out among them as a messenger, started the next morning—they got to his house about midnight, or 2 o'clock. Geary started immediately in the morning with Spotted Horse, and got to my house at 11 o'clock; riding between 60 and 70 miles during the day, for the purpose of giving me this information. I immediately notified the district commander, and put the recruits which were supposed to be subject to my command under his command, by an order; and any militia that might be organized was subject to his command for the purposes of defence. He sent express in every direction to notify the settlers. I telegraphed, and also sent messengers. It so happened that a militia company had gone down there, and were near that, and that a militia company had gone to Fort Lumpton, or near there.

The Indians came in at these different points on the second night, skulking along under the bluffs, where their trails were seen. They found the settlements all alarmed, and went back again, except at the head of Cherry creek, where they killed two or three and took quite a large number of cattle; and at Fort Lumpton they killed one man. And before Geary got back they stole some of his horses and the horses of one or two of his neighbors, and ran them off.

Question. At what time was this?

Answer. It must have been early in August.

Question. At what time was this hundred-days regiment organized?

Answer. Early in September.

Question. At what time was it mounted?

Answer. Some companies were mounted before the regiment was full; others were mounted subsequently, as they could get horses.

Question. How were horses obtained, and from whom?

Answer. The quartermaster of the department.

Question. Do you know anything further than you have stated in connexion with this attack upon Black Kettle and his band on Sand creek? Did you issue any orders, or take any part in any transaction having in view any such attack?

Answer. I did not know anything about it. After I got here, I got a letter from the secretary of the territory, saying it was rumored they were going there.

Question. Whom did "they" refer to?

Answer. Colonel Chivington and his force. I think he said it was surmised that they were going to Fort Lyon. It is proper for me to say that I understood they were going to make an expedition against the Indians. But I had no knowledge of where they were going.

Question. After Major Wynkoop left you in September, do you know what was done with these Indians?

Answer. I do not.

Question. Do you know what action the Indians took afterwards?

Answer. I do not.

Question. Do you know where they were encamped?

Answer. I accidentally heard—I had no official knowledge of the fact—that there were several hundred of them at Fort Lyon. The next day after this council I started for a place about 300 miles off, to hold a treaty with the Utes down on the Rio Grande, and was gone nearly a month.

Question. At what time did you start to come east?

Answer. I think I started on the 15th of November.

Question. Is Colonel Shoup yet in service?

Answer. No, sir; when I came away he was encamped at Bijou Basin, about 75 miles east of Denver, where they had been for a considerable length of time.

Question. How did he get out of the service?

Answer. His time expired, and he was regularly mustered out, so I understand.

Question. You have not been back since?

Answer. No, sir.

Question. Was there any property accounted for to you, or to any officer of the government, so far as you know, that was taken at Black Kettle's camp?

Answer. Not any. I would say, however, that any property the army captured they would not be likely to turn over to me.

I was asked if I knew of any depredations committed by these Indians, and I stated what was done in 1862. Before going further, I will say, that Black Kettle told me in that council that he and White Antelope had been opposed to depredations all the time, but could not control their tribes. They admitted that their tribes, that the Arapahoes and Sioux, had made a large number of attacks, and told me where each depredation I inquired about had been committed by the different tribes.

I gave to the committee of investigation on Indian affairs, the other day, a sketch of the minutes kept of that council. There was quite a large number of these depredations referred to and inquired of in that council, but not by any means all the depredations that were committed last summer.

The Cheyennes commenced their depredations early in the spring with the Arapahoes, Kiowas, Comanches, and Sioux. Agreeably to a previous treaty or council held by them in the winter of 1863 and 1864—which treaty was the consummation of an arrangement that the Sioux tried to make with our Indians in 1863, which I reported to the Indian bureau, and they sent me out authority to treat with them—I went to the head of the Republican, and spent about a month there trying to get them together, having my messengers out. Little Geary went to the camp of Bull Bear, Black Kettle, White Antelope, and a large number of others. The report of this attempt is published in my annual report for 1863.

The result of that failure was, that they told Mr. Geary, after agreeing first to come and see me, that they had made up their minds to have nothing more to do with us; that they did not want any more of our goods; that they might as well be killed as starved to death; that they were being driven out of their country by the whites; that they repudiated the treaty of Fort Wise, under which we were making preparations to settle them, as you will see by looking into my report, in which I give Geary's sworn statement.

After coming back a portion of these Indians ran together. You will observe that they made the treaty of 1861 together. A portion of them commenced committing depredations that fall. They stole a lot of horses, a portion of which we recovered in the autumn. A man who was present at their "big medicine" on the Arkansas, by the name of North, came to me privately and secretly from this band of Indians that committed depredations in November, 1863, within about twenty miles of Denver; he came to me from their camp, and made a statement which I forwarded to the War Department and to the Indian bureau, which is also in my annual report for this year.

North told me that the Kiowas, Comanches, Apaches, Cheyennes, a portion of the Arapahoes, and the Sioux, had held a council, at which he was present, and shook hands over it. That they would pretend to be friendly with the whites until they could get sufficient ammunition; then in the spring they would divide into little parties and commence a war on the whites. Early last spring the first depredation they committed was to steal one hundred and seventy-five head of cattle, which was done by the Cheyennes, from Irwin & Jackman, government contractors, for transportation across the plains. Irwin & Jackman's men followed them about twenty miles down Sand creek, until they struck off to the head of the Republican. They then came to Denver and reported to the military commander, Colonel Chivington, and requested a force to go with them to recover their cattle. That force was sent out, and after being gone a week or two they returned, having recovered about a dozen of the cattle, one soldier having been wounded. He returned for the want of subsistence, and was sent again, and went through to Fort Larned on the route. That was Lieutenant Ayres, and during the time he was gone he had a battle with the Indians, in which they drove him. They attacked him as he was passing through with his battery to Fort Larned, which is in Kansas. At that battle one of the Indians, who was said to be a very friendly Indian to the whites, was killed. He was said to be in favor of making peace, and preventing the battle, and was in the act of trying to pacify the Indians when he was shot. But Lieutenant Ayres's report has never been furnished to me, and consequently I cannot give the details of it; but this was the statement the lieutenant made when he got back. He got away from the Indians without being captured. They were in very large force. He got away and got to Fort Larned. That is the end of the effort to get back these cattle. He and the rest of his battery—he had a section of a battery, I think, two guns—was at Fort Larned for some time. But the commander there, who was said to be an intemperate man, was not on the alert; and the Kiowas and some other Indians, mainly Kiowas, captured the whole of the battery's horses, one hundred and forty, and ran them off right from the fort. While Satant, the commander of the Indians, was talking with the officer in command, making great professions of friendship at the time, they made this raid upon the battery's horses and got away with them.

I would say still further, that to give a description of all the depredations that were committed during the summer, and fall, and this winter, would require a statement which would be very extensive. I would like this, as there is an impression in the minds of people here that the Indian war out there has not amounted to much—I would like this, that this committee, for the purpose of ascertaining, would deputize somebody to gather the reports of the attacks, the number of people killed, and the amount of property destroyed during the past year.

By Mr. Gooch:

Question. With all the knowledge you have in relation to these attacks and depredations by the Indians, do you think they afford any justification for the attack made by Colonel Chivington on these friendly Indians, under the circumstances under which it was made?

Answer. As a matter of course, no one could justify an attack on Indians while under the protection of the flag. If those Indians were there under the protection of the flag, it would be a question that would be scarcely worth asking, because nobody could say anything in favor of the attack. I have heard, however—that is only a report—that there was a statement on the part of Colonel Chivington and his friends that these Indians had assumed a hostile attitude before he attacked them. I do not know whether that is so or not I have said all I have had to do with them. I supposed they were being treated as prisoners of war in some way or other.

I had a letter from General Curtis, after I got here, saying he was troubled to know what to do with so many nominal prisoners of war, as they were so expensive to feed there. The subsistence of the fort was short, and it was a long way to get subsistence, and through a hostile country, and he was troubled to know what to do with them.

Question. But from all the circumstances which you know, all the facts in relation to that matter, do you deem that Colonel Chivington had any justification for that attack?

Answer. So far as giving an opinion is concerned, I would say this: That the reports that have been made here, a great many of them, have come through persons whom I know to be personal enemies of Colonel Chivington for a long time. And I would rather not give an opinion on the subject until I have heard the other side of the question, which I have not heard yet.

Question. I do not ask for an opinion. Do you know of any circumstance which would justify that attack?

Answer. I do not know of any circumstance connected with it subsequent to the time those Indians left me and I started for another part of the country. It is proper for me to say, that these attacks during the summer, and up to the time I came away, were of very frequent occurrence. The destruction of property was very great. Our people suffered wonderfully, especially in their property, and in their loss of life. They murdered a family some twenty-odd miles east of Denver. The attacks by hostile Indians, about the time I came away, were very numerous along the Platte. There was an attack as I came in, about the month of November. It was in the evening, about sundown, and I passed over the ground in the night in the stage with my family, and a few days afterwards a party of emigrants, returning from Colorado, were murdered near the same ground, which was near Plum creek; and for a considerable length of time, immediately after I came in, the attacks were very numerous and very violent, until the stage was interrupted so that it has not been running since, until within a few days.

I started home and could not get there because there was no transportation. I came back here and shall return in a few days again. I mention this in order to do away with the impression that might exist that hostilities had ceased, and that this attack of Colonel Chivington had excited the recent hostilities.

These Indians told me, when they were there, that the Sioux were in large force on the head of the Republican, and would make an attack about the time I expected to come in. I delayed my coming in a short time on account of what they told me, and when I did come in I found some Indians commencing their depredations, which they continued about the month following, both before and after the attack made by Colonel Chivington. General Curtis wrote to me that he did not think Chivington's attack was the instigation of the hostilities perpetrated along the Platte.

Testimony of Mr. A. C. Hunt.

WASHINGTON, *March* 15, 1865.

Mr. A. C. HUNT sworn and examined.

By Mr. Loan:

Question. Where do you reside?

Answer. I reside at Denver, Colorado.

Question. What is your official position?

Answer. I am United States marshal for the district of Colorado. I have been in Denver since 1859.

Question. Do you know anything in connexion with the killing of the Indians at Sand creek, about the last of November, 1864?

Answer. I do not suppose I know anything that would be admissible as evidence. All I know is from general rumor, not being on the ground at all. I was in Denver when the regiment returned.

Question. Did you hear anything about it from Colonel Chivington, or any one of his command?

Answer. I heard an immense sight from soldiers in his command.

Question. State what they told you.

Answer. I also talked a long time with the guide, James Beckwith, after they returned.

Question. State anything that was said by any one connected with that transaction in regard to what was done.

Answer. I talked longer with Melrose, a private in Captain Baxtor's company, under Colonel Shoup. He gave me quite a history of the fight, and everything pertaining to it. He enlisted from the Arkansas. There is a general disposition, on the part of those who enlisted from that neighborhood, to cry down the whole transaction as being very badly managed, and very murderous. They made no secret of telling what had been done, but made no boast of it at all. They said they were heartily ashamed of it.

Question. State what they said was done.

Answer. According to their understanding, when they started out, they were enlisted for the purpose of fighting hostile Indians, there being any quantity of them on the plains. They knew nothing of their whereabouts. They went under the orders of Colonel Chivington, who led the command. They came within 80 miles of Fort Lyon, where they were halted for some days, and all communication stopped. No person, not even the United States mail, was permitted to go down the road for quite a length of time, until the forces which had been straggling back had all been collected together. When they did march to Fort Lyon they went very rapidly, taking every person about the fort by surprise, no person anticipating their coming at all. Their first movement was to throw a guard around the fort. That surprised the soldiers very much; they said they did not know the object of it. That night they were ordered to march again in a northeast direction. I think that and perhaps the next night they marched some 35 miles to fall upon this camp of Indians on Sand creek. None of the soldiers were posted as to what Indians they were fighting, or anything about it, until they got an explanation, after the attack was made, from various white men in the camp. Those white men told the soldiers that they were Black Kettle's band, who had been there for some time; a part of the time had been drawing rations from the fort—were, to all intents and purposes, friendly Indians. Beyond that I know that the colonel, as soon as the fight was over, came back to Denver. I met him the day he came in. The command afterwards returned in marching time. They had evidences of what they had been doing—among the rest, White Antelope's medal; I think they had about 20 of Black Kettle's scalps—quite that many, I think, were exhibited; they had White Antelope's commission, or something like that, from Commissioner Dole—something like a recommend; they had a thousand and one trophies in the way of finely worked buffalo robes, spurs, and bits, and things of that kind; all of which, I suppose, was contraband of war—they were taken on the field of battle.

Question. Did they say anything about how the attack was made, at what time, and under what circumstances?

Answer. I understood them to say it was made just at daylight. The Indians that were not armed almost all fled and escaped. The impression of the men I talked with was that they had killed over 100 of them; the impression of some others was that they had killed 400 or 500.

Question. Was anything said about killing women and children?

Answer. Yes, sir; they killed everything alive in the camp that they could get at. I believe that was part of the understanding, that none should be spared. I believe it is generally the understanding that you fight Indians in that way.

Question. What were those ornamented buffalo robes worth in the market?

Answer. They are very valuable—worth from $20 to $50 each.

Question. In whose possession did you see them?

Answer. They were most y in private hands—in the hands of the men who were in the fight; by permission, I suppose. I do not suppose there was any demand made for them by any person. I suppose each man who had one of them thought he was entitled to it.

Question. Is that the rule out there, that the soldiers of the United States are entitled to all they capture?

Answer. That is the only battle they have ever had; so that I do not know as there is any particular rule about that matter.

Question. How long did they say the fight continued?

Answer. I am under the impression now that they said it continued some two or three hours. That is my impression from the representations made by the parties engaged in the fight.

Question. How many Indians did they say were engaged in the fight?

Answer. It has been estimated that there were from 500 to 3,000 there. I suppose the agent knows almost exactly how many there were of them. They judge from the lodges, and there are from five to six in a lodge, so far as my experience goes. From the best information I could get there were from 100 to 120 lodges there.

Question. Was there anything said about the number that escaped?

Answer. A large proportion of them escaped; that was the supposition of the soldiers I talked with.

Question. In what way, on horseback or on foot?

Answer. Those of the warriors who had horses that they could get hold of escaped on horseback. The women and young ones, who had no horses, went on foot.

Question. Did they take any prisoners in that fight?

Answer. I never heard of any prisoners being taken that were brought in.

Question. Do you know whether they captured any property from the Indians?

Answer. I think they were possessed of no property except what I have mentioned.

Question. Did they have no horses, ponies, and mules?

Answer. Yes, sir; I saw a great many ponies. A New Mexican company was mostly mounted on ponies that they had captured. I saw them come in on Indian horses; they were poor, thin horses.

Question. Did you hear Colonel Chivington himself say anything about that transaction?

Answer. No, sir, except in a public speech he made afterwards, and in that he did not say much about it.

Question. Did he assign any reason why, under the circumstances, he attacked that band of Indians?

Answer. He said all the time that they were hostile Indians, and was very wroth with any of the community who knew anything about the Indians, who had been in the country a long while, who knew something about Black Kettle and White Antelope, and who denominated them friendly Indians, and who differed with him as to the policy of bringing those Indians down upon us at that time. He was very wroth with me particularly, and one or two others; and I suppose that was what brought forth the remarks that he made.

Question. What was his policy?

Answer. To exterminate the Indians.

Question. To kill them all?

Answer. Yes, sir, I should judge so; and that seemed to be quite a popular notion too.

Question. Did you have any means of knowing the reputation of Black Kettle and White Antelope?

Answer. We have always regarded Black Kettle and White Antelope as the special friends of the white man ever since I have been in the country.

Question. Do you know of any acts of hostility committed by them, or with their consent?

Answer. No, sir; I do not.

Question. Did you ever hear any acts of hostility attributed to them by any one?

Answer. No, sir.

By Mr. Gooch:

Question. Is there a general feeling among the whites there in favor of the extermination of the Indians?

Answer. That feeling prevails in all new countries where the Indians have committed any depredations. And most especially will people fly off the handle in that way when you exhibit the corpse of some one who has been murdered by the Indians. When they come to their sober senses they reflect that the Indians have feelings as well as we have, and are entitled to certain rights; which, by the by, they never get.

Question. Had there been any such acts committed by the Indians at that time?

Answer. No, sir; not for months. But last summer there were exhibitions that were horrid to tell, and there were terrible imprudences in consequence. Persons killed thirty or forty miles off were brought into Denver and exhibited there.

Question. There had been nothing of that kind for some time previous to this attack by Colonel Chivington?

Answer. No, sir.

Question. Do you know of any motive which actuated Colonel Chivington in making this attack?

Answer. It may be invidious in me to give my idea of his motive. I was entirely satisfied that his motive was not a good and virtuous one—so much so, that when I was where he stopped his command I wrote a letter to Judge Bennett, giving him my views about the matter, and telling him what I thought was his object. We regarded those Indians on the reservation as safe, and ought not to be attacked. That opinion, perhaps, was not shared by the community, though I presume the great majority of the command were aware of the Indians they were going to kill.

Question. If you have no objection, I would like you to state what you think was his motive.

Answer. I think it was hope of promotion. He had read of Kit Carson, General Harney, and others, who had become noted for their Indian fighting. I have no objection to state that.

Mr. Gooch. The reason why I ask these questions is, that this attack seems to us to be of such a character that we are anxious to ascertain, if possible, what could have been the motive which actuated an officer to make such an attack under the circumstances.

The witness. I have no doubt that what I have stated was one motive.

Papers submitted by Hon. H. P. Bennet, delegate in Congress from Colorado Territory.

WASHINGTON CITY, *March* 20, 1865.

SIR: I am compelled to leave to-night for New York, to be gone several days, and it will likely be impossible for me to appear before the committee at all. But, as you requested, I will furnish the committee with such official and unofficial documents as I have touching upon the "Sand creek affair."

Herewith enclosed please find the official reports of all the principal officers engaged in the transaction; also, a copy of Governor Evans's proclamation, after which the one-hundred-day regiment was raised; also, some slips cut from the "Rocky Mountain News," the organ of Governor Evans, and edited by the postmaster at Denver; also, find an extract from Secretary Elbert's message made to the legislature and published in the "Rocky Mountain News." All the foregoing papers I believe to be genuine copies of what they purport to be.

Very respectfully,

H. P. BENNET.

Hon. Mr. GOOCH.

Proclamation by Governor Evans, of Colorado Territory.

PROCLAMATION.

Having sent special messengers to the Indians of the plains, directing the friendly to rendezvous at Fort Lyon, Fort Larned, Fort Laramie, and Camp Collins for safety and protection, warning them that all hostile Indians would be pursued and destroyed, and the last of said messengers having now returned, and the evidence being conclusive that most of the Indian tribes of the plains are at war and hostile to the whites, and having to the utmost of my ability endeavored to induce all of the Indians of the plains to come to said places of rendezvous, promising them subsistence and protection, which, with a few exceptions, they have refusedto do:

Now, therefore, I, John Evans, governor of Colorado Territory, do issue this my proclamation, authorizing all citizens of Colorado, either individually or in such parties as they may organize, to go in pursuit of all hostile Indians on the plains, scrupulously avoiding those who have responded to my said call to rendezvous at the points indicated; also, to kill and destroy, as enemies of the country, wherever they may be found, all such hostile Indians. And further, as the only reward I am authorized to offer for such services, I hereby empower such citizens, or parties of citizens, to take captive, and hold to their own private use and benefit, all the property of said hostile Indians that they may capture, and to receive for all stolen property recovered from said Indians such reward as may be deemed proper and just therefor.

I further offer to all such parties as will organize under the militia law of the Territory for the purpose to furnish them arms and ammunition, and to present their accounts for pay as regular soldiers for themselves, their horses, their subsistence, and transportation, to Congress, under the assurance of the department commander that they will be paid.

The conflict is upon us, and all good citizens are called upon to do their duty for the defence of their homes and families.

In testimony whereof, I have hereunto set my hand and caused the great seal of the Territory of Colorado to be affixed this 11th day of August, A. D. 1864.

[SEAL.] JOHN EVANS.

By the governor:

S. H. ELBERT, *Secretary of Colorado Territory.*

OFFICIAL REPORTS OF OFFICERS ENGAGED IN THE AFFAIR OF SANDY CREEK, PUBLISHED IN THE ROCKY MOUNTAIN NEWS.

First report of Colonel Chivington.

HEADQUARTERS DISTRICT OF COLORADO,
In the field, on Big Bend of Sandy Creek, Col. Ter., Nov. 29, 1864.

SIR: I have not the time to give you a detailed history of our engagement of to-day, or to mention those officers and men who distinguished themselves in one of the most bloody Indian battles ever fought on these plains. You will find enclosed the report of my surgeon in charge, which will bring to many anxious friends the sad fate of loved ones who are and have been risking everything to avenge the horrid deeds of those savages we have so severely handled. We made a forced march of forty miles, and surprised, at break of day, one of the most powerful villages of the Cheyenne nation, and captured over five hundred animals; killing the celebrated chiefs One Eye, White Antelope, Knock Kno, Black Kettle, and Little Robe, with about five hundred of their people, destroying all their lodges and equipage, making almost an annihilation of the entire tribe.

I shall leave here, as soon as I can see our wounded safely on the way to the hospital at Fort Lyon, for the villages of the Sioux, which are reported about eighty miles from here, on the Smoky Hill, and three thousand strong; so look out for more fighting. I will state, for the consideration of gentlemen who are opposed to fighting these red scoundrels, that I was shown, by my chief surgeon, the scalp of a white man taken from the lodge of one of the chiefs, which could not have been more than two or three days taken; and I could mention many more things to show how these Indians, who have been drawing government rations at Fort Lyon, are and have been acting.

Very respectfully, your obedient servant,

J. M. CHIVINGTON,
Col. Comd'g Colorado Expedition against Indians on Plains.

CHAS. WHEELER, A. A. A. G.,
Headquarters District of Colorado, Denver.

Second report of Colonel Chivington.

HEADQUARTERS DISTRICT OF COLORADO,
Denver, C. T., December 16, 1864.

GENERAL: I have the honor to transmit the following report of operations of the Indian expedition under my command, of which brief notice was given you by my telegram of November 29, 1864:

Having ascertained that the hostile Indians had proceeded south from the Platte, and were almost within striking distance of Fort Lyon, I ordered Colonel Geo. L. Shoup, 3d regiment Colorado volunteer cavalry, (100-day service,) to proceed with the mounted men of his regiment in that direction.

On the 20th of November I left Denver and Booneville, C. T.; on the 24th of November joined and took command in person of the expedition which had been increased by a battalion of the 1st cavalry of Colorado, consisting of detachments of companies C, E and H. I proceeded with the utmost caution down the Arkansas river, and on the morning of the 28th instant arrived at Fort Lyon, to the surprise of the garrison of that post. On the same morning I resumed my march, being joined by Major Scott J. Anthony, 1st cavalry of Colorado, with one hundred and twenty-five men of said regiment, consisting of detachments of companies D, G and H, with two howitzers. The command then proceeded in a northeasterly direction, travelling all night, and at daylight of the 29th November striking Sand creek about forty (40) miles from Fort Lyon.

Here was discovered an Indian village of one hundred and thirty (130) lodges, composed of Black Kettle's band of Cheyennes and eight (8) lodges of Arapahoes, with Left Hand. My line of battle was formed with Lieutenant Wilson's battalion of the 1st regiment, numbering about 125 men, on the right, Colonel Shoup's 3d regiment, numbering about 450 men, in the centre, and Major Anthony's battalion, numbering 125 men, 1st regiment, on the left.

The attack was immediately made upon the Indian's camp by Lieutenant Wilson, who dashed forward, cutting the enemy off from their herd, and driving them out of their camp, which was subsequently destroyed.

The Indians, numbering from 900 to 1,000, though taken by surprise, speedily rallied and formed a line of battle across the creek, about three-fourths of a mile above the village, stubbornly contesting every inch of ground.

The commands of Colonel Shoup and Major Anthony pressed rapidly forward and attacked the enemy sharply, and the engagement became general, we constantly driving the Indians, who fell back from one position to another for five miles, and finally abandoned resistance and dispersed in all directions and were pursued by my troops until nightfall.

It may, perhaps, be unnecessary for me to state that I captured no prisoners. Between five and six hundred Indians were left dead upon the field. About five hundred and fifty ponies, mules and horses were captured, and all their lodges were destroyed, the contents of which has served to supply the command with an abundance of trophies, comprising the paraphernalia of Indian warfare and life. My loss was eight (8) killed on the field and forty (40) wounded, of which two have since died. Of the conduct of the 3d regiment (100-day service) I have to say that they well sustained the reputation of our Colorado troops for bravery and effectiveness; were well commanded by their gallant young Colonel, Geo. L. Shoup, ably assisted by Lieutenant Colonel L. L. Bowen, Major Hal Sayr and Captain Theodore G. Cree, commanding 1st, 2d and 3d battalions of that regiment

Of the conduct of the two battalions of the 1st regiment I have but to remark that they sustained their reputation as second to none, and were ably handled by their commanders, Major Anthony, Lieutenant Wilson and Lieutenant Clark Dunn, upon whom the command devolved after the disability of Lieutenant Wilson from wounds received.

Night coming on, the pursuit of the flying Indians was of necessity abandoned, and my command encamped within sight of the field.

On the 1st instant, having sent the wounded and dead to Fort Lyon, the first to be cared for, and the latter to be buried upon our own soil. I resumed the pursuit in the direction of Camp Wynkoop on the Arkansas river, marching all night of the 3d and 4th instant, in hopes of overtaking a large encampment of Arapahoes and Cheyennes, under Little Raven, but the enemy had been apprized of my advance, and on the morning of the 5th instant, at 3 o'clock, precipitately broke camp and fled. My stock was exhausted. For one hundred miles the snow had been two feet deep, and for the previous fifteen days—excepting on November 29 and 30—the marches had been forced and incessant.

Under these circumstances, and the fact of the time of the 3d regiment being nearly out, I determined for the present to relinquish the pursuit.

Of the effect of the punishment sustained by the Indians you will be the judge. Their chiefs Black Kettle, White Antelope, One Eye, Knock Knee, and Little Robe, were numbered with the killed and their bands almost annihilated. I was shown the scalp of a white man, found in one of the lodges, which could not have been taken more than two or three days previous. For full particulars and reports of the several commanders I respectfully refer you to the following copies herewith enclosed, of Colonel George L. Shoup, 3d regiment, December 6, 1864; Colonel Shoup, 3d regiment, December 7, 1864; Colonel L. L. Bowen, 3d regiment, November 30, 1864; Major Hal Sayr, 3d regiment, December 6, 1864; Captain Theodore G. Cree, 3d regiment, December 6, 1864; Major Scott J. Anthony, 1st regiment, December 1, 1864; Lieutenant Clark Dunn, 1st regiment, November 30, 1864; Lieutenant J. J. Kennedy, November 30, 1864.

If all the companies of the 1st cavalry of Colorado and the 11th Ohio volunteer cavalry, stationed at camps and posts near here, were ordered to report to me, I could organize a campaign, which, in my judgment, would effectually rid the country between the Platte and Arkansas rivers of these red rebels.

I would respectfully request to be informed, if another campaign should be authorized from here, whether I could employ one or two hundred friendly Utes, (Indians,) furnishing them subsistence, arms and ammunition for the campaign.

* * * * * * * * *

I am, general, very respectfully, your obedient servant,

J. M. CHIVINGTON,

Col. 1st Cavalry of Colorado, Commanding District of Colorado.

First report of Colonel Shoup.

HEADQUARTERS THIRD COLORADO CAVALRY,
In field, 100 miles below Fort Lyon, December 6, 1864.

CAPTAIN: In answer to your communication of this date, asking me to consult with the officers of my regiment, and report their opinion as to the propriety and willingness of themselves and the enlisted men under my command to continue this expedition against the Indians to the Smoky Hill and Republican, I have to say—

My "officers and men" will obey orders and go to the Smoky Hill and Republican, if the colonel commanding, after due deliberation, will so order. However, they are nearly all of the opinion, (the officers,) that an expedition to the above named streams at present must fail. This opinion is based upon the fact that their horses are worn out, and in an unserviceable condition; most of the animals would fail on the first forced march.

They are of the further opinion that many of these men will re-enlist to prosecute this campaign if we meet with no reverse and the men are not worn out and disheartened in a fruitless march just before the expiration of their term of enlistment.

All the above is fully indorsed by me; and while I am more than eager to duplicate the great victory of November 29, I think an expedition to the Smoky Hill and Republican, considering the worn-out condition of my horses, would prove more of a disaster than a success, at present; the failure of which would so dishearten my men, that no inducement could be held out that would cause them to re-enlist. All of which is most respectfully submitted.

GEORGE L. SHOUP,
Colonel 3d Colorado Cavalry.

Captain J. S. MAYNARD,
A. A. A. General, District of Colorado, in the field.

Second report of Colonel Shoup.

HEADQUARTERS DISTRICT OF COLORADO,
In the field, December 7, 1864.

DEAR SIR: I have the honor to report the part taken by my regiment, 3d Colorado cavalry, in the engagement with the Indians on Sand creek, forty (40) miles north of Fort Lyon, Colorado Territory, November 29, 1864.

I brought my regiment into action at sunrise. The first order given was to Captain John McCannon, company I, to cut off the Indians from their ponies on the south side of the village; this order was obeyed with great celerity and success. Captain McCannon captured about two hundred (200) ponies at the first dash, but being closely pressed by hundreds of Indians, sent the ponies to the rear, and opened a terrible and withering fire on the Indians, completely checking them, killing many, and causing them to retreat up Sand creek.

Captain O. H. P. Baxter, with his company G, was sent to re-enforce Captain McCannon. The two companies then fought the Indians up the south side of the creek for about two (2) miles, and at this point many of the Indians took refuge in the banks of the creek, where they had prepared rifle-pits. Captain McCannon, with his company, remained at that place until late in the afternoon, and was the last to leave the field of battle. His brave company killed twenty-six (26) Indians in one pit, and must have killed fifty (50) or more during the engagement. Company G, led by Captain Baxter and Lieutenant Templeton, pursued the demoralized and flying savages to the south and west, killing upwards of twenty Indians. Lieutenant W. E. Grinnell, with a detachment of 21 men of company K, fought during part of the engagement on the southwest side of the battle-field. This brave little detachment deserve honorable mention for their gallant conduct on the field. They lost one-fifth of their number, killed and wounded. At the opening of the engagement I led about four hundred (400) of my men up the north side of the creek and engaged the main body of the Indians, who were retreating to the west. I dismounted my men and fought them for some time on foot.

At this point Captain Talbott, of company M, fell severely wounded, while bravely leading his men in a charge on a body of Indians who had taken refuge on the banks on the north side of the creek. Here a terrible hand-to-hand encounter ensued between the Indians and Captain Talbott's men and others who had rushed forward to their aid—the Indians trying to secure the scalp of Captain Talbott. I think the hardest fighting of the day occurred at that point, some of our men fighting with club muskets; the 1st and 3d Coloradoans fighting side by side, each trying to excel in bravery, and each ambitious to kill at least one Indian. Many valuable lives of officers and men were saved by the bravery of others just as the fatal knife was raised to perform its work of death. Early in the engagement, Captain Nickols, with his company D, pursued a band of Indians that were trying to escape to the northeast; he overtook and punished them severely, killing twenty-five or thirty and captured some ponies.

Other companies of my regiment fought with zeal and bravery, but after 10 o'clock a. m. the battle became so general and covered so wide a field that it became necessary to divide my command into small detachments, sending them in all directions to pursue the flying Indians.

I am told by my officers and men that some of their comrades engaged the Indians in close combat. I am satisfied, from my own observation, that the historian will search in vain for braver deeds than were committed on that field of battle.

My loss is nine (9) men killed, one missing, supposed to be killed, and forty-four (44) wounded.

Captain Presley Talbott and Lieutenant C. H. Hawley are the only officers wounded of my regiment; Captain Talbott in left side, and Lieutenant Hawley in shoulder.

Enclosed herewith you will find copy of the reports of my battalion commanders to me. Aell of which is most respectfully submitted.

I am, sir, with great respect, your obedient servant,

GEORGE L. SHOUP,
Colonel 3d Colorado Cavalry.

Colonel J. M. CHIVINGTON, *Commanding District of Colorado.*

Report of Lieutenant Colonel Bowen.

SANDY CREEK, *November* 30, 1864.

SIR: I have the honor to enclose you the reports of the company commanders of the first battalion, commanded by myself, in the action of yesterday. I fully indorse all contained in these reports; all behaved well, each vieing with the other as to who could do the enemy the most injury. This, I think, can truly be said of the whole regiment. I was in position during the action to see most of the regiment, and did not see one coward. Permit me to congratulate you upon the signal punishment meted out to the savages on yesterday, "who so ruthlessly have murdered our women and children," in the language of the colonel commanding, although I regret the loss of so many brave men. The third regiment cannot any longer be called the "bloodless third."

From the most reliable information, from actual count and positions occupied, I have no doubt that at least one hundred and fifty Indians were killed by my battalion.

I cannot speak in terms of too high praise of all the officers and men under my command.

The war flag of this band of Cheyennes is in my possession, presented by Stephen Decatur, commissary sergeant of company C, who acted as my battalion adjutant.

Very respectfully,

LEAVITT L. BOWEN,
Lieut. Col. 3d Colorado Cavalry, Commanding 1st Battalion.

Colonel GEORGE L. SHOUP,
Third Regiment Colorado Cavalry.

Report of Major Sayr.

CAMP ———, *December* 6, 1864.

SIR: I have the honor to submit the following report of the part taken by my battalion in the action of November 29, on Sand creek. The battalion consisted of company B, Captain H. M. Orahood, First Lieutenant Charles H. Hawley, Second Lieutenant Harry Richmond, and sixty-four men; company I, Captain John McCannon, First Lieutenant Thomas J. Davis, and fifty-three men; company G, Captain O. H. P. Baxter, Second Lieutenant A. J. Templeton, and forty men; company K, Lieutenant W. E. Grinnell, and twenty-one men; making a total of 178 men. Company I was sent at the beginning of the action to the west of the field, where they remained during the day, much of the time sustaining a heavy fire from the enemy, who were secreted under a high bank, on the south side of Sand creek. This company did good service in preventing the escape of the Indians to the west. Companies B, G, and K, moved across the creek and went into the action on the north side of the creek and west of the Indian town, where they remained for several hours, doing good service, while under a heavy fire from the enemy, who were concealed in rifle-pits in the bed of the creek.

The action became general, and lasted from 6.30 a. m. until 1 p. m., when the companies divided into small squads and went in pursuit of the Indians, who were now flying in every direction across the plains, and were pursued until dark.

Both officers and men conducted themselves bravely. The number of Indians killed by the battalion, as estimated by company commanders, is about 175 to

200. Company B, Lieutenant Hawley, wounded in shoulder; private Marrion wounded in thigh; company I, three killed and three wounded; company G, none killed or wounded; company K, two killed and two wounded; making a total of five killed and seven wounded.

Hoping the above will meet your approval, I am, colonel, very respectfully, &c.,

HAL. SAYR,
Major Commanding 2d Battalion, 3d Colorado Cavalry.

Colonel GEORGE L. SHOUP,
Commanding Third Colorado Cavalry.

Report of Captain Cree.

CAMP SKEDADDLE, *December* 6, 1864.

SIR: I have the honor to report to you the part taken by the third battalion in the fight of the 29th of November. They first formed on the left of the regiment, in the rear of the village, then removed upon the right bank of the creek, near one-half mile; there dismounted and fought the red-skins about an hour, where the boys behaved like veterans.

After finding that we had done all the good that we could do there, removed companies D and E, (company F having gone with Colonel Bowen's battalion,) and moved to the right, across the hill, for the purpose of killing Indians that were making their escape to the right of the command, in which movement we succeeded in killing many. I then made a detail from company D, of fifteen (15) men, and sent them to capture some twenty (20) ponies, which I could see some four (4) miles to the right of the village; but before they reached the ponies some twenty Indians attacked them, when a fierce fight ensued, in which private McFarland was killed in a hand-to-hand engagement; but, like true soldiers, they stood their ground, killing five (5) Indians, and wounding several others.

The Indians finding it rather warm to be healthy, left. The boys pursued them some eight or ten miles, and finding that they could not overtake them, returned, bringing with them the ponies they were sent for. I then returned with the command to the village to take care of their killed and wounded companions.

Company E lost one killed and one wounded; company D, two killed and one wounded.

As for the bravery displayed by any one in particular, I have no distinctions to make. All I can say for officers and men is, that they all behaved well, and won for themselves a name that will be remembered for ages to come.

The number of Indians killed by my battalion is sixty (60.)

I am, colonel, yours truly,

T. G. CREE,
Captain Commanding 3d Battalion, 3d Colorado Cavalry.

Colonel GEORGE L. SHOUP.

Report of Major Anthony.

HEADQUARTERS, IN THE FIELD,
Battalion First Colorado Cavalry, December 1, 1864.

SIR: I have the honor to report that I left Fort Lyon, Colorado Territory, with detachments from companies D, G, and H, 1st Colorado cavalry, numbering one hundred and twenty-five men, and two howitzers, and joined Colonel Chivington's brigade one mile below Fort Lyon, at 8 o'clock p. m., November 28, and proceeded with his command, on Indian expedition, in a northeasterly direction, striking Sand creek at daylight of the 29th November, forty miles from

Fort Lyon, when we came upon a herd of Indian horses, and I was sent forward with my battalion to capture stock. After proceeding about one mile we came in sight of an Indian camp, some two miles further. I immediately sent word to the colonel commanding that an Indian camp was in sight, and proceeded with my command in the direction of the camp, which I reached just before sunrise. I found Lieutenant Wilson, with a detachment of 1st Colorado cavalry, upon the right and south of the camp, and Lieutenant Dunn, with a detachment of the 1st Colorado cavalry, posted upon the west bank of Sand creek, and opposite the camp, both commands keeping up a brisk fire upon the camp. Upon my nearing the camp upon the west side I was attacked by a small force of Indians posted behind the bank of the creek, who commenced firing upon me with arrows, and who had collected on the opposite side of camp. Colonel Chivington coming up at this time with Colonel Shoup's regiment, 3d Colorado cavalry, and two howitzers, charged through the camp, driving the Indians completely out of their camp and into the creek, in holes or rifle-pits dug in the sand. The fighting now became general. The Indians fought desperately, apparently resolved to die upon that ground, but to injure us as much as possible before being killed. We fought them for about six hours, along the creek for five miles.

The loss to my command was one killed and three wounded. The loss to the entire command, ten killed and forty wounded. Lieutenant Baldwin, commanding the section of howitzers, attached to my battalion, had a fine private horse shot from under him. Seven horses were killed from my command. The loss to the Indians was about three hundred killed, some six hundred ponies, and one hundred and thirty lodges, with a large quantity of buffalo robes, and their entire camp equipage.

The camp proved to be Cheyenne and Arapahoe Indians, and numbered about 1,100 persons, under the leadership of Black Kettle, head chief of the Cheyenne tribe. Black Kettle and three other chiefs were killed.

All the command fought well, and observed all orders given them. We camped upon the ground occupied by the Indians the day before, destroyed the entire camp of the Indians, and then pushed rapidly in a southeasterly direction, in pursuit of Little Raven's camp of Arapahoes, reported to be on the Arkansas river.

I am, sir, with much respect, your obedient servant,

SCOTT J. ANTHONY,
Major First Colorado Cavalry, Commanding Battalion.

A. A. A. General Colonel CHIVINGTON'S
Brigade, Indian Expedition.

Report of Lieutenant Kennedy.

HEADQUARTERS CO. C, FIRST COLORADO CAVALRY,
Camp, South Bend of Big Sandy, November 30, 1864.

COLONEL: I have the honor to make the following report of company C, 1st cavalry of Colorado, on the expedition against the Cheyenne Indians, in pursuance of special orders from headquarters, district of Colorado, No. 132, of November 13, 1864.

I left camp Wheeler, Colorado Territory, on the 20th of November, 1864, with forty-two men of company C, 1st cavalry of Colorado, en route for Fort Lyon, Colorado Territory, a distance of two hundred and forty miles, at which place I arrived on the 28th of November, 1864. I left Fort Lyon at eight (8) o'clock p. m the same day, with thirty-five (35) men of C company, under command of First Lieutenant Luther Wilson, commanding battalion 1st cavalry of Colorado, made a march of forty miles to South Bend of Big Sandy, Colorado Territory, at which place I arrived a little after daybreak on the morning of the 29th, where we came upon a large village of hostile Cheyenne Indians, numbering from nine hundred to one thousand, which we immediately attacked; after which a general engagement ensued, which lasted until 3 o'clock p. m., in which the Indians were defeated and nearly annihilated; after which we returned to the Indian village, which we helped to destroy, and then went into camp.

I had one private, Oliver Pierson, mortally wounded, (who has since died;) two privates, August Mettze and John B. Calhoun, severely wounded; Sergeant M. H. Linnell, saddler Elias South, and privates C. J. Ballou and William Boyls, slightly wounded. And I would most respectfully acknowledge to the colonel commanding the services rendered by my platoon commanders, sergeant John C. Turner and M. H. Linnell, and recommend them for their bravery during the entire engagement.

I am, sir, very respectfully, your obedient servant,

J. J. KENNEDY,

Second Lieut. 1st Colorado Cavalry, Commanding Co. C.

Colonel J. M. CHIVINGTON,
Commanding Indian Expedition.

Report of Lieutenant Dunn.

HEADQUARTERS CO. E, FIRST COLORADO CAVALRY,
Camp South Bend of Big Sandy, C. T., November 30, 1864.

COLONEL: I have the honor to make the following report of company E, 1st cavalry of Colorado, on an expedition against Indians.

On the 25th instant I left Camp Fillmore with my company, pursuant to Special Order No. 3, headquarters, District of Colorado, dated in the field November 23, 1864. I joined the column then in the field the same evening at Spring Bottom, thirty miles distant. I continued the march the next day under command of Lieutenant Wilson, commanding battalion of the 1st cavalry of Colorado. We reached Fort Lyon, seventy miles further down the Arkansas, on the 28th instant, about noon. About 7 o'clock the same evening I started from that place with eighteen men of my company, taking three days' cooked rations on our horses, and travelled in a northeasterly course. At daylight we came in sight of a large village of hostile Indians, Cheyennes and Arapahoes, numbering nine hundred or one thousand, nearly two miles north of us. We immediately proceeded to the attack by moving down a small ravine and making a charge on the village from the north side, taking the Indians completely by surprise. They rallied immediately and the engagement became general, and lasted till afternoon, when they were utterly routed and half their number left dead on the field.

We continued the pursuit till 3 o'clock p. m., when our horses being much fatigued, and our ammunition nearly exhausted, we returned to the village, which we helped to destroy, and then went into camp for the night.

I lost no men killed, and but two wounded. Sergeant Jackson had his hip broken, and private Mull was shot through the leg.

I am, sir, very respectfully, your obedient servant,

CLARK DUNN,

Second Lieut. 1st Colorado Cavalry, Commanding Co. E.

Colonel CHIVINGTON,
First Colorado Cavalry.

Editorial articles from the Rocky Mountain News, the organ of Governor Evans, and edited by Mr. William N. Byers, P. M. at Denver.

THE BATTLE OF SAND CREEK.

Among the brilliant feats of arms in Indian warfare, the recent campaign of our Colorado volunteers will stand in history with few rivals, and none to exceed it in final results. We are not prepared to write its history, which can only be done by some one who accompanied the expedition, but we have gathered from those who participated in it, and from others who were in that part of the country, some facts which will doubtless interest many of our readers.

The people of Colorado are well aware of the situation occupied by the third regiment during the great snow-storm which set in the last of October. Their rendezvous was in Bijou Basin, about eighty miles southeast of this city, and close up under the foot of the Divide. That point had been selected as the base for an Indian campaign. Many of the companies reached it after the storm set in; marching for days through the driving, blinding clouds of snow and deep drifts. Once there, they were exposed for weeks to an Arctic climate, surrounded by a treeless plain covered three feet deep with snow. Their animals suffered for food and with cold, and the men fared but little better. They were insufficiently supplied with tents and blankets, and their sufferings were intense. At the end of a month the snow had settled to the depth of two feet, and the command set out upon its long contemplated march. The rear guard left the Basin on the 23d of November. Their course was southeast, crossing the Divide and thence heading for Fort Lyon. For one hundred miles the snow was quite two feet in depth, and for the next hundred it ranged from six to twelve inches. Beyond that the ground was almost bare and the snow no longer impeded their march.

On the afternoon of the 28th the entire command reached Fort Lyon, a distance of *two hundred and sixty miles, in less than six days*, and so quietly and expeditiously had the march been made that the command at the fort was taken entirely by surprise. When the vanguard appeared in sight it was reported that a body of Indians were approaching, and precautions were taken for their reception. No one upon the route was permitted to go in advance of the column, and persons who it was suspected would spread the news of the advance were kept under surveillance until all danger from that source was past.

At Fort Lyon the force was strengthened by about two hundred and fifty men of the first regiment, and at nine o'clock in the evening the command set out for the Indian village. The course was due north, and their guide was the Polar star. As daylight dawned they came in sight of the Indian camp, after a forced midnight march of forty-two miles, in eight hours, across the rough, unbroken plain. But little time was required for preparation. The forces had been divided and arranged for battle on the march, and just as the sun rose they dashed upon the enemy with yells that would put a Comanche army to blush. Although utterly surprised, the savages were not unprepared, and for a time their defence told terribly against our ranks. Their main force rallied and formed in line of battle on the bluffs beyond the creek, where they were protected by rudely constructed rifle-pits, from which they maintained a steady fire until the shells from company C's (third regiment) howitzers began dropping among them, when they scattered and fought each for himself in genuine Indian fashion. As the battle progressed the field of carnage widened until it extended over not less than twelve miles of territory. The Indians who could, escaped or secreted themselves, and by three o'clock in the afternoon the carnage had ceased. It was estimated that between three and four hundred of the savages got away with their lives. Of the balance there were neither wouned nor prisoners. Their strength at the beginning of the action was estimated at nine hundred.

Their village consisted of one hundred and thirty Cheyenne and eight Arapahoe lodges. These, with their contents, were totally destroyed. Among their effects were large supplies of flour, sugar, coffee, tea, &c. Women's and children's clothing were found; also books and many other articles which must have been taken from captured trains or houses. One white man's scalp was found which had evidently been taken but a few days before. The chiefs fought with unparalleled bravery, falling in front of their men. One of them charged alone against a force of two or three hundred, and fell pierced with balls far in advance of his braves.

Our attack was made by five battalions. The first regiment, Colonel Chivington, part of companies C, D, E, G, H and K, numbering altogether about two hundred and fifty men, was divided into two battalions; the first under command of Major Anthony, and the second under Lieutenant Wilson, until the latter was disabled, when the command devolved upon Lieutenant Dunn. The three battalions of the third, Colonel Shoup, were led, respectively, by Lieutenant Colonel Bowen, Major Sayr, and Captain Cree. The action was begun by the battalion of Lieutenant Wilson, who occupied the right, and by a quick and bold movement cut off the enemy from their herd of stock. From this circumstance we gained our great advantage. A few Indians secured horses, but the great majority of them had to fight or fly on foot. Major Anthony was on the left, and the third in the centre.

Among the killed were *all* the Cheyenne chiefs, Black Kettle, White Antelope, Little Robe, Left Hand, Knock Knee, One Eye, and another, name unknown. Not a single prominent man of the tribe remains, and the tribe itself is almost annihilated. The Arapahoes probably suffered but little. It has been reported that the chief Left Hand, of that tribe, was killed, but Colonel Chivington is of the opinion that he was not. Among the stock captured were a number of government horses and mules, including the twenty or thirty stolen from the command of Lieutenant Chase at Jimmy's camp last summer.

The Indian camp was well supplied with defensive works. For half a mile along the creek there was an almost continuous chain of rifle-pits, and another similar line of works crowned the adjacent bluff. Pits had been dug at all the salient points for miles. After the battle twenty-three dead Indians were taken from one of these pits and twenty-seven from another.

Whether viewed as a march or as a battle, the exploit has few, if any, parallels. A march of 260 miles in but a fraction more than five days, with deep snow, scanty forage, and no road, is a remarkable feat, whilst the utter surprise of a large Indian village is unprecedented. In no single battle in North America, we believe, have so many Indians been slain.

It is said that a short time before the command reached the scene of battle an old squaw partially alarmed the village by reporting that a great heard of buffalo were coming. She heard the rumbling of the artillery and tramp of the moving squadrons, but her people doubted. In a little time the doubt was dispelled, but not by buffaloes.

A thousand incidents of individual daring and the passing events of the day might be told, but space forbids. We leave the task for eye-witnesses to chronicle. All acquitted themselves well, and Colorado soldiers have again covered themselves with glory.

THE FORT LYON AFFAIR.

The issue of yesterday's News, containing the following despatch, created considerable of a sensation in this city, particularly among the Thirdsters and others who participated in the recent campaign and the battle on Sand creek:

"WASHINGTON, *December* 20, 1864.

"The affair at Fort Lyon, Colorado, in which Colonel Chivington destroyed a large Indian village, and all its inhabitants, is to be made the subject of congressional investigation. Letters received from high officials in Colorado say that the Indians were killed after surrendering, and that a large proportion of them were women and children."

Indignation was loudly and unequivocally expressed, and some less considerate of the boys were very persistent in their inquiries as to who those "high officials" were, with a mild intimation that they had half a mind to "go for them." This talk about "friendly Indians" and a "surrendered" village will do to "tell to marines," but to us out here it is all bosh.

The *confessed* murderers of the Hungate family—a man and wife and their two little babes, whose scalped and mutilated remains were seen by all our citizens—were "friendly Indians," we suppose, in the eyes of these "high officials." *They* fell in the Sand creek battle.

The confessed participants in a score of other murders of peaceful settlers and inoffensive travellers upon our borders and along our roads in the past six months must have been *friendly*, or else the "high officials" wouldn't say so.

The band of marauders in whose possession were found scores of horses and mules stolen from government and from individuals; wagon loads of flour, coffee, sugar and tea, and rolls of broad cloth, calico, books, &c, robbed from freighters and emigrants on the plains; underclothes of white women and children, stripped from their murdered victims, were probably peaceably disposed toward *some* of those "high officials," but the mass of our people "can't see it."

Probably those scalps of white men, women and children, *one of them fresh, not three days taken*, found drying in their lodges, were taken in a *friendly*, playful manner; or possibly those Indian saddle-blankets trimmed with the scalps of white women, and with braids and fringes of their hair, were kept simply as mementoes of their owners' high affection for the pale face. At any rate, these delicate and tasteful ornaments could not have been taken from the heads of the wives, sisters or daughters of these "high officials."

That "surrendering" must have been the happy thought of an exceedingly vivid imagination, for we can hear of nothing of the kind from any of those who were engaged in the battle. On the contrary, the savages fought like devils to the end, and one of our pickets was killed and scalped by them the next day after the battle, and a number of others were fired upon. In one instance a party of the vidette pickets were compelled to beat a hasty retreat to save their lives, full twenty-four hours after the battle closed. This does not look much like the Indians had surrendered.

But we are not sure that an investigation may not be a good thing. It should go back of the "affair at Fort Lyon," as they are pleased to term it down east, however, and let the world know who were making money by keeping those Indians under the sheltering protection of Fort Lyon; learn who was interested in systematically representing that the Indians were friendly and wanted peace. It is unquestioned and undenied that the site of the Sand creek battle was the rendezvous of the thieving and marauding bands of savages who roamed over this country last summer and fall, and it is shrewdly suspected that somebody was all the time making a very good thing out of it. By all means let there be an investigation, but we advise the honorable congressional committee, who may be appointed to conduct it, to get their scalps insured before they pass Plum creek on their way out.

Extract from the message of Hon. S. H. Elbert, acting governor of Colorado Territory.

INDIAN WAR.

The before unbroken peace of our Territory has been disturbed, since the last spring, by an Indian war. Allied and hostile tribes have attacked our frontier settlements, driven in our settlers, destroyed their homes, attacked, burned, and plundered our freight and emigrant trains, and thus suspended agricultural pursuits in portions of our country, and interrupted our trade and commerce with the States. This has for the time seriously retarded the prosperity of our Territory.

At the commencement of the war the general government, taxed to the utmost in subduing the rebellion, was unable to help us, and it became necessary to look to our own citizens for protection. They everywhere responded with patriotism and alacrity. Militia companies were organized in the frontier counties, and secured local protection. Much credit is due to Captain Tyler's company of militia for the important service they rendered in opening and protecting our line of communication with the States.

In response to the call of the governor for a regiment of cavalry for hundred-day service, over a thousand of our citizens—the large majority of them leaving lucrative employment—rapidly volunteered, and in that short time, despite the greatest difficulties in securing proper equipments, organized, armed, made a long and severe campaign amid the snows and storms of winter, and visited upon these merciless murderers of the plains a chastisement smiting and *deserved.* The gratitude of the country is due to the men who thus sacrificed so largely their personal interests for the public good, and rendered such important service to the Territory; and their work, if it can be followed up with a vigorous winter campaign, would result in a permanent peace.

The necessity of such a campaign, and the imperative demand for immediate and complete protection for our line of communication with the States, has been, and is now being, earnestly urged on the government at Washington, and with a prospect of success. These efforts should be seconded by your honorable body with whatever influence there may be in resolution or memorial, setting forth the facts and necessities of our situation.

PAPERS FROM THE WAR DEPARTMENT.

WAR DEPARTMENT, ADJUTANT GENERAL'S OFFICE.
Washington, March 28, 1865.

SIR: In reply to your letter of the 15th instant, addressed to the Secretary of War, I have the honor to transmit herewith copies of the orders and reports called for in relation to Indian affairs in the department of Kansas, when commanded by Major General Curtis.

I am, sir, very respectfully, your obedient servant,

E. D. TOWNSEND,
Assistant Adjutant General.

Hon. D. W. GOOCH,
Acting Chairman Committee on Conduct of the War.

COLORADO SUPERINTENDENCY,
Denver, C. T., June 16, 1864.

SIR: You will immediately make necessary arrangements for the feeding and support of all the friendly Indians of the Cheyenne and Arapahoe Indians at Fort Lyon, and direct the friendly Comanches and Kiowas, if any, to remain at Fort Larned. You will make a requisition on the military commander of the post for subsistence for the friendly Indians of his neighborhood.

If no agent there to attend to this, deputize some one to do it. These friendly bands must be collected at places of rendezvous, and all intercourse between them and tribes or individuals engaged in warfare with us prohibited; this arrangement will tend to withdraw from the conflict all who are not thoroughly identified with the hostile movement, and, by affording a safe refuge, will gradually collect those who may become tired of war and desire peace.

The war is opened in earnest, and upon your efforts to keep quiet the friendly, as nucleus for peace, will depend its duration to some extent at least. You can send word to all these to come as directed above, but do not allow the families of those at war to be introduced into the camp. I have established a camp for our northern friendly bands on Cache-la-Poudre, and as soon as my plan is approved by the military I will issue a proclamation to the Indians; please spare no effort to carry out this instruction, and keep me advised by every mail of the situation.

Very respectfully, your obedient servant,

JOHN EVANS,
Governor and Ex-Officio Superintendent Indian Affairs.

Major S. G. COLBY, *Fort Lyon, Colorado Territory.*

A true copy:

W. W. DENISON,
Second Lieutenant 1st Colorado Veteran Cavalry, and Acting Regimental Adjutant.

U. S. MILITARY TELEGRAPH.

[By Telegraph from ————————, 186—.]

To ——— ———.

George Evans to Major Colby, at Fort Lyon, instructing him to make arrangements for feeding friendly Indians near Fort Lyon. General instructions about collecting together all friendly Indians at places of rendezvous, as a measure to stop the war with the red skins. Thinks by affording refuge of this kind that those at war now may become tired, and collect at those places, and sue for peace, &c.

ADJUTANT GENERAL'S OFFICE, *March* —, 1865.

Official:

——— ———,
Assistant Adjutant General.

EXECUTIVE DEPARTMENT, COLORADO TERRITORY,
Denver, June 29, 1864.

DEAR SIR: I enclose a circular to the Indians of the plains. You will, by every means you can, get the contents to all these Indians, as many that are now hostile may come to the friendly camp, and when they all do, the war will be ended. Use the utmost economy in providing for those who come in, as the Secretary of the Interior confines me to the amount of our appropriations, and they may be exhausted before the summer is out.

You will arrange to carry out the plan of the circular at Lyon and Larned.

You will use your utmost vigilance to ascertain how many of your Indians are hostile, where they are, and what plans they propose, and report to me by every mail at least. For this purpose you will enlist the active aid of Mr. John Smith and his son, and of such other parties as you may judge can be of essential service. Mr. C. A. Cook reports to me that Mr. Bent has given you important information in regard to the plans and strength of the hostile combinations on the plains.

Please be careful and report to me in detail all the reliable information you can get promptly, as above directed.

I have the honor to be, respectfully, your obedient servant,

JNO. EVANS,
Governor Colorado Territory and Superintendent Indian Affairs.

Major S. G. COLBY,
U. S. Indian Agent, Fort Lyon, Colorado Territory.

A true copy:

W. W. DENISON,
Second Lieutenant, 1st Colorado Veteran Cavalry,
Acting Regimental Adjutant.

COLORADO SUPERINTENDENCY, INDIAN AFFAIRS,
Denver, June 27, 1864.

To the friendly Indians of the plains:

Agents, interpreters, and traders will inform the friendly Indians of the plains that some members of their tribes have gone to war with the white people; they steal stock and run it off, hoping to escape detection and punishment.

In some instances they have attacked and killed soldiers and murdered peaceable citizens. For this the Great Father is angry, and will certainly hunt them out and punish them; but he does not want to injure those who remain friendly to the whites. He desires to protect and take care of them. For this purpose I direct that all friendly Indians keep away from those who are at war, and go to places of safety.

Friendly Arapahoes and Cheyennes belonging on the Arkansas river will go to Major Colby, United States Indian agent, at Fort Lyon, who will give them provisions, and show them a place of safety. Friendly Kiowas and Comanches will go to Fort Larned, where they will be cared for in the same way.

Friendly Sioux will go to their agent at Fort Laramie for directions. Friendly Arapahoes and Cheyennes of the Upper Platte will go to Camp Collins, on the Cache-la-Poudre, where they will be assigned a place of safety, and provisions will be given them.

The object of this is to prevent friendly Indians from being killed through mistake; none but those who intend to be friendly with the whites must come to these places. The families of those who have gone to war with the whites must be kept away from among the friendly Indians.

The war on hostile Indians will be continued until they are all effectually subdued.

JOHN EVANS,
Governor of Colorado and Superintendent of Indian Affairs.

A true copy:

W. W. DENISON,
Second Lieutenant 1st Colorado Veteran Cavalry,
Acting Regimental Adjutant.

ADJUTANT GENERAL'S OFFICE, *March* —, 1865.

Official:

——— ———,
Assistant Adjutant General.

FORT RILEY, *July* 23, 1864.

Major General H. W. HALLECK:

The Indian difficulties west of this point are serious, and I have come here to rally a force on the borders to repress the mischief. The stages not coming through, we have not definite intelligence. We only know that they have run off our stock from Larned and Walnut creek, murdering some men. Small parties of Indians have come within thirty miles of this place. I have ordered the quartermaster to buy horses to mount dismounted cavalry, and requested militia colonels to call out seven hundred militia to join me. In this way I hope to raise a thousand men. I go on to Saline to-morrow. I think stealing is the main object of the Indians.

S. R. CURTIS, *Major General.*

HEADQUARTERS OF THE ARMY, *March* 18, 1865.

Official:

D. C. WAGER, *A. A. G.*

SALINE, KANSAS, *July* 26, 1864, *via Leavenworth.*

General H. W. HALLECK:

The stage has just arrived from Laramie. The damage done by Indians amounts to ten teamsters killed, five wounded, two of them scalped, and the stealing of about three hundred cattle. Our posts are safe.

S. R. CURTIS, *Major General.*

HEADQUARTERS OF THE ARMY, *March* 18, 1865.

Official:

D. C. WAGER, *A. A. G.*

FORT LEAVENWORTH, *August* 8, 1864.

Major General HALLECK, *Chief of Staff:*

I have returned from Upper Arkansas. At Larned divided my force in all directions, going myself with those scouting southward towards Red river. Could not overtake Indians, but scared them away from Santa Fé route, where stages and trains move regularly. Have made district of Upper Arkansas, assigning General Blunt to command. Have increased and improved the organization of troops, giving stringent orders against allowing Indians inside of our line. Discharged militia, and directed continual caution. The Kiowas, Comanches and Big Mouth Arapahoes are evidently determined to do all the mischief they can. I hope no favor will be offered them by authorities at Washington till they make ample remuneration for their outrages.

S. R. CURTIS,
Major General.

HEADQUARTERS ARMY, *March* 18, 1865.

Official:

D. C. WAGER, *A. A. G.*

FORT LEAVENWORTH, *August* 10, 1864.

Major General HALLECK, *Chief of Staff:*

Indians have attacked and killed inhabitants on Little Blue, this side Fort Kearney, on overland stage route. Stage just arrived at Atchison without passengers. I have requested governor to send militia after them, and telegraphed commander of Kearney to come down on them if he has force, but forces are scarce in that region. Cannot some of General Sully's command move to Nebraska?

S. R. CURTIS,
Major General.

HEADQUARTERS ARMY, *March* 18, 1865.

Official:

D. C. WAGER, *A. A. G.*

HEADQUARTERS OF THE ARMY,
Washington, D. C., August 13, 1864.

Major General CURTIS, *Fort Leavenworth:*

The contractor of the overland mail line has represented through the Post Office Department that more protection against Indians is required along the line, and that two armed men should accompany each coach. He also asks that orders be given to the military not to use the grain, forage, and stores of the line.

Please see that these requests are carried out as far as you are able.

H. W. HALLECK,
Major General and Chief of Staff.

HEADQUARTERS OF THE ARMY, *March* 18, 1865.

Official:

D. C. WAGER, *A. A. G.*

FORT LEAVENWORTH, *August* 13, 1864.

General HALLECK:

Your despatch just received, and telegraphed to General Curtis, at Omaha. The following has just been received from General Mitchell, commanding district of Nebraska, to General Curtis, Fort Leavenworth:

"Just heard from a company of militia sent up the Little Blue from Kearney. They scoured the country for forty miles up and down the stream; found no Indians. I have parties out in every direction from each post chasing Indians. Everything will be done that I can do with my present force. I am raising militia as fast as I can; the governor has authorized the raising of twelve companies. I have received to-day —— toward one company in this vicinity, of staunch men.

"B. B. MITCHELL, *Brigadier General.*"

C. S. CHARLOTTE,
Major, A. A. G., Department of Kansas.

HEADQUARTERS ARMY, *March* 18, 1865.

Official:

D. C. WAGER, *A. A. G.*

OMAHA, *August* 16, 1864.

Major General H. W. HALLECK, *Chief of Staff:*

Yours of the 13th, concerning the furnishing of escorts for overland mail line to defend it against Indians, will be complied with. I am here to look after Indian troubles that are quite extensive on the line and against the border settlements. I have troops arriving on the Blue, where the mischief was greatest. General Mitchell telegraphs from Fort Kearney that he thinks that region is threatened by a large force of Indians collecting on the Republican. I am sending out militia in small parties to join forces which I have gathered below, and will soon be upon them, be they many or few.

S. R. CURTIS, *Major General.*

HEADQUARTERS ARMY, *March* 18, 1865.

Official:

D. C. WAGER, *A. A. G.*

OMAHA, *August* 18, 1864.

Major General H. W. HALLECK:

General Mitchell telegraphs from Fort Kearney that Captain Mussey encountered five hundred well-armed Indians on Elk creek, near Republican; had a fight; killed ten Indians, and lost two soldiers; drove Indians ten miles, but had to fall back, pursued by Indians, thirty miles.

S. R. CURTIS, *Major General.*

HEADQUARTERS ARMY, *March* 18, 1865.

Official

D. C. WAGER, *A. A. G.*

DENVER, *August* 18, 1864.

Hon. EDWIN M. STANTON, *Secretary of War:*

Extensive Indian depredations, with murder of families, occurred yesterday thirty miles south of Denver. Our lines of communication are cut, and our crops, our sole dependence, are all in exposed localities, and cannot be gathered by our scattered population. Large bodies of Indians are undoubtedly near to Denver, and we are in danger of destruction both from attack of Indians and starvation. I earnestly request that Colonel Ford's regiment of 2d Colorado volunteers be immediately sent to our relief. It is impossible to exaggerate our danger. We are doing all we can for our defence.

JNO. EVANS, *Governor.*

HEADQUARTERS ARMY, *March* 18, 1865.

Official:

D. C. WAGER, *A. A. G.*

DENVER, *August* 22, 1864.

E. M. STANTON, *Secretary of War:*

No government saddles within seven hundred miles from here; no government horses to mount hundred-days regiment of cavalry, nearly full. Unlimited information of contemplated attack by a large body of Indians, in a few days, along the entire line of our settlements. Order Captain Mullin, quartermaster here, to purchase horses, and Lieutenant Hawley, district ordnance officer, to purchase horse equipments. Necessity imperative.

JNO. EVANS,
Governor of Colorado Territory.

This application should be granted at once.

J. M. CHIVINGTON,
Colonel Commanding.

HEADQUARTERS ARMY, *March* 18, 1865.

Official:

D. C. WAGER, *A. A. G.*

HEADQUARTERS OF THE ARMY,
Washington, D. C., August 23, 1864.

Governor JOHN EVANS, *Denver, Colorado Territory:*

The Secretary of War directs me to say that a recent law requires all cavalry horses to be purchased under directions of Colonel Ekin, of the quartermaster's department. If there is such a pressing necessity that purchases cannot be made in time, the military authorities can resort to impressment. General Curtis is the proper judge of such necessity in his department.

H. W. HALLECK,
Major General, Chief of Staff.

HEADQUARTERS ARMY, *March* 18, 1865.

Official:

D. C. WAGER, *A. A. G.*

DEPARTMENT OF KANSAS,
Fort Kearney, August 28, 1864.

Major General HALLECK, *Chief of Staff*:

Indians in small bands continue to commit depredations, but seem more cautious moving westward. Have effectually scoured the country east of 99th meridian. Indians going west of settlements. Overland mail agents have withdrawn stock and gone east. I think they can run through with such escorts as I can furnish. Militia very tardy in coming forward, many turning back before reaching this point.

Some fifty murders have been committed by Indians on this line, and considerable private stock stolen, but government has lost but little.

S. R. CURTIS, *Major General.*

HEADQUARTERS ARMY, *March* 18, 1865.

Official:

D. C. WAGER, *A. A. G.*

HEADQUARTERS OF THE ARMY,
Washington, D. C., September 3, 1864.

Major General CURTIS, *Fort Kearney:*

The civil officers of Montana have asked for military escort to that Territory. The Secretary of War authorizes you to give such escort, if, in your opinion, you can spare troops for that purpose; but, first of all, the overland mail route and the frontier posts require protection from the Indians.

The Secretary of War authorizes you to raise hundred-days men in Nebraska, without bounties.

H. W. HALLECK,
Major General, Chief of Staff.

HEADQUARTERS ARMY, *March* 18, 1865.

Official:

D. C. WAGER, *A. A. G.*

DENVER, *September* 7, 1864.

Hon. EDWIN M. STANTON, *Secretary of War:*

Pray give positive orders for our second Colorado cavalry to come out. Have notice published that they will come in detachments to escort trains up the Platte on certain days. Unless escorts are sent thus we will inevitably have a famine in addition to this gigantic Indian war. Flour is forty-five dollars a barrel, and the supply growing scarce, with none on the way. Through spies we got knowledge of the plan of about one thousand warriors in camp to strike our frontier settlements, in small bands, simultaneously in the night, for an extent of 300 miles. It was frustrated at the time, but we have to fear another such attempt soon. Pray give the order for our troops to come, as requested, at once, as it will be too late for trains to come this season.

JOHN EVANS, *Governor.*

HEADQUARTERS ARMY, *March* 18, 1865.

Official:

D. C. WAGER, *A. A. G.*

CAMP OF SOLOMON'S RIVER,
Via Lawrence, Kansas, September 16, 1864.

Major General HALLECK, *Chief of Staff:*

I struck this river near 100th parallel; sent scouts south to head of Saline, finding no large body of Indians. Divided command; sent large portion up valley, to strike Ofallon's bluff; with remainder, two hundred and eighty-five, came down, scouring the country on all sides. Buffalo plenty. Indians only in small parties, escaping south. Shall reach settlements on Smoky Hill river to-morrow. No signs of great concentration of Indians. Bands of hunters steal and scalp, but can be routed by small armed force. Stage stations, ranches, and settlements must have enclosures for themselves and stock, and a few troops, carefully distributed, can protect settlements and lines of commerce.

S. R. CURTIS, *Major General.*

HEADQUARTERS ARMY, *March* 18, 1865.

Official:

D. C. WAGER, *A. A. G.*

HEADQUARTERS DEPARTMENT OF KANSAS,
Fort Leavenworth, September 19, 1864.

I am in receipt of a copy of letters from the honorable Secretary of the Interior and Commissioner of Indian Affairs, with your indorsement to take such action as I may "deem best." It is stated that I have ordered the Indians not to make their usual hunt. This is erroneous. I may have suggested that it would be dangerous for our friendly Indians to go, but I have desired the Pawnees to follow and operate when I had driven away the hostile bands. Yet I see great difficulty in discriminations, and also fear that some bands of our friendly Indians might mingle with foes if they come in proximity. If the friendly Indians could be united for the purpose of hunting and fighting with our troops, it would be easy to organize and so equip them as to avoid difficulty. In my recent reconnoissance I took about seventy-five Pawnees with me as scouts, and, to avoid mistakes, dressed them with a blowse and hats. It gave them a distinctive and graphic appearance, which could not be mistaken. Any other than an associate arrangement seems almost impossible.

I appreciate the importance of allowing or aiding the friendly Indians to hunt buffalo; but any general movement by them would lead to confusion and difficulty, not only with my troops, but with the border settlements; for the people, being terribly alarmed, would make very little difference in their resentment and raids.

I will do all I can to favor the friendly Indians in any rational arrangement to hunt the buffalo, and believe, with the honorable Secretary, that, properly associated with the troops, they would strengthen our efforts to suppress the hostile tribes.

I have the honor to be, general, your obedient servant,

S. R. CURTIS,
Major General.

Major General H. W. HALLECK, *Chief of Staff, Washington.*

HEADQUARTERS ARMY, *March* 18, 1865.

Official copy:

J. C. KELTON, *A. A. G.*

DENVER, *September* 19, 1864.

Hon. E. M. STANTON, *Secretary of War:*

Train with ordnance and ordnance stores en route to New Mexico, with mules, stolen by Indians at Fort Lyon, Colorado. We need such stores for 3d regiment Colorado volunteers, cavalry, one hundred day men, now full. Authorize me by telegraph to take them. Will not be used, if reach New Mexico, before next year. Indian warriors congregated eighty miles from Lyon, three thousand strong.

J. M. CHIVINGTON,
Colonel Commanding, District Colorado.

HEADQUARTERS ARMY, *March* 18, 1865.

Official:

D. C. WAGER, *A. A. G.*

HEADQUARTERS OF THE ARMY,
Washington, D. C., September 20, 1864.

Colonel CHIVINGTON, *Denver City:*

The chief of ordnance objects to the diversion of the train sent to New Mexico. You must make requisition for your wants in the usual way.

H. W. HALLECK,
Major General, Chief of Staff.

HEADQUARTERS ARMY, *March* 18, 1865.

Official:

D. C. WAGER, *A. A. G.*

DENVER CITY, *September* 22, 1864.

Major General HALLECK, *Chief of Staff:*

Have regiment 100 days men ready for field. Train on the way from Fort Leavenworth, but cannot get here in time because of the Indian troubles on the Platte route. Are four hundred miles back, and laid up. The time of this regiment will expire and Indians will still hold road. This is no ordinary case.

J. M. CHIVINGTON,
Colonel Commanding.

HEADQUARTERS ARMY, *March* 18, 1865.

Official:

D. C. WAGER, *A. A. G.*

HEADQUARTERS OF THE ARMY,
Washington, D. C., September 23, 1864.

Colonel CHIVINGTON, *Denver City:*

You will communicate your wants to your superior officer, General Curtis, at Fort Leavenworth.

H. W. HALLECK,
Major General, Chief of Staff.

HEADQUARTERS ARMY, *March* 18, 1865.

Official:

D. C. WAGER, *A. A. G.*

HEADQUARTERS OF THE ARMY,
Washington, D. C., September 24, 1864.

Major General CURTIS, *Fort Leavenworth:*

General Rosecrans has been directed to give you the regiment of Colorado cavalry at or near Kansas city. All your available forces, not required against western Indians, should be thrown south on the Fort Scott route. Large re-enforcements have been sent to the Arkansas river to cut off the enemy's retreat.

H. W. HALLECK,
Major General, Chief of Staff.

HEADQUARTERS ARMY, *March* 18, 1865.

Official:

D. C. WAGER, *A. A. G.*

FORT LEAVENWORTH, *September* 26, 1864.

Major General HALLECK:

Despatch received. Had already begun moving troops and supporting my southeast. But a full regiment of hundred-days men and part of the 1st Colorado going out this week. My main dependence must be in militia. If Price's forces come westward the militia are notified to be ready.

S. R. CURTIS, *Major General.*

HEADQUARTERS ARMY, *March* 18, 1865.

Official:

D. C. WAGER, *A. A. G.*

FORT LEAVENWORTH, *October* 7, 1864.

Major General HALLECK, *Chief of Staff*:

General Blunt came upon a party of Arapahoes and other hostile Indians, supposed to be four thousand, with fifteen hundred warriors, on the twenty-fifth ultimo. This was about one hundred miles west of Larned, in Pawnee fork. The Indians overpowered the advance, but the main force coming up routed and pursued them. Ninety-one dead Indians were left, and we lost two killed and seven wounded. General Blunt's force was less than five hundred. He pursued for several days.

S. R. CURTIS, *Major General.*

HEADQUARTERS ARMY, *March* 18, 1865.

Official:

D. C. WAGER, *A. A. G.*

HEADQUARTERS OF THE ARMY,
Washington, D. C., October 16, 1864.

Brigadier General CONNER, *Salt Lake City:*

Give all the protection in your power to the overland route between you and

Fort Kearney, without regard to department lines. General Curtis's forces have been diverted by rebel raids from Arkansas.

H. W. HALLECK,
Major General, Chief of Staff.

HEADQUARTERS ARMY, *March* 18, 1865.

Official:

D. C. WAGER, *A. A. G.*

HEADQUARTERS, *Fort Lyon, C. T.*, *November* 6, 1864.

SIR: I have the honor to report that I arrived at this post and assumed command November 2, in obedience to Special Orders No. 4, headquarters of district, October 17, 1864. Major E. W. Wynkoop, 1st cavalry of Colorado, was in command of the post. One hundred and thirteen lodges of Arapahoe Indians, under their chiefs Little Raven, Left Hand, Nervah, Storms, and Knock Knee, and numbering, in men, women and children, 652 persons, were encamped in a body about two miles from the post, and were daily visiting the post, and receiving supplies from the commissary department, the supplies being issued by Lieutenant C. M. Copett, assistant commissary of supplies, under orders from Major E. W. Wynkoop, commanding post.

I immediately gave instructions to arrest all Indians coming within the post, until I could learn something more about them. Went down and met their head chiefs, half way between the post and their camp, and demanded of them by what authority and for what purpose they were encamped here. They replied that they had always been on peaceable terms with the whites, had never desired any other than peace, and could not be induced to fight. That other tribes were at war, and, therefore, they had come into the vicinity of a post, in order to show that they desired peace, and to be where the travelling public would not be frightened by them, or the Indians be harmed by travellers or soldiers on the road.

I informed them that I could not permit any body of armed men to camp in the vicinity of the post, nor Indians visit the post, except as prisoners of war. They replied that they had but very few arms and but few horses, but were here to accept any terms that I proposed. I then told them that I should demand their arms and all the stock they had in their possession which had ever belonged to white men; they at once accepted these terms. I then proceeded with a company of cavalry to the vicinity of their camp, leaving my men secreted, and crossed to their camp, received their arms from them, and sent out men to look through their herd for United States or citizens' stock, and to take all stock except Indian ponies; found ten mules and four horses, which have been turned over to the acting assistant quartermaster. Their arms are in very poor condition, and but few, with little ammunition. Their horses far below the average grade of Indian horses. In fact, these that are here could make but a feeble fight if they desired war. I have permitted them to remain encamped near the post, unarmed, as prisoners, until your wishes can be heard in the matter; in the interval, if I can learn that any of their warriors have been engaged in any depredations that have been committed, shall arrest them, and place all such in close confinement.

I am of opinion that the warriors of the Arapahoes, who have been engaged in war, are all now on the Smoky Hill, or with the Sioux Indians, and have all the serviceable arms and horses belonging to the tribe, while these here are too poor to fight, even though they desired war.

Nine Cheyenne Indians to-day sent in, wishing to see me. They state that 600 of that tribe are now 35 miles north of here, coming towards the post, and 2,000 about 75 miles away, waiting for better weather to enable them to come in. I shall not permit them to come in, even as prisoners, for the reason that if I do, I shall have to subsist them upon a prisoner's rations. I shall, however, demand their arms, all stolen stock, and the perpetrators of all depredations. I am of the opinion that they will not accept this proposition, but that they will return to the Smoky Hill. They pretend that they want peace, and I think they do now, as they cannot fight during the winter, except where a small band of them can find an unprotected train or frontier settlement. I do not think it is policy to make peace with them now, until all perpetrators of depredations are surrendered up to be dealt with as we may propose.

The force effective for the field at the post is only about 100, and one company, (K, New Mexico volunteers,) sent here by order of General Carlton, commanding department of New Mexico, were sent with orders to remain sixty days, and then report back to Fort Union. Their sixty days will expire on the 10th of November (instant.) Shall I keep them here for a longer period, or permit them to return?

The Kiowas and Comanches, who have all the stock stolen upon the Arkansas route, are reported south of the Arkansas river and towards the Red river. The Cheyennes are between here and the Smoky Hill; part of the Arapahoes are near this post; the remainder north of the Platte. With the bands divided in this way, one thousand cavalry could now overtake them and punish some of them severely, I think, but with the force here it can only be made available to protect the fort. I shall not permit the Cheyennes to camp here, but will permit the Arapahoes now here to remain in their present camp as prisoners until your action is had in the matter.

I have the honor to be, very respectfully, your obedient servant,

SCOTT I. ANTHONY,
Major 1st Cavalry of Colorado, Commanding Post.

To ——————,
A. A. A. G. District of Upper Arkansas, Fort Riley, Kansas.

—

[Indorsed.]

HEADQUARTERS DISTRICT OF UPPER ARKANSAS,
Fort Riley, November 22, 1864.

Respectfully forwarded for the information of the general commanding, respectfully asking for instruction in regard to the Arapahoe Indians kept and fed as prisoners at Fort Lyon. Major Anthony has been instructed to carry out general field order No. 2, July 31, 1864, fully, until further instructions from department headquarters. I would also state that I have learned, unofficially, that on Saturday, the 12th instant, two white men were killed and five wagons destroyed near Fort Larned by a party of Indians numbering about thirty. Have written to commanding officer at Fort Larned in reference to it, and instructed him to report all cases of Indian depredations that may come to his knowledge.

B. I. HENNING,
Major 3d Wisconsin Cavalry, Commanding District.

FORT LEAVENWORTH, *December* 1, 1864.

Major General H. W. HALLECK, *Chief of Staff:*

I am informed by telegraph from Neosho crossing, about one hundred and twenty miles below Fort Scott, that the train carrying supplies to Fort Gibson is halted because of a large rebel force in front. This is beyond my department lines, and I am unable to do much, but have ordered a regiment of my troops under Colonel Moonlight to support the escort commanded by Major Phillips in going forward or back as circumstances seem to require. Indian troubles now demand all my force, and large numbers are crowding into Fort Lyon as prisoners of war, while others in small bands are attacking stages and trains. Under these circumstances, I cannot furnish escorts to carry provisions for Indians and troops beyond my department lines; and your attention is called to the necessity of furnishing General Steele with forces sufficient and in position to guard the lines to Fort Gibson and Fort Scott, or have the troops and Indians now there to fall back where they get provisions.

S. R. CURTIS, *Major General.*

HEADQUARTERS ARMY, *March* 18, 1865.

Official:

D. C. WAGER, *A. A. G.*

FORT LEAVENWORTH, *December* 8, 1864.

Major General H. W. HALLECK, *Chief of Staff:*

Colonel Chivington, after a march of three hundred miles in ten days, on the 29th returned. He came upon a Cheyenne camp of one hundred and thirty lodges at the south bend of Big Sandy, Cheyenne county, Colorado. He attacked at daylight, killing over four hundred Indians and capturing the same number of ponies. Among the killed are chiefs Black Kettle, White Antelope, and Little Robe. Our loss is nine killed and thirty-eight wounded. Our troops encountered snow two feet deep.

S. R. CURTIS,
Major General, Commanding.

HEADQUARTERS ARMY, *March* 18, 1865.

Official:

D. C. WAGER, *A. A. G.*

HEADQUARTERS DEPARTMENT OF KANSAS,
Fort Leavenworth, December 30, 1864.

Several papers have been referred to me concerning irregularities charged on General Blunt and others before I came in this command, and entirely outside. Yet, as some of the parties are in my command, I may do something if I can get men disconnected with Kansas affairs and worthy of credence. There is so much political and personal strife in our service, it is almost impossible to get an honest, impartial determination of facts.

A shift of troops, so as to put officers and men out of their own home localities, would greatly improve my command, and I wish especially that some of my Kansas regiments may be sent to the front and troops of other States sent to me. I have ordered the 11th Kansas to Colorado, far enough from their homes, but the 15th and 16th Kansas might well be changed.

The 1st Colorado, the 3d Colorado, and many companies of other regiments, have to be mustered out under the provisions of Circular No. 36.

I am also informed that Fort Smith and Fayetteville, in the department of Arkansas, are being evacuated. Fort Gibson, in the same department, is garrisoned with dismounted Indian troops, so that my southern border is more exposed than formerly.

The Indians on the plains continue to act in bands of fifty or one hundred at various points, and I desire to make new efforts to crush them during the latter part of winter. Under these circumstances, I feel it my duty to urge the sending of more troops of other States to aid in keeping open the overland lines, escort trains, put down the Indians, and strengthen the defences which overlook the enemy's approaches from Texas.

I have the honor to be, general, your obedient servant,

S. R. CURTIS, *Major General.*

Major General H. W. HALLECK,
Chief of Staff, Washington, D. C.

HEADQUARTERS ARMY, *March* 18, 1865.

Official copy:

J. C. KELTON, *A. A. G.*

HEADQUARTERS OF THE ARMY,
Washington, D. C., January 3, 1865.

GENERAL: Your communications proposing a winter's campaign against the Indians, and asking for more troops, were sent to General Grant immediately on their receipt. If he has acted on the matter, his orders have gone directly to you, as nothing on the subject has been received here.

I write this to inform you that the matter was duly attended to by me.

Very respectfully, your obedient servant,

H. W. HALLECK,
Major General, Chief of Staff.

Major General CURTIS,
Fort Leavenworth, Kansas.

HEADQUARTERS ARMY, *March* 18, 1865.

Official copy:

J. C. KELTON, *A. A. G.*

[Dated Denver, January 8, 1865.—Received January 9, 3 p. m.]

J. B. CHAFFEE, 45 *William:*

Urge the government to send troops on Platte route. Indians burning trains and slaying emigrants.

GEO. E. CLARK,
CHAS. A. COOK.

HEADQUARTERS ARMY, *March* 18, 1865.

Official copy:

J. C. KELTON, *A. A. G.*

NEW YORK, *January* 10, 1865.

DEAR JUDGE: I received the enclosed despatch this a. m. You cannot be too urgent with the Secretary of War, or the President, about our Indian troubles. Unless something is done to settle this trouble, we are virtually killed as a Territory. You can hardly realize, without seeing it, the large amount of machinery en route for our Territory to work the mines with. Everything in the way of supplies is exorbitantly high, all on account of the hazard of transportation. Emigration is limited on account of the danger of travel. It is peculiarly disastrous to us now because so many eastern capitalists have been and are investing in our mines, and are preparing to open and develop them.

I am inclined to the opinion that our administration, both civil and military, have failed to comprehend the situation. I mean Evans and Chivington. I think this whole difficulty could have been arrested; but this is nothing to the case now. This must be attended to immediately, or our prospects are blasted for some time to come, and the development of a rich mining country indefinitely postponed. For God's sake, urge some action. I can't come over just now, or I would give you my views regarding what action ought to be taken; but anything, so that some steps are taken to protect the line of travel.

There is no use to depend on General Curtis, Evans, Chivington, or any other politician.

Yours of the 9th received this morning.

Truly, &c.,

J. B. CHAFFEE.

HEADQUARTERS ARMY, *March* 18, 1865.

Official copy:

J. C. KELTON, *A. A. G.*

HEADQUARTERS OF THE ARMY,
Washington, D. C., January 11, 1865.

Major General CURTIS, *Fort Leavenworth:*

Statements from respectable sources have been received here that the conduct of Colonel Chivington's command towards the friendly Indians has been a series of outrages calculated to make them all hostile. You will inquire into and report on this matter, and will take measures to have preserved and accounted for all plunder taken from the Indians at Fort Lyons and other places.

H. W. HALLECK,
Major General, Chief of Staff.

HEADQUARTERS ARMY, *March* 18, 1865.

Official:

D. C. WAGER, *A. A. G.*

WAR DEPARTMENT, *January* 11, 1865.

Judge Bennet, delegate from Colorado Territory, presents a letter and telegram from J. B. Chaffee relative to the Indian depredations on the mail route to Colorado, and the general unsettled condition of the country, owing to the active hostility of the Indians, incited mainly by the recent attack of Colonel Chivington at Fort Lyons. The attention of the government is called to the immediate necessity of sending additional troops to that region to protect the route.

Respectfully referred to General Halleck.

By order of the Secretary of War.

JAS. A. HARDIE,
Colonel and Inspector General.

HEADQUARTERS ARMY, *March* 18, 1865.

Official copy:

J. C. KELTON, *A. A. G.*

HEADQUARTERS DEPARTMENT OF KANSAS,
Fort Leavenworth, January 12, 1865.

GENERAL: Your despatch of yesterday, directing me to investigate Colonel Chivington's conduct towards the Indians, is received, and will be obeyed. Colonel Chivington has been relieved by Colonel Moonlight, and is probably out of the service, under provisions of Circular No. 36, War Department.

Although the colonel may have transgressed my field orders concerning Indian warfare, (a copy of which is here enclosed,) and otherwise acted very much against my views of propriety in his assault at Sand creek, still it is not true, as Indian agents and Indian traders are representing, that such extra severity is increasing Indian war. On the contrary, it tends to reduce their numbers, and bring them to terms. Their bands are more united, perhaps, at this time than during the summer, but this results from their necessities and surroundings. They are in a destitute condition, and must, at this season of the year, resort to desperate measures to procure horses and provisions; hence we see a continual effort to overpower our little posts, or our trains and stages. Their lodges are now between the Arkansas and Platte, and they shift their assaults so as to attack to the best advantage. I am collecting and arranging troops near Fort Riley, but need more force to make another effort to destroy them. I will be glad to save the few honest and kindly disposed, and protest against the slaughter of women and children; although, since General Harney's attack of the Sioux many years ago at Ash Hollow, the popular cry of settlers and soldiers on the frontier favors an indiscriminate slaughter, which is very difficult to restrain. I abhor this style, but so it goes from Minnesota to Texas. I fear that Colonel Chivington's assault at Sand creek was upon Indians who had received some encouragement to camp in that vicinity under some erroneous supposition of the commanding officer at Lyon that he could make a sort of "city of refuge" at such a point. However wrong that may have been, it should have been respected, and any violation of known arrangements of that sort should be severely rebuked. But there is no doubt a portion of the tribe assembled were occupied in making assaults on our stages and trains, and the tribes well know that we have to hold the whole community responsible for acts they could restrain, if they would properly exert their efforts in that way. It is almost impossible to properly try officers in my command, if they have a high rank, my troops all being widely scattered and much employed.

I have the honor to be your obedient servant,

S. R. CURTIS, *Major General.*

HEADQUARTERS OF THE ARMY,
Washington, March 18, 1865.

Official copy:

——— ———, *A. A. G.*

GENERAL FIELD ORDERS No. 1.

[Extract.]

HEADQUARTERS DEPARTMENT OF KANSAS,
In the Field, Fort Ellsworth, July 27, 1864.

* * * * * * *

II. Hunters will be detailed for killing game, but the troops must not scatter and break down stock to chase buffalo. Indians at war with us will be the object of our pursuit and distinction, but women and children must be spared. All horses, ponies, and property taken will be placed in charge of Quartermaster P. C. Taylor, who will have it properly collected, or sent back to safe place for future disposition; this is necessary to prevent the accumulation of useless baggage.

* * * * * * *

By order of Major General Curtis.

JOHN WILLIAMS,
Assistant Adjutant General.

Official copy: JOHN WILLIAMS, *A. G. A.*

HEADQUARTERS OF THE ARMY,
Washington, March 18, 1865.

Official copy: ——— ———, *A. A. G.*

GENERAL FIELD ORDERS No. 2.

HEADQUARTERS DEPARTMENT OF KANSAS,
In the Field, Fort Larned, July 31, 1864.

I. At all military posts or stations west of the Kansas and Nebraska settlements in this department, stockades or abatis enclosures must be made for the troops and stock, and animals must be kept in such enclosures at night, and never herded during the day without distant and careful pickets, who can give warning of approaching enemies in time to preserve the stock from surprise.

II. Indians and their allies or associates will not be allowed within the forts except blindfolded, and then they must be kept totally ignorant of the character and number of our forces. Neglect of this concealment will be followed by the most severe and summary punishment.

Commanders of forts and stations will furnish escorts according to their best judgments, keeping in view the safety of their own posts, the stage or public property to be guarded, and the preservation of the horses.

These precautions must not be relaxed without permission of the commander of the department, and all officers, of whatever grade, will report promptly to the nearest and most available assistance, and to district and department headquarters, any patent neglect of this order, or any palpable danger to a command.

The industry and skill displayed by Lieutenant Ellsworth, and the troops under his command, in the erection of a block-house and other protection for his troops and animals at Smoky Hill crossing, deserve special commendation, while the negligence exhibited elsewhere, especially at this post, while under its former commander, is deprecated and denounced.

By command of Major General S. R. Curtis.

JOHN WILLIAMS,
Assistant Adjutant General.

Official:

JOHN WILLIAMS, *A A. G.*

HEADQUARTERS OF THE ARMY,
Washington, March 18, 1865.

Official copy:

——— ———, *A. A. G.*

HEADQUARTERS DEPARTMENT OF KANSAS,
Fort Leavenworth, January 30, 1865.

GOVERNOR: Yours of the 20th is just received, and I telegraph the latest news. I was provoked at the course taken by the commanding officer at Julesburg, who took his entire force to escort prisoners through, leaving that post for a few days entirely vacated. I have telegraphed a proper rebuke, and trust this will not again occur. None of my military stations have been disturbed. They are all intact, and generally too strong to be taken by assault. All we need is three or four regiments, which it seems to me will be sufficient. Most of these I would keep moving in the country infested by foes. I fear your Interior Department will make me trouble, by proposing military evolutions which conflict with my own. After traversing most of the plains last summer, up the Arkansas, up the Platte, and near the head of every stream between these rivers, my personal knowledge, coupled with that obtained from my officers, is abundant to enable me to understand the matter, and I am only desirous of doing what I consider necessary to make a finish, as near as may be, of these troubles. But I cannot carry on war on other people's plans. I want no fancy movements, such as occurred last summer, when one of your militia companies marched down the line, passing my troops, and claiming to have "opened the overland route," as though others had not been over most of the places on the Blue, and on Plum creek and elsewhere, where most of the losses had transpired. This move of Chivington against the bands that had been congregated on Sand creek, at the instance of Major Wynkoop, was also an inspiration of over-zeal which did not emanate from my headquarters. I name these things, governor, to secure unity of action, not to find fault.

On every occasion last summer I took the field promptly, and, although I did not get to Denver, I was at the slaughter-ground near Larned on the Arkansas, and on the Plum and Blue on the Platte, making overland journeys between, with active, efficient forces extending over two thousand miles; so that my zeal and energy cannot be doubted. I protest my desire to pursue and punish the enemy everywhere, in his lodges especially; but I do not believe in killing women and children who can be taken, and, if need be, camped east of the Mississippi, where they can be kept and cared for. I always did and do consider the Ash Hollow massacre a monstrous outrage, but the promotion and laudation that followed that transaction should excuse the indiscretion and cruelty of excited and outraged frontier soldiers, who have always heard Ash Hollow warfare extolled as the very brilliant point of glorious Indian warfare.

In my first movement last summer, when in pursuit of the Indians, I tried to restrain this plan of warfare, by issuing an order against the massacre of women and children, believing that taking such captive and bringing them away would just as effectually mortify and annoy the Indian robbers and warriors. Let me say, too, that I see nothing new in all this Indian movement since the Chivington affair, except that Indians are more frightened and keep further away. By pushing them hard this next month, before grass recruits their ponies, they will be better satisfied with making war and robbery a business. I would send into their lines some friendly, reliable Arapahoes and Cheyennes, and separate tribes, so as to save such as may be willing to make peace and fight the bad Indians.

Such are my views. I am not anxious to have the job of operating matters; but while I have command, I want unity of action, or no cross or counter currents. I have written this, because I see by telegraph that matters are spoken of as being organized at Washington, where I fear less is known of details.

I am, governor, yours truly,

S. R. CURTIS, *Major General.*

His Excellency Governor JNO. EVANS, *Washington, D C.*

HEADQUARTERS OF THE ARMY,
Washington, March 18, 1865.

Official copy:

——— ———, *A. A. G.*

HEADQUARTERS DEPARTMENT OF KANSAS,
Fort Leavenworth, January 30, 1865.

GENERAL: Governor Evans writes me, that he fears Chivington's conduct at Sand creek may embarrass military matters on the plains. I have written him fully, and enclose you a copy of my letter.

There is no new feature in these Indian troubles, except that Indians seem more frightened. More forces and more prudence will keep the lines open and subdue the hostile tribes. Some accounts of great combinations go the rounds; but I put no confidence in such stories.

The Indians of the plains are generally robbers and murderers, and act only from motives of hunger and avarice in their assaults, and by fear in their forbearance.

Settlements have increased, and our lines of communication have become more convenient for their assaults, till they become more troublesome and venturesome. The carelessness of emigration invited their assaults. It is folly to attribute the Indian troubles to the wrongs committed by white men. While we may condemn these, it is really more indulgence than cruelty that endured and continues their warfare. They have no great armies; they are not combined; their action is in separate bands of separate tribes. A thousand men with light artillery can whip their greatest possible combinations; but it is desirable to have three or four more regiments, so that a movable force of say two thousand can take a shifting attitude, going to a central point and throwing out detachments as circumstances seem to require. Such a force must follow the buffalo, as the Indians do, and must not go beyond reasonable proximity to the lines of travel, but remain near enough to the little posts that guard the travel and trains that follow the routes up the Platte and up the Arkansas.

I send you a map of the overland route to the mountains with stations marked. I have required our troops to erect defences against Indian assaults, and a few men can in this way hold position, and a few more accompany the stage or train to adjacent stations. Such forts cost nothing of consequence, and have already saved men and stores in several instances.

Forces are necessary on these lines and in the edge of settlements; but a movable force generally stationed between the Platte and Arkansas, as I have suggested, and nearest the eastern settlements where it can be most economically supplied, will, in my judgment, be the proper organization for the country. I have in a former letter expressed my purpose to do all I can to continue the campaign during the winter.

I specially urge the extension of the telegraph at least to Riley. The advantage will, in my judgment, greatly exceed the cost. I need connexion with the Indian and buffalo range, so I can direct matters on the Platte to correspond with intelligence arriving from the Santa Fe route. Our telegraph company can extend the line with only a cost of about ten thousand dollars; but it is proper to say my request last season was disapproved by the honorable the Secretary of War, and this is a renewal of the request.

I have the honor to be, general, your obedient servant,

S. R. CURTIS,
Major General.

Major General H. W. HALLECK,
Chief of Staff, Washington, D. C.

P. S.—*February* 2.—I delayed this for the map, which does not satisfy me, and will be delayed a few days for revision. I have ordered all possible force to Julesburg, where Indian difficulties continue. I have information, also, that a council of the chiefs have determined to try to draw off troops from the Arkansas line, by attacking the Platte line. I have to act in view of their shifting assaults.

S. R. CURTIS, *Major General.*

HEADQUARTERS OF THE ARMY,
Washington, March 18, 1865.

Official copy:

HEADQUARTERS OF THE ARMY,
Washington, D. C., February 1, 1865.

GENERAL: I transmit herewith a copy of a letter from General Conner in regard to the defence of the overland mail route, and also several papers from General Curtis on this subject.

These papers and others were, on their receipt, forwarded to Lieutenant General Grant, and have been returned without any instructions from him, so far as I am informed.

It is therefore presumed that he deems the large cavalry force in the department of Kansas as sufficient for present purposes, without taking others from active duty in the field.

It is proper to state in this connexion, that others report these stories of Indian hostilities as greatly exaggerated, if not mostly gotten up for purposes of speculation; and respectable authorities assert that they are encouraged by the agents of the Overland Mail Company, in order to cover their frequent failure to transport the mails according to contract.

Be this as it may, it is highly important that the roads to New Mexico, Colorado, Utah and Idaho should be properly protected from Indian hostilities, so that there may be no interruption in the transmission of supplies and the mails.

You will transmit these papers, with the necessary instructions, to General Dodge, who will give the whole matter his immediate care and attention.

Very respectfully, your obedient servant,

H. W. HALLECK,
Major General, Chief of Staff.

Major General JOHN POPE,
St. Louis, Missouri.

HEADQUARTERS ARMY, *March* 18, 1865.

Official copy:

J. C. KELTON, *A. A. G.*

SENATE CHAMBER,
February 13, 1865.

SIR: We are appointed by the Committee on Indian Affairs of the Senate a sub-committee to confer with the President and yourself on the subject of transferring the Indian country, with one tier of counties of western Arkansas, to the Missouri–Kansas Department. We refrain from giving reasons or argument, believing you are already of opinion the change should be promptly made, and merely submit the request.

Yours, &c.,

JAMES HARLAN,
J. H. LANE.

Hon. E. M. STANTON,
Secretary of War.

N. B.—I saw General Grant Saturday night, who informed me he had no objection to the change.

J. H. LANE.

We earnestly recommend that the Indian troops now in the service in the Indian country be mustered out of the service with their arms in time to raise a crop for their destitute families this season, if other troops are substituted.

JAMES HARLAN,
J. R. DOOLITTLE,
M. S. WILKINSON,
B. GRATZ BROWN,
C. R. BUCKALEW,
Committee on Indian Affairs.

HEADQUARTERS ARMY, *March* 18, 1865.

Official copy:

J. C. KELTON, *A. A. G.*

WAR DEPARTMENT,
January 23, 1865.

Case of application of Ben Holladay that General Curtis may be ordered to re-enforce Julesburg (crossing of the Platte) immediately.

Referred to Major General Halleck, chief of staff.

By order of the Secretary of War.

JAMES A. HARDIE,
Colonel and Inspector General.

HEADQUARTERS OF THE ARMY,
March 18, 1865.

Official copy:

J. C. KELTON,
Colonel and Assistant Adjutant General.

[From Julesburg, dated 14.—Received January 16, 1865.]

BEN HOLLADAY:

I arrived here to-day with fifteen (15) men; shall try and hold station; soldiers all gone; only the wounded; station badly torn up; messenger robbed; great deal of property destroyed.

R. R. THOMAS,
Division Adjutant.

HEADQUARTERS OF THE ARMY,
March 18, 1865.

Official copy:

J. C. KELTON,
Colonel and Assistant Adjutant General.

[Dated New York 21, 1865.—Received Washington, January 21, 1865.]

(Care of Senator POMEROY, 15th and F sts.)

Reuben Thomas telegraphs cannot hold Julesburg. If he does not the Indians have conquered the country, from Kearney to Denver, beyond hope this winter.

BEN HOLLADAY.

HEADQUARTERS OF THE ARMY,
March 18, 1865.

Official copy:

J. C. KELTON,
Colonel and Assistant Adjutant General.

[Dated New York 21, 1865, 11 o'clock.—Received Washington, January 21, 1865.]

To GEORGE B. JOLIS, care of Senator POMEROY:

Try to have order sent to Curtis or Mitchell to help them at Julesburg, or he will abandon.

B. HOLLADAY.

HEADQUARTERS OF THE ARMY,
March 18, 1865.

Official copy:

J. C. KELTON,
Colonel and Assistant Adjutant General.

FORT LYON, COLORADO TERRITORY,
January 15, 1865.

SIR: In pursuance of Special Order No. 43, headquarters, district of Upper Arkansas, directing me to assume command of Fort Lyon, as well as to investigate and immediately report in regard to late Indian proceedings in this vicinity, I have the honor to state that I arrived at this post on the evening of the 14th of January, 1865, assumed command on the morning of the 15th of January, 1865, and the result of my investigation is as follows:

As explanatory, I beg respectfully to state that, while formerly in command of this post, on the 4th day of September, 1864, and after certain hostilities on the part of the Cheyenne and Arapahoe Indians, induced, as I have had ample proof, by the overt acts of white men, three Indians (Cheyennes) were brought as prisoners to me, who had been found coming toward the post, and who had in their possession a letter written, as I ascertained afterwards, by a half-breed in the Cheyenne camp, as coming from Black Kettle and other prominent chiefs of the Cheyenne and Arapahoe nations, the purport of which was that they desired peace, had never desired to be at war with the whites, &c., as well as stating that they had in their possession some white prisoners, women and children, whom they were willing to deliver up providing that peace was granted them. Knowing that it was not in my power to insure and offer them the peace for which they sued, but at the same time anxious, if possible, to accomplish the rescue of the white prisoners in their possession, I finally concluded to risk an expedition with the command I could raise, numbering one hundred and twenty-seven men, to their rendezvous, where I was informed they were congregated to the number of two thousand, and endeavor by some means to procure the aforesaid white prisoners, and to be governed in my course in accomplishing the same entirely by circumstances. Having formerly made lengthy reports in regard to the details of my expedition, I have but to say that I succeeded, procured four white captives from the hands of these Indians, simply giving them in return a pledge that I would endeavor to procure for them the peace for which they so anxiously sued, feeling that, under the proclamation issued by John Evans, governor of Colorado and superintendent of Indian affairs, a copy of which becomes a portion of this report, even if not by virtue of my position as a United States officer, highest in authority in the country included within the bounds prescribed as the country of the Arapahoe and Cheyenne nations, I could offer them protection until such time as some measures might be taken by those higher in authority than myself in regard to them. I took with me seven of the principal chiefs, including Black Kettle, to Denver city, for the purpose of allowing them an interview with the governor of Colorado, by that means making a mistake of which I have since become painfully aware—that of proceeding with the chiefs to the governor of Colorado Territory, instead of to the headquarters of my district, to my commanding officer. In the consultation with Governor Evans, the matter was referred entirely to the military authorities. Colonel J. M. Chivington, at that time commander of the district of Colorado, was present at the council held with these Indian chiefs, and told them that the whole matter was referred to myself, who would act toward them according to the best of my judgment, until such time as I could receive instructions from the proper authorities. Returning to Fort Lyon, I allowed the Indians to bring their villages to the vicinity of the post, including their squaws and pappooses, and in such a position that I could at any moment, with the garrison I had, have annihilated them, had they given any evidence of hostility of any kind, in any quarter.

I then immediately despatched my adjutant, Lieutenant W. W. Denison, with a full statement, to the commanding general of the department, asking for instructions; but in the mean while various false rumors having reached district headquarters in regard to my course, I was relieved from the command of Fort Lyon, and ordered to report at headquarters. Major Scott J. Anthony, 1st cavalry of Colorado, who had been ordered to assume command of Fort Lyon, previous to my departure held a consultation with the chiefs, in my presence, and told them that though acting under strict orders, under the circumstances, he could not materially differ from the course which I had adopted, and allowed them to remain in the vicinity of the post, with their families, assuring them perfect safety until such time as positive orders should be received from headquarters in regard to them. I left the post on the 25th day of November, for the purpose of reporting at district headquarters. On the second day after leaving Fort Lyon, while on the plains, I was approached by three Indians, one of whom stated to me that he had been sent by Black Kettle to warn me that about two hundred Sioux warriors had proceeded down the road between where I was and Fort Larned, to make war, and desired that I should be careful; another evidence of these Indians good faith. All of his statement proved afterwards to be correct. Having an escort of twenty-eight men, I proceeded on my way, but did not happen to fall in with them.

From evidence of officers at this post, I understand that on the 27th day of November, 1864, Colonel J. M. Chivington, with the 3d regiment of Colorado cavalry (one-hundred-days men) and a battalion of the 1st Colorado cavalry. arrived at Fort Lyon, ordered a portion of the garrison to join him, under the command of Major Scott J. Anthony, and against the remonstrance of the officers of the post, who stated to him the circumstances of which he was well aware, attacked the camp of friendly Indians, the major portion of which were composed of women and children. The affidavits which become a portion of this report will show, more particularly than I can state, the full particulars of that massacre. Every one whom I have spoken to, either officer or soldier, agrees in the relation that the most fearful atrocities were committed that ever were heard of. Women and children were killed and scalped, children shot at their mothers' breasts, and all the bodies mutilated in the most horrible manner. Numerous eye-witnesses have described scenes to me, coming under the eye of Colonel Chivington, of the most disgusting and horrible character; the dead bodies of females profaned in such a manner that the recital is sickening; Colonel J. M. Chivington all the time inciting his troops to these diabolical outrages. Previous to the slaughter commencing he addressed his command, arousing in them, by his language, all their worst passions, urging them on to the work of committing all these atrocities. Knowing himself all the circumstances of these Indians resting on the assurances of protection from the government, given them by myself and Major Scott J. Anthony, he kept his command in entire ignorance of the same; and when it was suggested that such might be the casé he denied it, positively stating that they were still continuing their depredations, and laid there threatening the fort. I beg leave to draw the attention of the colonel commanding to the fact established by the enclosed affidavits, that two-thirds or more of that Indian village were women and children, and he is aware whether or not the Indians go to war taking with them their women and children. I desire also to state that Colonel J. M. Chivington is not my superior officer, but is a citizen mustered out of the United States service; and also, that at the time this inhuman monster committed this unprecedented atrocity he was a citizen, by reason of his term of service having expired, he having lost his regulation command some months previous.

Colonel Chivington reports officially that between five and six hundred Indians were left dead upon the field. I have been informed by Captain Booth, district inspector, that he visited the field and counted but sixty-nine bodies, and by others who were present that but a few, if any, over that number were killed, and that two-thirds of them were women and children. I beg leave to further state, for the information of the colonel commanding, that I have talked to every officer in Fort Lyon, and many enlisted men, and that they unanimously agree that all the statements I have made in this report are correct.

In conclusion, allow me to say that from the time I held the consultation with the Indian chiefs on the head-waters of Smoky Hill, up to the date of the massacre by Colonel Chivington, not one single depredation had been committed by the Cheyenne and Arapahoe Indians. The settlers of the Arkansas valley had returned to their ranches from which they had fled, had taken in their crops, and had been resting in perfect security under assurances from myself that they would be in no danger for the present, by that means saving the country from what must inevitably become almost a famine were they to lose their crops; the lines of communication were opened and travel across the plains rendered perfectly safe through the Cheyenne and Arapahoe country. Since this last horrible murder by Colonel Chivington the country presents a scene of desolation. All communication is cut off with the States except by sending large bodies of troops, and already over a hundred whites have fallen as victims to the fearful vengeance of these betrayed Indians. All this country is ruined. There can be no such thing as peace in the future but by the total annihilation of all the Indians on the plains. I have the most reliable information to the effect that the Cheyennes and Arapahoes have allied themselves with the Kiowas Comanches, and Sioux, and are congregated to the number of five or six thousand on the Smoky Hill.

Let me also draw the attention of the colonel commanding to the fact stated by affidavit, that John Smith, United States interpreter, a soldier, and a citizen, were present in the Indian camp, by permission of the commanding officer of this post—another evidence to the fact of these same Indians being regarded as friendly; also, that Colonel Chivington states, in his official report, that he fought from nine hundred to one thousand Indians, and left from five to six hundred dead upon the field, the sworn evidence being that there were but five hundred souls in the village, two-thirds of them being women and children, and that there were but from sixty to seventy killed, the major portion of whom were women and children.

It will take many more troops to give security to travellers and settlers in this country, and to make any kind of successful warfare against these Indians. I am at work placing Fort Lyon in a state of defence, having all, both citizens and soldiers, located here employed upon the works, and expect soon to have them completed, and of such a nature that a comparatively small garrison can hold the fort against any attack by Indians.

Hoping that my report may receive the particular attention of the colonel commanding, I respectfully submit the same.

Your obedient servant,

E. W. WYNKOOP,
Major Com'g 1st Colorado Cavalry and Fort Lyon.

Lieutenant J. E. TAPPAN,
Act'g Ass't Adj't General, District of Upper Arkansas.

ADJUTANT GENERAL'S OFFICE, *March*, 1865.

Official:

——— ———,
Assistant Adjutant General.

FORT LYON, COLORADO TERRITORY,
January 15, 1865.

Personally appeared before me John Smith, United States Indian interpreter, who, after being duly sworn, says:

That on the 4th day of September, 1864, he was appointed Indian interpreter for the post of Fort Lyon, and has continued to serve in that capacity up to the present date; that on the 4th day of September, 1864, by order of Major E. W. Wynkoop, commanding post of Fort Lyon, he was called upon to hold a conversation with three Cheyenne Indians, viz: One Eye, and two others, who had been brought in to the post that day; that the result of the interview was as follows: One Eye, Cheyenne, stated that the principal chiefs and sub-chiefs of the Cheyenne and Arapahoe nations had held a consultation and agreed to a man, of the chiefs and sub-chiefs, to come or send some one who was well acquainted with the parties at the post, and finally agreed to send himself, One Eye, with a paper written by George Bent, half-breed, to the effect that they, the Cheyennes and Arapahoes, had and did agree to turn over to Major E. W. Wynkoop, or any other military authority, all the white prisoners they had in their possession, as they were all anxious to make peace with the whites, and never desired to be at war. Major E. W. Wynkoop then asked One Eye, he having lived among whites, and known to have always been friendly disposed towards them, whether he thought the Indians were sincere, and whether they would deliver the white prisoners into his (Major Wynkoop's) hands. His reply was, that at the risk of his life he would guarantee their sincerity. Major Wynkoop then told him that he would detain him as a prisoner for the time, and if he concluded to proceed to the Indian camp he would take him with him and hold him as a hostage for their (the Indian's) good faith.

One Eye also stated that the Cheyenne and Arapahoe nations were congregated, to the number of two thousand, on the head-waters of the Smoky Hill, including some forty lodges of Sioux; that they had rendezvoused there, and brought in their war parties for the purpose of hearing what would be the result of their message by which they had sued for peace, and would remain until they heard something definite. Major Wynkoop told One Eye that he would proceed to the Indian camp and take him with him. One Eye replied that he was perfectly willing to be detained a prisoner, as well as to remain a hostage for the good faith of the Indians, but desired the major to start as soon as possible, for fear the Indians might separate.

On the 6th day of September I was ordered to proceed with Major Wynkoop and his command in the direction of the Indian encampment. After a four days' march, came in sight of the Indians, and one of the three Indians before mentioned was sent to acquaint the chiefs with what was the object of the expedition, with the statement that Major Wynkoop desired to hold a consultation with the chiefs. On the 10th day of September, 1864, the consultation was held between Major Wynkoop and his officers, and the principal chiefs of the Cheyenne and Arapahoe nations. Major Wynkoop stated through me, to the chiefs, that he had received their message; that acting on that, he had come to talk with them; asked them whether they all agreed to and indorsed the contents of the letter which he had in his possession, and which had been brought in by One Eye. Receiving an answer in the affirmative, he then told the chiefs that he had not the authority to conclude terms of peace with them, but that he desired to make a proposition to them to the effect that if they would give him evidence of their good faith by delivering into his hands the white prisoners they had in their possession, he would endeavor to procure for them peace, which would be subject to conditions that he would take with him what principal chiefs they might select, and conduct them in safety to the governor of Colorado, and whatever might be the result of their interview with him, return them in safety to their tribe.

Black Kettle, the head chief of the Cheyenne nation, replied as follows:

That the Cheyenne and Arapahoe nations had always endeavored to observe the terms of their treaty with the United States government; that some years previously, when the white emigration first commenced coming to what is now the Territory of Colorado, the country which was in possession of the Cheyenne and Arapahoe nations, they could have successfully made war against them, the whites. They did not desire to do so—had invariably treated them with kindness, and had never, to their knowledge, committed any destruction whatever; that until the last few months they had gotten along in perfect peace and harmony with their white brethren, but while a hunting party of their young men were proceeding north, in the neighborhood of the South Platte river, having found some loose stock belonging to white men, which they were taking to a ranch to deliver them up, they were suddenly confronted by a party of United States soldiers and ordered to deliver up their arms. A difficulty immediately ensued, which resulted in the killing and wounding several on both sides.

A short time after this occurrence took place, a village of pappooses, squaws and old men, located on what is known as the Cedar cañon, a short distance north of the South Platte river, who were perfectly unaware of any difficulty having occurred between any portion of their tribe, Cheyenne, and the whites, were attacked by a large party of soldiers, and some of them killed and their ponies driven off. After this, while a body of United States troops were proceeding from the Smoky Hill to the Arkansas river, they reached the neighborhood of Sean Bears' band of the Cheyenne nation. Sean Bears', second chief of the Cheyennes, approached the column of troops alone, his warriors remaining off some distance, he not dreaming that there was any hostility between his nation and the whites. He was immediately shot down, and fire opened upon his band; the result of which was a fight between the two parties. Presuming from all these circumstances that war was inevitable, the young men of the Cheyenne nation commenced to retaliate by committing various depredations all the time, which he, Black Kettle, and other principal chiefs of the Cheyenne nation, was opposed to, and endeavored by all means in their power to restore pacific relations between that tribe and their white brethren, but at various times, when endeavoring to approach the military post for the purpose of accomplishing the same, were fired upon and driven off. In the mean time, while their brothers and allies, the Arapahoes, were on perfectly friendly terms with the whites, and Left Hand's band of that nation were camped in close vicinity to Fort Larned, Left Hand, one of the principal chiefs of the Arapahoe nation, learning that it was the intention of the Kiowas on a certain day to drive off the stock from Fort Larned, proceeded to the commanding officer of that post and informed him of the fact. No attention was paid to the information he gave, and on the day indicated the Kiowas run off the stock. Left Hand again approached the post with a portion of his warriors, for the purpose of offering his services to the commanding officer there to pursue and endeavor to regain the stock from the Kiowa Indians, when he was fired upon and was obliged hastily to leave.

The young men of the Arapahoe nation, supposing it was the intention of the whites to make war upon them as well as the Cheyennes, also commenced retaliating as they were able, and against the desire of most of their principal chiefs, who, as well as Black Kettle and other chiefs of the Cheyennes, were bitterly opposed to hostility with the whites.

He then said that he had lately heard of a proclamation issued by the governor of Colorado, inviting all friendly disposed Indians to come in to the different military posts, and that they would be protected by the government. Under these circumstances, although he thought the whites had been the aggressors and forced the trouble upon the Indians, and anxious for the welfare of his people, he had made this last effort to communicate again with the military authority, and he was glad he succeeded.

He then arose, shook hands with Major Wynkoop and his officers, stating that he was still, as he always had been, a friend to the whites, and, as far as he was concerned, he was willing to deliver up the white prisoners, or anything that was required of him, to procure peace, knowing it to be for the good of his people, but that there were other chiefs who still thought that they were badly treated by the "white brethren," who were willing to make peace, but who felt unwilling to deliver up the prisoners simply on the promise of Major Wynkoop that he would endeavor to procure them peace. They desired that the delivering up the white prisoners should be an assurance of peace. He also went on to state that even if Major Wynkoop's proposition was not accepted there by the chiefs assembled, and although they had sufficient force to entirely overpower Major Wynkoop's small command, from the fact that he had come in good faith to hold this consultation, he should return unmolested to Fort Lyon.

The expressions of other chiefs were to the effect that they insisted upon peace as the conditions of their delivering up the white prisoners.

Major Wynkoop finally replied that he repeated what he had said before, that it was not in his power to insure them peace, and that all he had to say in closing was that they might think about his proposition, that he would march to a certain locality, distant twelve miles, and there await the result of their consultation for two days, advising them at the same time to accede to his proposition as the best means of procuring that peace for which they were anxious.

The white prisoners were brought in and turned over to Major Wynkoop before the time had expired set by him, and Black Kettle, White Antelope, and Bull Bear, of the Cheyenne nation, as well as Nevah Nattanee, Borcu, and Heap Buffalo, of the Arapahoe nation, all chiefs, delivered themselves over to Major Wynkoop. We then proceeded to Fort Lyon, and from there to Denver, Colorado Territory, at which place Governor Evans held a consultation with these chiefs, the result of which was as follows:

He told them he had nothing to do with them; that they would return with Major Wynkoop, who would reconduct them in safety, and they would have to await the action of military authorities. Colonel Chivington, then in command of the district, also told them that they would remain at the disposal of Major Wynkoop until higher authority had acted in their case. The Indians appeared to be perfectly satisfied, presuming that they would eventually be all right as soon as these authorities could be heard from, and expressed themselves so. Black Kettle embraced the governor and Major Wynkoop, and shook hands with all the other officials present, perfectly contented, deeming that the matter was settled. On our return to Fort Lyon I was told by Major Wynkoop to say to the chiefs that they could bring their different bands, including their families, to the vicinity of the post until he had heard from the big chief; that he preferred to have them under his eye and away from other quarters, where they were likely to get into difficulties with the whites.

The chiefs replied that they were willing to do anything Major Wynkoop might choose to dictate, as they had perfect confidence in him. Accordingly, the chiefs went after their families and villages and brought them in; they appeared satisfied that they were in perfect security and safety after their villages were located, and Major Wynkoop had sent an officer to headquarters for instructions. He, Major Wynkoop, was relieved from command of the post by Major Scott J. Anthony, and I was ordered to interpret for him, Major Anthony, in a consultation he desired to hold with these Indians. The consultation that then took place between Major Anthony and these Indians was as follows:

Major Anthony told them that he had been sent here to relieve Major Wynkoop, and that he would from that time be in command of this post; that he had come here under orders from the commanders of all the troops in this country, and that he had orders to have nothing to do with Indians whatever, for they heard at headquarters that the Indians had lately been committing depredations, &c., in the very neighborhood of this post, but that since his arrival he had learned that these reports were all false; that he would write to headquarters himself and correct the rumor in regard to them, and that he would have no objection to their remaining in the vicinity of Sand creek, where they were then located, until such a time as word might be received from the commander of the department; that he himself would forward a complete statement of all that he had seen or heard in regard to them, and that he was in hopes that he would have some good news for the Indians upon receiving an answer, but that he was sorry that his orders were such as to render it impossible for him to make them any issues whatever.

The Indians then replied that it would be impossible for them to remain any great length of time, as they were short of provisions. Major Anthony then told them that they could let their villages remain where they were and send their young men out to hunt buffalo, as he understood that the buffaloes had lately come close in. The Indians appeared to be a little dissatisfied with the change in the commanders of the post, fearing that it boded them no good; but having received assurances of safety from Major Anthony, they still had no fears of their families being disturbed.

On the 26th of November I received permission from Major Scott J. Anthony, commanding post, to proceed to the Indian village on Sand creek for the purpose of trading with the Indians, and started, accompanied by a soldier named David Louderback, and a citizen, Watson Clark. I reached the village and commenced to trade with them. On the morning of the 29th of November the village was attacked by Colonel J. M. Chivington with a command of from nine hundred to one thousand men. The Indian village numbered about one hundred lodges, counting altogether five hundred souls, two-thirds of whom were women and children. From my observation, I do not think there were over sixty Indians that made any defence. I rode over the field after the slaughter was over and counted from sixty to seventy dead bodies, a large majority of which were women and children, all of whose bodies had been mutilated in the most horrible manner. When the troops first approached, I endeavored to join them, but was repeatedly fired upon, as also the soldier and the citizen with me.

When the troops began approaching, I saw Black Kettle, the head chief, hoist the American flag over his lodge, as well as a white flag, fearing there might be some mistake as to who they were. After the fight Colonel Chivington returned with his command in the direction of Fort Lyon, and then proceeded down the Arkansas river.

JOHN S. SMITH,
U. S. Interpreter.

Sworn and subscribed to at Fort Lyon, Colorado Territory, this 27th day of January, 1865.

W. P. MINTON,
Second Lieut. 1st New Mexico Vols., Post Adjutant.

ADJUTANT GENERAL'S OFFICE,
March —, 1865.

Official:

—— ——, *A. A. G.*

FORT LYON, COLORADO TERRITORY,
January 16, 1865.

Personally appeared before me Lieutenant James D. Cannan, 1st New Mexico volunteer infantry, who, after being duly sworn, says:

That on the 28th day of November, 1864, I was ordered by Major Scott J. Anthony to accompany him on an Indian expedition as his battalion adjutant. The object of that expedition was to be a thorough campaign against hostile Indians, as I was led to understand. I referred to the fact of there being a friendly camp of Indians in the immediate neighborhood, and remonstrated against simply attacking that camp, as I was aware that they were resting there in fancied security, under promises held out to them of safety from Major G. W. Wynkoop, from commander of the post of Fort Lyon, as well as by Major S. J. Anthony, then in command. Our battalion was attached to the command of Colonel J. M. Chivington, and left Fort Lyon on the night of the 28th of November, 1864. About daybreak on the morning of the 29th of November we came in sight of the camp of the friendly Indians aforementioned, and was ordered by Colonel Chivington to attack the same, which was accordingly done. The command of Colonel Chivington was composed of about one thousand men. The village of the Indians consisted of from one hundred to one hundred and thirty lodges, and, as far as I am able to judge, of from five hundred to six hundred souls, the majority of whom were women and children.

In going over the battle-ground the next day, I did not see a body of man, woman, or child but was scalped; and in many instances their bodies were mutilated in the most horrible manner, men, women, and children—privates cut out, &c. I heard one man say that he had cut a woman's private parts out, and had them for exhibition on a stick; I heard another man say that he had cut the fingers off of an Indian to get the rings on the hand. According to the best of my knowledge and belief, these atrocities that were committed were with the knowledge of J. M. Chivington, and I do not know of his taking any measures to prevent them. I heard of one instance of a child a few months old being thrown in the feed-box of a wagon, and after being carried some distance, left on the ground to perish. I also heard of numerous instances in which men had cut out the private parts of females, and stretched them over the saddle-bows, and wore them over their hats, while riding in the ranks. All these matters were a subject of general conversation, and could not help being known by Colonel J. M. Chivington.

JAMES D. CANNAN,
First Lieutenant 1st Infantry, New Mexico Volunteers.

Sworn and subscribed to before me this 27th day of January, 1865, at Fort Lyon, Colorado Territory.

W. P. MINTON,
Second Lieut., 1st New Mexico Vols., Post Adjutant.

Deposition of Lieutenant Cannan, 1st New Mexico Volunteers.

Was ordered by Major Anthony to accompany him as his adjutant on an Indian expedition—object, thorough campaign. States that he referred to the camp of friendly Indians, and remonstrated against attacking that camp.

About daybreak, November 29, Colonel Chivington ordered the attack; gives particulars of the barbarities of our men, cutting out *privates, &c.*

ADJUTANT GENERAL'S OFFICE, *March* —, 1865.

Official:

——————— ———————,
Assistant Adjutant General.

FORT LYON, COLORADO TERRITORY,
January 16, 1865.

Personally appeared before me Captain R. A. Hill, 1st New Mexico volunteer infantry, who, after being duly sworn, says:

That, as an officer in the service of the United States, he was on duty at Fort Lyon, Colorado Territory; at the time there was an understanding between the chiefs of the Arapahoe and Cheyenne nations and Major E. W. Wynkoop with regard to their resting in safety with their villages in the vicinity of Fort Lyon until such time as orders in regard to them could be received from the commanding general of the department; that after Major Wynkoop being relieved from the command of Fort Lyon, Colorado Territory, the same understanding existed between Major Scott J. Anthony and the aforesaid Indians; that, to the best of his knowledge and belief, the village of Indians massacred by Colonel J. M. Chivington on the 29th day of November, 1864, were the same friendly Indians heretofore referred to.

R. A. HILL,
Captain 1st Infantry, New Mexico Volunteers.

Sworn and subscribed to before me this 27th day of January, 1865.

W. P. MINTON,
Second Lieut. 1st Infantry, New Mexico Vols. Post Adjutant.

Deposition of Captain R. A. Hill, 1st New Mexico infantry.

Was on duty at Fort Lyon at time these Indians were camping near said fort; that they were then, by permission of Major Wynkoop and Major Anthony, waiting until instructions could be received from headquarters how to act in their case.

To the best of his knowledge, these Indians were the same massacred by Colonel Chivington November 29.

ADJUTANT GENERAL'S OFFICE, *March* —, 1865.

Official:

———— ————,
Assistant Adjutant General

FORT LYON, COLORADO TERRITORY,
January 27, 1865.

Personally appeared before me Second Lieutenant W. P. Minton, first regiment, New Mexico infantry volunteers, and Lieutenant C. M. Cossitt, first cavalry of Colorado, who, after being duly sworn, say:

That on the 28th day of November, 1864, Colonel J. M. Chivington, with the third regiment of Colorado cavalry (one-hundred-days men) and a battalion of the first cavalry of Colorado, arrived at this post, and on the 29th of November attacked a village of friendly Indians in this vicinity, and, according to representations made by others in our presence, murdered their women and children, and committed the most horrible outrages upon the dead bodies of the same; that the aforesaid Indians were recognized as friendly by all parties at this post, under the following circumstances, viz:

That Major E. W. Wynkoop, formerly commander of the post, had given them assurances of safety until such time as he could hear from the commanding general of the department in consequence of their having sued for peace, and given every evidence of their sincerity by delivering up the white prisoners they had in their possession, by congregating their families together and leaving them at the mercy of the garrison of Fort Lyon, who could have massacred them at any moment they felt so disposed; that upon Major Wynkoop being relieved from the command of Fort Lyon and Major Scott J. Anthony assuming command of the same, it was still the understanding between Major Anthony and the Indians that they could rest in the security guaranteed them by Major Wynkoop.

Also, that Colonel J. M. Chivington, on his arrival at the post of Fort Lyon, was aware of the circumstances in regard to these Indians, from the fact that different officers remonstrated with him, and stated to him how these Indians were looked upon by the entire garrison; that, notwithstanding these remonstrances, and in the face of all these facts, he committed the massacre aforementioned.

W. P. MINTON,
Second Lieut. 1st Infantry, New Mexico Volunteers.
C. M. COSSITT,
First Lieutenant 1st Cavalry of Colorado.

Sworn and subscribed to before me this 27th day of January, 1865.

W. W. DENISON,
Second Lieutenant 1st Colorado Veteran Cavalry,
Acting Regimental Adjutant.

ADJUTANT GENERAL'S OFFICE, *March* —, 1865.

Official:

———— ————,
Assistant Adjutant General.

FORT LYON, COLORADO, *January* 27, 1865.

Personally appeared before me Samuel G. Colley, who, being duly sworn, on oath deposes and says:

That he is now, and has been for the past three years, United States agent for the Arapahoe and Cheyenne Indians.

That in the month of June last he received instructions from Hon. John Evans, governor and ex-officio superintendent Indian affairs for Colorado Territory, directing him to send out persons into the Indian country to distribute printed proclamations, (which he was furnished with,) inviting all friendly Indians to come in to the different places designated in said proclamation, and they would be protected and fed. That he caused the terms of said proclamation to be widely disseminated among the different tribes of Indians under his charge, and that in accordance therewith a large number of Arapahoes and Cheyennes came into this post, and provisions were issued to them by Major E. W. Wynkoop, commanding, and myself.

That on the 4th day of September last two Cheyenne Indians (One Eye and Manimick) came into this post with information that the Arapahoes and Cheyennes had several white prisoners among them that they had purchased, and were desirous of giving them up and making peace with the whites.

That on the 6th day of September following Major E. W. Wynkoop left this post with a detachment of troops to rescue said prisoners; and that after an absence of several days he returned, bringing with him four white prisoners which he received from the Arapahoe and Cheyenne Indians. He was accompanied on his return by a number of the most influential men of both tribes, who were unanimously opposed to war with the whites, and desired peace at almost any terms that the whites might dictate.

That immediately upon the arrival of Major Wynkoop at this post large numbers of Arapahoes and Cheyennes came in and camped near the post.

Major Wynkoop selected several of the most prominent chiefs of both nations and proceeded to Denver to council with Superintendent Evans; after his return he held frequent councils with the Indians, and at all of them distinctly stated that he was not empowered to treat with them, but that he had despatched a messenger to the headquarters of the department, stating their wishes in the matter, and that as soon as he received advices from there he would inform them of the decision of General Curtis respecting them.

That until that time, if they placed themselves under his protection, they should not be molested. That the Indians remained quietly near the post until the arrival of Major Anthony, who relieved Major Wynkoop.

Major Anthony held a council with the Indians, and informed them that he was instructed not to allow any Indians in or near the post, but that he had found matters here much better than he had expected, and advised them to go out and camp on Sand creek until he could hear from General Curtis. He wished them to keep him fully advised of all the movements of the Sioux, which they promptly did.

He also promised them that as soon as he heard from General Curtis he would advise them of his decision.

From the time that Major Wynkoop left this post to go out to rescue the white prisoners until the arrival of Colonel Chivington here, which took place on the 28th of November last, no depredations of any kind had been committed by the Indians within two hundred miles of this post.

That upon Colonel Chivington's arrival here with a large body of troops he was informed where these Indians were encamped, and was fully advised under what circumstances they had come in to this post, and why they were then on Sand creek. That he was remonstrated with both by officers and civilians at this post against making war upon those Indians. That he was informed and fully advised that there was a large number of friendly Indians there, together with several white men who were there at the request of himself (Colley) and by permission of Major Anthony. That notwithstanding his knowledge of the facts as above set forth, he is informed that Colonel Chivington did, on the morning of the 29th of November last, surprise and attack said camp of friendly Indians, and massacre a large number of them, (mostly women and children,) and did allow the troops under his command to mangle and mutilate them in the most horrible manner.

S. G. COLLEY,
United States Indian Agent.

Sworn and subscribed to before me this 28th day of January, 1865, at Fort Lyon, Colorado Territory.

W. P. MINTON,
Second Lieut. 1st Infantry, New Mexico Vols., Post Adjutant.

HEADQUARTERS DEPARTMENT OF THE MISSOURI,
St. Louis, ——— —, 186—.

Deposition of Samuel G. Colley, United States agent for the Arapahoe and Cheyenne Indians, says that in June last, obedient to instructions from Governor Evans, Colorado Territory, he distributed printed proclamations through the Indian country, inviting all friendly Indians to come to the different places designated in said proclamation. That the Indians in question came to Fort Lyon; provisions were issued to them by Major Wynkoop. That two of the chiefs reported they had several white prisoners which they purchased, and which they wished to give up. That Major Wynkoop, on the 6th of September, went and rescued the prisoners. On his return, was accompanied by influential men of both tribes unanimously for peace at any terms almost the whites might dictate. Major Wynkoop proceeded with the chiefs to council with Governor Evans. Major Wynkoop repeatedly stated that he had not the power to treat with them, but was waiting instructions from General Curtis, and until that time he would protect them. These Indians kept the commander of the post fully advised of the movements of the Sioux. No depredations were committed within two hundred miles of the post while these Indians were in the vicinity of the post.

Upon Colonel Chivington's arrival he was informed where the Indians were and advised of the circumstances that brought them. He was remonstrated with by officers and civilians against making war. Notwithstanding Colonel Chivington's knowledge of these facts, on the 29th November he surprised and attacked said camp of friendly Indians, killed a large number, mostly women, and allowed his troops to mangle and mutilate bodies.

Deposition of Lieutenants Minton and Cossitt.

Colonel Chivington, with 3d Colorado cavalry and battalion of 1st Colorado cavalry, attacked, on the 29th November, a village of friendly Indians, and, according to representation, murdered women and children in horrible manner. Indians were recognized friendly. They were there and on assurance from

Major Wynkoop of safety. Indians earned the friendship by giving up white prisoners. Colonel Chivington was acquainted with circumstances, and was remonstrated with against, &c.

ADJUTANT GENERAL'S OFFICE, *March* —, 1865.

Official:

——— ———,

Assistant Adjutant General.

FORT LYON, COLORADO TERRITORY,
January 27, 1865.

Personally appeared before me Private David Louderback, 1st cavalry of Colorado, and R. W. Clark, citizen, who, after being duly sworn, say:

That they accompanied John Smith, United States Indian interpreter, on the 26th day of November, 1864, by permission of Major Scott J. Anthony, commanding post of Fort Lyon, Colorado Territory, to the village of the friendly Cheyenne and Arapahoe Indians, on Sand creek, close to Fort Lyon, Colorado Territory, he, John Smith, having received permission to trade with the aforesaid friendly Indians; that on the morning of the 29th day of November, 1864, the said Indian village was attacked, while deponents were in the same, by Colonel J. M. Chivington, with a command of about 1,000 men; that, according to their best knowledge and belief, the entire Indian village was composed of not more than 500 souls, two-thirds of which were women and children; that the dead bodies of women and children were afterwards mutilated in the most horrible manner; that it was the understanding of the deponents, and the general understanding of the garrison of Fort Lyon, that this village were friendly Indians; that they had been allowed to remain in the locality they were then in by permission of Major Wynkoop, former commander of the post, and by Major Anthony, then in command, as well as from the fact that permission had been given John Smith and the deponents to visit the said camp for the purpose of trading.

R. W. CLARK,
DAVID H. LOUDERBACK.

Sworn and subscribed to before me this 27th day of January, 1865.

W. P. MINTON,
Second Lieut. New Mexico Vols., Post Adjutant.

Deposition of David Louderback, 1st Colorado cavalry, and R. W. Clark, citizen.

They were in camp of Indians with John Smith, interpreter, who had permission to trade with the Indians. On the morning of 29th November camp was attacked by Colonel Chivington's command of 1,000 men, while they were in camp; dead bodies of women and children were horribly mutilated; that it was their understanding, and general understanding of garrison Fort Lyon, that these Indians were friendly; that they were allowed to remain there by Major Wynkoop and Major Anthony.

ADJUTANT GENERAL'S OFFICE, *March* —, 1865.

Official:

——— ———,

Assistant Adjutant General.

WAR DEPARTMENT, *February* 14, 1865.

Resolutions of Kansas legislature, requesting the Secretary of War to place a sufficient force under General Curtis to enable him to protect the Kansas frontier and the overland and Santa Fé routes.

Referred to General HALLECK, chief of staff, February 14, 1865.

Copy sent to General GRANT some days ago.

H. W. HALLECK,
Major General, and Chief of Staff.

HEADQUARTERS OF THE ARMY,
March 18, 1865.

Official:

J. C. KELTON, *Colonel, A. A. G.*

CONCURRENT RESOLUTIONS in relation to the overland travel and the settlers upon the frontier.

Whereas the Indian massacres which occurred upon the border of our State during the summer and fall of 1864, and which are now being re-enacted by the hostile tribes of Indians upon the overland route to California, Nevada, and New Mexico, and the Territories of Colorado and Idaho, interfere and retard the settlement and development of the mineral resources of these Territories, and interrupt the overland communication to and from the Pacific and the Territories of Colorado and Idaho; and whereas the military force on said route is entirely inadequate and insufficient to chastise the hostile tribes of Indians, and to keep them from committing their murderous attacks upon emigrants to those Territories and Pacific States, and to keep the line of communication open from the Missouri river, in the State of Kansas, to said States of California and Nevada, and Territories of Colorado and Idaho and New Mexico; and whereas it is necessary to the settlement of the northern and western portion of our State that the hostile tribes of Indians be prevented, if possible, from committing their murderous attacks upon our frontier settlers and the overland mail: Therefore

Be it resolved by the house of representatives of the State of Kansas, (the senate concurring therein,) That the Secretary of War be, and he is hereby, requested to place a sufficient military force in the hands of Major General Curtis, commanding this department, to enable him to give sufficient and ample protection to the frontier of Kansas and the overland and Santa Fé routes.

Resolved, That the secretary of state be instructed to forward copies of this preamble and resolution to the Secretary of War and our senators and representatives in Congress.

Passed by both houses.

D. M. EMMERT, *Chief Clerk.*

I, R. A. Barker, secretary of state, do hereby certify that the above is a true and correct copy of a concurrent resolution, the original of which is on file in my office.

In testimony whereof, I have set my hand and affixed the official seal of my office this 21st day of January, A. D. 1865.

R. A. BARKER,
Secretary of State.

HEADQUARTERS OF THE ARMY, *March* 18, 1865.

Official copy:

J. C. KELTON,
Colonel and Assistant Adjutant General.

HEADQUARTERS DISTRICT OF COLORADO,
Denver, February 13, 1865.

GENERAL: The condition of military affairs in this Territory for the last three months has caused quite a stir at home, and a very great commotion abroad, and justly so. To enable you to properly appreciate the wants and necessities of this people, so as to apply a remedy; to arrive at a desirable conclusion as to the cause of existing hostilities on the part of the Indians; to define my position as district commander, and to lay before you the many difficulties and embarrassments which I have had to contend against since assuming command, as well as to inform you of the steps taken, and the means provided for carrying out the behests of the government and protection of this Territory, I deem it my duty, *first duty*, to give you a concise history of events which may be relied upon for present information and future guidance. Had I been possessed of certain facts from *reliable sources* when I assumed command of this district, on the 4th of January, but a little over a month ago, it might have been possible to arrange matters so as to have fended off part, at least, of the present troubles, which will have (if not, indeed, already) one good effect, viz: to change the policy of the government respecting the treatment of the Indians on the plains. Whatever may have been the origin of the present difficulties, whether the white men or the red were the aggressors, matters not now. We are in every respect the superior of the Indians, and can afford to wage a war of their own choosing, even to extermination.

When I assumed command of this district there were but about two hundred (200) men all told, and they were scattered over an area of three hundred (300) miles, and yet with this command, I was expected to protect the route from Denver to Julesburg, a distance of one hundred and ninety (190) miles, while only forty (40) of the two hundred (200) soldiers were on that line, stationed forty (40) miles from Denver. The balance were on the Arkansas river and at Fort Garland. My district extends about sixty (60) miles on the overland route from Denver, and yet I am called upon to protect as far as Julesburg, in the northeast corner of Colorado Territory, with no troops at my command, while on the north there are plenty, as also from Julesburg to Kearney, which, in my opinion, from what I have seen of them, and heard from reliable sources, had better be sent to some new field of operations. I have special reference to the stations from Kearney to Julesburg. I cannot say who is to blame for this, but it is not the less true. I see every reason why the district of Colorado should embrace the Territory, and none for it being as it now stands defined. Fort Lyon was not in my command when I arrived here, and has but lately been added, which gives me about two hundred and fifty (250) more effective men in the district, but not for operations on the overland route, as they are needed in the southern portion of the Territory to protect the Santa Fé route.

About the end of December, 1864, the 3d regiment Colorado cavalry (one-hundred-days men) were mustered out of the service, thus denuding the district of troops, and at a time, too, when the Indians had suffered an overwhelming defeat, or been subjected to a wholesale massacre at the hands of Colonel Chivington, then commanding district; (I give you these distinctions, as the people here are divided on the question;) at a time when the Indians were burning for revenge on the white men, women, and children, in retaliation for the killed by Colonel Chivington, commanding, for it is useless to deny this fact; at a time when the severity of the winter prevented the making of a campaign with any hope of success on our side, even had the troops been at my command. In view of these facts, and knowing, as he did, that the Territory would be exposed to Indian assaults and depredations, while denuded of troops, I question much the policy and propriety of the Sand creek battle fought by Colonel Chivington on the 29th of November, 1864. This matter is now under investigation by a commission appointed under instructions from Major General Curtis, so that in course of time it will speak for itself.

After having become possessed of all these facts, I looked around to see what could be done in the premises to save the country. I first made a statement to Major General Curtis, which, by the way, has never been acknowledged, and impressed upon him the necessity for making certain changes and of hurrying out re-enforcements. Finding no response or relief from that quarter, I next called upon the governor regarding the turning out of the militia, which was deemed impracticable, owing to the fact that the law has so many defections. I then suggested to the legislature, which was in session, the propriety of amending the militia law, but no answer came or action taken. In consultation with the governor and other prominent men of the Territory, it was deemed most expedient and best to urge the passage of a bill issuing territorial bonds, which could be cashed at par by moneyed men, and the same used to pay volunteers a bounty for three (3) months' service, and purchase horses on which to mount them, (for there are none in the quartermaster's hands, nor any money to purchase them with;) and these men were to be placed under my command, and used in opening and keeping open the overland stage route. The house and council could not agree on this bill; so after over two weeks' delay, and no good resulted from their action, I was compelled to proclaim martial law, shut up all houses of business, stop all labor and traffic, and keep matters so until they furnished me three hundred and sixty (360) mounted men, which I would arm and equip. These men are now being raised, and I expect by the 20th to have the most of them in the field. My position has been, and is, anything but a pleasant one—isolated from all support, a stranger in the land, cut off from all communication, threatened and attacked by hostile Indians, being in a community divided against itself, and compelled to proclaim martial law, with not a man at my back to enforce obedience to the same; yet I have succeeded by first stirring up the public mind, and preparing it for the result which had to follow, unless I chose to back down, and yield my authority, which no living soldier will do.

I enclose, for your information on this subject, copies of a correspondence between myself, the governor, and the legislature on these troubles, also an article from the Journal, a newspaper published in the mountains, which will define to you my position, and show you what I have had to contend with. I made it my business to visit the mountains officially on the very day when excitement was at the highest pitch. On the day but one after that article was written I addressed a meeting of about fifteen hundred (1,500) citizens, in which I pointed out to them at whose door the blame lay, the duties they owed themselves and the government, and my reasons for proclaiming martial law. I was unanimously sustained, and that night one hundred and twenty (120) men were sworn in for three months. This was the quota required by the governor to fill my call.

I enclose you a copy of the order establishing martial law, as also the governor's call in accordance therewith. To assert your authority *here,* in trying cases, is very different from asserting it in any other portion of the Union.

Men of influence and wealth in the east are interested to a very great amount in the mining companies, so that they readily obtain an official ear in Washington to a one-sided story, which invariably works injustice to those in authority and responsible. I therefore respectfully ask, general, that you forward this, or a copy, to Washington, that I may stand right on the record.

I am not afraid to assume any responsibility commensurate with the surrounding circumstances, and which is for the good of the service; but I *am* afraid of the snake-like winding of *hypocrisy,* backed by a grovelling, sensual desire. If men will adhere to truth, I will cheerfully abide every issue.

In the hope this will prove satisfactory and of use to you in your administration, and satisfy your mind regarding my position and the steps I have taken in the premises,

I have the honor to remain, very respectfully, your obedient servant,

T. MOONLIGHT,
Colonel 11th Kansas Cavalry, Commanding.

Major General G. M. DODGE,
Commanding Department of the Missouri,
Fort Leavenworth, Kansas.

HEADQUARTERS DISTRICT OF COLORADO,
Denver, January 7, 1865.

SIR: As matters now stand in this district (having in a manner no troops) there is great danger of being overrun by the Indians. Troops could at the present time be raised better than at any other time, and now is the time we require them. Will you, as acting governor, communicate with the authorities on the subject (the governor being in Washington) to obtain this authority? It is of immense importance to the Territory, and the only way to receive speedy relief from the danger surrounding, and prevent starvation.

I submit this for your consideration and action, and my name may be used by you in this connexion on your despatches.

Very respectfully, your obedient servant,

T. MOONLIGHT,
Colonel 11th Kansas Cavalry, Commanding.

Hon. SAMUEL H. ELBERT.

HEADQUARTERS DISTRICT OF COLORADO,
Denver, C. T., January 8, 1865.

SIR: Owing to the depredations of Indians, we are, at present, shut up from telegraphic communications with the east, and, therefore, beyond the reach of immediate support from any quarter, leaving us to ourselves to act in the premises. Should the troubles continue, I will be constrained to call on the able-bodied men to muster for the protection of the line of transportation. If you have any special views on the subject, I would be pleased to have them.

Very respectfully, your obedient servant,

T. MOONLIGHT,
Colonel 11th Kansas Cavalry, Commanding.

Hon. S. H. ELBERT,
Secretary and Acting Governor.

HEADQUARTERS DISTRICT OF COLORADO,
Denver, January 9, 1865.

GENTLEMEN: Learning that the legislative body of Colorado Territory is now in session, I respectfully suggest for your consideration the propriety of immediately reorganizing the militia law. Your country is in a manner isolated from the balance of the federal government, on which you depend for supplies. Your line of transportation is now inoperative, and it devolves upon you, the representatives of the people, to take a step in a direction that will insure you, at least, an active and efficient militia force to guard over your interests. As matters now stand, the militia must be called out sooner or later, and I make these suggestions that there may be no misunderstanding between the civil and military.

Gentlemen, pardon my intrusion, I mean it for your good.

Very respectfully, your obedient servant,

T. MOONLIGHT,
Colonel 11th Kansas Cavalry, Commanding.

SPEAKER OF THE HOUSE OF REPRESENTATIVES,
Colorado City, Colorado Territory.

HEADQUARTERS DISTRICT OF COLORADO,
Denver, January 17, 1865.

SIR: By reason of the scarcity of troops in this district, our natural enemies the Indians, have possessed themselves of our lines of communication. They have burned ranches, killed innocent women and children, destroyed government property wherever it was found, driven off the stage stock, killed the drivers and passengers travelling on the coaches; in short, they are making it a war of extermination. We may look in vain for such timely military assistance as will protect the lives and property of settlers; nor can we hope for an eastern communication this winter, unless the citizens of the Territory band themselves together in a military organization, and spring to arms at your call as chief executive. The blood of the innocent and unoffending martyrs cries aloud for vengeance, and starvation stares in the face the living. You nor I cannot longer remain inactive, and be considered guiltless. It devolves upon the militia, as matters now stand to open the overland route, and keep it open until troops can be had from the east to make war on these savages of the plains, until there remains not a vestige of their originality. On behalf of the general government, and on my own responsibility, (trusting to the justice of the cause for my own protection,) I will furnish carbines to the first mounted and accepted company, and rifled weapons of improved pattern to all the balance; also, rations for the same as United States troops, and forage for the animals, with the proper allowance of transportation, and also horse equipments. My scouts inform me that the Indian spies are now prowling around the very skirts of this place, so that, in addition to your call for militia for field service, the city companies should at once be placed on a war footing, having daily drills, with appointed places of rendezvous, that we may not be caught napping.

I am, very respectfully, your obedient servant,

T. MOONLIGHT,
Colonel 11th Kansas Cavalry, Commanding.

Hon. S. H. ELBERT,
Acting Governor, Colorado Territory.

HEADQUARTERS DISTRICT OF COLORADO,
Denver, January 25, 1865.

SIR: I have the honor to acknowledge the receipt of your communication of yesterday, from Golden City, making inquiries as to the number of troops in this district, and the disposition made of them. I will cheerfully give you the desired information.

At Fort Lyon, which has lately been placed in my district, there are about 300 men. The mustering officer, Captain J. C. Anderson, has but returned after completing the organization of the 1st regiment, by consolidating it into six maximum companies. About forty men are at Fort Garland, but these now will be increased to 100. About forty men are at Camp Fillmore, but these will be increased to 100 also, as companies will be stationed together at posts so remote. One company will be stationed here of 100 men in place of the stragglers now doing duty. One company will be divided and stationed at Bijou Basin and Living Springs. This leaves only two companies at Fort Lyon. In addition to these, there are about seventy-five (75) recruits of the 2d Colorado; part of them are now at or near Junction, and the balance will join in a few days. There are about sixty men now at Valley Station, but these must be changed, owing to the new organization. There are about 500 men, all told, for duty, scattered from Fort Lyon, *via* Garland, Fillmore, Denver, and on route to Valley Station, a distance of about 450 miles.

The committee will see from this that so widely spread are the troops, that, even in a case of emergency, it would not be possible to get together more than 200 men in thirty-six hours.

Trusting this may be of service to you in your proceedings, I remain, very respectfully, your obedient servant,

T. MOONLIGHT,
Colonel 11th Kansas Cavalry, Commanding.

D. H. NICHOLS,
Chairman of Committee on Military Affairs.

HEADQUARTERS DISTRICT OF COLORADO,
Denver, January 31, 1865.

SIR: I have been looking eagerly and waiting patiently for the passage of the bill which was designed to relieve the people of this Territory from the ravages of the Indians. That bill was introduced at my suggestion, as the most feasible of all plans to raise troops rapidly and voluntarily for the opening of the overland route, and the keeping of it open until succor could arrive from the States. The Indians are every day becoming more desperate, and to-day there stands not a ranch, out of the many that were between Valley Station and Julesburg, and but very few on this side, and all since the introduction of that bill. I trusted implicitly in the patriotism and fidelity of the legislature, and that their wisdom and judgment would at once foresee the necessity of taking steps to defend their homes, their little ones, and the property of the people whom they represent. Am I mistaken? God forbid! Yet every indication of late seems to blight my fondest hopes. I cannot longer await the action of your honorable body, for this night's despatches from Junction inform me that about three thousand (3,000) Indians are marching up the Platte on both sides. Unless the legislature, within forty-eight hours, does something to relieve suffering humanity, and save this country from ruin and devastation, I will be compelled, much against my will, to proclaim martial law, shut up all houses of business, and force every man able to bear arms into the ranks, and send them out to protect their brethren, kill off the Indians, and establish permanent communication with the east. I cannot quietly look on and perform my duty to *this people, my country, and my God.*

I have weighed this matter well in my own mind, and what I have stated is my firm resolve, with a lingering hope that your honorable body will yet, and immediately, save this Territory from destruction, and themselves from the indignation of an infuriated people.

I have the honor to remain, very respectfully, your obedient servant,

T. MOONLIGHT,
Colonel 11th Kansas Cavalry, Commanding.

SPEAKER OF THE HOUSE OF REPRESENTATIVES, *Golden City.*

HEADQUARTERS DISTRICT OF COLORADO,
Denver, February 4, 1865.

DEAR SIR: I send this communication by special messenger, and respectfully ask that an answer to this, as well as that of January 31, ultimo, be returned. Time passes, and the danger increases—hence the urgency of my request.

I have been informed from various sources that a portion of the house took exceptions to my letter of the 31st of January, as being threatening and coercive in its tone. Permit me to say that nothing was further from my mind or intention. Liberty is a boon I prize too highly to wilfully deprive others of its blessing, and the course that I fear I must pursue for the salvation of this people is forced upon me by a combination of circumstances which, in my humble opinion, the legislature might, within the past two weeks, have scattered to the winds. This they have not done; therefore I must do something.

On invitation of your honorable body, and on the speaker's stand, in their presence, did I make known my feelings on the Indian question. There I urged the passage of that bill, and there I told them that I was opposed to martial law. My acts have not belied my words; but the time has come when "patience ceases to be a virtue," and when inactivity is a wilful "dereliction of duty." So far, I have been patient in the extreme, though not inactive. I have nothing to retract in my letter of January 31, but will adhere closely to my decision. I may err in addressing the house, and not the council. Should such be the case, it must be attributed to my ignorance of parliamentary rules, for I suppose that a measure of this kind would be acted upon in joint ballot.

I have the honor to be, very respectfully, your obedient servant,

T. MOONLIGHT,
Colonel 11th Kansas Cavalry, Commanding.

Hon. SPEAKER OF HOUSE OF REPRESENTATIVES,
Golden City, Colorado Territory.

HEADQUARTERS DISTRICT OF COLORADO,
Denver, Colorado Territory, February 6, 1865.

SIR: I have the honor to acknowledge the receipt of your communication of the 4th instant, (in behalf of the house of which you are an honorable member,) in which I am informed that the bill authorizing the issuing of $200,000 bonds for the purpose of mounting the militia called for, paying the bounty, &c., was *not* likely to pass; and also that a bill was likely to pass, (superseding the bond bill,) giving bounties to men who would enlist in the two Colorado regiments now in the field, and also that it had been represented to the house, as coming from me, that a sufficient number of men could be obtained in this way, so as to avoid the necessity of proclaiming martial law.

In reply, I would state that I am very sorry the bond bill did not pass over two weeks ago, for, to my mind, it was the surest and most honorable way that men could be raised and horses procured. I have never stated that a sufficient number of men could be enlisted for the old regiments, so as to meet the exigencies of the case; and even could these men be persuaded to enlist, I have not at present the horses on which to mount them. I should be pleased to see a bill pass authorizing the payment of a liberal bounty to recruits for the 1st and 2d Colorado regiments, for I think the regiments might be recruited up to the maximum; but I am sorry to say that such a bill at this late hour would not meet the necessities of the times. Men and horses must be had immediately, or else we must yield ourselves living sacrifices to inhuman savages; and who of us all are prepared to do this? I beg of you not to defeat the bounty bill because of the lateness of the hour which gave it birth, for, in my estimation, it will be of great assistance and good. I am more than sorry that I have now no other alternative but to proclaim martial law and suspend all business until a sufficient number of men (mounted) are had to open the overland road and protect the frontier settlers of the Territory. When I modified martial law, as it existed under the former district commander, I never expected to be compelled to recreate it with renewed severity.

Accept my thanks for your courtesy, and believe me, with esteem and respect, your obedient servant,

T. MOONLIGHT,
Colonel 11th Kansas Cavalry, Commanding.

Hon. E. T. HOLLAND,
Chairman of Military Committee.

HEADQUARTERS DEPARTMENT OF THE MISSOURI,
St. Louis, Missouri, March 9, 1865.

A true copy:

J. F. BENNETT, *A. A. G.*

ADJUTANT GENERAL'S OFFICE, *March* —, 1865.

Official:

—— ———, *A. A. G.*

Testimony of Colonel J. M. Chivington.

Interrogatories propounded to John M. Chivington by the Joint Committee on the Conduct of the War, and answers thereto given by said Chivington reduced to writing, and subscribed and sworn to before Alexander W. Atkins, notary public, at Denver, in the Territory of Colorado.

1st question. What is your place of residence, your age and profession?

Answer. My place of residence is Denver, Colorado; my age, forty-five years; I have been colonel of 1st Colorado cavalry, and was mustered out of the service on or about the eighth day of January last, and have not been engaged in any business since that time.

2d question. Were you in November, 1864, in any employment, civil or military, under the authority of the United States; and if so, what was that employment, and what position did you hold?

Answer. In November, 1864, I was colonel of 1st Colorado cavalry, and in command of the district of Colorado.

3d question. Did you, as colonel in command of Colorado troops, about the 29th of November, 1864, make an attack on an Indian village or camp at a place known as Sand creek? If so, state particularly the number of men under your command; how armed and equipped; whether mounted or not; and if you had any artillery, state the number of guns, and the batteries to which they belonged.

Answer. On the 29th day of November, 1864, the troops under my command attacked a camp of Cheyenne and Arapaho Indians at a place known as Big Bend of Sandy, about forty miles north of Fort Lyon, Colorado Territory. There were in my command at that time about (500) five hundred men of the 3d regiment Colorado cavalry, under the immediate command of Colonel George L. Shoup, of said 3d regiment, and about (250) two hundred and fifty men of the 1st Colorado cavalry; Major Scott J. Anthony commanded one battalion of said 1st regiment, and Lieutenant Luther Wilson commanded another battalion of said 1st regiment. The 3d regiment was armed with rifled muskets, and Star's and Sharp's carbines. A few of the men of that regiment had revolvers. The men of the 1st regiment were armed with Star's and Sharp's carbines and revolvers. The men of the 3d regiment were poorly equipped; the supply of blankets, boots, hats, and caps was deficient. The men of the 1st regiment were well equipped; all these troops were mounted. I had four 12-pound mountain howitzers, manned by detachments from cavalry companies; they did not belong to any battery company.

4th question. State as nearly as you can the number of Indians that were in the village or camp at the time the attack was made; how many of them were warriors; how many of them were old men, how mauy of them were women, and how many of them were children?

Answer. From the best and most reliable information I could obtain, there were in the Indian camp, at the time of the attack, about eleven (11) or twelve (12) hundred Indians; of these about seven hundred were warriors, and the remainder were women and children. I am not aware that there were any old men among them. There was an unusual number of males among them, for the reason that the war chiefs of both nations were assembled there evidently for some special purpose.

5th question. At what time of the day or night was the attack made? Was it a surprise to the Indians? What preparation, if any, had they made for defence or offence?

Answer. The attack was made about sunrise. In my opinion the Indians were surprised; they began, as soon as the attack was made, to oppose my troops, however, and were soon fighting desperately. Many of the Indians were armed with rifles and many with revolvers; I think all had bows and arrows. They had excavated trenches under the bank of Sand creek, which in the vicinity of the Indian camp is high, and in many places precipitous. These trenches were two to three feet deep, and, in connexion with the banks, were evidently designed to protect the occupants from the fire of an enemy. They were found at various points extending along the banks of the creek for several miles from the camp; there were marks of the pick and shovel used in excavating them; and the fact that snow was seen in the bottoms of some of the trenches, while all snow had disappeared from the surface of the country generally, sufficiently proved that they had been constructed some time previously. The Indians took shelter in these trenches as soon as the attack was made, and from thence resisted the advance of my troops.

6th question. What number did you lose in killed, what number in wounded, and what number in missing?

Answer. There were seven men killed, forty-seven wounded, and one was missing.

7th question. What number of Indians were killed; and what number of the killed were women, and what number were children?

Answer. From the best information I could obtain, I judge there were five hundred or six hundred Indians killed; I cannot state positively the number killed, nor can I state positively the number of women and children killed. Officers who passed over the field, by my orders, after the battle, for the purpose of ascertaining the number of Indians killed, report that they saw but few women or children dead, no more than would certainly fall in an attack upon a camp in which they were. I myself passed over some portions of the field after the fight, and I saw but one woman who had been killed, and one who had hanged herself; I saw no dead children. From all I could learn, I arrived at the conclusion that but few women or children had been slain. I am of the opinion that when the attack was made on the Indian camp the greater number of squaws and children made their escape, while the warriors remained to fight my troops.

8th question. State, as nearly as you can, the number of Indians that were wounded, giving the number of women and the number of children among the wounded.

Answer. I do not know that any Indians were wounded that were not killed; if there were any wounded, I do not think they could have been made prisoners without endangering the lives of soldiers; Indians usually fight as long as they have strength to resist. Eight Indians fell into the hands of the troops alive, to my knowledge; these, with one exception, were sent to Fort Lyon and properly cared for.

9th question. What property was captured by the forces under your command? State the number of horses, mules and poneys, buffalo robes, blankets, and also all other property taken, specifying particularly the kinds, quality, and value thereof.

Answer. There were horses, mules, and poneys captured to the number of about six hundred. There were about one hundred buffalo robes taken. Some of this stock had been stolen by the Indians from the government during last spring, summer and fall, and some of the stock was the property of private citizens from whom they had been stolen during the same period. The horses that belonged to the government were returned to the officers responsible for them; as nearly as could be learned, the horses and mules that were owned by private citizens were returned to them on proof of ownership being furnished; such were my orders at least. The poneys, horses, and mules for which no owner could be found, were put into the hands of my provost marshal in the field, Captain J. J. Johnson, of company E, 3d Colorado cavalry, with instructions to drive them to Denver and turn them over to the acting quartermaster as captured stock, taking his receipt therefor. After I arrived in Denver I again directed Captain Johnson to turn these animals over to Captain Gorton, assistant quartermaster, as captured stock, which I presume he did. Colonel Thos. Moonlight relieved me of the command of the district soon after I arrived in Denver, that is to say, on the —— day of ———, A. D. 186–, and I was mustered out of the service, the term of service of my regiment having expired. My troops were not fully supplied with hospital equipage, having been on forced marches. The weather was exceedingly cold, and additional covering for the wounded became necessary; I ordered the buffalo robes to be used for that purpose. I know of no other property of value being captured. It is alleged that groceries were taken from John Smith, United States Indian interpreter for Upper Arkansas agency, who was in the Indian camp at the time of the attack, trading goods, powder, lead, caps, &c., to the Indians. Smith told me that these groceries belonged to Samuel G. Colby, United States Indian agent. I am not aware that these things were taken; I am aware that Smith and D. D. Colby, son of the Indian agent, have each presented claims against the government for these articles. The buffalo robes mentioned above were also claimed by Samuel G. Colby, D. D. Colby and John Smith. One bale of buffalo robes was marked S. S. Soule, 1st Colorado cavalry, and I am informed that one bale was marked Anthony, Major Anthony being in command of Fort Lyon at that time. I cannot say what has been done with the property since I was relieved of the command and mustered out of service. There was a large quantity of Indian trinkets taken at the Indian camp which were of no value. The soldiers retained a few of these as trophies; the remainder with the Indian lodges were destroyed.

10th question. What reason had you for making the attack? What reasons, if any, had you to believe that Black Kettle or any other Indian or Indians in the camp entertained feelings of hostility towards the whites? Give in detail the names of all Indians so believed to be hostile, with the dates and places of their hostile acts, so far as you may be able to do so.

Answer. My reason for making the attack on the Indian camp was, that I believed the Indians in the camp were hostile to the whites. That they were of the same tribes with those who had murdered many persons and destroyed much valuable property on the Platte and Arkansas rivers during the previous spring, summer and fall was beyond a doubt. When a tribe of Indians is at war with the whites it is impossible to determine what party or band of the tribe or the name of the Indian or Indians belonging to the tribe so at war are guilty of the acts of hostility. The most that can be ascertained is that Indians of the tribe have performed the acts. During the spring, summer and fall of the year 1864, the Arapaho and Cheyenne Indians, in some instances assisted or led on by Sioux, Kiowas, Comanches and Apaches, had committed many acts of hostility in the country lying between the Little Blue and the Rocky mountains and the Platte and Arkansas rivers. They had murdered many of the whites and taken others prisoners, and had destroyed valuable property, probably amounting to $200,000 or $300,000. Their rendezvous was on the headwaters of the Republican, probably one hundred miles from where the Indian camp was located. I had every reason to believe that these Indians were either directly or indirectly concerned in the outrages which had been committed upon the whites. I had no means of ascertaining what were the names of the Indians who had committed these outrages other than the declarations of the Indians themselves; and the character of Indians in the western country for truth and veracity, like their respect for the chastity of women who may become prisoners in their hands, is not of that order which is calculated to inspire confidence in what they may say. In this view I was supported by Major Anthony, 1st Colorado cavalry, commanding at Fort Lyon, and Samuel G. Colby, United States Indian agent, who, as they had been in communication with these Indians, were more competent to judge of their disposition towards the whites than myself. Previous to the battle they expressed to me the opinion that the Indians should be punished. We found in the camp the scalps of nineteen (19) white persons. One of the surgeons informed me that one of these scalps had been taken from the victim's head not more than four days previously. I can furnish a child captured at the camp ornamented with six white women's scalps; these scalps must have been taken by these Indians or furnished to them for their gratification and amusement by some of their brethren, who, like themselves, were in amity with the whites.

11th qnestion. Had you any, and if so, what reason, to believe that Black Kettle and the Indians with him, at the time of your attack, were at peace with the whites, and desired to remain at peace with them?

Answer. I had no reason to believe that Black Kettle and the Indians with him were in good faith at peace with the whites. The day before the attack Major Scott J. Anthony, 1st Colorado cavalry, then in command at Fort Lyon, told me that these Indians were hostile; that he had ordered his sentinels to fire on them if they attempted to come into the post, and that the sentinels had fired on them; that he was apprehensive of an attack from these Indians, and had taken every precaution to prevent a surprise. Major Samuel G. Colby, United States Indian agent for these Indians, told me on the same day that he had done everything in his power to make them behave themselves, and that for the last six months he could do nothing with them; that nothing but a sound whipping would bring a lasting peace with them. These statements were made to me in the presence of the officers of my staff whose statements can be obtained to corroborate the foregoing.

12th question. Had you reason to know or believe that these Indians had sent their chief and leading men at any time to Denver city, in order to take measure in connection with the superintendent of Indian affairs there, or with any other person having authority, to secure friendly relations with the whites?

Answer. I was present at an interview between Governor Evans on the part of the whites, and Black Kettle and six other Indians, at Camp Weldmar, Denver, about the 27th of September, 1864, in which the Indians desired peace, but did not propose terms. General Curtis, by telegraph to me, declined to make peace with them, and said that there could be no peace without his consent. Governor Evans declined to treat with them, and as General Curtis was then in command of the department, and, of course, I could not disobey his instructions. General Curtis's terms of peace were to require all bad Indians to be given up, all stock stolen by the Indians to be delivered up, and hostages given by the Indians for their good conduct. The Indians never complied with these terms.

13th question. Were those Indians, to your knowledge, referred by the superintendent of Indian affairs to the military authorities, as the only power under the government to afford them protection?

Answer. Governor Evans, in the conference mentioned in my last answer, did not refer the Indians to the military authorities for *protection*, but for *terms of peace*. He told the Indians "that he was the peace chief, that they had gone to war, and, therefore, must deal with the war chiefs." It was at this time I gave them the terms of General Curtis, and they said they had not received power to make peace on such terms, that they would report to their young men and see what they would say to it; they would like to do it, but if their young men continued the war they would have to go with them. They said there were three or four small war parties of their young men out on the war path against the whites at that time. This ended the talk.

14th question. Did the officer in command of Fort Lyon, to your knowledge, at any time extend the protection of our flag to Black Kettle and the Indians with him, and direct them to encamp upon the reservation of the fort?

Answer. Major E. W. Wynkoop, 1st cavalry, Colorado, did, as I have been informed, allow some of these Indians to camp at or near Fort Lyon, and did promise them the protection of our flag. Subsequently he was relieved of the command of Fort Lyon, and Major Anthony placed in command at that post, who required the Indians to comply with General Curtis's terms, which they failed to do, and thereupon Major Anthony drove them away from the post.

15th question. Were rations ever issued to those Indians either as prisoners of war or otherwise?

Answer. I have been informed that Major Wynkoop issued rations to the Indians encamped near Fort Lyon while he was in command, but whether as prisoners of war I do not know. I think that Major Anthony did not issue any rations.

16th question. And did those Indians remove, in pursuance of the directions, instructions, or suggestions of the commandant at Fort Lyon, to the place on Sand creek, where they were attacked by you?

Answer. I have been informed that Major Anthony, commandant at Fort Lyon, did order the Indians to remove from that post, but I am not aware that they were ordered to go to the place where the battle was fought, or to any other place.

17th question. What measures were taken by you, at any time, to render the attack on those Indians a surprise?

Answer. I took every precaution to render the attack upon the Indians a surprise, for the reason that we had been chasing small parties of them all the summer and fall without being able to catch them, and it appeared to me that the only way to deal with them was to surprise them in their place of rendezvous. General Curtis, in his campaign against them, had failed to catch them; General Mitchel had met with no better success; General Blunt had been surprised by them, and his command nearly cut to pieces.

18th question. State in detail the disposition made of the various articles of property, horses, mules, ponies, buffalo robes, &c., captured by you at the time of this attack, and by what authority was such disposition made?

Answer. The horses and mules that had been stolen from the government were turned over to the officer who had been responsible for the same; and the animals belonging to Atzins was returned to them upon proof being made of such ownership. The animals not disposed of in this way were turned over to Captain S. J. Johnson, 3d regiment Colorado cavalry, with instructions to proceed with the same to Denver, and turn them into the quartermaster's department. After the command arrived in Denver, I again directed Captain Johnson to turn over the stock to Captain C. L. Gorton, assistant quartermaster, at that place. The buffalo robes were turned into the hospital for use of the wounded as before stated.

19th question. Make such further statement as you may desire, or which may be necessary to a full understanding of all matters relating to the attack upon the Indians at Sand creek.

Answer. Since August, 1863, I had been in possession of the most conclusive evidence of the alliance, for the purposes of hostility against the whites, of the Sioux, Cheyennes, Arapahoes, Camanche river, and Apache Indians. Their plan was to interrupt, or, if possible, entirely prevent all travel on the routes along the Arkansas and Platte rivers from the States to the Rocky mountains, and thereby depopulate this country. Rebel emissaries were long since sent among the Indians to incite them against the whites, and afford a medium of communication between the rebels and the Indians; among whom was Gerry Bent, a half-breed Cheyenne Indian, but educated, and to all appearances a white man, who, having served under Price in Missouri, and afterwards becoming a bushwhacker, being taken prisoner, took the oath of allegiance, and was paroled, after which he immediately joined the Indians, and has ever since been one of their most prominent leaders in all depredations upon the whites. I have been reliably informed that this half-breed, Bent, in order to incite the Indians against the whites, told them that the Great Father at Washington having all he could do to fight his children at the south, they could now regain their country.

When John Evans, governor of Colorado Territory, and ex officio superintendent of indian affairs, visited by appointment the Cheyenne Indians on the Republican fork of the Kansas river, to talk with them in regard to their relations with the government, the Indians would have nothing to say to him, nor would they receive the presents sent them by the government, but immediately on his arrival at the said point the Indians moved to a great distance, all their villages appearing determined not to have any intercourse with him individually or as the agent of the government.

This state of affairs continued for a number of months, during which time white men who had been trading with the Indians informed me that the Indians had determined to make war upon the whites as soon as the grass was green, and that they were making preparations for such an event by the large number of arrows they were making and the quantity of arms and ammunltion they were collecting; that the settlers along the Platte and Arkansas rivers should be warned of the approaching danger; that the Indians had declared their intention to prosecute the war vigorously when they commenced. With very few troops at my command I could do but little to protect the settlers except to collect the latest intelligence from the Indians' country, communicate it to General Curtis, commanding department of Missouri, and warn the settlers of the relations existing between the Indians and the whites, and the probability of trouble, all of which I did.

Last April, 1864, the Indians, Cheyennes, Arapahoes, and others, commenced their depredations upon the whites by entering their isolated habitations in the distant parts of this territory, taking therefrom everything they desired, and destroying the balance; driving off their stock, horses, mules and cattle. I sent a detachment of troops after the Indians to recover the stolen property, when the stock, &c., being demanded of them they (the Indians) refused to surrender the property so taken from the whites, and stated that they wanted to fight the troops. Again, when a few weeks after the country along the Platte river, near Fremont's orchard, became the theatre of their depredations, one Ripley, a ranchman, living on the Bijon creek, near camp Sanborn, came into camp and informed Captain Sanborn, commanding, that his stock had all been stolen by the Indians, requesting assistance to recover it. Captain Sanborn ordered Lieutenant Clark Dunn, with a detachment of troops, to pursue the Indians and recover the stock; but, if possible, to avoid a collision with them. Upon approaching the Indians, Lieutenant Dunn dismounted, walked forward alone about fifty paces from his command, and requested the Indians to return the stock, which Mr. Ripley had recognized as his; but the Indians treated him with contempt, and commenced firing upon him, which resulted in four of the troops being wounded and about fifteen Indians being killed and wounded, Lieutenant Dunn narrowly escaping with his life. Again, about one hundred and seventy-five head of cartle were stolen from Messrs. Irwin and Jackman, government freighters, when troops were sent in pursuit toward the headwaters of the Republican. They were fired upon by the Indians miles from where the Indians were camped. In this encounter the Indians killed one soldier and wounded another. Again, when the troops were near the Smoky Hill, after stock, while passing through a canon, about eighty miles from Fort Larned, they were attacked by these same Cheyenne Indians, and others, and almost cut to pieces, there being about fifteen hundred Indians. Again, when on a Sunday morning the Kiowas and Camanches were at Fort Larned, to obtain the rations that the commanding officer, on behalf of the government, was issuing to them, they, at a preconcerted signal, fired upon the sentinels at the fort, making a general attack upon the unsuspecting garrison, while the balance of the Indians were driving off the stock belonging to the government, and then as suddenly departed, leaving the garrison afoot excepting about thirty artillery horses that were saved; thus obtaining in all about two hundred and eighty head of stock, including a small herd taken from the suttler at that post.

Again, a few days after this, the Cheyennes and Arapahoes Indians, with whom I had the fight at Sand creek, meeting a government train bound for New Mexico, thirty miles east of Fort Larned, at Walnut creek, who, after manifesting a great deal of friendship by shaking hands, &c., with every person in the train, suddenly attacked them, killing fourteen and wounding a number more, scalping and mutilating in the most inhuman manner those they killed, while they scalped two of this party alive, one a boy about fourteen years of age, who has since become an imbecile. The two persons that were scalped alive I saw a few days after this occurred. Though it occurred within sight of Fort Zarah, the officer commanding considered his command entirely inadequate to render any assistance. But we think we have related enough to satisfy the most incredulous of the determined hostility of these Indians; suffice it to say that during the spring, summer, and fall such atrocious acts were of almost daily occurrence along the Platte and Arkansas routes, till the Indians becoming so bold that a family, consisting of a man, woman, and two children, by the name of Hungate, were brutally murdered and scalped within fifteen miles of Denver, the bodies being brought to Denver for interment. After seeing which, any person who could for a moment believe that these Indians were friendly, to say the least, must have strange ideas of their habits. We could not see it in that light

This last atrocious act was referred to by Governor Evans in his talk with the Cheyennes and Arapahoes Indians on about the 27th day of September, 1864, at Denver, Colorado Territory. The Indians then stated that it had been done by members of their tribe, and that they never denied it. All these things were promptly reported to Major General S. R. Curtis, commanding department, who repeatedly ordered me, regardless of district lines, to appropriately chastise the Indians, which I always endeavored to do. Major General S. R. Curtis himself and Brigadear General R. B. Mitchell made campaigns against the Indians, but could not find them; the Indians succeeded in keeping entirely from their view. Again, Major General J. P. Blunt made a campaign against the Indians; was surprised by them, and a portion of his command nearly cutto pieces.

Commanding only a district with very few troops under my control, with hundreds of miles between my headquarters and rendezvous of the Indians, with a large portion of the Sante Fe and Platte routes, besides the sparsely settled and distant settlements of this Territory, to protect, I could not do anything till the 3d regiment was organized and equipped, when I determined to strike a blow against this savage and determined foe. When I reached Fort Lyon, after passing over from three to five feet of snow, and greatly suffering from the intensity of the cold, the thermometer ranging from 28 to 30 degrees below zero, I questioned Major Anthony in regard to the whereabouts of hostile Indians. He said there was a camp of Cheyennes and Arapahoes about fifty miles distant; that he would have attacked before, but did not consider his force sufficient; that these Indians had threatened to attack the post, &c., and ought to be whipped, all of which was concurred in by Major Colley, Indian agent for the district of the Arkansas, which information, with the positive orders from Major General Curtis, commanding the department, to punish these Indians, decided my course, and resulted in the battle of Sand Creek, which has created such a sensation in Congress through the lying reports of interested and malicious parties.

On my arrival at Fort Lyon, in all my conversations with Major Anthony, commanding the post, and Major Colley, Indian agent, I heard nothing of this recent statement that the Indians were under the protection of the government, &c.; but Major Anthony repeatedly stated to me that he had at different times fired upon these Indians, and that they were hostile, and, during my stay at Fort Lyon, urged the necessity of my immediately attacking the Indians before they could learn of the number of troops at Fort Lyon, and so desirous was Major Colly, Indian agent, that I should find and also attack the Arapahoes, that he sent a messenger after the fight at Sand creek, nearly forty miles, to inform me where I could find the Arapahoes and Kiowas; yet, strange to say, I have learned recently that these men, Anthony and Colly, are the most bitter in their denunciations of the attack upon the Indians at Sand creek. Therefore, I would, in conclusion, most respectfully demand, as an act of justice to myself and the brave men whom I have had the honor to command in one of the hardest campaigns ever made in this country, whether against white men or red, that we be allowed that right guarranteed to every American citizen, of introducing evidence in our behalf to sustain us in what we believe to have been an act of duty to ourselves and to civilization.

We simply ask to introduce as witnesses men that were present during the campaign and know all the facts.

J. M. CHIVINGTON,
Lieu't Col. 1st Cavalry of Colerado, Com'd'g Dist. of Colerado.

Sworn and subscribed to before me this 26th day of April, 1865.

ALEXANDER W. ATKINS,
Notary Public.

ICE CONTRACTS.

Testimony of Mr. Addison Gage.

WASHINGTON, *February* 6, 1864.

Mr. ADDISON GAGE sworn and examined.

By Mr. Gooch:

Question. Where is your place of residence?

Answer. Boston, Massachusetts.

Question. What is your occupation? How long have you been engaged in your present business, and to what extent?

Answer. I have been twenty-five years in the ice business, and that is my business now. I think the average amount of my business for twenty years past would reach 75,000 tons of ice a year. The business of Addison Gage & Co. is confined to the city of Boston, and shipping ice from Boston. I have been interested for a great many years, in connexion with others, in supplying the cities of Charleston, South Carolina, Savannah, Georgia, Mobile, Alabama, and New Orleans with ice.

Question. Have you supplied any ice to the government at New Orleans since its recapture by our forces?

Answer. From some time in June, 1862, to about the first of April, 1863, I supplied the hospitals in New Orleans under written contract with the Surgeon General.

Question. Do you recollect what you received per ton for your ice?

Answer. I had $1 50 per hundred pounds, delivered daily, as they required.

Question. Delivered to the hospitals, or delivered to them to be taken to the hospitals?

Answer. Sometimes it was delivered by us at the hospitals, and sometimes delivered at the ice-house. We delivered it at the hospitals immediately in the city. Those outside of the city would send their ambulances or wagons to the ice-house for it.

Question. You delivered it at $1 50 per hundred pounds at the hospitals within the city proper, where it was wanted, and it was carried by the government from the ice-house to the hospitals outside of the city?

Answer. Yes, sir.

Question. Do you know the amount of ice you delivered, or the amount of your bills for ice during that period?

Answer. I cannot now give the exact amount. But the whole amount I received from the government for ice during that time was inside of $2,000.

Question. Did you supply all the ice the government required during that time?

Answer. I think I supplied all the ice that was required for the hospitals there, with the exception of perhaps some eight days that I was out of ice, and I cannot say now that I, or my partner there, did not bring the ice during that time and deliver it to the hospitals; at least, with that exception, I delivered all the ice that was required.

Question. Have you been supplying the government with ice during the past year at New Orleans?

Answer. Not to the government, but I supplied ice in New Orleans.

Question. At what rate did you deliver ice in New Orleans during last year?

Answer. The price of ice during the last year varied considerably. During 1863 the price was $2 per hundred pounds. But at one time, in consequence of vessels making very long passages, the price went up very high. I think ice was sold as high as $100 a ton, delivered in New Orleans. But that was only for a short time—for two or three weeks.

Question. Was your contract with the government an open contract? Were you continuing to supply them without limit as to time?

Answer. I think so; I think it merely stated that I was to supply them. Either party, I think, could dissolve the contract at any time by giving notice.

Question. When did that contract terminate, and under what circumstances?

Answer. We were notified about the first of April, I think, that the government had ice of their own, and did not wish us to furnish it to them any longer.

Question. Did you know, prior to that time, that the government had advertised for ice for New Orleans?

Answer. Yes, sir.

Question. Tell us all you know in relation to that.

Answer. Some time in February, 1863, a gentleman calling himself Major Tiffany, representing that he had been connected with the government, and was a sort of agent for the government, called at our office in Boston and asked if I was going to put in any bid for supplying ice, under the proposals then out to supply the government with ice. I informed him that I did not think I should; that, with the exception of New Orleans, I did not care to supply ice, and as I was already supplying the government there as low as I could afford to do it, I did not think I would put in any bid at all, for I did not suppose the government would give a higher price for ice without first ascertaining whether I would continue to supply at the rates for which I was then supplying ice. He stated that he should have the giving out of those contracts, as he had got up the advertisements, and if I wanted any of them I must get them through him, as he had the management of that business. I declined to put in any bid, and never did.

Question. Do you know who did supply the government with ice at New Orleans?

Answer. This Major Tiffany.

Question. Do you know at what rate and in what manner?

Answer. He informed me that he supplied it at the rate of $22 50 per ton, putting it in at invoice weight, less 15 per cent. wastage on the passage.

Question. Where delivered, and how?

Answer. He delivered it on board the vessels alongside the levee in New Orleans, charging for the quantity invoiced as put in when the vessels were loaded, less 15 per cent.

Question. Did the government discharge the vessels, or did he discharge them?

Answer. The government discharged the vessels, and paid demurrage, allowing four days to discharge each vessel.

Question. What would be the ordinary wastage of ice in shipping it as that was shipped, and from the points where that was shipped?

Answer. That is a question I cannot answer accurately, for this reason: ice cannot be well loaded where these parties loaded that ice. Ordinarily for vessels loading ice in Boston and taking it to New Orleans the wastage during the winter months would probably be 15 per cent., and during the summer months 30 per cent. But the wastage upon cargoes shipped as those were would, in the ordinary course of business during the year, be more than three times that, probably, and I do not know but what more, in consequence of their being loaded by inexperienced men, not acquainted with the proper manner of packing ice on board vessels, and the inconvenience of getting proper packing material where those vessels were loaded in the State of Maine.

Question. Do you know what was done with this ice after it was delivered at the levee at New Orleans?

Answer. It was put into one of my ice-houses.

Question. Have you any knowledge of the vessels in which that ice was shipped—the amount they carried?

Answer. I have not, except of one. There was one—I cannot give the name of it now, because I did not bring my memorandum with me—whose invoice was nearly, if not quite, double the amount she could carry, as I was informed in New Orleans by the officer who discharged her. But that can be very easily ascertained, because a man experienced in loading vessels with ice can tell the tonnage within a very few tons; he can measure it almost as accurately as the ice could be weighed.

Question. Do you know anything about the time required to discharge any of those vessels?

Answer. Not of my own knowledge; I only know from report.

Question. What would have been a fair price for furnishing ice under that contract according to its terms?

Answer. I should have been willing to have taken the contract at the time he took it, and delivered the ice there at invoice weight, as he delivered it, for $11 or $12 a ton, and I would have had the quantity certified to which I should put on board the vessels at Boston. The freight would have been about $8 a ton, and the ice from $3 to $4 a ton; and I would have conducted the business as I usually do it, have had good ice and shipped it in good order; and as I should have put up that ice, the loss by wastage on the passage to New Orleans would not have been over 15 per cent. during the winter months, and not over 30 per cent. during the summer months.

Question. I find, from evidence furnished this committee by the War Department, that it cost the government $91,108 30 to supply ice to the hospitals in New Orleans during the year 1863. You say you supplied ice to the hospitals there from June, 1862, to April, 1863, and the whole amount of your bills with the government for that was less than $2,000?

Answer. Yes, sir.

Question. Can you explain to the committee how it is that there is such a remarkable difference in the cost of ice for those hospitals during the time in which you supplied it, and during the time in which it was supplied by this contractor, Tiffany?

Answer. In the first place, the ice never was properly shipped; the quantity that the government paid for probably never was put on board the vessels. In the next place, they took an ice-house and opened it just as often to furnish what little a hospital wanted as it would have been to furnish four times as much, or any large quantity. And the wastage in opening an ice-house is relatively the same to take out a very small quantity as to take out a large quantity. The percentage of waste is much less in delivering a large quantity of ice than in delivering a small quantity. The manner in which the government has done their business is not the same that individuals would follow. As ice dissolves into water very rapidly when the thermometer stands at 90°, it generally goes very quick if it is not taken care of. I have no other knowledge of my own in regard to the matter. There are probably various other causes which tended to increase the cost.

Question. Do you know whether the ice delivered there under that contract was treated as free ice—delivered very freely to everybody who wanted it?

Answer. I was informed so when I was down there, but I do not know how reliable that information was.

Question. What would have been the best and most economical way for the government to have supplied ice to its hospitals in New Orleans?

Answer. To have bought it of the dealers, day by day, as they did in 1862. There were plenty of dealers there who would have contracted to keep ice on hand.

Question. At what rate could the government have been supplied with ice there?

Answer. I should have continued to have supplied ice to the hospitals during the year 1863 for the same that I supplied it in 1862, if they had not stopped me. If I had had to make a new contract for 1863, I think I should not have agreed to supply ice at less than $40 a ton.

Question. Deliver it as you were then delivering it?

Answer. As I delivered it in 1862.

By Mr. Odell:

Question. Do you count by the long or short ton?

Answer. The short ton—2,000 pounds.

By the chairman:

Question. What, in your judgment, would it have cost the government for ice there had you supplied them during 1863 upon the terms at which you supplied it in 1862?

Answer. From the knowledge I have of the number of hospitals in New Orleans I do not believe it would have cost the government over $5,000 for the year 1863; at any rate, it could not possibly have been $10,000.

By Mr. Gooch:

Question. Do you mean to say that what cost the government $91,108 30, under the contract with Tiffany, could have been furnished by you for from $5,000 to $10,000?

Answer. That is what I mean to say; and allow me to say that the amount stated to have been paid to Major Tiffany does not include the rent of the ice-house, the expense of discharging the ice from the vessels, and the expense of men to take care of the ice-house and deliver the ice.

Question. Could you, or not, in your opinion, have supplied the government with all the ice they needed in New Orleans last year for what it cost the government to take care of and deliver ice after it was delivered to them under this contract?

Answer. I would have been willing to furnish them with all the ice they wanted there, delivered daily, for what it cost the government beyond the amount paid the contractor; that is, $3,000 for the ice-house, which the government have to pay me; then discharging the ice—it costs me a dollar a ton, invoice weight, to get the ice from the vessel into the ice-house; and then the expense of the men to take care of the ice-house and deliver the ice. That last item depends upon the amount delivered. He keeps four men in the ice-house to deliver this year, and if he does not deliver more than 200 or 300 pounds a day it comes higher.

Question. Why did you not put in a bid for that contract?

Answer. Because when Major Tiffany called upon me he represented himself as an agent of the government, and as having this in his control, so that no bid could be received except through him.

By Mr. Harding:

Question. He was the man who finally got the contract?

Answer. Yes, sir.

By Mr. Gooch :

Question. Do you know whether he called on other ice dealers in New England ?

Answer. He told me that he had.

Question. Did any dealer you know of bid for this contract ?

Answer. I think not.

By Mr. Odell :

Question. Did you see the advertised proposals ?

Answer. Yes, sir.

Question. Why did you not bid ?

Answer. For the reasons I have already given. I supposed at the time that the government would not alter the contract in New Orleans and pay a higher price without first taking some steps to find out whether I would continue to furnish it as I was then doing it. He represented that no contract could be given out except with his sanction. I therefore determined to have nothing to do with it.

Question. Did you understand him to be in the employ of the government at that time ?

Answer. Yes, sir, from his representations.

Question. By whom were these advertisements for ice signed ?

Answer. By Surgeon General Hammond, I think ; they may have been signed by Mr. Smith as acting Surgeon General.

Question. Did Mr. Tiffany's name appear at all in the advertisement ?

Answer. No, sir. He brought the advertisement into my office when he came in, and wanted to know if I had seen it. I told him I had.

Question. And the result of that interview with Major Tiffany induced you not to bid for the contract ?

Answer. Yes, sir.

Question. Did you suppose there was no use in bidding ?

Answer. It was that, taken in connexion with the situation that I held in New Orleans in supplying ice. I told him that there was no other point I cared about, and I would let the matter rest and see how it would come out. I think if I had not been supplying the government in New Orleans, and had wished to do so, I should have put in a bid ; but having things represented to me as they were, and not being exactly satisfied with the man, I concluded not to mix myself up with it in any way.

Question. Was the advertisement for any other points than New Orleans ?

Answer. Yes, sir ; the whole coast, clear down, I think.

Question. During the time you supplied ice to the government, did you fail to comply with any of its requirements ?

Answer. Only for the few days I have referred to.

Question. Was that a time when there was a pressure upon the hospitals ?

Answer. No, sir ; and I do not know but my man there furnished it all the time ; but I would not like to state that positively.

Question. Was the government induced to make other arrangements from any failure on your part ?

Answer. No, sir ; after the eight days were out my ice arrived, and I had plenty of ice from that time, and continued to supply it to the government all the time.

Question. Were you complained of to the government at any time during the time of your contract ?

Answer. Not at all.

Question. So far as you know, your manner of conducting business with the government was entirely satisfactory to the parties who had knowledge of it ?

Answer. Yes, sir.

By the chairman:

Question. Did the Surgeon General give any reason for taking the contract from you and giving it to other parties?

Answer. No, sir. The medical purveyor, or the man who had charge there, said that the government had their own ice, or that their own ice had arrived, and they would take no more from me after that time.

By Mr. Odell:

Question. Did they take your ice-house by agreement with you?

Answer. No, sir; they said that military necessity required them to take the ice-house. I had two or three there, and had not used this one to put ice in since I built it.

By Mr. Gooch:

Question. Do you know what would have been a fair price for ice supplied to the hospitals in New York and vicinity during the last year?

Answer. The only knowledge I have of delivering ice in New York is at David's island, where I think is the largest hospital. It would cost about five dollars a ton, invoice weight, there.

Question. Was there anything during the last season to cause any variation in the price of ice purchased in open market in New York?

Answer. Yes, sir; the price of ice varied very much last season in consequence of the government using or wasting so much, and of there not being an over-stock of ice. The price during the summer went up to a high rate—higher than I have ever known before.

Question. What was the maximum price in Boston, where you were familiar with it?

Answer. In the month of August I sold it as high as fifteen dollars a ton on board the vessel.

Question. For how long a time did that rate continue?

Answer. For only two or three weeks.

Question. What would have been a fair price during the last year to have delivered, say, eighty tons of ice at Annapolis, Maryland?

Answer. The way I have generally delivered there, it would be about five dollars a ton. I am basing these prices upon the idea that the contracts were made at the time the proposals advertised they should be made—not at a time during the summer, because there was a great change in the price.

Question. What would have been a fair price for, say, 3,500 tons of ice delivered here in Washington during the last year—I mean delivered in the vessel at the wharf, and taken out by the government?

Answer. Between six and seven dollars a ton.

Question. What would it have cost per ton to have got it into the ice-house?

Answer. I could not state, because, though I know where the government ice-house is here, I do not know the facilities for discharging vessels there.

Question. Properly stored and taken care of, how many people would 3,500 tons of ice have supplied in the city of Washington last year?

Answer. I should not want to state that, because I have no data to go upon.

Question. What would have been a fair price for delivering 1,428 tons of ice at Fortress Monroe during last year according to the terms of the advertisement you have already referred to?

Answer. These contracts were not given out according to the terms of the advertisement; if I recollect now, the advertisement was for delivering so much ice at these places. After making the contract, it was changed so as to take the ice at invoice weight. The way we understood the advertisement, it was to deliver ice at those place at so much, weighed there; whereas the contracts, after they were awarded, were changed to taking the ice at invoice weight, with certain percentage allowed for wastage from places of loading to the places of discharging, so that there was no chance for anybody to bid understandingly, the advertisement was so ambiguous. According to the terms of the proposal ice would be worth about the same at Fortress Monroe as at Washington—perhaps a little less.

Question. Did the government suffer much by this difference between the terms of the contracts and the terms of the proposals?

Answer. Yes, sir, very much.

Question. What would have been a fair price for delivering ice at Newbern last year? Understand that in all these cases the ice is to be taken from the vessels by the government.

Answer. Between eight and nine dollars a ton, I should think.

Question. What would have been a fair price, under the terms of this proposal, for delivering say 1,762 tons of ice last year at Hilton Head?

Answer. About the same price as at Newbern. The freight would have been about the same. The ice would have cost no more when invoiced.

Question. What would have been a fair price for the delivery of three hundred and twelve tons of ice at Key West last year?

Answer. About eleven dollars a ton; about the same as at New Orleans, because the freight would have been about the same, and the ice would have been worth about the same on board the vessel.

Question. What would have been a fair price for the delivery of four hundred tons at Pensacola, Florida?

Answer. About the same as at New Orleans—from eleven to twelve dollars a ton. It is the freight that makes the difference; the ice is worth no more on the vessel.

Question. Do you know anything about what was done with the ice at Pensacola last year?

Answer. The medical purveyor, who has charge now of the ice-houses at New Orleans, told me that he was at Pensacola last year when that cargo of ice arrived there. The government had no place in which to put it, and they dug a hole in the sand and buried it up, and in four days the ice was all gone.

By Mr. Harding:

Question. How long could the ice have been kept in the vessel?

Answer. Ice can be packed in a vessel so as to stay six months; but packed as that was it probably would not have lasted very long.

By the chairman:

Question. Would an ice merchant, who had contracted to be paid for what was put on board, be likely to take much pains in packing or storing the ice?

Answer. That would depend somewhat upon the character of the man.

By Mr. Gooch:

Question. Are you familiar with the delivery of ice at Baton Rouge?

Answer. I am constantly sending ice, by the hogshead, from New Orleans to Baton Rouge.

Question. What would ice cost per ton delivered at Baton Rouge—say a cargo of 325 tons?

Answer. When we are selling ice in New Orleans at $2 per 100, we charge packed to go up the river, to any of those points, half a cent a pound extra—that is, $2 50 per 100 pounds. The men who take it up there to sell again usually add about fifty per cent. to that, in order to make their profit in retailing in those places. A cargo of 325 tons, towed to Baton Rouge by the government, could be delivered there at about $300 more the cargo than it would cost at New Orleans.

Question. Have you any information as to whether this cargo of ice was towed up by the government?

Answer. I do not know of my own knowledge. I was told that it was.

Question. Are you familiar with the price of ice at St. Louis, Cairo, Louisville, Nashville, Memphis, or Vicksburg?

Answer. I am not.

Question. Can you inform the committee whether or not this J. C. Tiffany has been known in the ice trade?

Answer. He never has until the last year.

Question. Has A. T. Edgerton been known to the ice trade?

Answer. Never until the last year.

Question. Do you know what the business of these men has been heretofore?

Answer. Not of my own knowledge. Mr. Tiffany said he had been connected with the army.

Question. Did he say in what capacity?

Answer. He remarked that in so many months he had had so many millions of dollars of government money pass through his hands. I supposed from what he said that he was a paymaster, though he did not use that word.

Question. Have you any knowledge at all of Mr. Edgerton?

Answer. From information that I received from himself—nothing very definite—I think he has been a speculator following the army; a sutler, or something of that kind.

Question. Is there any connexion between Edgerton and Tiffany that you know of?

Answer. Mr. Edgerton told me that he was interested in all contracts taken with Tiffany.

Question. Have you any knowledge of any recent contracts made, or proposed to be made, by the War Department for the supplying of ice for this year? If so, state all that you know about it.

Answer. I have. On the 31st day of December last, my son and partner made a contract with J. W. Parrish & Co., of St. Louis. The person they made the contract with was George C. Hadley, who signs himself "for Parrish & Co." He represented that he had made a contract with the government—though the contract had not then been completed—to put 3,000 tons of ice into the ice-house at New Orleans at $25 a ton, measured in the house in New Orleans. My son took that contract from him at $18 75 per ton; the ice to be put in between now and the 1st of May next, measured and paid for as soon as put into the house. The house is to be furnished by me, and the government is to take the ice with the free use of the house.

Question. What have Parrish & Co. to do with the ice after you have put it into your ice-house, and it is ready for delivery?

Answer. Nothing at all.

Question. Does the government accept the ice as you store it in your ice-house, or is it to be delivered by Parrish & Co.?

Answer. The government receives the ice in the ice-house; and it is their ice and ice-house as long as the ice lasts.

By the chairman:

Question. So that the difference between what the government contracted to pay, and what you have agreed to deliver it for, is so much clear gain to Parrish & Co.?

Answer. Yes, sir; $18,750.

By Mr. Odell:

Question. In fulfilling this contract have Parrish & Co. any expenditure to make?

Answer. None at all. I should have bid for this contract had I seen the advertisement.

By Mr. Gooch:

Question. How did it happen that you did not see the advertisement?

Answer. It was only advertised in the western papers.

Question. In your judgment, for what amount can the government hospitals in New Orleans and vicinity be supplied with ice from the New Orleans market for the present year?

Answer. Not to exceed $10,000.

Question. That includes all the ice that would be necessary?

Answer. Yes, sir.

Testimony of Mr. L. J. Middleton.

WASHINGTON, *February* 9, 1864.

Mr. L. J. MIDDLETON sworn and examined.

By Mr. Gooch:

Question. What is your residence; your present business; and how long have you been engaged in it?

Answer. My place of residence is this city. My business is dealing in ice; and this is the ninth year, I think, that I have been engaged in it.

Question. Can you tell me about what quantity of ice you dispose of in a year in this place—that is, how much do you deliver to your customers?

Answer. We buy in the neighborhood of 10,000 tons; we do not sell more than half of it, or very little more.

Question. What proportion of the population in this city do you supply?

Answer. I really cannot tell.

Question. Do you and Mr. Godey supply the city of Washington?

Answer. I believe we do pretty much. I do not think that for the last two or three years there has been anybody but Mr. Godey and myself in the business.

Question. At what season of the year do you contract for your ice, and where?

Answer. We contract as soon as the ice-cutting is over; about this time of the year generally. We generally purchase our ice in Boston, sometimes in Maine; but we generally purchase in Boston, because the ice is packed better, and the freight is a little lower in Boston, and more easily obtained.

Question. Where is the quantity of your ice determined? That is, do you take it by the amount put on board the vessels in Boston?

Answer. We suppose it to be weighed in Boston; we know nothing about that part of it. We generally deal with men whom we can rely upon. They say: We have sent you, per bill of lading, so many tons of ice, and we take it for granted that it is so. Of course when we weigh it here we do not find so much, on account of the loss.

Question. Is there any difference between ice packed in Boston and ice packed in Maine?

Answer. I think we get more from the ice packed in Boston. In Maine the ice does not sometimes come out in good shape; some pieces are six feet, some three, and some two feet long; there is no regular shape to it. In Boston it is gauged to about twenty-two inches, and it packs much better in the vessel. And it is packed more nicely in Boston; in Maine they do not take that trouble. As to weighing it, I do not know how it is done in Maine; I do not know that it is done at all; it is measured, perhaps.

Question. Do you remember what your ice cost you last year, here in your ice-house?

Answer. Under the first contract that we made it cost us about $6 a ton here.

Question. Could you have contracted at that time for all that you wanted?

Answer. Yes, sir. The cost of ice here depends upon the freights; they vary sometimes, but at that time freight was from $2 50 to $3 a ton.

Question. Do you remember what you paid for ice in Boston last year under your contract?

Answer. The contract price was $2 50 a ton from January until May, $3 a ton from May to July, and $3 50 a ton after July for the balance of the contract. The freights varied from $2 50 to $5 a ton, but not often as high as $5. It averaged, I suppose, about $3.

Question. Can you tell me what would be the average percentage of waste during the year between Boston and this place, when the ice is delivered and put into your ice-house in this city?

Answer. I have never made an exact calculation, but it is supposed that the waste between Boston and here is 10 per cent. It depends very much upon the time the vessel stays out; they sometimes stay out a month, and when you get into the river, where the water is warm, it wastes a great deal. If you make a quick passage the waste is not so much. We have estimated it to be in the neighborhood of 10 per cent. on an average.

Question. At what rate per pound did you deliver ice here during last year?

Answer. We sold it last year, in the beginning, to the government hospitals at 75 cents per 100 pounds, before this contractor commenced; the ice weighed and delivered at my office. We sold it to our regular customers for about the same price, delivered about in the city. We had to raise it, because our contractor in Boston failed to perform his part, and we were compelled to buy elsewhere, and charged a cent a pound.

Question. At what rate could you have supplied the hospitals from your ice-house during the last season?

Answer. I proposed to do it for 75 cents per 100 pounds, or $10 a ton, put up in my ice-house, and the key of the house handed to the medical purveyor.

Question. Weighed as it was put into the ice-house?

Answer. Yes, sir. I will say that I am very glad I did not get the contract, for I should have lost money by it. Still I should have carried it out if I had got it.

Question. Do you know why your proposal to supply at 75 cents per 100 pounds and deliver as wanted was not accepted by the government?

Answer. I do not. I put in my proposal about half an hour before the time for opening the bids. I did not remain to see them opened; but I called upon Dr. Smith the next day and asked if he could tell me who was the successful bidder. He said it had been given to Mr. Godey by the medical purveyor, but the bid was not exactly acceptable. I did not learn why it was not acceptable. He said he thought the contest was between a Mr. Tiffany and myself. I told him that if I got the contract I should comply with it, and do everything I could to give satisfaction. He told me that the bids had to be re-examined; that there was some difficulty about them, but I should know the next day. I called upon Dr. Smith the next day, and said that I wanted to know about the matter in order to make my arrangements in time. He said he would let me know in the afternoon. I received a note from him that afternoon, stating that Mr. Tiffany's bid was so far below mine that he should be obliged to give it to him.

Question. Have you a copy of your proposal under that advertisement?

Answer. Yes, sir. This is it.

"WASHINGTON, D. C., *February* 23, 1863.

"We, the undersigned, propose to furnish the medical and hospital department of the army, until the first day of January, 1864, with all the ice required at Washington, District of Columbia, stored in suitable ice-houses, for $10 per ton of 2,000 pounds; the ice gathered in Massachusetts and Maine, and of the best quality.

"Or we propose to deliver it to the hospitals and other places to be supplied within the limits of Washington and Georgetown, and in the immediate vicinity, the amount required at 75 cents per 100 weight.

"L. J. MIDDLETON,
"WILLIAM W. RUSSELL,
"*Firm of L. J. Middleton & Co.*

"We have ample facilities for storing 10,000 tons."

Question. There was to be no charge to the government for the use of the ice-house?

Answer. No, sir. I had a house that would hold from 2,000 to 2,500 tons, which I presumed would be sufficient, at any one time, to supply all that the government would want. I do not now recollect whether the government got any ice from us at a dollar the 100 pounds. But our prices were put up after the difficulty with our folks in Boston, who had a short allowance of ice, and therefore failed to perform their contract. The government ran out of ice, and sent to me. I told them I would charge them $1 a hundred-weight, or, if they wished, I would run them a cargo. They preferred to borrow a cargo, which they returned.

Question. Mr. Tiffany received the contract?

Answer. Yes, sir.

Question. Do you know what arrangements were made by Mr. Tiffany, or where the ice was stored here?

Answer. It was deposited in the government ice-house, as I understood it; the way was this: I called upon Dr. Smith to know about the matter; he said the government would have a house of its own very shortly, and they intended to allow Mr. Tiffany $2 a ton more for the ice, and the house would belong to the government after the contract ended. I asked how much ice was wanted; he said he did not know—2,000 or 3,000 tons. I said if they allowed $2 a ton for the house it would cost a great deal of money. He said the government would want an ice-house. I have been near enough to the house to see through it. It is at the foot of 11th street. It was not made very tight; but I have not examined it very closely.

Question. From the examination that you have given it, are you of the opinion that it was a suitable place in which to store ice?

Answer. No, sir. I do not think it was tight enough to secure ice, for unless ice is kept from the air, you might as well keep it out of doors, perhaps better; for the wind would cut it all to pieces, and there would be no telling but what it would melt in twenty-four hours.

Question. Will you describe that ice-house as nearly as you can?

Answer. I have never examined it very closely, and I should not like to trust my eyes in regard to it. If I expected to get anything like the amount out of a house again that I put in it, I would put a house up as we do, in this way: we usually build houses with two walls, three feet apart, filled in with tan or sawdust to exclude the sun and air. I do not know what was the thickness of this house.

Question. What would an ice-house suitably built have cost, sufficiently large to have held 3,000 tons of ice?

Answer. I built one on my wharf two years ago, a very nice one, one of the best in the city—except, perhaps, that of Mr. Godey, who has put one up in the best style—which cost from $1,800 to $2,000; it could contain from 1,800 to 2,000 tons of ice.

Question. How much would this ice-house contain that Mr. Tiffany built?

Answer. I have not examined it closely; perhaps a thousand tons or something like that.

By Mr. Odell:

Question. Was it built on government land, or on private land?

Answer. I cannot state; I have never made any inquiries about the matter. It is down about the 11th street wharf. I have not been there since the house was built but once, and that was an accidental visit.

By Mr. Gooch:

Question. How is it—could you or not have supplied the government with ice, delivered from your own ice-house, very much cheaper than they could obtain it from a house kept by themselves, taking out only what was wanted for use?

Answer. Yes, sir; there is a great difference. When we deliver it we sustain the loss, and the government does not.

Question. The taking out a large quantity of ice does not waste more than taking out a small quantity?

Answer. No, sir. We take all the loss from the time it leaves Boston until we serve it out to our customers. We proposed to deliver it to the government at 75 cents per 100 pounds, delivered at the hospitals in the city, weighed there, of course, that they may be satisfied.

Question. Have you at any time supplied the hospitals here?

Answer. Yes, sir.

Question. During what period?

Answer. I supplied them in 1862, until the army left Harrison's landing. I had an order from the Surgeon General to supply ice to the hospitals here. I have forgotten the price, but I think it was 75 cents per 100 pounds; I do not know but what it may have been 60 cents; in fact, I believe it was. I saw a copy of an order, when the ice was brought up from Harrison's landing, sent to all the hospitals by the medical director, requiring them to purchase their ice from Mr. Godey, or to get it from him; I do not know what arrangement was made exactly; it was government ice, though. I said nothing about it, but squared up my books, made out my bills, &c., and settled up with the government, and I had nothing more to do with the hospitals until last spring. I commenced then again without any formal proposal; they came to me and asked if I would sell them ice, and I said "Yes, at 75 cents per 100 pounds," and I did so until June or July, but I did not supply them after that.

Question. Did you during that time supply all the hospitals?

Answer. No, sir; I think Mr. Godey had a part of them.

Question. Can you give us copies of your bills—the amounts of ice delivered and the prices charged?

Answer. I think so. The bills are on my books and I can copy them. You mean for 1863, I believe?

Question. Yes, sir. And I should like for you to state about the year before. State to us what you supplied to the hospitals for such and such a time, and at what prices.

Answer. They settled up with me every month, and it would be an easy matter to give that statement.

Question. Which is the most economical way in which the government can supply itself with ice for hospitals in Washington and its vicinity?

Answer. I think the cheapest plan is to purchase the ice from the dealers, and let contracts alone. We can furnish them with all the ice they want at a specified rate. It would not cost half what it would for the government to buy it and deliver it themselves.

Question. How is it that you can furnish it cheaper than the government can supply itself?

Answer. Because the government takes the loss, and not the dealers. If you contract it at $10 a ton at the ice-house, you will not get more than half of it really. Now, we employ our own teams to supply it through the town, and they can as well take the hospitals in their turn. We charge individuals a cent a pound for 16, 18, or 20 pounds a day. We charge the government a cent a pound and deliver it to the hospitals every day, giving them 600, 800 or 1,000 pounds a day, and we take the loss, and not the government.

Question. You are acquainted with all the principal ice dealers of the country?

Answer. Yes, sir; with most of them.

Question. Are you acquainted with Goslow & Scott as ice dealers?

Answer. No, sir.

Question. Do you know J. C. Tiffany as an ice dealer?

Answer. No, sir; I never heard of him until last year.

Question. Do you know A. Tracy Edgerton or J. W. Parrish & Co. as ice dealers?

Answer. No, sir.

WASHINGTON, *February* 10, 1864.

Mr. L. J. MIDDLETON recalled and examined.

By Mr. Gooch:

Question. Have you prepared the statement asked for by the committee showing the amount of ice furnished to the hospitals in Washington and vicinity by you during the years 1862 and 1863?

Answer. Yes, sir; this is the statement:

Ice furnished the following hospitals in 1862 *and* 1863 *by L. J. Middleton & Co.*

1862.

Clifburn Hospital, 5,400 pounds of ice from May 23 to June 31, at 75 cents	$40 50
Douglas Hospital, 65,800 pounds of ice from July 1 to September 30, at 50 cents	279 89
Eckington Hospital, 35,400 pounds of ice from May 26 to November 18	177 00
Patent Office Hospital, 9,800 pounds of ice from May 26 to June 26, at 50 cents. This bill was not collected. Surgeon in charge left and never heard from	
Eruptive Fever Hospital, 11,900 pounds of ice from May 26 to September 30, at 50 cents	89 25
St. Elizabeth Hospital, 10,087 pounds of ice from June 7 to August 30, at 75 cents	75 65
Insane Hospital, 9,242 pounds of ice from July 7 to October 27, at 75 cents	69 31
Casparis Hospital, 11,700 pounds of ice from July 6 to August 30, at 75 cents	87 25
Ascension Hospital, 4,000 pounds of ice from June 18 to August 18, at 60 cents	24 00

Ninth Street Church Hospital, 3,200 pounds of ice from July 5 to August 8, at 75 cents	$21 20
Epiphany Church Hospital, 17,700 pounds of ice from June 20 to August 31, at 60 cents	106 20
13th Street Baptist Church Hospital, 15,500 pounds of ice from June 28 to August 31, at 50 cents	75 00
Unitarian Church Hospital, 5,300 pounds of ice from July 1 to August 15, at 50 cents	26 00
Judiciary Square Hospital, 54,200 pounds of ice from July 1 to August 31, at 50 cents	271 00
Union Chapel Hospital, 4,800 pounds of ice from July 7 to August 31, at 50 cents	24 00
Armory Square Hospital, 73,850 pounds of ice from July 1 to September 30, at 50 cents	369 25
Columbia College Hospital, 26,949 pounds of ice from August 12, to September 30, at 50 cents	134 75
Small hospitals: Providence; Ebinezer Church; Odd-Fellows' Hall; Trinity Church; Capitol; about	200 00
	2,070 25

1863.

Judiciary Square Hospital, 3,200 pounds of ice from June 1 to June 8, at 75 cents	$24 00
Kalorama Hospital, 1,035 pounds of ice from June 1 to June 13, at 75 cents	7 76
Post Hospital, (Camp Barry,) 9,100 pounds of ice from June 1 to October 31, at $1	91 00
Mount Pleasant Hospital, 4,630 pounds of ice from May 15 to June 10, at 75 cents	34 72
Campbell Hospital, 9,340 pounds of ice from May12 to June 8, at 75 cents	68 55
Harewood Hospital, 20,800 pounds of ice from May 12 to June 11, at 75 cents	156 00
Finley Hospital, 10,275 pounds of ice from May 11 to June 11, at 75 cents	77 05
Emory Hospital, 12,464 pounds of ice from May 5 to June 10, at 75 cents	124 62
St. Aloysius Hospital, 5,800 pounds of ice from May 2 to June 7, at 75 cents	43 50
Stanton Hospital, 14,566 pounds of ice from June 1 to June 8, at 75 cents	109 24
	736 49

Question. About what percentage of the year's supply of ice would be used during the months of May, (the last seven days of May,) June, July, and August?

Answer. I could not tell exactly. But we generally call the ice season five months; that is about as much as we can get out of the year. The rest of the year is scarcely profitable at all, unless it happens to be a very warm fall. I think we delivered two-thirds and more of our whole year's work in that time.

Testimony of Mr. Walter Godey.

WASHINGTON, *February* 9, 1864.

Mr. WALTER GODEY sworn and examined.

By Mr. Gooch:

Question. What is your present business, how long have you been engaged in it, and where is it carried on?

Answer. My business is the ice business; I have been in it five years last October; my place is in Georgetown, in this District.

Question. You carry on the ice business in Georgetown and Washington?

Answer. Yes, sir.

Question. Did you see the government advertisement for ice last year?

Answer. Yes, sir.

Question. Have you a copy of your bid?

Answer. I did not bring it with me.

Question. Do you remember the terms of your bid for supplying ice?

Answer. Yes, sir.

Question. Will you state them?

Answer. I agreed to furnish all the ice they would want in the hospitals in the District, they hauling it, at $14 a ton, weighed to them every morning as they got it.

Question. Did you make any other offer?

Answer. No, sir; not for the hospitals here. I agreed to furnish ice at Alexandria and Fortress Monroe at $13 a ton, by bill of lading, the government to take charge of the ice as it was delivered.

Question. Were you to be paid for the amount put on board the vessels where you purchased the ice?

Answer. I think I agreed to give it to them at that price, weighed at the different points.

Question. Did you agree to deliver it as they wanted day by day, or were you to deliver it by the cargo?

Answer. I was to deliver it here in Washington day by day as it was wanted.

Question. How at other points?

Answer. At the other points they were to take the cargo that I ordered to them.

Question. Will you furnish the committee with a copy of your proposal?

Answer. I think I have it at home; I may have left it at the medical purveyor's office. I had two as good men as there are in our town for securities. The contract was at first awarded to me by Mr. Johnson. An estimate was made under the proposals submitted by Mr. Tiffany, Middleton, and myself, and it was shown by the calculation that my proposal was some $8,000 to $10,000 better than that of Mr. Tiffany. I fought the matter with Dr. Smith for a month. He said, "Mr. Godey, I know you, and I know Mr. Middleton; but this Tiffany I do not know. But we have given Tiffany the contract, and we do not like to take things back." I said, "Doctor, I will bring you a statement from the office, of your own clerks, showing that you will save $8,000 or $10,000 to the government by taking my bid." Said he, "We will investigate the whole matter." I went there from time to time to see about it. I went to the office and got a statement of the saving to the government under my bid and showed it to him. He said, "We do not do business haphazard; we have competent clerks here to attend to it, and there is no such loss in ice." I then said, "Doctor, I do not suppose it is worth while for me to come in very often here." He said, "I will have the thing investigated." After a time I went there again, and he went into the Surgeon General's office, and said a few words, and came out again, and said to me, "We have thoroughly investigated the matter, and I do not see that there is any cheating in it." I bade him "good morning," and came away.

Question. Were the terms on which you proposed to furnish the ice better than those of any other bidder?

Answer. I do not know what Mr. Middleton's bid was. But the contract was at first awarded to me.

Question. Were you present when the bids were opened.

Answer. Yes, sir.

Question. Where were they opened?

Answer. At the medical purveyor's office.

Question. By whom were they opened?

Answer. By Mr. Henry Johnson, then acting medical purveyor.

Question. And was it declared by him that the contract was yours?

Answer. Yes, sir.

Question. And it was then refused to you by Dr. Smith, and this conversation subsequently occurred as you have stated.

Answer. Yes, sir. If you will look at the books of the office where the accounts of the hospitals are kept, and take the amount of ice delivered to the hospitals, and the amount of ice shipped here, you will see for yourselves that there would have been from $8,000 to $10,000 saved on my bid.

Question. For the hospitals in the city of Washington and vicinity?

Answer. Yes, sir. I happened to be at the office about a month ago; the clerk there is a very clever fellow, and I wanted to know what the ice cost them. He told me that there was so much ice shipped, and so much ice delived to the hospitals. My bid was $14 a ton weighed to them here. They paid $9 45 a ton by bill of lading. I made the difference to be about $10,000. Their own books will show that.

Question. Have you furnished ice to the hospitals here during any period; and if so, when?

Answer. I furnished ice, from the commencement of the hospitals here, for the same time Mr. Middleton furnished.

Question. For how long a time?

Answer. Up to this contract, except a year ago last fall, when they had some come up here with the army from Harrison's landing.

Question. Can you give us the periods during which you furnished ice, and the amount per month?

Answer. Yes, sir.

Question. At the time you were furnishing ice, was there anybody else but Mr. Middleton furnishing ice to them?

Answer. No, sir; I believe not.

Question. Did you and he furnish to the hospitals all the ice required?

Answer. Yes, sir; and the stewards told me they were never better accommodated or better supplied.

By the chairman:

Question. Where do you get your ice?

Answer. From Boston and Maine; principally from Boston, when there is a good supply there.

By Mr. Gooch:

Question. Do you know at what rate you could have contracted for ice, making your contract as early in the season as February or March?

Answer. I bought some 1,600 tons of ice in February, shipped in March and April, and it cost me $2 a ton in Boston. I contracted for 5,000 tons, but did not get this contract, and therefore did not take but 1,600 tons.

Question. What does it cost you to ship ice from Boston to this place?

Answer. From $2 to $3 and $3 50 a ton.

Question. According to the season of the year in which it is shipped?

Answer. Yes, sir. Later in the season ice got higher, and when my contract run through I bought at higher prices. Of course, if I had got this contract I should have got a larger supply.

Question. What would be the ordinary amount of waste between Boston and here in ice?

Answer. I have weighed it in June, July, and August, and I always find that I lose about 25 per centum.

Question. And to points further south the waste would be greater?

Answer. I should think so. Get it on early in the season, it comes on dry, and you do not lose so much.

Question. What, in your opinion, is the best and most economical way in which the government can furnish ice to the hospitals in Washington and vicinity?

Answer. From the dealers here, I think.

Question. Purchasing daily?

Answer. Yes, sir; you get your net weight then, and we have all the losses.

Question. The government can have what it wants, and pay for what it uses?

Answer. Yes, sir.

Question. Which ice turns out best here, ice packed in Boston, or ice packed in Maine?

Answer. The Boston ice. I have been treated very badly in Maine ice. Last year, when they got short, the firm I deal with in Boston bought ice in Maine and shipped it to me. And, instead of their weighing their ice there, I understand they measure it. There were two cargoes came here, one said to be 300 tons, which I weighed and had but 102 tons; the other cargo of 250 tons, and I did not get 90 tons out of it.

By the chairman:

Question. What was the occasion of such great waste?

Answer. Well, they did not put it in the vessel.

By Mr. Gooch:

Question. Do you know where the government kept its ice here last summer?

Answer. They kept it on the 11th street wharf.

Question. Do you know the house that the ice was kept in?

Answer. I have seen it.

Question. By whom was it built?

Answer. I understood that it was built by Tiffany, and that he got more per ton for his ice on that account.

Question. How much more?

Answer. I understood it was $2 a ton until the house was paid for.

Question. Was the house a suitable one, and properly built for storing ice?

Answer. No, sir; I have been up to it. The house is built with scantling or joists, about eight inches wide, and stuffed with sawdust, or hay, or any trash. It was no house to keep ice in, that is certain. I would not put a pound of ice in such a house as that. I looked at it a month ago when I was down by there, and the roof had sunk down considerably. I am myself a carpenter by trade, and know what kind of work it is. If you will look at the houses built by me and Mr. Middleton, and then at the one Tiffany built, you will see the difference at once.

Question. Can you tell what that house ought to have cost?

Answer. That house cost, I should judge, from $1,200 to $1,400; mine has cost me nearly $3,000.

By Mr. Loan:

Question. Would you have lost money in furnishing ice to the government under the contract you proposed?

Answer. If we make a contract——

Question. That is not my question. Would you have lost money under the contract you proposed?

Answer. No, sir.

Question. How can you make a profit and furnish ice to the government cheaper than it can furnish its own ice?

Answer. We fill our ice-houses up, and are generally taking it out and putting it in all the time. We keep our ice moving; our cargoes do not stand long, not more than a week or so. If the government puts a large quantity of ice in an ice-house, and use but a small quantity daily, the ice is wasting all the time. But our ice is constantly moving. It would not do for us to keep a cargo on hand more than a week or two, because we should lose our profits. The faster we can push our ice out the better for us. If you put all your ice into an ice-house you will be subject to a dead waste there. If you put up a thousand tons and let it lay there two, or three, or four months, you are losing all the time. We put up a thousand tons and it lasts us three or four weeks; there is the difference.

Question. What is the percentage of loss by wastage in ice-houses per month?

Answer. I could not tell that.

Question. Are there any other advantages in favor of the dealer—any other reasons why you should make it profitable in preference to the government?

Answer. Where we supply it, the government is not bothered with a check against each hospital, or with men to handle the ice. We keep the men ourselves to attend to the business, and thus that much is saved to the government.

Question. Are there any other means of saving that you can state?

Answer. I do not think of any now.

By the chairman:

Question. Do not men who transact business for themselves generally do it better and with less waste than government agents do?

Answer. Yes, sir, certainly.

By Mr. Gooch:

Question. Are you acquainted with the principal ice dealers in the country?

Answer. I know a great many of them.

Question. Do you know Gosner & Scott, or J. C. Tiffany, or A. Tracy Edgerton, or Parrish & Co., as ice dealers?

Answer. No, sir, I do not.

WASHINGTON, *February* 10, 1864.

Mr. WALTER GODEY recalled and examined.

By Mr. Gooch:

Question. Have you prepared the statement asked for by the committee, of the amounts of ice furnished by you to the hospitals in this city?

Answer. Yes, sir, this is it:

Ice delivered to different hospitals in Washington and vicinity in 1862 *by Walter Godey.*

	Pounds.
Seminary hospital	28, 915
Clifford hospital	121, 450
Carver hospital	149, 690
Mount Pleasant hospital	102, 560
Columbian College	30, 490

Stone hospital	19, 800
Ryland Chapel	7, 795
Camp Sprague	43, 955
Emory hospital	62, 529
Union hospital	23, 382
8th Street hospital	3, 060
Ascension Church, 9th street	5, 250
" " 10th street	5, 300
Corner 6th and E streets	3, 180
Corner 6th and D streets	3, 285
Georgetown College	5, 760
Waters's Warehouse	3, 575
Presbyterian Church	1, 132
Total	621, 108
Tons	$310\frac{1108}{2000}$

By Mr. Loan:

Question. What price did you charge the government for this ice?

Answer. I charged sixty cents per 100 pounds, or twelve dollars a ton.

Question. What quantity of ice was brought up with the army of the Potomac and stored in your ice-house at the time you have mentioned?

Answer. I cannot state positively now; but I think it was between 600 and 700 tons. It was not weighed; that is merely my judgment, for I would not weigh the ice at my own expense. I made rather a loose bargain. I paid for discharging the ice, and gave my house to store it in, for which I was to receive one ton of ice out of every two tons.

By Mr. Gooch:

Question. Did you take one ton of ice out of every two tons for the use of your ice-house?

Answer. Yes, sir.

Question. Did the balance of the ice supply the hospitals for the rest of the season?

Answer. Yes, sir, until the spring.

Question. Do you concur with Mr. Middleton in what he has said about the length of the ice season?

Answer. Yes, sir.

Testimony of Mr. Robert A. Payne.

WASHINGTON, *February* 10, 1864.

Mr. ROBERT A. PAYNE sworn and examined.

By Mr. Loan:

Question. What is your place of residence?

Answer. Georgetown, District of Columbia.

Question. In what capacity were you engaged in March, 1863?

Answer Chief clerk to the medical purveyor.

Question. Will you examine this contract (contract with J. C. Tiffany) and state if you were in the office at the time that contract was made?

Answer. Yes, sir; I was.

Question. Will you state what you know about the advertisement for this contract, and the bids in relation to it, and everything attending it, up to the final consummation of that contract, so far as you remember?

Answer. All that I can state is, that proposals were advertised for in due form for furnishing ice. There were some five or six bidders for the places embraced in Tiffany's contract.

Question. State who they were.

Answer. Mr. Godey, of Georgetown, was the principal bidder for Washington, Georgetown, Aquia Creek, and Fortress Monroe. Mr. Middleton was a bidder for Washington, but I have no recollection whether he made any further bids. I think there were several other bidders for Washington, but I do not recollect their names now.

Question. Were you present when the bids were opened?

Answer. Yes, sir; upon opening the bids we at the office decided that Mr. Walter Godey, of Georgetown, was the lowest bidder for Washington. I think Mr. Tiffany was in the office at the time, but he immediately went out; where he went I do not know. But after the notice from our office was sent down to the Surgeon General's office that the bids had been opened and we had awarded to Mr. Godey the contract for furnishing ice to Washington, and I do not know but what of Aquia Creek and the other points, the thing was afterwards changed at the Surgeon General's office and the contract given to Mr. Tiffany.

Question. Do you know what reasons induced this change?

Answer. I understood that Dr. Smith, the Assistant Surgeon General at the time, said that he thought that Mr. Tiffany's bid was the lowest. But we were universally of the opinion—and I made out several statements myself that would convince any youngster of 12 or 13 years of age—that Mr. Godey's proposition was the cheapest for the government by some $15,000 or $20,000. And the result has proved it to be so, as I have understood since Mr. Tiffany furnished the ice. Mr. Godey's proposition, I think, was to furnish the ice and deliver it at $13 or $14 a ton. I do not recollect what Mr. Tiffany's proposition was; but this contract will show. (Reads:)

"That for each and every ton of ice delivered at Washington, D. C., and accepted by the medical officer in charge, the said J. C. Tiffany shall receive the sum of $10 50."

Then there was an arrangement that he should be paid per bill of lading, and also paid for building an ice-house, and also paid for wagoning this ice. All this made a difference, so that under this contract the loss to the government was some $10,000 or $15,000, and I do not know but more. As I said before, I made out several statements showing the whole cost under the different proposals. And I think that at the time there was also a bid for New Orleans lower than the one put in by Mr. Tiffany; in fact, I am almost confident of it.

Question. Can you state who the party was who submitted a lower bid for New Orleans?

Answer. I cannot. We made out a written statement for the Surgeon General, setting forth who were the bidders and what were their bids.

Question. What do you know in regard to the ice-house that was built by Mr. Tiffany?

Answer. I do not know much about it; I know that it was a long time in being built, and that we had to purchase ice from dealers here—from Mr. Middleton and Mr. Godey—for some two or three months after the contract was given out to Mr. Tiffany. I have understood that the ice-house was very poorly put up.

Question. Have you any knowledge upon that matter?

Answer. No, sir; I was down there while it was being built, but I have no been there since it was built.

Question. Do you know the capacity of that house?

Answer. I do not.

Question. You do not know why this change was made, and the contract given to Mr. Tiffany?

Answer. No sir; I do not know the reasons for changing it, further than I understood at the time that Dr. Smith conceived Mr. Tiffany's bid to be the lowest.

Question. The paper you sent to the Surgeon General's office was not referred back to your office for further explanation?

Answer. No, sir; after we had given them the list of bidders, they sent for the proposals, and we sent them.

Question. Was it the usual practice for the Surgeon General's office to act upon your decisions upon these questions, or was it usual for them to review your decisions?

Answer. As far as I can recollect, this was the only contract ever given out at that office.

Question. Do you know of any reason why the quantity of ice should have been increased in Washington at that time over what it had been prior to that time—you had been purchasing but a very small quantity of ice previously?

Answer. Yes, sir.

Question. What necessity, if any, was there for increasing the quantity?

Answer. I do not think there was any; and I do not know that the quantity of ice delivered and used was actually increased. I think, from what I understood at the time, that ice was brought here by Mr. Tiffany without orders from any person. As I understood, no orders came from Mr. Johnson, or the medical director, for so much ice. I think the contract says the ice is to be furnished from time to time in such quantities as required. I know of no reason for the increase, further than I believe there was some ice shipped to the army of the Potomac. I know that the year previous we occasionally sent ice to the army of the Potomac while I was there in the office.

Question. Under Tiffany's contract?

Answer. No, sir.

Question. Do you know of any reason why the quantity of ice required should be increased under Tiffany's contract?

Answer. No, sir, further than I imagine, if there was an increase, it was because of ice being shipped to the army of the Potomac, as we had been in the habit of doing the season before; but I do not know that that was done. One reason why the consumption of ice the year before was smaller was, I think, that when General McClellan came up from the Peninsula with the army of the Potomac they brought up some ice, which was all turned over to Doctor Lamb.

Question. What quantity was brought up?

Answer. I cannot tell you. I only know that there was a great discrepancy between the bills of lading and the amount of ice turned over to us from the army of the Potomac. We understood from the captains of vessels that the ice had laid there a long time and had lost by melting. In fact, Doctor Lamb has never receipted for any of the ice yet, and says he will not because there was such a discrepancy.

Question. Were there any orders given to Mr. Tiffany under his contract to furnish ice for any parties that you know of?

Answer. No, sir.

Question. Who received the ice from Mr. Tiffany under this contract?

Answer. It is made the duty of the medical director to receive the ice under the contract.

Question. Who did receive it, in fact? Do you know?

Answer. That I do not know.

Question. You have no means of knowing what quantity was delivered?

Answer. No, sir; I have not. I only know that a great many hospitals were complaining about the quantity of ice delivered; that it was smaller than the quantity proposed to be delivered by Mr. Tiffany's man who had charge of the ice-house. The whole arrangement was very blundering. The government paid for their ice, put it in their own ice-house, and Mr. Tiffany sent it out in his own wagon, by his own man. The hospitals complained that they received their ice at unseasonable hours; instead of getting it at eight or nine o'clock in the morning, they got it in the afternoon, at four or five o'clock. I think the medical director receipted for the ice as it was received here on the vessels.

By Mr. Odell:

Question. Did he receive the ice?

Answer. He must have received it if he receipted for it.

Question. Who is responsible for the amount of ice received?

Answer. The medical director is responsible for receiving as many tons as the bill of lading called for. It is his duty.

By Mr. Loan:

Question. Is he the man who did receive it, and receipt for it?

Answer. I think so.

Question. Who was he?

Answer. It was Doctor R. O. Abbott.

Question. Do you know what quantity of ice was actually received?

Answer. No, sir, I do not.

Question. You were not connected with that part of the business?

Answer. No, sir. The whole arrangement was at first intended by the Surgeon General to have been turned over to the medical director. And at all the other posts further down south I believe that is done.

By the chairman:

Question. Is this contract of Tiffany's made according to usage and custom in such matters?

Answer. I do not know. I am not very conversant with making contracts.

By Mr. Loan:

Question. Where are you now?

Answer. In the Provost Marshal General's office.

Question. How came you there?

Answer. I left the medical director's office, and then went in under Colonel Fry.

By Mr. Gooch:

Question. Is this a copy of the advertised proposals under which bids were received for ice last year at the time to which you have referred?

Answer. Yes, sir.

The following is the copy referred to:

PROPOSALS FOR ICE.

MEDICAL PURVEYOR'S OFFICE,
Washington, January 22, 1863.

Sealed proposals will be received at this office until Monday, the 23d day of February, 1863, at twelve (12) o'clock m., for furnishing the medical hospital department until the 1st day of January, 1864, with a supply of pure ice, to be delivered at the following places, viz:

Hilton Head, South Carolina; Newbern, North Carolina; Fortress Monroe, Virginia; Pensacola, Florida; Nashville, Tennessee; New Orleans, Louisiana;

St. Louis, Missouri; Cairo, Illinois; Washington, District of Columbia; Memphis, Tennessee.

As the quantity required at the respective posts is not precisely known, bidders will state the quantity of ice they can furnish, where it is gathered, price per ton of 2,000 pounds, and within what period they can furnish the amount of their bids; although it is desirable that bidders should propose to furnish the whole amount required at any one of the places proposed to be supplied.

Bidders will state what facilities they possess, if any, for storing the ice at the posts they propose to supply.

The ice must be of the best quality, subject to the inspection and approval of the officer in charge of the post where it is delivered. The full name and post office address of the bidder must appear in the proposal.

If a bid is made in the name of a firm the names of all the parties must appear, or the bid will be considered as the individual proposal of the party signing it.

Proposals from disloyal parties will not be considered, and an oath of allegiance must accompany each proposition.

Proposals must be addressed to Henry Johnson, M. S. K., U. S. A., and Acting Medical Purveyor, Washington, D. C., and should be plainly marked "Proposals for Ice."

The ability of the bidder to fill the contract, should it be awarded to him, must be guaranteed by two responsible persons, whose signatures are to be appended to the guarantee, and said guarantee must accompany the bid.

The responsibility of the guarantors must be shown by the official certificate of the clerk of the nearest district court, or of the United States district attorney.

Bonds in the sum of five thousand dollars, signed by the contractor and both his guarantors, will be required of the successful bidder upon signing the contract.

Form of guarantee.

We, ——, of the county of ——, and state of ——, and ——, of the county of ——, and State of ——, do hereby guarantee that —— —— is able to fulfil the contract, in accordance with the terms of his proposition, and that, should his proposition be accepted, he will at once enter into contract in accordance therewith.

Should the contract be awarded him we are prepared to become his securities.

(To this guarantee must be appended the official certificate above mentioned.)

The Surgeon General reserves to himself the right to reject any or all bids that he may deem too high or unsuitable.

HENRY JOHNSON, M. S. K., U. S. A.,
Acting Medical Purveyor.

Testimony of Mr. Manchester Eldridge.

WASHINGTON, *February* 10, 1864.

Mr. MANCHESTER ELDRIDGE sworn and examined.

By Mr. Gooch:

Question. What is your present business, and how long have you been engaged in it, and where?

Answer. I have been in Alexandria about ten years. I have been engaged in what is generally termed the commission and shipping business; but owing to the war I was compelled to change my business somewhat, and two years ago I went into the ice business, and have followed it until the present time. I was in it season before last and last season, and am now engaged in it, in connexion with my other business.

Question. Have you furnished any ice to the government or governmen hospitals during this period? If so, how much have you furnished, and for what periods?

Answer. Season before last I furnished ice to all the hospitals in Alexandria. I also furnished a great deal to the army; at one time I sent out some thirty odd tons, at the time of the defeat of General Pope.

Question. Can you give the committee the accounts from your books?

Answer. Yes, sir, I can do so; but I came away in a great hurry this morning and did not have time to prepare myself.

Question. Will you prepare for the committee a statement of all the ice delivered by you to the government or to government hospitals, and the months in which it was delivered?

Answer. I think I can give such a statement very nearly, and will do so.

Question. Who supplied the ice last year to the government hospitals and for government purposes in Alexandria?

Answer. I supplied them, I think, up to about the 20th of June; it might have been to nearly the first of July. I do not now remember the exact date at which I ceased to supply the government. After that it was supplied by the contractor.

Question. By what contractor?

Answer. I cannot answer that positively. I had supplied the hospitals the year before, and the surgeons seemed all to be very well satisfied with the manner in which I had done it. Several times I had been called upon at 10 or 11 o'clock at night for ice when there had been wounded brought in, and I had gone to the ice-house and delivered to them what ice they wanted. They took no more ice from day to day than they wanted; when it would be weighed out to them on the pavement, where they could see it weighed if they wished. Last year I made application to supply ice again to the hospitals. They said that so far as they were concerned they had been perfectly satisfied with me, and hoped I would get the order to do it again. But they said there had been an intimation that there would be a contract, and told me that if I desired to supply them, I better see the Surgeon General or the medical purveyor about it. I came to Washington and went to the Surgeon General's office, but I must say I did not have much opportunity to speak with him. He merely said there was going to be a contract. I also made an application to the medical purveyor, and he told me the same thing—that there was to be a contract, and that the contractor would supply Alexandria; that is, that they had given out a contract for Washington to supply all the ice necessary for the army and the hospitals around Washington, and Alexandria would be included and supplied by the same contractor. I therefore gave the matter up, and did not pretend to try any further.

Question. At what price per 100 pounds did you sell ice to the government year before last?

Answer. I think I supplied the hospitals for 75 cents a 100 pounds for the whole season.

Question. And at what price did you supply the government with ice last year, so far as you supplied any?

Answer. At the same price I think. I am under the impression that I did not raise on them at all, up to the time they quit getting ice of me.

Question. At what price would you have continued to supply ice to the government last year?

Answer. The probability is that I would have taken a contract to supply the hospitals during the season at $1 per 100 pounds.

Question. Delivered where?

Answer. Delivered at the hospitals as they wanted it. We got more than that for our ice during the season.

Question. Do you know in what manner ice was taken from Washington to Alexandria to be supplied there?

Answer. The surgeons told me that they received it at very great inconvenience sometimes. At times it was brought down on a tug-boat and put out on the wharf. Afterwards, I think it was delivered from their own wagons.

Question. Would there necessarily be a great amount of wastage in taking ice from Washington to Alexandria?

Answer. I should suppose there would be. I have on several occasions been compelled to call on Washington for ice in order to keep going. I would sometimes have a cargo out over time. In one instance I came to Washington and got ice, and took it down to Alexandria at very great inconvenience and extra expense, in order that the hospitals should not be short of ice, and I have generally found that not much less than fifty per cent. ran away between Washington and Alexandria in transporting it. Probably a small amount put on board a tug-boat and run right down would not waste so much. And I generally calculate on about twenty-five per cent. loss in distributing from the ice-house around to the inhabitants. But what we got from Washington from time to time generally turned out with not much less than fifty per cent. loss.

Question. When you supplied the hospitals did you deliver the ice at your ice-house, or at the hospitals?

Answer. It is weighed out at each hospital, and it is charged with what it weighs there.

Question. Do you know anything about the manner in which ice was supplied to the government by the contract last year?

Answer. I heard something about it from other parties. I bought a cargo of ice loaded at Gardiner, Maine, and when it arrived here I went on board the vessel, the schooner Marshall Perrin, Captain Gibbs. I said to the captain: "Did you see this ice weighed in?" Said he, "I did." I asked: "Do you think I got good weight?" He replied, "I think you did, very good weight, indeed:" I said: "It is important, when I am paying so high a price for ice, and such high freight, that I should get all I pay for." He said: "I think you have. The man who loaded this ice seems to be a very fair man. But if you had to pay as much freight on your ice as government is paying other parties, you might have cause to complain." I asked him why he said that. He said: "The vessels that were trading there for the government told me they carried more ice than they ever had carried or possibly could carry coal." Now, generally, so far as my knowledge goes, a vessel cannot carry much more than two-thirds as many tons of ice as they can carry tons of coal. The ice would fill the vessel long before she had loaded her full number of tons. Ice does not load a vessel heavy at all.

Question. In your opinion, in what way can the government supply itself with ice most economically for hospital use?

Answer. I think there is no better way than for the government to make a contract with somebody on the spot already in the ice business, or take it at the ruling prices during the season from the dealers in the vicinity.

Question. During the time you were supplying ice to the government did you furnish all that was wanted—all that was required at the hospitals?

Answer. Yes, sir. There was once or twice that I run out of ice on account of the vessels having extremely long passages; but, notwithstanding that, I went to great expense and great trouble to get it elsewhere, in order that the hospitals should not fall short. And I had letters from the head surgeons of the three departments in Alexandria last year giving me very high recommendations; and I also had one this year.

Question. Will you explain why an ice dealer in the vicinity can supply the government with ice cheaper than it can be supplied in any other way?

Answer. From the fact that he is already in the business, has made all his preparations for supplying ice to the citizens, and it comes right in in connexion with his regular business to supply the hospitals. I supplied the government with ice year before last at less prices than I supplied the inhabitants; and so I did last year, so far as I did supply the hospitals. It does not make much difference to me whether I get two or three cargoes more or less. I can get it a little cheaper, perhaps, by taking two or three cargoes more. But the outfit and every arrangement for supplying ice are already prepared by ice dealers in the business, and all the expense attending the ice business is partially paid by distributing ice to the inhabitants.

WASHINGTON, *February* 12, 1864.

Mr. MANCHESTER ELDRIDGE recalled and examined.

By Mr. Gooch:

Question. Have you brought with you the accounts which the committee asked of you when you were here before?

Answer. I have brought the account of the ice furnished the hospitals in 1862 as near as I can get it. I find that one or two memorandum books have been lost; the accounts were kept in little memorandum books. I presume the account will not be far either way from the amount furnished for that year. I have also made it up for the year 1863 to the time we quit furnishing ice, in June. For 1862 the amount of ice furnished the hospitals in Alexandria was about 320,000 pounds, which, at three-quarters of a cent per pound, would amount to $2,400. For the year 1863, until July 20, it was about 60,000 pounds, amounting to $450. I have calculated it at three-quarters of a cent per pound, though for some of it we charged a cent a pound.

Question. When did you commence to furnish ice to the hospitals in Alexandria?

Answer. In June, 1862, and furnished it all that season, and up to July 20, 1863.

Question. During that period did you furnish to the hospitals all the ice that they required?

Answer. I did. Here are some certificates from the surgeons there—all except one, who has left—in relation to the manner in which I supplied the hospitals with ice:

"HEADQUARTERS 2D DIVISION, U. S. GENERAL HOSPITAL,
"*Alexandria, Virginia, January* 9, 1864.

"SIR: It affords me pleasure to state that Messrs. Eldridge & Co. supplied this hospital with ice during the season of 1862 and a portion of 1863 in a manner entirely satisfactory; indeed, much more so than by the system adopted afterwards.

"Very respectfully,

"T. RUSH SPENCER,
"*Surgeon United States Volunteers, in Charge.*

"HENRY JOHNSON,
"*M. S. K., Acting Medical Purveyor, Washington, D. C.*"

"1ST DIVISION GENERAL HOSPITAL,
"*Alexandria, Virginia, February* 12, 1864.

"This is to certify that Mr. M. Eldridge supplied this hospital last summer with ice until about the 20th of July, and that his supply was regular, of good quality, and every way satisfactory.

"CHARLES PAGE,
"*Surgeon United States Volunteers, in Charge.*"

"3D DIVISION UNITED STATES GENERAL HOSPITAL,
"*Alexandria, Virginia, February* 12, 1864.

"I cheerfully represent that Mr. M. Eldridge's supply of ice and dealings with the hospital have always been honorable and satisfactory.

"EDWIN BENTLEY,
"*Surgeon United States Volunteers, in Charge.*"

The witness. During 1862 the hospitals were constantly full of sick and wounded. There never has been, since I have been there, such a number of wounded and sick men in the hospitals as there was in 1862.

Testimony of Dr. R. O. Abbott.

WASHINGTON, *February* 11, 1864.

Dr. R. O. ABBOTT sworn and examined.

By Mr. Gooch:

Question. What is your present rank and position in the army?

Answer. I am a surgeon in the army of the United States, and medical director for the department of Washington, at present.

Question. Have you any knowledge in relation to the manner in which the government has been supplied with ice for hospital purposes, &c., since this war began?

Answer. Only so far as this department is concerned.

Question. Over what period of time does your knowledge extend in regard to this department?

Answer. From about June, 1863, until the present time.

Question. Only that portion of time covered by the contracts made last year?

Answer. That is all.

Question. Will you state to the committee all the knowledge you have in relation to that matter?

Answer. A contract was made with Mr. Tiffany, of Maine, at $10 50 per ton, less 10 per cent., to be delivered here—making about $9 45 per ton. He was to have $3 a ton for freight. The ice was to be loaded in Maine, and the bill of lading sworn to was to be the voucher upon which it was to be receipted for here. I think the cargoes I received, in all, amounted to nearly 4,000 tons, which arrived here in eight or ten different schooners; and, upon ascertaining that they had arrived, and that the ice had been discharged into the government ice-house, I always receipted the bill upon this sworn invoice and affidavit. Mr. Tiffany contracted to build an ice-house and to put the ice in it, and then deliver it from there to the hospitals at 50 cents a ton upon requisitions approved by me. That arrangement went on until about September, when I found that he could not well deliver the ice to the hospitals, and that part of the agreement was broken by common consent, and the surgeons sent to the ice-house for their ice. They made requisitions for the amount of ice needed for each month, which I approved. Those requisitions were then taken to the ice-house and deposited with Mr. Hull, Mr. Tiffany's agent, and with a hospital steward that I had down there, and the ice was given out on those requisitions from time to time until they were filled. Out of 4,000 tons delivered in that way, I suppose I did not get over 1,600 tons, owing to the want of knowledge in the parties who managed the ice. There still remains in the government ice-house about 400 tons. But I knew, nothing of the contract until I was called upon to receive the first cargo.

Question. Why could not Mr. Tiffany carry out his contract and deliver the ice to the hospitals?

Answer. There was nothing said about his delivering it at certain hours, and the hospitals were so far apart that, during the long summer days especially, it was very late before he made his rounds; and it was found t be more convenient to send our own wagons for the ice.

Question. You only received the bill of lading?

Answer. I received the bill of lading and ascertained that the ice had arrived and been put into the government ice-house. The bill of lading was sworn to.

Question. You had no knowledge of the amount that the vessels actually discharged here?

Answer. No, sir, except in one instance. Mr. Middleton, of this city, was very anxious to exchange a cargo of ice; he was expecting some which had not arrived, and the government ice-houses were full. I agreed to let him have a cargo, weight for weight; and I know that in weighing that one cargo it fell short considerably over 10 per cent.

Question. How much over?

Answer. The cargo, I think, was 350 tons, and I do not think I got over 300 tons.

Question. Do you remember what you did get?

Answer. I got about 300 tons, I think.

By Mr. Odell:

Question. How many tons of that cargo did you pay for?

Answer. I must have receipted for the full amount, 350 tons, less ten per cent. I took the bill of lading as it was sworn to, without inquiry.

By Mr. Gooch:

Question. Who has those bills of lading?

Answer. I retained copies of them in my office; the originals were given to Mr. Tiffany to be enclosed with his vouchers.

Question. Can you furnish this committee with copies of those bills of lading, and will you do so?

Answer. Yes, sir.

Question. Do you know of any person who has any knowledge of the actual amount of ice that was received under this contract?

Answer. It is known at the Surgeon General's office.

Question. I mean any one who has personal knowledge of the amount of ice Mr. Tiffany really delivered here; not the amount he contracted to deliver, or the amount the bills of lading called for, but the actual amount delivered here.

Answer. Nobody but myself.

Question. The ice was not weighed here when received?

Answer. No, sir, except in the one instance I have mentioned. The waste was so very great in the ice-house that it was impossible to get at anything like a correct estimate. It was weighed only when given out to the hospitals.

By Mr. Odell:

Question. Do you know whether there was any agent at the point of shipment to ascertain the quantity put on board the vessels?

Answer. I do not know. I knew nothing about it until it arrived here. In fact, I did not know I was to receipt for the ice until the first cargo arrived. I was not previously notified.

Question. You took no measures yourself, either at the point of embarcation or the point of delivery, to ascertain if the quantities agreed with the quantities called for by the bills of lading?

Answer. I did not, as the contract stated the voucher was to be sworn to, and I was to receipt accordingly.

Question. Where were those bills of lading sworn to?

Answer. In Maine, the place of shipment.

Question. By whom?
Answer. By Mr. Tiffany himself.
Question. Did the captain of the vessel swear to them?
Answer. I am not so certain about that.

By Mr. Gooch:

Question. Did you have in your possession a copy of the contract with Tiffany?
Answer. I did not. I read the copy of the contract in the Surgeon General's office.
Question. Here is an extract from the contract:
"All the ice delivered under this contract to be subject to the inspection and approval of the medical officer in charge of the post where it is delivered, and such as does not conform to the specifications set forth in this contract shall be rejected."
Was it not your duty under that article to see that this ice was inspected?
Answer. I sent officers down from my office several times to inspect it, and the surgeons universally reported to me that the quality of the ice was very good indeed. They said that it was very fine clear ice, and I had no reason to believe that it was not.

By Mr. Julian:

Question. That relates to the quality only?
Answer. Yes, sir; the quality was to be determined by the sworn vouchers.

By Mr. Gooch:

Question. What, in your judgment, is the best manner for the government to supply itself with ice?
Answer. To make contracts for ice to be delivered at the hospitals where needed, not at the government ice-house.
Question. Do you mean at each hospital?
Answer. Contract that each hospital shall make requisition for the amount of ice they want; the requisition for each month to be left with the contractor; the ice to be called for day by day, delivered and weighed at each hospital until the requisition is filled.

By Mr. Julian:

Question. Get the ice from the dealers in the city here?
Answer. Yes, sir.

By Mr. Odell:

Question. Do you arrive at the conclusion that that is the best way from any experience that you have had?
Answer. From the experience of the past season, for the work is too great in putting it in the hands of parties who are not acquainted with ice.

By Mr. Gooch:

Question. Why was the change made last year from the previous practice?
Answer. I understood that contracts had been given out for many points where there were no dealers, and where the government took the ice by the cargo and furnished the ice-houses, and it was made a sort of general rule. But I am convinced that in places where there are dealers it is better to buy of the dealers.
Question. Was there any necessity for blending this city, and Baltimore and New York, &c., with those remote places where there are no dealers in ice?
Answer. I cannot say. I think the Surgeon General will not contract again except in the way I recommended.
Question. Has there been any failure on the part of dealers here to supply any quantity and quality required for the use of the hospitals?

Answer. None that I am aware of. I recollect that when I first came to this city as medical director I found that the hospitals were in the habit of buying ice where they could get it cheapest, and paying for it out of the hospital fund. But provisions rose in price so rapidly, and became so expensive, that they had to do away, as far as possible, with purchasing ice with the hospital fund. I had nothing to do with that at all. They bought ice just as they bought anything else that was needed.

Question. How did the number of patients in the hospitals in 1862 compare with the number in 1863?

Answer. In the fall of 1862, and early in 1863, there were more patients here than there have been at any other time. I think there were then 22,000 sick and wounded in this city. I could give the statistics of the number of patients from the time I took hold of the office here, but not before.

Question. The greatest number of patients that have ever been in the hospitals here in any year was prior to 1863, in June?

Answer. Yes, sir; I think so; there were a great many patients brought in here after the second Bull Run battle.

Question. Do you know when the delivery of ice under this contract of Tiffany commenced?

Answer. I think it commenced in April, 1863, if my memory serves me.

Question. When did the government require the greatest amount of ice in this department; prior to April, 1863, or since that time?

Answer. Since that time, I think. During the cold season, of course, we do not use much ice. Last summer was an exceedingly hot summer, and they used a great deal of ice.

Question. Was not the number of patients in the hospitals here in 1862 greater than at any other period?

Answer. I cannot speak as to that, for I was not here in the summer of 1862, but the number of patients would not be a criterion by which to judge the amount of ice required, except you take it in connexion with the season. The season is the criterion. During the warm months, of course, the most ice is consumed, while during the winter months comparatively little is required. I have found that in the summer months it was necessary to take from 2 to 2½ pounds of ice from the ice-house in order to give a pound or so to the hospitals.

By Mr. Odell:

Question. And before this contract system all that loss was saved to the government?

Answer. Yes, sir; and that was the reason I reported against the contract system.

By Mr. Gooch:

Question. Would not any man of ordinary intelligence know that ice delivered at the hospitals day by day, as required, at 75 cents per 100 pounds, would be very much cheaper for the government than to purchase it by the cargo at $10 50 a ton invoice weight at place of shipment in Maine, with 10 per cent. discount for wastage in transporting it here?

Answer. It would seem that any one who had ever thought upon the subject and knew anything about ice would see that.

Question. Were there any complaints from the hospitals while Tiffany was delivering ice under his contract?

Answer. There were complaints, particularly from the hospitals in Alexandria, who complained that they never got half the ice they ought to have got. It was put on a boat and carried down there, and exposed a great deal. By mutual consent that part of the contract was set aside.

By Mr. Odell:

Question. Were the hospitals, generally, satisfied with Mr. Tiffany's manner of supplying ice, as to time, quantity, &c.?

Answer. They were not; the most of them, I think, preferred to send for the ice themselves.

The bills of lading referred to in the foregoing testimony were transmitted to the committee, with the following indorsement:

MEDICAL DIRECTOR'S OFFICE,
February 12, 1864.

Respectfully forwarded, as requested.

These bills of lading comprise all received from Mr. J. C. Tiffany, except the bill of lading of the schooner Richmond, whereof N. T. Dill was master, which has been mislaid. The Richmond was freighted with 140 tons of ice, one of the first cargoes received.

R. O. ABBOTT, *Surgeon U. S. A.,*
Medical Director, Department of Washington.

Six days' time was allowed for discharging cargo, and after that $12\frac{1}{2}$ cents per registered ton allowed for demurrage.

Abstract of supply of ice for Washington, D. C., furnished under contract with J. C. Tiffany.

Date.	Place of shipment.	Name of vessel.	Name of captain.	No. of tons per invoice.
1863.				
June 1	Gardiner, Me...	Schr. Thomas C. Bartlett...	Winchester Card	*$127\frac{11}{40}$
3	......do........	Schr. October	Bartlett Morse	*156
3	......do........	Schr. Golden Rod	Norman Bishop	*118
3	......do........	Schr. Exeter	Abram Snow.........	*148
6	......do........	Schr. Olivia Buxton	Samuel J. Williams..	*130
8	......do........	Schr. Abbott Lawrence	Cyrus T. Fuller.....	†265
8	......do........	Schr. Martha	Alpheus Baxter	†230
17	......do........	Brig Whitaker	Joseph W. Handy ..	†262
18	......do........	Schr. Hudson...............	Charles S. Brown ...	‡257
20	......do........	Schr. Hannah Matilda.....	John Price	§$355\frac{5}{37}$
Aug. 13	......do........	Brig Forrester	James Murray	‖$180\frac{947}{2000}$
19	......do........	Schr. Mary Ella............	Charles W. Talpey..	¶$186\frac{1}{2}$
21	......do........	Schr. Jennie Morton........	J. G. Hufnagel.......	**413
26	......do........	Brig Isadora...............	G. B. Hussey........	††264
28	......do........	Schr. Thomas Martin	Jabez Lyon	‡‡176
Sept. 5	......do........	Schr. Louie F. Smith......	E. W. Cobb	‡‡372
9	......do........	Schr. H. N. Farnham......	D. W. Smith	‡‡300

*Invoice sworn to by the captain, and John McCartney, agent, before Barker A. Neal, for J. C. Tiffany.
†Invoice sworn to by the captain, and John McCartney, agent, before William T. Hall, for J. C. Tiffany.
‡Invoice sworn to by the captain, and John McCartney, agent, before Barker A. Neal, for J. C. Tiffany.
§Invoice sworn to by the captain, and John McCartney, agent, before Jacob Smith, for J. C. Tiffany.
‖Invoice sworn to by the captain, and John McCartney, agent, before Nutting and J. T. Robinson, for J. C. Tiffany.
¶Invoice sworn to by the captain, and John McCartney, agent, before Barker A. Neal, for J. C. Tiffany.
**Invoice sworn to by the captain, and John McCartney, agent, before George C. Morrell and J. T. Robinson, for J. C. Tiffany.
††Invoice sworn to by the captain, and John McCartney, agent, before George C. Morrell, for J. C. Tiffany.

Testimony of Mr. Henry Johnson.

WASHINGTON, *February* 11, 1864.

Mr. HENRY JOHNSON sworn and examined.

By Mr. Gooch:

Question. Will you state if you are now in the employ of the government, and how long you have been so employed, and in what capacity?

Answer. I have been employed in the capacity of medical storekeeper since about the 1st of November, 1862. I was assigned to duty as acting medical purveyor of Washington about the 10th of November, 1862, and have been so employed since that time.

Question. Have you any knowledge of the manner in which the government has been supplied with ice since you have held your present position?

Answer. Yes, sir. Proposals were advertised for, bids received, and contracts drawn up under the bids according to the proposals.

Question. Will you state fully to the committee all the knowledge you have in relation to that matter?

Answer. Advertisements were given out, and the proposals were received and opened by myself, and contracts were awarded, according to our decisions, to the lowest bidders. It then rested for the final decision of the Surgeon General, who had the approval or disapproval of our awards. In this city, for the last year, the proposals were forwarded to the Surgeon General's office for his decision, and he awarded the contract to Mr. J. C. Tiffany, instead of to the one I had decided to be the lowest bidder, as he said, because he thought Mr. Tiffany's bid the cheapest. I afterwards went to Dr. Smith, who was the representative of the Surgeon General, and stated that I thought my award for Washington city was lower than the one he had made in reference to Mr. Tiffany, and I stated my reasons. Mr. Godey, to whom I awarded it, had agreed to weigh the ice at the ice-house for the hospitals at $13 a ton. I told Dr. Smith that I thought the wastage on the ice would be probably so great that the proposition of Mr. Godey was the cheaper one, and I endeavored to show him why I thought so. That in shipping ice there was considerable loss, 25 or 30 per cent.; and that the government would have to pay for the ice-house; while Mr. Godey had an ice-house of his own, and submitted to all this loss himself, delivering and being paid for just the amount of ice required. He replied that he had good calculators in his office, and seemed to think that Mr. Tiffany's proposal was the cheapest.

Question. Do you remember the amount of Mr. Tiffany's bid?

Answer. His bid was, I think, $10 50 per ton shipped, with 10 per cent. off for wastage.

Question. Do you know what Mr. Tiffany was to have for building an ice-house?

Answer. He was to have a dollar and a half per ton in Washington.

Question. So that he was to receive about $9 45 a ton; then the price of the ice-house added would make it $10 95 per ton.

Answer. Yes, sir; but that would depend upon how much ice was required for the season.

Question. Could there, in your judgment, be an honest difference of opinion as to which of those two bids was the more advantageous to the government at that time?

Answer. It was a matter I knew nothing about. I merely took the word of Mr. Godey, and of disinterested parties who wrote to me at the time, stating that the loss of ice in shipping and transporting would be 25 or 30 per cent. I mentioned that to Dr. Smith, and he said that he could not consider those things; that the parties were probably interested.

Question. Did you have more than one conversation with Dr. Smith, or the Surgeon General, about that matter?

Answer. I do not think I went to see him more than once. As they had made the decision I did not think it worth while to go there again about it.

Question. Had they decided the matter peremptorily when you saw them, rejecting the bid of Mr. Godey?

Answer. They had decided, stating that they had made a calculation in their office, and had come to the conclusion that Mr. Tiffany's bid was lowest.

Question. Is this the advertisement issued by you, and under which proposals were received? (Showing witness the advertisement at close of testimony of Mr. Robert A. Payne.)

Answer. Yes, sir.

Question. Do you know whether the terms were changed in making the contract with Mr. Tiffany?

Answer. I do not know that they were.

Question. In the fourth item of the contract with Mr. Tiffany I find this:

"All the ice delivered under this contract to be received and paid for as per bill of lading, fifteen per cent. being deducted from the face of bill of lading for wastage on ice delivered at Pensacola, Florida, and New Orleans, Louisiana, and ten per cent. deducted on ice delivered at Washington, D. C."

Is that in accordance with your advertised proposals? If so, point out where, in the advertisement, that is suggested or provided for?

Answer. The propositions were not all in conformity to the advertisement; but then they were taken in reference to the lowest bidders.

Question. Have you the various propositions that were submitted?

Answer. I have not.

Question. Who has them?

Answer. They were withdrawn from my office by order of the Surgeon General, and forwarded to the War Department. I made a request that they may be returned to me in order to be filed.

Question. This provision in the contract was not specially provided for in your advertisement?

Answer. No, sir.

Question. Do you know whether there was any such suggestion as that, or any provision for that article, in Mr. Tiffany's proposal?

Answer. I really forget all about the forms of his proposals.

Question. By whom was that contract drawn?

Answer. It was drawn by my clerk, in my office.

Question. Between whom were the terms of the contract agreed upon?

Answer. The contract was based upon the proposals of Mr. Tiffany, after they had been accepted at the Surgeon General's office. We were ordered to make the contract with Mr. Tiffany.

Question. Is this contract drawn precisely in accordance with the terms of his proposals?

Answer. I think so.

Question. Are you positive on that point?

Answer. I think it was as near as we could possibly get it.

Question. Had you any knowledge in relation to the ice business?

Answer. No, sir; I have had no experience in it.

Question. Then how did you know what would be a proper percentage for waste?

Answer. I knew nothing about it. I had to go according to the proposals.

Question. How could you tell which proposition was best if you knew nothing of the rate of wastage of ice in being transported and delivered?

Answer. The matter was left to me to decide in drawing up the proposals, and I had to do the best I could. I had no judgment in the matter of the contracts. As I said before, that was left entirely to the decision of the Surgeon General; and his decision was final. I recommended Mr. Godey's bid, because he took upon himself the whole matter of loss and wastage in shipping and putting the ice into the ice-house.

Question. Then are we to understand that you made this contract with Mr. Tiffany in compliance with the order of the Surgeon General?

Answer. Yes, sir.

Question. You did not make it because, in your opinion, it was the best for the government?

Answer. No, sir.

Question. You did not make it because you believed that particular contract to be best, but because you were ordered to make it?

Answer. Because I was ordered to do so.

Question. Did you receive any instructions from the Surgeon General in relation to the terms of the contract?

Answer. No, sir; we had to take just such terms as he had proposed in his bid. Upon those terms the contract was based.

Question. Do you remember whether any of the other bids contained terms similar to that?

Answer. There was a party of the name of Cheeseman, I think—I will not be positive about the name—who made a proposal similar to that, offering to supply ice at so much for New Orleans.

Question. Do you remember what percentage he proposed to allow for wastage?

Answer. I do not think he allowed any wastage at all.

Question. Then it was not like this?

Answer. It was similar to it in some respects.

Question. But in this respect of wastage it was not like it?

Answer. No, sir.

Question. Did you know Mr. Tiffany?

Answer. No, sir.

Question. Do you know whether he had ever been engaged in the ice business?

Answer. I know nothing at all about him.

Question. Where did you first see him?

Answer. He came in my office and asked some questions about this ice business. That is about the first I saw of him.

Question. Do you issue advertisements and receive proposals for other things besides ice?

Answer. I have done so, but the matter has been cancelled by the Surgeon General. I advertised for proposals to furnish hospital furniture. I received proposals, and forwarded them to the Surgeon General's office; but it was decided there to be inexpedient to act upon them. It was thought that the things could be purchased to greater advantage in the open market. I also prepared the advertisement for ice this year.

Question. Did your agency in this ice matter cease when you had made out the contract, or were you bound to receive it and superintend its delivery?

Answer. I had nothing to do with that. It was left to the medical director to receive the ice.

Question. Your agency terminated with the execution of the contract?

Answer. Yes, sir; that is, so far as this: The medical director received all the ice, and was accountable for its quality, &c.; but I had a hospital steward assigned to duty to take charge of the ice-house, and he reported to me and to Dr. Abbott; but I received none of the ice, and did not examine any of it; it was all receipted for by the medical director's department.

Question. Who made the contract for building the ice-house?

Answer. That was included in Mr. Tiffany's proposition.

Question. At whose suggestion was that item about the ice-house inserted?

Answer. He inserted in his proposition that he would build the ice-house at a dollar and a half a ton.

Question. That was a part of his proposition?

Answer. Yes, sir.

Question. Did you purchase any ice or make any arrangements for the purchase of ice before these contracts?
Answer. No, sir.

By Mr. Odell:

Question. Did the medical director understand the nature of this contract?
Answer. I should suppose so.

By Mr. Gooch:

Question. Was a copy of this contract furnished to the medical director?
Answer. I furnished none. I had a copy in my office, and a copy was furnished to the Surgeon General, and one to the Second Comptroller.

By Mr. Odell:

Question. Did you in making this contract institute any means, through the medical department or otherwise, to ascertain that the terms of the contract were complied with as to quantity and quality?
Answer. No, sir; that was left entirely to the medical director. It was his duty to receive it, and it was for him, I suppose, to take the proper means to ascertain that.

By Mr. Gooch:

Question. What was the name of the hospital steward you sent to take charge of the ice-house?
Answer. Ezra Holden, I think; he is still in charge of the ice-house.
Question. Did you make this contract (handing witness a copy) with A Tracy Edgerton?
Answer. Yes, sir.
Question. By whom was that contract awarded to him?
Answer. That was awarded on my own decision, accepted and approved by the Surgeon General.
Question. Were there any other proposals to furnish ice at the places embraced in this contract beside the proposal of Edgerton?
Answer. I think there were.
Question. Have you in your possession the proposals in this case?
Answer. No, sir; I have no proposals at all. They were all withdrawn.
Question. Where do you understand those proposals now to be?
Answer. In the office of the Secretary of War, I presume. I have a letter here in reference to that matter. I made a request that the proposals be returned to my office, in order that I might file them in the returns of my office according to law. This is the answer I received:

SURGEON GENERAL'S OFFICE,
Washington City, D. C., August 17, 1863.

SIR: Your communication of the 14th instant, requesting that certain proposals for ice may be returned to your office, has been received.
You are respectfully informed that these proposals were sent to the Secretary of War on the 28th of April last, and have not yet been returned.
Very respectfully, your obedient servant,

JOSEPH R. SMITH,
Acting Surgeon General.

HENRY JOHNSON, *M. S. K., U. S. A., Washington, D. C.*

Question. Will you state to us what you understand to be the meaning of the sixth item in this contract with A. Tracy Edgerton? "That payment shall be made from time to time upon receipted bills of lading and duplicate accounts certified to by the medical officer in charge of the post where it is delivered."

Answer. The bill of lading accompanied the account as evidence upon which to base the correctness of the account. The account is made out in duplicate and certified to by the medical officer in charge of the post where it is delivered.

Question. What was that certificate to be?

Answer. Something in this form, I suppose: "I certify that the above account is correct and just, and that the ice was received as specified," or "as stated," or "that the ice was received by me"—something to that effect, to be attached below the account.

Question. Do you expect the bill of lading and certificate to agree in amount?

Answer. Yes, sir.

Question. That the receipt shall be for just so many tons as the bill of lading called for?

Answer. This is a different form from the proposal of Mr. Tiffany; there is no deduction for wastage; and the contractor agrees to deliver a certain amount of ice to each of these points.

Question. Then the bill of lading and the certificate would not agree as to quantity?

Answer. That would depend upon the receipt of the medical officer. If he received the amount on the bill of lading, of course he would have to acknowledge it to be correct.

Question. You understand that contract to call for the delivery of 2,000 pounds of ice per ton at each of these points?

Answer. Yes, sir.

Question. It is not sufficient that so many tons at 2,000 pounds per ton shall be stated on the bill of lading?

Answer. No, sir, it is that so much ice shall be delivered at the ice-house.

Question. Why did you put in the provision in relation to the bill of lading?

Answer. I presume the proposal read in that way—to take the receipted bill of lading.

Question. That would not prove anything, would it?

Answer. Yes, sir; if the officer received so many tons, at 2,000 pounds per ton, according to the bill of lading, he should receipt for it.

Question. Have you not knowledge enough of the ice business to know that no vessel can deliver in a southern port as many tons of ice as are put on board the vessel in New England?

Answer. I know that very well. But Mr. Edgerton stated to me that, in order to invoice the full quantity of ice at these points, he should put 2,240 pounds to the ton on board the vessel, and by the time it reached the point of delivery he had no doubt that 2,000 pounds would be delivered at the ice-house. Still that was a matter that was to be decided by the receiving officer.

Question. Can you tell who suggested that particular clause of the contract?

Answer. I presume it was suggested by the proposal.

Question. Do you understand by payment being made upon the receipt of the medical officer, that so much ice has been received under that bill of lading?

Answer. Yes, sir.

Question. That there was receipted for on the bill of lading the amount actually delivered?

Answer. Yes, sir; that, I presume, is it.

Question. Then why did you have your conversation with Mr. Edgerton in relation to his putting on board 2,240 pounds to the ton, in the expectation that it would hold out 2,000 pounds at the time of delivery, if it was to be then weighed, and the exact amount received to be receipted for?

Answer. He merely made that remark in conversation. I told him he would have to deliver the actual quantity stated; and he said there would be no difficulty about that, because he could put the ice on by the long ton, and by the time it reached the point of delivery the wastage would not make it less than 2,000 pounds to the ton. It was merely in conversation that that matter was mentioned. I enjoined upon him that he was bound to deliver 2,000 pounds to the ton.

Question. The amount of wastage would depend very much upon the post at which it was delivered?

Answer. Yes, sir.

By Mr. Odell:

Question. Have you any knowledge of the principle upon which Mr. Edgerton's accounts were settled; whether he was paid for the whole amount called for by the bill of lading, or for the amount actually delivered?

Answer. I have no knowledge of that. I paid pretty much all the bills. They were all audited in the Surgeon General's office, and sent to me with an order on them to pay.

Question. Do you know upon what principle those bills were audited?

Answer. I do not. They had the contract in the Surgeon General's office, and they should have been audited according to the contract.

Question. You say you do not know whether the full amount called for by the bill of lading was paid for, or only the amount actually delivered?

Answer. I do not.

Question. Having made the contract yourself, and knowing the terms of it, should you not, as a good business man, have seen whether you paid for more ice than was actually delivered?

Answer. When an account has been examined in the Surgeon General's office, and comes to me with an order on it to pay it, I do not know that I have any right to question the matter further. The Surgeon General is my superior officer, and I must obey his orders. It does not do for me to question his orders.

Question. I understand that you must obey his orders. But I understand another thing: that, as you made the contract, if you thought it was not complied with, you should have called the attention of the Surgeon General to that fact.

Answer. I should have done so if I had thought there was anything wrong about the matter.

Question. Your answer is that you did not examine into that fact.

Answer. I have no doubt it was done by my clerk, who has my instructions to audit every account that comes in.

By Mr. Gooch:

Question. Do you remember in what paper these advertisements for proposals for ice were inserted?

Answer. I could not recall them just now.

Question. In what portions of the country?

Answer. All over the country: in Boston, New York, Philadelphia, Baltimore, Washington, Ohio, Wisconsin, and, I think, in Illinois.

Question. Was this contract with Parrish & Co. [showing witness a copy] made by you?

Answer. Yes, sir.

Question. Were there any other contracts for ice made by you except with Tiffany, Edgerton, and Parrish & Co.

Answer. No, sir.

Question. Do you know whether there were any other proposals to furnish ice at the points covered by the contract with Parrish & Co.?

Answer. I think there must have been; there were a great many proposals in.

Question. Were any proposals, so far as you know, rejected merely for informality?

Answer. Yes, sir; I think there were several that were informal; probably informal so far as the want of a certificate—some evidence to show the ability of the party bidding to comply with the contract if awarded to him. There were several informalities in many of the proposals.

Question. Did you have any conversation with any one in relation to the terms of that advertisement before it was published?

Answer. Do you mean in relation to the form of the advertisement?

Question. Yes, sir.

Answer. The matter was submitted to the Surgeon General's office for decision, and he ordered me to advertise; the advertisement was drawn up by me.

Question. Was it changed in the Surgeon General's office?

Answer. I think not.

Question. Did any persons call on you, or have any interview with you, in relation to that advertisement before it was sent by you to the Surgeon General's office, or after?

Answer. No, sir. The Surgeon General directed me to draw up an advertisement for ice, and I did so, and immediately forwarded it to his office for approval, and it was returned after approval.

Question. When did you first see Mr. Tiffany?

Answer. About the first time I saw Mr. Tiffany——

Question. I want *the* first time you saw him, not *about* the first time.

Answer. It was some time between inserting the advertisement and receiving the proposals.

Question. Had you not seen him before that time?

Answer. No, sir.

Question. When did you first see Mr. Edgerton?

Answer. About the same time.

Question. Had you any conversation with either of them before issuing the advertisement?

Answer. No, sir.

Question. Nor with Mr. Parrish?

Answer. No, sir; I did not know either of the parties.

Question. Have you made any contracts for ice for the coming year?

Answer. No, sir.

Question. Have you issued any advertisements?

Answer. Yes, sir.

Question. How many?

Answer. I have inserted the same advertisement in 14 or 15 different papers. The bids will be opened on the 25th of this month.

Question. Have you changed the terms of the advertisement in any way?

Answer. Yes, sir. The first one was withdrawn, and a second one inserted, more in detail, and asking for more information.

Question. Why was the first withdrawn?

Answer. I do not know. An order was sent to me from the Surgeon General's office to withdraw it, without intimating any reason for it.

Question. Who prepared the second proposals now issued?

Answer. I prepared them, based upon instructions given to me from the Surgeon General's office.

Question. You changed the advertisement according to instructions given to you by the Surgeon General?

Answer. Yes, sir.

Question. Were you not notified, in that connexion, that the advertisement which you had issued was so indefinite that it would be impossible for any intelligent man to bid under it?

Answer. No, sir; I received no notice of that kind. I was ordered to withdraw it, and I did so, according to orders, without asking any reason for it. There were one or two parties who wanted to put in proposals who stated that the matter was indefinite; but at the same time the information called for by the advertisement could be received from the medical officers at the different points. It was impossible for me to know the amount required, or whether there were ice-houses at the different points. That information could be obtained from the medical directors at the different points.

Question. Would it not have been very much more business-like for you to advertise what facilities the government had, and to inform persons, who desired to bid, whether the ice was to be received by the cargo or by the pound, and whether it was to be distributed by them or by the government?

Answer. I think the better plan is that the ice should be distributed to the various hospitals as required, and the actual weight delivered there receipted for. It appears to me that that would be the better plan. I think that by that plan the government would save all the loss in shipping and transporting it, and the expense of storing it and taking care of it, and make the party who receives the contract responsible for all that thing. The ice-dealer knows what the wastage would be, and can put in his proposals at such a price as would be proper under the circumstances.

Question. Have you made any such recommendation to the Surgeon General?

Answer. I made that recommendation when I drew up the first proposals. I had a consultation with him about it, and suggested that plan, and he also thought that would be the better plan, and I accordingly drew up the proposals.

Question. The second proposals?

Answer. The first ones.

Question. It did not contain that.

Answer. It did not state the amount required.

Question. It did not state whether the ice was to be delivered at the hospitals or where.

Answer. It was to be delivered at the hospitals at this point.

Question. Did your first advertisement so state?

Answer. Yes, sir.

Question. Have you a copy of it?

Answer. Not with me.

Question. Did your first advertisement specify that the contractor was to deliver the ice at each of the hospitals in the vicinity of the several points named?

Answer. Yes, sir. The form of that advertisement was similar to the one I now have in, except in regard to certain portions of the country north of this.

Question. Can you state, of your own knowledge, how the hospitals were supplied with ice before these contracts?

Answer. I cannot state positively.

Testimony of Dr. Joseph R. Smith.

WASHINGTON, *February* 12, 1864.

Dr. JOSEPH R. SMITH sworn and examined.

By Mr. Gooch:

Question. What is your rank and position in the army, and where have you been stationed since the commencement of the war?

Answer. I am a surgeon in the United States army; I was taken prisoner in Texas at the beginning of the war, and when I came north on parole I was stationed in Georgetown in charge of the hospitals there, from July, 1861, until July, 1862, when I was put on duty in the Surgeon General's office as principal assistant in that office; I remained there until September, 1863, when I was ordered west; I have been serving since as medical director of the army of Arkansas.

Question. Have you any knowledge of the manner in which the government has been supplied with ice for hospital purposes, &c.?

Answer. Yes, sir.

Question. State to the committee what knowledge you have in relation to it.

Answer. While I was in charge of the hospitals in this city, the ice was purchased from the hospital fund; some time in the winter of 1862 and 1863, the Surgeon General directed advertisements to be put in the paper for supplying ice at different points in the country, where there were troops and hospitals. In answer to those advertisements, bids were received and contracts were made with several parties, whose names I do not now recollect, with the exception of three, Mr. Edgerton, Mr. Tiffany and Mr. Parrish.

Question. By whom, or under whose directions, were the contracts made with those parties?

Answer. Under direction of the Surgeon General.

Question. Who examined the proposals received in response to the advertisements, and who awarded the contracts?

Answer. The proposals were first taken, I think, to the medical purveyor in this city, who examined them and made a decision in the matter. Then they were brought by him to the Surveyor General's office and brought to me. I happened to be busy at the time. I requested Dr. Alden, who was an assistant in the office, and whose business it was to take charge of contracts, requisitions, and things of that kind, to come down in the evening and look them over. He came down in the evening and we looked them over; after having decided which we thought to be the cheapest, they were presented the next day to the Surgeon General, who directed the contracts to be made accordingly.

Question. Were any of the awards changed that were made by the medical purveyor, Mr. Johnson?

Answer. I think three or four were.

Question. Will you state what awards you changed, and the reasons for the change?

Answer. I do not recollect which were changed; they were changed because it was thought in the office that the bids he took were not the most advantageous to the government.

Question. Was there a change made awarding the contract to Mr. Edgerton?

Answer. I do not now recollect.

Question. Was there a change made awarding the contract to Mr. Tiffany?

Answer. Yes, sir.

Question. Was there a change made awarding the contract to Mr. Parrish?

Answer. I do not recollect.

Question. Was there a change made awarding the contract to Gosnell and Scott?

Answer. I do not recollect.

Question. Do you remember to whom Mr. Johnson awarded the contract which was subsequently awarded to Mr. Tiffany?

Answer. I do not.

Question. The change was made by you and Dr. Alden?

Answer. The examination was made by us, and the next day the matter was submitted to the Surgeon General, and he directed a contract to be as was deemed most advantageous.

Question. In accordance with your recommendation?

Answer. Yes, sir.

Question. Had you or Dr. Alden any knowledge in relation to the ice business?

Answer. No, sir.

Question. Then how could you determine which contract was the most advantageous, and why did you change the award made by the medical purveyor?

Answer. We examined the terms of the proposals.

Question. Take for instance this department. If I remember rightly, Mr. Tiffany offered to furnish ice for $10 50 per ton, invoice weight, as per bill of lading, delivered here by the cargo—that is, the weight at the point where it was loaded into the vessels, with ten per cent. discount, was to be accepted as the weight here. Do you remember that such were the terms of his contract?

Answer. I do not remember exactly; they were something of that character.

Question. Mr. Godey, of this city, offered to furnish ice, weighed out every morning at his ice-house, at $14 a ton, and Mr. Middleton, of this city, offered to supply ice at seventy-five cents per hundred pounds, delivered at the hospitals every morning. Do you remember anything about that?

Answer. I do not recollect the exact prices; but I recollect that the ice-dealers here proposed to deliver ice at the hospitals, or from their ice-houses.

Question. Had you not sufficient knowledge of the ice business to know that it was more advantageous to the government to have the ice delivered at the hospital at 75 cents per 100 pounds than to take it at the invoice weight loaded in Maine at $10 50 per ton, with only 10 per cent. off for wastage, the government having to take it from the vessel, put it into an ice-house built by themselves, and deliver it here by themselves, suffering all the loss?

Answer. The decision that was made was that which was supposed to be the best for the government, after considering the matter.

Question. Did you consult anybody?

Answer. Yes, sir.

Question. Did you consult any ice-men, or any person who had any knowledge of the ice-business?

Answer. I talked with Mr. Godey about it for one. I know Mr. Godey very well, for he had been supplying the hospitals when I was in charge of them, and also supplied my own family with ice. I think I talked with Mr. Middleton upon the subject.

Question. Did they not both tell you that it was more economical for the government to take ice at the rate at which they offered it?

Answer. They both thought their bids were the best.

Question. Then it was not in accordance with their advice that you changed the award the medical purveyor had made to Mr. Godey, and gave the contract to Mr. Tiffany?

Answer. I did not ask their advice on the subject. I inquired of them in reference to various points, among those concerning wastage in vessels. There was great discrepancy in reference to the amount of wastage in the statements of the different persons whom I asked.

Question. Did anybody fix it as low as 10 per cent.?

Answer. Yes, sir.

Qnestion. Any ice man?

Answer. I forget who.

Question. Did you have any conference with Mr. Tiffany in relation to the matter?

Answer. Yes, sir; Mr. Tiffany came to the office when the awards had been made by Mr. Johnson, and represented what he considered the facts of the case,

Question. Had you known Mr. Tiffany before?

Answer. No, sir; I never had any other conference with him.

Question. Was there any change made in the contract differing from the proposals made by Mr. Tiffany? If so, state what was that change, and why it was made

Answer. I do not recollect any. If there was any, if I should hear it mentioned, I probably would remember it.

Question. Did his original proposition contain a clause providing that the ice should be taken by the weight in Maine, at 10 per cent. discount?

Answer. I do not remember the terms of his contract.]

[A copy of the contract with Mr. Tiffany was then shown to the witness, upon examining which, he said—]

I do not recollect any change from the terms of the proposal.

Question. Had you not sufficient knowledge of the ice business to know that it would be more economical to the government to have its ice delivered to it in Washington in such quantities as it wanted, from an ice-dealer here, at $14 a ton; or delivered at the hospitals in such quantities as were required day by day, at $15 a ton, than it would be for the government to pay for it at the rate of $9 45 a ton in Maine, and then suffer all the loss that would result by wastage in transporting it from Maine to this place, then put it into an ice-house here, and deliver it from the ice-house in such quantities as might be wanted by the hospitals; adding thereto the expenses of building the ice-house, and the taking the ice to the hospitals?

Answer. It was my opinion after consultation ———. I recollect now that I consulted the medical storekeeper, Mr. Johnson, on the subject, after having sent for him, and told him the views of the office upon the subject, and he agreed that the contract which was adopted by the Surgeon General's office was the most advantageous one.

Question. I will state that we understand the testimony of Mr. Johnson to be exactly the reverse; that he urged Mr. Godey's proposal in preference to that of Mr. Tiffany.

Answer. I do not recollect that he did that.

Question. Do you remember that he did assent to the contract with Tiffany?

Answer. I remember distinctly that he did, after talking the matter over.

Question. Where is Dr. Alden, the gentleman with whom you consulted?

Answer. I think he is in Philadelphia. He was assistant surgeon, on duty in the Surgeon General's office.

Question. Do you know whether Mr. Tiffany was a man who had been in the ice business prior to that time?

Answer. I do not; I know nothing about that but what he said. He said that he had delivered some ice previously to the army of the Potomac.

Question. Have you any knowledge in relation to the delivery of ice under any of these contracts?

Answer. No, sir.

Question. Have you any knowledge of the manner in which New Orleans was being supplied with ice at the time this contract was made?

Answer. I do not think it was being supplied; I do not know that it was.

Question. You have no knowledge on that point?

Answer. No, sir.

Question. Have you any knowledge in relation to the manner in which ice was being supplied at that time, or had been previously supplied, at the other places covered by these contracts?

Answer. I recollect now that some ice had been ordered to Hilton Head from a firm in Boston, on an intimation being given to the office that ice was needed there; I think that was under some previous contract, before I entered the Surgeon General's office; but I do not know. I am under the impression that a majority of the hospitals throughout the country purchased their ice from the hospital fund.

Question. From ice-dealers in the vicinity?

Answer. Yes, sir.

Question. Is there anything else in connexion with this matter that you wish to state?

Answer. I do not know; I wish to give the committee any information I have.

Mr. Gooch. I have asked you questions in relation to the points brought in question.

The witness. When bills were brought in, questions came up for discussion, such as demurrage, the number of working days, and such as are referred to the office for decision.

Question. You mean, under these contracts?

Answer. Yes, sir. I understand that contracts are now being made to furnish ice to the hospitals in the west. I received a notification from the Assistant Surgeon General's office, inquiring how much ice was needed at Little Rock, where I was stationed.

By Mr. Loan:

Question Do you know where the proposals for this contract which Mr. Tiffany took were drawn up and by whom?

Answer. I think by Mr. Johnson, the medical purveyor; I am not certain about that.

Question. By whose direction?

Answer. Under the general directions which he received from the Surgeon General's office to make out proposals.

Question. Do you know whether the terms of the advertisement were prescribed to Mr. Johnson by the Surgeon General, or any other person?

Answer. As I recollect it, Mr. Johnson was directed to prepare an advertisement and put it in the papers. He made it out himself and brought it, or a copy of it, to the Surgeon General's office, and it was approved.

Question. Do you know at whose suggestion the manner of furnishing ice was changed from the daily supplies obtained from Mr. Godey and Mr. Middleton to the system of obtaining it under contracts?

Answer. I do not know. All these things were discussed from time to time in the Surgeon General's office, and had been discussed a great many times; and the Surgeon General directed the proposals to be issued.

Question. Can you tell about what quantity of ice was furnished monthly to the hospitals in this city and Georgetown by Mr. Godey and Mr. Middleton while they furnished it?

Answer. I do not know. When I was in charge of Seminary hospital, in Georgetown, we purchased about 200 pounds a day.

Question. I believe you have stated that you have no means of knowing the motives for changing the manner of supplying ice?

Answer. Congress had made an appropriation for ice which had not been done previously. The hospital funds were believed to be unable to supply sufficient ice for the hospitals, so that the Surgeon General determined to furnish it from the medical appropriation.

Question. Do you know that the Surgeon General assigned that as a reason for the change?

Answer. Yes, sir; I know that he said so. In talking the matter over that was the reason given.

Question. Upon what basis was it that the quantity of ice was so largely increased under the contract with Mr. Tiffany?

Answer. The medical director in this city, as elsewhere, in every other place where ice was furnished, was required to report the probable amount needed for the sick in his charge; and it was on that data that the quantity was ordered.

Question. By whom was it ordered?

Answer. By the medical purveyor, generally; or, in some cases, where letters, calling for ice, came from the medical directors to the Surgeon General's office, it was ordered from there.

Question. Do you remember to have seen any such orders?

Answer. I do not remember, certainly. I think I did, several.

Question. Could you state about what quantities were named in those orders?

Answer. No, sir; that can be ascertained from the office. The orders and letters are on file, about that time, calling for about that amount of ice.

Question. Did you have anything to do with originating this contract, in prescribing its terms in any way, or in determining its acceptance? If so, state precisely what part you took in the transaction.

Answer. All that I did was what I have already stated. When the contracts were brought in for the scrutiny of the Surgeon General, I looked them all over in conjunction with Dr. Alden.

Question. And recommended their acceptance by the Surgeon General?

Answer. No, sir; I selected those I deemed the most advantageous to the government, and took them to the Surgeon General.

Question. Did you recommend the acceptance of those you reported to him?

Answer. Yes, sir; that is, I recommended them as the best contracts.

Question. That is what I mean.

Answer. I deemed those that we selected the most advantageous to the government.

Question. And recommended them to the Surgeon General to be accepted?

Answer. Well, I had nothing to do in any way with the matter of recommending at that time. The Surgeon General directed the contracts to be made.

Question. How came you in possession of these contracts?

Answer. I was the principal assistant in the Surgeon General's office. All the papers that came into the Surgeon General's office came to me.

Question. For what purpose?

Answer. To do what was proper in the case; to send such as required the action of the Surgeon General to be presented to him; to send others to proper officers for consideration.

Question. Why did you undertake to determine on the relative merits of these bids?

Answer. Because there were a great many people came into the office; every ice-dealer who had made a bid came in, each advocating the merits of his own proposal; and where there was so much dispute about it I deemed it worthy the attention and consideration of the Surgeon General. I looked them over and took them to him.

Question. You looked them over at your own suggestion, not because you deemed it your duty to do so?

Answer. I considered it my duty to do it.

Question. And having discharged that duty, you reported to the Surgeon General those that you deemed it most advisable to accept?

Answer. I took all the bids in to him.

Question. What was your recommendation, if any?

Answer. I made no recommendation on the subject. I informed the Surgeon General which contracts I deemed most advantageous to the government. He looked them over also, and directed them to be so awarded.

Question. By whom was the ice received which was delivered by Mr. Tiffany?

Answer. I think the medical purveyor, Mr. Johnson, did. I do not know It may possibly have been the medical director, Dr. Abbott. It was one of the two.

Question. What position does Dr. Abbott hold?
Answer. He is the medical director of this department.
Question. Are you able to state the quantity of ice ordered from Mr. Tiffany under this contract?
Answer. I have not the slightest idea. It is on record, however. I would state here that when I ordered ice I had no individual action in the matter. My action was by order of the Surgeon General.
Question. You acted under his directions, I suppose. But I wanted to know to what extent those orders were.
Answer. I do not know.
Question. Have you any means of knowing whether Mr. Tiffany advised the form of this proposal, or the terms of the contract, or anything of that kind, in advance of the time of the contract being completed?
Answer. I do not know that he did.
Question. Had you seen him prior to the acceptance of this contract, or prior to the time his bid was put in, and had any conversation with him in regard to this matter?
Answer. No special conversation.
Question. Did you have any conversation with him?
Answer. Mr. Tiffany had come into the office; all the ice-dealers had come into the office and spoken upon the subject. I recollect that Mr. Tiffany came into the office once and recommended that the date for the reception of the ice be hastened, on account of the probabilities of the ice season being over; which was not done, however.
Question. Is that the only conversation you remember to have had with Mr. Tiffany?
Answer. Yes, sir.

Testimony of Dr. David L. Magruder.

WASHINGTON, *February* 15, 1864.

Dr. DAVID L. MAGRUDER sworn and examined.

By Mr. Gooch:

Question. What is your position in the army?
Answer. I am a surgeon of the United States army.
Question. Where are you stationed?
Answer. At Louisville, as medical director.
Question. Have you any knowledge of the manner in which the government has supplied itself with ice since the war began?
Answer. The last year I knew there was a contract made by the Surgeon General with J. W. Parrish & Co., of St. Louis, to supply ice to the general hospitals of the west, I believe; but as to the terms of that contract I could not say. I was then medical director for St. Louis, that is, the department of Missouri.
Question. Had you anything to do with that contract, or the making of it?
Answer. No, sir, nothing at all. The contract was made and sent out, and I had nothing to do with it but to sign the papers when received, and to prove the receiving by the acting medical purveyor.
Question. Do you know when and where the contract was made?
Answer. Here, in Washington.
Question. You have no knowledge of its terms?
Answer. I have seen a copy of the contract of it, but I really did not notice it. All I had to do was to see, as medical director of the department, that it was not improperly issued.

Question. Did you receive the ice under that contract?

Answer. No, sir.

Question. Who did receive it?

Answer. The man who did receive it was Mr. Robert T. Creamer, medical storekeeper, and acting medical purveyor in St. Louis.

Question. Have you any knowledge of any other contract?

Answer. Yes, sir; the contract made this year was made by me, under instructions from the Acting Surgeon General.

Question. Who was the Acting Surgeon General at that time?

Answer. Dr. Joseph K. Barnes.

Question. When did you receive instructions from him?

Answer. The instructions were dated November 27, and I received them a few days afterwards, probably on the 1st or 2d of December. I will not be positive as to the exact day; but on the 4th of December I advertised proposals in the papers for bids.

Question. For the supply of what points did you advertise, and in what papers did you insert the advertisement?

Answer. This is a copy of the advertisement:

"ARMY MEDICAL PURVEYOR'S OFFICE,
"*Louisville, Kentucky, December* 4, 1863.

"Proposals will be received at this office until December 20, 1863, for furnishing ice to all the United States general hospitals at the west (those of the division of the Mississippi, and of the department of the Gulf upon the Mississippi and its tributaries) in such quantities as may be required for the use of the sick and wounded during the year 1864.

"In all cases the ice to be well packed and stored in properly constructed ice-houses previous to the 15th of April, 1864, at such points nearest the hospitals as may be designated from this office.

"The ice either to be delivered by actual weight of issues to the hospitals by the contractors, or by inspection and measurement by the issuing officer, (on or before the 1st of May, 1864,) who will then receipt for actual contents of ice-houses.

"D. L. MAGRUDER,
"*Surgeon United States Army, Medical Purveyor.*"

That advertisement was put into the Cincinnati Gazette, the Louisville Journal, the Chicago Tribune, the St. Louis Union, and the St. Louis Democrat.

Question. Who determined the papers in which the advertisement was inserted?

Answer. A list of papers in which I might advertise was sent me from the Surgeon General's office.

Question. And you selected from the list such papers as you thought advisable?

Answer. I selected what I thought the best papers in the list sent to me in each city west. I supply the department of the west. I do not advertise in eastern papers, because there are medical purveyors in the cities of New York and Philadelphia.

Question. Did you advertise for ice in any of the New England, New York, or other eastern papers?

Answer. No, sir; I advertised in none of them.

Question. Why did you not advertise in some of the eastern papers?

Answer. I had no particular orders to do so. The fact is, the only articles I supply are articles produced or manufactured in the west. All drugs and articles of that kind, I get my requisitions on the purveyors of New York and Philadelphia. After putting this advertisement in the papers I have mentioned,

I wrote a letter, December 7, to the Acting Surgeon General, stating what I had done, specifying the papers in which I had put the advertisement, and stated that I had limited the time of receiving proposals to the 20th of December, giving my reasons for doing so. I then asked whether what I had done was correct; if any alteration was required in the advertisement; whether the time allowed was too short; and if anything else was required, I wished to be instructed in regard to it.

Question. When was the advertisement first inserted?

Answer. On the 4th of December.

Question. Why did you allow only sixteen days for receiving proposals?

Answer. I gave my reasons in this letter of December 7, which is on file in the Surgeon General's department and in the War Department. I have not a copy of the letter with me. I did so because, as I understood, the crop of ice in the west has to be gathered during the latter part of December and the early part of January. After that time there is always a thaw, and ice gathered after it has thawed and becomes porous is not so merchantable.

Question. You were not to receive the ice before the 20th of December, but only the proposals?

Answer. Only the proposals.

Question. The ice was not to be received at that time?

Answer. No, sir. The ice would have to be cut in the latter part of December and the early part of January.

Question. My question is, Why did you limit the time of receiving proposals to the 20th of December, thereby allowing only sixteen days for proposals to be sent in under this advertisement?

Answer. I gave the reasons for that in my letter of the 7th of December.

Question. I do not care what reasons you gave the Surgeon General. I ask you now what reasons you had for limiting the time in that way?

Answer. I did so for the reason that I thought it would require some time for the contractor, whoever he should be, to cut his crop of ice, and get his barges to put the ice in. As I understand from all the ice men in the west, the ice is usually cut in the Upper Illinois river and in Lake Pepin, and has to be cut in a particular portion of the year, and some time and preparation are required by a man who has a large contract of this kind.

Question. Did it make any difference to the government whether it was supplied with ice that had already been cut, or cut after the proposals were received?

Answer. No, sir. I did not look upon it in that light. When the contract was given out the weather was rather bad for ice. We had bids from Chicago, St. Louis, and Louisville; I do not recollect that we had any from Cincinnati.

Question. The weather being bad at that time, made the short time you allowed for proposals to come in the more unfavorable instead of favorable for the government, did it not?

Answer. The ice business was something I never had had anything to do with, and I did not wish to make the contract, and did not make it at that time. I wrote and sent on this letter of December 7, in reply to the instructions I had got from my chief, and the best light I had.

Question. Have you given all the reasons you can for limiting the time for receiving proposals to sixteen days, under that heavy contract?

Answer. That was the only reason; I have forgotten the exact terms of my letter.

Question. Did you confer with anybody in relation to this matter?

Answer. No, sir; that was my own idea.

Question. You had no conversation with anybody?

Answer. No, sir; not on that point.

Question. You say you were ignorant of the ice business?
Answer. Yes, sir.
Question. And you determined this question without any consultation with any one who had any knowledge of the subject?
Answer. I had talked with persons in Louisville—ice men; and I had seen ice men the year before in St. Louis, and some of them had been in Louisville that year.
Question. With whom had you talked about these proposals?
Answer. I did not talk with any one about these proposals; I only talked with them about ice being cut in the early part of the year, and they all agreed with me.
Question. Why did you not advertise in the eastern papers—in New England and New York papers?
Answer. I never advertise in eastern papers for anything I purchase.
Question. Did you not know that New Orleans, and that vicinity, had always been supplied with ice from New England?
Answer. No, sir; I did not.
Question. Did you have any knowledge in relation to that subject?
Answer. No, sir.
Question. Do you know from what point New Orleans has been supplied with ice?
Answer. No, sir; I am not aware of that.
Question. If you had known that New Orleans had always been supplied with ice from New England, would you have deemed it proper to have confined your advertising to the western papers?
Answer. No, sir; probably not.
Question. Ought you not, before assuming to determine the papers in which to advertise for ice, have ascertained the points from which the places could be best supplied?
Answer. All I can say is, that after I put the advertisement in these papers I wrote to my chief for instructions as to whether there should be any change in what I had done.
Question. Did you receive any reply?
Answer. I received a reply dated December 11, to the effect that what I had done was satisfactory, and that nothing else was necessary.
Question. How many proposals did you receive in response to this advertisement?
Answer. I think there were eleven of them; I will not be certain.
Question. Can you tell us from whom they were received?
Answer. I could not now give their names. They are all on file in the office of the Assistant Secretary of War, Mr. Dana.
Question. He has all the proposals?
Answer. Yes, sir.
Question. Can you name the points covered by this advertisement?
Answer. All the general hospitals in the west?
Question. Yes, sir.
Answer. I could name the points where there are general hospitals. They are Cincinnati and vicinity, Camp Denison, Camp Chase, Cleveland; Louisville and vicinity, embracing Jeffersonville and New Albany, Indiana; Madison and Evansville, Indiana; Nashville, Memphis, Cairo, Mound City, Jefferson Barracks, in St. Louis; Quincy, Illinois; Keokuk, Iowa; also New Orleans, Natchez, Vicksburg, and Little Rock.
Question. Did your proposals cover all these points, or were these proposals for each particular point?
Answer. As I understood the instructions I had, the proposals covered every place.

Question. Do you mean by that that you were to award the contract to the man whose proposal was the lowest for all the points together?

Answer. Yes, sir; that is the way I understood it.

Question. Would it not have been very much better to have had a distinct proposal for each point, and to have taken that which was lowest for each particular place?

Answer. I presume it might have been.

Question. Did not the proposals show it would have been? That is, I mean this: could you not have selected from the different proposals parties to have supplied each particular point, and have obtained the supply for the government cheaper than you now have done?

Answer. I could not tell that unless I had the proposals before me, for I have forgotten now what they were.

Question. The award was to Parrish & Co.?

Answer. Yes, sir.

Question. You made the award?

Answer. Yes, sir.

Question. Do you know whether they were the lowest for supplying each particular hospital?

Answer. They were a great deal the lowest for the whole together.

Question. Were they the lowest for each particular hospital?

Answer. That I could not state now. There was one lower bid for St. Louis, and one lower bid for Mound City. I do not recollect any others.

Question. You recollect that there were lower bids for St. Louis and Mound City?

Answer. Yes, sir; for those particular places. But they were bids from men whom I did not know. They did not offer any bond; the bid was on a little slip of paper, without any reference to anybody; and I did not know the men at all.

Question. Did you reject those bids on account of informality?

Answer. No, sir; I sent all the bids on to Washington; enclosed them all to the Surgeon General, and asked for further instructions. I wrote that I did not feel authorized, under the instructions I had, to make a contract where it was for so large an amount, and therefore I did not care to assume the responsibility.

Question. Who made the award?

Answer. I made an award, under the instructions of my chief. On the 21st of December, after all the bids had come in, I enclosed all the bids to the Surgeon General. I stated that I did not think that the instructions were specific enough to warrant me to make a contract for so large an amount of ice; I enclosed all the bids to him for his action, and for further instructions.

Question. Before making the award?

Answer. Yes, sir.

Question. What instructions did you receive?

Answer. The bids were all returned to me, and I was instructed to make a contract which I should think the most advantageous for the government.

Question. Did your instructions confine you to the making of one contract for all the points, or were you left at liberty to make contracts for the respective points?

Answer. The way I construed it was, that I should make a contract the most advantageous for the government, which I did.

Question. The most advantageous contract for the government would have been to have let each man supply that point which he would supply the cheapest, would it not?

Answer. I construed it as I made the award.

Question. I ask if it is not the fact that it would have been the most advantageous for the government to have let each man supply the point he would have supplied the cheapest?

Answer. It probably might have been, but I did not look at it so.

Question. Is it not a mathematical certainty that it would have been?

Answer. (After a pause.) I made the contract, subject to the approval of my chief. After I had drawn up the contract with the best light I had, I wrote to my chief that I had made an agreement with J. W. Parrish & Co., but it would not be binding on either party unless approved by himself.

Question. If they were the lowest bidders, and if their bid was the most advantageous to the government, why did you hesitate to make the contract, after having received the instructions to do so?

Answer. There was a great deal of trouble about ice last year, and I did not want to have anything to do with the matter, if possible. I wanted to send the matter on here and let the contract be made in Washington, so that I should not be come upon for it. As medical purveyor, the supply of ice was not usually in my province. My business is with drugs, hospital property, &c. For that reason I sent the matter back here for approval, because I knew that where one man got the contract, every one else who bid would be disappointed and feel sore on the subject, and I did not care about being held responsible for it, and therefore the award I made was forwarded here to Washington. I sent all the papers, everything connected with it—all the bids, all my correspondence, and all the correspondence of the Surgeon General, and enclosed them to the Secretary of War.

Just before I left Louisville to come here I received a telegram from Mr. Dana, the new Assistant Secretary of War, stating that in the place of the contract I had made with Parrish & Co., one would be drawn up by the solicitor of the War Department. I had done the best I could, but they desired to close the doors against all possible frauds by the use of technical terms that I had no knowledge of. That contract was drawn up. I have never seen it. It was sent out to Louisville for my signature, to take the place of the one I had made, and which had been approved by the Surgeon General. Before that contract arrived I was ordered here as a witness before this court-martial. Since I have been here I have been told unofficially that the contract sent out was, in substance, like the one I had made.

Question. You have not executed that contract?

Answer. No, sir; it still remains unexecuted. It may be now in Louisville, or it may have been returned to the Secretary of War.

Question. It requires your signature to execute it?

Answer. I do not know what it requires now. I act under instructions, and until I get another telegram from the Secretary of War, or additional authority from the Surgeon General, I shall take no further action.

Question. I see that your advertisement contains the following clause:

"The ice either to be delivered by actual weight of issues to the hospitals by the contractors, or by inspection and measurement by the issuing officer, on or before the 1st of May, 1864, who will then receipt for the actual contents of ice-houses."

Which of these conditions is executed in the contract?

Answer. It is to be delivered in the ice-houses and taken by actual measurement.

Question. Is the ice then to be delivered to the hospitals by the contractor or by the government?

Answer. After the government has received the ice from the contractor, it delivers it to its hospitals.

Question. The contractor has nothing to do with the ice after he has put it n the ice-houses, had it measured, and delivered it to the government?

Answer. No, sir; those provisions in the advertisement are taken almost verbatim from my letter of instructions from the Surgeon General's office. My letter of instructions was as follows:

"SURGEON GENERAL'S OFFICE,
"*Washington City, D. C., November* 27, 1863.

"DOCTOR: You are instructed to advertise for proposals for furnishing ice for all the United States general hospitals at the west, those of the divisions of the Mississippi and of the department of the Gulf, upon the Mississippi and its tributaries, in such quantities as may be required for the use of the sick and wounded during the year 1864. In all cases the ice to be well packed in properly constructed ice-houses (previous to the 15th of April) at such points nearest the hospitals as, upon consultation with medical disbursing officers at St. Louis, Cairo, Cincinnati, Nashville, Memphis, Vicksburg, and elsewhere, you may consider most advantageous.

"The ice to be delivered by actual weight of issues to hospitals by contractors, or by inspection and measurement by the issuing officer, on the 1st of May, 1864, who will then receipt for the actual contents of ice-houses.

"In those few cases where it may be found necessary to contract for delivery from barges during the summer, you will carefully protect the United States by so wording contracts that only the amount of ice actually delivered, as shown by receipts of medical officers, will be paid for.

"It is believed that an immense saving can thus be effected upon the expenditures for ice of past year, and your attention is particularly directed to the importance of such a reduction. The reports of Medical Storekeeper Stevens, and propositions of Parrish & Co., and of Alger, are enclosed.

"Very respectfully, your obedient servant,

"C. H. CRANE,
"*Surgeon United States Army.*

"By order of the Acting Surgeon General.

"Surgeon D L. MAGRUDER, U. S. A.,
"*Medical Purveyor, Louisville, Ky.*

The propositions referred to there were those which had nothing to do with this contract.

Question. Propositions made before the advertisement?

Answer. Yes, sir; before there was any advertisement at all. They were sent to me from Washington; they had nothing to do with the bids at all.

Question. "In all cases the ice to be well packed and stored in properly constructed ice-houses, prior to the 15th of April, 1864, at such points nearest the hospitals as may be designated." Who provided the ice-houses?

Answer. The contractor.

Question. Did not the government own ice-houses at some of these points?

Answer. Not that I know of.

Question. Was the price of building the ice-houses to be a part of the price of the ice?

Answer. Of course the contractor had to furnish the ice-houses, and had to build them.

Question. Then, as by the terms of your proposals, an ice-house was to be built at every point where it was needed. What is meant by having ice delivered from barges?

Answer. That is, if it should be found necessary to do so. Last year ice was taken to Vicksburg and other places on the river in barges and delivered from them. That is what is meant by that; but there will probably be none of that this year.

Question. There is no stipulation in your advertisement for proposals in relation to delivery of ice from barges?

Answer. No, sir; not now, but, as it says there, it may be found necessary during the summer.

Question. There is nothing said about it in your proposals?

Answer. I looked upon it that that could be advertised for afterwards. I could not make a contract at that time to deliver ice from barges during the summer, because I did not then know of any place at which to deliver it. We are not fighting on the Mississippi now anything like we were last year.

Question. That would not be provided for in any of the bids which you would receive in response to that advertisement?

Answer. No, sir.

Question. So that without a separate, independent bargain it could not come into the contract?

Answer. No, sir; I construed that to be a separate thing from the other, according to my instructions, that it might be with any other contractor. For that reason I did not embrace it in the advertisement.

Question. Left it to be made a separate contract if necessary?

Answer. Yes, sir; if it should be needed. I did not think we should need any such thing. Last year they bought a great deal of ice, at a high price, during the hot months, and took it down in barges, and it all melted before they got to use it.

Question. Can you furnish to us, or inform us where we can obtain, the correspondence between you and the Surgeon General in relation to this contract; also copies of the proposals received by you in response to this advertisement, and a copy of the contract as made by you?

Answer. I sent all those things to the Secretary of War from Louisville; everything, I believe, that I had in my possession in connexion with that matter. I kept copies of all but the bids, and they are now on file in my office in Louisville. But they are all on file in the Surgeon General's office, and the office of Assistant Secretary Dana.

Question. Have you any knowledge of the time usually allowed in advertisements for ice in so large quantities as this calls for?

Answer. No, sir; I have not. As I have already told you, I was ignorant on the subject of ice; it was a matter altogether foreign to my business.

Question. Do you know what the contract you made with Parrish & Co. would probably amount to?

Answer. No, sir; that was one difficulty; I could get no data. I had to issue that proposal, although I did not know what each hospital would want. A circular has been sent out now, the responses to which will fix the amount needed for each hospital. By them I can ascertain the number of bids in each hospital; and north of a certain latitude a half a pound a day, and south of it a pound a day of ice is allowed to each man. That is a circular letter which has been addressed to me since I have been here. Before I came away I had not received letters from all the general hospitals, although I had addressed circular letters to them noting the quantity of ice they would need for the coming year.

Question. Did you receive any proposals in response to this advertisement of the 20th of December?

Answer. I think there were two which came in afterwards, which I forwarded to the Secretary of War. I am certain there was one; it was a bid to supply all the ports north of the Ohio for $16 a ton, while the bid of Parrish & Co. was $10 a ton.

Question. Can you tell whether, under the terms of the Chicago Ice Co., the ice is to be taken after it has been delivered into the ice-houses, or whether it is to be taken as weighed out at the hospitals?

Answer. I think it is to be taken by the load, and receipted for out of their cars. They deliver at some places by cars. I think that is the way; however, that is on file. I did not tax my memory with it, but sent all the papers to Mr. Dana's office.

By Mr. Loan:

Question. At what time on the northern and northwestern waters is ice usually gathered and secured?

Answer. I am under the impression that it is during the latter part of December and the early part of January. I have lived up on the Upper Mississippi, and that is the time we always gathered our ice there. I used to have charge of a hospital there, and they usually allowed me to superintend the cutting of the ice and putting it away, as the principal portion of it was intended for the sick of the garrison; and we always cut the best ice at that time.

Question. Where were you stationed then?

Answer. I was at Fort Pierre Choteau and at Fort Randall for nearly six years. From the 1st to the 10th of January was the time when we cut the best ice; for in the latter part of January and in February we had a thaw which made the ice porous.

Question. At what points must ice necessarily be procured for the supply of all places north of Cairo?

Answer. You can get good merchantable ice north of Quincy.

Question. Procured from the waters that empty into the Mississippi?

Answer. From the tributaries of the Mississippi; yes, sir.

Question. In advertising for this ice, did you take into consideration the security of procuring the necessary means to obtain so large a supply of ice, and was that one of the reasons that induced you to fix the time of receiving the bids at as early a date as possible?

Answer. That is the very reason which I stated in my letter to the Surgeon General; that the man who should take so large a contract as that must have a great many hands in his employ, must have the means to cut his ice, and must get the barges to ship it in.

Question. Is the period for gathering the crop of ice a limited one?

Answer. I think merchantable ice is obtained from about the 20th of December to the 12th or 15th, perhaps the 20th of January.

Question. It ought to be received during that time?

Answer. Yes, sir; I think so.

Question. Were you instructed to let the contract for all the points to one man, or were you to make several contracts?

Answer. I construed it to mean the best contract for all the points.

Question. Did you receive special bids for each point?

Answer. Yes, sir; I received bids for each point.

Question. Were the points designated and known at the time the bids were put in?

Answer. Yes, sir; the bids mentioned them. There were three bids from St. Louis firms; they all designated in their bids the different points—St. Louis, Memphis, Nashville, Louisville, &c.; some of them designated more and some less places. I think there were three bids for New Orleans.

Question. Separate bids?

Answer. Yes, sir; of three firms; but the bid of Parrish & Co. was the only one at $25 a ton.

Question. Do you remember whether there were separate bids put in for each of these places?

Answer. I think there were only eleven bids in all.

Question. And how many points were to be supplied?

Answer. I think there were some 24 points in all to be supplied.

Question. How many of these bids covered the supply of all the points?

Answer. No one covered them all except that of Parrish & Co.

Question. There were three bids for supplying New Orleans?

Answer. I think so; two others, besides Mr. Parrish, from St. Louis.

Question. Mr. Parrish put in a bid to supply all the points?

Answer. Yes, sir: including New Orleans.

Question. He made no separate bid for New Orleans, independent of his general bid?

Answer. No, sir.

Question. Did the other parties make separate bids for New Orleans?

Answer. No, sir; they included other points.

Question. What other points?

Answer. Vicksburg, Memphis, Nashville, Louisville, St. Louis, and other places.

Question. Was there any special bid for any individual place, separate and apart from the others? For instance, did any one put in just one bid for New Orleans, or for any other one place?

Answer. No, sir; nobody.

Question. All the bids included the furnishing ice to more than one point?

Answer. There may have been one bid for supplying Louisville.

Question. Do you remember any other for any other point?

Answer. No, sir, I do not.

By Mr. Gooch:

Question. Did not the bidders specify the prices at which they would deliver ice at each particular point?

Answer. Yes, sir; all specified the prices at each point.

Question. Then if you felt bound, as I think you say you did, to give the contract to the man who was the lowest bidder for all the points, and Parrish & Co. being the only bidder for all the points, the contract went to them without any competition?

Answer. You might construe it in that way. But I gave it to them as the most comprehensive bidder, and thought I was doing the best for the government. As he was the lowest bidder for nearly all the points, and the most comprehensive one, I awarded it to him, subject, of course, to the approval of my chief. In my letter enclosing the contract to him I specifically stated that.

Question. Had there been a bid to supply New Orleans for $20 a ton, Mr. Parrish's bid being for $25 a ton, would you have felt bound, under your instructions, to have awarded the contract to him?

Answer. There was no bid of that kind.

Question. But there were other points for which there were bids lower than the one of Mr. Parrish.

Answer. I construed it that I was to award the contract to the best bidder—that is, the most comprehensive one—the one under which I could do the best for the government.

Question. The most comprehensive bid, from the very nature of the case, would be the one that covered all the points?

Answer. Yes, sir.

Question. And did not the fact that there were bids for particular points, not including all the points, show that they did not understand that the man who bid honestly for all the points in the aggregate was to receive the contract, and did understand that the honest bidder for each particular point was to receive the contract for that point?

Answer. I do not know what they understood. I think I should have referred particular bids to Washington, as I did the other bids. New Orleans is very far out of my province. There is a regular medical purveyor at New Orleans whom I do not supply with anything. I do not know where he gets his supplies. However, the department of the Gulf is embraced in my instructions.

By Mr. Odell:

Question. You did not feel that you had authority, without reference and further instructions, to accept a bid at $20 a ton for New Orleans alone?

Answer. I can tell what I did. In the first place I sent all the bids to Washington. I did not want to make the contract, because it was something foreign to my duties, and I knew there would be trouble about it, and I did not wish to have myself involved in it in any way. I did the best I could, as I thought, for the government.

Question. But were you competent, under your instructions, to have received a bid proposing to supply New Orleans alone at a lower price than Mr. Parrish's bid, which covered the whole, and to have awarded the contract for New Orleans on that bid?

Answer. I do not know whether I would have awarded the contract; I think it probable I should not have done it; I should most likely have sent it on to Washington. All the bids were before the solicitor of the War Department and Assistant Secretary Dana; and, as I have understood, they have drawn up a new contract with Parrish & Co., the wording I used having been changed, because I did not put in the legal technicalities. But the contract is for the same amount, and covers the same grounds that mine did, I understand. That new contract was sent out to me for signature; but I have not yet signed it, because, before it got there, I was called here for this court-martial; and since then, I understand, there has been a telegram sent out there to stop my signing it; why, I do not know. But I shall have nothing to do with ice until I get further instructions, which I hope I shall not get.

Testimony of Hon. John A. Bingham.

WASHINGTON, *February* 16, 1864.

Hon. JOHN A. BINGHAM sworn and examined.

By the chairman:

Question. The committee have called you here in reference to a certain order from the Surgeon General's department relating to the purchase of hospital supplies from the Sanitary Commission.

Answer. I will state to the committee that I understood the memorandum shown me by the Sergeant-at arms to ask me to bring with me a *duces tecum* issued to Dr. R. O. Abbott. I have not that in my possession or control at all; but I am free to state to the committee that in the præcipe for a subpœna for Mr. Abbott, who, I understand, has some control at least over the hospitals in and about Washington city—in that præcipe I prayed the Adjutant General to issue a subpœna *duces tecum* to Abbott to bring all orders issued by him during the month of June, 1863, directing supplies for the hospitals to be purchased of the Sanitary Commission.

Question. Has that been returned?

Answer. I am not yet advised that it has been returned, nor have I seen it. My orderly has said that it has been served, but I have not seen the writ, and do not know.

Question. Has any order from the Surgeon General to Dr. Abbott, directing him to purchase chickens, eggs, butter, and such things, from the Sanitary Commission, come into your possession?

Answer. Nothing has come into my possession except what purports to be a copy of a circular issued in June, 1863, by Abbott, which circular, among other things, directs the persons to whom it is addressed to purchase eggs, poultry, &c., of the Sanitary Commission; directing on what days, and at what places, in or about Washington, to apply for the same. The circular concludes with the statement that the Surgeon General directs that the purchase of those articles shall be made only from the Sanitary Commission, or words to that effect. That is all the information I have on that subject.

I will state that, in order to make my answer more complete, I will, when I return to my room, abstract the exact language of that circular, in so far as it refers to the Surgeon General and the supply of those articles, and send it to the committee.

That is all the information I have on that subject, except the hearsay which informed me of the fact that there was such a circular, which, of course, was sought by myself and received confidentially.

Question. Have you any evidence of what has been done under that order?

Answer. Not as yet; the witness has not appeared in court. [The court-martial in the case of Surgeon General Hammond, of which the witness is the judge advocate.]

Question. Can you give us the names of witnesses who are supposed to know anything about the proceedings under that order?

Answer. I am not able now to do so, because I did not push my inquiry further than to ascertain who it was who issued the circular, in order to reach him and make him tell me.

Question. From whom did the circular purport to emanate?

Answer. From R. O. Abbott.

Question. Addressed to whom?

Answer. It did not name any person, but seems to be a circular; it is headed "circular."

By Mr. Gooch:

Question. A printed circular?

Answer. The copy I have is not printed.

By the chairman:

Question. You have not the original circular?

Answer. No, sir; that is what I have ordered Abbott to bring into court. He has not answered yet; he will to-morrow, I suppose.

Subsequently the witness forwarded the following papers to the committee:

[Circular.]

MEDICAL DIRECTOR'S OFFICE,
Washington, June 23, 1863.

SIR: On and after Friday next the Sanitary Commission will be prepared to furnish the hospital under your charge, at cost prices, with mutton, poultry, milk, butter, eggs, vegetables, dried fruits, &c., &c.

These supplies will be delivered from the store-house of the Express Company, New Jersey avenue, opposite front of passenger station Baltimore railroad, at any time between sunrise and 11 a. m. You will accordingly send your hospital wagon to this point with the order for delivery of such articles as you may require—(see enclosed form)—signed by yourself.

The amount to be received on Friday and Saturday will be the amount stated in your reply to the circular of June 9, from this office, as then required for the use of your hospital.

The amount required for Sunday will be ordered on Friday morning, and thereafter orders for supplies will always be given two days in advance of the time the supplies are needed.

The Surgeon General directs that the purchase of such supplies will be made from no other source except in cases of emergency.

Very respectfully, your obedient servant,

R. O. ABBOTT,
Surgeon U. S. A., Medical Director, Dep't Washington.

Copy of form referred to in the foregoing circular.

The Sanitary Commission is requested to purchase the following supplies for —— hospital, to be delivered at Adams' Express Company's office, corner New Jersey avenue and C street, Washington, next —— day —— 1863.

Articles.	Quantity.	Articles.	Quantity.
Butter, print..............pounds.		Carrots ....bushels.	
roll ....do...		Turnips ....do...	
tub ....do...		Onions......................do...	
Mutton ....do...		Beets ....do...	
Lamb ....do...		Apples ....do...	
Poultry ....do...		Potatoes ....do...	
Veal ....do...		Parsnips ....do...	
Lard ....do...		Potatoes, sweet ....do...	
Fish, fresh ....do...		Herbs..................bunches.	
salt ....do...		Celery ....do...	
Apples, dried ....do...		Oyster plant................do...	
Turkeys, dressed...........do...		Oysters.................gallons.	
Ducks, " ....do...		Cranberries...............quarts.	
Geese, " ....do...		Cabbage ....heads.	
Pork, fresh ....do...		Mackerel, No. 1.........barrels.	
Peaches, dried ....do...		No. 2...........do...	
Eggs ....dozens.		No. 3...........do...	
Squash, Boston.............do...		Chickens, live ....pairs.	
Oranges ....boxes.		Geese, live ....do..	
Lemons.....................do ..		Ducks, live.................do..	
Rutabaga ....bushels.		Turkeys, live ....do..	

———— ————,
Surgeon in charge.

WASHINGTON, ——————, 1863.

SURGEON GENERAL'S OFFICE,
Washington City, D. C, February 8, 1864.

SIR: In conformity to the request of the "Joint Committee on the Conduct and Expenditures of the War," forwarded by you on the 5th instant, I have the honor to transmit herewith copies of all the contracts made by this department for ice since the 1st of January, 1862.

Very respectfully, your obedient servant,

JOS. K. BARNES,
Acting Surgeon General.

Hon. EDWIN M. STANTON,
Secretary of War.

[Circular letter.]

SURGEON GENERAL'S OFFICE,
Washington, D. C., February 6, 1864.

Ice provided from the appropriation for the medical department is exclusively for the use of the sick in general and post hospitals, and will not, under any circumstances, be issued, or otherwise disposed of, to officers or soldiers not actually under treatment in them. The most rigid economy must be observed in the issue and use of ice so supplied. Issues to hospitals will be made upon the estimate of one pound daily, per patient, at Washington and points south of it; half a pound daily, per patient, at all points north of Washington, which, with proper care, will be found an ample allowance. Medical directors will give such orders as will insure compliance with these instructions.

Very respectfully, your obedient servant,
By order of the Acting Surgeon General,
C. H. CRANE, *Surgeon U. S. Army.*

Articles of agreement made this twenty-fifth day of February, eighteen hundred and sixty-three, between Henry Johnson, medical storekeeper United States army, and acting medical purveyor, Washington, D. C., of the one part, and A. Tracy Edgerton, of the city of New York, and State of New York, of the other part,

Witnesseth: That the said Henry Johnson, medical storekeeper United States army, for and on behalf of the United States of America, and the said A. Tracy Edgerton, for himself, his heirs, executors and administrators, have mutually agreed, and by these presents do mutually covenant and agree, to and with each other, in the manner following, viz:

First. That the said A. Tracy Edgerton shall deliver at Hilton Head, South Carolina, Newbern, North Carolina, and Fortress Monroe, Virginia, the whole amount of ice required to be consumed at each respective point and vicinity.

Ice to be in quality A No. 1, gathered in Maine, and delivered at two thousand (2,000) pounds to the ton.

Second. That for each and every ton delivered at Hilton Head, South Carolina, and accepted by the medical officer in charge, the said A. Tracy Edgerton shall receive the sum of $11.

Third. That for each and every ton of ice delivered at Newbern, North Carolina, and accepted by the medical officer in charge, the said A. Tracy Edgerton shall receive the sum of ten dollars and fifty cents ($10 50.)

Fourth. That for each and every ton of ice delivered at Fortress Monroe, Virginia, and accepted by the medical officer in charge, the said A. Tracy Edgerton shall receive the sum of eight dollars and seventy-five cents ($8 75.)

Fifth. All the ice delivered under this contract to be subject to the inspection and approval of the medical officer in charge of the post where it is delivered, and such as does not conform to the specifications set forth in this contract shall be rejected.

Sixth. That payment shall be made from time to time upon receipted bills of lading, and duplicate accounts certified to by the medical officer in charge of the post where it is delivered.

Seventh. No member of Congress shall be admitted to any share herein, or any benefits to arise therefrom.

Eighth. It is further agreed that the said A. Tracy Edgerton will allow three working days for discharging each cargo at either one of the points before mentioned, without extra charge; after that time, demurrage to be allowed by the said Henry Johnson, medical storekeeper United States army as per charter-party of the vessel or bill of lading.

In witness whereof, the undersigned have hereunto placed their hands and seals the day and date above written.

HENRY JOHNSON. [SEAL.]
A. TRACY EDGERTON. [SEAL.]

Witnesses:
WM. H. YEATON.
ROBERT A. PAYNE.

SURGEON GENERAL'S OFFICE, *February*, 1864.

A true copy from the records.

W. C. SPENCER,
Assistant Surgeon United States Army.

Articles of agreement made this fifth day of March, 18C3, between Henry Johnson, medical storekeeper United States army, and acting medical purveyor, Washington, D. C., on the one part, and Joseph W. Parrish and William S. Huse, comprising the firm of Joseph W. Parrish & Co., of the city of St. Louis, State of Missouri, of the other part,

Witnesseth: That the said Henry Johnson, medical storekeeper United States army, for and on behalf of the United States of America, and the said Joseph Parrish and William S. Huse, comprising the firm of J. W. Parrish & Co., for themselves, their heirs, executors and administrators, have mutually agreed, and by these presents do mutually covenant and agree, to and with each other, in the manner following, viz:

First. That the said J. W. Parrish & Co. shall deliver at Memphis, Tennessee, Nashville, Tennessee, St. Louis, Missouri, and Cairo, Illinois, the whole amount of ice required to be consumed at each respective point and vicinity during the remainder of the year 1863. Ice to be in quality A No. 1, and delivered at two thousand (2,000) pounds to the ton.

Second. That for each and every ton of ice delivered at Nashville, Tennessee, and accepted by the medical officer in charge, the said J. W. Parrish & Co. shall receive the sum of twenty-five dollars ($25.)

Third. That for each and every ton of ice delivered at St. Louis, Missouri, and accepted by the medical officer in charge, the said J. W. Parrish & Co. shall receive the sum of sixteen dollars ($16.)

Fourth. That for each and every ton of ice delivered at Cairo, Illinois, and accepted by the medical officer in charge, the said J. W. Parrish & Co. shall receive the sum of twenty dollars ($20)

Fifth. That for each and every ton of ice delivered at Memphis, Tennessee, and accepted by the medical officer in charge, the said J. W. Parrish & Co. shall receive the sum of twenty dollars ($20.)

Sixth. All the ice delivered under this contract to be subject to the inspection and approval of the medical officer in charge of the post where it is delivered, and such as does not conform to the specifications set forth in this contract shall be rejected.

Seventh. That payment shall be made from time to time upon receipted bills of lading, and duplicate accounts certified to by the medical officer in charge of the post where it is delivered.

Eighth. No member of Congress shall be admitted to any share herein or any benefit to arise therefrom.

Ninth. It is further agreed that the said J. W. Parrish & Co. will allow three

(3) working days for discharging each cargo at either one of the points before mentioned; after that time demurrage to be allowed by the said Henry Johnson, medical storekeeper United States army, as per charter-party or bill of lading of the vessel.

In witness whereof, the undersigned have hereunto placed their hands and seals the day and date above written.

HENRY JOHNSON, [SEAL.]
Medical Storekeeper U. S. A., Act'g Med. Purveyor.
J. W. PARRISH & CO. [SEAL.]

Witnesses:
R. A. PAYNE.
FRANK L. SLADE.

SURGEON GENERAL'S OFFICE, *February*, 1864.

A true copy from the records.

W. C. SPENCER,
Assistant Surgeon United States Army.

Articles of agreement made this sixth day of March, eighteen hundred and sixty-three, between Henry Johnson, medical storekeeper United States army, and acting medical purveyor, Washington, D. C., of the one part, and J. C. Tiffany, city of New York, State of New York, of the other part,

Witnesseth: That the said Henry Johnson, medical storekeeper United States army, for and on behalf of the United States of America, and the said J. C. Tiffany, for himself, his heirs, executors, and administrators, have mutually agreed, and by these presents do mutually covenant and agree, to and with each other, in the manner following, viz:

Specification.—That the said J. C. Tiffany shall deliver at New Orleans, La., Pensacola, Fla., and Washington, D. C., the whole quantity of ice required to be consumed at each respective point and vicinity during the remainder of the year eighteen hundred and sixty-three (1863;) ice to be in quality A No. 1, and delivered at two thousand (2,000) pounds to the ton; to be well stored in the vessels at the point of shipment, according to the most approved method, and subject while stowing to the inspection of an agent of this department.

First. That for each and every ton of ice delivered at New Orleans, Louisiana, and accepted by the medical officer in charge, the said J. C. Tiffany shall receive the sum of twenty-two dollars and fifty cents ($22 50.)

Second. That for each and every ton of ice delivered at Pensacola, Florida, and accepted by the medical officer in charge, the said J. C. Tiffany shall receive the sum of twenty-two dollars and fifty cents ($22 50.)

Third. That for each and every ton of ice delivered at Washington, District of Columbia, and accepted by the medical officer in charge, the said J. C. Tiffany shall receive the sum of ten dollars and fifty cents ($10 50.)

Fourth. All the ice delivered under this contract to be received and paid for as per bill of lading, fifteen (15) per cent. being deducted from the face of bill of lading for wastage on ice delivered at Pensacola, Florida, and New Orleans, Louisiana, and ten (10) per cent. deducted on ice delivered at Washington, District of Columbia.

Fifth. Bill of lading of each cargo of ice to be sworn to before United States district attorney, clerk of the district court, or notary public, at the point of shipment, by the said J. C. Tiffany and the captain of the vessel.

Sixth. All the ice delivered under this contract to be subject to the inspection and approval of the medical officer in charge of the post where it is delivered, and such as does not conform to the specifications set forth in this contract shall be rejected.

Seventh. That payment shall be made from time to time upon receipted bills of lading and duplicate accounts certified to by the medical officer in charge of the post where it is delivered.

Eighth. It is further agreed that the said J. C. Tiffany will build ice-houses on the plan herewith attached, (provided they shall be wanted,) charging therefor two dollars and fifty cents ($2 50) per ton according to the tonnage of the house if built at Pensacola, Florida, or New Orleans, Louisiana, and one dollar and fifty cents ($1 50) per ton according to the tonnage if built at Washington, District of Columbia, the United States furnishing the ground therefor.

Ninth. And the said J. C. Tiffany shall store the ice in the said ice-houses and deliver therefrom daily at the various hospitals in Washington, District of Columbia, and vicinity, the daily amount of ice required at such hospitals, and shall receive therefor fifty cents per ton additional for each and every ton so stored and delivered. The ice to be well stored in the ice-houses according to the most approved method, subject at all times to the inspection of an agent of this department.

Tenth. No demurrage to be allowed for any detention of vessels delivering ice at Washington, District of Columbia.

Eleventh. No member of Congress shall be admitted to any share herein, or any benefit to arise therefrom.

Twelfth. And it is further agreed that the said J. C. Tiffany will allow five (5) working days for discharging cargo at Pensacola, Florida, New Orleans, Louisiana; after that time demurrage to be allowed by the said Henry Johnson, medical storekeeper, as per charter-party and bill of lading of the vessel.

In witness whereof, the undersigned have hereunto placed their hand and seals the day and date above written.

HENRY JOHNSON, [SEAL.]
Medical Storekeeper U. S. A., Act'g Med. Purveyor.
J. C. TIFFANY. [SEAL.]

Witness:
ROBERT H. PAYNE.
FRANK L. SLADE.

SURGEON GENERAL'S OFFICE, *February* 8, 1864.

A true copy from the records.

W. C. SPENCER,
Assistant Surgeon United States Army.

This contract entered into this third day of April, eighteen hundred and sixty-three, between J. T. Head, surgeon United States army, an officer in the service of the United States of America, of the one part, and Jarrett Gosnell and Samuel C. Scott, both of Louisville, in the State of Kentucky, of the other part,

Witnesseth: That the said Surgeon J. T. Head, for and on behalf of the United States of America, and the said J. Gosnell and Samuel C. Scott, for themselves, their heirs, executors, and administrators, have mutually agreed, and by these presents do mutually covenant and agree, to and with each other, as follows, viz:

That the said party of the second part shall deliver, properly packed in such ice-houses at Louisville as shall be designated by the said Surgeon J. T. Head, United States army, five hundred tons of good, firm, clear ice, on or before the fifteenth day of May, 1863, the unavoidable casualties of navigation only excepted.

That the said party of the first part shall pay or cause to be paid to the said party of the second part fifteen dollars for each and every ton of two thousand pounds of ice so delivered, the weight to be determined by water-gauge at Louisville: provided, if the necessary barges for the conveyance of said ice from Beaver, Pennsylvania, to Louisville, Kentucky, shall be furnished by the United States of America, then the said party of the second part shall refund the hire of said barges to an amount not to exceed two dollars for each and every ton of ice so delivered. That in case of failure or deficiency in quantity or quality of the ice stipulated to be delivered, then the said Surgeon J. T. Head, United States army, or the medical director, shall have power to supply the deficiency by purchase, and the said party of the second part shall pay the cost.

No member of Congress shall be admitted to any share herein, or any benefits to arise therefrom.

(The words "at Louisville" interlined before signing.)

J. T. HEAD, [SEAL.]
Surgeon United States Army.
JARRETT GOSNELL. [SEAL.]
SAMUEL C. SCOTT. [SEAL.]

Signed, sealed, and delivered, in presence of—
ELIJAH GLASSCOKE.
SAM'L L. EWING.

SURGEON GENERAL'S OFFICE, *February*, 1864.

A true copy from the records.

W. C. SPENCER,
Assistant Surgeon United States Army.

[Proposal.]

CHICAGO ICE COMPANY TO UNITED STATES.

We will deliver on board cars at any railroad depot in that city, ice packed as hereinafter described, in any quantity as may be required of us not to exceed in all four thousand tons, we to receive pay for the same at the rate of five dollars per ton weighed here, payable monthly at Chicago. Or we will deliver said ice or any part thereof, packed as hereinafter described, at any of the following named places, viz: Cincinnati, Ohio; New Albany, Indiana; Cairo, Illinois; East St. Louis, Illinois; we to receive pay for the same at the following rates, viz: $10 50 (ten and a half dollars) per ton for full car-loads of ten tons, weight at Chicago; $14 (fourteen dollars) per ton for shipments of less than ten tons and over two tons, weight at Chicago; $17 (seventeen dollars) per ton, for shipments of less than two tons, weight at Chicago. (Memorandum.—The increase of price in the last two stipulations is occasioned by difference in freight charged by railroad.) It being understood that we are to receive pay for all ice delivered by us at the above named places monthly in Chicago, and that we are to furnish a correct account monthly of all ice shipped by us to the respective places above named.

We will pack said ice in cars as follows, viz: First spreading upon the floor of car a layer of sawdust or fine shavings, six inches deep; next, and upon said shavings, a layer of ice, leaving a space of six inches between the edges of said layer of ice and the sides of the car; said space to be filled with sawdust or fine shavings; next a second layer of sawdust or fine shavings six inches deep on the top surface of said first layer of ice, and in like manner each successive layer of ice in car, covering the whole with a layer of sawdust or shavings eight inches deep. Or we will pack said ice, or any part thereof, if required, in boxes or tierces, as follows, viz: first, spreading on the bottom of said boxes or tierces a layer of sawdust or fine shavings; next, filling said boxes or tierces with ice, leaving a space of four inches around the sides and top of ice; said space to be filled with sawdust or fine shavings; said boxes or tierces to be properly closed and strongly hooped. We will deliver said ice at any time or times during the year 1862. All ice furnished by us to be lake ice, from eleven to eighteen inches thick. Our Lake Michigan ice-houses adjoin the Union depot of the Illinois Central railroad, Michigan Central railroad, and the Chicago, Burlington and Quincy railroads; and our Crystal Lake ice-houses are situated alongside the track of the St. Louis, Alton and Chicago railroads; and the ice contained in either of these houses can be loaded direct upon the cars of the said roads without delay of cartage, rehandling or breakage.

We have been engaged in shipping ice south and elsewhere for the last twelve years.

Respectfully,

H. H. BLAKE, *Secretary Chicago Ice Company.*

CHICAGO, *May* 7, 1862.

This proposal was approved and accepted by the Surgeon General.—(See letter to Mr. Blake, May 23, 1862.)

A true copy from the records.

W. C. SPENCER, *Assistant Surgeon U. S. A.*

SURGEON GENERAL'S OFFICE, *February* 8, 1864.

This contract, entered into this 31st day of May, 1862, between Surgeon General William A. Hammond, of the United States army, and Messrs. Addison Gage & Company, witnesseth: That, for the consideration hereafter mentioned, the said Addison Gage & Company promise and agree to deliver to the agents of the United States medical department at Charleston and Savannah (when in possession of the authorities of the United States) a good and wholesome quality of ice.

It is understood that the ice is to be delivered during the coming summer months in such quantities as the agents of the United States medical department at the above-mentioned places may need and call for, and at such times as they, the said agents, may designate.

The said Addison Gage & Company further agree to deliver a good and wholesome quality of ice at New Orleans and Mobile, (when in possession of the authorities of the United States,) subject to the same stipulations hereinbefore mentioned as to quantity, quality, &c., and as to the delivery of ice at the aforesaid Atlantic ports. And the said Surgeon General promises and agrees, on behalf of the United States, to pay or cause to be paid to the said Addison Gage & Company the sum of one dollar and twenty-five cents for each hundred pounds of good and wholesome ice delivered as aforesaid at Charleston and Savannah; and the Surgeon General promises and agrees, on behalf of the United States, to pay or cause to be paid to the said Addison Gage & Company the sum of one dollar and fifty cents for each and every hundred pounds of good and wholesome ice delivered, as aforesaid, at New Orleans and Mobile.

WILLIAM A. HAMMOND,
Surgeon General.

ADDISON GAGE & CO.

Witness to signature of Addison Gage & Co., J. CARTER CUTTER.

A true copy from the records.

W. C. SPENCER, *Assistant Surgeon U. S. A.*

SURGEON GENERAL'S OFFICE, *February*, 1864.

Statement of ice used by the medical and hospital department of the army during the year 1863.

Where delivered.	Quantity.	Price.	Amount.	Total.	Remarks.
		Ton.			
New York	$2\frac{400}{2000}$ tons, at	$4 00	$8 80		Open market.
	$187\frac{1445}{2000}$ tons, at	4 50	844 75		Do.
	$31\frac{1340}{2000}$ tons, at	6 00	183 72		Do.
	314 tons, at	7 00	2,198 00		Do.
	$203\frac{1550}{2000}$ tons, at	10 00	2,037 75		Do.
	20 tons, at	12 00	240 00		Do.
	$761\frac{635}{2000}$			$5,513 02	
Annapolis, Md	80 tons, at	10 00		800 00	No contract.
Washington, D. C.	$3,310\frac{350}{2000}$ tons, at	10 50	34,756 84		Contract with J. C. Tiffany, of New York.
	1 ice-house		1,500 00		Do ... do ... do.
	For distributing ice to hospitals in and around Washington		525 00	36,781 84	
Fortress Monroe, Va.	$1,428\frac{441}{2000}$ tons, at	8 75	12,494 30		Contract with A. T. Edgerton, of New York.
	Demurrage		460 00		Do ... do ... do.
	Sundries		92 50	13,046 80	Do ... do ... do.
Newbern, N. C.	699 tons, at	10 50	7,339 50		Do ... do ... do.
	Demurrage		269 00		Do ... do ... do.
	Sundries		63 79	7,672 25	Do ... do ... do.
Hilton Head, S. C.	1,762 tons, at	11 00	19,382 00		Do ... do ... do.
	Demurrage		3,439 60	23,821 60	Do ... do ... do.
Key West, Fla.	$312\frac{1600}{2000}$ tons, at	22 50		7,038 00	Contract with J. C. Tiffany, of New York.
Pensacola, Fla.	$399\frac{443}{2000}$ tons, at	22 50	8,982 49		Do ... do ... do.
	Demurrage		63 15	9,045 64	Do ... do ... do.

Place	Quantity		Rate	Amount	Total	Remarks
New Orleans, La.	3,874 $\frac{560}{2000}$	tons, at	22 50	87,171 30		Do. do. do.
		Demurrage		3,937 00		Do. do. do.
					91,108 30	
Baton Rouge, La.	328 $\frac{188}{2000}$	tons, at	22 50	7,401 14		Do. do. do.
		Demurrage		1,566 72		Do. do. do.
					8,967 86	
St. Louis, Mo.	3,629 $\frac{1000}{2000}$	tons, at	16 00		58,071 00	Contract with J. W. Parrish & Co., of St. Louis.
Cairo, Ill.	547	tons, at	20 00		10,940 00	Do. do. do.
Louisville, Ky.	599	tons, at	15 00	8,985 00		Contract with Gosnell & Scott, of Louisville.
		Minus barge-hire		600 00		Do. do. do.
					7,385 00	Do. do. do.
Nashville, Tenn.	497	tons, at	25 00		12,425 00	Contract with J. W. Parrish & Co., of St. Louis.
Memphis, Tenn.	3,667 $\frac{1666}{2000}$	tons, at	20 00	73,356 66		Do. do. do.
	313 $\frac{1000}{2000}$	tons, at	60 00	18,810 00		No contract.
					92,166 66	
	3,981 $\frac{666}{2000}$	tons.				
Vicksburg, Miss.	1,072	tons, at	75 00	80,400 00		Horace Holton.
	345	tons, at	60 00	20,700 00		White & Co.
					101,100 00	
	1,417	tons.				
Total	23,625 $\frac{1883}{2000}$	tons			485,882 97	

JOS. K. BARNES,
Acting Surgeon General U. S. A.

SURGEON GENERAL'S OFFICE, *February* 5, 1864.

ARMY MEDICAL PURVEYOR'S OFFICE,
Louisville, Ky., December 7, 1863.

COLONEL: I have the honor to acknowledge the receipt of your letter of instructions in regard to advertising for proposals for ice to be furnished for the general hospitals at the west for the year 1864; also the reports of Military Storekeeper Stevens, and propositions of Parrish & Company, and Alger, for furnishing ice.

On the 4th instant I caused an advertisement, as per enclosed slip, to be inserted in five newspapers of the principal cities of the west, (viz: Louisville Journal, Cincinnati Gazette, Chicago Tribune, and the Democrat and Union, of St. Louis.)

I limited the time for the reception of bids to the 20th instant, for the reason that the ice should all be cut and stored in barges during the latter days of this month or in January, before the thaw of February, for ice cut after that time will not keep well.

I thought it would be better, also, that the contract might be made as early this month as possible, to allow the contractors, whomsoever they might be, ample time to make their preparations for filling so large a contract with northern ice, the only kind, I think, merchantable in this climate.

Should you think any alteration in the advertisement necessary, or that the time is too short, I respectfully request that you will notify me as soon as practicable.

Very respectfully, your obedient servant,

D. L. MAGRUDER, U. S. A.,
Surgeon and Medical Purveyor.

Colonel JOS. K. BARNES, U. S. A.,
Medical Inspector General and Acting Surgeon General,
Washington, D. C.

MEDICAL PURVEYOR'S OFFICE,
Louisville, Ky., January 9, 1864.

I certify that the above is a true copy.

D. S. MAGRUDER, U. S. A.
Surgeon and Medical Purveyor.

SURGEON GENERAL'S OFFICE,
Washington City, D. C., December 11, 1863.

SIR: I am directed to acknowledge the receipt of your communication of the 7th instant, and, in reply, to inform you that your action in regard to the procurement of ice for the ensuing year is entirely satisfactory.

Very respectfully, your obedient servant,

C. H. CRANE,
Surgeon United States Army.

By order of the Acting Surgeon General.

Surgeon D. L. MAGRUDER, U. S. A.,
Medical Purveyor, Louisville, Kentucky.

MEDICAL PURVEYOR'S OFFICE,
Louisville, Ky., January 9, 1864.

I certify that the above is a true copy.

D. S. MAGRUDER,
Surgeon United States Army, Medical Purveyor.

SURGEON GENERAL'S OFFICE,
Washington City, D. C., December 25, 1863.

SIR: In reply to your letter of the 21st instant, enclosing "proposals for furnishing ice" for the ensuing year, &c., I am instructed to return the "bids," and to direct you to award the contract as may be deemed by you most advantageous to the service.

These offers are considered fair and reasonable by the Acting Surgeon General.

Very respectfully, your obedient servant,

C. H. CRANE,
Surgeon United States Army.

By order of the Acting Surgeon General.

Surgeon D. L. MAGRUDER, U. S. A.,
Medical Purveyor, Louisville, Kentucky.

MEDICAL PURVEYOR'S OFFICE,
Louisville, Kentucky, January 9, 1864.

I certify that the above is a true copy.

D. S. MAGRUDER,
Surgeon United States Army, Medical Purveyor.

ARMY MEDICAL PURVEYOR'S OFFICE,
Louisville, Kentucky, January 1, 1864.

COLONEL: I have the honor to enclose herewith a contract with J. W. Parrish & Co. for furnishing ice to all the general hospitals at the west; the contract subject to your approval in every part before it will be binding. I have inserted a clause in the first article which requires the appointment of one or more competent persons as ice inspectors, who will inspect and measure the ice after it is stored in the ice-houses, and report its condition, quality, and quantity to the officer receiving it.

I was induced to do it for the reason that, at many of the points where ice will be delivered, the officer receiving it may be ignorant of either the proper mode of packing or measuring the ice. If you should see fit to make or suggest any alteration, please inform me when you return the contract.

When approved, I will have a copy duly signed by both parties sent to your office for file, as also to the Assistant Surgeon General in this city.

Very respectfully, your obedient servant,

D. L. MAGRUDER,
Surgeon United States Army, Medical Purveyor.

Colonel JOS. K. BARNES,
Acting Surgeon General U. S. A., Washington, D. C.

MEDICAL PURVEYOR'S OFFICE,
Louisville, Kentucky, January 9, 1864.

I certify that the above is a true copy.

D. S. MAGRUDER,
Surgeon United States Army, Medical Purveyor.

ARMY MEDICAL PURVEYOR'S OFFICE,
Louisville, Kentucky, January 9, 1864.

SIR: I have the honor to enclose copy of telegram despatched to you of this date.

Very respectfully, your obedient servant,

D. S. MAGRUDER,
Surgeon United States Army, Medical Purveyor.

Hon. EDWIN M. STANTON,
Secretary of War, Washington, D. C.

LOUISVILLE, *January* 9, 1864.

Your telegram of yesterday relating to ice awards received. All papers connected therewith will be sent by mail to-day.

D. L. MAGRUDER,
Surgeon United States Army, Medical Purveyor.

Hon. EDWIN M. STANTON,
Secretary of War, Washington.

ARMY MEDICAL PURVEYOR'S OFFICE,
Louisville, Kentucky, January 12, 1864.

SIR: I have the honor to enclose herewith contract with J. W. Parrish & Co., of St. Louis, Missouri, made December 30, 1863, and approved and returned by Acting Surgeon General January 7, 1864.

This contract, which had not been returned before my letter of 9th instant, was received at this office last night.

I enclose also copy of letter from Acting Surgeon General's office, approving and returning it to this department.

Very respectfully, your obedient servant,

D. S. MAGRUDER,
Surgeon United States Army, Medical Purveyor.

Hon. E. M. STANTON,
Secretary of War, Washington, D. C.

CHICAGO, *January* 26, 1864.

DEAR SIR: Your telegraph was received late Friday evening. Saturday morning I instituted inquiries, but before inquiry could be made at their offices the principal packers were off superintending their work. Memorandum was left, asking of each the best terms upon which they would put up 1,500 tons, or more, of best quality ice, to be taken by me at any time I chose previous to the first of October, payment to be made immediately on my receiving satisfactory certificates of storage. They furnish storage without charge. Yesterday the dealers sent in their bids. Wadhams & Co. have their ice-houses about six miles from town, at Calumet, on the Illinois Central railroad. The ice is very pure and clear, and they have one ice-house containing about 1,500 tons, well put up, which they offered to sell to me at $2 a ton, with the liberty to let the ice lie there till 1st of November. They will furnish more at same rate, if desired. The ice can be obtained from there with little more, if any, expense than if housed in the city, and if wanted to go down the Mississippi, is as well located as possible. The dealers all say that the wastage by 1st of September is never less than half. The same firm offered to furnish it on board cars at any depot in Chicago, if taken before the end of September, at $4 a ton, they to be paid for what they deliver when placed by them on board of the cars. Or they will sell it to the 1st June at $2 50 per ton; to 1st July, $3 50; to 1st August, $4; afterwards at $4 50 per ton. This last proposition seems to contradict their first one, but was not intended to do so, as they will sell it at $4 during September. In case you should prefer to buy it in the ice-house, they will load it in cars to be furnished by you, well packed in shavings or sawdust, at fifty cents per ton.

The Chicago City Ice Company offer to furnish the ice at any time before the 1st of October, in any amount desired, well packed on board cars to be furnished by you, at $4 a ton, at either the Illinois Central, Michigan Central, or Chicago, Alton and St. Louis depots in this city. Their ice is Crystal Lake ice—considered the very best. The Michigan Central depot is the proper place to have the ice loaded in case you want to send it to Cincinnati, Louisville, or any point on the Ohio river; the Illinois Central, in case you want to send it to Cairo or down the Mississippi; the Chicago, Alton and St. Louis, the proper place if you want to send it to St. Louis. Payment to be made on satisfactory certificates of amounts when placed on board the cars. I consider this offer desirable.

These terms were offered on the supposition that I was purchasing for the Sanitary Commission, although no such representation was made. As president of the Sanitary Commission, I bought very heavily from these dealers last year; they, of course, inferred I was bargaining for the commission on the present occasion. Had they supposed it was on government account, the charge undoubtedly would be heavier.

Command my services in this matter as you may require.

The offers of the other dealers were all higher.

Very respectfully, yours, &c.,

MARK SKINNER.

Hon. C. A. DANA,
Assistant Secretary of War.

SURGEON GENERAL'S OFFICE,
Washington City, D. C., February 8, 1864.

SIR: In conformity with the request of the Joint Committee on the Conduct and Expenditures of the War, forwarded by you on the 5th instant, I have the honor to transmit herewith copies of all the contracts made by this department for ice since the first of January, 1862.

Very respectfully, your obedient servant,

JOS. K. BARNES,
Acting Surgeon General.

Hon. EDWIN M. STANTON,
Secretary of War.

Bids received at the office of D. L. Magruder, medical purveyor at Louisville, Ky., for furnishing ice to the United States general hospitals of the west, for the year 1864, in such quantities as required.

No. of proposal.	Parties bidding.	Delivered at all points above St. Louis, Mo.	Delivered at St. Louis.	Delivered at Cairo, Ill., and all points between Saint Louis and Cairo.	Delivered at Memphis, Tenn., and all other points between Cairo and Memphis.	Delivered at Vicksburg, Miss., and all points between Memphis and Vicksburg.	Delivered at Natchez, Miss., and all points between Vicksburg and Natchez.	Delivered at New Orleans, and all points between Natchez and New Orleans.	Delivered at Louisville, Ky., and all points on the Ohio river between Cincinnati and Cairo, Illinois.	Delivered at Cincinnati, O., and all points between Pittsburg and Cincinnati.	Delivered at Nashville, Ten., and all points on the Cumberland river from Smithland to Nashville.	Delivered at Columbus, Ky.
		P. ton.	*P. ton.*	*Per ton.*	*Per ton.*	*Per ton.*	*Per ton.*	*Per ton.*	*Per ton.*	*Per ton.*	*Per ton.*	*P. ton.*
1	Josiah W. Bissell, of St. Louis	......	$14 00	$22 00	$27 00	$40 00	$42 00	$30 00	$24 00	$26 00	$40 00	$24 00
1½	John S. Andrews, of Waukegan, Ill.	......	15 00	23 50	24 00	37 50	41 00	30 00	24 50	27 00	39 00	......
2	Thos. Walker & Co., of Pittsburg	......	......	20 00	25 00	....	....	....	....	....	35 00	......
3	L. O. Goodell & Frank L. Coppelle, of Louisville	......	8 50	18 00	25 00	35 00	....	....	....	....	....	......
4	J. D. Harmon, of Chicago	......	......	17 50	....	....	....	....	....	....	....	......
5	W. P. Hahn, of Louisville	......	......	....	....	....	....	....	20 00	....	....	......
6	C. Stone, of New York	......	......	20 00	20 00	....	....	25 00	....	....	40 00	......
7	Thomas Alger, of Pittsburg	......	......	....	22 50	....	....	....	....	....	....	......
8	........do..........do	......	......	....	....	....	....	....	....	....	39 00	......
9	........do..........do	......	......	20 00	....	....	....	....	....	....	....	......
10	J. W. Parish & Co., of St. Louis	$10 00	15 00	20 00	25 00	30 00	30 00	25 00	20 00	20 00	30 00	25 00
11*	Chicago Ice Company, of Chicago	......	16 00	16 00	....	....	....	....	16 00	....	....	......
12*	Conrad & Stevens, of Nashville	......	......	....	....	....	....	....	....	....	20 00	......

* Received after time advertised for closing bids.

SURGEON GENERAL'S OFFICE,
Washington City, D. C., February 13, 1864.

SIR: In reply to your communication of the 12th instant, I have the honor to enclose a copy of the instructions given to Surgeon Magruder, U. S. A., November 27, 1863, to advertise for proposals for ice for all that section of country, the absolute wants of which he, as senior medical purveyor stationed at Louisville, in direct relation with the Assistant Surgeon General, would be most conversant with. To economize expenditure by controlling the estimates, and to have the river depots available for any emergency, it was considered advisable to include so much of the department of the Gulf as was upon the Mississippi and its tributaries in one general system of supply, under the supervision of this officer.

That the advertisements were not inserted in the eastern papers arose from this consolidation of the supply through Surgeon Magruder, who informs me that he gave them the same publicity as his advertisements for other articles. There was no intention of confining the proposals to any section, nor was the necessity for advertisement at the east anticipated.

Very respectfully, your obedient servant,

J. K. BARNES,
Acting Surgeon General.

Hon. C. A. DANA,
Assistant Secretary of War, War Department.

SURGEON GENERAL'S OFFICE,
Washington City, D. C., November 27, 1863.

DOCTOR: You are instructed to advertise for proposals for furnishing ice for all the United States general hospitals at the west, those of the division of the Mississippi, and of the department of the Gulf upon the Mississippi and its tributaries, in such quantities as may be required for the use of the sick and wounded during the year 1864.

In all cases the ice to be well packed in properly constructed ice-houses, (previous to the 15th of April,) at such points nearest the hospitals as, upon consultation with medical disbursing officers at St. Louis, Cairo, Cincinnati, Nashville, Memphis, Vicksburg, and elsewhere, you may consider most advantageous.

The ice to be delivered by actual weight of issues to hospitals by contractors, or by inspection and measurement by the issuing officer, on the 1st of May, 1864, who will then receipt for the actual contents of ice-houses. In those few cases where it may be found necessary to contract for delivery from barges during the summer, you will carefully protect the United States by so wording contracts that only the amount of ice actually delivered, as shown by receipt of medical officer, will be paid for. It is believed that an immense saving can thus be effected upon the expenditures for ice of past year, and your attention is particularly directed to the importance of such a reduction.

The reports of Medical Storekeeper Stevens, and propositions of Parrish & Co., and of Alger, are enclosed.

By order of Acting Surgeon General.

Very respectfully, your obedient servant,

C. H. CRANE, *Surgeon U. S. A.*

Surgeon D. L. MAGRUDER, U. S. A.,
Medical Purveyor, Louisville, Ky.

SURGEON GENERAL'S OFFICE,
January 9, 1864.

A true copy:

C. H. CRANE, *Surgeon U. S. A.*

SURGEON GENERAL'S OFFICE,
Washington City, D. C., January 7, 1864.

SIR: I am directed by the Acting Surgeon General to return the contract made by you with J. W. Parrish for furnishing ice for all the United States general hospitals in the west, for the year 1864, approved.

The insertion of clause for appointment of competent person or persons as ice inspector or inspectors is deemed an excellent suggestion, and is highly approved by the Acting Surgeon General.

By order of Acting Surgeon General.

Very respectfully, your obedient servant,

C. H. CRANE,
Surgeon U. S. A.

Surgeon D. L. MAGRUDER,
Medical Purveyor, Louisville, Ky.

MEDICAL PURVEYOR'S OFFICE,
Louisville, Ky., January 12, 1864.

I certify that the above is a true copy.

D. L. MAGRUDER,
Surgeon U. S. A., Medical Purveyor.

OFFICE U. S. MILITARY TELEGRAPH,
War Department.

The following telegram received at Washington 9.15 p. m., January 23, 1864, from Chicago, dated January 23, 1864:

Hon. C. A. DANA, *Assistant Secretary of War:*

On Monday I think I can furnish you with precise information. Your despatch only reached me late last evening, and I cannot get the exact figures to-day, owing to absence of parties.

MARK SKINNER.

OFFICE U. S. MILITARY TELEGRAPH,
War Department.

The following telegram received at Washington 1.15 p. m., January 23, 1864, from Cleveland, Ohio, dated January 23, 1864:

Hon. C. A. DANA, *Assistant Secretary of War:*

In Mr. Stone's absence have made inquiries. Ice can be furnished here well covered and protected for three (3) dollars per ton.

If competition is created by advertising for proposals it could probably be procured for less. One dealer offers to furnish fifteen hundred (1,500) tons already stored at that price, on condition that it be measured and accepted by the fifteenth of March, free of rent or storage.

W. E. CLARKE,
P. M. Secretary to C. E. Stone.

WAR DEPARTMENT, WASHINGTON CITY,
January 21, 1864.

In relation to the award of contract for furnishing ice to all the United States general hospitals at the west and southwest for the use of the sick and wounded during the year 1864.

December 4, 1863, Surgeon D. L. Magruder, medical purveyor at Louisville, Kentucky, by order of the Acting Surgeon General, advertised for proposals as follows:

"Proposals will be received at my office until December 20, 1863, for furnishing ice to all the United States general hospitals at the west (those of the division of the Mississippi and of the department of the Gulf upon the Mississippi, and its tributaries,) in such quantities as may be required for the use of the sick and wounded during the year 1864.

"In all cases the ice to be well packed and stored in properly constructed ice-houses previous to the 15th of April, 1864, at such points nearest the hospitals as may be designated from this office.

"The ice either to be delivered by actual weight of issues to the hospitals by the contractors, or by inspection and measurement by the issuing officer (on or before the 1st of May, 1864,) who will then receipt for the actual contents of ice-houses.

"D. L. MAGRUDER,

"*Surgeon United States Army, Medical Purveyor.*"

Eleven bids were received, and the contract, with the consent of the Acting Surgeon General, awarded to Parrish & Co., at the following rates:

Per ton delivered at		New Orleans	$25 00
"	"	Natchez	30 00
"	"	Vicksburg	30 00
"	"	Helena	30 00
"	"	Memphis	25 00
"	"	Columbus, Kentucky	25 00
"	"	Nashville	30 00
"	"	Cairo	20 00
"	"	Paducah	20 00
"	"	Evansville	20 00
"	"	Louisville	20 00
"	"	Cincinnati	20 00
"	"	St. Louis	15 00
"	"	Jefferson Barracks	15 00
"	"	Quincy	10 00
"	"	Keokuk	10 00
"	"	Madison	10 00
"	"	Chicago	10 00
"	"	Columbus, Ohio	10 00
"	"	Cleveland	10 00

This firm supplied the western and southwestern hospitals with ice during last season, and appeared to have fulfilled their duties, under great disadvantages, faithfully and honorably.

Their facilities for furnishing the ice promptly are very superior; and as they are the only bidders who offer to furnish *all* the hospitals with ice, it is supposed that the medical purveyor awarded them the contract as "most advantageous to the service."

The following is a list of the bids presented at lower rates:

Josiah W. Bissell, of St. Louis, offers to deliver at Columbus, Kentucky, at $24, and at St. Louis at $14, both bids $1 less than Parrish & Co.; bids of deliveries at eight other points, all higher than Parrish & Co. Satisfactory security offered.

John S. Andrews, of Waukegan, Illinois, offers to deliver at Memphis at $24, $1 less than Parrish & Co.; bids of deliveries at eight other points, all higher than Parrish & Co. Satisfactory security offered.

Goodell & Chappell, of Louisville, offers to deliver at Cairo at $18, ($2 less than Parrish & Co.,) and at St. Louis at $8 50 ($6 50 less than Parrish & Co.) Two other bids higher than Parrish & Co. No security offered.

J. D. Harman, of Chicago, offers to deliver at Cairo at $17 50, ($2 50 less than

Parrish & Co.) One other bid higher than Parrish & Co. Will not deliver later than forty days from acceptance of contract. Security offered.

C. Stone, of New York city, offers to deliver at Memphis $20, ($5 less than Parrish & Co.) Three other bids higher than Parrish & Co. No security offered.

Thomas Alger, of Memphis, offers to deliver at Memphis $22 50, ($2 50 less than Parrish & Co.) Two other bids higher than Parrish & Co. No security offered, but is recommended by responsible parties as an experienced and reliable ice dealer.

After the awarding of the contract two very advantageous offers were received, viz:

Chicago Ice Company, who proposed to deliver at any time between April and December, 1864, from railroad cars at Cairo, at $16 per ton, or $4 less than Parrish & Co.

Conrad & Stevens, at Nashville, who propose to deliver the ice required at that post, at $20 per ton, or $10 less than Parrish & Co.

Both these parties offer satisfactory security.

OFFICE U. S. MILITARY TELEGRAPH,
War Department.

The following telegram received at Washington 2.15 p. m., January 24, 1864, From Springfield, Illinois, dated January 23, 1864:

CHARLES A. DANA, *Assistant Secretary of War:*

Worth as you propose, one dollar and three quarters to two (2) dollars per ton, contracted for now at Quincy.

JACKSON GRIMSHAW.

OFFICE U. S. MILITARY TELEGRAPH,
War Department.

The following telegram received at Washington 8 p. m., January 25, 1864, from Columbus, Ohio, dated January 25, 1864:

Hon. C. A. DANA, *Assistant Secretary of War:*

Supply of ice here limited. Dealers offer it at from three (3) to four dollars per ton in store.

GEO. B. WRIGHT,
United States M. Ord.

OFFICE U. S. MILITARY TELEGRAPH,
War Department.

The following telegram received at Washington 1.30 p. m., January 25, 1864, from Cleveland, Ohio, dated January 25, 1864:

Hon. C. A. DANA, *Assistant Secretary of War:*

The party who, as I informed you, offered to furnish ice for three dollars per ton, has called and offered it at fifty cents less, or two (2) dollars and a half ($\frac{1}{2}$) per ton.

C. STONE.

OFFICE U. S. MILITARY TELEGRAPH,
War Department.

The following telegramr eceived at Washington 9.10 p. m., January 25, 1864, from Chicago, dated January 25, 1864:

Hon. CHAS. A. DANA, *Assistant Secretary of War:*

Parties will furnish fifteen hundred (1,500) tons best quality ice, free of storage until November, for two dollars a ton, payment to be made as soon as satisfactory storage certificates are furnished.

They will also furnish it on board cars at either the Illinois Central depot, the Michigan Central depot, or the St. Louis depot, at any time before first October, for four dollars a ton.

This last offer is the best, as the wastage in houses is full half by September.

I write by to-day's mail. It is not suspected that I inquire on government account.

MARK SKINNER.

ARMY MEDICAL PURVEYOR'S OFFICE,
Louisville, Ky., January 9, 1864.

SIR: In compliance with instructions contained in your telegram received this morning, I have the honor to enclose herewith all the papers connected with contracts for furnishing ice to the general hospitals at the west, marked and designated as follows, viz:

A.—Letter of instructions from Acting Surgeon General, received December 1, 1863.

B.—My letter of December 7, 1863, acknowledging receipt of instructions—reporting having put advertisement in certain papers; also, giving reasons for limiting time for receiving proposal to 20th December, 1863, and asking to be notified as soon as possible, should any alteration be thought necessary, or the time too limited.

C.—Letter from Acting Surgeon General, approving my action.

D.—My letter of December, 21, 1863, to Acting Surgeon General, enclosing *all bids* received previous to, and opened upon that day, deeming instructions received insufficient to warrant making contract; hence, referred them for decision and further instructions; also, adding some remarks in relation to bids, and quantity of ice wanted at a few points.

E.—All the bids put in on or before December 21, 1863, numbered respectively from one to eleven, (1—11.)

F.—Bids which came to hand after those coming in on the 21st had been forwarded to Washington.

G.—Letter from Surgeon General's office, December 25, 1863, returning bids, and directing me to award the contracts as I might deem most advantageous to the service; also, adding that the bids were considered fair and reasonable.

H.—My letter to Acting Surgeon General, January 1, 1864, enclosing draught of contract with J. W. Parrish & Co., of St. Louis, Mo., for furnishing ice for the general hospitals of the west; said contract to be subject to approval of Surgeon General, in every part, before binding either party; also, giving reasons for inserting clause in the first article, in relation to ice inspector, and asking its approval, &c.

The above are all the papers now in my hands, relating to ice contracts.

The draught of the contract with Parrish & Co., which was enclosed to the Acting Surgeon General on the 1st of January, instant, has not been returned to this office.

Very respectfully, your obedient servant,

J. S. MAGRUDER,
Surgeon U. S. A., Medical Purveyor.

Hon. EDWIN M. STANTON,
Secretary of War, Washington, D. C.

Messrs. Addison Gage & Co., extensive ice dealers in Boston, made a sub-contract with the St. Louis firm, to fill their contract for supplying New Orleans with ice at $6 a ton less than the original government contract price; giving an estimated profit to the St. Louis party of $25,000 for New Orleans alone. The firm of Gage & Co. stands high in the mercantile community for honesty and fair dealing. They are the largest ice-dealers in New England, and are now desirous of contracting *directly with the government* for supplying the department of the Gulf at the same price they were to supply New Orleans "second-handed" for; and that price *was the lowest* the St. Louis party could get any responsible New England dealer to contract for.

Messrs. G. & Co. have made arrangements to ship several cargoes to New Orleans immediately.

Messrs. Gooch, Hooper, Rice, and other Massachusetts members of Congress, know the firm well, and will vouch for its ability and high-toned honor.

WAR DEPARTMENT,
Washington City, January 27, 1864.

SIR: On December 5, 1863, Doctor D. L. Magruder, medical purveyor at Louisville, Kentucky, under orders from the Surgeon General, advertised for proposals to furnish ice to all the United States general hospitals in the military division of the Mississippi and in the department of the Gulf, upon the Mississippi and its tributaries. This advertisement was answered by eleven bidders, and on December 20, according to the terms of the advertisement, the contract was awarded to J. W. Parrish & Co., of St. Louis, they being, on the whole, the lowest bidders.

After the contract had been approved by the Surgeon General, and signed by both Doctor Magruder and the contractors, its execution was suspended and the papers transferred to Washington.

I have carefully examined these papers, and have repeatedly conversed upon the matter with Mr. J. W. Parrish, but have not discovered any evidence of fraudulent design or dishonest practice in the making of the contract. It also appears that Parrish & Co. were the contractors there last year, and faithfully executed their contract at considerable loss.

It is true that the advertisements appear to have been ill-judged in requiring all the hospitals to be furnished under one contract, and that better terms might, perhaps, have been made had the vast territory in question been divided into districts; but, on the other hand, it is indispensable that the contractors should be men, in respect of whom there can be no fear of failure. To deal with one contractor is also more convenient than to deal with many.

Since the papers have been in my hands, I have ascertained that ice can be procured in the northwestern States, for use in the hospitals there, at about one-half the prices stipulated in this contract; but it should be remembered that at these places the quantities needed are very limited, and when the contract was made, the amount of this season's ice crop was still uncertain. The contractors who took the risk ought not to be deprived of their profits because their venture proves fortunate.

A bid for the quantity needed at Nashville, at a price 33⅓ per cent. less than that of the contractors, was not considered by Doctor Magruder, for the reason that it was offered after the time for receiving proposals had expired. For the same reason he excluded a bid for supplying Cairo and Jeffersonville at a price more favorable than that of the contract. This last bid, however, must have been excluded, even had it been in season, for the reason that it proposed to furnish ice in railway cars only, and not in ice-houses.

Messrs. Addison Gage & Co., of Boston, who represent that they have bargained with Parrish & Co. to supply the quantity contracted for at New Orleans, at $6 per ton less than the contracted price, (namely, at $19 per ton, instead of $20 per ton,) now propose that the government shall ignore the contract with Parrish & Co., so far as New Orleans is concerned, and make a new contract with them at the lower rate.

Being satisfied that the agreement with Parrish & Co. was honestly made, and that, considering the risk involved, the prices were not extravagant, I recommend that the contract be confirmed. But the stipulations in the papers executed o not appear sufficiently precise and guarded to secure faithful fulfilment, and I therefore also recommend the execution of new and amended papers for that object.

I have the honor to be, sir, very respectfully, your obedient servant,

C. A. DANA,
Assistant Secretary of War.

Hon. EDWIN M. STANTON,
Secretary of War.

WAR DEPARTMENT,
Washington, D. C., February 3, 1864.

DEAR SIR: I acknowledge with many thanks the receipt of your letter of January 26, with regard to the price of ice at Chicago. The contract which had previously been made at Louisville has been confirmed, but the information afforded by your letter, as well as by your previous telegrams, has been of very great value to us.

I remain yours, very respectfully,

C. A. DANA,
Assistant Secre'ary of War.

Hon. MARK SKINNER,
Chicago, Illinois.

Testimony of Dr. R. O. Abbott.

WASHINGTON, *February* 18, 1864.

Dr. R. O. ABBOTT sworn and examined.

By the chairman:

Question. What is your rank and position in the army?

Answer. I am a surgeon in the United States army, and medical director of Washington.

Question. Have you any relation to or connexion with the Sanitary Commission?

Answer. Nothing whatever; I have no connexion with it in any way.

[The copy of the circular appended to the testimony of Hon. John A. Bingham was then read to the witness.]

Question. Was a circular to the effect of the one just read to you issued by you at the time indicated?

Answer. Yes, sir; and it was based on an order received by me from the Surgeon General, very similar to the circular issued by me.

Question. What was the object of that order and circular?

Answer. There was a great deal of difficulty at that time about supplying the hospitals with vegetable food especially, so as to vary the diet properly; and I think this proposal was made to the Surgeon General that they should run this car, and supply everything needed at cost prices, lower than market rates at that time, and delivered in the city. That, I believe, was the only object at the time. We found great difficulty indeed, at that time, in procuring vegetables here.

Question. One would have supposed that would have led you to seek the open market everywhere.

Answer. They certainly sold at that time cheaper than the market rates. I have been lately inquiring into the matter, with a view to see if the arrangement should be continued; and I find that in many articles, such as poultry, mutton, and one or two vegetables, they are still below the rates of local dealers here. In some of the vegetables the local dealers are now selling somewhat lower than the Sanitary Commission.

Question. What enables the Sanitary Commission to afford these things cheaper than they can be found elsewhere?

Answer. That I do not know. I know nothing whatever of their movements. I supposed at the time that it was for a charitable purpose that they started this thing; that they did not intend to make any profit, but it was one of the outlets for spending their money for the soldiers.

Question. I will say that, without knowing much about it, I had supposed the Sanitary Commission was a charitable institution for the purpose of receiving and distributing the things given them by the charitable from time to time. Do you know whether that was so or not?

Answer. It is a very much more extensive commission than that. They employ a large number of paid agents and inspectors, and make a large number of suggestions and reports of every character. They do a little of everything; they do not limit themselves, so far as I understand, to any one object, but wherever they think they can do good they put in train their operations.

Question. On how large a scale are they doing business; or what is the extent of their business, so far as you know?

Answer. In this particular line?

Question. I mean all their operations.

Answer. I am not prepared to say; I had hardly anything to do with the commission. I did not at first like the manner in which they commenced operations, because under their guise of charitable object I thought I recognized a disposition to grasp and assume control of everything. For that reason I did not give them as hearty a support as I otherwise would have done; and I have had little or no dealing with the institution in any way.

Question. As you understand it, they buy and sell all kinds of commodities for the army?

Answer. I know they do in this instance, and I think they have done so elsewhere. At least I think so; but I am not certain of that. They have their own reasons for it, I suppose.

Question. Do you know their manner of keeping accounts, so as to guarantee to the public any assurance of the proper application of what they receive?

Answer. I do not; I have never attended one of their meetings, or looked at any of their books.

Question. What was the reason for the last clause of this circular, forbidding the hospitals purchasing supplies from any other source than the Sanitary Commission, except in case of emergency?

Answer. That was the order to me; I do not think the order contained any reference to any emergency. As far as I now recollect, I think the order was that purchases should be made from no other source. I put in the clause about emergency myself, because I saw at once that if the supply car should be detained, or anything like that occur, there might an emergency arise requiring supplies to be obtained elsewhere.

Question. You interpolated that because you thought an exigency might happen that would require it?

Answer. Yes, sir.

Question. What was the object of that restriction?

Answer. I suppose, in order that they should have sufficient support to enable them to carry on the scheme. I myself rather favored the plan at the time, for the reason that the surgeons complained of the difficulty of procuring these things. I thought I had reason to suspect that the local dealers were bribing the stewards of the hospitals to deal with them. I could not prove it, but from indirect information that reached me I was inclined to believe that of them.

Question. Had you any conversation with the Surgeon General on the subject of this plan of procuring supplies?

Answer. Very little; the conversation I had with him did not amount to much. I think that I approved the plan when suggested to me, as far as I can remember.

Question. Will you state what the plan was, as far as you can remember?

Answer. That the Sanitary Commission should purchase all the hospitals needed in Philadelphia, where the market was good, and furnish them at rates equally as low if not lower than the local dealers were furnishing the same articles to the hospitals. We could not, at that time, purchase the variety of vegetables we wanted without paying enormously high for them.

Question. Are you sure the commission always furnished those articles cheaper than they could be obtained from other sources?

Answer. I think that, as a general rule, they have done so. Latterly I have been inquiring into the matter again to see if I could modify it with advantage in any way. I have had reports from some of the surgeons, and I find that in some of the articles they are yet lower than the local dealers; in other articles they are about equal to, and in some cases higher than, the local dealers. For instance, I think you can purchase potatoes of the local dealers a few cents per bushel cheaper than the commission furnishes them.

Question. Do you know what this Sanitary Commission does with the specific articles furnished them by the benevolent of the country for charitable purposes?

Answer. I believe they distribute a large portion of them to the hospitals. I understand that they give very freely when asked. I think that, generally speaking, they want money more than articles in kind.

Question. Do you understand that they convert these articles received in kind into money and then purchase other articles?

Answer. No, sir; I have no reason to think so.

Question. They make their purchases with money received from charitable sources?

Answer. Yes, sir. They receive a great many things in kind which they distribute.

Question. You have no knowledge of the extent of their business, you have said?

Answer. None whatever. I have never mixed myself up with them in any shape or way. I have never had any dealings with them except in this one instance, and then by direction of the Surgeon General, and occasionally giving them orders for transportation at the request of other medical directors; that is, under general order of the War Department.

Question. Was the Surgeon General authorized to designate the source from which these things should be purchased to the exclusion of all other sources?

Answer. I do notknow, except that he as sumed that authority, supposing it to be best. I do not know any law upon the subject. I suppose he assumed it from his general authority as Surgeon General.

Question. I think you say he never explained to you the reason for restricting these purchases to the Sanitary Commission?

Answer. No, sir; he never did. But I assumed that the reason was in order to give them sufficient encouragement and support to enable them to carry out the scheme.

Question. Would not purchases be made to better advantage by taking the competition of the open market?

Answer. I think not. I think that you will find that, on the whole, they have sold below market rates here.

Question. Do you know any particular advantages that the Sanitary Commission had for making their purchases, or why they could afford to supply those articles cheaper?

Answer. Only that they did not pretend to make any profit whatever on them. They have their agents to buy and send here, and they sell for exactly what the articles cost them. The dealers, of course, want to make their profit.

Question. They had their agents in the city of Philadelphia to make purchases for them?

Answer. Yes, sir; I sent the articles here every day.

Question. You say you do not know the extent of their dealings or purchases?

Answer. I could very readily give it for the supply of the hospitals here by taking the different orders of the surgeons from time to time. It varies continually according to the number of patients. On some one day there may be 200 patients transferred to the hospital, and five or six days afterwards they may be removed. The rations of the hospital is a matter which is left entirely with the surgeon.

Question. Did the Surgeon General have any dealings with this Sanitary Commission any further than related to the supply of the hospitals?

Answer. Not that I am aware of.

By Mr. Gooch:

Question. When this circular was issued was it understood that there was to be any concealment about it, or was it an open transaction?

Answer. I think it was open.

Question. Was there any effort made to conceal it from the public, either on the part of the Surgeon General or of the Sanitary Commission?

Answer. Not at all, so far as I know. The local dealers knew it very soon.

Question. Did it become generally known?

Answer. I think it must have been.

Question. The reason for it was that you could not get here exactly the articles you needed, and therefore the Surgeon General made an arrangement with the Sanitary Commission to supply those articles, they being able to do it better than anybody else, and being willing to do so without making any profit on the articles?

Answer. That was my understanding of the matter at the time.

Question. And you give it as your opinion that the hospitals have been better and more economically supplied by that arrangement than by any other?

Answer. I think so from the time it was started to the present moment. I think that is the general opinion, too, as expressed to me by the surgeons in charge of the hospitals.

By the chairman:

Question. Did the War Department know of this order?

Answer. I do not know that they did.

Question. How long was business done under this circular or order?

Answer. They are still doing it, and have done so since last June. Latterly I have been making inquiry to see if it should be longer continued, and I find that they still supply many articles, such as poultry, mutton, &c., cheaper than the local dealers do. But I find that I can purchase from the local dealers some of the vegetables cheaper than the Sanitary Commission can supply them. For instance, I find I can purchase potatoes of local dealers four or five cents cheaper er bushel than I can of the Sanitary Commission.

By Mr. Odell:

Question. On the whole, what is the result of your investigation?

Answer. On the whole, the arrangement with the Sanitary Commission has been of advantage to the hospitals. And I have every reason to believe that the whole thing was entered into in good faith on both sides, and for the advantage of the hospitals.

Testimony of Mr. E. T. Fowler.

WASHINGTON, *February* 26, 1864.

Mr. E. T. FOWLER sworn and examined.

By Mr. Gooch:

Question. What is your occupation and place of residence?

Answer. I am an ice-dealer, and reside at Medford, Massachusetts.

Question. Do you know anything in relation to the manner in which the government was supplied with ice last year?

Answer. All I know was simply about the loading and measurement of the vessels, which was the measurement of the entire hold of the vessel, without allowing anything for damage or for the projections of the deck. The amount the vessel would carry was determined by that measurement. They just went to the ice-house and ran in the ice as it happened. I was shipping ice at the same time, and at the same point. If Mr. Tiffany wanted a vessel, I could not get one, because I was putting in my ice by weight, and he had some 20 per cent. more by his measurement than I did by mine. The parties who owned the vessel stated at the time that that was the reason. A vessel rated at 200 tons could not possibly be made to hold more than 150 tons of ice.

Question. At what place was this?

Answer. Gardiner, Maine.

Question. Were you shipping ice from that place at the same time?

Answer. Yes, sir; I was shipping to different parts of the south.

Question. Who made this measurement that you speak of?

Answer. D. C. Palmer, of Gardiner.

Question. What is his business?

Answer. A surveyor of lumber; that is all I know.

Question. Had he any connexion with Mr. Tiffany?

Answer. None that I know of. He was usually a fair man, but the only surveyor in the place that would have anything to do with it, because it was a fraud. I know one party who refused to measure in that way, and assigned that as the reason, although afterwards he had some connexion with Mr. Tiffany.

Question. He refused because he considered it a fraud?

Answer. Yes, sir, he so stated to me.

Question. Was Mr. Tiffany there at the time?

Answer. He was there off and on; his agent was there all the time; there and at Richmond.

Question. Knowing the registered tonnage of a vessel, can you determine with accuracy the number of tons of ice she will carry?

Answer. She will carry of ice about four-fifths of her registered tonnage; a little more, perhaps. We generally measure a vessel by taking the number of tons of coal she will carry as the standard of measurement, and she will carry 20 per cent. more coal than anything else, and these bills of lading for ice (referring to bills of lading of Mr. Tiffany) would, all of them, I think, overrun the tonnage in coal from 15 to 20 per cent.; whereas they should have fallen short that amount; that is, the bills of lading for those vessels of Mr. Tiffany call for at least 25 per cent. more ice than the vessels could possibly carry; certainly more than I could get in by weighing the ice.

Question. Do you know anything about the manner in which this ice was stowed in these vessels?

Answer. I presume it was fairly stowed; I do not know anything to the contrary.

Question. Of how many vessels or cargoes of ice did you have knowledge?

Answer. Mr. Tiffany was shipping there all through the months of June and July; perhaps twenty vessels.

Question. Do you know whether the rule you have referred to was the rule adopted in all the shipments of ice?

Answer. Yes, sir.

Question. Do you know who supplied Washington with ice last year?

Answer. Yes, sir; Mr. Tiffany.

Question. Do you know where the ice was stowed here?

Answer. Yes, sir.

Question. State all you know in regard to that.

Answer. The examination of the ice-house which I made convinced me that it was an entirely unfit place in which to store ice. The filling between the walls was such that air would be admitted freely, which, of course, would lead to a waste of the ice.

Question. By whom was that ice-house built?

Answer. By Mr. Tiffany, as I understand.

Question. In which to store the ice he furnished the government?

Answer. Yes, sir; Mr. Tiffany said that in draughting the bills of lading he had his own way, and had them so draughted to suit his own purposes.

Question. Do you know whether the vessels which Tiffany loaded with ice were filled as full as they could be?

Answer. I do not know; I did not see them, but I heard it reported that they were not very particular about that.

Question. Can you tell what would be a fair price for ice delivered on board a vessel to be supplied to this station, and to the various points along the coast, for which ice has been advertised recently?

Answer. At the other end of the route, at Boston, the price is about \$2 50 a ton; \$2 25 is the very lowest it can be bought for.

Question. How is it in Maine?

Answer. You can get it in Maine for about half a dollar a ton less.

Question. What would it cost for freight from Boston and from Maine?

Answer. There is 30 per cent. difference in the freight between Boston and Maine.

Question. What would it cost per ton from Boston to be delivered in Washington?

Answer. The freight would be about \$3 a ton from Maine, perhaps a little more, and about \$2 from Boston.

Question. Then what would be the wastage in bringing the ice here, stowing it in the ice-house, and delivering it to the hospitals?

Answer. About one-half, 50 per cent.

Question. What would be the cost of cartage per ton to put it in the ice-house here and deliver it to the hospitals?

Answer. Somewhere from \$2 50 to \$3 a ton, as they might call for it.

Question. Then what would be the lowest price that ice could be furnished here, delivered at the hospitals from time to time as required?

Answer. From \$11 to \$12 a ton would be the lowest.

Question. What would it be at Fortress Monroe?

Answer. It would be a little cheaper there than here; by the cargo it would cost about \$9 a ton.

Question. What at Norfolk?
Answer. Very little difference; perhaps $10 a ton.
Question. What at Newbern, North Carolina?
Answer. From $15 to $16.
Question. And at Hilton Head?
Answer. About $11 or $12.
Question. What would be the cost of ice delivered in the ice-house here?
Answer. About $7 a ton; the wastage would not be as much as in the other cases.

Testimony of Mr. A. Tracy Edgerton.

WASHINGTON, *February* 26, 1864.

Mr. A. TRACY EDGERTON sworn and examined.

By Mr. Gooch:

Question. Where is your place of residence, and what is your occupation?
Answer. My place of residence is Cypress avenue, Long Island; I have no occupation at present.
Question. What has been your occupation or business?
Answer. Importing brandies and gins.
Question. Have you ever been in the ice business?
Answer. I have.
Question. From what time to what time, and to what extent?
Answer. In 1862 and 1863.
Question. Have you had anything to do with the ice business, excepting so far as you were connected with supplying ice to the government?
Answer. Yes, sir; I sold to outside parties last summer.
Question. Where, and to what extent?
Answer. In Philadelphia and Baltimore, but to no great extent.
Question. To what extent?
Answer. Two cargoes; one for Philadelphia, and one for Baltimore.
Question. Then you never had been in the ice business until you went into it for the purpose of supplying the government?
Answer. No, sir.
Question. When did you first furnish ice to the government?
Answer. In the summer of 1862.
Question. To what extent?
Answer. Two vessels.
Question. Where?
Answer. One at Norfolk, and one on the Peninsula.
Question. What were the terms of your contract?
Answer. There was not any contract. It was a private sale.
Question. You sold two cargoes to the government at private sale, and that was all you sold to the government in 1862?
Answer. Yes, sir.
Question. Was there any trouble in relation to that ice between you and any officer of the government? If so, state what it was.
Answer. I had some difficulty with Colonel Baker here, about the ice sold on the Peninsula. It was said that I charged the government half a cent per pound for the ice more than I agreed to sell it for. That was all the difficulty.
Question. How was it settled?
Answer. It was settled by refunding a half a cent per pound; that is the way it now remains.

Question. From whom did you receive your money?
Answer. From the Surgeon General's department.
Question. To whom did you refund the money?
Answer. To Colonel Baker.
Question. With whom was the bargain made for the ice?
Answer. To Dr. Charles H. Tretler, medical director of the army of the Potomac.
Question. To whom was the ice delivered?
Answer. To the surgeons of the army corps and to the hospitals and transports.
Question. Was your bargain made in writing?
Answer. I think it was partly by telegraph and partly in writing. The papers are all together.
Question. Have you the telegrams and the written contract?
Answer. I have not. I deposited them with my vouchers.
Question. Where did you deposit them?
Answer. In the Surgeon General's office.
Question. How happened it that Colonel Baker had anything to do with your contract for ice?
Answer. It arose out of a dispute with other parties. Dr. Tretler was the medical director of the army of the Potomac. I telegraphed to him—he was at Savage Station at the time—if he wanted the ice, and he telegraphed back he would take it; and it was distributed at different places, as ordered by the medical directors of the different corps. I afterwards saw Dr. Tretler, and he gave me a written order to send the balance of the cargo by cars to Savage Station. That written order, the telegraphic communications, and everything of the kind, were handed in with the vouchers.

A party whom I had taken out in the trip, because we did not agree in the settlement of our business transactions, sent a person to Washington to state that I had charged half a cent a pound more for the ice than I had agreed to sell it for. Now, there is everything in the papers to show the true state of the facts; all the different receipts, vouchers, orders, and everything of the kind, are together. I have endeavored to get at the papers to find out what the charge was, but have not been able to do so.

Question. From whom did you receive payment?
Answer. From the quartermaster's department; that is, I passed my claim to Jay Cooke & Co., and they made the collection.
Question. How long was it after this money was paid over to you that you were called upon to refund?
Answer. Within two or three months.
Question. State the particulars of the transaction.
Answer. My brother-in-law, David S. Weinbrenner, of Philadelphia, paid the money over to Colonel Baker.
Question. Who made the demand for the money to be refunded, and when and where?
Answer. I was in Baltimore, and an officer came over to bring me to Washington.
Question. Who was that officer?
Answer. His name was Morris. He is now at Fortress Monroe, I believe.
Question. What office did he hold?
Answer. He was attached to Colonel Baker's department.
Question. Do you know his rank, or given name?
Answer. They called him major. I do not know his given name. He brought me on here, and took me to Colonel Baker's office.
Question. What took place there?
Answer. They took me into a back room, took my watch and my money out

of my pockets, took my ring off my finger, took every paper I had on my person, took off my boots, and sent me to Capitol prison.

Question. What was said at the time? Did they inform you what that was done for?

Answer. They asked me if I had charged the government a half a cent a pound more than I had agreed to take for the ice, and I told them I had not. They told me I would have an examination the next day, but I never had any examination. My brother-in-law was telegraphed to come on. He came, and I saw him twice at the Old Capitol prison, but only for a minute or two. The next night after I was taken to the prison I was taken out and taken down to Colonel Baker's office, and some questions asked me in regard to the same things—questions of the same nature as before. I was then remanded to the Old Capitol. My brother-in-law paid to Colonel Baker the difference of half a cent a pound, and some long time afterwards I was released without any examination in the case in any manner, shape, or form.

Question. How long a time after?

Answer. I was in the Old Capitol prison eight weeks.

Question. Do you know whether anybody else but Colonel Baker and his men had any knowledge of your arrest? I mean any other officer of the government.

Answer. I do not know. There was an outsider, a man by the name of Henry, said to me in Baltimore that if I would pay the money then and there the thing would be settled. I told him I would not do it.

Question. What was the amount?

Answer. I think it was about $1,500; I cannot tell exactly.

Question. What was the man's name?

Answer. Edwin Henry; he is now a quartermaster.

Question. Had you had any personal connexion with him?

Answer. Yes, sir; he had been a customer of mine years before, but had failed and owed me money.

Question. Do you know how he happened to be present at your arrest?

Answer. He said he had come down with officer Morris, if possible, to settle the matter; that if I would settle up the matter of difficulty between another party and myself, these things could all be settled.

Question. Settle up with whom?

Answer. The party I went in with in this ice business. At one time when I was in New York, the party said to me, "Will you advance half the money and load a vessel with ice and send it down to the army?" He persuaded me into it. After the vessel was loaded, I had to make all the disbursements; and after the party got down there, I found that he was an habitual drunkard, and I had to take hold and do everything myself. There had been an agreement that we should share the profits equally. After we returned I told him I would not do that, because he had advanced no money and had done nothing; that I would only pay him so much. From that arose all the trouble; a person was sent to Washington by him to make all this difficulty, because I would not pay this outside party what he wanted.

Question. Do you mean to say that when Colonel Baker's officer, Major Morris, went to Baltimore to arrest you, there went with him a Mr. Henry, then a civilian and now a quartermaster, who told you there, that if you would pay to this man in partnership with you in this ice business the amount he claimed, that would end the matter?

Answer. Yes, sir.

Question. And you refused to do that?

Answer. Yes, sir.

Question. And you were then brought here and put in prison?

Answer. Yes, sir; the next day.

Question. Was there any proposition of that kind made to you afterwards, or any intimation made to you by any person that you could be let off by settling up with your partner in the ice business?

Answer. No, sir.

Question. Was Major Morris present when Henry made this proposition to you?

Answer. No, sir; he was at the hotel. I met Henry in the street, and he asked me to go and take a drink with him; I did not care about it, but finally consented. We went to the Fountain Inn hotel, on Light street, where he introduced me to Major Morris. Then Henry took me one side up stairs, when this conversation took place.

Question. Then what was done?

Answer. I told him that I did not believe any such thing; I insisted that he was humbugging me, and told him to go down and get his papers. He went down, then came up again, and then went down again. I felt convinced he was trifling with me, and I left the hotel by the back way. The next day I was in a store on Gay street on some business, and two officers came in there and arrested me.

Question. Who were they?

Answer. I do not know their names.

Question. Was either of them Major Morris?

Answer. No, sir; they conducted me to the provost marshal's office, and Major Morris came in there. Then one of the officers who arrested me, Major Morris and myself came down to Washington together.

Question. After you got out of the Capitol prison, did you communicate the fact of your arrest to any officer of the government in Washington?

Answer. No, sir, not to a soul; because when I got out they had my papers, my watch and my ring, and it took me a long time to get them.

Question When, where, and from whom did you get them?

Answer. I got them through Judge Knox, of Philadelphia; I think Mr. Wood, the superintendent of the prison, was the cause of the return of my watch and ring. When I left the Old Oapitol, Mr. Wood said to me "There is the order for your release." I asked "From what department?" He said, "I cannot show you; but you can go when you please, and where you please." I said, "Mr. Wood, I have letters and papers in the hands of Colonel Baker, and my watch, ring and money are there;" said he "You better go straight home now, and I will see that you get them." I saw Judge Knox with my brother-in-law, and he wrote for the return of those things, and Colonel Baker wrote back, so Judge Knox told me, that they had been returned. I wrote either to Mr. Wood or to the clerk of the Cld Capitol, and he wrote back word that they had called upon Colonel Baker, and Colonel Baker said they had been returned; and I got them in the course of a week afterwards. I was told that if I went up there after my watch and ring I would be locked up again.

Question. Who told you that?

Answer. Parties in the Old Capitol—I cannot tell their names; but parties who had been under arrest there, and when they got out, had gone after their property and been sent back again.

Question. Have you ever been to the Surgeon General, or to any other officer, and requested to see your contract and telegrams, in order to determine whether or not you had taken more for your ice than you were entitled to?

Answer. I came on with my brother-in-law to Washington, and we went to Judge Advocate Turner, and asked to see the order for arrest and the papers in the case; I think we called twice. The first day we were promised that we should see them the next day. We went the next day, but we did not see them. I understood that there were no papers—that is, that there was no order for the arrest, or anything of that kind. My brother-in-law wrote to the judge advocate about it, and a letter came back with this indorsement on it: "Referred for information to the Secretary of War."

Question. Did you ever ask to see your contract and telegrams?

Answer. I told Colonel Baker——

Question. Did you ever satisfy yourself whether that money had been wrongfully taken from the government by you?

Answer. It had not been.

Question. Did you ever examine the telegrams and contract so as to determine whether or not there was an error in the amount received by you from the government?

Answer. No, sir. I have had no chance to see them.

Question. Have you ever applied to the Surgeon General for them?

Answer. I put them in some quartermaster's department, and I have not seen them since.

Question. Did you furnish any ice to the government last year?

Answer. I did; to three different places.

Question. What places?

Answer. Norfolk, Virginia; Newbern, North Carolina, and Hilton Head, South Carolina.

Question. Was any one connected with you in your contracts last year?

Answer. No, sir.

Question. You had no connexion with Mr. Tiffany in those contracts?

Answer. No, sir.

Question. Did you know Mr. Tiffany?

Answer. I met him in Mr. Johnson's office prior to the contracts, and he spoke to me, and I remembered having met him before.

Question. Had you any acquaintance with the Surgeon General or any one in his office?

Answer. Not at the time I took the contract; nor with any one in the medical purveyor's department.

Question. You saw the advertisement for ice?

Answer. Yes, sir.

Question. Did you hand in your proposal in response to that?

Answer. Yes, sir; to Mr. Henry Johnson, medical purveyor.

Question. What were the terms of your proposition?

Answer. I offered to furnish ice for $8 50 to Norfolk, $10 50 to Newbern, and $11 to Hilton Head.

Question. To be delivered into the ice-houses there?

Answer. No, sir; to be delivered by bill of lading.

Question. The weight to be taken as per bill of lading?

Answer. Yes, sir.

Question. At the point where it was loaded?

Answer. Yes, sir.

Question. Was that your original proposition?

Answer. It was so understood before the contract was given to me.

Question. Was that in your original proposition?

Answer. That I cannot say; a copy of it is on file.

Question. Do you not now remember in relation to your original proposition?

Answer. I do not think anything definite is stated in it, except that I proposed to furnish ice at those places at such and such prices.

Question. You proposed to deliver ice at those points at the prices you have stated?

Answer. Yes, sir.

Question. And you expected your ice to be weighed there?

Answer. No, sir; my understanding was that it was to be taken by bill of lading; that was my expectation in making my figures.

Question. From what point or points did you ship your ice?

Answer. From Herring gut, Goose creek, and Southport, Maine.

Question. Can you tell in what vessels you shipped ice?

Answer. I can name some of them.

Question. Give us the names.

Answer. The Means; two vessels called the Fish, the O. N. Francis. I do not think I could remember them all.

Question. Did you fulfil your contract?

Answer. Yes, sir.

Question. Did you supply Newbern with all the ice required there?

Answer. Yes, sir.

Question. Was not the government obliged to buy ice of an ice dealer in Newbern?

Answer. No, sir. The government took a cargo of my ice and used it for private purposes, and I had to wait some two or three months before I got my money.

Question. Did you ship ice to Newbern by the schooner Magnet?

Answer. I did not.

Question. The statement has been made that you shipped ice to Newbern by the schooner Magnet; that the bill of lading called for 93 tons, and that it was surveyed when it got there, and only $17\frac{800}{2000}$ tons found in it.

Answer. I know nothing of that kind ever took place.

Question. And that there was another cargo by another vessel, the bill of lading for 125 tons, and only 43 tons arrived.

Answer. There was nothing of that kind.

Question. What medical officer received your ice there?

Answer. Dr. Snelling, the most of it.

Question. Did you hear any complaint from Dr. Snelling in relation to your ice?

Answer. No, sir.

Question. Did you hear any complaint from any officer of the government authorized to receive your ice?

Answer. No, sir.

Question. How did you determine the quantity of ice put on board the vessels?

Answer. It was weighed on board.

Question. It was not determined by the measurement of the hold of the vessels?

Answer. No, sir. I never heard of measuring ice on board a vessel in that way.

Question. Who superintended the loading of your ice?

Answer. The parties from whom I bought it. The parties I bought it of weighed it themselves, and I paid them in accordance to that weight.

Question. From what persons did you purchase ice?

Answer. From Mr. Gore, of Boston; George W. Gilmore, of Southport, Maine; and Mr. Carleton, of Rockport, Goose creek, Maine.

Question. Did you pay for the same number of tons of ice that you charged the government for?

Answer. Yes, sir.

Question. Can you furnish us with the names of the vessels by which you shipped your ice, the tonnage of each vessel, and the quantity of ice on board each vessel?

Answer. I can do it, but it will take some time.

Question. Will you do so?

Answer. Yes, sir.

Question. Did you take anything else in the holds of the vessels in which you shipped ice?

Answer. Two or three times I put some small packages of butter for the hospitals in on top of the ice to keep it cool; nothing else.

Question. Did you, at any time, purchase a cargo of ice, or a portion of a cargo, at Hilton Head?

Answer. Yes, sir; of Mr. Darling.

Question. What did you do with it?

Answer. I sold it to the government.

Question. At what price, and on what terms?

Answer. Just the same price as I contracted for. I asked the medical department if they wanted it; they said they did, and I sold it to them.

Question. It was taken by bill of lading?

Answer. Yes, sir.

Question. Was any alteration or change made in the bill of lading?

Answer. I took the bill of lading from the gentleman I bought it of.

Question. Was there any change or alteration made in that bill of lading?

Answer. I cannot say. I do not think there was.

Question. Do you not know whether there was or not?

Answer. I do not think there was. I do not know.

Question. Did you not make out a new bill of lading?

Answer. There was a bill of lading made out, because he had other stuff on board the vessel; and I think he made out a separate bill of lading for the ice.

Question. Who made it?

Answer. It was made either by the captain or by Mr. Darling.

Question. Was Mr. Darling on board?

Answer. He was out there on board the vessel at that time.

Question. The government took that ice by bill of lading?

Answer. Yes, sir.

Question. How did you get at the quantity of ice on board the vessel?

Answer. I took what they told me it was.

Question. What evidence did you furnish to the government of the quantity of ice you furnished from that vessel?

Answer. I do not know of any evidence furnished except the statement they gave me.

Question. You were to deliver ice by bill of lading?

Answer. Yes, sir.

Question. And the government took this ice from this vessel on your contract?

Answer. Yes, sir.

Question. How were you to determine the quantity of ice it had on board?

Answer. From what they stated at the time.

Question. From what who stated?

Answer. The parties who had it there—Mr. Darling and the captain.

Question. Do you remember what evidence you furnished the government of the quantity of ice on board that vessel?

Answer. I think the bill of lading was all.

Question. Did you furnish them that bill of lading?

Answer. Yes, sir.

Question. Was it the original bill of lading?

Answer. No, sir.

Question. What was it?

Answer. I bought it by bill of lading; the bill of lading given me there.

Question. It was not a bill of lading, was it, but a bill of the ice?

Answer. I think it was a bill of lading.

Question. Did you have the original bill of lading?

Answer. No, sir.

Question. Then what did you have?

Answer. I had the bill of lading made for me there.

Question. Who made it?

Answer. I cannot tell which of them made it.

Question. How long had the vessel been there?

Answer. I think I bought the ice the day the vessel got there.

Question. Do you know how long the vessel was there before the ice was discharged?

Answer. I do not know; some time.

Question. The ice had wasted a great deal?

Answer. No, sir; I think not. It was very fine ice.

Testimony of Mr. J. C. Tiffany.

WASHINGTON, *March* 26, 1864.

Mr. J. C. TIFFANY sworn and examined.

By Mr. Gooch:

Question. What was your business prior to 1862?

Answer. I was an agent of the quartermaster's department, in this city. I have been the president of a joint-stock company for putting up machines for the saving of fuel; I have also been a farmer.

Question. What has been your business since that time?

Answer. I have been engaged in shipping ice.

Question. When were you an agent for the quartermaster's department?

Answer. I think it was in November, 1861, that I had charge of the Sixth street government depot here in Washington.

Question. By whom were you engaged in that capacity?

Answer. General Van Vliet sent me to Colonel Rucker, and Colonel Rucker sent me down there.

Question. Have you at any time supplied ice to the government?

Answer. Yes, sir.

Question. When?

Answer. In 1862, at the time the army was on the Peninsula, at Harrison's landing.

Question. How did you supply it—under contract?

Answer. The first ice was ordered.

Question. By whom?

Answer. The medical director of the army of the Potomac, approved by the Surgeon General. That was the first ice furnished by me.

Question. Did you furnish any ice the next year under contract?

Answer. I did.

Question. State the circumstances under which the contract was made by you.

Answer. In the fall of 1862, when they were getting ice, I told them if they would like to have it supplied by contract I would do so. I was referred to the Surgeon General. I believe I wrote out a contract. They afterwards informed me that, by order of the Secretary of War, all contracts had to be advertised, and that I might put in my proposition then. That was the first I heard of it. I think the bids were opened on the 23d of February, 1863, and the contracts for New Orleans, Pensacola, Key West, and Washington were awarded to me as the lowest bidder.

Question. With whom did you have your conversation in the Surgeon General's office in relation to the contract before the advertisement?

Answer. I think it was with Surgeon Smith, who had a room there next to the Surgeon General's office.

Question. Can you state to the committee the terms of the proposal you made in response to the advertisement?

Answer. The one that was executed?

Question. Yes, sir.

Answer. As near as I can recollect, I agreed to furnish the ice at New Orleans and Pensecola, and anywhere thereabouts that it was taken, for $22 50 a ton, with 15 per cent. off for wastage; and at Washington for $10 50 a ton, with 12 or 15 per cent. off for wastage; I cannot tell positively the exact prices, but the contract will show it.

Question. Were not the terms of your proposition changed after it was sent in?

Answer. No, sir; not that I know of. They wanted the ice delivered in Washington at the hospitals, and I told them I would delivered it at 50 cents a ton additional to the contract. That was all the change that was made, as far as I know. They wanted an ice-house pen, and I agreed to put it up at such a price; all that had nothing to do with the supplying of the ice. There was no alteration at all made in the terms for the delivery of the ice.

Question. Were you present when the proposals were opened by the medical storekeeper, Mr. Johnson?

Answer. Yes, sir.

Question. Were you announced as the lowest bidder?

Answer. No, sir; it was not announced at all then who was the lowest bidder.

Question. Was it not said by Mr. Johnson, when the bids were opened, that the contract would be awarded to somebody else?

Answer. Yes, sir; it was awarded to Mr. Godey at a certain price.

Question. How happened it that that award was changed?

Answer. I bid lower than Mr. Godey did, and I felt that I had been wrongly ruled out. I went over to the Surgeon General's office, where Mr. Johnson had announced that his award would be submitted for approval.

Question. With whom had you any conversation at the Surgeon General's office?

Answer. With Mr. Smith. Mr. Smith ordered all the proposals to be sent over to the office. I believe the Surgeon General ordered Mr. Smith to have them all sent for. They were sent over for examination. They asked me then if my proposal had been sent over. It was not there, and they sent again for all of them, and asked me to come back at 2 or 3 o'clock, I think, and they would look them over, and see whether the award was correct or not; I came back, but I really do not remember whether they gave me an answer then, or the next day; I am under the impression that it was the next day, but I cannot state positively about it.

Question. Do you remember the terms of Mr. Godey's bid?

Answer. I believe it was thirteen dollars and something a ton.

Question. What was he to do?

Answer. To deliver it to the hospitals.

Question. What were you to do?

Answer. I was to deliver it at the ice-house at $9 45 a ton, after the deduction for wastage, delivered on the wharf; and deliver it at the hospitals for 50 cents a ton additional.

Question. You were to deliver the ice on the wharf at $9 45 a ton?

Answer. Yes, sir; with the wastage off.

Question. Do you consider that your proposal was lower than his—he to de liver at the hospitals at $13 a ton, and you to deliver at the wharf at $9 45?

Answer. I considered it certainly a great deal cheaper; I do not think it would cost $2 50 a ton to deliver it at the hospitals.

Question. What would be the wastage to deliver the ice at the hospitals?

Answer. That would depend a great deal upon circumstances.

Question. What was the wastage?

Answer. It was pretty large.

Question. What was the actual percentage of wastage?

Answer. The way things were managed, I judge the ice wasted pretty nearly three-fourths.

Question. As you delivered it yourself?

Answer. I delivered it as it was ordered; I had nothing to do but to draw it. I suppose, when it went out in the morning, you might deliver 80 or 90 pounds out of a hundred; in the middle of the day you would not deliver so much.

Question. You say the wastage was three-fourths?

Answer. Yes, sir, altogether, for the ice-house was open almost all the time.

Question. Was the ice-house properly built—one suitable for ice?

Answer. I believe it was.

Question. Who had the control of the ice-house?

Answer. There was an orderly sent down there by the medical director, or somebody else; I do not know whom.

Question. You had the whole control of delivering while you carried on that part of the business?

Answer. Yes, sir; I agreed to deliver it at the hospitals for 50 cents a ton; a great many of them would not take the ice when carried there, but said they would rather send their own teams for it.

Question. Is it your opinion, with the knowledge you have of the ice business, that it is for the interest of the government to pay $9 45 a ton for ice delivered on the wharf in Washington, in preference to paying $13 a ton for ice delivered at the hospitals?

Answer. It would be better for them, if it was properly managed, to pay that for its delivery on the wharf. I do not think the government has acted very wisely in their contracts. I think they could do a great deal better. I told Dr. Abbott here, even when I was delivering the ice, that it would be better to have the regular dealers in the cities to supply them; and where they wanted ice in places where there were no regular dealers, the government should ship it for themselves. That is the only true way of doing business so far as I know anything about it. I do not think any new man can go into a place and deliver ice as well as those who are used to the place. I delivered all that was called for. But when they came in the middle of the day for ice, you must have the doors of the ice-house open, and the heat will get in so that you might almost as well have your ice out of doors.

Question. Knowing these facts, how could you be of the opinion that it was better for the government to accept of your proposals to furnish ice delivered on the wharf here at $9 45 a ton, and then send it out to the hospitals, instead of paying $13 a ton for it delivered at the hospitals?

Answer. I supposed the hospitals would draw their own ice, and that all their ambulances, or whatever they sent for it, would be sent in the morning and take the ice then, so that the ice-house would not be open except in the morning. That was the way I advised them to do, and I finally got them to adopt that in September, although I had been to a great expense in getting horses and carts. I told them all along that they were wasting too much ice, and that they should get down there before sunrise in the morning, get what ice they wanted, and then shut the ice-house up; that by that means they would save a great deal.

Question. Do you not think that the wastage of the ice from the time it is delivered on the wharf until it is delivered to the consumer would be at least 25 per cent.?

Answer. I could not tell you; I have not done anything more than ship it here; I have not dealt in it here; I do not know what the wastage here is.

Question. Do you know what considerations operated upon the mind of the Surgeon General or his assistant to induce them to change the award that had been made by Mr. Johnson?

Answer. I do not know; I never had any conversation with them about that, except to urge that my bid was the lowest. I never saw the Surgeon General but twice that I know of; and I do not think I ever talked with him more than twenty minutes.

Question. Did you have anything to do with preparing the advertisements for ice?

Answer. No, sir.

Question. Did you ever represent to any person that you had anything to do with the preparation of the advertisement?

Answer. No, sir.

Question. Did you call on Addison Gage & Co., in Boston, at any time?

Answer. I did; twice.

Question. Did you represent to them that it was no use for them to bid for ice; that whoever took contracts would have to get them through you?

Answer. No, sir; I never told them any such thing. Some time last summer I received a letter from the Secretary of War, stating that Mr. Gage had written a letter to some senator about that. I wrote, in reply, that nothing of the kind had been said. Mr. Gage said that he intended to put in a bid, and refused to contract for ice with me at New Orleans for $35 a ton delivered. I told him I had seen the advertisement, but I did not say I had anything to do with giving the contracts.

Question. For what purpose did you call on Mr. Gage?

Answer. To get ice.

Question. For what purpose did you want ice?

Answer. To sell.

Question. To whom?

Answer. To any person who wanted to buy it. I had been supplying ice the year before; but that year there was very little chance to supply ice.

Question. Had you supplied it to any one but the government?

Answer. No, sir, not before 1863; but I had made contracts to supply ice to others.

Question. What contracts?

Answer. At New York, Newark, Philadelphia, and some in Baltimore.

Question. With whom?

Answer. I had made a contract to supply some ice to the Knickerbocker Ice Co., with Freeman & Co., Newark, and I sent a load to Mr. Barnum, of Baltimore.

Question. Were they private individuals, or connected with the government?

Answer. Private individuals.

Question. Had you made a contract prior to that time?

Answer. I do not know that I had made any prior to that time. I was determined to go into the ice business, and wanted to get a supply of ice I could control.

Question. Did you tell the ice-dealers in New England that you were to have these contracts with the government?

Answer. Not that I know of. I told them I was going to put in bids for the contract; and they told me they were going to do so. I never made any representation to any one that I was going to have the contract any way, for I never had any assurance from any person that I was going to get it.

Question. From what point or points did you ship your ice?

Answer. I shipped some from New York, some from Boston, and some from the Kennebec river, in Maine.

Question. Will an ordinary vessel carry as many tons of ice as her registered tonnage?

Answer. Yes, sir; generally a little more. Some vessels will carry a great deal more, some not quite so much as their register. It depends upon how they are built. A profitable ice vessel will carry more than her registered tonnage.

Question. Was the ice you shipped weighed or measured?

Answer. Some was weighed and some was measured.

Question. At what points was it weighed and at what points measured?

Answer. On the Kennebec river we weighed a great deal; and we measured some there. It depended upon the facilities whether the ice was weighed or was measured. At some places where we got ice, the houses where it was put up were so arranged that we could weigh it as well as not; at others the facilities were not so great, and we measured it.

Question. You paid so much per ton, then, for the number of tons put on board the vessels?

Answer. Yes, sir.

Question. Who superintended the loading the ice into the vessels?

Answer. Mr. John McCartney superintended the most of it. I believe two or three cargoes were superintended by a man named Charles F. Dodge, and a Mr. Barker Neal superintended some of them.

Question. Where do those men reside?

Answer. Mr. McCartney resided at Newton, or Newtown, Long Island. I do not know where Mr. Dodge is now. He had been in the army as quartermaster of the 52d Pennsylvania regiment, but had left on account of his health, and had been residing in Williamsburg, Pennsylvania, I believe. He talked about going into the produce business, but I do not know whether he has or not. Mr. Barker Neal resided at Gardiner.

Question. Did these three men superintend the loading of all your ice?

Answer. I believe they did. I do not now remember that anybody else superintended any.

Question. Did you superintend the loading of any yourself?

Answer. No, sir; I did not. I was in New York a great deal, but used to go down there often.

Question. Was any ice weighed here that was received?

Answer. I could not tell whether there was any weighed here or not.

Question. Was any weighed to your knowledge?

Answer. I do not know that there was. The contract was that the loading should be subject to the inspection of a government agent. I do not know whether there was any there or not. When the government wanted ice they ordered a load of it, and I went there and loaded it.

Question. When the government wanted ice they notified you to send it?

Answer. Yes, sir.

Question. You understood, by the terms of your contract, that a government inspector was to superintend the loading of it?

Answer. That it was subject to that inspection, if they choose to send an agent there to do it.

Question. Was there any such inspection?

Answer. No, sir, not to my knowledge. I have never heard that there was any such inspection.

Question. The only evidence the government had that you shipped the quantity of ice, for which you were paid, was the bill of lading, sworn to by the captain of the vessel?

Answer. Yes, sir. I took the accounts of my agents for that. The captain of the vessel knew what he had.

Question. You paid for the number of tons he swore to in the bill of lading?

Answer. I did, and was paid for the ice at the same rate.

Question. Of whom did you purchase this ice?

Answer. I purchased some ice in New York of the Knickerbocker Ice Company. All I purchased in Boston was purchased of Daniel Draper & Sons; in Bath, I purchased of Colonel Harding; in Richmond, Maine, I bought of Allen & Maxwell, or of their agent, H. S. Hagar; and I bought some in Gardiner of a man by the name of Stevens—Mr. Barker Neal, who measured the ice for me, knows his first name—I do not; and I bought some of a man named William Sturtevant, of Richmond, though I think he had his ice at Gardiner, or on the river; and I bought some ice of a man by the name of Carhart, but it afterwards turned out to belong to Addison Gage & Co., of Boston. It seems that Carhart sold it to Gage, and I paid Gage for it.

Question. Have you named all the persons of whom you bought ice?

Answer. As far as I now remember. That amounted to a great deal of ice.

Question. Whom were you supplying with ice besides the government?

Answer. I sent some to the Knickerbocker Ice Company, of New York; some to Freeman, of Newark, New Jersey; some to a man in New Brunswick, New Jersey—I forget his name; some to Kershaw & Co., in Philadelphia, somewhere from 4,000 to 5,000 tons; and then I sent off a lot to a man by the name of Lloyd, who shipped it to Hilton Head and Charleston bar; I believe he resides somewhere in Pennsylvania, but he came up from Beaufort then.

Question. Can you tell from your books the amount of ice you furnished to each one of the parties you have named?

Answer. I think I can.

Question. Have you your books with you?

Answer. No, sir.

Question. Will you forward to us the amount of ice you furnished to each of those parties?

Answer. Yes, sir, if I can make it out. I think it would amount to about the same that I sold to the government.

Question. What did you pay per ton for this ice?

Answer. All the way from $2 50 to $4 a ton.

Question. What was the lowest you paid?

Answer. I think $2 50 was the lowest; I will not be positive about that; but I can find out.

Question. What did you pay per ton for freight?

Answer. On an average from $3 to $3 50 to Washington. The vessels that went to New Orleans I chartered by the month to go out and back.

Question. You paid no vessels by the ton except those that went to Washington?

Answer. No, sir; because it was a short voyage. I would pay them so much per ton to come out, and they would find their own freight back. But there was so little freight to come back from New Orleans that I had to charter the vessels by the month out and back, or else pay so much for freight per ton that I would rather run the risk of getting freight back.

Question. Did you ship any ice to Pensacola?

Answer. Yes, sir.

Question. Do you know what was done with the ice you shipped there?

Answer. One of the vessels, after she arrived there, was ordered to go to New Orleans and discharge her ice there. Another vessel discharged her ice at Pensacola.

Question. Do you know what was done with the ice discharged at Pensacola?

Answer. I do not; they did not order me to put up any ice-house there. I sent the ice down there, and I understood that they put it in Fort Pickens; but I do not know.

Question. Are you interested in any ice contracts with the government now?

Answer. I have no contracts for ice with the government now.

Question. Are you interested in any contracts that other people have?

Answer. Mr. Hull asked me to furnish him some ice to be sent to Annapolis. He wanted to make a bid; and I agreed to furnish him ice at so much per ton.

Question. When you were delivering ice in Washington, did you deliver it at any other places, or to any other parties than the hospitals?

Answer. Yes, sir.

Question. To whom?

Answer. To several parties; I sent some to Mr. Smith; some to Dr. Abbott's place; some to the officers in the War Department; and, I believe, I sent some to parties connected with Riggs & Co., bankers; only a few tons altogether.

Question. What ice was it you sent to Riggs & Co.?

Answer. I made a request that I might be allowed to have 25 tons of ice, which should be deducted from the bill of lading, that I might have it to use as I wished, and the request was granted by the department, and I sent it around to those parties.

Question. What was this ice sent for—as a matter of business, or as a present?

Answer. I never charged them anything for the ice; there was no understanding about its being a present or anything of the kind. I do not know whether I sent any to the Surgeon General or not. I know the parties in the medical department all insisted that they should pay for the ice. I think I asked to have the control of 25 tons; I am not positive about the amount.

Question. That is, you were to take 25 tons, and have it deducted from your bill?

Answer. Yes, sir; and for which the government never paid me.

Question. You have no knowledge of the amount of ice actually delivered at any of the points to which you shipped it?

Answer. No, sir; because I never heard of any of it being weighed after delivery. It was a matter they could do just as they chose about. I should not have objected to having the ice weighed at all. I know what I sent.

Question. Do you know what would be a fair percentage for wastage?

Answer. There is a great deal of difference about that. I have sent ice down to Matanzas, and when it got there and was unloaded, even the sap of the ice was not melted off. Then again, I have sent ice which wasted very much. It depends a great deal upon the temperature of the water, the heat of the sun, and the time of the year; in summer time it wastes the most, of course. It wasted more last summer than I ever knew it before.

Question. How much per cent. do you think it wasted last year in shipping it to Washington?

Answer. I do not know what it wasted. We protected it pretty well by putting lumber and hay on as a deck load. I should think it came very well; it looked pretty well when it was opened. I got some of the persons here to inspect some vessels, for I wanted them to be satisfied that the ice they were getting was good. I suppose it was all good. I agreed to furnish them first quality ice, and I did send them last year the best ice in the United States. I do not believe there was ever any better ice cut than I sent.

Question. If I have understood you correctly, you have stated that the government can supply itself with ice more economically by purchasing it from the dealers in the neighborhood, if they got it at reasonable rates, than by shipping it and storing it for themselves?

Answer. For this reason, yes, sir; that the parties the government have to take care of the ice know so little about it that the wastage amounts to a great deal more than the difference in price; and my opinion now is, that if the government had taken their ice from Mr. Godey, at $13 a ton, they would have got it a little cheaper than it turned out as they got it from me. But, as a general thing, I think, if they had gone out into the market and bought it, instead of from Mr. Godey or me, it would have cost them more, for ice went up very high last season. I sold it at my ice-house for the same price that I delivered it here. I think, at the same time, the government can do better to have their ice supplied from the dealers, in the large places where there are dealers. Where there are no regular dealers, I think the government should buy their own ice at so much a ton on board the vessel, load it for themselves, and attend to it for themselves. I offered to supply the government this year at so much a ton, put on board vessels, paying a government weigher five cents per ton for weighing it; I would do that for $1 75 per ton, and I would then have made more money than by any other contract.

Question. At what place did you propose to load it in that way?

Answer. At Richmond, Maine.

Statement of ice shipped to government.

Date.	Name of vessel.	Destination.	Registered tonnage.	Tons ice.
1863.				
April 1	Schr. Robert Caldwell	New Orleans	447	503
11	Schr. Queen of the South	....do	445	455
13	Ship Lisbon	....do	$502\frac{27}{95}$	$496\frac{1950}{2000}$
17	Bark Scotland	....do	384	$38\frac{1976}{2000}$
18	Ship Flora Southard	Pensacola	524	515
28	Brig Stephen Duncan	New Orleans	287	328
29	Bark Argean	....do	450	513
Mar. 24	Ship Clara Ann	Pensacola	420	$469\frac{1350}{2000}$
May 23	Schr. Richmond	Washington	....	140
29	Brig Abbott Lawrence	....do	200	265
June 1	Schr. T. C. Barlette	....do	....	$127\frac{11}{40}$
3	Schr. Golden Rod	....do	....	118
3	Schr. Exeter	....do	....	148
3	Schr. October	....do	....	156
5	Brig Almon Rowell	Key West	280	368
6	Brig Whitaker	Washington	....	262
6	Schr. Olivia Buxton	....do	....	130
8	Schr. Martha	....do	....	230
10	Schr. Hudson	....do	....	257
20	Schr. Matilda	....do	....	$355\frac{5}{37}$
30	Schr. L. F. Smith	....do	....	372
30	Ship May Flower	New Orleans	....	1,233
Aug. 11	Schr. Mary Ella	Washington	210	$186\frac{1000}{2000}$
13	Brig Isadora	....do	....	264
13	Brig Forrester	....do	....	$180\frac{947}{2000}$
13	Schr. Jennie Morton	....do	....	413
13	Schr. H. N. Farnham	....do	302	325
22	Schr. Thomas Martin	....do	145	176
23	Ship Lisbon	New Orleans	$502\frac{27}{95}$	464
	Total	....	....	$9,888\frac{143}{2000}$

RICHMOND, *February* 23, 1864.

SIR: Above you have the class, name, and destination of the vessels, with the registered tonnage of those had on charter-party. Those not having registered tonnage marked were taken on rates, or so much per ton, for amount actually put on board, voyage to Washington being too short to take vessels by the month, and there being no return freights from Washington. The ship May Flower was sent out to a market, but the government wanted it, in fact took it, although ice was bringing fifty dollars per ton in New Orleans at that time. The ship registers about 1,000 tons, but I only took the hold for ten thousand dollars out to New Orleans; but the owner, James Hagar, swore upon a suit that she carried 1,500 tons, and was under-registered, as is the case with most vessels. The ice for New Orleans was loaded mostly in New York by the Knickerbocker Ice Company; the Scotland and Lisbon in Boston by D. Draper & Sons. The balance was loaded on the Kennebec river in Maine, and from ice I bought by the house-full, and also put up myself, I paying for what I bought by the bill of lading; the ice put in being weighed or measured by a regularly appointed weigher. The government sent no one to inspect the loading that I know of; but I took the medical director, Dr. R. O. Abbott, to see some cargoes examined and opened, with which he was satisfied. The ice was of the very first quality. I do not think it the best plan for the government to buy ice delivered in ice-houses, but in large places to buy ice delivered at the hospitals at so much per hundred weight; and for all other points I should advise to buy the ice put on board the vessel where they can get it the best and cheapest, furnish their own vessels, or have them taken up for them; let the ice be inspected and weighed by a weigher sworn before the United States district court, and the government will save all that the contractors make.

Very respectfully, your obedient servant,

J. C. TIFFANY

Hon. B. F. WADE.

ROSECRANS'S CAMPAIGNS.

IN THE HOUSE OF REPRESENTATIVES OF THE UNITED STATES, *February* 6, 1865.

On motion of Mr. GARFIELD.

Resolved, That the Committee on the Conduct of the War be directed to make a full investigation and report upon the military campaigns of Major General W. S. Rosecrans, from the beginning of his service in Western Virginia to the conclusion of his recent campaign in Missouri.

Attest:

EDWARD McPHERSON, *Clerk*.

WASHINGTON, *April* 22, 1865.

Major General W. S. ROSECRANS sworn and examined.

By the chairman:

Question. What is your present rank and position in the army, and what positions have you held in the army since the commencement of the rebellion?

Answer. My first military service in this war was as volunteer engineer and acting aide-de-camp to General McClellan, during which I laid out camp Dennison and visited Philadelphia to examine Justus's arm factory, and Washington to urge that prompt provision be made for paying and clothing our Ohio troops, many of the officers and men, from leaving home so promptly, being in great destitution.

On my return from Washington I found awaiting me a commission as chief engineer of the State of Ohio, under a special law then recently passed authorizing such an officer, with the rank, pay and emoluments of a United States colonel of engineers.

I accepted, but explained to Governor Dennison that this office would keep me from active service at a time when my military training and information would be of great service to our noble young men who were flying to arms and would be subjected to numberless hardships and hazards arising solely from ignorance and inexperience in the military service.

A few days after he sent me a commission as colonel of the 23d Ohio volunteer infantry, which I accepted, and repairing to Columbus, reported for duty as commandant of the encampment of three years' volunteers, which I named Camp Chase, and commanded until I was surprised by the receipt of an appointment, dated May 16, 1861, as brigadier general in the regular army; and almost immediately thereafter of an order from General McClellan to report to him at Cincinnati for further orders.

On my arrival in Cincinnati I found I was to accompany him into Western Virginia, into which, after the defeat and dispersion of the rebels under Porterfield, at Philippi, General Robert S. Garnett had entered for the purpose of teaching the loyal Union men proper deference to the will of their liege masters, the slaveholders, east of the Blue Ridge.

I served in this grade long after colonels had been promoted to major generals for camp service; and finally, the day after the battle of Iuka received an appointment of major general of volunteers, to rank from the 16th day of September, 1862, the date of which was subsequently changed to March 21, 1862, probably to avoid the inconvenience in placing me in command of Buell's army, in which were major generals of senior rank.

In this grade I have since served.

Question. You have read the resolution of the House of Representatives, directing inquiry in relation to your campaigns. Will you give the committee a statement embracing all that you may deem essential to a full understanding of the subject-matter contained in the resolution?

Answer. In reply to this interrogatory, I shall endeavor to narrate, from memory, the principal events of my campaigns, referring as far as possible to my official reports and correspondence with the general-in-chief and War Department for details, and omitting what is purely personal, or belongs to private memoirs, so that my narrative, with those official documents, will give the narrative of those military movements with which I have been directly connected.

For clearness and convenience I will refer to my letter of April 5 to your chairman, for the names of persons whose testimony would be likely to be valuable in ascertaining the truth, and will quote or indicate what papers ought to be before the committee for consideration and made a part of my testimony.

I now proceed to my campaigns.

Of the campaign in Western Virginia in 1861, I have to state that as soon as Garnett entered West Virginia he moved, with his main column, to Laurel Hill, on the Beverly and Webster road, 17 miles north of Beverly; while General Pegram, with a considerable column—seizing the pass over Rich mountain, on the Beverly and Ripley turnpike—covered Garnett's communications, with his base at Staunton.

General McClellan, having ordered General Morris with all his available force to confront Garnett, moved from Camp Dennison to Parkersburg 22d June, 1861, where he assembled three small brigades and two batteries. I was ordered to accompany him, and at Parkersburg placed in command of a provisional brigade, consisting of the 8th and 10th Indiana and the 17th and 19th Ohio volunteer infantry, three months' service. Moving McCook's and Schleick's brigades to Grafton, he left me in command at Parkersburg, whence, under his orders, I moved to Clarksburg on the 28th, and immediately advanced to Duncan's farm, 15 miles distant on the road to Buckhannon, where I encamped and reported for orders.

General McClellan having determined that General Morris should watch the motions of Garnett, while he, with the remainder of his available force, should move by the way of Buckhannon and Rich mountain to Beverly, permitted me to occupy Buckhannon, which I did by a night march; and on my arrival found, contrary to our information and belief, that the citizens were mainly loyal, and that the place had never been in the hands of the enemy for more than a few hours.

As soon as General McClellan's troops had concentrated at this point and his supplies came up, he moved, reaching Roaring creek, at the foot of the western slope of Rich mountain, about 3 o'clock p. m. of the second day, where the command went into camp in a drenching rain. Reconnoitring the enemy, he was found posted in a strong natural position on the turnpike near the foot of the mountain—his right covered by an almost impenetrable laurel thicket—his left resting high up on the spur of the mountain, and his front defended by a log breast-work, in front of which was an abatis of fallen timber. As the second in rank, the command of the camp devolved on me, and my first duty was to know the locality. I soon learned that a young man named Hart, whose father kept a tavern in the gap at the top of Rich mountain, was loyal, and had been seen in our camp; and that, having herded cattle, he knew the mountains thoroughly, which fact I reported to Lieutenant Poe, chief engineer at General McClellan's headquarters, suggesting that search should be made for this young man and his information obtained.

On the 9th July, General McClellan, having completed his preparations, ordered a reconnoissance in force, which was made by McCook's brigade, supported by my own, and resulted in disclosing the great strength of the enemy's position without ascertaining his numbers. On returning from this reconnoissance, General McClellan directed me to occupy the front with my brigade, which was to lead in the attack he intended to make the next morning. Having made the necessary dispositions, on returning to my tent an officer of my command informed me that he had found young Hart. Being brought to my tent, the young man informed me that the enemy's camp was $2\frac{3}{4}$ miles west of his father's house at the top of the mountain, where they had their hospital and commissary stores; that it was possible to reach the top of the mountain by a circuitous route through the forest around the enemy's left to a point within a mile and a half of the gap, whence there was a practicable sled and cart road to his father's house. He stated he had no doubt he could conduct a body of troops to this point, even in the night, but that they could not take with them any artillery. I immediately repaired to the tent of General McClellan with this information, showed him a sketch, and explained it. I then asked him if he desired to see young Hart, and at his request brought the young man to his tent, where the general questioned him very carefully. I then sent Hart to my tent to await orders, and said to the general: "Now, general, if you will allow me to take my brigade I will take this guide and, by a night's march, surprise the enemy at the gap, get possession of it, and thus hold his only line of retreat. You can then take him on the front. If he gives way we shall have him; if he fights obstinately I will leave a portion of the force at the gap and with the remainder fall upon his rear." Colonel Marcy, chief of staff, at once fell in with my suggestion, and the general, after an hour's deliberation, assented, stating that as one of my regiments (the 17th Ohio) was absent, he would give me the 13th Indiana, Colonel Jeremiah Sullivan; and then inquired about what time I thought I could reach the point, which was a matter of importance to know, so as to time his attack. I said I supposed I might be able to reach it by 10 o'clock on the morning of the 10th, and that I thought he could safely begin his attack on that supposition. But it was finally decided that, as unforeseen obstacles might arise to retard the time of my reaching the gap, I should take Burdsall's cavalry and send a message back every ten minutes, reporting progress, while he was to hold his troops in readiness to commence the attack the moment he heard the noise of my firing. I then gave him the following as my proposed arrangement: "The troops to be formed in front of his quarters at 3 o'clock in the morning, and to enter the forest at the front line of our pickets at daylight with one day's rations." To this arrangement he assented, and an invitation to Colonel Lander to accompany me completed the programme.

The troops entered the forest in the morning in a terrible rain-storm. As it was now daylight, and the enemy might discover our movements, on consultation with the guide and Colonel Lander, who accompanied him, it was deemed best to incline much further to the right than had been at first intended, which lengthened the route. At 11 a. m., weary and wet, the column halted on the brink of a deep valley, the opposite side of which was the last ascent, except a small one, before reaching the road that would bring us to an open wood with a gentle descent three-quarters of a mile to the object of our march. From this point I despatched to General McClellan stating this fact, and that, owing to the excessive roughness of the road, almost impassable for horses, and to the fatigue of the animals, I should not send another despatch until I had something of importance to communicate. Down through this gorge, and toiling slowly up the opposite ascent, the head of the column arrived at, within a short distance of the top of the mountain, a cleared field, after eleven hours' marching, at about 1 p. m., where, halting, the men were directed to rest and lunch, while, with the guide and Colonel Lander, I reconnoitred our position.

To the east, though apparently near our feet, though seven miles distant, lay Beverly. Cavalry horses were hitched in the streets; the end of a tented encampment appeared on the right, partly hidden by the mountain; wagons were passing, all indicating the presence of a considerable force in Beverly. Beyond the depression in the open ground in front of us was a low wooded crest which we had to ascend, and thence it was but a short mile to Hart's tavern. At two o'clock the column, closed in mass, was moved noiselessly and swiftly across the open ground into the edge of the forest, and thence, after some difficulty in finding the way, wound up the hill to the top of the crest, which it reached about half past two o'clock, in a terrific shower, and was fired upon by the enemy's advanced guard. The 10th Indiana rapidly advanced, inclining to the right, along the crest of a steep declivity overlooking the Beverly road, halted and formed in line of battle just out of range of the enemy's musketry. The 8th Indiana, under my orders, halted in column, while the 13th Indiana, following the 10th, formed on its left and occupied a spur of the mountain covered by a thicket overlooking the field in front of the enemy's position. The 19th Ohio halting faced towards the enemy's encampment in the direction of which lay a broad well-trodden way.

The enemy, posted behind log breastworks nearly parallel to the road, opened upon us with artillery from a point on each of his flanks, while the sharpshooters occupied the line of fence in front of his position. Owing to a mistake in its movements the 13th Indiana took forty minutes to get into the proper position and to occupy the thicket in front of our left; so that it was forty minutes after three o'clock before our line of battle was ready to advance. All this time the enemy was firing on us with his artillery, which, however, did us but little damage, most of the shots going over the heads of the troops, while we could do nothing but annoy them by our skirmishers. When the line was ready to move, I brought down the 8th Indiana, and directed it, taking advantage of the cover on the right of our line, to make its way to and capture the artillery on the enemy's left. By mistake Colonel Benton took the direction of the centre. He was then directed to take advantage of a roll in the ground and charge another gun of the enemy's towards our left. Misunderstanding this, he passed through an interval between the wings of the 10th, and began deploying in front of its left. I directed him to remain in that position, and the colonel of the 10th to form his left wing in column on the left platoon, and be ready to charge the enemy's line in due time. The whole line advanced. Colonel Sullivan had been ordered to take a portion of the 13th, which had remained in column for want of space, and moving around on the left of the field, to charge the enemy's battery on the right. Comprehending the rawness of our troops, and desirous of putting an end to the artillery fire as soon as possible, I placed myself at the head of this charging column of the 13th Indiana and urged it forward at a double-quick. Colonel Sam Beatty, of the 19th Ohio, conforming the movement of his command to that of our advancing line, took advantage of the first opening to form half of his regiment in line of battle, and delivered a terrific volley opportunely—just as the charging column of the 13th had got within about a hundred yards of the enemy's breastworks. At this the enemy began to waver. A second volley from the 19th threw him into confusion, whereon our whole line, charging with a terrific shout, leaped the enemy's breastworks and pursued his fugitive army into the woods. The battle was over. The enemy's dead and wounded covered the ground. Two pieces, the only artillery he had, fell into our hands. Flushed with success, our troops scattered very much through the woods, and it became a matter of critical importance to reassemble them without delay. This was substantially accomplished by a little after six o'clock. While the troops were reassembling, a quartermaster of the 44th Virginia was captured down the road towards Beverly, who reported that his regiment had reached a point within three-quarters of a mile of the battle, but did not dare to come up. This, and what had been seen from the top of the mountain, made it evident that our position was an isolated point between the rebel intrenched camp on the west and another force of unknown strength in the vicinity of Beverly. No firing was heard in the direction of the intrenched camp. No attack had therefore been made by General McClellan. There was no assurance of succor from that quarter; nothing to prevent the enemy taking his measures to overwhelm us without the possibility of prevention from our main body. What was to be done? We could not go to Beverly, for we were already separated from our command by the enemy, whose strength had been stated to me by ——— and McC. as probably from 5,000 to 8,000 men. It was too late to undertake an advance on the enemy's camp, distant nearly three miles of a road skirted by almost impenetrable thickets of underbrush. In this emergency Captain Conklin was detailed to take charge of the captured pieces of artillery, and the troops were placed in position to prevent a surprise and to defend themselves from attack coming either from the enemy's camp or from Beverly. By the time these dispositions were made it was dark. Meanwhile a messenger had been sought among our cavalry, and none could be found who would undertake to carry word to General McClellan. The night was dark, cold, and rainy. The wounded of both sides filled all the outhouses, and were huddled together in a tavern; in fact, every building was used to keep them from the inclemency of the weather. The troops turned out six times during the night, on account of the picket firing on the front, expecting an attack of the enemy. At three o'clock in the morning a prisoner was brought in, from whose answers I inferred that the enemy were attempting to evacuate, and accordingly made disposition to move on them at daylight, which was done. On reaching the enemy's camp our advance discovered a white flag, and soon it was surrendered with all that remained of Pegram's force, about a hundred and seventy men, with all their artillery, transportation, camp and garrison equipage, and quartermaster's stores. Pegram, with the remainder of his force, had escaped during the night to the north of us with the intention of reaching General Garnett; but the news of the capture of the gap, which had been carried to Beverly by the 44th Virginia, was despatched that night to Garnett, whose position was, as I have before stated, seventeen miles north of Beverly. General Morris was in his front to prevent his advance, and he could retreat only by Beverly on the turnpike, or take an inferior road in a northeast direction through a rough country down Cheat river and strike the northwest Virginia turnpike, which leads from Clarksburg to Winchester, near the Maryland line. He chose the latter, apprehensive that he would be intercepted by our force coming over Rich mountain. On the next morning, at seven o'clock, General Morris began to pursue him. This movement cut off the retreat of Pegram, who sent in a flag of truce and surrendered to General McClellan, who, on the morning of the 11th, as soon as he had learned of the capture of the rebel camp, marched through it to Beverly, and thence followed the 44th Virginia, and whatever other rebels had retreated by the turnpike, towards Staunton, continuing the pursuit to the top of Cheat mountain.

The committee will remember that General Morris overtook the rear guard at Carrick's ford, where, during a sharp skirmish, Garnett fell, and his troops, continuing their retreat, finally escaped to Winchester. Thus, by the capture of the gap at Rich mountain, the keystone was knocked from the rebel arch of defence, and they were driven from Western Virginia.

I forbear to take notice of the various reports and statements concerning this battle which have been privately and publicly circulated. The committee will find the facts here stated substantially in my official report, which is of that of the four regimental commanders who accompanied me in that expedition—Colonel Jerry Sullivan, 13th Indiana, now brigadier; Colonel Samuel Beatty, 19th Ohio, now brigadier; Colonel Benton, 8th Indiana, now brigadier; and Colonel (afterwards brigadier general) Manson, and is hereby made a part of my testimony.

As no explanation was ever, to my knowledge, given for the failure of our main force to attack the enemy on the 10th, it is proper to say that while we were seizing the gap, not only was the firing of the enemy's artillery heard, but the musketry and cheers of our own men in the final charge on the enemy's line were heard by the men in the camp, a mile and a half in rear of our main force.

It should also be added, that so strong was the impression that our column had met with disaster in the conflict at the gap, that General McClellan sent his chief of staff from the front back to the camp to arm all the teamsters, lest the enemy, after having destroyed my brigade, should fall upon and cut the main body to pieces.

As it is probably known to some members of the committee that sundry reports of this battle, at variance in many material points with its true history as here given, were in circulation in Washington duing the latter end of 1861 and the early part of 1862, I have been careful to enter into details, giving all the facts of importance in relation to the actions of the general commanding, his staff officers, and those who served with me in the affair.

By Mr. Gooch :

Question. Do you know any reason why General McClellan did not make an attack, with the force immediately under him, in his front, as was contemplated when you left him?

Answer. I know of no reason why he did not, and of no reason why he should not have done so.

Question. If he had made that attack, as was contemplated between you and him, in your opinion what would have been the result?

Answer. The enemy, having made no attack on his front, had despatched to the gap one half of his artillery and a considerable force in addition to that usually stationed there. The probabilities are that, had the attack in front been made, we should have beaten the enemy and destroyed or captured nearly his entire force that day, instead of allowing them to run away through the woods, individually or in squads, during the night subsequent to the capture of the gap, as they did. At all events General McClellan was bound, as a military man, to have made the attack in his front, for the purpose of preventing the enemy from falling on me with too heavy a force.

Question. Do you know whether General McClellan has ever assigned any reason why he did not make the attack, as contemplated between you and him ?

Answer. The only reason I have ever seen assigned is contained in his official report, published as a campaign document, and prefaced by the remark that he had not, until recently, had in his possession the necessary papers to enable him to write a report of the campaign of Western Virginia. In that report he says :

"About half past two the firing which we had heard in the direction of the gap, and which apparently receded, ceased. Shortly afterwards an officer appeared in the rebel camp and made a speech. We could not hear the words, but from the cheers which followed many supposed it had fared badly with our detachment. Immediately ordered roads to be cut and guns got into position, intending to open the next morning, in order to relieve Rosecrans."

I am quoting from memory and may not give the words exactly, but I give the substance. General McClellan adds that he was delayed by accidents the next morning in opening, until the arrival of a messenger announcing the capture of the rebel camp. This is all I have ever seen or heard from him in reference to the matter.

Question. If he had supposed that the enemy was getting the better of you, why should he have delayed until the next morning before commencing the attack?

Answer. Such a mode of relieving me was the surest way to enable the enemy to destroy me. The only sure relief he could have given would have been to attack the enemy the instant he heard the first firing.

Question. I understand you to say you expected to reach the top of the mountain by 10 o'clock in the morning. In reality you did not arrive there until half past two o'clock in the afternoon. Why was that?

Answer. In reply to General McClellan's question about what time I thought I could reach the top of the mountain I stated that I thought 10 o'clock would be the latest. That was on the supposition that I should start as soon as possible after our then conversation. But, as I have already stated, it was, on the suggestion of General McClellan, determined that the head of the column should not quit the main road and enter the forest at our front picket line until daylight. A further cause of delay, which has been stated, was this: that, owing to the fact that we were undertaking this march mainly in the day-time, General Lander thought, on consultation with the guide, and I decided, that it would be wiser to take a more circuitous route, passing further from the enemy. This lengthened our march, making it over ten hours.

Question. How far distant from you were General McClellan and the main body of our army at the time you were engaged with the enemy?

Answer. In a straight line it was probably two miles; by road it was two and three-quarter miles to the rebel lines, and our troops were formed in line of battle in front of the rebel lines just out of the range of their fire.

Question. When he must have known from the sound of your guns, if in no other way, when you commenced your attack upon the enemy and the continuance of the fight?

Answer. Certainly.

Question. How many men had General McClellan under his command, including the force which accompanied you?

Answer. I do not know exactly, but believe at least between 6,000 and 7,000 effective men.

Question. How many men did you take with you when you made your movement to the top of the mountain?

Answer. Either 1,743 or 1,843; I forget which. My official report shows the number, and is made a part of my testimony.

On the 23d July, a gloomy, rainy day, I went to the tent of General McClellan, who read to me a despatch in nearly these words:

"We have been badly beaten; our army is in full retreat—a most wonderful transformation of a well-appointed army into a rabble.

"WINFIELD SCOTT."

General McClellan then informed me that General Scott had ordered him to Washington, directing him to turn over the command of his department to me.

Question. How many troops were there in the army of West Virginia at the time General McClellan was called to Washington and you were placed in command, and what was their condition?

Answer. There were ten regiments of three-years troops in West Virginia, east of the Kanawha valley. They were newly raised, and as a matter of course without drill or experience. There was one battalion of cavalry and two batteries of artillery, one of them mountain howitzers, manned by regulars.

The strength of those regiments would average about eight hundred men. In the Kanawha valley there were about 2,700 men under General Cox. In all there were probably 11,000 men scattered all over West Virginia.

The gloom of our late disaster was made deeper to me by the announcement of this new and weighty responsibility which devolved on me. Imagination pictured the swift and fierce pursuit of our helpless fugitives from Bull Run, and the ferocious triumph of the enemies of our government. It was evident to me that Western Virginia would soon feel the effects of their activity, to meet which we then had but ten regiments of three-years men east of the Kanawha, the services of the three-months men having already expired or being about to expire. General McClellan left me a memorandum of what he had proposed to enable the troops to hold, acting on the defensive, Western Virginia. The main points of defence were to fortify and hold Gauley pass from the Kanawha valley towards Lewisburg, Cheat Mountain pass, on the Beverly and Staunton road, and Red House pass, on the northwestern Virginia turnpike, leading from Clarksburg to Winchester. I accompanied him to Grafton, and during the ride he spoke appreciatingly of the difficult task devolved on me of defending a mountain country like this, where my troops must be scattered and isolated from each other, and promised to send me as many instructed staff officers as possible. I immediately addressed myself to the task of meeting the anticipated coming invasion of the rebels. General Cox was instructed to proceed to the north of Gauley and fortify that pass. To Brigadier General J. J. Reynolds was confided the defence of the Cheat Mountain pass, which included that of the road leading from Huttonsville to Lewisburg, which was closed by a line of field-works at a place called Elkwater, a few miles south of Huttonsville. Colonel Lorin Andrews, with three and a half regiments, was posted on the northwestern Virginia turnpike, near the point where it crossed the north branch of the Potomac, where, under the direction of Captain Merrill, of the engineers, he threw up some field-works.

Soon the news oozed through every pore of society that, acting on the defensive in front of Washington, the rebels intended to make an offensive campaign to recover possession of Western Virginia; that to General Lee was to be confided the accomplishment of this work. Dismay and alarm pervaded the State, even reached Washington, and came to me in friendly warnings from more than one of the departments of the government. Nor was it long before these rumors received confirmation. General Lee, appearing in General Reynolds's front with a flag of truce, proposed the exchange of some of our men captured at Bull Run for the prisoners of war captured by us at Rich mountain and Beverly and paroled by order of General Scott. A heavy force appeared menacing us in front at Cheat mountain, while another column, coming from Warm Springs by the way of Huntersville, appeared in front of Elkwater. Meanwhile General Cox, from the Kanawha valley, informed me that while General Wise was advancing on his position at the mouth of the Gauley by the Lewisburg and Kanawha turnpike with a force variously estimated at from five to eight thousand men, he had information that General Floyd with another column was advancing from Lewisburg with the intention of crossing Gauley above him, and either attacking our depots at Weston and Clarksburg, or making his rear on the Kanawha river in the vicinity of Charlestown.

I at once despatched General Cox instructions to remove his sick and all public property, not absolutely necessary, from the valley, and if compelled to leave, to retire fighting towards the northwestern Virginia railroad, with a view to concentration, in case of necessity, with General Reynolds and other troops further east. The post at New Creek station was turned over to Colonel Biddle, of General Burk's command, and that on the northwest road stripped of all save a nominal force to re-enforce General Reynolds.

The governor of Ohio, at this time apprehending disaster to us, sent us the

28th, 47th, and 30th, raw regiments of three-years troops. I also assembled all the troops that could be spared, seven regiments and a half, three of which had just received their arms, and marched from Clarksburg, by way of Weston, Bulltown, and Sutton, to meet General Floyd, who, having crossed Gauley, had attacked and overwhelmed Colonel Tyler, of the 7th Ohio, at Cross Lanes, a distance from Clarksburg of 117 miles and about 20 miles above General Cox's position at the mouth of the Gauley.

Our column crossing Big Birch mountain on the 10th September, 1861, encamped at its foot, ten miles above Somerville, on the ground from which we had driven Floyd's outposts. Here the citizens reported that Floyd, with from 15,000 to 20,000 men, was encamped below Somerville, near Cross Lanes, on the north side of the Gauley. We could not stop to count numbers. Our only alternatives were to fight and whip or pass him and unite with General Cox. Accordingly at 3 o'clock the next morning our column began to move, and by 1 o'clock p. m., after a march of fifteen miles, halted two miles from the enemy's intrenched position, having thus far had only a little skirmishing. While resting, cavalry, of which we had but two companies, and staff began to reconnoitre. Firing between the enemy's advanced guard and the head of our column soon followed, and by half past two o'clock Colonel Lytle was in the camp of the rebel Colonel Reynolds, who had retreated into the thick forest, the entrance to which, marked with numerous paths leading from to the rear, satisfied me that the citizens' reports of the enemy being intrenched were probably correct. I therefore directed the leading brigade, (Benham's,) consisting of three of my best regiments, to advance cautiously, but firmly, and to feel the enemy's position. Unfortunately, its commander, excited and impressed with the idea that the enemy was retreating, though emphatically cautioned to beware of masked batteries, advanced through the forest, without deploying skirmishers, until the head of the column emerged in front of an intrenched line, and a battery of seven or eight pieces behind a parapet, where it received a terrific artillery and musketry fire, which brought it to a stand. This sudden and fierce fire caused the commander to send for re-enforcements and artillery. Despatching orders for the other four regiments to follow and halt at the edge of the woods, I proceeded to the front and reconnoitred to the enemy's position. Meanwhile Colonel Robert McCook, whose brigade followed next, sent a portion of the 9th Ohio to our right, where it also drew the enemy's artillery, accompanied by heavy volleys of musketry. His line was found to extend across a bend in the Gauley river, its flanks resting upon almost inaccessible precipices five or six hundred feet above the Gauley. I now prepared for the assault, and to that end sent Colonel W. S. Smith, with the 13th Ohio, supported by the 28th Ohio, under Colonel Mohr, to our left, where he reported he could find cover from the enemy's musketry until within about fifty yards of his flank, whence he thought he could ascend to the height on which their breastworks were built, and, by a sudden rush, take them. It was sunset before the fierce firing at that point indicated that Smith's column was at work. Meanwhile Colonel McCook had formed the 9th and 47th Ohio as a storming column, to be supported by the 10th Ohio, to attack the battery on the enemy's centre. The troops were much jaded, and to inspire them with spirit I told them I would lead them myself. At this time the firing on our left receded, showing our attack there had not succeeded. It was also dusk, and an officer brought the report that our column, under Colonel Smith, had found it impracticable in the darkness and depth of the ravine to accomplish its work. It therefore became necessary to defer the attack until morning. Taking good care to leave the impression that we were immediately in their front, and ready for the attack, the troops were quietly and carefully withdrawn to a good position, just out of reach of the enemy's fire, where, exhausted with the marching and fighting of the day, they lay down on their arms. At five o'clock next morning Colonel

Ewing, from the advance, brought in a contraband, who stated that during the night the enemy had withdrawn across the Gauley, destroyed the foot-bridge and sent the ferry-boats over the falls, leaving only a small portion of his troops on the north side. Orders were immediately given to advance, and Colonel Ewing took possession of the camp and the few prisoners he could find skulking through the woods unable to make their escape. Orders were immediately given to drive the enemy from the opposite side of the river, and hold the ferry, which, under General Benham, was to be put in condition for crossing our troops as rapidly as possible. The Gauley, for a distance of nearly twenty-five miles, rushes through a chasm cut in the rocks from five to eight hundred feet deep, with precipitous sides, the current, except at a very few places, being two swift to cross, even with a skift. Carnifex ferry, at the mouth of Meadow river, a southern tributary of the Gauley, is a level reach about two hundred and fifty yards long and one hundred and twenty-five yards wide, above and below which the water dashes over the rocks white with foam. The descent from the north side is by a winding road about a mile and a half in length from the line of the enemy's intrenchment. It was extremely difficult to obtain materials, and it took twelve days to replace the ferry-boats the enemy had destroyed. Meanwhile General Cox, from the mouth of the Gauley, despatched that after Wise had skirmished heavily with his advanced guard, he retired towards Lewisburg, and that he, General Cox, should cross the Gauley in pursuit. I replied that he should advance carefully, until we could get the means to cross and join him. He obeyed the instructions, and so soon as a single small ferry-boat was ready, General McCook, with two and a half regiments, by working night and day for forty-eight hours, crossed and joined him at the head of the Sunday road. It was also our misfortune to have been compelled to move so light that our ammunition and provisions were both nearly exhausted, and the trains to replenish them, which had been directed to follow us, were so delayed by the terrible rains which set in the night after the battle that they did not reach us for nine days thereafter. And the country was unable to supply us, which would have so long delayed, even had we not been hindered by want of means of crossing the Gauley. The enemy having retreated towards Lewisburg, General Cox followed him, taking possession of one or two lines of intrenchments on his way, and reaching the top of Mount Sewell, where I joined him on the 28th, leaving orders for the remainder of my troops to follow as rapidly as possible. It was pending this movement, when General Lee, learning that I was marching to attack Floyd, attempted to force Reynolds from his position at Cheat mountain, but was badly beaten. From that time he seemed to be in observation, awaiting the result of the operations under Floyd and Wise. General Reynolds, with rare intelligence and sagacity, kept him perpetually harassed, until finally the battle of Carnifex ended the enemy's operations in the Kanawha valley.

General Lee next determined to concentrate all his forces on the Lewisburg road to oppose the advance of our victorious troops. When, therefore, we reached the top of Mount Sewell, we found him strongly posted in front of us, intrenched with an army of about 14,000 men; we had in our advance on his front 5,300 men and four and a half regiments coming up from the rear. One of the most terrible storms ever known in Western Virginia set in. Eighteen horses perished in one night at headquarters. The Gauley rose fifty feet. Forage, clothing, and commissary stores at its mouth, down the Kanawha, in spite of our utmost exertions, were damaged or swept away by the flood. The roads became almost impassable. The country between the mouth of Gauley and Mount Sewell, a distance of thirty-eight miles, never abundantly supplied, was now almost destitute of forage. It was evident that as, all told, we could not number to exceed 8,500 effectives, we had no reasonable chance of driving Lee, with near twice that number, from an intrenched position, nor could we have compelled Lee to retire. Would it have been advisable to advance any further at that season of the year, when it was impossible to have subsisted either animals or men, and when, moreover, we had nothing to accomplish by an advance of a small column far into the interior, beyond support and in proximity to the enemy's great rail communications. Having spent two or three days in examining the country with a view to future operations, the troops were withdrawn to the vicinity of the Gauley, where prompt measures were taken to supply them with clothing, an imperative necessity, from the fact that the continual marching during the past four months, and their remoteness from depots of supplies had rendered it impracticable heretofore, and the troops were so naked that in one regiment I counted one hundred and thirty-five men without pantaloons on parade. This position was held because it covered all the country in its rear, and still threatened and compelled the enemy to watch us. While thus occupied I learned from various sources that General Lee had determined to drive us from our posisition by sending a column through Raleigh Court House to strike the Kanawha below us, and cut off our supplies, while he should take advantage to attack us on our front, and desperately damage us in the retreat to which he expected to force us. Knowing the country better than General Lee, I felt certain his column west of the river would be obliged to take the route by Fayette Court House over Cotton mountain, and strike the river opposite the mouth of the Gauley, where our rear guard was posted, and took my measures accordingly. Nor was I disappointed. On the 27th October the head of Floyd's column, passing through Fayetteville, seized the road opposite Miller's ferry, where lay McCook's brigade, and the next day opened with his artillery from the top of Cotton mountain, a distant and comparatively harmless fire on our position and depots at the mouth of Gauley. Between our forces and Floyd's ran New river, through a narrow chasm from seven hundred to a thousand feet deep, cut in the rocks. The water whirls and foams through this channel, with but two short level reaches in twenty-five miles. One of these, at Miller's ferry, the enemy watched. About four miles above was a small pool, known as Townsend's ferry, to which there was a descent by a foot-path and a small ascent leading from the opposite side to the plateau, southeast of Fayetteville. Having satisfied myself of the possibility of using this as a place of crossing by which to surprise the enemy, I ordered the means therefor to be prepared, which consisted in sawing down the trees to avoid noise, and lowering by ropes over the cliffs materials for two ferries, one formed of wagon boxes laid side by side across two parallel poles, to which they were bound by two others lying on the tops of the boxes and secured to the lower ones by rope lashings. Over this was stretched canvas paulin. The other was what is known in the west as a bull-boat, covered with the paulin. These were to be passed to and fro by a rope stretched across the river, which here was not too wide to admit of it. The work was pushed with the utmost secrecy and despatch, under the direction of Major (now Major General) Crawford, and during a continued rain of seventy hours. The plan of operations was as follows: The brigade which lay next above General Cox's, at the mouth of Gauley, passing down secretly to a point six miles below, being re-enforced by troops brought up from Charlestown and other points on the river below, was secretly to cross the Kanawha at the mouth of Loup creek, and lie concealed until our preparations as above described were made for the crossing. When that was done, General Cox was to commence skirmishing with the enemy, whose artillery had been driven from the front of Cotton hill.

The commander of the Loup creek force was to send a column of 1,000 men across the mountain to Cassidy's mill, four miles west of the enemy's position, and about the same distance from Fayetteville, which lay seven and a half miles in his rear, and while this detachment was on its way was to march with the remainder of his forces up the river, and, in conjunction with General Cox's troops, to drive the enemy from Cotton hill, and prepare to attack him in his encampment on Laurel creek at its southern base. As soon as his detachment should have reached the mill this attack was to begin. While thus drawing the enemy's attention, General Schenck was to move simultaneously to cross New river with 2,700 men at Townsend's ferry and seize the enemy's line of retreat near Fayetteville, announcing the success of this operation to the command in the enemy's front. Thus Floyd's force would be hemmed in beyond the possibility of escape. To be in readiness for any movement of General Lee co-operating with Floyd by attacking us on the Lewisburg road, thorough watch was to be kept on that road towards Mount Sewell, and McCook's brigade with our artillery was to hold it, or a point near Hawk's Nest, which offered such difficulties to the advance of an enemy as would have enabled him to hold General Lee for at least twenty-four hours. Our troops on the west side, having taken Floyd, were, in that case, to march to Bowyer's ferry, cross New river seven miles south of Fayetteville, and place themselves, 6,000 strong, on the Lewisburg road in the rear of Lee's position, which would have put him wholly in our power. The execution of this plan proceeded until the ferry-boats were ready; but the exceedingly violent rains had raised New river so that the small level reach at Townsend's ferry disappeared, and the river there, as elsewhere, was but a torrent, over which it was impossible even to ferry a skiff. When this became certain General Schenck's command was ordered to move with all possible despatch to the mouth of Gauley, and cross the Kanawha at the falls, where means were in readiness.

On the morning of November 11, General Cox's troops attacked and drove the enemy's advance guard from Cotton hill, where the head of the Loup creek column arrived before noon, and pushed on over the mountain, attacked the enemy's rear guard at Laurel creek, his main body having retired from his encampment there to Dickinson's farm, three miles further south. At 12 o'clock on the same day the detachment, 1,300 instead of 1,000 strong, arrived at Cassidy's mill, on the flank and rear of the enemy, and there waited for orders while watching for the advance of Lee on the east side of the mill, and the movement of our columns over the river, as well as that of General Schenck, who, by marching all night, reached the mouth of Gauley on the morning of the 12th, and began crossing. Our column on the enemy's front, on the side of the mountain, lay on their arms from four o'clock in the afternoon of the 11th until the next morning, though its commander had ample and explicit orders. Hearing nothing from that front until late in the morning of the 12th, at 10 o'clock I despatched Captain W. F. Rainolds, topographical engineers, aide-de-camp, to ascertain what was the matter. At about 2 p. m. he found the command about half a mile south of the foot of the mountain, lying on their arms, and after inquiry as to what was the matter, rode to the front beyond our advanced skirmishers to some hastily-built breastworks, thrown up by the enemy at Dickinson's farm, opposite Miller's ferry, the day before, and found them deserted. Returning, he informed our commander, who expressed surprise, and immediately set about ordering a move. But the column only reached the enemy's deserted camp at about 11 o'clock that night, when it halted. Meanwhile the detachment at Cassidy's mill, instead of moving across to Fayetteville, only three or four miles distant, was ordered to march four miles down the stream to join the rear of this column, seven miles and a half north of Fayetteville, which it did. The enemy had retreated about midnight of the 11th, an advanced guard hearing the movement, which was not more than three miles from the main body, and reporting the same to the column headquarters as early as 2 a. m. of the 12th. This put Floyd about twenty-four hours ahead. Our troops halted here, and the commander, General Benham, sent me the following despatch, viz:

"ONE MILE FROM DICKINSON'S—11½ p. m.

"General ROSECRANS: I push forward with the chance of catching Floyd's train. Do not let me be interfered with, although he has a long start. Two great blunders, made by my two best officers, have put me twelve hours behind Floyd. I should have been only twelve hours had it not been for this. I intend to take his train. It is safe for all to come on, as I am pushing to Raleigh.

"Respectfully, &c."

On the forenoon of the 14th our advance came up with the enemy's rear guard, with which it had a smart skirmish. Meanwhile General Schenck, with his command, had followed as rapidly as possible, and, being senior in rank, was ordered on to assume the command until my arrival on that side of the river. General Schenck sent his adjutant general, Major Piatt, to the front to ascertain the condition of affairs, and sent all the subsistence he could get forward on unharnessed train animals to supply our hungry men, who were out of rations, and to give such orders as might be deemed prudent in the premises. The major met a messenger from General Benham with despatches to General Schenck, informing him that he had information which led him to believe Lee, with a considerable force, was at Bowyer's, urging General Schenck to come and meet him, and proposing that their united forces should proceed at once in that direction. But, proceeding to the front, the major ascertained that our troops were exhausted, out of rations, and in the then condition of the roads could neither be supplied nor had they much prospect of catching the enemy or his trains, which, of course, were sent in advance of his retreating forces. Moreover, a terrible snow and rain storm came on; the roads became desperate, and it was perfectly manifest that further pursuit would be much more likely to damage us than the enemy. Under these circumstances General Schenck gave orders to discontinue pursuit and return to Fayetteville, where supplies could reach him, and whence, subsequently, I ordered all troops, except General Schenck's, to return to their old positions. Thus Floyd escaped; but his column had retreated in a most demoralized condition, leaving some ammunition and camp equipage behind.

General Lee did not carry out the plan of attack he had originally proposed on the Lewisburg road, the condition of the roads between us and Mount Sewell having interposed almost insuperable obstacles; and, moreover, General Lee himself having been called about that time east under orders for Charleston, most of Lee's troops retiring from the position in front of Mount Sewell to an intrenched camp at Meadow Bluff; while Floyd's troops went to Dublin Station, on the Southwest Virginia and Tennessee railroad. Thus ended the enemy's campaign against us in Western Virginia—in defeat and failure—and the people, during the winter, established an effective civil government, which has ever since continued.

Question. Did you make the exchange of prisoners proposed by General Lee; and if not, why not?

Answer. When General Lee proposed the exchange on grounds of humanity, I declined to make it, because I saw that he desired to get these mountaineers, who knew that country, and which would immediately add so many men to his available strength, in exchange for men captured at Bull Run, which would add nothing to my strength, and, in fact, could not even serve with my command. I stated to General Lee that unless he could remedy this inequality there could be no exchange; and there was none.

It is due to history to state to the committee that the foregoing minutes of the affair at Cotton hill against Floyd have been given because interested parties have attempted, through various channels, directly and indirectly, to falsify history, and conceal misbehavior which was reported in the form of charges to the Adjutant General of the army. While preparing to make this statement my attention was directed to the "Rebellion Record," for dates which had escaped my memory, where I observed, among others, a statement on page 384, vol. III or IV, copied from the New York World, which I take occasion here to pronounce a tissue of errors and falsehoods. Soon after these closing events of the campaign here executed, I received orders to send twelve regiments to General Buell, and then repairing to Wheeling, established my headquarters there for the winter. On the 6th of December, satisfied that the condition of the roads over the Alleghanies into Western Virginia, as well as the scarcity of subsistence and horse-feed, would preclude any serious operations of the enemy against us until the opening of spring, I began quietly and secretly to assemble all the spare troops of the department in the neighborhood of the Baltimore and Ohio railroad, under cover of about 5,000 men I had posted at Romney, with the design of obtaining General McClellan's permission to take nearly all these troops, and suddenly seize, fortify and hold Winchester, whereby I should at once more effectually cover the northeastern and central parts of Western Virginia, and at the same time threatening the left of the enemy's position at Manassas, compelling him to lengthen his line of defence in front, the army of the Potomac and throw it further south. That I might more fully lay my views before the general commanding, I requested his permission to visit him at Washington, whither I proceeded about the 28th of December, and found General McClellan sick of typhoid fever. Before an interview could be had with him on the subject Stonewall Jackson, with a column of 10,000 men, began an advance in the direction of Cumberland, which threatened such serious consequences that, although ordered to send all my troops to General Lander, and to remain personally idle, I was obliged to return to Wheeling for the purpose of seeing this order executed and supplies and subsistence sent to General Lauder. But before I left I had a conversation on the subject with General Fitz J. Porter, who was regarded as the confidential adviser of General McClellan. I found that to my plan was opposed an old stereotyped idea, that it "would lead to changing the theatre of the war," and that at least a portion of what I desired to have done on the eastern boundary of my department, with nearly all my available troops, had been confided to General Lander. I directed my attention to perfecting the details for the execution of a cherished plan of seizing and occupying or destroying the Southwest Virginia and Tennessee railroad between Lynchburg and Knoxville, for which I had begun to prepare during the summer of 1861, until General Lee furnished me with other occupation. To this end I completed an experimental train of three hundred pack-mules, and by that demonstrated the fact that during winter I could transport stores from Clarksburg to Huttonsville at one-third of the cost per pound which it required to carry them in government wagons from Webster to Beverly, a distance of sixteen miles less. The great difficulty of moving through these mountainous regions, where subsistence for troops cannot be found, being in transportation, I conceived the idea of using pack-trains instead of wagons, for many reasons, among others, that they are less cumbrous, are not necessarily confined to the few wagon roads, and can carry their maximum load as well over bad places as over good roads. One of the chief difficulties in organizing pack-trains being to procure packers, I directed the quartermasters to employ one for each regiment, and the commanding officers to cause all their teamsters to be drilled thoroughly in packing. I subsequently submitted to the Secretary of War a plan of a campaign for the employment of my command during the spring and summer of 1862, based on the supposed movement of the army of the Potomac, which having been examined by him and by General McClellan, was by both those officers, in autograph letters, highly complimented. But on the 6th April, 1862, I was relieved from the command of the department by Major General John C. Frémont, and did not have the opportunity to carry it into execution. As the civil administration of a department commander is an important element of duty, in closing the statement of my campaign in Western Virginia it will be proper to say that the people of Western Virginia gave testimony to their satisfaction with my administration by a unanimous vote of thanks from both houses of the legislature, which was passed during the session of 1861–'62.

The Ohio legislature also testified its appreciation of my services in that campaign by a unanimous vote of thanks.

Having turned over the command of the department to General Frémont, in obedience to orders, I repaired to Washington and reported to the Secretary of War, who reiterated his compliments on the plan of campaign I had proposed, and expressed his regret at not being able to confide to me its execution. On the evening after my arrival the Secretary sent for me to come to his office, and informed me that he desired to send me in search of Blencker's division, wrote a letter of instructions to that effect, and also directed me to visit the headquarters of General Banks and confer with him, reporting progress from each telegraph station to the War Department. I mention this as a circumstance of significance in what follows. I left the next morning for Harper's Ferry, and reached Winchester the same evening, despatching messengers from two or three points on my route in search of General Blencker's division. At Winchester I learned that General Blencker, having arrived at Berry's ferry, in attempting to cross his men by means of the old ferry-boat, had, unfortunately, by its careening and sinking, lost some thirty-five men. I immediately wrote, informing him of my orders and directing him to march to Snicker's ferry, lower down on the Shenandoah, where we had a flying bridge, and cross there. I arrived at Woodstock the evening of the 18th April, and informed General Banks of my mission. As my instructions did not indicate any subject for conference, the general and myself concluded that it was to be *ad libitum*, and therefore took up the military situation. After considering the position and numbers of McDowell's, Banks's, and Frémont's forces, I said to General Banks, "What force has the enemy in front of you?" He replied, "Between 8,000 and 13,000." I then said, "Our entire forces under yourself, General McDowell and General Frémont are at present having no decided influence on the contest between General McClellan's forces and the rebels on the Peninsula. You are in the great valley which has always been an abundant source of rebel supplies. Your line of communication is covered by the Blue Ridge and the Shenandoah, and therefore comparatively safe. It seems to me Blencker's crossing the Shenandoah to go to General Frémont, whence he will have to return, is a waste of time. What do you think of the following: Blencker not to cross the Shenandoah, but to march to Sperryville and seize Luray gap; McDowell to advance to Culpeper. Jackson and Ewell will immediately retreat to Staunton or Rockfish and Brown's gaps. You can then advance to Harrisonburg. General Frémont can order Milroy to march from Beverly and meet his column moving from New Creek station, on the Beverly and Staunton turnpike, whence the entire command of the three departments can be put in communication and concentrated: yours and General Frémont's seizing Staunton, and making it your depot, can move on Charlotte, at which point General McDowell can join you. This will give a combined army of 46,000 men, with ample detachments—near 20,000 men—to cover your lines of communication. You will have the control of the forage and beef of the great valley, and the remainder of your supplies and your ammunition can be wagoned from Winchester. This army will be sufficient to take Gordonsville and compel the enemy to detach a large army of observation to watch your movements and fight you, or to lose the line—the defensive line of the James river and his connexion with Lynchburg. If he detach an army of observation we have accomplished our purpose, and General McClellan can beat the remainder of his forces and occupy Richmond. If he does not, you will compel him to evacuate Richmond. If he attempts to fall on you with his entire force, he could not reach Gordonsville in less than four days, which would give ample time to prepare for him; and as you will have the control of the mountain passes, and of the great valley, your army could be dislodged from it only by a long campaign. Thus all these troops, which at present weigh not a feather in the great contest, will be brought to aid in bringing it to a successful conclusion."

General Banks having approved this plan, which it was thought proper to lay before his division commanders, I left the next morning for Strasburg, whence I telegraphed it in cipher to the Secretary of War, stating that General Banks had requested me to say it met his entire approbation. To carry it out it was necessary that Blencker's orders to cross the Shenandoah should be promptly revoked. Receiving no order from the Secretary of War, Blencker's movement *was* continued across the Shenandoah. This command was found in the most wretched condition—unfed, unclothed, unshod and unpaid—between 800 and 1,000 men barefooted, the cavalry and artillery horses unshod, and the whole command requiring a new outfit to prepare it for a campaign. Its condition was promptly reported to the War Department, and orders were given to forward the supplies; but a terrible flood in the Potomac, which swept away the Harper's Ferry bridge and prevented the crossing of the river for eight days, delayed their arrival. When finally prepared, I conducted them to General Frémont, and forthwith returned to Washington, about the 16th of May, where I received orders to join General Halleck, to whom I hastened, hoping to arrive in time for the great battle, then thought to be impending in front of Corinth. I arrived at his headquarters on the 22d May, and on the 23d was directed to report to General Pope, who was then expecting General Jeff. Davis and General Asboth's commands from Pea Ridge. They arrived, were consolidated into divisions, and placed under my orders. On the 26th and 27th I was assigned to the command of Paine's and Stanley's divisions of the troops under General Pope, which were known as the army of the Mississippi. At 1 o'clock on the morning of the 28th I was called to General Pope's headquarters, who informed me that he had just received a despatch from General Halleck, stating that the enemy was massing heavily on our left, and would probably attack us in the morning. He therefore desired that I should go to the front and prepare, which I did. At 4 o'clock a. m. the discharge of a solitary heavy gun from the direction of Corinth seemed to announce the beginning of the contest, but a succession of reports soon followed, which satisfied me the enemy were blowing up their magazines. I immediately ordered General Stanley to send two regiments towards Corinth by the road in his front, General Paine to do the same on his, and despatched word to General Pope to this effect. Soon came the announcement from Paine's front of the occupation by our troops of a fort belonging to the enemy, with which we had a fierce cannonade the day before. Both these advances from my command reached Corinth about a quarter past 7 o'clock, where I soon after joined them. I found the place had been evacuated during the night, the enemy having destroyed or carried away most of his ammunition and provisions, but leaving a considerable quantity of old tentage and wagons. At 9 o'clock I received orders to return my command to camp for rations, and then immediately to start in pursuit of the enemy on the Danville road. By 11 o'clock that night the head of my column halted at the Tuscumbia, where our cavalry had been checked by the enemy's rear guard. The Tuscumbia at this point ran through a low swampy bottom, in a narrow muddy channel, rendering the passage across it very difficult except at the bridge, which they had burnt.

The next morning General Pope arrived to supervise the operations of forcing a passage, which the enemy still held, and sent me with General McPherson to reconnoitre the country for a camp-ground, in obedience, as he said, to the orders of General Halleck, who had directed him to pursue until he was satisfied he could do the enemy no further damage, and then returning go into camp in that vicinity. On my return, about 3 o'clock p. m., a fierce artillery and musketry fire at the Tuscumbia startled General Pope's headquarters. The general directed me to go to the front and force the passage. I arrived there just before sunset, and having reconnoitred the ground, made my arrangements to pass by a surprise during the night. But the enemy having delayed us twenty-four hours quietly decamped, and by daylight our troops were rebuilding the bridge, which was ready for the crossing of our artillery before 12 o'clock m. My infantry reached Rienzi the same evening. Our cavalry pushed on to Booneville, whence General Gordon Granger despatched me before daylight that the enemy was still retreating, and shortly afterwards that he had taken possession of Booneville, with a number of prisoners, and that the enemy had crossed Twenty Mile creek, the bridge over which they were destroying. I pushed on with my command to Booneville, and thence made reconnoissances to the front at several points over a front of twelve miles, finding the enemy in force at each point, which results I reported to General Pope on his arrival the next morning, where he was joined by General Buell, whose command (the army of the Ohio) arrived during the afternoon and night and took position on our right, towards Blackland. In this position we lay until the 11th of June, when General Buell marched to Alabama and Tennessee, and we returned to camp Clear Creek, six miles below Corinth, where we arrived on the 12th or 13th of June.

General Pope receiving a leave of absence, the command of the army of the Mississippi devolved on me, as the next in rank, whereupon I directed General Sheridan, with a brigade of cavalry, to take post at Booneville, at which point we had previously a battalion. A day or two after his arrival the rebel General Chalmers, with eleven regiments and parts of regiments of cavalry, attacked him ; but such was the vigor and energy with which Sheridan handled his troops, one regiment of which was armed with revolving rifles, that the enemy were defeated, and this defeat gave our cavalry, consisting of only four regiments, the mastery of country within the scope of its travel from that time forth, and constituted an epoch in its history in that region.

The seven days' fight before Richmond caused General Halleck to be ordered to Washington, and General Pope to be in command of the army in Virginia. I then became permanent commander of the army of the Mississippi, which remained in camp some weeks, during which I instituted the plan of constructing "*information maps.*" This consisted in making a skeleton map from the best map to be had of the country, and placing upon it the results of *inquiries* and *the information* obtained from scouts, spies, citizens, and all other sources. This map was then photographed and distributed among our subordinate commanders, with instructions to complete and correct it, as well as for use in directing their operations ; and the more surely to accomplish this, each brigade was to detail an officer for topographical duty. This, I believe, originated that system, which was subsequently carried to great perfection in the army of the Cumberland, and has been one of the most useful agencies in the handling of large bodies of troops in countries comparatively unknown to us, and of which no accurate maps had been made.

About the 20th of August I received orders to send two divisions of my command to Tennessee to re-enforce General Buell. Paine's, (afterwards Palmer's and Davis's,) commanded by General Mitchell, were ordered ; the latter crossing the Tennessee at Eastport—the former at Tuscumbia. Stanley's division moved from camp Clear Creek to protect the line of the railroad between Corinth and Tuscumbia, and the operation of crossing.

While I was at Tuscumbia a telegram reached me from General Grant, that the rebels appeared to be moving north ; that a heavy cavalry force had attacked Bolivar and cut the line of the railroad between that and Jackson. The crossing of Paine's division now being completed, Stanley was directed to return at once to Iuka, where out of the refugee contrabands I organized a detachment of colored engineer troops into platoons of twenties and companies of a hundred, each *hiring* officers. Things were now beginning to wear a threatening aspect. It was evident, by the enemy's movements, that they were about to commence an offensive campaign. I accordingly returned from Iuka to my old encampment at Clear creek, leaving a rear guard to protect the sending of the stores which had been brought up from Eastport to Corinth. Colonel R. C. Murphy, 8th Wisconsin, who was charged with this duty, learning that the rebels were moving on Iuka, hastily abandoned the place, which was occupied by the enemy's cavalry, followed soon after by General Price's entire command. The precipitancy of Colonel Murphy's movements left it a matter of doubt whether the enemy's infantry occupied the place. A reconnoissance in force was made on it by Colonel (now Major General) Mower, who drove in the enemy's pickets on his main force in line of battle at Iuka, and settled the question of the enemy's presence there with infantry, cavalry, and artillery; which information having been sent to General Grant, the department commander, he determined to attack, ordered General Ord to move to Burnsville, and brought all the spare troops under Ross from Bolivar to re-enforce him.

Burnsville is a small town, seven and a half miles west of Iuka, on the Memphis and Charleston road near its crossing over Yellow creek. General Grant thought my command should join General Ord's, and that, while the latter moved towards Iuka on the north, mine should take the south side of the railroad. I represented to him that as our chances of success lay in the celerity of our movements, and as one of my divisions was at Jacinto, nine miles south of Burnsville, on the Tuscumbia road, and as the country along the railroad on the south side, full of morasses and covered with brush, would be difficult to operate in, it would probably be better that, with Stanley's division, I should join Hamilton's at Jacinto, and, moving with the two by the Tuscumbia road, should get possession of the rebels' line of retreat, south of Iuka, by seizing and holding both the Fulton and Jacinto roads, which at Iuka were only a mile and a half apart, and the ground there being highly favorable for the operation, while General Ord's entire force should attack Price in front, and thus put him completely in our power. To this General Grant assented, and on the 18th Stanley's division was concentrated at Jacinto, which point it reached at 9 o'clock p. m., ready to bivouac. Immediately on my arrival there I established a line of courier posts to General Grant's headquarters at Burnsville, to which point he had gone at 12 o'clock on the 18th, advising him of our arrival and of the establishment of the line of courier posts. I also notified him that the troops being somewhat fatigued, and the distance to Iuka being nineteen and a half miles, we would probably not reach that place the next day before 2½ o'clock, but certainly would not be later than 4½ p. m. At 3 o'clock next morning the troops were called up, and began to move as soon thereafter as possible, taking nothing but ammunition, ambulances, and the rations in their haversacks. At seven in the morning I despatched General Grant that the troops were off in good spirits, the advance at least six miles on its way, and that we should undoubtedly arrive at Iuka as early as 4 o'clock p. m. He was also informed that a line of courier posts would be continued every two or three miles, to connect my headquarters with his, so as to afford certain and rapid intercommunication. At 12 o'clock the head of Hamilton's column reached the forks of the Iuka and Tuscumbia roads, seven and a half miles from Iuka, having skirmished with the enemy's cavalry for the last two miles, when his division advanced, driving the enemy's skirmishers all before him. I here ascertained that the Fulton road crossed the Tuscumbia four and a half miles east of this point, and that there were no cross-roads between it and that leading hence to Iuka, by which columns advancing on them separately could certainly and safely communicate with each other, and also that the enemy's strength was believed to be between 20,000 and 30,000 strong. I therefore determined that it would be unsafe to move Stanley's division up the Fulton road, whereby I should divide my command, consisting of only four brigades, into two columns, not within supporting distance of each other, and despatched General Grant our progress, condition, and this my determination, with the reasons therefor. Here General Grant's aids, Colonels Lagon and Dickey, joined me; asked the news; inquired if I believed the rebels were in Iuka in force—if I thought they would fight—if I intended to attack, and if I did not apprehend that unless we hurried up they would retreat. I informed them that our information warranted the belief that the enemy were in force and would fight; that, as a matter of course, I should attack on my arrival, but that it was now near 1 o'clock; that we were within seven miles of Iuka, *and ought to hear the guns of the other column*, and I was surprised that we did not. Colonel Lagon suggested that "perhaps General Grant expected me to attack first;" to which I replied that such was not the understanding, and, moreover, that it would be very bad policy to allow the enemy's attention to be first attracted towards his line of communication, to seize and secure which was the object of my movement; that Hamilton's division was already pushing up—he could hear the firing of the skirmishers in the distance—and Stanley's division would follow promptly. Receiving word that the way was open for Stanley's division, we left this point, Colonels Lagon and Dickey accompanying us to the front, where we arrived at about 4 o'clock, and the battle opened on a rough brushy point, near the top of which was the coveted cross-road leading over to the Fulton road, of which we wished to gain possession. Our troops moved rapidly into line, lying down until the enemy's position could be ascertained. They opened on us in a few minutes with grape and canister. From that time till nightfall the battle raged furiously. The enemy poured down upon us in overwhelming numbers. They could be seen moving across the fields from the railroad near the Iuka and Burnsville road. Nothing in that quarter appeared to attract their attention. Hamilton's division barely held its ground, sometimes gaining and sometimes losing a little. Mower's brigade of Stanley's division was ordered in on the right of Hamilton's, while Fuller's was held in reserve. Just after sunset the enemy came down in a terrific attack on Mower, but was driven back. A second and still more powerful assault was made. The conflict was short but terrible. In half an hour their column was repulsed, after every round of ammunition had been expended by Mower's men. Our troops, which had ceased fighting, lay down on the ground, the enemy within three hundred yards of us. Out of sixteen, eleven of our regiments had been in action. There was no news from General Grant. The enemy had fought us with superior numbers. What next was to be done? Quietly placing a brigade in the front line, and withdrawing Hamilton's division to replenish their ammunition and take position in reserve, I despatched General Grant an account of the conflict and present condition of affairs, and at the same time sent a reconnoitring party to our right to ascertain the mode of crossing the swampy ground which skirted the field to the east of us, and to examine the heights beyond with a view to their occupation with our artillery, which, owing to the nature of the ground, could not be brought into action with effect. By 11½ p. m. these dispositions were made. Going frequently to the front I heard the enemy cutting, chopping, driving stakes, halting and aligning their men. I also heard the movement of the train in the distance towards the southeast, and artillery moving apparently along the very heights I desired to occupy, and from which my reconnoitring party had not returned. This gave me no little uneasiness. Going to the front at 3 a. m. I heard the voices of drivers of artillery or ambulance trains, evidently anxious and in haste, and returning, gave orders that our troops should be called and have their breakfast, so as to move at daylight, which was done, Stanley's division leading. As our skirmishers advanced the enemy fled. Their dead and wounded were lying on the ground in front of us. Our troops pushed forward, and the rebels retired towards Iuka, into which Stanley soon sent a shot, causing the rebels there to move hastily. What we at first suspected *might* be a change of position we now became satisfied was a retreat. All our cavalry, a regiment and a half, were immediately ordered to move in on the flank of the Fulton road, and Stanley's division to follow with all possible despatch. Hamilton's, instead of moving up to Iuka, was ordered to face about, march back to the forks of the road, and, taking the Tuscumbia road, if possible, to fall on the enemy's flank. These dispositions concluded, and our troops having passed through Iuka, I was suddenly startled by the sound of music, and looking, beheld the head of General Grant's column entering the place. No explanation was then or subsequently made of the cause which prevented that column from attacking the enemy in front the day before, save that they did not hear our guns. General Grant directed a brigade of his troops to occupy Iuka, and take care of the hospital and public property, and that I should pursue the enemy as far as I thought it likely to result in any benefit to us or injury to them; and we accordingly pushed them till nightfall, when, overworked with the last two days' and nights' marching and fighting, our troops halted for the night; satisfied that the enemy, by marching all night, would probably reach Bay Springs, twenty-five miles south of the Tuscumbia road, by next morning, and that they would thence move as rapidly as possible to the Mobile and Ohio road, near Tupelo, all of which proved true. And our rations being exhausted, and the country towards Bay Springs destitute, I was satisfied that further pursuit with our infantry would be utterly unavailing, and directed the cavalry to follow the enemy, and my command to return the next day to Jacinto, advising General Grant, who approved the movement.

On this day, the 20th of September, I received my appointment as major general of volunteers. On the 23d, General Grant, having been made department commander, confided to me the command of the district of Corinth, with my headquarters at that place, to which I immediately repaired, and where I found McKean's and Davies's divisions. During the summer I had made it a point, whenever I visited General Grant's headquarters, to suggest that the great line of fortifications ordered by General Halleck, about a mile and a half in front of Corinth, in the construction of which our troops were employed during the hot weather, was utterly useless to our small command, and urged the construction of a line in the immediate vicinity of Corinth, which could be defended by a comparatively small force, to cover our depots, to which suggestion General Grant had finally acceded, giving Captain Prime orders at once to begin it. To the completion of this line I directed my attention, increasing the number of my contraband engineer laborers, who, under the efficient command of Captain (now Colonel) Gaw, United States colored volunteers, repaired all the bridges and roads in the vicinity of the town, and felled the timber in front of the new line of intrenchments we had begun, looking westward. Rumors soon reached me that the enemy, under Van Dorn, whom Price had joined with his discomfited command, were about to make a grand campaign to drive us out of Mississippi, western Tennessee, and Kentucky, and thus co-operate with Bragg's movement into Kentucky, in seizing, as they intended, the line of the Ohio road. I accordingly ordered the troops from Jacinto to the vicinity of Corinth, and they had but just arrived when these rumors ripened into certainty by positive information that the enemy had reached Ripley, half way between the Mobile and Ohio and the Mississippi Central roads, where they were encamped, forty thousand strong. This information was communicated to General Grant.

On the 1st of October the head of the enemy's column made its appearance at Pocahontas, twenty miles west of Corinth, on the Memphis and Charleston road, where they seized Davis's bridge, across the Hatchie. From this point they could move to Bolivar, and thence to Jackson, seventy miles north of Corinth, or could strike the railroad from Corinth to Jackson, at Purdy or Bethel, about thirty miles north of Corinth. As Jackson was the headquarters of the department and the depot for our ordnance stores, and the garrisons of Jackson and Bolivar were neither of them equal to that at Corinth, which I knew had a reputation with the enemy of being fortified, I thought it was their interest to move at once on Bolivar and Jackson, and expected only a demonstration on Corinth, which I prepared to meet, punish, and pursue. This same preparation would equally secure us if their main attack should be Corinth. Instead of a demonstration on us, it proved a real attack. On the night of the 2d the head of the enemy's column drove our advance from Chewalla, ten miles distant, and followed it. In the morning, at 1 o'clock, orders were despatched to our troops to move at 3 a. m. to their positions, as indicated in the orders, on the south and west of Corinth, which they reached shortly after daylight. The enemy on the Chewalla road early began to pursue our troops, who were ordered to fall back slowly and steadily. All the division commanders were informed that it was desirable they should hold against the enemy's pressure until he had fully developed himself, in a favorable position for an offensive movement on our part. The enemy pushed steadily in, and by 11 o'clock it became apparent that, instead of a feint, the enemy was in full force. About 3 o'clock in the afternoon he had been pressed mainly into the wooded angle between Memphis and Charleston and the Corinth and Jackson railroads, and had advanced within range of the defensive line under construction. The opportune moment appeared now at hand, and I directed General Hamilton, whose division was on our right, beyond the range of the enemy's operations, to face to the westward, and move on to the enemy's flank and rear. Colonel Ducat, who carried the order and a sketch showing the mode of the movement, returned from Hamilton's headquarters, a mile and a half distant, stating that the general could not understand without further explanation. This led to such a delay that it was 5 o'clock before his division was fairly in movement on the enemy. But no sooner had the movement begun to develop itself than its effect became most obvious on the front of General Davies's division, which had been heavily pressed, and on which the enemy immediately relaxed his efforts, and appeared to be greatly disturbed, attempting to make dispositions to meet our troops, the left brigade of which, under Sullivan, about dusk became sharply engaged with them. It was now too late to carry out the operations. The day's fighting had developed the fact that we were vastly outnumbered. I determined on a readjustment of our lines for a final battle, making use of what was available in the new line of defence and dispositions to prevent the enemy from turning our right. This was accomplished by 3 a. m. of the 4th. Between 3½ and 4 o'clock the enemy opened his batteries furiously from a point in front of battery Robinett, but in the course of an hour he was silenced and driven from his position. Our troops, thus aroused from their brief rest, which could scarcely be called slumber, nerved themselves for the coming fight, the brunt of which came on about 10 o'clock, when the enemy charging our right centre, Davies's division gave way, but speedily rallied, and with the aid of Hamilton's division and a cross-fire from battery Robinett, poured in a fire so destructive that the enemy were thrown into confusion and finally driven from this part of the field; at the same time he also charged battery Robinett, but was thoroughly repulsed, after two or three efforts, and retired to the woods. With our inferior numbers of exhausted troops we stood on the defensive, sending skirmishers to the front and expecting another charge from the enemy, till about 3 o'clock p. m., when, finding that their skirmishers yielded to ours, we began to push them, and by 4 o'clock became satisfied that they intended to retire from our immediate front; but so superior was their strength that I could not believe they would altogether abandon the operation. By 6 p. m. our skirmishers had pushed theirs back five miles, but our troops, having now been marching and fighting for nearly two days and nights, and the weather being excessively hot, were nearly exhausted. I rode over the field and explained to them, in person, that the enemy had received a bloody repulse; that, except those on the skirmish line, all should at once lie down to rest, while rations for five days were being issued to them, and at the earliest hour of morning we would start in pursuit. Just before sunset McPherson arrived with five fresh regiments, sent down by General Grant to re-enforce us. The following orders were given for the pursuit:

"HEADQUARTERS ARMY OF THE MISSISSIPPI,
"*3d Division, District of West Tennessee, Corinth, October* 4, 1862.

"GENERAL: The general commanding directs that you furnish your command with three days' rations and one hundred rounds of ammunition. Let your animals be well watered and supplied with forage or turned out to graze.

"Be prepared to move at daylight.

"H. G. KENNETT,
"*Lieutenant Colonel and Chief of Staff.*

"Brigadier General MCPHERSON."

Brigadier Generals McKean, Davies, Hamilton, and Stanley furnished with copies of above.

Under this order McPherson moved the next morning and pushed the enemy, with whose rear guard he soon came up and began fighting, but the roughness of the country and narrowness of the roads made progress slow; the whole command, however, pressed up closely to our advance. The enemy attempted to delay our advance by flag of truce borne by a burial party of several hundred men. McPherson directed this party to stand aside and wait orders, on the ground that, as fighting was going on, it could not be suspended without direct orders from me. I at once despatched that the burial party should remain until further orders, and to inform General Van Dorn that his wounded would be cared for and his dead buried as humanity and the rules of war required.

Night found McPherson at a distance of fifteen miles from Corinth, where he had a skirmish with the enemy about sunset, on the ascent to Davis's hill. At 3 o'clock on the next morning I visited his front, directed him to push the enemy as soon as it was light, and returned to visit the divisions along the road, and to give direction for the return of one of the division trains, which, by misunderstanding, had accompanied it, and was much in the way. About 7 o'clock a staff officer from the front came back bearing a rebel stand of colors, and informed me that the enemy's attempt to force the passage of the Hatchie at Davis's bridge had been completely foiled by General Ord. Despatches from General Grant and General Ord also reached me to the same effect. These facts communicated to our troops filled them with enthusiasm, and they pushed on after the enemy, who had crossed the Hatchie twelve miles south of Davis's bridge, at Crum's mill, and afterwards fired the mill and bridge. Our advance, on their arrival, began bridging the place, which, by the use of the dam, was soon accomplished, and McPherson crossed; the other troops followed as closely as possible. Ordering 30,000 rations to Chewalla, and eighty wagon-loads in the direction of Ripley, covered by Hamilton's division, which, to save time, was ordered to move south on the Blackland road east of the Hatchie, till he reached the Ripley and Rienzi road, I despatched General Grant the condition of affairs, and sent, also, a despatch to General Hurlbut, at Davis's bridge, informing him of the enemy's condition, and requesting him to inform General Sherman what had happened. That night we pushed our infantry within three miles of Ripley. The enemy was exhausted; his cavalry, eighteen regiments strong, gave way everywhere to our four little regiments. Numbers of deserters and stragglers were scattered through the woods in all directions, and were constantly being picked up by our men. Our cavalry went into Ripley, while the enemy's infantry laid down within cannon-shot of it on the south, without molesting it. These facts, and many others, showing that the enemy considered himself thoroughly whipped, satisfied me he was in our power unless he received large re-enforcements, which could only come from Bragg, or the Atlantic seaboard. Mississippi was in our hands. The enemy had concentrated all his available force for an offensive movement, had been thoroughly beaten at Corinth, and had then retreated, blowing up his ammunition wagons and caissons, their men throwing away their camp and garrison equipage in the flight. The weather was cool; the roads were dry, and likely to be so for a month to come. Corn was ripe, and, as yet, untouched. We had three millions of rations in Corinth, and ammunition for six months. There was but one bridge injured on the Mobile and Ohio road, and it could be put in running order by a regiment in half a day. The enemy were so alarmed, when Hamilton sent a reconnoissance to Blackland, they vacated Tupalo, burning even the bacon which they could not take away on the first train. I had eighty wagon-loads of assorted rations which had reached me that night at Ripley, and had ordered the thirty thousand from Chewalla to Hurlbut.

Impressed with these views, on receipt of General Grant's despatch of 8.30 p. m., October 7, at Jonesboro, declining to let Hurlbut move with me in the pursuit because we were not strong enough, I despatched him as follows:

"HEADQUARTERS, JONESBORO, MISS.,
"*October* 7, 1862—midnight.

"Major General GRANT,
"*Jackson, Tennessee:*

"Yours, 8.30 p. m., received. Our troops occupy Ripley. I most deeply dissent from your views as to the policy of pursuit. We have defeated, routed, and demoralized the army which held the lower Mississippi valley. We have the two railroads leading south to the Gulf, through the most populous parts of this State, into which we can now pursue them by the Mississippi Central, or Mobile and Ohio road. The effect of returning to our old position will be to give them up the only corn they have in the country west of Alabama, including Tuscumbia valley, and to permit them to recruit their forces, advance and re-occupy their old ground, reducing us to the occupation of a defensive position, barren and worthless, on a long front, of which they can harass us until bad weather precludes any effectual advance except along the railroads, where time, fortifications, and rolling stock will render them superior to us.

"Our force, including what can be spared with Hurlbut, will garrison Corinth and Jackson, and enable us to push them. Our advance will cover even Holly Springs, which will be ours when we want it. All that is needful is, to combine, push, and whip them. We have whipped and should now push to the wall all the forces in Mississippi, and capture the rolling stock of the railroads west of the Alabama and Mobile. Bragg's army alone could repair the damage we have it in our power to do them. But I beseech you to bend everything to push them while they are broken, weary, hungry, and ill supplied. Draw everything from Memphis to help move on Holly Springs. Let us concentrate and appeal to the governors of the States to rush down some twenty or thirty new regiments to hold in our rear, and we can make a triumph of our start.

"Respectfully and truly,

"W. A. ROSECRANS,
"*Major General.*"

In reply to this I received an order from the general commanding, directing me to desist from pursuit, and return, with my command, cautiously, but promptly, to Corinth, which I promptly acknowledged and obeyed, though I stated that I most deeply dissented from the policy, for reasons given in my despatch from Jonesboro. And, to carry out his orders to the letter my movements were conducted with such care and secrecy that the enemy did not know for a week what we had been doing, or that we had retreated to Corinth.

Thus terminated the enemy's campaign against us between the Tennessee and Mississippi. In it we fought very superior numbers, as will appear from my official report, wherein the provost marshal's list shows we had taken prisoners from fifty-three regiments of infantry, eighteen regiments of cavalry, and sixteen batteries of artillery. Our own force in the fight was about 15,700 infantry and artillery, and about 2,500 effective cavalry.

My official report of the battle of Corinth, which I hereby make a part of my testimony, gives the details of the engagement.

Nine days after I returned from the pursuit of Price I was relieved from the command of the army of the Mississippi, and directed to report at Cincinnati for orders, where I found a despatch from the general-in-chief directing me to proceed to the headquarters of Major General Buell, and, showing that order to him, take command of his army. Without inquiring the reasons for this unusual mode of relieving an officer from so important a command, I proceeded to execute the order, and on the 27th of October, 1862, assumed command of the army of the Ohio, and of the department of the Cumberland, which was to be all of Tennessee east of the Tennessee river.

I proceeded to Bowling Green, in the vicinity of which all the army had been ordered to concentrate, except three divisions which had pursued Bragg into the Cumberland mountains, and which, under Crittenden, halted at Glasgow. Instituting an inspection, and finding that the troops required shoes and clothing, orders were promptly given to supply them, and further movement delayed until that was accomplished. It was now about the 1st of November. Many of the troops, raw regiments suddenly thrown into the field, had suffered much in health and strength from losses incident to overwork and unaccustomed exposure. The cavalry were badly armed, imperfectly equipped, and, as a body, without experience or *esprit de corps*, having hitherto, for want of confidence in them, been employed chiefly in picket, vidette, and escort duty, and regarded as too weak to play any important part in an offensive campaign. The military situation was as follows: Bragg, after the battle of Perryville, retreated to Knoxville, his army suffering indeed from the hardships of the march and the weather and from the demoralization incident to the failure to realize their hopes of remaining in Kentucky, but still formidable.

Our garrison at Nashville, beleaguered by Forrest's cavalry, overwhelmingly superior in numbers to ours, and supported by Breckinridge's command of infantry with six batteries of artillery, were reduced to stinted rations, and had stripped the country within their control of its forage. The railroad between Bowling Green and Nashville was badly broken. Both the tunnels, the roofs of which had been supported by piles of cord-wood lying on the tops of trestles, by the burning of this wood, had been badly damaged and caved in nearly throughout the entire length. The entire transportation belonging to the army, on inspection, was found to be about sufficient, with good roads, to supply subsistence for a distance, at the utmost, of forty or fifty miles from its depots. What was to be done? General Halleck, in a long letter of instructions, directed me to march to East Tennessee, a distance of over two hundred and forty miles, over mountains, traversed by but few roads, far separated from each other, and often rough, narrow, and difficult, near the beginning of the inclement season of the year, the country being substantially bare of forage and subsistence along the road and East Tennessee itself having been stripped by the rebel army of most of its forage and subsistence, either for transport by rail to Virginia, or in supplying Bragg's and Buckner's troops with a cavalry force. Moreover, could we have transported our army immediately into East Tennessee, and had our trains and the roads been sufficient to transport its supplies, our cavalry was too weak in numbers to protect these trains and keep open our communications. These, moreover, would have left open the route with a good railroad from Chattanooga to Nashville, and thence on into Kentucky. Under these circumstances I deemed the project of marching into East Tennessee impracticable, and accordingly determined to move at once to Nashville, relieve our garrison there, repair the railroad, and establish and replenish a good depot of supplies at that point, whence, moreover, the route for an advance to East Tennessee would be better than from Bowling Green. Accordingly, McCook, with three divisions, reached Nashville on the 7th of November; Thomas followed, taking possession of the line of railroad from Bowling Green to Gallatin, and charged to have it put promptly in repair, while Crittenden, with three divisions, moved from Glasgow, by Scottsville, across the Cumberland, to Lebanon, Tennessee. I immediately put to work all the means of transportation at our disposal to haul supplies from Mitchellsville to Nashville while the road was being repaired, and by the 26th of November had succeeded in getting five day's supplies in advance for our command, and bringing down ammunition enough to put all our troops, including the Nashville garrison, in fighting condition. I assembled the cavalry within the infantry lines in a mass, appointed Major General Stanley its commander, and, having inspected, informed them it was my intention to procure them first-class arms, and then to expect from them fighting worthy of our arms and country; and to infuse into them the cavalry spirit, I arranged to give them an opportunity for combat where evident superiority would insure their success, and had the pleasure soon to witness the happiest results. I communicated to the general-in-chief the facts just stated; but before we could get the railroad repaired, the first train over which came through on the 27th of November, I received an urgent letter pressing me to move forward. In reply, I explained that it must be evident to him an advance at that time offered us no advantages, because, with our present means of transportation, we could do very little more than to subsist our troops at Nashville, distant one hundred and eighty-three miles from our base at Louisville; that to advance would be to expose Nashville and what little we had there, as well as our line of communication, to interruption from the enemy's superior cavalry, and thus put us on limited supplies; that the enemy was advancing towards Nashville—Bragg with all his army and reported re-enforcements from Longstreet—and that every mile these rebels travelled towards us, before reaching the point of conflict, was to us an advantage and to them a disadvantage; and since our true objective, the enemy's army, was approaching us, therefore, while we were obliged to wait the completion of the railroad, we need not regret it, since it was increasing our chances of success. From the 27th of November to the 25th of December the Louisville and Nashville road pushed down all the supplies which it could carry in the then condition of its equipment and want of water-tanks. The general replied that there were urgent political reasons for my advance, and that he had been requested by the President to designate my successor. To this I replied, substantially restating the necessities of our situation, and reiterating my opinion that the country was gaining by the course I was pursuing; that my appointment to that command having been made without any solicitation from me or my friends, if the President continued to have confidence in the propriety of the selection he must permit me to use my judgment, and be responsible for the results; but if he entertained doubts, he ought at once to appoint a commander in whom he could confide, for the good of the service and of the country, without delay. This seemed satisfactory, for I received no further communication on the subject.

As soon as we had twenty days' rations in advance in Nashville, I prepared to move on the enemy, who, through representations which I had caused to be made, had been induced to believe we dare not advance from Nashville, and had gone into a slightly intrenched camp at Murfreesboro with his main force, while Hardee's corps took post at Triune, 17 miles west of Murfreesboro, from whence, by the aid of his cavalry, he could control all the roads leading south from Nashville, and keep and hold all the foraging country outside of our infantry lines from us, unless we gathered it by a formidable foraging party, seldom, if ever, less than a brigade.

I had another object in persuading the enemy I did not intend to advance until spring, which was to induce him to send off a portion of his cavalry. In this I was successful. Morgan was sent to Kentucky to operate on my communications, and Forrest went to West Tennessee to operate on General Grant's, who was on the march by land to Vicksburg.

Taking advantage of this large diminution of their cavalry force, on the 26th of December the army began to move. The outline plans of the advance and of the resulting battle of Stone river are briefly these:

Crittenden's corps to advance by the Murfreesboro turnpike to Lavergne; McCook's, on the Nolansville turnpike, to Nolansville, and take the pass there from Hardee, whose corps held it; Thomas to move by the Franklin turnpike, and cross to Nolansville, threatening Hardee's flank, which, with McCook's movement, it was presumed would dislodge and cause Hardee to join the main rebel force, which we expected to fight us either at Stewart's creek or in front of Murfreesboro.

To provide for the former case, Thomas was to cross from Nolansville to Stewart's creek and meet Crittenden there; McCook was to move towards Murfreesboro by the Wilkinson turnpike; while Thomas and Crittenden took the main turnpike towards Murfreesboro.

Our movements were successful on the night of the 30th, after skirmishing with the enemy's advance for six or seven miles on each road on the 29th and all day on the 30th. At the close of that day we were all in position on the enemy's front, and had determined the general distribution of his troops.

The plan of the battle was, that our right should hold its position; Thomas, the centre, with a division in reserve; and Crittenden, with two divisions, should cross Stone river, beat Breckinridge, and from his position enfilade or take in reverse the enemy's centre and left, on which Thomas would press with crushing weight, and thus roll up his forces on the left, which would leave them but little chance of escaping total destruction. For details I refer to my official report, which I hereby make a part of this testimony.

The official report states why, after the pursuit, the army was halted at Murfreesboro instead of being pushed further into the interior of the country. The committee's attention may, perhaps, well be directed to the following facts bearing on the question of an advance at that time beyond Murfreesboro: Before the railroad could be opened from Nashville our troops were obliged to live on short rations, and that the transportation, in the desperate condition of the roads, was not sufficient fully to supply them. That, in addition to the enemy's superior numbers of cavalry, he had been re-enforced, by General Van Dorn, with six or seven thousand cavalry from Mississippi. With such a force it would have been impossible for us to have maintained our communications at any distance materially greater from our depots than Murfreesboro.

It will also appear from that report, and from the testimony of others, that such is the nature of the soil from Murfreesboro south to the Tennessee river that in winter grand movements are next to impossible.

Had we possessed a superior cavalry, with which to have beaten the enemy's, and afterwards to have threatened his communications and assured the citizens of Tennessee of our protection to our friends and condign punishment to our enemies, we could undoubtedly have expelled Bragg from Middle Tennessee. Fully conscious of this, I made every effort to have the cavalry well mounted and well armed, and the urgency of my solicitation was so great that I incurred the displeasure of the War Department, which was manifested, as will appear, in the copies of correspondence which is herewith submitted and made a part of my testimony.

During the winter, with our utmost endeavor, it became utterly impossible to get an adequate supply of long forage, the consequence being that our team and cavalry horses suffered badly, and nearly one-half of our cavalry-men were dismounted. When spring arrived, and the roads had become settled, a movement, which the country expected, and which would have given the officers and men of our command, including myself, pleasure and promised renown, was proposed. I felt it my duty to sacrifice all personal gratification, and even to fall in the estimation, temporarily, of the country and friends who had high hopes and expectations of the army of the Cumberland, to secure General Grant, in his operations before Vicksburg, from the consequences of compelling Bragg to retire, when it would not be possible for us so to pursue as to prevent him from re-enforcing Johnston, whose relative numbers to our troops under General Grant was deemed more formidable than I subsequently learned it to have been. The confidence of the country in the army of the Cumberland seems to have reconciled it to a delay, the cause for which the mass of its citizens could not understand.

The propriety of this delay, if not its necessity, will appear from the copies of my letters to the War Department and general-in-chief, herewith submitted and made part of my testimony.

I may add that General Burnside's co-operation promised by the general-in-chief, and very desirable, failed us. The magnitude of the movement across the barren mountains, and the destitution of the country into which we would debouch, made it evident that we could not, with any reasonable hope of success, attempt to seize Chattanooga and East Tennessee until new corn came in to furnish forage for at least cavalry and artillery horses, and until the railroad could be completed to the Tennessee river. Such being the case, it is evident that since we could not successfully pursue the enemy into Georgia, were we to compel him to retire from Middle Tennessee, it was our interest, and offered us the greatest chances of safety against any use the enemy might in that case make of his troops against General Grant, to keep him as far away from the general, and as near to us, as possible; and, besides, it would increase our chances of striking him a damaging blow when the time came. The motives General Bragg had for remaining in Middle Tennessee, in our immediate front, Shelbyville and Tullahoma, were most influential. He had many Tennessee troops who did not desire to quit the State; he was in a better country for forage and subsistence than would be the country in the rear of his position at Chattanooga; he had the prestige of commanding a great advance, and the natural desire of a commander to retain his prestige and the troops who gave him confidence and the means of success; he was, moreover, flattering himself that he was doing a most useful work in preventing re-enforcements from going to Grant from the army of the Cumberland.

News of the favorable progress and probable speedy termination of the siege of Vicksburg, and the arrival of our cavalry horses, decided the time for our movement on Bragg's army, which held an intrenched camp at Shelbyville, with another fortified position at Tullahoma, eighteen miles further south, on the Nashville and Chattanooga railroad. The plan was to seize the gap covering his front and right flank, turn Shelbyville by the way of Manchester, and, moving on his communications in rear of Tullahoma, compel him to come out and fight on our own ground, or retreat by a disadvantageous route.

The movement began about the 24th of June, and, despite one of the most remarkable periods of rain which had been known at that season for many years in Tennessee—such that a corps did not march more than five miles per day—was eminently successful.

In nine days we drove the enemy from two fortified positions, which gave us possession of Middle Tennessee—a campaign conducted in one of the most extraordinary rains ever known in Tennessee at that period of the year, over a soil that became almost a quicksand. Our operations were retarded thirty-six hours at Hoover's gap, and sixty hours at and in front of Winchester, which alone prevented our getting possession of the enemy's communications and forcing him to very disastrous battle.

Our losses were only 560 men killed, wounded, and missing.

The enemy retreated across mountains and across the Tennessee river at Bridgeport, where he destroyed the railroad bridge and his pontoon bridge at the mouth of Battle creek. For the details of this campaign, so decisive and important in its results, I refer to my official report on file at the War Department, which is hereby made a part of this testimony. It will show that to dislodge the enemy from Middle Tennessee cost us only 560 men *hors de combat*. Every effort was immediately directed to the repairing of the railroad from Murfreesboro to the Tennessee river, to which point we sent a small advance of infantry and cavalry. By the 25th of July we were able to send through a supply train, and General Sheridan was then directed to occupy Stevenson with two brigades, and sent the third brigade of his division to Bridgeport. The next object was to establish a depot at Stevenson and replenish it with supplies, to repair the Tracy City road, a branch which runs up to the Sewanee coal mine in the Cumberland mountains, so as to put supplies at that point in case the army should operate by the Sequatchie valley. These preparations also were pushed with the utmost vigor. We were now about to undertake what would have been a great operation in any war—to move over a range of mountains, to cross a great river, and then two other ranges of mountains, before reaching the vital point of the enemy's position or seriously endangering his line of communication. To carry both provisions and forage for our animals in such an expedition was simply impossible. It was necessary either to move slowly and complete the railroad for hauling our supplies, or to wait until the new corn should be fit to use. I chose the latter, as it gave us the advantage of being able to operate so as to deceive the enemy, and, crossing the river, seize the mountain passes by stratagem, instead of giving him an opportunity to oppose us. It was also the dictate of military prudence to provide an adequate force for keeping up our communications as the distance from our depots lengthened, as well as to meet the concentration which it was the enemy's obvious interest to make on our army in order to attack it at the remotest distance from its base, and where it should have the greatest number of obstacles in case of disaster.

But about this time, 25th of July, the general-in-chief began to manifest great impatience at the delay in the movement on Chattanooga, notwithstanding he was informed of the cause, and was, moreover, aware that General Burnside, whose co-operation was justly expected, was not ready to co-operate in the movement. About this time I also sent General Rousseau to Washington with a letter to the Secretary of War, to the general-in-chief, and one to the President, representing the importance of adequately supporting the advance we were about to make, and of preparing the means for making it efficient in damaging the enemy after we should reach Chattanooga, and suggesting, among other modes, that of allowing General Rousseau to avail of the offers of the governors of Pennsylvania, Massachusetts, and some others, to raise for him veteran mounted troops to serve in the department of the Cumberland for the purpose of relieving the troops otherwise necessary to secure the railroad bridges and depots in the rear as we advanced. I received from the President, in reply, a letter commending the wisdom of the suggestions in my letter; but the Secretary of War not only gave them an unfavorable reception, but went so far as to say he would be damned if he would give me another man. General Rousseau said he was satisfied my official destruction was but a question of time and opportunity; the *will* to accomplish it existed, and that it was no use to hope for any assistance from the War Department.

Under these circumstances—having discharged my duty by stating the facts, which called for ample provision to support the movement, to my military superiors—I silently pushed, as I had previously been doing, preparations for the advance on Chattanooga with the army of the Cumberland alone, stating to the general-in-chief what I was doing, and proposed to do, and that if this was not satisfactory I wished to be relieved from the command of the army.

Accordingly, on the completion of the Tracy City road the army of the Cumberland began its movement for the possession of Chattanooga. The first thing to be done was to deceive the enemy as to our real point of crossing, which had to be selected in proximity with our depot of ammunition and supplies at Stevenson. Accordingly, by secret information, and by the open movement of Crittenden's corps, and by the demonstrations made by detachments from it, and from our cavalry, the whole extending from Blythe's ferry down to Decatur, Alabama, 150 miles of front, as well as by the concealment of the movement of the main force to the vicinity of Stevenson and Battle creek, the enemy was persuaded we intended to cross above Chattanooga, and made his dispositions accordingly.

For the details of the campaign by which we succeeded in crossing the Cumberland mountains, the Tennessee river, Sand mountains, and Lookout range, in the face of an army whose business it was to oppose us, and, finally, in getting possession of Chattanooga, the great objective point, notwithstanding the enemy had been re-enforced by a number of troops equal to that of our entire army, I refer the committee to my official report of the battle of Chickamauga, which I hereby make a part of my testimony.

The points to which I wish to direct the attention of the committee, in reference to this campaign, are—

First. That I was fully aware of the magnitude and difficulties of the movement; that I made known, so far as I thought duty required and circumstances permitted, these views to General Halleck, the Secretary of War, and even to the President; that subsequent events—that is to say, the time necessarily consumed in the campaign—fully showed that it could not have been undertaken with reasonable hopes of success earlier, on account of the necessity of having forage for our animals, and the impossibility of transporting that forage and the more necessary ammunition and subsistence, which we were compelled to carry over these mountains, and that the necessity of supporting the movement by additional forces, to which the attention of the general-in-chief and the War Department had been directly and indirectly invited, was amply demonstrated by the fact that the enemy did concentrate upon and attempt to crush the army of the Cumberland, and that this attempt was anticipated by me, and ought to have been expected by the general-in-chief and the War Department.

I would also call the attention of the committee to the fact that General Burnside's co-operation was left on the footing of an independent movement, and that in consequence of the want of unity between these movements the army of the Cumberland and the interests of the nation were greatly and needlessly imperilled at Chattanooga. I desire also to direct attention to the contrast in the manner in which our movement on Vicksburg and Missionary ridge were supported to show that the authorities at Washington by their action in these cases recognized the principle which was violated in the case of this movement, and thus bear testimony to the greatness of the mistake they made in not suitably supporting the movement of the army of the Cumberland in this great campaign.

In his annual report for 1863, the general-in-chief says:

"It seemed useless to send any more troops into East Tennessee and Georgia, on account of the impossibility of supplying them in a country which the enemy had nearly exhausted. General Burnside's army was on short rations, and that of the Cnmberland inadequately supplied. General Rosecrans had complained of his inadequate cavalry force, but the stables of his depots were overcrowded with animals, and the horses of his artillery, cavalry, and trains were dying in large numbers for want of forage."

This statement is wholly untrue of any period after the 1st of May, and therefore ought not to have been stated in the way it was. I was perfectly able to feed all the cavalry horses needed in my movement on Chattanooga. It conveys a very erroneous idea of the facts when applied to the previous period from my arrival at Nashville until the campaign of Tullahoma; for the general-in-chief well knows, and the official correspondence submitted shows, that the only reason we could not command adequate supplies of long forage for our animals during that period was *because our cavalry force was too weak to go and get it.* Had we possessed a sufficient cavalry force, we should have had all the forage of every description we wanted. Not only so, but my correspondence with the general shows the control of Middle Tennessee, and all its resources, would have been ours, with adequate cavalry force to have driven the rebel cavalry from it or put them behind their infantry lines.

I will also call the attention of the committee to the spirit of the report of the general-in-chief, wherein he implies that the battle of Chickamauga was a consequence of a wild scheme of advance into Georgia undertaken by me without just warrant of prudence or authority.

The general is very much mistaken in this matter. I well remember my surprise on receiving the following from General Halleck, directing me to occupy Dalton, and the passes to the west of it, at the moment when every nerve was tense with energy and anxiety to get my troops out of those passes and concentrated on the Lafayette and Chattanooga road, *twenty miles north of Dalton,* in time to cover Chattanooga and prevent the enemy from falling on and beating us in detail:

HEADQUARTERS OF THE ARMY,
Washington, D. C., September 11, 1863.

Major General ROSECRANS, *Chattanooga:*

General Burnside telegraphs from Cumberland gap that he holds all East Tennessee above Loudon, and also the gaps of the North Carolina mountains. A cavalry force is moving towards Athens to connect with you.

After holding the mountain passes on the west, and Dalton, or some other point on the railroad, to prevent the return of Bragg's army, it will be decided whether your army shall move further south into Georgia and Alabama.

It is reported here by deserters that a part of Bragg's army is re-enforcing Lee. It is important that the truth of this should be ascertained as early as possible.

H. W. HALLECK,
General-in-Chief.

To meet controversy directly on this point, I will state that no "wild" or other scheme of advance into Georgia was ever entertained by me, nor anything beyond the capture and firm possession of Chattanooga contemplated, save a sharp pursuit moving lightly to injure the enemy *should we find him hastily retreating in a condition to be injured* north of Oostenaula. To show what an estimate was put upon the securing of Chattanooga as a base for future operations, getting an opening into Georgia, and shutting out the enemy from the coal region and from East Tennessee, the committee will find that, before crossing the Tennessee on this march, I contracted with very responsible parties, one, to complete the railroad bridge across the Tennessee before the 1st day of October; the other, to complete the *Running-Water bridge* by the 1st day of November, and that the battle was fought on the 18th, 19th, and 20th of September. Speaking from memory as to the dates of these contracts, but the contracts are on file and will show the dates.

The committee will observe from my official report that we began to cross the Tennessee on the 28th of August, and that, therefore, we were twenty-two days out from our depots; our army having to carry in that campaign ammunition for two great battles and twenty-five days' subsistence, which was done and pronounced by General Meigs to be not only the greatest operation in this war, but a great thing in any war.

My official report will, I think, sufficiently show, that it would have been impossible for my command to have got possession of Chattanooga by direct force. There is a bare possibility that by crossing the Tennessee above Chattanooga at some suitable point where the enemy could not directly oppose us, and being re-enforced by Burnside's command, we might have captured the place by a battle; but when it is remembered that on much more favorable ground, with greater relative superiority of force, our army was forty two days in front of Vicksburg, it may well be doubted whether the army of the Cumberland could have wrested Chattanooga from Bragg's force alone by any other than the means adopted, namely, the powerful demonstration on his lines of communication made at a time when yet he had not been joined by Johnston's and Longstreet's commands, which added between 40,000 and 50,000 to his strength. At all events, it was my best judgment at the time that in that way only could we succeed in dislodging Bragg from Chattanooga and obtaining possession of it; and General Garfield, if not other members of my staff, will remember and bear witness that two of my most anxious and sleepless nights were spent, one in Lookout valley, the other in Chattanooga, watching Bragg, and hoping that his movements would permit the concentration of our army east of Lookout, between him and Chattanooga. Fortunately for us, his re-enforcements were not up, and our possession of the two passes, over Lookout, at Frick's and Cooper's gaps, and the position of McCook's corps, and the cavalry threatening to enter Broomtown valley, induced him to retire behind Pigeon mountain, with headquarters at Lafayette.

It has been a popular impression, possibly encouraged if not believed in high military quarters, that because a portion of our command, including myself, entered Chattanooga, that we had possession of it with our army, in the sense of being so established there, so that we could have retained it without a battle.

This is an error into which no good military mind cognizant of the facts could for a moment fall. Bragg was compelled or induced to fall back from Chattanooga by the menacing attitude of Thomas's corps at Frick's and Cooper's Gap, twenty-six miles south, and of McCook's, with the cavalry corps at Valley Head, forty-two miles from Chattanooga. Crittenden's corps, a part of which was employed in making the demonstration above Chattanooga, and the remainder in watching and covering the pass over the extremity of Lookout, passed into Chattanooga when Bragg fell back, and repaired at once to that point to ascertain the movement of the enemy; and all that was done was done promptly, and to that end only. And the instant these movements were discovered, and the enemy was found to have retired slowly towards Lafayette, not a moment was lost in making the necessary disposition, first, to secure our troops against being cut up in detail; and, secondly, to effect a most expeditious concentration at an eligible point between the enemy and Chattanooga, the goal of our efforts. It was our good fortune to succeed in concentrating on the afternoon of the 18th, but the tardy arrival of McCook's corps came near being fatal to us.

For the events which followed I refer the committee to my official report, calling attention only to one point which is not therein sufficiently elaborated. Forgetting my past record, and influenced by the calumnies put in circulation, it has been thought that I needlessly or languidly forsook the field of battle on the 20th. The facts are as follows: Immediately on the arrival of McCook's troops at the encampment of Thomas, at the foot of Frick's gap, all our spare trains, including those of Crittenden's corps, were ordered into the valley of Chattanooga creek, which lies at the eastern base of Lookout mountain, both for safety and forage. The troops, infantry and artillery, as my official report shows, were pushed with all possible vigor (marching all night) eastward to get possession of the Lafayette road. Our cavalry was ordered to connect with our right, and extend westward to cover those trains from the enemy's cavalry;

and the guards were increased by Post's brigade of Davis's division, McCook's corps, which had been left behind to conduct its train. When the breach on the right of our lines occurred at midday of the 20th, this train, with all our spare subsistence and other supplies lay along the valley of Chattanooga creek, from near the front some four or five miles; and as the distance from the point where the enemy had penetrated our infantry lines to the flank and rear of the train was only three or four miles, they were in the most critical condition, and it became a matter of the utmost importance to put it out of the enemy's reach. When, therefore, I reached the vicinity of Rossville, and became satisfied that though cut off from the main body of our army, which held the centre and left, General Thomas with five brigades, three of Sheridan's and two of Davis's, we still held the field in front of Thomas, two things were to be done: first, to ascertain the condition of affairs at the front; the other, to have this train moved to a place of security. This latter required that the orders should be given for its being pushed and secured north of Chattanooga creek, the only passage over which was by a very rickety bridge near a hundred feet long and thirty or forty feet high, and to order the movement of the train to that place, and send orders to General Mitchell, commanding the cavalry, advising him of the condition of affairs, and directing him to make such dispositions as would most securely effect the movement of the train and cover it from the enemy's enterprises; while at the same time, as a part of the general dispositions for the continuance of battle, he must be advised to put himself in connexion with our right in the new position it had been compelled to take after its repulse from the field at the widow Glen's house. Having explained this to General Garfield, my chief of staff, it was determined that the movement to the front, being less complicated, should be performed by him, while I made the dispositions and gave the orders just spoken of. Nor was I unmindful of the consideration that, as the security of Chattanooga was the essential thing, my duty as commanding general required that I should look to the ground with a view to the eventualities of being driven from the field of battle, where we were so vastly outnumbered, and that I should make such dispositions as would enable us to hold that place and to subsist our troops until we could be re-enforced. As it was possible that the enemy's cavalry might penetrate the rough country on the right of our line, and cut telegraphic and other communications, south of the river, with Bridgeport and the north, and in pursuance of a duty I have always imposed on myself, to keep the government candidly informed of the exact posture of affairs, I deemed it proper to telegraph to Washington the events of the day.

Out of the performance of these two duties, dictated by candor and a pure desire to do the best for the country, unjust and sycophantic men have undertaken to construct the means of injuring my military reputation.

As my official report of the battle substantially closes with the firm possession of Chattanooga, I will here state what seems of importance:

That it was abundantly established by information gained before and during the battle of Chickamauga, and confirmed by subsequent information and events, that we were outnumbered very nearly two to one in that battle. As my determination was to hold what we had gained, at all hazards and to the last extremity, all my dispositions were at once directed to that end. I concentrated the forces within a defensive line sufficiently contracted to defy the enemy's power, and fortified it without delay. I at the same time used every possible effort to provide bridges by which our troops and trains could communicate with the north side of the river, from which our line of communication with Bridgeport would be comparatively safe, while, against the superior numbers of the enemy, its maintenance on the south side of the river was practically out of the question.

General Halleck in his annual report says I abandoned the passes of Lookout mountain, leaving the public to imagine that these passages were within the possible control of my army, and their abandonment not justified as a military measure. I call the attention of the committee to the fact that one of these passes was 42 miles south of Chattanooga, and the next nearest 26 miles south of Chattanooga, and the nearest at the extremity of Lookout mountain in front of our lines. This latter may have been the one which gave rise to his report; and if so, it ought to have been so stated. I was satisfied that I could not hold even *this* pass and Chattanooga at the same time if the enemy did his duty, and therefore withdrew my troops from it, but established batteries on the other side of the river, which rendered it practically of little if any use to them. Subsequent events amply justified the wisdom of this decision, for the enemy, with a division and a half, were unable to hold it against General Hooker, and it was their attempt to cover this point which was one of the causes of their being beaten so easily at Missionary ridge. In General Grant's official report of the battle of Missionary ridge, I think—for I have not the document—there is an implication that when he assumed command there was great danger of my abandoning Chattanooga. Nothing could be more mistaken or unjust to me than such an impression. All my actions and sentiments were utterly at variance with the idea of giving up that point, which I had won, and the possession of which formed an epoch in the war. I mention facts on this subject, viz: as early as the 4th of October, fourteen days after the battle, I called the attention of General Thomas and General Garfield to the map of Chattanooga and vicinity, and, pointing out to them the positions, stated that as soon as I could possibly get the bridge materials for that purpose, I would take possession of Lookout valley, opposite the passage over the extremity of the mountain, and fortify it, thus completely covering the road from there to Bridgeport, on the south side as well as the river, and giving us practical possession and use of both, as well as of Lookout valley; because, by means of a fortified tête-de-pont, after our fortifications at Chattanooga were completed, we could easily concentrate our whole force to fight the enemy if he entered Lookout valley, and that within less than two hours' march, while he could not approach us in force with artillery without making a circuit over Lookout mountain, by way of Frick's and Stevens's gaps, 26 miles southeast, which would take two or three days.

An interior line of fortifications was laid out and put in course of construction, designed to cover our depots with a garrison of one or two divisions against all the forces the enemy could bring. I had, moreover, ordered the construction of small steamboats and barges at Bridgeport to run thence to Chattanooga, two of which were well advanced when the army crossed on its advance into Georgia; and, from the 23d of September, my correspondence and my staff officers will testify that I was urging the quartermaster, Captain Edwards, who had the work in hand, to hasten its completion, which it was hoped would be the case by the time we were ready to take and hold Lookout valley. To effect this General Hooker was directed to concentrate his troops at Stevenson and Bridgeport, and advised that as soon as his train should arrive, or enough of it to subsist his army ten or twelve miles from his depot, he would be directed to move into Lookout valley to take possession of that; and every effort was made to complete the pontoons, &c., to connect that with our troops at Chattanooga. On the 19th of October I examined the river, and selected a point for the crossing of the bridge at Ferry to connect Hooker's with the forces at Chattanooga. I moreover directed General W. F. Smith to reconnoitre the shore above Chattanooga, with a view to that very movement on the enemy's right flank which was afterwards made by General Sherman.

On the 19th of October, on my returning from selecting the position of the pontoon bridge, I received orders to turn over the command of the army of the Cumberland to Major General Thomas, repair to Cincinnati, and report from there by letter to the Adjutant General for orders. Convinced that this would excite profound sorrow and discontent in the army of the Cumberland, which my continued presence, after it became known, would increase, and that this would be detrimental to the public service in the presence, as we were, of the enemy, I determined to forego the gratification of receiving the parting adieus of those with whom I had shared so many toils and successes. I left the next morning shortly after daylight, before the order was known. The committee will probably desire to know what communication took place between me and General Burnside during my movement on Chattanooga. I have before stated that a co-operation between him and myself, arranged with a view to the Tullahoma campaign, was prevented by re-enforcements ordered from Burnside's command to Vicksburg. When his troops were returned, he arranged to move on East Tennessee, communicated to me his plan for a movement into East Tennessee, but it was independent of mine, and though intended to be contemporary, was likely and actually proved to be unavailing to assist my movement for want of unity of object and command. It was from the first obvious that the moment we seriously threatened Chattanooga all the forces in East Tennessee would probably abandon it and join General Bragg to oppose us. General Burnside's as an independent command, as was to have been expected, was little or no use, for the moment we threatened to cross the Tennessee above Chattanooga Buckner began to retire from the north towards Loudon, and when we threatened Bragg's communications south of Chattanooga, he precipitately abandoned the whole of East Tennessee and joined General Bragg.

General Halleck, in his official report for that year, quotes at length orders given on the 12th, 13th, and 14th of September to Burnside, at Knoxville, General Hurlbut, at Memphis, and General Sherman, at Vicksburg, to re-enforce the army of the Cumberland, but fails to state that on the 14th of September I telegraphed the general asking if he had reason to believe Bragg had been re-enforced from Virginia, and that on the 15th he telegraphed in reply that no re-enforcements had gone south to Bragg, only a few regiments to Charleston. More, the accompanying correspondence shows that an apprehension existed in Washington even as late as the 11th of September that Bragg was re-enforcing Lee. The committee will no doubt inquire how orders to troops at such distant points at that date could have brought any support to the army of the Cumberland, which began its life and death struggle on the 18th, only six days from the earliest of his orders. I will also state to the committee that Longstreet's movement to support Bragg was known to General Peck as early as the 6th, and that Colonel Jacques, 73d Illinois, endeavored to communicate the fact that Longstreet's corps was going to Bragg, to the authorities at Washington, so long before the battle that he was able to wait ten days in vain in Baltimore for a hearing, and then to reach us and take part in the battle of Chickamauga.

As I have narrated the principal events *not* prominently developed in my official report, (a copy of which, and some official letters, I have made a part of my testimony before the committee, in relation to the campaign of Chickamauga,) I forbear to notice and reply to the various erroneous and diverse rumors and statements which have found more or less publicity; but I think it due to justice and the discipline of the army, as well as to the country, whose servants are thereby implicated, to state that General Woods, whose official report of his part in the battle, comprising near seventy pages foolscap, was duly forwarded to Washington by me, was, after I was relieved from command of the army of the Cumberland, permitted access to my official report and allowed to send a letter to Washington direct, without furnishing me a copy of it; and that his letter was received without notice to me, and quoted by the general-in-chief, as to some extent, a rival authority, and subsequently furnished from the War Department to the press as an accompaniment to my official report of the battle; and that, when I complained of it, no redress or apology was offered therefor, nor was my letter of correction published until the lapse of some two months thereafter.

CORRESPONDENCE WITH THE WAR DEPARTMENT.

Major General Halleck to Major General Rosecrans.

WASHINGTON, D. C., *July* 14, 1863.

Burnside has been frequently urged to move forward, and cover your left in entering ast Tennessee. I do not know what he is doing. He seems tied fast to Cincinnati.

H. W. HALLECK, *Commander-in-Chief.*

For Major General Rosecrans.

WASHINGTON, *August* 5, 1863.

The orders for the advance of your army, and that its progress be reported daily, are per-nptory.

H. W. HALLECK.

Major General Halleck to Major General Rosecrans.

WASHINGTON, *August* 20, 1863.

It has been reported for some days that some portion of Bragg's army has been sent ot chmond to re-enforce Lee. It is important that the truth of this report be ascertained early as possible.

H. W. HALLECK, *Major General.*

Major General Halleck to Major General Rosecrans.

WASHINGTON, *August* 25, 1863.

Burnside, when last heard from, was at Mount Vernon, moving towards Knoxville. He is directed to move forward as rapidly as possible, and to keep you posted in regard his operations. Grant's movements at present have no connexion with you.

H. W. HALLECK.

Major General Halleck to Major General Rosecrans.

WASHINGTON, *September* 2, 1863.

Burnside is at Montgomery, moving on Kingston ; the enemy expected to be concentrated Loudon.

HALLECK.

Major General Halleck to Major General Rosecrans.

WASHINGTON, *September* 6, 1863.

I have heard nothing from Burnside since his despatch of August 31, the substance of ich was sent to you. His instructions were to advise you of his movements, and con-ct as soon as possible with your left. There is no reason now to suppose that any of e's troops have been detached, except, perhaps, a small force at Charleston.

H. W. HALLECK, *Major General.*

Major General Halleck to Major General Rosecrans.

WASHINGTON, *September* 6, 1863.

You give no information of the position of Bragg and Buckner ; if they have united, it is portant that you and Burnside unite as quickly as possible, so that the enemy may not ack you separately.

H. W. HALLECK, *Major General.*

Major General Halleck to Major General Rosecrans.

WASHINGTON, *September* 11, 1863.

Burnside telegraphs from Cumberland gap that he holds all East Tennessee above udon, and also the gap of the North Carolina mountains. A cavalry force is moving vards Athens to connect with you. After holding the mountain passes on the west and

Dalton, or some other point on the railroad, to prevent the return of Bragg's army, it will be decided whether your army shall move further south into Georgia and Alabama. It is reported here by deserters that a part of Bragg's army is re-enforcing Lee. It is important that the truth of this should be ascertained as early as possible.

H. W. HALLECK, *Commander-in-Chief.*

By order of Secretary of War to Major General Rosecrans.

WASHINGTON, *September* 12, 1863.

Following telegram is sent for your information, by order of Secretary of War, from Memphis, 5 p. m., September 9. A gentleman just in from Mobile reports that all of Johnston's force has gone to join Bragg at and near Chattanooga. I think the report true, from the source I received it, and from the fact that the country south of Corinth is full of regular cavalry making some movement.

S. A. HURLBURT, *Major General.*

" *Major General Halleck to Major General Rosecrans.*

" WASHINGTON, *September* 13, 1863.

" There is no intention of sending Burnside into North Carolina. He is ordered to move down and connect with you.

" Should the enemy attempt to turn your right flank through Alabama, Chattanooga should be turned over to Burnside and given away, or such part of it as may not be required there should move to prevent Bragg from re-entering Middle Tennessee. Hurlbut will aid you all he can, but most of Grant's available force is west of the Mississippi.

" HALLECK."

Major General Halleck to Major General Rosecrans.

WASHINGTON, *September* 21, 1863—3 p. m.

Nothing heard from Burnside since the 19th ; he was then sending to your aid all his available force. It is hoped that you will hold out till he can re-enforce you. He was directed to connect with you ten days ago, and the order has been reported several days since. I can get no reply from Hurlbut or Sherman.

H. W. HALLECK, *Major General.*

President Lincoln to Major General Rosecrans.

WASHINGTON, *September* 23, 1863.

Below is Bragg's despatch, as found in the Richmond papers. You see he does not claim so many prisoners or captured guns as you were inclined to concede. He also confesses to heavy loss.

An exchanged general of ours, leaving Richmond yesterday, says two of Longstreet's divisions and his entire artillery, and two of Pickett's brigades and Wise's legion have gone to Tennessee. He mentions no other.

A. LINCOLN.

" CHICKAMAUGA RIVER, *September* 20, *via Ringold*, 21*st.*

" Major General COOPER, *A. Gen.:*

" After two days' hard fighting we have driven the enemy, after a desperate resistance from several positions, and now hold the field, but he still confronts us. The losses are heavy on both sides, especially on our officers. We have taken over 20 pieces of artillery and some 2,500 prisoners.

"BRAXTON BRAGG."

WASHINGTON, D. C., *September* 24, 1863—3 a. m.

Major General ROSECRANS,

Comd'g Dept. of Cumberland:

In addition to the expected assistance to you from Burnside, Hurlbut and Sherman, with fourteen or fifteen thousand men from here, will be in Nashville in about seven days. The government deems it very important that Chattanooga be held till re-enforcements arrive.

H. W. HALLECK, *Commander-in-Chief.*

WASHINGTON, D. C., *September* 30, 1863—10 a. m.

Major General ROSECRANS,
Comd'g Army of Cumberland:

The advance of Grant's re-enforcements were on their way from Vicksburg to Memphis on the 22d. Hurlbut was directed to report their movement from day to day, but he is probably unable to do so, having no telegraphic communication. Moreover, it is probable that all mail boats were sent to Vicksburg for troops. I have no communication with Burnside since he left Knoxville. Communicate to him directly what you wish him to do.

H. W. HALLECK, *Commander-in-Chief.*

WASHINGTON, D. C., *September* 24, 1863—10 a. m.

Major General ROSECRANS,
Comd'g Dept. of Cumberland.:

The corps of 14 to 15,000 men to be sent you from here has the usual amount of artillery, but no cavalry; if the artillery is not deemed necessary, the railroad transportation will be greatly diminished. Please answer.

H. W. HALLECK, *Commander-in-Chief.*

WASHINGTON, D. C., *October* 12, 1863—10 a. m.

Major General ROSECRANS,
Comd'g Dept. of Cumberland:

Captain Comstock is sick. Sherman is moving east of Corinth ; where he now is I do not know ; no telegraphic communication with him. Have heard nothing of Burnside since the 7th. If he is not moving down you must look to the passes of the Tennessee river above Chattanooga. Lee's army is again moving northward.

H. W. HALLECK, *Commander-in-Chief.*

WASHINGTON, D. C., *September* 28, 1863—10.5 a. m.

Major General ROSECRANS:

Grant's forces were ordered to move to Memphis, Corinth, Tuscumbia, to Decatur, and thence, as might be necessary, to co-operate with you. Supplies were to be collected at Corinth before they arrived ; as the rolling stock is only sufficient to carry baggage and supplies, the troops must march the whole distance. The order was issued on the 18th, and steamboats went to Vicksburg to bring up the troops; they calculated to be able to communicate with you in fourteen days from that time. Since then nothing has been heard of them, there being no telegraph lines. The troops from here will probably reach you first.

H. W. HALLECK, *Commander-in-Chief.*

MURFREESBORO, *January* 14, 1863.

Major General HALLECK, *Washington, D. C.:*

I must have cavalry or mounted infantry. I could mount infantry had I horses and saddles. The saddles I had ordered have been delivered so very slowly, that now, after four months, I have only a few hundred more than have been required for the use of the cavalry. With mounted infantry I can drive the rebel cavalry to the wall, and keep the roads open in my rear. Not so now. I must also have some bullet-proof light-draught transports for the Cumberland. Will you authorize the purchase of saddles and horses for mounting, when requisite, 5,000 more infantry?

W. S. ROSECRANS, *Major General.*

MURFREESBORO, *February* 1, 1863.

Major General HALLECK, *Washington, D. C.:*

I have direct information that Joe Johnston arrived at Tullahoma on the 27th ultimo. Van Dorn, who was sent in command of the rebel cavalry in Mississippi, has been ordered over here to subsist on the country and interrupt our communication. To meet this emergency we must bring down all the cavalry available, and add to it the mounting of a brigade of infantry for backing and expeditionary purposes. If you will back me up, I am determined to command the country, instead of giving it up to the enemy. I shall ask you things as they are needed. General Wright thinks the 2d Ohio cavalry at Columbus, and the 10th at Cleveland, are not at his disposal. I advised him otherwise, but not having heard from him, advise you of it. Our first want will be arms. Don't be weary at my importunity. No economy can compare with that of furnishing revolving arms ; no mode of recruiting will so promptly and efficaciously strengthen us. I am about to establish n elite battalion in each brigade, composed of the soldiers from each company. One commissioned and five non-commissioned officers from each regiment, and one field officer for the brigade, to be selected for superior and soldierly bearing in battle and on duty. I promise them the best of arms, when I can get them, and will mount them for rapid field movements, like flying artillery. Will you please aid me to get the arms—even instalments, to show they will come some day, will answer. We must create military ardor.

W. S. ROSECRANS, *Major General.*

MURFREESBORO, *February* 2, 1863.

Hon. E. M. STANTON, *Washington, D. C.:*

I telegraphed the commander-in-chief that 2,000 carbines or revolving rifles were required to arm our cavalry. He replied as if he thought it a complaint. I telegraph you also to prevent misunderstanding. I speak for the country when I say that 2,000 effective cavalry will cost the support of nearly four thousand, say five thousand dollars per day. But this is the smallest part of our trouble. One rebel cavalryman takes, on an average, three of our infantry to watch our communications, while our progress is made slow and cautious, and we command the forage of the country only by sending large train guards. It is o prime necessity, in every point of view, to master their cavalry. I propose to do this, first by so arming our cavalry as to give it its maximum strength ; second, by having animals and saddles temporarily to mount infantry brigades for marches and enterprises. We have now one thousand cavalrymen without horses, and two thousand without arms. We don't want revolvers so much as light revolving rifles. This matter is so clearly, in my mind, of paramount public interest, that I blush to think it necessary to seem to apologize for it. I do hope the government will have confidence enough in me to know I never have asked, and never will ask, anything to increase my personal command. Had this been understood when I went with Blencker's division, this nation might have been spared millions blood and treasure.

W. S. ROSECRANS, *Major General.*

MURFREESBORO, *February* 2, 1863.

Major General H. W. HALLECK, *Washington, D. C.:*

I am surprised that you mistake my meaning. I do not complain. I point the way to victory. I tell you how I think this force is to be created and maintained at slight expense. This war demands such consideration, and many more, to save the waste of human life. Already our thinned regiments testify to this, and show no substantial gain from recruiting. I wish to be understood as making no complaints. The great point I make is that the government pays costs of troops, without getting the benefit of their strength. The other is, no matter what the government has done or left undone for this army, policy and duty demand means to meet the coming emergency. Why should the rebels command the country which, with its resources, would belong to our army, because it can muster the small percentage of six or eight thousand more cavalry than we? I want superior arms to supply the place of numbers. Give revolving rifles in place of pistols. We must have cavalry arms, and the difference between best and worst is more than one hundred per cent. on the daily cost of the troops. Excuse my earnestness in this matter; I probably see it much more clearly than I can explain.

W. S. ROSECRANS, *Major General.*

MURFREESBORO, *March* 6, 1863.

GENERAL: Yours of the first instant, announcing the offer of a vacant major generalship in the regular army to the general in the field who first wins an important and decisive victory, is received. As an officer and a citizen, I feel degraded at such an auctioneering of honors. Have we a general who would fight for his own personal benefit, when he would not for honor and his country? He would come by his commission basely in that case, and deserve to be despised by men of honor. But are all the brave and honorable generals on an equality as to chances? If not, it is unjust to those who probably deserve most.

W. S. ROSECRANS, *Major General.*

Major General H. W. HALLECK,
Commander-in-Chief, Washington, D. C.

MURFREESBORO, *March* 20, 1863.

Brigadier General L THOMAS,
Adjutant General U S Army, Washington, D. C :

Duty compels me to recall the attention of the War Department to the necessity of more cavalry here. Let it be clearly understood that the enemy have five to our one, and can therefore command the resources of the country and the services of the inhabitants. To supply in some measure our deficiency, I asked leave to mount some infantry; it was granted to the extent of five thousand. I have mounted about two thousand; I now ask authority to add to these two thousand a detail of one hundred and forty picked men from each brigade, which will give me the means of picketing all our ordinary lines, and thus enable me to mass the cavalry for expeditions. Early action is vitally important.

W. S. ROSECRANS, *Major General.*

MURFREESBORO, *March* 29, 1863.

Major General HALLECK, *Washington, D. C.:*

General Rousseau would undertake to raise eight or ten thousand mounted infantry; thinks he could succeed in two months I think the time very propitious, and that his influence would be healthful on butternuts and lukewarms If you can arm, you can doubtless mount them, and they would be of great avail in the future. I recommend that he be charged with raising these men, if deemed advisable, without delay.

W. S. ROSECRANS, *Major General.*

MURFREESBORO, *April* 24, 1863.

Hon. E M. STANTON, *Secretary of War:*

Cavalry horses are indispensable to our success here. We have always been without the control of the country, except for a short distance beyond our infantry lines, and all the forage and horses the country could furnish have thus fallen into the hands of the enemy; they subsist on the country by having five to our one of mounted force. Out of our nominal cavalry force we have not more than forty per cent. available for want of horses; the fruits of victory when gained will be lost for want of mounted force to pursue. This has been stated and reiterated to the department, but horses have not been obtained. No saving of prices paid by the contracting system can compensate for the losses we have thus sustained and are sustaining. Prices should be paid that will give us good horses, and that rapidly. Authority might wisely be given to your chief quartermaster to purchase at reasonable prices wherever he can obtain them. General Stanley is now waiting in Louisville with twelve hundred (1,200) dismounted cavalry to bring down horses None there.

W. S. ROSECRANS.

MURFREESBORO, *April* 26, 1863.

Major General H. W. HALLECK,
Commander-in-Chief, Washington, D. C.:

GENERAL: Your letter of the 20th instant is received. If I have used the telegraph freely, it has been through an anxious desire to do my duty, and insure that by no fault of mine should things go unattended to, which my experience has shown may be the case, even with the most able and zealous officers, without reminders. That I am very careful to inform the department of my successes, and of *all* captures from the enemy, is not true, as the records of our office will show. That I have failed to inform the government of my defeats and losses is equally untrue, both in letter and spirit. I regard the statement of these two propositions of the War Department as a profound, grievous, cruel, and ungenerous official and personal wrong. If there is any one thing I despise and scorn it is an officer's blowing his own trumpet, or getting others to do it for him I had flattered myself that no general officer in the service had a clearer record on this point than I have. I shall here drop the subject, leaving to time and Providence the vindication of my conduct, and expect justice, kindness, and consideration only from those who are willing to accord them.

Accept for yourself, personally, my cordial thanks for your kindness, both personal and official.

Very respectfully, your obedient servant,

W. S. ROSECRANS, *Major General, Commanding.*

MURFREESBORO, *April* 26, 1863.

Brigadier General THOMAS, *Adjutant General, Washington:*

Inform the general-in-chief I have from a letter of Colonel Hill, commanding a brigade in the rebel army, that Joe Johnston has got 18,000 re-enforcements, of which 5,000 had already arrived on the 19th instant, and that he would have 30,000 in all by the 7th proximo; he says it is the intention of the rebels to advance on us if we do not advance on them; if we return into fortifications they will cross into Kentucky and seize Columbus, and so on. They intend to get there before Grant can arrive. Our expedition to cut the Georgia railroad promises to succeed. Dodge took Tuscumbia on the 24th, and was to take Florence on the 26th. Bragg has occupied the line of Duck river; his re-enforcements hold Tullahoma. My expedition to McMinnville succeeded. Report by mail, under late instructions to save expense.

W. S. ROSECRANS, *Major General.*

HEADQUARTERS DEPARTMENT OF THE CUMBERLAND, *July* 24, 1863.

Major General HALLECK:

Your despatch received. All is very good. Your views accord with my own. All your suggestions about baggage and rations have been anticipated and carried out from the beginning of our movement, and are now being carried out with all the energy of which we are capable. We never think of moving with any but minimum baggage, nor of taking anything but essential parts of rations, but to move our troops beyond our means of supply would break down and disable both men and horses without result. This I am sure you do not desire. Any disappointment that may be felt at the apparent slowness of our movements would be readily removed by a knowledge of the obstacles and true military appreciation of the advantages of not moving immediately. I confess I should like to avoid such remarks and letters as I am receiving lately from Washington, if I could do so without injury to the public service. You will, I think, find the officers of this army as anxious for success, and as willing to exert themselves to secure it, as any member of the government can be. As to subsistence being drawn from the country over which we are to travel to Chattanooga, it was always barren with but few fertile spots. These spots have been gleaned and scraped by rebels with a powerful cavalry force ever since last winter. We shall get some hay and cattle in the region of Fayetteville, Huntsville, and south of there; none south or east of us.

W. S. ROSECRANS, *Major General.*

We shall move promptly, and endeavor not to go back. What move from Grant will affect us?

HEADQUARTERS DEPARTMENT OF THE CUMBERLAND,
Murfreesboro, May 10, 1863.

GENERAL: Your letter of the 1st instant, on the subject of cavalry horses, was yesterday received, and carefully considered. I thank you for taking pains to write so fully. I will explain to you with equal care the true state of the case in this army, for I find you have fallen into quite a number of errors on the subject.

1st. It is a fact that up to the 1st instant our total supply of cavalry horses was as follows:

Cavalry horses on hand	6,537
Mounted infantry	1,938
Total	8,475
Less, at least one-quarter, are not serviceable	2,119
Making cavalry mounted not over	6,356

But when these troops are called out we have at no time been able to turn out more than 5,000 for actual duty. The other cavalry horses, reported by Colonel Taylor, were—

Escorts and orderlies	2,028
Unserviceable in Nashville	975
	3,003

You will thus see that we have not the cavalry you suppose. We are using the most strenuous and unremitting efforts to increase in care of horses, and the efficiency of this arm

2d. But I must call your attention to the fact, that this small cavalry force, effectively not half that required for a permanent garrison of infantry equal to that of this army, have to furnish pickets, scouts, and couriers for Fort Donelson, Clarksville, Nashville, Gallatin, Carthage, and the front of this army from Franklin to this place, twenty-eight miles. You may thus form some idea of the labor imposed on our cavalry, and how our horses are worn out so rapidly.

3d As to the actual work of this arm, besides the routine labor, you will find it has had some expedition or fight in mass nearly every week, and as yet without a single failure.

4th. As to expeditions, we have not a sufficiently strong cavalry force to drive that of the enemy to the wall, or to risk detachments for the enterprises of which you speak to the rear of the rebels. The one which I did send out under Colonel Streight, in spite of our precautions, was captured by the superior cavalry force of the enemy detached from Granger's front at Franklin, where Van Dorn has still left about four to our one.

5th As to forage, our want is for long forage, and is owing to the impossibility of getting transportation either by water or rail. You must remember we are two hundred and twenty miles from our base of supplies at Louisville. You may rely on it, I am fully alive to all you have suggested, and ask for nothing which I am not fully satisfied will be an ample economy to the service. Had we a cavalry force equal to that of the enemy, we would have commanded all the forage of the country—commanded information of its inhabitants, upon whose fears we, instead of they, would thus be able to operate.

As to the comparative number of cavalry in our and other armies, I am sure you are mistaken as to Russia, at least, which has 80,000 regular cavalry, while all the outpost, picket, and courier duty is done by regular cavalry. But even were it otherwise, I know what cavalry would do for us here, and am not mistaken in saying that this great army would gain more from 10,000 effective cavalry than from 20,000 infantry.

W. S. ROSECRANS, *Major General, Commanding.*

Brigadier General M. C. MEIGS,
Quartermaster General U. S. Army, Washington, D. C.

MURFREESBORO, *June* 21, 1863.

GENERAL: In your favor of the 12th instant you say you do not see how the maxim of not fighting two great battles at the same time applies to the case of this army and Grant's Looking at the matter practically, we and our opposing forces are so nearly separated that for Bragg materially to aid Johnston he must abandon our front substantially, and then we can move to an ultimate work with more rapidity and less waste of material or natural obstacles If General Grant is defeated, both forces will come here, and then we ought to be near our base. The same maxim that forbids, as you take it, a single army fighting two great battles at the same time (by the way a very awkward thing to do) would forbid this nation engaging all its forces in the great west at the same time, so as to leave without a single reserve to stem the current of possible disaster This is, I think, sustained by military and political considerations. We ought to fight here if we have a strong prospect of winning a decisive victory over the opposing force, and upon this ground I shall act. I shall be careful not to risk our last reserve without strong ground to expect success.

Very respectfully, your obedient servant,

W. S. ROSECRANS, *Major General.*

Major General HALLECK,
Commander-in-Chief, Washington, D. C.

WINCHESTER, *July* 26, 1863.

Hon. E. M. STANTON, *Secretary of War:*

As you approve of General Rousseau's suggestion and views as to the advantage of raising an additional amount of force of ten thousand men to operate against the rebels from this direction, I have sent him to Washington with letters to yourself and General Halleck, and directed him to lay before you the plan which he has of obtaining from the disciplined troops recently mustered out of the service in the east such a mounted force as would enable us to command the country south of us and control its resources, cut off the enemy's means of drawing supplies from the country, destroy his lines of communication, and restore law and order to the entire country from which we have expelled the insurgents—a thing now impossible, because no one desires to avow his sentiments for fear the rebel cavalry or guerillas will wreak vengeance on him. At the expense of repeating what I have so often laid before the War Department when urging the necessity of cavalry arms for the force we actually had in pay, but badly armed and mounted, I beg leave to state:

1st. An adequate cavalry force would have given us control of all Middle Tennessee, with all its forage, horses, cattle and mules, and driven the enemy from it, without the battle of Stone river, and re-established civil order.

2d. It would save us five thousand infantry now guarding our lines of communication, and the attendant expense.

3d. We could have destroyed the enemy's lines of communication and compelled him to relinquish East Tennessee and Chattanooga and returned to Atlanta.

4th. We could have developed, by giving protection to the Union sentiment, which does not manifest itself much beyond the limits of our infantry lines, for fear of calling down the vengeance of the rebel cavalry and guerillas, whose superior numbers and knowledge of the country have hitherto given almost exclusive control of it. As we advance we shall have the same condition of things renewed on our front, and must take with us a superior cavalry force to insure success. We should, moreover, require additional mounted force to control the country, protect the roads in our rear, exterminate guerillas, and give confidence to the population, who will then readily furnish us with supplies and give us information that will aid us to put down brigandage, and thus relieve us from the necessities of detachments of infantry guards at many points where otherwise they will be indispensbale. The importance of General Rousseau's mission may be inferred from the value I attach to cavalry force to operate in connexion with this army. To all these uses of cavalry I will add another no less important. Should we succeed in disorganizing the enemy's force, a powerful cavalry force will enable us to harass and destroy his communications, and thus make him an easy prey.

Very respectfully, your obedient servant,

W. S ROSECRANS, *Major General.*

WINCHESTER, *July* 26, 1863.

GENERAL: When General Rousseau was in Washington last winter he laid before the War Department the immense advantage of having a large mounted force to operate against the rebels in these regions. He says the plan was looked upon with favor, but as speedy success and efficient service involved the taking one division of infantry from this army, it was not deemed expedient to order it into execution. The losses and delays which have attended the operations of this army since I assumed command have been so frequently presented to you and the War Department that I deem it proper merely to allude to them, and to say that the increasing area covered by our operations, the extension of our lines of communication, as well as the great advantages to be reaped from the proper use of cavalry on the enemy's lines of communication, his supply trains and foraging parties, render an increase of our mounted force more than ever desirable. It is also essential to enable us to command the forage and subsistence which the country can furnish. Before we can expect the inhabitants of the country to show any disposition to supply us, we must be able to give them reasonable assurance of protection against the rebel cavalry and guerillas.

Had we been able to do this, it would have changed entirely the military and political aspects of Tennessee, and the rebels could have been driven from it last autumn without a battle. General Rousseau, with the approval of General Thomas, suggested that with the large number of disciplined troops recently mustered out of service in the east it would be easy to raise ten thousand men for mounted service. Deeming the attainment of such a result of the highest moment, and believing that if the plan should be approved General Rousseau would be able to render more efficient service in carrying it out than in any other possible way, I order him to Washington to lay the matter before you and the War Department for such action as may be deemed best.

Very respectfully, your obedient servant,

W. S. ROSECRANS, *Major General, Commanding.*

Major General H. W. HALLECK,
Commander-in-Chief.

WINCHESTER, *August* 4, 1863.

Major General HALLECK, *Washington, D. C.:*

Your despatch ordering me to move forward without further delay, reporting the movement of each corps until I cross the Tennessee, is received. As I have been determined to cross the river as soon as practicable, and have been making all preparations and getting such information as may enable me to do so, without being driven back like Hooker, I wish to know if your order is intended to take away my discretion as to the time and manner of moving my troops.

W. S. ROSECRANS, *Major General.*

WINCHESTER, TENN., *August* 7, 1863.

Major General HALLECK, *Washington, D. C.*:

Your despatch received. I can only repeat the assurance given before the issue of the order. This army shall move with all the despatch compatible with the successful execution you wish. We are pressing everything to bring up forage for our animals; the present rolling stock of the road will hardly suffice to keep us day by day here, but I have bought fifty more freight cars, which are arriving. Will advise you daily.

W. S. ROSECRANS, *Major General.*

HEADQUARTERS DEPARTMENT OF THE CUMBERLAND,
Stevenson, August 23, 1863.

Major General HALLECK, *Washington, D. C.*:

Corps remain same. Crittenden's advance occupies Poe's tavern and a point six miles from Chattanooga. Wilder's report, received to-day, confirms last night's report; he says he sunk one of the steamboats, damaged the other. Our loss one wounded, four horses killed. Rebels hold the fords and ferries from Washington, down to Shell Mound, which we seized last night. Means of crossing getting ready. Wilder reports, saw enemy take away nine engines in one train, two hauling the rest; thinks they are evacuating Chattanooga. I think they are a little confused.

W. S. ROSECRANS, *Major General.*

Official:

R. S. THOMS, *A. D. C.*

STEVENSON, *August* 24, 1863—11.50 p. m.

Major General HALLECK, *Washington, D. C.*:

Nothing further from the left, except that enemy are reported as having moved up two brigades to Blythe's ferry, Tennessee. Have heard nothing from Burnside. Would like to know if Grant is to do anything to occupy Johnston's attention. No changes in my position to-day.

W. S. ROSECRANS, *Major General.*

Official;

R. S. THOMS, *A. D. C.*

HEADQUARTERS DEPARTMENT OF THE CUMBERLAND,
Stevenson, August 29, 1863.

Major General HALLECK, *Washington, D. C.*:

Pontoon bridge across at Caperton's ferry; two brigades over; cavalry forded at two places. Brannan's advance crossed at Battle creek; Reynolds's advance at Shell Mound. Reports not in yet, but suppose we have one hundred prisoners; no fighting to amount to anything.

W. S. ROSECRANS, *Major General.*

Official:

R. S. THOMS, *A. D. C.*

HEADQUARTERS DEPARTMENT OF THE CUMBERLAND,
Stevenson, Alabama, September 2, 1863.

Major General HALLECK, *Washington, D. C.*:

Our trestle gave way at the Bridgeport bridge this afternoon, and seven hundred feet of bridge fell into water; no loss, save one mule and damage to contents of a few wagons. All Sheridan's division and his artillery had passed over before the accident. Crittenden's corps is crossing in boats, and McCook's infantry advance has probably reached Valley Head. The cavalry will reach Rawlinsville by to-morrow night. Burnside's position from you is all we have, save rebel rumors that he has Knoxville. If he is not much involved, I think our move will wholly relieve him.

W. S. ROSECRANS, *Major General.*

HEADQUARTERS DEPARTMENT OF THE CUMBERLAND,
Stevenson, Alabama, Septmeber 3, 1863.

Major General HALLECK, *Washington, D. C.*:

The bridge was repaired to-day at noon; trains have been passing over since that time; most of the troops are now over. No report from General McCook, who probably reached Valley Head with his head division to-day, and possibly has seized Winston's gap; none from the cavalry at Rawlinsville. Have you any news from Burnside; any reason to think forces will be sent from Virginia to East Tennessee; any that Johnston has sent any force up this way? Thomas will be at Trenton, McCook at Valley Head, and Crittenden between Whiteside and Trenton, communicating with Thomas to-morrow night. We shall seize the gaps in Lookout mountain at Frick's and Winston's, while we threaten Chattanooga by the river road.

W. S. ROSECRANS, *Major General*

CAVE SPRING, *September* 5, 1863.

H. W. HALLECK, *General-in-Chief, Washington, D. C.:*

Except one division, (opposite Chattanooga,) 14th, 20th, and 21st army corps, are now across the river; by to-morrow night they will be in position in Lookout valley, extending from Rawlinsville to within six miles of Chattanooga. The rebels prepared a pontoon bridge at Chattanooga last night, with the apparent intention of crossing. I have ordered General Granger to bring up all the available reserves to Bridgeport and Stevenson, leaving minimum garrison at all posts.

W. S. ROSECRANS, *Major General.*

Official:

J. A. GARFIELD, *Brigadier General, Chief of Staff.*

HEADQUARTERS DEPARTMENT OF THE CUMBERLAND,
Trenton, Georgia, September 6, 1863.

H. W. HALLECK, *General-in-Chief, Washington, D. C.:*

I reached this place to-day. Crittenden has pushed up, near the point of Lookout mountain; enemy still in force in Chattanooga, threatening to cross the river. All reports concur that Johnston and Breckinridge are with Bragg. Buckner is closing down, and has destroyed the bridge at Loudon. Enemy attempting to-day to obstruct passes of Lookout mountain; some skirmishing at Davis's gap; twelve rebels captured. Lookout mountain is a formidable mountain, even more so than Raccoon, (just crossed,) one thousand feet high, and but three passes in forty miles. No word from Burnside.

W. S. ROSECRANS, *Major General.*

Official:

J. A. GARFIELD, *Brigadier General, Chief of Staff.*

HEADQUARTERS DEPARTMENT OF THE CUMBERLAND,
Trenton, Georgia, September 7, 1863.

Major General HALLECK, *Washington, D. C.:*

Your despatch of yesterday received with surprise. You have been often and fully advised that the nature of the country makes it impossible for this army to prevent Johnston from combining with Bragg. When orders for an advance of the army were made, it must have been known that those two rebel forces would combine against it, and to some extent choose their place of fighting us. This has doubtless been done, and Buckner, Bragg and Johnston are all near Chattanooga. The movement on East Tennessee was independent of mine. Your apprehensions are just, and the legitimate consequences of your orders. The best that can now be done is for Burnside to close his cavalry down on our left, supporting it with his infantry, and, refusing his left, threaten the enemy without getting into his grasp, while we get him in our grip and strangle him or perish in the attempt.

W. S. ROSECRANS, *Major General.*

Official:

C. GODDARD, *A. A. G.*

TRENTON, GEORGIA, *September* 9, 1863.

Major General HALLECK, *General-in-Chief, Washington, D. C.:*

I did not in my last telegraph lay enough stress on uniting Burnside's cavalry with mine. The two combined can control the country far into the interior and prevent the enemy from gathering the crops. I would respectfully urge this upon your attention.

W. S. ROSECRANS, *Major General.*

HEADQUARTERS DEPARTMENT OF THE CUMBERLAND,
Chattanooga, September 12, 1863—12 m.

Major General HALLECK, *Washington, D. C.:*

Hurlbut despatches that the country south of Corinth is full of regular cavalry. He is induced to believe that a general movement of all the available force of the enemy is being made on this army. Hurlbut ought to cover that flank. It is reported from several sources that even Loring's division has been moved up and is at Atlanta. Burnside ought to send his infantry down in this direction. The enemy has concentrated at Lafayette and attacked one of Thomas's columns in the Chickamauga valley, west of Dug gap, compelling it to fall back to Stevens's gap.

W. S. ROSECRANS, *Major General.*

Official:

J. P. DROUILLARD, *Captain and A. D. C.*

HEADQUARTERS DEPARTMENT OF THE CUMBERLAND,
Chattanooga, September 12, 1863—12 m.

Major General HALLECK, *Washington, D. C.:*

I think it would be very unwise in present attitude of affairs for General Burnside to make any move in direction of North Carolina; it would leave my left flank entirely unprotected and open the way into Kentucky; all forces should now be concentrated in this direction. I trust I am sufficient for the enemy now in my front, but should he fall back to the line of the Coosa, the roads from there are short and comparatively good to the Tennessee, where it is necessary for me to cross two ranges of mountains over very barren, rough and difficult roads to reach the Tennessee, and then move from 30 to 50 miles to reach the flank of a column moving from Gunter's landing or Whitesburg on Nashville. It is desirable to have that avenue shut up. Cannot you send a force from the army of Tennessee to do it.

W. S. ROSECRANS, *Major General.*

Official:

R. S. THOMS, *Captain and A. D. C.*

HEADQUARTERS DEPARTMENT OF THE CUMBERLAND,
Near Gordon's Mill, Georgia, September 16, 1863.

Major General HALLECK, *Washington, D. C.*:

From information derived from various sources from my front, I have reason to believe what you assert in your despatch of yesterday, 4. 30 p. m, is true, and that they have arrived at Atlanta at last. Push Burnside down.

W. S. ROSECRANS.

Official:

F. S. BOND, *Major and A. D. C.*

CRAWFISH SPRING,
September 18, 1863—1. 30 p. m.

Major General HALLECK, *Washington, D. C.:*

Everything indicates that the enemy are determined to make every effort to overthrow this army. What we need most is to have our flanks well covered. You do not say how soon Hurlbut is to move. Please advise what orders he has received, and from whence he is to draw subsistence. Even a movement in Tuscumbia valley would be of great importance at this time. Enemy demonstrating on our front now. We occupy line of West Chickamauga; our cavalry on right covers Stevens's gap.

W. S. ROSECRANS, *Major General.*

HEADQUARTERS DEPARTMENT OF THE CUMBELAND,
September 19, 1863—8 p. m.

Major General HALLECK, *Washington, D. C.:*

We have just concluded a terrific day's fighting and have another in prospect for to-morrow. The enemy attempted to turn our left, but his design was anticipated, and sufficient force placed there to render his attempt abortive. The number of our killed is considerable; that of our wounded very heavy. The enemy was greatly our superior in numbers; among our prisoners are men from some thirty regiments; we have taken two cannon and lost seven (7.) The army is in excellent condition and spirits, and by the blessing of Providence the defeat of the enemy will be total to morrow. The battle-ground was densely wooded, and its surface irregular and difficult. We could make but little use of our artillery.

W. S. ROSECRANS,
Major General Commanding.

CHATTANOOGA, *September* 21, 1863.

To the PRESIDENT *of the United States:*

After two days of the severest fighting I ever witnessed, our right centre was beaten. The left held its position until sunset. Our loss is heavy, and our troops worn down. The enemy received heavy re-enforcements. Every man of ours was in action on Sunday, and all but one brigade on Saturday. Number of our wounded large, compared with that of the killed. We took prisoners from two divisions of Longstreet. We have no certainty of holding our position. If Burnside could come immediately, it would be well; otherwise he may not be able to join us unless he comes on the west side of the river.

W. S. ROSECRANS, *Major General.*

MORRISTOWN, *September* 21, 1863.

General HALLECK:

Your despatch of the 20th received. Before I knew of the necessity of sending immediate assistance to Rosecrans, I had sent a considerable portion of my force to capture or drive out a large force of the enemy under General Sam Jones, stationed at the road from Bristol to Jonesboro, which amounts to at least 1,000 men. I had an ample force on the way to have, in all probability, accomplished this object quickly, when the urgent despatches from Rosecrans and yourself caused me to send back Brigadier General Whicks's divisions and Colonel Woolford's brigade of cavalry with orders to move as rapidly as possible until they joined Rosecrans's left flank. Colonel Byrd was ordered to Athens with his cavalry brigade; soon after occupied Knoxville, and was afterwards ordered to send a portion of his force to Cleveland, which he did, but was driven out of there three days ago. Colonel Woolford's brigade joining him will increase the force to over three thousand men, but they are now ordered to move down at once and attack Forrest, who is said to be occupying Cleveland. There is great difficulty in crossing forces above the Holston, as we have no pontoon bridge ready yet. One is being built at Loudon, which will be finished in a day or two, after which troops can cross and recross rapidly. General White's infantry division will follow down to support his cavalry as rapidly as possible. The advance of the 9th army corps will be here to-night, and will be at once put in motion down the road. The force under Jones, at Zollicoffer, is over 6,000, and I have but about that number opposed to him. Nothing but provost guards are left at Knoxville, Loudon, and this place. All the force at Cumberland gap will be brought down; I have not left a single guard at my lines. When you remember the size of our force, the amount of work which it has had to do, and the length of line occupied, you will not be surprised that I have not helped Rosecrans; more particularly, as I was fully impressed with the truth of the statement that Bragg was in full retreat. It has not seemed possible for me successfully to withdraw my force from the presence of Jones until we should be beaten back or captured; yet upon the receipt of your despatch, if it were possible to get our force from there down to Rosecrans within three or four days, I would make the attempt, and shall, at the risk of being too late, order every available man in that direction. I am sure that I am disposed to give him every possible assistance. I sincerely hope he will be able at least to check the enemy for seven or eight days, within which time I will be able to make a considerable diversion in his favor. I hope my action will meet with the approval of the department.

A. E. BURNSIDE, *Major General.*

CHATTANOOGA, *September* 21, 1863.

Major General HALLECK, *Washington:*

A man of company C, Tennessee artillery, deserted from Mobile September 1. When he left, garrison was but — Alabama regiments and three batteries, one of six guns, two of four guns, and two hundred cavalry. Joe Johnston's army all came here, except one division. Nineteen forts around city, mounting three siege guns each, 32-pounders and larger, besides three field guns two miles down bay from city; three batteries heavy guns; two rams in bay, six heavy guns each. On Pensacola side, three batteries heavy guns; forts all manned. Saw colonel and lieutenant colonel from Little Rock; said Arkansas army was very much demoralized; they said Bragg would not hold Chattanooga, but draw Rosecrans across the river and overwhelm him with numbers; said if rebels were successful at Chattanooga their cause would be greatly encouraged; if whipped there and at Charleston, confederacy was gone. Three thousand home guards were at Mobile. Officers said they feared they would turn against them if place were attacked; home guards and Tennessee battery said they would not fire a shot if they could help it; force at Mobile fear advance by Banks; one division of Johnston's army between Meridian and Selma, ready to go to Mobile or Chattanooga, as required; five thousand cavalry at Pollard, Alabama, to guard against raids; no other force beyond there between Atlanta and Montgomery. There are three floating batteries in harbor of Mobile, well manned: if necessary, they intend to sink them to obstruct the navigation; new breech-loading Whitworth gun on point near Fort Morgan.

W S. ROSECRANS, *Major General.*

HEADQUARTERS DEPARTMENT OF THE CUMBERLAND,
Chattanooga, September 23, 1863.

A. LINCOLN, *President:*

We hold this point, and cannot be dislodged except by very superior numbers and after a great battle. Immediate disposition should be made for covering our communication by ordering down every available man from Kentucky to Bridgeport and Stevenson, and having all re-enforcements you can send hurried up.

W. S. ROSECRANS, *Major General.*

Official:

FRANK S. BOND, *A. D. C.*

HEADQUARTERS DEPARTMENT OF THE CUMBERLAND,
Chattanooga, September 27, 1863.

Major General HALLECK, *Washington:*

The enemy is in our front, out of cannon range, three corps, the fourth out towards Tyners; no news from Burnside; every effort being made to secure our communications. Report of Roddy and Jesse Forrest, with four or five thousand cavalry, in vicinity of Fort Donelson; cannot the Corinth mounted force look after them? What are the orders of the troops from Grant; which way will they come; cannot they push head of column to Athens, Alabama, immediately? Please answer soon, stating what can be done to cover the flank of our railroad line from Roody and Forrest, and others in West Tennessee. No more.

W. S. ROSECRANS, *Major General.*

CHATTANOOGA, *September* 29, 1863.

Major General HALLECK, *Washington. D. C.:*

I would not advise the withdrawal of our forces from East Tennessee. Kingston should be strongly garrisoned, the bulk of the troops concentrated for movement in any direction, and cavalry thrown this way to co-operate with us. If forces from Mississippi and Potomac reach us soon, and with the expected strength, it will be sufficient for our success. It is now too late for Burnside to do more than protect our flank, but his forces should be held in readiness to help us in case of emergency. Do not hear from Grant's troops.

W. S. ROSECRANS, *Major General.*

HEADQUARTERS DEPARTMENT OF THE CUMBERLAND,
Chattanooga, September 29, 1863.

General HALLECK:

Please send the infantry by brigade as fast as possible; let the artillery follow at leisure. The great point is to have troops at Stevenson and Bridgeport, to secure those points and the railroad. We can hold this point if we can keep up communication and supplies. Hurlbut must secure us from an advance from Rome by Governor Brown.

W. S. ROSECRANS, *Major General.*

HEADQUARTERS DEPARTMENT OF THE CUMBERLAND,
Chattanooga, October 1, 1863.

Major General HALLECK, *Washington, D. C.:*

All quiet here. Enemy on our front. Our wounded coming in. Raining heavily. River begins to rise. Roads will be awful. Enemy's cavalry forced passage at several points below Kingston; thought to be moving towards McMinnville. Another cavalry column crossed below Gunter's landing, reported at New Market yesterday; they will aim to destroy the railroad communication. Our cavalry concentrated to oppose the column between us and Kingston. As I often advised, more mounted force will be needful to cover an advance, or even hold our own. I must have an able cavalry commander; Stanley is much disabled; Mitchell also. Cannot you send me John Buford? No news from Sherman. Despatches from Burnside, dated yesterday afternoon at Knoxville; no mention made of movement of enemy now between us. Regret he did not move his cavalry, as I suggested, between his right and our left; he says he will soon move according to programme subjoined, but nothing subjoined came; says it has been submitted to you.

W. S. ROSECRANS, *Major General.*

HEADQUARTERS DEPARTMENT OF THE CUMBERLAND,
Chattanooga, October 8, 1863—11.30 a. m.

Major General HALLECK, *Washington, D. C.:*

Despatch about Burnside received; no news received from him since the first. Rebel cavalry took McMinnville on fourth, crossed the railroad between Duck river and Murfreesboro, and sacked Shelbyville on the 1st. General Hooker's disposition of infantry promises to secure most vital points of railroad. Rebels tore up rails near Wartrace and vicinity and burned trestle-bridge of considerable magnitude. Mitchell, with the cavalry, overtook rebels yesterday morning near Shelbyville. Reported killed, one hundred; captured, two hundred, and three pieces of artillery, and in hot pursuit. Enemy has superior numbers and better horses; our men the *morale*, aided by the fresh cavalry on the railroad. Hope we shall irreparably damage them; enemy still on our front. No news from Sherman.

W. S. ROSECRANS, *Major General.*

Official:

R. S. THOMS, *Captain and A. D. C.*

HEADQUARTERS DEPARTMENT OF THE CUMBERLAND,
Chattanooga, October 4, 1863—1 p. m.

Major General HALLECK, *Washington, D. C.:*

Following despatches were sent to Burnside: 3 div.—11; September 30—12; September 30; October 2. This morning I received the following, October 4, (book tel. rec'd.) What more he could expect from me to induce him to move, or what I may hope from him in covering my left flank, after all this, I cannot tell. By his failure hitherto to close to our left, we have lost four hundred wagons and a large number of our mules, and the post of McMinnville, a train of eleven cars, and what other mischief they will yet do. I fear he will not assist us in pursuing the rebels, who are in heavy force, and doubtless mean to do all possible mischief to the railroad, and sweep around on Burnside's communication and come out in East Tennessee or Virginia.

W. S. ROSECRANS, *Major General.*

HEADQUARTERS DEPARTMENT OF THE CUMBERLAND,
Chattanooga, October 11, 1863.

Major General HALLECK, *Washington, D. C.:*

Our cavalry pushing rebels; have not heard from them for two days. Roddy with 1,000 mounted rebels attacked the tunnel guards near Cowan; succor from Stevenson repulsed them; Hooker thinks they would try to join Wheeler. Rebel rumors are that the head of Ewell's column reached Dalton yesterday; will know by to-morrow. Rebels deeply feel the necessity of retaking this place. No news from Sherman; are his, or any other troops, really coming to this army?

W. S. ROSECRANS, *Major General.*

Official.

R. S. THOMS, *Captain and A. D. C.*

HEADQUARTERS DEPARTMENT OF THE CUMBERLAND,
Chattanooga, October 12, 1863—3 p. m.

Hon. A. LINCOLN, *President United States:*

Line from here to Kingston is long; our side is barren mountain; rebel side has railroad. Our danger is subsistence; we cannot bring up Hooker to cover our left against a crossing above us, for want of means to transport provisions and horse-feed. Enemy's side of valley full of corn. Every exertion will be made to hold what we have and gain more, after which we must put our trust in God, who never fails those who truly trust.

W. S. ROSECRANS, *Major General.*

HEADQUARTERS DEPARTMENT OF THE CUMBERLAND,
Chattanooga, October 12, 1863—3 p. m.

Major General HALLECK, *Washington, D. C.:*

Despatches received. Reported enemy building pontoons near here. Jeff. Davis was here on the 10th. We watch the river high up, but cannot extend to Kingston without great danger. Burnside ought to hold Kingston with strong fortifications and substantial garrison—cavalry to cover the river below. Kingston should be the last point of East Tennessee surrendered, except the Cumberland gap. From there our forces can act in better concert than from any other point by the Cumberland. Mill Spring, when water is up, has a good line of retreat, and commands Loudon. No time should be lost in this matter. No further news from cavalry raid or our cavalry.

W. S. ROSECRANS, *Major General.*

HEADQUARTERS DEPARTMENT OF THE CUMBERLAND,
Chattanooga, October 13, 1863—7.30 p. m.

Major General HALLECK, *Washington, D. C.:*

Jeff. Davis was on our front Saturday and Sunday. He told the troops he would give them 30,000 re-enforcements; he would sacrifice Richmond and Charleston before he would lose this place, and bid them be of good cheer; they should be in Kentucky by November.

Some re-enforcements are now arriving at Dalton, and one division of Vicksburg prisoners, under Stevenson, is on our front. A deserter, one of the Jackson prisoners, had a paper sending him to duty, alleging his parole to have been irregular. They are building pontoons. Raining very steadily.

W. S. ROSECRANS, *Major General.*

HEADQUARTERS DEPARTMENT OF THE CUMBERLAND,
Chattanooga, October 15, 1863.

Major General HALLECK, *Washington, D. C.:*

It is of prime necessity that we should have an efficient and able chief of cavalry, and that every possible exertion should be made to swell our mounted force. I fear that rebel cavalry force has crossed the river west of us, and without serious damage. We must have mounted force to keep it in check, or it will paralyze this army, and compel it to retire from its position.

W. S. ROSECRANS.

HEADQUARTERS DEPARTMENT OF THE CUMBERLAND,
Chattanooga, October 15, 1863—1 p. m.

Major General HALLECK, *Washington, D. C.:*

If Sherman is to give us any real help, his force must not be more remote than Athens. All the rebel cavalry that can be spared from vidette duty is on that flank, and they will overpower and wear ours out, unless we have increased mounted force soon.

W. S. ROSECRANS, *Major General.*

HEADQUARTERS DEPARTMENT OF THE CUMBERLAND,
Chattanooga, October 16, 1863—5.30 p. m.

Major General HALLECK, *Washington, D. C.:*

Evidence increases that the enemy intend a desperate effort to destroy this army. They are bringing up troops to our front. They have prepared pontoons and will probably operate on our left flank, either to cross the river and force us to quit this place and fight them, or lose our communication. They will thus separate us from Burnside. We cannot feed Hooker's troops on our left, nor can we spare them from our right depots and communications; nor has he transportation. The rains have raised the river and interrupted our pontoon bridge; the roads are very heavy. Our future is not bright. Had we the railroad from here to Bridgeport—the whole of Sherman's and Hooker's troops brought up, we should not probably outnumber the enemy. This army, with its back to barren mountains, roads narrow and difficult, while the enemy has the railroad and the corn in his rear, is at much disadvantage. To secure this position, at least, McMinnville should be made a strong fortified depot; Kingston the same; and for ulterior operations, twenty or thirty thousand more troops put into Tennessee at easy points to cover the railroad and subsist until called to the front for advance on the enemy. Additional cavalry force is indispensable to a good future for this army. Burnside must be within supporting distance of us; if we lose this point his hold on East Tennessee is gone; if we hold it, the rebs cannot make much use of the country above, and we shall dispossess them.

W. S. ROSECRANS, *Major General.*

HEADQUARTERS ARMY OF THE CUMBERLAND,
Chattanooga, October 17, 1863.

Major General H. W. HALLECK,
General-in-Chief, Washington, D. C.:

The following despatch has just been received from Brigadier General Crook, commanding 2d cavalry division, dated Rogersville, Alabama:

"I have the honor to inform you that the chase is over. I would have despatched you from the different points, but the rebels left concealed parties along to pick up any couriers that I might send back, and my command was so small that I could not send large parties. I have had three fights with the enemy since I left Sequatchie valley, whipping them very badly each time. The last battle ended at Farmington, Tennessee, where I fought Wheeler's entire command with only two brigades. I cut his force in two, scattering a large portion of it, capturing four pieces of artillery, one thousand stand of small-arms, two hundred and forty prisoners, besides the wounded. As I push on after the enemy immediately, I have not been able to ascertain the number of their killed and wounded, but it was very heavy; they were scattered over a distance of fifteen miles from this, on. Their retreat was a perfect rout, their men deserting and straggling over the country. I pressed them with great vigor, but their horses being better than mine I was only able to come up with a couple of regiments at Sugar creek, left to detain me. I made a charge on them, capturing some fifty of them, and scattering the remainder in the mountains. When within eight miles of the river I struck the gallop, but when I reached the river I found they had all crossed at a ford some three miles above Lamb's ferry, where they could cross twelve abreast. I never saw troops more demoralized than they were, and I am satisfied that their loss in the raid was not less than 2,000. No fears need be entertained of their making another raid soon.

"GEORGE CROOK."

W. S. ROSECRANS.

Official:

C. GODDARD, *A. A. G.*

WASHINGTON, *April* 24, 1865.

General W. S. ROSECRANS'S examination continued.

By the chairman:

Question. At what time did you assume command of the department of Missouri?

Answer. I assumed command of the department of Missouri on the 28th of January, 1864.

Question. Please give us an account, in your own way, of your administration there—all the facts that you deem material.

Answer. Immediately on assuming command of the department, I addressed myself to ascertaining its military and civil condition. I found that St. Louis was the great depot for quartermaster and subsistence stores for supplying our armies on the Mississippi, Red river, in Kansas and the Indian territories, and one of the depots for supplying the army in Tennessee. The troops of the department consisted of four regiments of three-year volunteers, and ten regiments of Missouri State militia, so-called because, while mustered into the service of the United States and paid by the United States as three-year volunteers, they were not liable to be taken out of the State. There were also at the cavalry depot some three or four regiments of three-year volunteer cavalry, and it was made a stopping place for the veteran cavalry going home and returning from home to the field. There was also a part of a regiment of heavy artillery, which was in process of organization, called the 2d Missouri heavy artillery. The Missouri State militia consisted of nine regiments of mounted men, and one regiment of infantry. The mounted men supplied their own horses. Orders were given, soon after my arrival, that no more horses should be purchased and supplied them. These troops were scattered over the State; at Springfield and through that district; at Rolla and through that district; at Pilot Knob, Cape Girardeau, Jefferson city, Sedalia, Macon city, and St. Joseph, north of the Missouri river. There was also a force of Missouri militia called "provisionally enrolled militia," about 2,800 in number, on duty in northwest Missouri. They were called by the Union men "pawpaw militia," because, as they alleged, it was composed of persons who had been in the brush and lived upon pawpaws, until organized with other rebels to watch the Union men.

Question. Were they considered disloyal?

Answer. They were composed in a great measure of disloyal people, or people who had been disloyal, and quite a number of them had been in Price's army and had returned. They had been armed by the State government, because it was alleged that the Union people of the region either perpetrated outrages upon the property of peaceful secessionists, or permitted thieves and rascals to do so; and these men were armed in self-defence and pledged to obey the laws of the State and of the United States. I found that the "pawpaw militia" was one of the great objects of irritation. I found that "the radicals," as the ultra Union men were called, and the rebel sympathizers and disloyalists at the back of the conservatives, and using the conservatives when they could as their mouth-piece, were very much excited against each other. The principal question appeared to be whether this "pawpaw militia" was to be disbanded, and, as the conservatives alleged, given up to violence and outrage or whether they were to be trusted, and, as the Union men alleged, allowed to domineer over the Union men and keep them in subjection. It was believed by the Union men that they intended, the moment the opportunity offered, to join the invading army, which was expected, and had been threatened and promised before I arrived in Missouri, and was a constant matter of expectation from the time I arrived until the invasion was consummated. I heard both sides very patiently, and satisfied myself that the apprehensions of the Union men in regard to the "pawpaw militia" were well founded. I therefore, upon understanding the condition of affairs, immediately represented to the government at Washington the condition of affairs, and that in order to pacify this section of the State, which was in a state of great excitement, and to prevent murder and bloodshed, it was desirable that a regiment at least of troops well disciplined and well officered, and coming from some other State, should be sent to me. In the mean time I sent for the great friends and leaders of the "pawpaws," to say that I would leave them until I could get troops of this sort, provided their behavior warranted it, and I hoped they would endeavor to prove that they could be trusted. The government did not assent to my views. General Grant sent out General Hunt, under the impression that there were many more troops in Missouri than we needed there. General Hunt having gone over the State, expressed to me the belief that the inhabitants would behave themselves, and that there was no danger of any outbreak, and that he did not think that even the troops there were needed. In the mean time, ascertaining that the Union men saw arms coming into north Missouri more plentifully than for two or three years previous, and that among secessionists, and that in consequence of that they began to suspect that there was some move on foot, I took measures to ascertain what could be the cause of this purchasing of arms by the rebels, and the secret movements into which the Union men said they found it difficult to penetrate. It was not long before I found that there was some secret organization going on in north Missouri, in the shape of lodges; that the leaders of this organization were rebels, and that they met in Union settlements and in remote places, even in the brush and woods. I also found that it was currently talked in the counties of Howard, Boone, Calloway, Carroll, and Ray, along the river, slave-holding counties, between citizens of loyal sentiments and disloyalists, that the loyalists had pretty nearly had their time, and that it would soon come to an end, and then the disloyal men would have their time. This, and a great many other circumstances of a similar nature, satisfied me that it was something more than appeared on the surface which brought arms into north Missouri, and that these lodges had something more in view than merely political organization opposed to the administration.

In order to reach the bottom of the matter I succeeded in obtaining a very intelligent physician, who had been down south a great deal, to act as our agent, and sent him with a roving commission to do as he pleased in north Missouri, directing his attention to the circumstances which I have just mentioned. In a short time he made his way into one of their lodges, and from that time advanced, and finally obtained a ritual from the grand commander of the State, which settled the character of the organization, and at the same time showed that our men were thoroughly in with them. The ferreting out of the organization and its purposes was then placed completely in the hand of the provost marshal, the late Colonel Sanderson, who used to consult with me every night. Means were organized to test the accuracy of our information in various ways. For this purpose we extended into Illinois, Indiana, and Kentucky, and finally traced it to New York. We sent an agent to Canada to attend a convention of grand commanders which was to be held at Sandwich some time in April, 1864.

My official report, which is with the Judge Advocate General in Washington, will show the history of this matter. This commission, and all the details of which I have already made mention, as well as others subsequently resulting from agencies which we put to work, in four or five weeks demonstrated that the organization at in Missouri was called "The Order of American Knights," or "Sons of Liberty," a name given to the association after Vallandigham was elected supreme commander of the north, which election took place on the 22d of February, 1864; that the organization had in view a grand conspiracy to overthrow the Union cause and secure the triumph of the rebels and their sympathizers, embracing the following points: First, the return of Vallandigham to attend the democratic convention at Chicago, on the 4th of July; preparations to defend him from all arrests, and to take occasion from that to rise in all the States wherein the order existed and seize the reins of government, get the officials out of the way, and get the arsenals, forts, and public property; that these plans were known to the south, to a similar association, the supreme commander of which was General Stirling Price; that the rebels to co-operate with this movement were to invade Missouri under Price; that the American Knights in Missouri, about 23,000 strong, were to rise and join him; that Kentucky was to be invaded by Morgan's or some other force; and that the north was to be invaded by the way of Cumberland valley—probably by way of Gettysburg.

Having about a thousand pages of testimony, obtained in the way I have just mentioned, I wrote a note to General Garfield, in Washington, requesting him to state to the President that I had this; and to say, that as the time for the denouement was approaching rapidly, and that as the thing was not in a sufficiently perfect state to take action on without submitting it to him, more particularly as it concerned not only my own department, but the whole west of the nation, I wished permission from him to send a staff officer, who understood the subject, with the fragments of the testimony we had collected, to lay the whole matter before him, and answer such questions as the President desired to put; that I made this request, not because I doubted my right to send a staff officer to Washington, but because, when I had before sent a staff officer on a similar occasion on business of importance, he had been arrested by the Secretary of War, and I did not wish to subject another officer unnecessarily to such an indignity.

The President telegraphed me to send the depositions and information by mail. I wrote him that it was of such a nature that it would not be safe to transmit it by mail. He then suggested that it be sent by express. I then wrote him as well as I could, that it might be giving an opportunity to the society to find out what we were doing, and gave the reason why I could not send it in that way. He then sent his secretary, Major Hay, who came out to Missouri. As soon as he read over the fragmentary testimony he hastened back and reported to the President, then in Philadelphia, the condition of affairs.

In the meanwhile the period approached when the mischief was to begin. In Missouri, about this time, at one of their lodge meetings, when a principal man of St. Louis was present, a resolution was offered to commence the assassination of Union officers in St. Louis, beginning with the provost marshal, and then wind up with a grab at department headquarters. The resolution was laid over without objection until the next meeting, apparently because they wished to get ready. I then caused the arrest of the commander, who had been, and was then, I believe, the Belgian consul—of the deputy grand commander, the grand secretary, the lecturer, and thirty or forty of the principal conspirators throughout the State, and lodged them in the Gratiot street prison, awaiting the orders of the President as to what should be done—what should be the general policy, to meet the schemes of the organization. These men were simply permitted to make a statement under oath before the provost marshal, wherein every man of them swore distinctly that he did not know anything whatever of the existence of such an organization.

Instead of receiving the orders of the President, I received a despatch from Secretary Stanton ordering me to report why I arrested the Belgian consul, and directing me to restore him to liberty, return his papers to him, and to state to the War Department how it came to pass that I had done such a thing. He said these were the President's orders. I replied to the Secretary that, had the President known the circumstances of the case, he never would have issued that order. I respectfully requested a suspension of the order until Major Hay returned and reported to the President.

In the meanwhile, to avoid any possible difficulty in the matter, I sent the Provost Marshal General, with as much testimony as had been put into shape, to Illinois to submit it to Judge Daniels, who, in company with Governor Yates, read it over carefully, and telegraphed the President immediately that it was of the greatest importance, and that he ought by all means to see it.

About two weeks afterwards I got a despatch from the President, saying that if I had not done anything about releasing the Belgian consul I had better not do anything.

Question. Had you done anything?

Answer. No, sir, I had not. I would not have released him; I would have been relieved from duty myself before I would have released him. About this time I ascertained through the lodges that Vallandigham, suspecting that some information about his organization had got abroad, had determined to return to Ohio at an earlier period than was contemplated in their original project; that he would be a candidate for delegate from Butler county to the Chicago convention, and would make a speech in Hamilton on the 15th of May. Satisfied that this would be the case, I sent a stenographic reporter, who obtained a letter of credence from the Chicago Times, and who arrived on the ground in time to receive Mr. Vallandigham and report his speech, a copy of which he sent to the Chicago Times, the original of which he carried, by my order, to Governor Brough and General Heintzelman, whom I had telegraphed what was going to take place.

No orders came from the President until the time approached for the Chicago convention so nearly that I became alarmed, lest they should not get the information I had about the invasion of Pennsylvania. I determined to send an officer to Governor Curtin with the evidence, and a letter requesting him to examine it in company with one or two other leading men, and to see that the information it contained was made of use. The officer went to Harrisburg and laid the papers before Governor Curtin. Mr. Meredith, the attorney general of the State, General Couch, and General Cameron were called in. Fully impressed with the importance of the information, they despatched a special messenger to Washington with letters to Mr. Seward, General Garfield, and Senator Convers, who took the papers to the President. One week after that the invasion of Pennsylvania began, as the evidence predicted it would.

In the meanwhile I thought it my duty to permit to be prepared, from the evidence on hand, a synopsis of our information, which was published in the Missouri Democrat and other western papers, for the purpose of anticipating as far as we could the plans of this organization. Judge Holt came out some time after this and read over all the papers with me, and returned to Washington as fully impressed as I was with the magnitude of the mischief with which we had been threatened.

The committee remembers that the democratic convention at Chicago was postponed; but operations in Missouri, under the plans, could not be postponed. The thieves and the rascals in the northwest hoisted the rebel flag in Platte county, and commenced operations on the 7th of July. From that time until after the expiration of the invasion and the expulsion of Price, there was nothing but murder and rapine wherever they could operate.

Question. Do I understand correctly that you had ascertained that the State of Missouri was to be invaded by Price before he came there?

Answer. Yes, sir; that was the rumor there when I first arrived. The organization gained strength day by day; that is to say, I became daily more and more convinced and satisfied that the rebel portion of Missouri felt satisfied that Price would invade that State.

Question. Do you suppose his invasion was intended to be in concert with the plans of these secessionists you have mentioned?

Answer. I have no doubt it was. Not only that, but he supposed himself to be a kind of master of their movements; he supposed the societies to be acting under his guidance in a certain measure, and paving the way for him, informing him as thoroughly as they could what they would do. They had an organization to run horses to him, to carry pistols in small quantities to him and to the recruits and guerillas in Arkansas. They kept up a regular mail with him.

Question. Did you learn from your evidence in any way that he belonged to this order of knights?

Answer. He was the supreme commander of the order south; and the order was instituted in Missouri mainly by a man who was called the deputy high priest, commissioned by him to do it.

Question. Who was he?

Answer. One Douglass.

Question. A resident of Missouri?

Answer. Yes, sir, who had been in the rebel army, and had come back to Missouri some nine months or a year before.

Question. You have stated that Secretary Stanton arrested one of your messengers on the way here with information. Why was that done?

Answer. He arrested my senior aid who brought letters to General Halleck and General Grant respecting the condition of Missouri, and the measures which I thought immediately necessary there to be of advantage to the government and to the Stâte. He was arrested on the pretence that he had no permission to come here, under an old order that no officer should visit Washington without permission from the Secretary of War. Major Bond returned home under arrest; and considering that the shortest way to get rid of his arrest would be to have him tried, I ordered his trial by a court composed of the highest officers in Missouri, Major General Pleasonton being president. That court unanimously and honorably acquitted him.

Question. Did the authorities refuse to receive the information you sent by him?

Answer. They never answered any of the letters, although they were important—so much so that I should like to submit copies of them to the committee.

Question. I wish you would submit them in connexion with this testimony.

Answer. I have gone through a sort of history of our discovery of this secret society, and what was the end of it. I will now return to the military arrangements and what I proposed to do.

I proposed to the government, in the first place, that the citizen provost marshals, who were scattered all over the State, who had been used as tools of political factions, and had created a distrust of all military authority and of all just action, should be replaced by good officers, taken from those not fit for active service on account of disability, headed by a provost marshal of the same sort. I proposed, secondly, that there should be sent four or five regiments of troops, well disciplined and well officered, but belonging to other States, to be posted in the most disturbed districts of the State, where collisions between the Unionists and the—I might almost say—conservatives were imminent; and also for the purpose of enabling me to reorganize the Missouri State militia, and put it upon the basis of the three-years service. Thirdly, that inasmuch as the principal use of those troops beyond guarding the depots was to secure the citizens of the State in tilling the ground, and as the principal danger to them lay from Price's army south, and from his emissaries who came up to pave the way for his purposes and get recruits for him, all the spare troops of Missouri, those of Arkansas and those of Louisiana, should be combined under one command to operate against the enemy, drive him out west of Mississippi, and sweep them down from the Arkansas river to the Gulf.

I sent General Ewing to have an interview with General Sherman, to whose division the department of Arkansas belonged, and requested him to see General Grant; and I wrote a letter to the War Department, dated the 10th of March, proposing this, which letter I should like the committee to see. General Sherman agreed with my plan, and presented it to General Grant at Nashville, who then appeared to think favorably of it; but he reserved his decision until he arrived at Washington, from whence he had me informed that no other movements would take place west of the Mississippi than those then about to commence, viz., the Red river expedition, under General Banks, and Steele's co-operative expedition.

After the massacre at Fort Pillow the four regiments of three-years troops were taken away from St. Louis, which was also stripped of all the three-years cavalry which could be turned out from the cavalry bureau. This subtraction of all regular troops, just about the time the order of American Knights had planned their insurrection, made it necessary to make some provision against accident. To that end I obtained authority from the Secretary of War to raise twelve-months volunteers for the defence of the State, and under that authority I called for eleven regiments. As my personal popularity was of some use, we succeeded in raising the regiments and organizing them during the summer and early part of the fall.

Although the invasion by Price did not take place as early as it had been threatened, from the first to the middle of July, it was only deferred until corn was ripe enough. In the mean time the secret societies, and the soldiers from Price's army, recruiting through their instrumentality in the rebel districts of Missouri, kept up a guerilla war which was very harassing to the citizens. The account of the campaign against General Price and its result, are so fully given in my official report, that I think it best to have that taken as a part of my testimony.

Question. Have you a copy of that report?

Answer. Yes, sir; and I will furnish it to the committee. To what is therein stated, I can now add from various reports founded on rebel authority, that I am satisfied General Price lost in that campaign between 18,000 and 19,000 men. The report, which appeared in both the New York Herald and New York Tribune, some time in March, obtained, I believe, from Henry S. Foote, states that they report a loss of 19,500 men.

Question. In connexion with your account of this conspiracy of the American Knights, I will ask you who were the leaders of the organization in Missouri, so far as you ascertained?

Answer. In my official report which, is in Judge Holt's office, there is a full list of the leaders throughout the State. I would suggest that that be made a part of my testimony.

Question. For what reason were you ultimately removed from that command?

Answer. No reason was ever assigned to me, nor have I ever, directly or indirectly, heard of any reason for it until within the last six weeks. I have lately heard, from three or four different sources, that I was removed at the personal request of General Grant, who was supposed, by the parties giving me that information, to be extremely hostile to me. As no occasion for any such hostility has ever been given by me, so far as I know, I am at a loss to understand it. General Grant's chief of staff, General Rawlins, visited me after the close of the campaign of General Price. He mixed freely with the citizens, and took the pains to volunteer the statement, in my office, in the presence of various members of my staff, that he was satisfied that things had been managed wonderfully well during that campaign; that few could have done as well, and probably none better.

Question. Has there been any misunderstanding between you and General Grant at any time?

Answer. Never. On one occasion, when some of his staff told my staff that he was under the impression that the newspaper correspondents who, in 1862, attacked him in the Chicago Tribune and other papers, had received some countenance at my headquarters, I had a conversation with him upon the subject. He expressly stated that he did not suppose it came from me; and after conversation with him, in which I answered him that there was not the slightest foundation for such a feeling, he not only expressed himself satisfied, but we parted, promising continued friendly intercourse wherever duty might throw us.

Question. Was there any complaint or remonstrance from the authorities here in regard to any part of your administration?

Answer. Never a complaint, never a remonstrance, never the slightest inquiry from any one except the President, early in my administration, concerning the order which I published requiring preachers holding conventions to take the oath of allegiance, if they had not already done so. About that Mr. Lincoln wrote me a letter asking some explanations, and, among others, how I could reconcile it to require the oath of allegiance of preachers, and allow political meetings to take place without requiring those who took part in them to take the same oath. To this I replied that political meetings were open to surveillance, while religious convocations were not; that if I sent a man to their religious convocations to exercise a surveillance over them, and prevent them from using their meetings as a clock for political iniquity, it would be an interference with their religious freedom. I therefore required of them to assure me, under oath, that they were not going to do any mischief to the government in their convocations, and the President appeared to be satisfied.

Question. Among the religious denominations were any of them of secession proclivities?

Answer. The southern Methodists were regarded as extremely so, and it was at the suggestion of some southern Methodists who were loyal that that order was published. It was made general, however, so that no religious bodies could assemble without first taking the oath of allegiance; believing that those who were loyal would have no objection to do that, and that those who were disloyal would be compelled to hold no meetings, or to put themselves under a bond of good behavior.

Question. That applied to all religious societies?

Answer. Yes, sir; the southern Methodists said that a large number of preachers, who had run off to Arkansas, would participate in this meeting, and that they would pave the way for Price.

PAPERS FROM THE WAR DEPARTMENT.

WAR DEPARTMENT,
Washington, May 15, 1865.

SIR: I have the honor to transmit herewith, in compliance with your request of the 24th ultimo, copies of the following documents:

Reports of General McClellan and General Rosecrans of the battle of Rich Mountain, Virginia, with accompanying sub-reports.

Reports of General Grant and General Rosecrans of the battle of Iuka, Mississippi, and of the battle of Corinth.

Report of General Rosecrans of his campaign in Missouri.

Your obedient servant,

EDWIN M. STANTON,
Secretary of War.

Hon. B. F. WADE,
Chairman Committee on the Conduct of the War, Washington.

BATTLE OF RICH MOUNTAIN.

HEADQUARTERS DEPARTMENT OF THE OHIO,
Buckhannon, Virginia, July 3, 1861.

GENERAL: Yours of the 2d has reached me. After questioning your messenger and hearing his full story, I confess that I do not share your apprehensions, and that I am not a little surprised that you feel the defense of Philippi so hazardous and dangerous an operation.

If four thousand (nearly) of our men, in a position selected and fortified in advance, with ample time to examine the ground carefully and provide against any possible plan of attack, are not enough to hold the place against any force these people can bring against it, I think we had better all go home at once. If we cannot fight in position, I am much mistaken as to our men.

I have, however, in deference to your views, ordered the 6th Ohio on temporary duty with you until the crisis is past, although I believe they can be employed to more advantage at other points.

This is all the re-enforcement I can now spare. As to the one or two squadrons of efficient cavalry asked for by Captain Benham, it seems hardly necessary for me to repeat that I have only one and a half companies, such as they are, and that more important duty is for them here.

You have only to defend a strong position, or, at most, to follow a retreating enemy. I fear you do not share the confidence I feel in our men, and that you regard their cavalry as more dangerous than I do.

I feel that these men of ours can be worked up to any deed of daring, that their leaders can make them cool under fire, and that a couple of good companies of infantry can drive off all their cavalry in this mountainous country. I propose taking the really difficult and dangerous part of this work on my own hands. I will not ask you to do anything that I would not be willing to do myself. But let us understand each other: I can give you no more re-enforcements. I cannot consent to weaken any further the really active and important column which is to decide the fate of the campaign. If you cannot undertake the defence of Philippi with the force now under your control, I must find some one who will. I have ordered up Latham's company, all of "Keys's" cavalry that are fit to take the field, and the 6th Ohio. Do not ask for further re-enforcements; if you do, I shall take it as a request to be relieved from your command and to return to Indiana.

I have spoken plainly; I speak officially. The crisis is a grave one, and I must have generals under me who are willing to risk as much as I am, and be content to risk their lives and reputation with such means as I can give them. Let this be the last of it. Give me full details as to the information you obtained—not mere rumors, but facts—and leave it to my judgment to determine what force you need. I wish action now, and determination.

I am, sir, very respectfully, your obedient servant,

GEORGE B. McCLELLAN, *Major General, Commanding.*

General T. A. MORRIS, *Philippi.*

HEADQUARTERS DEPARTMENT OF THE OHIO, *Beverly, Va., July* 10, 1861.

Official copy:

S. WILLIAMS, *Assistant Adjutant General.*

HEADQUARTERS DEPARTMENT OF THE OHIO,
Buckhannon, Virginia, July 6, 1861.

GENERAL: The major general commanding directs that you advance from your present position to-morrow morning and take up a position within two miles of the enemy, near Elliott's farm—in preference on the south side of Barker's Mill run, on the heights in rear of William Yeager's house. It is deemed preferable to avoid the defile north of the Elliott house by crossing the river somewhere near the nineteen-mile post from Beverly, and re-crossing at the ford where the middle fork road crosses, just at the position to be occupied. Your train may remain at Philippi, under a sufficient escort, until you have occupied your new position. You will move prepared to force any opposition offered, and will at all hazards accomplish the object proposed. Occupy Beelington by a strong advanced guard, and place a strong detachment to cover the paths leading from the rebel camp to the left flank of your position. From this position push out strong infantry reconnoissances to ascertain the exact position, condition, and movements of the enemy. Watch them closely day and night, have everything ready to pursue them should they retreat, and follow them up closely in that event.

Make extended reconnoissances, calculated to give the impression that the main attack is to be made by you, and use all efforts to retain them in their present position. Arrange your hour of starting from Philippi so that you will, by an easy march, reach the vicinity of Elliott's within an hour or two after sunrise. Let your advanced guard be of infantry, strong, and near the main column. Do not push out any advanced cavalry patrols. A strong advanced guard will move from here to-morrow morning to occupy the middle fork bridge; by the next day the Roaring creek bridge will be taken, and perhaps on the same day the town of Beverly will be occupied. The general is delayed by the non-arrival of supplies, but hopes to occupy Beverly on Tuesday, at latest—probably on Monday. He asks you to do all in your power to hold the enemy in check in the present position, and to induce them to believe that you will make the main attack, the object being to cut them off at Beverly.

I have the honor to be, sir, very respectfully, your obedient servant,

S. WILLIAMS, *Assistant Adjutant General.*

Brigadier General T. A. MORRIS, *Commanding at Philippi.*

HEADQUARTERS DEPARTMENT OF OHIO, *Beverly, Va., July* 16, 1861.

Official copy:

S. WILLIAMS, *Assistant Adjutant General.*

HEADQUARTERS, AT MR. KETTLE'S HOUSE,
Near Tygart's, Vally River, six miles from Beverly, July 12, 1861.

SIR: I write to state to you that I have, in consequence of the retreat of General Garnett, and the jaded and reduced condition of my command, most of them having been without food for two days, concluded, with the concurrence of a majority of my captains and field officers, to surrender my command to you to-morrow as *prisoners of war.* I have only to add, I trust they will only receive at your hands such treatment as has been invariably shown to the northern prisoners by the south.

I am, sir, your obedient servant,

JNO. PEGRAM,
Lieutenant Colonel P. A., C. S., Commanding.

COMMANDING OFFICER *of Northern Forces, Beverly, Virginia.*

HEADQUARTERS, DEPARTMENT OF THE OHIO,
Beverly, Virginia, July 13, 1861.

SIR: Your communication dated yesterday, proposing to surrender as prisoners of war the force assembled under your command, has been delivered to me.

I will receive you, your officers and men, as prisoners, and I will treat you and them with the kindness due to prisoners of war, but it is not in my power to relieve you or them from any liabilities incurred by taking arms against the United States.

I am, sir, respectfully, your obedient servant,

GEO. B. McCLELLAN,
Major General U. S. Army, Commanding Department.

JOHN PEGRAM, Esq.,
Styling himself Lieutenant Colonel P. A., C. S.

HEADQUARTERS, DEPARTMENT OF THE OHIO,
Beverly, Virginia, July 13, 1861.

Official copy:

S. WILLIAMS, *Assistant Adjutant General.*

CHEAT RIVER CAMP,
Corrick's Ford, eight miles south of Saint George, Va., *July* 13, 1861.

SIR: In accordance with your directions this morning, I took command of the advance guard of your column, consisting of the 14th Ohio, Colonel Steadman, with one section of Colonel Barnett's artillery, the 7th Indiana, under Colonel Damon, and the 9th Indiana, Colonel Milroy, in all about 1,800 men, and with this force, as instructed, I started from near Leedsville at about 4 a. m. to pursue the army of General Garnett, which consisting, as we learned, of 4,000 to 5,000 men, and four to six cannon, had retreated from the north side of Laurel mountain, near Beelington, the day before yesterday.

It being ascertained that the enemy had retired towards the village of "New Interest," and thence, as was supposed, over a mountain road leading to Shaffer fork or main branch of the Cheat river, to St. George, the troops were brought rapidly forward on their route, so as to reach the entrance of the mountain road, about seven miles' march, at about 6 o'clock.

A short distance after entering this path the passage was found to be obstructed by large trees, recently felled in about twelve to fifteen places, and in nearly every defile for three or four miles; but the information that was from time to time received that this force, which had some fifeen hours the start of us from Beelington, were now only four or five miles in advance, encouraged our efforts, and though for nearly the whole time the rain was pouring in torrents, and the clayey roads almost impassable in many places, the spirit of the troops, without exception, as it came under my eye, was such as to bear them most rapidly onward. Under all these trials, superadded to that of hunger with the greater part of them for the previous fifteen or twenty hours, at about noon we reached Kaler's, or the first ford of the Shafer branch or main Cheat river, having within the previous two or three miles fired at and driven in several pickets of the enemy, protecting those who were forming the barricades, and at one place we broke up a camp where the meals were being cooked.

At the ford near Kaler's, and at about one-half the distance to another ford, which we afterwards met with about one mile further on, we saw the baggage train of the enemy apparently at rest. This I proposed to attack as soon as strengthened by the arrival of Steadman's 2d battalion, with Dumant's regiment, when the thoughtless firing of a musket at our ford; set the train rapidly in motion, and long lines of infantry were formed in order of battle to protect it. In a few minutes, however, the arrival of Barnett's artillery, with Dumant close upon it, enabled the commander to push forward in its original order. But the train and its guard had retired, leaving only a few skirmishers to meet us at the second ford, where, however, quite a rapid firing was kept up by the advance regiment, and the artillery opened for some minutes to clear the adjacent woods the more completely of the enemy. We then continued our march rapidly to this ford, and as we approached it we came upon their trains the last half of it just crossing in the river. The enemy was found to have taken a strong position with his infantry and artillery, upon a precipitous bank of some fifty to eighty feet in height upon the opposite side of the river. While our own ground was upon the low land, nearly level with the river, Steedman's regiment in the advance, opened its fire most gallantly upon them, which was immediately returned by their strong force of infantry and by their cannon, upon which Barnett's artillery was ordered up, and opened upon them with excellent effect.

As I soon perceived a position by which their left could be turned, six companies of Colonel Dumant's regiment were ordered to cross the river, about three hundred yards above them, to pass up the hill obliquely from our right to their left, and take them in rear. By some mistake, possibly in the transmission of the order, this command crossed at about double this distance, and turned at first to their right, which delayed the effect of this movement. After some fifteen minutes, however, this error was rectified, and the hill being reported as impracticable, this command, now increased to the whole regiment, were ordered down to the ford under close cover of this hill on their side, and then to take them directly in front at the road.

The firing of Steedman's regiment and of Milroy's, now well up and in action, with repeated and rapid discharges of the artillery during this movement, decided the action at once. As Dumant reached the road, having passed along and under their whole front, the firing ceased, and the enemy fled in great confusion, Dumant's regiment pursuing them for about one mile further, having a brisk skirmishing with their rear for the first half of that distance, during which General Garnett was killed

The enemy would still have been followed up most closely, and probably to the capture of a large portion of their scattered army, but this was absolutely impossible with our fatigued and exhausted troops, who had already marched some eighteen miles or more in an almost incessant violent rain, and the greater part of them without food since the evening, and a portion of them even from the noon of yesterday, so warm had been the pursuit on their hasty retreat from Laurel mountain, twenty-five miles distant. The troops were therefore halted for food and rest at about 2 p. m. The result of the action proves to be the capture of about forty loaded wagons and teams, (being nearly all their baggage trains, as we learn,) and including a large portion of new clothing, camp equipage, and other stores, their headquarters papers, and military chest; also, two stands of colors, and one fine rifled piece of artillery.

While the commanding general, Robert S. Garnett, is killed, his body being now cared for by us, and fifteen or twenty more of the enemy are killed, and nearly fifty prisoners are taken, our own loss is two killed, and six or seven wounded, one dangerously.

In concluding this report, I feel it my duty to state that just as the action was closing, the head regiment of the body of the troops under yourself, though starting, as I learn, three hours later, (the 6th Indiana, under Colonel Crittenden,) came up to the field in excellent order, but unfortunately too late to aid us in the battle.

The conduct of those gallant officers, Colonels Barnett, Steedman, Dumant, and Milroy, with the steady perseverance of their officers and men, in their long and arduous march, suffering from hunger, rain, and cold, with their gallantry in action, was most heroic, and beyond all praise of mine. Their country only can appreciate and reward their services.

I have the honor to be, sir, very respectfully, your obedient servant,

H. W. BENHAM, *Captain of Engineers,*
Chief Engineer Department of the Ohio and Commanding Advance Column.

General T. A. Morris,
Commanding United States Forces.

Sir: I reported yesterday, at about 6 a. m., the progress of the forces of my command in pursuit of the enemy retreating from Laurel hill.

The pursuit was continued through the day in the same order as stated in my report of yesterday morning, viz: Steedman's 14th Ohio in advance, with two sections of Barnett's artillery; next Dumant's 7th Indiana, and Milroy's 9th Indiana.

These regiments, as I reported, started in pursuit from our resting place near Leedsville at about 4 o'clock in the morning, under the immediate command of Captain Benham. The remainder of the column were on the march by 5 o'clock a. m. A drizzling rain commenced about 6 o'clock, which by 9 became quite heavy.

The enemy left the main turnpike and turned towards Cheat river, crossing two branches of the Laurel mountain over a narrow and difficult road Owing to the heavy rain the roads were rendered very difficult for the men and the few wagons of ammunition and provisions. By 11 o'clock the rain became a drenching storm, and continued for several hours, the roads in the mountains becoming nearly impassable. At 2 o'clock the whole command were up to the position which we now occupy.

For details of the operations of the advance column I refer you to the report of Captain Benham.

The attention of the commanding general is particularly called to the gallant bearing of the regiments which led the advance. I would also call attention to the fact that the entire command commenced the pursuit on a few minutes' notice, without time to prepare even a day's rations for the haversacks.

I ordered four wagons to be loaded with hard bread and pork, to follow the command. These four wagons, with the additional rations put in with the ammunition, is all the provisions the command has had since leaving Burlington, except some beeves procured in this vicinity. The march of yesterday was from eighteen to twenty miles.

When it is considered that we have put to flight a force equal to our own, and have pursued him night and day for thirty hours, almost without provisions, over a mountainous and difficult road, and part of the time through a drenching storm, we may feel sure that our cause must be successfully maintained by men who show such gallant bearing and soldierly endurance.

Justice to a gallant soldier compels me to say that, from Philippi to the routing of the enemy at this place, too much praise cannot be bestowed on Captain Benham, and I take this occasion to thank him for the invaluable service he has rendered me I must also call attention to the services of Major W. Gordon, now of the 11th regiment of infantry, United States army. Major Gordon volunteered a private in the 9th Indiana regiment, was promoted sergeant major in the same regiment, and two weeks since received the appointment of major in the regular army. Owing to the position of the enemy in front of the brigade in which he was serving as sergeant major, he requested to be retained until the issue should be settled. Acting yesterday as my volunteer aid with the advance column, Captain Benham testifies to his gallantry and invaluable services during the entire day, and more especially in the face of the enemy.

I am, sir, very respectfully, your obedient servant,

T. A. MORRIS, *Brigadier General, Commanding.*

Major SETH WILLIAMS,
Assistant Adjutant General, Department of the Ohio.

HEADQUARTERS ARMY OF OCCUPATION, WESTERN VIRGINIA,
Camp near Huttonsville, July 14, 1861.

COLONEL: I have the honor to submit, for the information of the commanding general, the following report of the operations of the forces under my command from the time of my leaving Grafton:

Previous to my departure from Grafton I became satisfied that a large body of the rebel army (supposed to consist of six or seven thousand men, under Brigadier General Robert S. Garnett, formerly of the United States army) occupied an intrenched position at Laurel hill, about thirteen miles south of Philippi, on the turnpike leading to Beverly, with the apparent intention of making a determined stand at that point. Whereupon I at once resolved to push on with all the available force at my disposal, and endeavor, by making a rapid detour through Buckhannon, to reach Beverly and strike their rear, cutting off their supply communication from Staunton.

As soon as I had concentrated my forces at Buckhannon, I moved forward, and at the same time ordered General Morris to advance from Philippi and take a commanding position about a mile and a half distant, and directly opposite the enemy's works, thereby enabling him to divert their attention from me, also to watch their movements and be in position to act promptly after I had reached their rear at Beverly.

General Morris promptly responded to my order and secured the proper position with but slight resistance, and I pushed forward with my column as rapidly as my means of transportation would permit

On the evening of the 9th instant I arrived at Roaring creek, near the base of Rich mountain, where I found the enemy, in considerable force, had destroyed a bridge, and were strongly intrenched at a point where the road enters a defile leading up the mountain, about two miles distant from my camp. On the morning of the 10th I ordered a reconnoissance in force, consisting of the 9th and 4th Ohio volunteers and Loomis's battery, under the supervision of Lieutenant Poe, topographical engineers. This was pushed within two hundred yards of the enemy's guns, and resulted in the loss of one man killed and one wounded, but the dense thickets with which their works were surrounded prevented the attainment of much positive or satisfactory information. It served, however, to confirm my previous supposition that the intrenchments were held by a large force, with several guns in position to command the first approaches, and that a direct assault would result in a heavy and unnecessary l ss of life. These considerations at once determined me to make an effort to turn their flank and commence the attack from the rear. Accordingly I ordered General Rosecrans to move at 4 o'clock in the morning with the 19th Ohio, the 8th, 10th, and 13th Indiana regiments, and Burdsall's dragoons, to cut his way through the almost impenetrable thickets of brush to the lofty summit of Rich mountain, at Hart's farm, about five miles distant, and to move thence at once down the turnpike road and attack the intrenchments in rear, and, during the progress of his march, to communicate with me every hour. The remainder of the force under my command to be held in readiness to assault in front as soon as Rosecrans's musketry should indicate that he was immediately in their rear. The order to General Rosecrans to attack the rear of the enemy's lower intrenchments was not carried out, but his brigade remained at Hart's farm during the remainder of the day and night, and I received no communication from him after about 11 o'clock a. m., when he was still distant about a mile and a half from Hart's farm.

About the time I expected the general to reach the rear of their intrenchments I moved up all my available force to the front and remained, in person, just in rear of the advance pickets, ready to assault when the indicated moment should arrive. In the mean time I sent Lieutenant Poe to find such a position for our artillery as would enable us to command the works. Late in the afternoon I received his report that he had found such a place. I immediately detailed a party to cut a road to it for our guns, but it was too late to get them into position before dark, and, as I had received no intelligence whatever of General Rosecrans's movements, I finally determined to return to camp, leaving merely sufficient force to cover the working party. Orders were then given to move up ten guns with the entire available infantry at daybreak the following morning. As the troops were much fatigued, some delay occurred in moving from camp, and just as the guns were starting intelligence was received that the enemy had evacuated their works and fled over the mountains, leaving all their guns, means of transportation, ammunition, tents, and baggage behind. Then, for the first time since 11 o'clock the previous day, I received a communication from General Rosecrans giving me the first intimation that he had taken the enemy's position at Hart's farm, from which it appeared that he, with great difficulty, and almost superhuman efforts on the part of his men, had forced his way up the precipitous side of the mountain, and at about 1 p. m. reached the summit, where he encountered a portion of the enemy's forces, with two guns in position behind earth and log works, affording protection to their men.

The attack was commenced by the enemy with heroic spirit and determination. They opened upon the advance of our column with volleys of musketry and rapid discharges of canister, killing several of our men and at first throwing them into some confusion. They however soon rallied and returned a brisk and accurate fire, which told with terrible effect in the enemy's ranks, killing and wounding nearly every man at their guns. The troops then advanced, continuing their well-directed fire until they drove the enemy from their position and caused them to take flight down the turnpike towards their intrenchments at the base of the mountain.

The troops then encamped on the battle-field at about 2 o'clock p. m., and remained there until the following morning, when I made a rapid march and occupied Beverly. I here learned that General Garnett, as soon as he discovered we were approaching his rear and had cut off his retreat in this direction, abandoned his intrenchments at Laurel hill, leaving his tents and other property, and had made a hasty retreat in the night over a rough country road leading towards St. George. General Morris had been repeatedly instructed by me to keep a close watch upon Garnett's movements, and to be ready the moment he retreated to follow him up vigorously with all his available force and crush him if possible; but, much to my surprise, when he discovered that Garnett had escaped, he only sent a portion of his force about eight miles, and then halted it for several hours to communicate with me and bring up re-enforcements.

This detention gave Garnett the opportunity to get far in advance, and had it not been for the rapid and well-directed march of the advance conducted by Captain Benham, it is believed that the rebel general would have escaped unharmed. Captain Benham is entitled to great praise for his prompt and energetic movement upon Garnett's rear, the result of which will be seen from his report enclosed. This shows that General Garnett and about twenty others of the enemy were killed, and fifty prisoners, two stands of colors, and one rifled cannon taken, besides the baggage train and a large amount of other property. I take very great pleasure in recommending Captain Benham to the special notice of the general-in-chief.

Immediately after learning that Garnett had retreated, I ordered Brigadier General Hill (commanding at Grafton) to assemble all his disposable force and endeavor, by a rapid march upon Saint George or West Union, to cut off the retreat of the rebels; but I have not yet heard the result of his movement. My last advices this evening report General Hill's advance within four miles of the retreating rebels.

I have not time now to notice individual acts of merit and bravery displayed in the recent conflicts, but shall take an early opportunity of presenting them to you in detail. I cannot, however, let the present occasion pass without making mention of the services of Brigadier General Rosecrans in conducting his command up the very precipitous sides of the mountains and overcoming the formidable obstacles which impeded his progress; also, for the very handsome manner in which he planned and directed his attack upon the rebels at Hart's farm, carrying them after a stout and determined resistance. I also consider it due to my volunteer aide-de-camp, Colonel F. W. Lander, to speak of his services in this connexion. He (by the request of General Rosecrans) accompanied his column, and by his experience assisted materially in conducting the troops over a most difficult country, and displayed extraordinary activity and courage in the battle. He escaped unhurt, having the horse under him disabled by a canister shot.

I pursued the retreating rebels yesterday as far as Cheat river, and became satisfied that they would not stop short of Staunton. I therefore returned to this camp, which commands the communication between eastern and western Virginia over the Staunton and Parkersburg turnpike.

General Garnett's command, when last heard from, were retreating in great confusion near the north branch of the Potomac on the road leading from West Union to Williamsport.

I trust I will not be regarded as merely conforming to a formula when I expres the great obligations due to my personal and general staff, who by their good judgment, untiring energy and cool conduct, have enabled me to overcome the inevitable difficulties of an imperfect and hasty organization, and to accomplish whatever good results have been achieved. As far as I have myself observed and learned from their officers, the conduct of the volunteers who participated in the actions at Rich mountain and at Carrick's ford was unexceptionable. They invariably displayed an ardent desire to meet the enemy, and great gallantry in action, and, in my judgment, all they require to make good and reliable soldiers is a little more drill and discipline.

The results of the action at Rich mountain, as nearly as can be ascertained, were as follows: Our loss in killed, 12; wounded, 59; no prisoners. The loss of the enemy in killed, 135; wounded and prisoners, (not yet reported,) as near as can be determined, between 800 and 900. Two brass 6-pounder cannon, a large number of muskets, two stands of colors, and other property, were taken. Two 6-pounder brass cannon were captured at the lower intrenchments, with a large wagon train, with horses and a large number of tents. But the really important results of these operations are the complete rout and annihilation of the rebel forces, the capture of one and the death of the other of their leaders, that this portion of Western Virginia is entirely freed from their presence and that there is now not one seingle organized band of the rebels on this side of the mountain north of the Kanawha valley.

After my arrival at Beverly I received a note from Colonel Pegram containing a proposition to surrender his command as prisoners of war. This note, with my reply, are enclosed. His command, consisting of 33 commissioned officers and 560 men, are now prisoners.

I am, sir, very respectfully, your obedient servant,

GEORGE B. McCLELLAN, *Major General U. S. Army.*

Colonel E. D. TOWNSEND, A. A. G.,
Headquarters of the Army, Washington, D. C.

HEADQUARTERS 1ST BRIGADE U. S. VOLUNTEER MILITIA,
Beverly, Virginia, July 19, 1861.

MAJOR: In obedience to the order of the major general commanding, I have the honor to submit the following report of the operations of the 1st brigade, consisting of the 8th and 10th Indiana volunteer militia, the 13th Indiana U. S. volunteer infantry, and 19th Ohio U. S. volunteer militia, which resulted in dislodging the rebel forces from their intrenched position at camp Garnett on Rich mountain.

After the armed reconnoissance was over, by direction of the major general I ordered the 8th Indiana to bivouac in advance of the camp at Roaring creek, and the 10th and 13th into camp.

About 10 p. m. I came to the headquarters with a plan for turning the enemy's position. The general, having considered it and heard the information on which it was based, was pleased to direct me to carry it out, and for that purpose ordered Colonel Sullivan, of the 13th Indiana, and Burdsall's cavalry, temporarily attached to the brigade, and that the movement should begin at daylight on the next morning.

The troops were ordered to parade in silence under arms, without knapsacks, with one day's rations in their haversacks and their canteens filled with water. By inadvertence the assembly was sounded in the 19th Ohio regiment and lights put in several tents, when I discovered it; but they were promptly extinguished.

The pickets relieved, the regimental camps and guards with the sick, and a few men of each company remaining, orders were given that the reveille should be beaten at the usual hour, and the column formed and moved forward in the following order and strength:

First. 8th Indiana, under Benton	242	strong.
Second. 10th Indiana, under Manson	425	"
Third. 13th Indiana, under Sullivan	650	"
Fourth. 19th Ohio, under Beatty	525	"
Total infantry	1,842	
Fifth. Burdsall's cavalry	75	
Aggregate	1,917	

Colonel Lander, accompanied by the guide, led the way through a pathless forest over rocks and ravines, keeping far down on the southeastern declivities of the mountain spurs and using no axe, to avoid discovery by the enemy, whom we supposed would be on the alert by reason of the appearance of unusual stir in our camp and the lateness of the hour. A rain set in about 6 a. m. and lasted until about 11 o'clock a. m., with intermissions, during which the column pushed cautiously and steadily forward, and arrived at last and halted in rear of the crest on the top of Rich mountain, hungry and weary with an eight-hours' march over a most unkindly road. They lay down to rest, while Colonel Lander and the general examined the country. It was found that the guide was too much scared to be with us longer, and we had another valley to cross, another hill to climb, another descent beyond that to make, before we could reach the Beverly road at the top of the mountain. On this road we started at 2 o'clock and reached the top of the mountain after the loss of an hour's time, by mistake in the direction of the head of the column, in rectifying which the 10th Indiana took the advance.

Shortly after passing over the crest of the hill, the head of the column, ordered to be covered by a company deployed as skirmishers, was fired on by the enemy's pickets, killing Sergeant James A. Taggart and dangerously wounding Captain Christopher Miller, of the 10th. The column then advanced through dense brushwood, emerging into rather more open brushwood and trees, when the rebels opened a fire of both musketry and 6-pounders, firing some case shot and a few shells.

The 10th advanced and took position at A, Plan No. 1, with one company deployed as skirmishers covering its front. The 8th advanced and halted in column of fours at B. The 13th advanced to C, in an old road, where it was ordered to occupy the heights, with three companies at *d d d*, and skirmish down the hill, keeping strong reserves on the top; three companies were ordered back to E, to cover the debouch up the valley on the left; the companies of the remainder were to fill the space in the line marked ⊤|⊤|⊤, the remaining two companies standing in column at ⁂. The 19th Ohio came down the road and halted in column at H.

Owing to misunderstanding orders, Colonel Sullivan occupied the hill with his whole regiment, and it took forty minutes to correct the error and get into the proper position as indicated. The command forward was then given, and another company from the right of the 10th deployed as skirmishers, leaving an interval through which the 8th could pass in column and charge the rebel battery on the left of their position at Z as soon as our fire had told properly. At the same time Colonel Sullivan was to take his four companies and charge around the road on the left. After an advance of fifty yards and some heavy firing from our line, the enemy showed signs of yielding, and I gave orders to the 8th and sent them to the colonel of the 13th, to charge in column. The 8th made a mistake and got into line at B, where, in consideration of their abundant supplies of ammunition, I left them.

The 13th went into column at D, Plan 2. Seven companies of the 19th Ohio deployed into line at H and delivered two splendid volleys, when the enemy broke. Meanwhile I rode round to the 13th and drove them in to charge up across the road, as shown at L. The 10th charged by fours at J. The 8th came down and charged upon the rebel front at K.

The battle was over, the enemy dispersed, one piece of cannon taken at A, another at B, and their dead and wounded scattered over the hill-side.

Learning from a captive that the 44th Virginia and some Georgia troops and cavalry were below, and finding it too late to continue the operations against the rebels' position that evening with troops as much exhausted as were ours, and threatened, too, by succors, the troops were bivouacked in the position shown on Plan No. 2—Lieutenant Colonel Hollingsworth going down on the ridge with six companies to the position mentioned, within half a mile of the rebel pickets.

The two brass 6-pounders captured were put in order, and, under command of Captain Conckle, 19th Ohio, placed—one looking down the Beverly road at C, the other at *d*, looking towards camp Garnett.

During that rainy night our men bivouacked cheerfully, and turned out with great promptitude whenever the rebels by their movements alarmed our pickets. About 3 o'clock in the morning of the 12th our pickets brought in a prisoner from the rebel camp, from whom I learned their forces were disorganized and probably dispersing. This determined the dispositions for the attack on the camp. I ordered Colonel Beatty, with all the 19th, to proceed along the ridge and take their position on the south side of the road, and directed Burdsall's cavalry, accompanied by one company of the 10th Indiana, to reconnoitre down the road. Colonel Sullivan, with the 13th, was to follow the movement promptly, and by his skirmishers to clean the hill-side north of the road.

These orders were obeyed, and, finding the position abandoned, Burdsall's cavalry and company C, 10th Indiana regiment, entered the camp about 6 o'clock a. m., where they found and took prisoners ten (10) officers, five (5) non-commissioned officers, fifty-four (54) privates, the descriptive list of which is hereto attached, and marked A. Colonel Beatty entered the upper camp about the same time and occupied it, taking charge of the property, among which were two brass 6-pounders, and some eighty tents, four caissons, and one hundred (100) rounds of ammunition. Colonel Sullivan, of the 13th Indiana, came in and occupied the camp on the north side of the road, and took charge of the horses, wagons, tents, tools, and implements of the rebels there.

The 8th and 10th Indiana were left in possession on the battle-field, and were charged with the duty of burying the dead. They remained until next morning, the 13th, when the whole force moved forward to their present encampment at Beverly.

Having given the details, I close my report by the following

SUMMARY OF THE MOVEMENT.

With strong detachments from the 19th Ohio, the 8th, 10th, and 13th Indiana, and Burdsall's cavalry, amounting to 1,912 rank and file, I set out at 5 a. m. of the 11th, and by a circuitous route through a trackless mountain forest reached the Beverly road at the top of Rich mountain, where I found the enemy advised of my approach, and in force with two 6-pounders, field-pieces, and infantry, from various circumstances judged to have been from 800 to 1,200 strong, though probably not all of them in action. We formed at about 3 o'clock, under cover of our skirmishers, guarding well against a flank attack from the direction of the rebels' position, and after a brisk fire, which threw the rebels into confusion, carried their position by a charge, driving them from behind some log breastworks, and pursued them into the thickets on the mountain. We captured twenty-one (21) prisoners, two brass 6-pounders, fifty stand of arms, and some corn and provisions. Our loss was twelve (12) killed, and forty-nine (49) wounded.

The rebels had some twenty (20) wounded on the field. The number of the killed we could not ascertain, but subsequently the number of burials reported to this date is one hundred and thirty-five, (135,) many found scattered over the mountain. Our troops were informed that there were one or two regiments of rebels towards Beverly, and finding the hour late, bivouacked on their arms, amid a cold, drenching rain, to await daylight, when they moved forward on the enemy's intrenched position, which was found abandoned by all except sixty-three (63) men, who were taken prisoners.

We took possession of two brass 6-pounders, four caissons, and one hundred rounds of ammunition, two kegs and one barrel of powder, 19,000 buck and ball cartridges, two stands of colors, and a large lot of equipments and clothing, consisting of 204 tents, 427 pairs pants, 124 axes, 98 picks, 134 spades and shovels; all their train, consisting of 29 wagons, 75 horses, 4 mules, and 60 pairs harness.

The enemy finding their position turned, abandoned intrenchments which taken by the front would have cost us a thousand lives, and dispersed through the mountains, some attempting to escape by the way of Laurel hill, and others aiming for Huttonsville. Among the former were the command of Colonel Pegram, which, unable to join the rebels at Laurel hill, surrendered to the major general on the 13th. Our loss in the engagement, killed and wounded, is shown in the statement hereto appended, marked B. The list of prisoners taken is shown in the paper hereto appended, marked D. The invoice of property captured and turned over to the post quartermaster is hereto annexed, marked E.

In closing this report, I deem it proper to observe that, considering the rawness and inexperience of both officers and men, the fact that one-fourth were on picket guard the previous evening, and had made a most fatiguing march through the rain, and with only inadequate supplies of food, their conduct was admirable.

Among those who are entitled to special mention are Colonel Lander, who, with the guide, led the way into the very midst of the action; Colonel Manson, of the 10th Indiana, who was everywhere along his line, inspiring the men by his voice and presence, and who bravely led the charge of his regiment.

Colonel Benton was ready to obey orders, and moved among his men with alacrity.

Colonel Sullivan charged with his command as the rebels were dispersing, and captured several of the prisoners. Major Wilson, of the 8th, was conspicuous for coolness and promptitude of action. Lieutenant Colonel Colgrove, of the 8th, deserves especial mention for his coolness while forming his lines of the regiment under fire. Major Foster, of the 13th, showed coolness and self-possession in forming a portion of his men under the fire of the cannon.

My thanks are due Captain Kingsbury, my assistant adjutant general, and to Captain A. Irwin Harrison, for their valuable and efficient aid in carrying orders under fire.

The 10th Indiana was under fire for an hour and a half.

The 19th Ohio distinguished itself for the cool and handsome manner in which they held their post against a flank attack, and for the manner in which they came into line and delivered their fire near the close of the action.

I consider Colonel Beatty to have managed his men well, and to have been ably seconded by Colonel Hollingsworth and Major Buckley.

For the individuals who distinguished themselves under the eyes of their regimental commanders, I respectfully refer to the report of the colonels of regiments herewith submitted.

Very respectfully, your obedient servant,

W. S. ROSECRANS,
Brigadier General United States Army.

Major S. WILLIAMS, *A. A. G.*,
United States Army, Headquarters Army of West Virginia.

HEADQUARTERS OF THE ARMY OF OCCUPATION,
West Virginia, July 23, 1861.

MAJOR: Herewith please find report of the affair at Rich mountain, July 11. The map which should accompany it will be forwarded you to-morrow.

Very respectfully, your obedient servant,

W. S. ROSECRANS,
Brigadier General United States Army.

Major S. WILLIAMS, *Assistant Adjutant General.*

B.

List of wounded in the 1*st brigade, army of West Virginia, under Brigadier General Rosecrans, in the affair at Rich mountain, July* 11, 1861.

10*th regiment of Indiana volunteer militia.*—James R. M. Briant, lieutenant colonel; W. C. Wilson, Major; Chris. Miller, company A, captain; ——— Conklin, company H, captain; John Brower, company D, lieutenant.

Commissioned officers wounded	5
Non-commissioned and privates	51
Total wounded	56
Total non-commissioned officers and privates killed	12
Total killed and wounded	68

8*th Indiana regiment.*—Franklin M. Slobaugh, company A, 2d corporal, Joseph Funk, company A, private; William H. Keller, company A, 1st sergeant; G. W. Shane, company B, 4th sergeant; Henry L. Powell, company B, private; C. W. Reid, company C, private; Andrew Ridenour, company C, private; Ashbury Kerwood, company C, private; John Walker, company C, private; Frederick Coppersmith, company C, private; Park Strahan, company E, private; Samuel Williams, company E, private; William Lamb, company F, private; Benjamin Curtis, company G, private; Lemuel Cuzick, company H, private; Jacob Saibors, company H, private; Jacob Beroth, company H, private; Jesse King, company H, private; M. M. Stevenson, company I, 1st sergeant; James Buchanan, company I, private; Andrew Stutzman, company I, private; Frank Hall, company K, 2d sergeant; Samuel DeVaughn, company K, private.

10*th Indiana regiment*—William Stokes, company A, private; William Manburn, company A, private; Chauncey Thompsôn, company A, private; Frank M. Bryant, company A, private; Thomas C. Truit, company A, private; Noah Kick, company A, private; Lent

Sanders, company F, private ; Howe Husel, company F, private ; H. T. Everhart, company F, private ; James W. Gwin, company D, private ; Aaron ———, company D, private ; John Cunghaw, company D, private ; Henry Rank, company D, private ; Henry Young, company D, private ; Daniel Lander, company I, private ; William Singleton, company I, private ; Reuben Wesco, company I, private ; George W. Brooks, company K, private ; Reilly Woods, company K, private ; Henry McGill, company H, private.

13th Indiana regiment.—Charles Crumbo, company A, private ; Henry Loop, company E, private ; Charles Paff, company E, private ; Durban Mathews, company E, private ; Isaac Thornburg, company H, private ; James Carnagan, company H, private ; James Thompson, company G, private ; John Fordzee, company G, private.

List of casualties in the 1st brigade, army of occupation, West Virginia, under Brigadier General Rosecrans, in the affair at Rich mountain, July 11, 1861.

8th Indiana regiment.—Philander Wiseheart, company B ; Joseph Beck, company G, private ; James H. Emmett, company H, private.

10th Indiana regiment.—James A. Taggert, company A, private ; Samuel Yocum, company F, private ; R. R. Ellington, company E, private.

13th Indiana regiment.—James Blazer, company A, private ; John Powell, company B, corporal ; John F. Warner, company B, corporal ; William Riffle, company E, private ; Patrick Welsh, company G, private ; Allen Thompson, company H, private.

Received, Beverly, Virginia, July 15, 1861, of Captain C. N. Goulding, quartermaster brigade Ohio and Indiana United States volunteer militia, commanded by General Rosecrans, being property captured from the enemy at Rich mountain, July 12, 1861—

890 muskets.
42 rounds 6-pounder shot, fixed.
60 rounds 6-pounder shot, case.
1 keg blasting powder.
1 keg rifle powder.
1 barrel common powder.
18,000 musket cartridges, calibre 69.
1,000 musket cartridges, calibre 54.
1 can powder.
4 6-pounder brass cannon.
4 caissons.
84 axes.
98 picks.
11 pick handles.
98 picks and handles.
19 axes, (hand.)
1 mallet.
1 auger.
104 shovels.
30 spades.
585 cartridge-boxes.
84 tents.
84 sets tent poles.
6 unfinished tents.
60 harness.
157 cotton haversacks.
30 oil-cloth haversacks.
21 knapsacks.
67 canteens.
427 pantaloons.
1 trunk.
1 chest.
¾ keg of nails.
3 drums.
75 horses.
4 mules.
2 spring wagons.
5 Conestoga wagons.
1 four-horse common wagon.
19 two-horse common wagons.
21 tents in company I, 13th regiment Indiana volunteer militia.

Received, Beverly, July 15, 1861, of C. N. Golding, quartermaster brigade Ohio and Indiana United States volunteers, militia, commanded by Brigadier General Rosecrans—

40 tin cups.
25 tin plates.
20 coffeepots.
14 tin pans.
12 tin buckets.
71 wooden buckets.
8 frying pans.
6 quart cups.
3 ovens and seven lids.
4 skillets.
6 camp kettles.
5 wash pans.
3 saucepans.
2 baking pans.
2 brass kettles.
3 tin dippers.
2 sieves.
1 teakettle.
1 artillery bucket.
1 wooden can.
1 hatchet.
1 hand axe.
81 tents.
81 sets tent poles.

BATTLE OF CORINTH.

HEADQUARTERS 13TH ARMY CORPS, DEPARTMENT OF THE TENNESSEE,
Lagrange, Tennessee, November 13, 1862.

COLONEL: I have the honor to transmit herewith Brigadier General Thomas J. McKean's report of the part taken by the sixth division in the battle of Corinth. It was not in at the time of forwarding other reports.

I am, colonel, very respectfully, your obedient servant,

U. S. GRANT, *Major General.*

Colonel J. C. KELTON,
Assistant Adjutant General, Washington, D. C.

HEADQUARTERS ARMY OF THE MISSISSIPPI,
THIRD DIVISION DISTRICT OF WEST TENNESSEE,
Corinth, October 25, 1862.

MAJOR: I have the honor to submit, for the information of the major general commanding the district, the following report of the battle of Corinth:

PRELIMINARIES.

The rumors which followed the battle of Iuka were, that Price had marched to the vicinity of Ripley, and was being joined by Van Dorn with all the available rebel forces in north Mississippi, for the purpose of capturing Corinth, or breaking our line of communication, and forcing us to retreat towards Columbus. These rumors gained strength until the first of October, when strong cavalry scouts, sent out for the purpose, demonstrated the fact that the rebels were moving in force from Ripley, via Ruckersville, and that the main body was at Pocahontas.

The question then was, where would they strike the main blow? Equally favorably situated to strike Bolivar, Bethel, Jackson, or Corinth—which would it be?

Unfortunately for me, there was no map of the country northwest of this place to be found, therefore I could not tell whether to expect a strong demonstration here, to hold us in suspense while the blow was struck elsewhere or *vice versa*. Rumors that the attack was to take the direction of Jackson or Bolivar, via Bethel, were so rife, and the fortifications of Corinth were so well known to the rebels, that I had hopes they would undertake to mask me, and, passing north, give me an opportunity to beat the masking force and cut off their retreat. This hope gained some strength from the supposed difficulties of the country lying in the triangle formed by the Memphis and Charleston, the Mobile and Ohio railroads, and Cypress creek.

To be prepared for eventualities, Hamilton's and Stanley's divisions were placed just beyond Bridge creek, the infantry outposts were called in from Iuka, Burnsville, Rienzi and Danville, and the outpost at Chewalla retired to near Alexander's, and strengthened by another regiment and a battery, early on the morning of the second.

During that day evidences increased, showing the practicability of the country northwest of us, and disclosed the fact, not before known, that there were two good roads from Chewalla eastward, one leading directly into the old rebel intrenchments, and the other crossing over into the Pittsburg Landing road.

Accordingly, the following disposition of the troops for the 3d was ordered at half past one a. m. of that day, viz:

There being indications of a possible attack on Corinth immediately, the following dispositions of troops will be made: General McKean, with his division, will occupy his present position; General Davis will occupy the line between the Memphis and the Columbus roads; General Hamilton, with his division, will take position between the rebel works on the Purdy and on the Hamburg roads, and General Stanley will hold his division in reserve at or near the old headquarters of Major General Grant.

The respective divisions will be found in two lines, the second line being either in line of battle, or close column by division, as circumstances may require.

The troops were ordered to move towards their positions with one hundred rounds of ammunition, and three days' rations per man, by 3 o'clock a. m.

These dispositions were made, and the troops at 9 o'clock on the morning of the third occupied the positions shown on the accompanying map: Hamilton on the right, Davis in the centre, McKean on the left, with an advance of three regiments of infantry and a section of artillery under Colonel Oliver, on the Chewalla road, at or near Alexander's, beyond the rebel breastworks.

The cavalry was disposed as follows, (see map accompanying Colonel Minzer's report :)

A battalion at Burnsville, one at Rory's mill, on the Jacinto and Corinth road. Colonel Lee, with the 7th Kansas and part of the 7th Illinois, at Kossuth and Boneyard, watching the rebels' right flank. Colonel Hatch and Captain Wilcox on the east and north fronts, covering and reconnoitring.

The reasons for these dispositions flow obviously from the foregoing explanations of our ignorance of the northwesterly approaches, and of the possibility that the rebels might threaten us on the Chewalla, and attack us by the Smith's Bridge road on our left, or go round and try us with his main force on the Purdy, or even Pittsburg Landing road.

The general plan, which was explained to the division commanders, verbally, in the morning, was to hold the enemy at arm's length, by opposing him strongly in our assumed positions, and when his force became fully developed, and he had assumed position, if we found it necessary to take a position which would give us the use of our batteries and the open ground in the immediate vicinity of Corinth, the exact position to be determined by events and the movements of the enemy.

OPERATIONS OF THE BATTLE ON THE 3D OF OCTOBER.

Early in the morning the advance under Colonel Oliver found strong indications that the presence under which he had retired on the second came from the advancing foe, and accordingly took a strong position on the hill near the angle of the rebel breastworks with his three regiments and a section of artillery.

By 9 o'clock the enemy began to press them sharply and outflank them. Brigadier General McArthur, whom I had requested to go to the front, reported wide-spread but slack skirmishing, and said the hill was of great value to test the advancing force. I ordered him to hold it pretty firmly with that view.

About 10 o'clock word came that the enemy were pressing the point hotly, and that re-enforcements were required, or they must yield the position. Supposing its importance was properly understood, and that it was held in subordination to the general views of its use, which had been explained, I directed General Davies to send up from his position two regiments.

But it proved that General McArthur had taken up four more regiments from McKean's division, and was contesting the ground almost as for a battle. It was probably this which induced General Davies to ask permission to rest his right on the rebel intrenchments, and to which I consented, adding the verbal order to Lieutenant Colonel Ducat that he might use his judgment about leaving his present for that position, but in no event must he cease to touch his left on McArthur's right.

The advance was made to the breastwork, as shown on the drawing, but leaving an interval between McArthur and Davies's left. The enemy developed his forces along that line. McArthur retired from his position, which gave the rebels an opportunity to advance behind Davies's left, and forced it, after obstinate resistance, to fall back rapidly about a thousand yards, losing two heavy guns.

Our troops fought with the most determined courage, firing very low. At 1 p. m., Davies having resumed the same position he had occupied in the morning, and McArthur's brigade having fought a heavy force, it became evident that the enemy were in full strength, and meant mischief. McKean, with Crocker's brigade, had seen only skirmishers; there were no signs of any movements on our left, and only a few cavalry skirmishers on our right. It was pretty clear that we were to expect the weight of the attack to fall on our centre, where hopes had been given by our falling back.

Orders were accordingly given to McKean to fall back to the next ridge beyond our intrenchments, to touch his right on Davies's left; for Stanley to move northward and eastward, to stand in close echelon with McKean, but nearer town. General Hamilton was ordered to face towards Chewalla, and move down until his left reached Davies's right. Davies was informed of these dispositions, and told to hold his ground obstinately, and then when he had drawn them in strongly, Hamilton would swing in on their flank and rear, and close the day. Hamilton was carefully instructed on this point, and entered into the spirit of it.

Owing to loss of time in conveying orders to Generals McKean and Davies, the orders were less perfectly conformed to, but nothing materially injurious resulted therefrom.

But, owing to the tremendous force with which the enemy pressed Davies back, Stanley was called with his division into the batteries, and sent a brigade under Colonel Mower to support Davies, whose right had at last become hotly engaged. Mower came up while Davies was contesting a position near the White House, and Hamilton began to swing in on the enemy's flank, across the Columbus railroad, through a very impracticable thicket, when night closed in and put an end to the operations for the day.

The details of the heroic deeds of the troops of Davies's division, of McArthur's and Oliver's brigades, as well as those of Sullivan's brigade, of Hamilton's division, will be found in the accompanying sub-reports.

THE DISPOSITIONS FOR THE BATTLE OF 4TH OCTOBER.

We had now before us the entire army which the rebels could muster in northern Mississippi, Van Dorn commanding—Price's army, Van Dorn's army, Villipigne, and the remnants of Breckinridge's corps. They were in the angle between the Columbus and the Memphis roads. Our left was comparatively free, our right very assailable; they outnumbered us probably two to one.

THE PLAN.

Was to rest our left on the batteries extending from battery Robinett, our centre on the slight ridge north of the houses, and our right on the high ground covering both the Pittsburg and Purdy roads, while it also covered the ridge road between them, leading to their old camp.

McKean held the extreme left; Stanley, with his well-tried divison, batteries Williams and Robinett, the Memphis railroad and the Chewalla road, extending nearly to the Columbus road. Davies's tried divison was placed in the centre, which was retired, reaching to battery Powell. Hamilton's staunch fighting division was on the right, with Dillon's battery, supported by two regiments posted on the prolongation of Davies's line. The design of General Hamilton was to use the hill where the batteries stood against an approach from the west, where Sullivan found the enemy on the last evening. Against my better judgment, expressed to him at the time, I yielded to his wishes, and allowed the occupation as described.

Early in the evening I called the chiefs of divisions together, and explained to them these plans, and having supervised the positions, retired at three a. m. of the fourth to take some rest. I was soon aroused by the opening of the enemy's artillery, which he had planted within six hundred yards of battery Robinett.

THE BATTLE.

This early opening gave promise of a hot day's work, but the heavy batteries and the 10th Ohio, placed north of General Halleck's old headquarters, silenced them by 7 o'clock, and there was an interval of an hour, which was employed in going over our lines.

About 9 o'clock the skirmishers which we had sent into the woods on our front, by their hot firing, proclaimed the presence of their forces preparing for the assault. Soon the heads of their columns were seen emerging to attack our centre—on Davies first, Stanley next, and Hamilton last. The drawing shows these positions, and is referred to for the sake of brevity.

I shall leave to pens dipped in poetic ink to inscribe the gorgeous pyrotechny of the battle, and paint in words of fire the heroes of this fight, the details of which will be found graphically depicted in the accompanying sub-report.

I will only say that when Price's left bore down on our centre in gallant style their force was so overpowering that our wearied and jaded troops yielded and fell back, scattering among the houses. I had the personal mortification of witnessing this untoward and untimely stampede.

Riddled and scattered, the ragged head of Price's right storming columns advanced to near the house, north side of the square, in front of General Halleck's headquarters, when it was greeted by a storm of grape from a section of Immell's battery, soon re-enforced by the 10th Ohio, which sent them whirling back, pursued by the 5th Minnesota, which advanced on them from their position near the depot.

General Sullivan was ordered and promptly advanced to support General Davies's centre. His right rallied and retook battery Powell, into which a few of the storming column had penetrated, while Hamilton having played upon the rebels on his right, over the open space effectively swept by his artillery, advanced on them, and they fled. The battle was over on the right.

During all this the skirmishers of the left were moving in our front. A line of battle was formed on the ridge, as shown in the drawing. About twenty minutes after the attack on the right, the enemy advanced in four columns on battery Robinett, and were treated to grape and canister until within fifty yards, when the Ohio brigade arose and gave them a murderous fire of musketry, before which they reeled and fell back to the woods. They, however, gallantly reformed and advanced again to the charge, led by Colonel Rogers, of the 2d Texas.

This time they reached the edge of the ditch, but the deadly musketry fire of the Ohio brigade again broke them, and at the word charge, the 11th Missouri and 27th Ohio sprang up and forward at them, chasing their broken fragments back to the woods. Thus by noon ended the battle of the 4th of October.

After waiting for the enemy's return a short time, our skirmishers began to advance, and found that their skirmishers were gone from the field, leaving their dead and wounded. Having ridden over it, and satisfied myself of the fact, I rode over all our lines, announcing the result of the fight in person, and notified our victorious troops that after two days of fighting, two almost sleepless nights of preparation, movement, and march, I wished them to replenish their cartridge-boxes, haversacks, and stomachs, take an early sleep, and start in pursuit by daylight.

Returning from this, I found the gallant McPherson with a fresh brigade on the public square, and gave him the same notice, with orders to take the advance.

The results of this battle briefly stated are :

We fought the combined rebel forces of Mississippi, commanded by Van Dorn, Price, Lovell, Villipigne, and Rust, in person, numbering, according to their own authorities, 38,000 men. We signally defeated them with little more than half their numbers, and they fled, leaving their dead and wounded on the field. The enemy's loss in killed was fourteen hundred and twenty-three officers and men; their loss in wounded, taking the general average, amounts to fifty-six hundred and ninety-two.

We took twenty-two hundred and sixty-eight prisoners, among whom are one hundred and thirty-seven field officers, captains and subalterns, representing fifty-three regiments of infantry, sixteen regiments of cavalry, thirteen batteries of artillery, and seven battalions; making sixty-nine regiments, seven battalions and thirteen batteries, besides separate companies. We took also fourteen stands of colors, two pieces of artillery, thirty-three hundred stand of small-arms, forty-five thousand rounds of ammunition, and a large lot of accoutrements.

The enemy blew up several ammunition wagons between Corinth and Chewalla, and beyond Chewalla many ammunition wagons and carriages are destroyed, and the ground was strewn with tents, officers' mess chests, and small-arms. We pursued them forty miles in force, and sixty miles with cavalry.

Our loss was only three hundred and fifteen killed, eighteen hundred and twelve wounded, and two hundred and thirty-two prisoners and missing.

It is said the enemy was so demoralized and alarmed at our advance, they set fire to the stores at Tapello, but finding we were not close upon them, they extinguished the fire and removed the public stores, except two car-loads of bacon, which they destroyed.

To signalize in this report all those officers and men whose action in the battle deserves mention, would unnecessarily lengthen this report. I must, therefore, refer to the subreports and special mentions, and to a special paper herewith, wherein those most conspicuous to the number of one hundred and nine officers and men are mentioned.

W. S. ROSECRANS, *Major General.*

GENERAL ROSECRANS'S REPORT OF BATTLE OF IUKA.

HEADQUARTERS DEPARTMENT OF THE TENNESSEE,
Jackson, Tennessee, October 25, 1862.

COLONEL : I have the honor to transmit herewith my official report of the "battle of Iuka," fought on the 19th day of September, 1862, and the following official papers relating to the same, viz :

1st. General Rosecrans's report of the battle, and the following enclosures, viz: 1. General Hamilton's report of the part taken by the 3d division, and twelve (12) enclosures. 2. General Stanley's report of the part taken by the 2d division, and fifteen (15) enclosures. 3. Colonel Mizner's report of the part taken by the cavalry division, and four (4) enclosures. 4. Colonel Lathrop's report of the part taken by the artillery. 5. Captain Simmons's report of the commissary stores captured at Iuka. 6. Captain Taylor's report of the quartermaster's stores captured. 7. Medical director's report of the killed, wounded, and missing. 8. Provost marshal's report of the enemy's killed, wounded, and paroled prisoners. 9. Chief of ordnance's report of the quantity and kind of ordnance and ordnance stores captured.

2d. Major General Ord's report of the part taken by the forces under his command.

3d. The report of Surgeon John G. F. Holston, medical director, of the number of wounded.

4th. Report of Brigadier General Lenoman, and four enclosures.

I am, colonel, very respectfully, your obedient servant,

U. S. GRANT, *Major General.*

Colonel J. C. KELTON,
Assistant Adjutant General, Washington, D. C.

HEADQUARTERS ARMY OF THE MISSISSIPPI,
THIRD DIVISION OF THE DISTRICT OF WEST TENNESSEE,
Corinth, Mississippi, September 29, 1862.

MAJOR: Having received the reports of the commander of the troops, lists of stores and prisoners captured, I hasten to lay them before the major general commanding, with the following

REPORT OF THE BATTLE OF IUKA.

Mower's able reconnoissance on the 15th, on the Burnsville road, to within two miles of Iuka, with other information, having established the fact that Price occupied that place with a force of about twenty-eight regiments of infantry, six batteries, and a strong body of cavalry, you resolved to attack, and gave orders for Ord's and Ross's commands to concentrate at Burnsville, while I prepared to do the same at Jacinto.

I telegraphed you proposing that the force from Burnsville should attack the rebels from the west and draw them in that direction, and that I would move in on their rear by the Jacinto and Fulton roads and cut off their retreat. Your approval of the plan having been received, I ordered Stanley to concentrate his division at Jacinto on the 18th, where they had all arrived by 9 o'clock p. m. I despatched you that evening, from Jacinto, of the arrival of Stanley's troops, jaded by a long march, and that in consequence of it we would not be able to reach Iuka until half past two of the 19th.

The whole column—consisting of Stanley's and Hamilton's divisions, with five batteries—moved by daybreak of the 19th on the Tuscumbia road towards Barnett's. I despatched you at 7 a. m. that it had moved forward in good spirits and time, and that I hoped to reach Iuka by half past 2 p. m. We reached Barnett's (a distance of twelve miles) by noon, having driven the enemy's cavalry pickets some two or three miles. Here Sanborn's brigade, of Hamilton's division, took the lead, the rest of Hamilton's division came next, and Stanley's division followed. The advance drove the enemy's cavalry skirmishers steadily before them, until we arrived within a mile and a half of Iuka, near the forks of the Jacinto road and cross-roads leading from it to the Fulton road. Here we found their infantry and a battery, which gave our advance guard a volley. Hamilton, pushing his first brigade rapidly forward up the narrow road on the right hand, leading from the church at the forks, found them astride it around the brush on the rough wooded knoll, (see accompanying map,) placing Sands's battery on the only available ground. The action opened immediately with grape and canister from the enemy's battery, directed at ours, and sharp musketry fire from his skirmishers.

Having inspected General Hamilton's dispositions on the front and found them good, I ordered Colonel Mizner to send a battalion of the 3d Michigan cavalry to reconnoitre our right, and Colonel Perezel, with the 10th Wisconsin infantry and a section of artillery, to take position on our left on the road leading north. The remainder of Hamilton's division formed in rear of the first line, and the head of Stanley's division (in column) stood below the hospital, awaiting the developments on the front before being moved into line. The position of the troops at this time—say, 5 p. m.—is shown very nearly on the map.

The enemy's line of infantry now moved forward on the battery, coming up from the woods on our right on the 5th Iowa, while a brigade showed itself on our left and attempted to cross the road towards Colonel Perezel. The battle became furious. Our battery poured in a deadly fire upon the enemy's column advancing up the road, while their musketry concentrated upon it soon killed or wounded most of our horses. When within one hundred yards they received a volley from our entire line, and from that time the battle raged furiously. The enemy penetrated the battery, were repulsed, again returned, were again repulsed, and, finally, bore down upon it with a column of three regiments, and this time carried the battery. The cannoniers were many of them bayoneted at their pieces. Three of the guns were spiked. In this last charge, the brigade of Texans which had attempted to turn our left, having been repulsed by Perezel, turned upon the battery and co-operated in the charge. The 48th Indiana, which lay in its track, was obliged to yield about one hundred yards, where it was supported by the 4th Minnesota, and held its position until relieved at the close of the fight by the 47th Illinois.

The 5th Iowa maintained its position on the right against a storm of fire from the rebel left and centre, and even when the battery was carried its left yielded but slightly, when Boomer, with a part of the 26th Missouri, came up to its support, and maintained its position to the close of the fight.

About this time it was deemed prudent to order up the 1st brigade of Stanley's division, which went forward with a shout. The 11th Missouri, filing into the woods, took its position on the right of the 5th Iowa, slightly in its rear. Here the rebels made a last desperate attempt with two Mississippi brigades. As the first came bearing down upon the

11th Missouri, when within twenty paces, an officer from the rebel ranks sprung forward and shouted, "Don't fire upon your friends, the 37th Mississippi." He was answered by a volley, which drove them back in confusion. The second brigade followed, and, in the dusk of evening and the smoke of battle, reached the very front of the Missouri 11th. The roar of musketry was terrific; but Mower met the shock and stood firm. The rebels re-recoiled, and the firing ceased throughout the line.

The troops rested on their arms. The 39th Ohio and the 47th Illinois held the front, slightly in rear of the position of the advance regiments, which were withdrawn to replenish their ammunition. The 11th and 26th Missouri took position in a depression of the ground, in the open field, in rear of the woods in which the fight had occurred. The 10th Iowa and the 80th Ohio held our left, on the road running north, at 8 p. m.

During the early part of the night the enemy made great noise, as if chopping and constructing batteries. There was much moving of troops; commands of halting and aligning were heard, as if massing on our front.

Profoundly disappointed at hearing nothing from the forces on the Burnsville road, and not knowing what to expect, it became my duty to make dispositions for the battle next morning, as if we were alone. To this end, Stanley's batteries were brought into position in the field south of the hospital, on advantageous ground, and a line was selected for the infantry, in case the enemy should attack us in heavy force; while Hamilton's division, having borne the brunt of the battle, was ordered to the rear, in the next field below, with the intention of moving it thence across the field to the east through the strip of woods, to attack the enemy's left.

The enemy's trains were heard from midnight, moving in a southeasterly direction, and it became evident that he was providing for its safety.

Day dawned: no firing on the front. Our skirmishers, advancing cautiously, found the enemy had retired from his position. Skirmishers were immediately pushed forward, and Stanley's column ordered to advance upon Iuka. When within sight of the town, discovering a few rebels, he ordered some shells to be thrown. They were a few stragglers from the enemy's rear guard, his entire column having gone by the Fulton road. Taking possession of the town and the stores left there, General Stanley's column pushed on in pursuit.

The cavalry advanced by the intermediate road between the Fulton and Jacinto roads Hamilton's division faced about and marched by Barnett's, following the enemy until night, when, finding themselves greatly distanced, the pursuit was discontinued, and our troops returned the next day to Jacinto, while the rebel column continued its flight by Bay Springs and Marietta to its old position on the Mobile and Ohio railroad.

The enemy left his dead on the field, part of them gathered for interment, and his badly wounded in the hospital at Iuka. His loss was—

Killed	265
Died in hospital (of wounds)	120
Left in hospital	342
Estimated number of wounded removed	350
Prisoners	361
Total loss	1,438

Among his killed were General Little and Colonel Stanton; how many other officers we do not know. Among his wounded were twenty-six commissioned officers.

Our loss consists of—

Commissioned officers killed	6	
Commissioned officers wounded	39	
Commissioned officers missing	1	
Total	46	
		46
Enlisted men killed	138	
Enlisted men wounded	559	
Enlisted men missing	39	
Total	736	
		736
Total		782

Some of the missing have returned.

Among the ordnance stores captured, as will be seen by the accompanying exhibit, were 1,629 stand of arms and a large number of equipments, a quantity of quartermaster and commissary stores, and thirteen thousand rounds of ammunition.

Having thus given a detailed narrative of the battle, with sub-reports, appended statements, and a map, I conclude with the following brief recapitulation:

We moved from Jacinto at 5 a. m., with nine thousand men, on Price's forces at Iuka; after a march of eighteen miles, attacked them at half-past 4 p. m.; fought them on unknown and disadvantageous ground, with less than half our forces in action, until night put a stop to the contest. Having lost about two hundred and sixty-five (265) killed, seven or eight hundred wounded, three hundred and sixty-one prisoners, over sixteen hundred stand of arms, and a quantity of quartermaster and commissary stores, the rebels retreated precipitately during the night towards Bay Springs Our troops pursued them fifteen miles, and, finding themselves distanced, gave up the pursuit and returned to Jacinto.

After the detail of our operations, it is with pride and pleasure I bear testimony to the cheerfulness and alacrity of both officers and men during the march, and their courage and energy in action. With insignificant exceptions, it was all that could be asked.

Among the infantry regiments deserving special mention are the 5th Iowa, which, under its brave colonel, (Matthias,) withstood the storm of triple fire and triple numbers; the 26th Missouri, which nobly sustained the 5th Iowa; the 11th Missouri, which, under the gallant Mower, met and discomfited two rebel brigades, and, having exhausted every cartridge, held its ground until darkness and the withdrawal of the rebels enabled him to replenish; the 16th Iowa, the 4th Minnesota, the 48th Indiana, and 10th Iowa, who shared in the combat, and the 47th Illinois, the 39th Ohio, and others, who fought in the front or supported the rest. Sands's 11th Ohio battery, under command of Lieutenant Sears, behaved nobly. The fearful losses sustained by this battery (16 killed, 44 wounded) shows their unyielding obstinacy in serving the battery. The cavalry—3d Michigan and 2d Iowa—covered our flanks, reconnoitred our front, whipped the vastly superior numbers of Armstrong's cavalry, under the protection of their infantry, and kept them there during the battle and retreat. I must not omit to mention the eminent services of Colonel Du Bois, commanding at Rienzi, and Colonel Lee, who, with the 7th Kansas and part of the 7th Illinois cavalry, assured our flank and rear during the entire period of our operations.

Among the officers of the command who deserve special mention are Brigadier General Hamilton, commanding the 3d division, who took the advance and held the front in the battle; Brigadier General Stanley, who never failed to yield the most efficient and unwearying support and assistance; Brigadier General Sullivan, commanding the 2d brigade of Hamilton's division, whose determined courage rises with, and has always proved equal to, the occasion; Colonel Sanborn, commanding the 1st brigade of the same division, whose conduct in his first battle was highly creditable; Colonel Eddy, 48th Indiana, and Colonel Matthias, 5th Iowa; Colonel Boomer, 26th Missouri, wounded in the action; Colonel Mower, whose gallantry is equalled only by his energy; and numerous others, whose names appear conspicuously in the accompanying reports, are commended to the favorable notice of the major general commanding. Besides officers of the line and their respective staffs, I must not omit to acknowledge the services of the able and indefatigable chief of cavalry, Colonel Mizner. Colonel Lathrop, chief of artillery, also rendered services contributing much to the general strength and efficiency of his arm. Captain Temple Clark, assistant adjutant general, Greenwood and Goddard, my aids, were very gallant and indefatigable in the discharge of their duties. The energy, painstaking, and care of Surgeon A. B. Campbell, and the medical officers who attended the wounded, deserve most honorable mention.

W. P. ROSECRANS, *Major General.*

Major JOHN A. RAWLINS, A. A. G.,
District of West Tennessee.

HEADQUARTERS THIRD DIVISION ARMY OF THE MISSISSIPPI,
September 23, 1862.

SIR: I have the honor to report that my division, the 1st brigade leading, marched from Jacinto, on the morning of the 19th instant, to attack the enemy at Iuka. One-half mile west of Barnett's the advanced pickets of the enemy were first encountered in a deep ravine; a battalion of the 3d Michigan cavalry, by dismounting a body of skirmishers, soon drove the enemy from his cover. Soon after passing Barnett's the cavalry were thrown to the rear and a battalion of the 5th Iowa deployed as skirmishers. From this time out our advance was warmly contested. The enemy's sharpshooters occupied every position of defence, making the last five miles of the march a steady contest, a constant skirmish. At Mrs. Moore's house, four (4) miles from the battle-ground, the action became quite hot.

Lieutenant Schranne, of the Benton hussars, one of my body-guard, was mortally wounded, and a number of our skirmishers killed or wounded. The enemy was steadily driven before us, and with constant loss. When within two miles of the battle-field the battalion of the 5th Iowa skirmishers was relieved by an equal force of the 26th Missouri, and the forward movement of the column pressed. When the head of the column had reached a point on the brow of a hill at the cross-roads, two (2) miles from Iuka, it was halted for the purpose of reconnoitring and the line of skirmishers pushed rapidly forward. This line had not advanced more than three hundred (300) yards when they came upon the enemy drawn up in great force and occupying a strong position along a deep ravine running transversely with the main road and behind the crest of the hill.

I was in position just behind the line of skirmishers and saw at a glance that the moment for action had come. The skirmishers were driven back on the head of the column, and the attack by the enemy immediately begun. The ground occupied by the head of my column was on the brow of a densely wooded hill, falling off abruptly to the right and left; the underbrush and timber were too thick to admit of deployments, and the most that could be done was to take a position across the road by marching the leading regiments into position by a flank movement. This was done under a heavy fire of musketry and grape, canister and shell. The 11th Ohio battery was with difficulty got into position on the crest of the hill, where it could command the road in front of us. The 5th Iowa, under the brave Matthias, being the leading regiment, was first in position in the woods to the right of the road, with its left resting near the battery. The 26th Missouri, under the resolute Boomer, immediately took position on the right of the 5th Iowa; the next regiment in the column, the 48th Indiana, under its brave Colonel Eddy, took position on the left of the road, a little in advance of the battery, and with its left thrown forward so as to cover the open field on their left with their fire. This was the position when the battle opened on our side. I directed each of these regiments into position myself, and they were taken by the troops, under a heavy fire, with the steadiness of veterans determined to conquer. The battle thus opened with but three (3) regiments in position. The rebels were commanded by Major General Sterling Price in person, who had arrayed against us no less than eighteen (18) regiments. I saw the importance of holding the position we had assumed, and gave each regimental commander orders to hold every inch of ground at every hazard; as the remaining regiments of the 1st brigade came up the hill I threw them into position to protect the flanks of our little line of battle, the 4th Minnesota, under Captain Le Gro, and the 16th Iowa, Colonel Chambers, the former on the left and the latter on the right of the line, in rear, "*en echelon.*"

The battle at this time had become terrific; the enemy in dense masses bore down in front, on the right and left, showing a determined purpose to envelop and crush the little line in front. The ground admitted of no more forces being brought into action in front, and our position must be held, or the enemy once forcing it, his overwhelming masses would have passed over the hill and fallen on our unformed column in the rear. Brigadier General Sullivan having reached the rear of the battle-ground with the head of his brigade, placed one of his regiments, the 10th Iowa, under the gallant Perezel, with a section of the 12th Wisconsin battery, on the road across the ravine and open field on our extreme left, and finding no more of his forces could be brought into immediate action, placed them in position in reserve and came gallantly to the front asking to be of service. I immediately placed him in charge of the right of the line in front, with instructions to hold the ground and see that the right flank was not turned by the heavy force of the enemy moving in that direction. Colonel Sanborn, in command of the first brigade, most gallantly held the left in position, until, under a desolating carnage of musketry and canister, the brave Eddy was cut down, and his regiment, borne down by five times their numbers, fell back in some disorder on the 80th Ohio, under Lieutenant Colonel Bartelson. The falling back of the 48th exposed the battery; as the masses of the enemy advanced the battery opened with canister at short range, mowing down the rebels by scores, until, with every officer killed or wounded, and nearly every man and horse killed or disabled, it fell an easy prey. But this success was short-lived. The hero Sullivan rallied a portion of the right wing, and with a bravery better characterized as audacity, drove the rebels back to cover. Again they rallied, and again the battery fell into their hands, but with the wavering fortunes of this desperate fight, the battery again fell into our hands, and with three of its guns spiked, and the carriages cut and splintered with balls, it is again ready to meet the foe. While these events were transpiring along the road, the brave General Stanley had come to the front, and joining his personal exertions to mine, the regiments that had fallen into disorder were rallied and held in position to the close of the battle. One of Stanley's regiments, the 11th Missouri, coming up fresh and eager for action, was pushed in to the right, where, uniting its efforts with the 5th Iowa and 26th Missouri, it made a most gallant fight, and aided much, first, in holding our ground against the enemy, and afterwards in driving him back in confusion to the cover of the ravine from which the attack was begun. An attempt to turn my left flank, by a heavy force of the enemy moving up the open field and ravine on my left, was most signally repulsed by Colonel Perezel with the 10th Iowa and a section of Immell's battery. So bravely was this attempt repulsed that the enemy made no more attempts in that direction. After this repulse the 4th Minnesota was withdrawn from the left and ordered to report to General Sullivan on the right, where it did good service to the close of the action.

This completed the movements in the front, and the battle was fought and won in this position. The 39th Ohio, of Stanley's division, coming up during the heat of the contest, could not be placed in position to take an active part, owing to the want of ground, and was placed in reserve near the log church. From 5 p. m. until darkness prevented distinguishing friend from foe, the battle was fought along the road, and to the right of it, by the 5th Iowa, the 26th Missouri and 11th Missouri, with a bravery which scarcely admits of a parallel.

The enemy, confident in the heavy forces they had deployed, pushed on with frantic desperation, but they were met by a greater heroism, and though often rallied and driven to the charge, they were as often met and hurled back to their cover. Against this little front the fiercest of the battle was waged. Colonel Boomer was cut down by a terrible wound, but his regiment held their ground undismayed. The 5th Iowa, under its brave and accomplished Matthias, held their ground against four times their numbers, making three desperate charges with the bayonet, driving back the foe in disorder each time, until, with every cartridge exhausted, it fell back slowly and sullenly, making every step a battle-ground, and every charge a victory. Night alone closed the contest, and left us in possession of the field so bravely won.

For a detailed report of the operations of each regiment I respectfully refer you to the reports of subordinate commanders herewith submitted.

I am indebted for able and cheerful assistance rendered by Brigadier General Stanley, whose division, with the exception of one regiment, the 11th Missouri, being in rear, could not take an active part. General Stanley had come to the front and tendered his services.

To the commanders of brigades, Brigadier General J. C. Sullivan, whose personal exertions and bravery contributed very largely to our success, and to Colonel J. B. Sanborn, who, in this his first battle, exhibited a coolness and bravery under fire worthy a veteran, I am greatly indebted.

These commanders, Stanley, Sullivan and Sanborn, I cordially commend to the favorable notice of the government. The reports of brigade and regimental commanders do justice to those who were conspicuous in this daring contest. I cordially unite in all they have said, and, were it in my power, would do personal honor in this report to every hero.

To my personal staff I am under the deepest obligations; Captain R. M. Sawyer, assistant adjutant general, Captain D. P. Allen, assistant commissary subsistence, Lieutenants E. T. Pearce and W. F. Wheeler, aides-de-camp, bore my orders through the thickest of the battle. Intelligent, capable and brave, their gallant conduct is worthy of, and will receive, the honor rightly their due.

My division surgeon, J. E. Lynch, was unceasing in his efforts in his own department, and to his energy and skill the greatest credit is due for the prompt and efficient care of the wounded.

Captain Allen, in carrying orders along the line, came upon one of the enemy's regiments, but by his coolness and courage escaped from a murderous fire, though with a terrible wound; Lieutenant Wheeler received a slight but honorable wound, while bearing orders in the face of the enemy; Captain Borcherdt, commanding my personal escort, did excellent and gallant service in rallying men to their standards. He was seriously hurt by the fall of his horse.

Much of the time I was without a single officer of my staff, and was forced to send messages by orderlies; two of these, Corporals White and Hill, did excellent service, and I beg to commend them to the notice of the general commanding.

To the commanders of batteries, Lieutenant Sears and Lieutenant Immel, the highest praise is due for unyielding bravery, and the skill with which their pieces were handled. Lieutenant Sears was severely wounded, and left his guns only when his officers, men and horses were nearly all killed and disabled, and when the battery was fairly in the enemy's hands.

In closing this report I shall be permitted to embody this summary:

On the 19th instant my division marched nineteen (19) miles; fought a desperate battle with seven regiments against a rebel force under General Price of not less than eighteen regiments; won a glorious victory; lying at night on their arms on the field their valor had won, and the following morning chased the fleeing enemy for fifteen miles, until, worn out with labor and fighting, and famished for want of food, the pursuit was discontinued only when the powers of nature were exhausted. The records of war may well be challenged to produce a victory under circumstances and odds so desperate. No words of mine can add lustre to the brilliancy of this victory, and no award of praise given to those who were miles away from the battle-field will detract from the glory justly due to those heroes who won this audacious victory.

The fearful list of killed and wounded in the few regiments actively engaged shows with what heroism and desperation this fight was won.

I say boldly, that a force of not more than 2,800 men met and conquered a rebel force of 11,000 on a field chosen by Price, and a position naturally very strong and with its every advantage inuring to the enemy.

A list of casualties is herewith submitted.

It is known that 263 rebel bodies were buried on and near the field. All their severely wounded, numbering over 400, fell into our hands. The number of able-bodied prisoners who fell into our hands is large.

I report with the greatest satisfaction but twenty-six (26) missing from my command.

Over eight hundred (800) stand of arms were gathered on the battle-field, mostly of improved patterns, showing that the rebels are not wanting in this essential means of making war.

The dead of my division number	135
The wounded of my division number	527
Missing	26
Of my staff and escort, officers wounded	4
" " " private killed	1
	693

Respectfully submitted:

C. S. HAMILTON,
Brigadier General, Commanding 3d Division.

Lieutenant Colonel H. G. KENNETT, *Chief of Staff.*

HEADQUARTERS 1ST BRIGADE, THIRD DIVISION,
Army of the Mississippi, September 21, 1862.

SIR: I have the honor to report that, in pursuance of your orders of the 17th instant, I moved my command, consisting of the 5th Iowa infantry, 26th Missouri infantry, 48th Indiana infantry, 4th Minnesota infantry, 16th Iowa infantry, and 11th Ohio battery, at four o'clock a. m., in an easterly direction, to a point on the Tuscumbia road one mile west of the junction of the Pontotoc road with the same, without meeting with any opposition. At this point I disposed of my command in order of battle, and posted a strong guard on my front and flanks, and awaited further orders.

In pursuance of your orders of two o'clock a. m. of the 19th instant, I moved my command in an easterly direction on the Tuscumbia road, preceded by the 3d Michigan cavalry. When I had advanced about three miles I fell upon the enemy's pickets, who fired briskly at the advanced cavalry and retired across a clearing into a thick growth of timber and brush, and continued their fire as the cavalry advanced, so rapidly that it was deemed prudent to have a portion of the cavalry dismount and advance as infantry skirmishers. It being desirable at this time to conceal from the enemy all our force except the cavalry, I advanced in this manner to the point where the road leading from Iuka to Bay Springs crosses the Tuscumbia road, and halted, disposing of my command in the best manner possible, in my judgment, to receive an attack from any quarter, and posted guards south, east, and north. I had hardly accomplished this when I received your further orders to move forward immediately toward Iuka. I at once drew in my guards and took up my line of march on the Iuka road, preceded as before by cavalry. When I had advanced about two miles the firing of the enemy's pickets was so rapid and well sustained that under your orders I threw out four companies of the 5th Iowa infantry as skirmishers. These companies moved forward to their task with great alacrity, and soon succeeded in driving the enemy's pickets from a strong position they had selected in a house by the road-side, and advanced steadily, driving them for three hours, killing two of them and seriously wounding one, at least.

At this time (about four o'clock p. m.) I relieved the companies skirmishing from the gth Iowa by four companies of the 26th Missouri infantry, who went forward with the 5reatest cheerfulness, and continued to drive in the enemy's pickets rapidly till they reached a point a little more than a mile from Iuka, where they met the enemy drawn up in line of battle in strong force, about eighteen thousand infantry, with cavalry and artillery, and drew the fire from nearly his whole line The enemy almost instantaneously opened his batteries upon us and commenced advancing his line, and rendered the most rapid movements and formations necessary to prevent him enveloping my whole command.

I immediately caused the 5th Iowa infantry to file to the right of the road and form in order of battle, with the right wing slightly refused, to prevent it, as far as possible, from being flanked on that wing before other troops could be brought up.

The 11th Ohio battery was brought into position immediately on the left of this regiment, the 48th Indiana infantry on its left, with the left wing slightly refused, and the 4th Minnesota in the prolongation of this line; this line was upon the crest of a ridge. These regiments were ordered to hold their positions at all hazards until further orders. The 26th Missouri infantry was formed in order of battle below the crest of the ridge, with its left nearly in rear of the centre of the 5th Iowa, and its right retiring from the front line, with orders to Colonel Boomer, commanding, to move immediately to the right of the 5th Iowa, should the enemy make his appearance in that direction, but with discretionary authority to move to the relief of any point the most strongly assailed.

The 16th Iowa infantry was formed in order of battle below the crest of the hill, with its right in rear of the left of the 5th Iowa and the battery, and the three right companies of the 48th Indiana, masking the balance of its front and about twenty yards in advance, this formation being made to support the battery. All these formations and movements were made under a steady fire of canister from the enemy's batteries, and hardly had the disposition of the troops been made when the enemy came forward with his whole force and formed in front of the battery three battalions deep. I immediately ordered the battery to open fire and the infantry to commence firing. The battery fired with great rapidity and with extraordinary accuracy of aim, which, in conjunction with the volleys of musketry from the regiments in the front line, threw the enemy into confusion, and thus in his first attempt to take the battery the enemy was repulsed with heavy loss. The firing of his musketry during this advance was very rapid and quite destructive, and caused the battalion on the left of the battery to waver and the right to fall back. The enemy soon reformed, and with renewed vigor and cheers came on to the assault again, and was again repulsed by the well-directed fire of the battery, and the volleys and charges made by the 5th Iowa.

The three companies of the 5th Iowa flanking the battery had by this time become so unmasked by the loss of men that it seemed impossible for the regiment or the battery to hold out, and Colonel Boomer, of the 26th Missouri, immediately brought up four companies of his command and formed them in line under the most galling fire on the right of the battery and left of the 5th Iowa. The firing of the enemy at this time had become so destructive that Colonel Boomer promptly proceeded to bring up the balance of his command with great gallantry and personal bravery, but fell severely wounded before reaching his command, and was carried from the field. I had during this time been making the greatest efforts, in conjunction with the general commanding the division and members of the staff and field officers of the regiment, to bring back the regiment placed upon the left of the battery to its first position. During these efforts Colonel Eddy, commanding the regiment with the greatest valor, fell severely wounded and was carried from the field. The fire was so galling it was found impossible to bring this regiment again on to this line.

Colonel Chambers, commanding the 16th Iowa infantry, had already fallen and been carried from the field, and it did not at this time seem prudent to move the 2d line of battle in rear of the battery. I proceeded to the left flank of the whole line with a view of drawing in that battalion in support of the battery, but the enemy had then appeared in its front, and was engaging it with musketry. There was no alternative but for the battery, the 5th Iowa, and the four companies of the 26th Missouri to fight the battle out with nearly the whole force of the enemy concentrated on that point, and nobly did they do this.

The infantry on the right continued to fire and charge upon the enemy under their gallant leader, Colonel Matthias, until their whole forty rounds of ammunition was exhausted, and until it was too dark to distinguish one object from another, and until one half of all the men that had been taken upon the line upon the right of the battery were killed or wounded.

The battery at the same time, under command of the gallant Lieutenant Sears, held out, if possible, with still greater desperation, firing until all canister shot was exhausted, and more than one-half of his men and nearly all his horses had been killed or wounded. After this, the enemy came upon the ground where it was stationed, but did not remove the battery from the field.

The position where the remaining companies of the 26th Missouri were left had become very much exposed to the enemy's fire, and the lieutenant colonel, in his discretion, and without orders, removed them to an open field, to the right of the 5th Iowa, and there formed them in order of battle, where they remained for the night.

The enemy making no further appearance on my left, I withdrew the 4th Minnesota infantry from that wing, and ordered them to move forward and occupy the ground originally occupied by the battery and the left of the 5th Iowa. They promptly moved forward to within a few yards of this position, when they received a heavy volley of musketry from one of the regiments of the second brigade, which caused them to hault and lie down. The regiment occupied this position until a quarter past 8 o'clock, when it was relieved by General Sullivan, with one of the regiments of the 2d brigade.

I am happy to report that, with the single exception of the battalion on the left of the battery, each regiment obeyed every order with alacrity, and held every position assigned them until directed to vacate them ; and, in the case of the exception above named, I deem it proper to state, that the enemy's fire, in that position, was so severe that veteran troops even could hardly be expected to hold it. The brigade was in order of battle soon after the close of the engagement, ready for action on the following morning.

Every regiment conducted itself with coolness and deliberation, and in no case fired' except when the enemy appeared in full view, and then with deliberate aim, but were subjected to four full volleys from regiments of other brigades of our own troops in the rear.

I forward herewith the reports of the commanders of the respective regiments of my brigade, containing full lists of casualties of the respective commands.

The official report of the 11th Ohio battery will be forwarded at an early day, the only officer able to be on duty since the battle, having been constantly engaged in refitting his battery for service.

I regret that, in an action occupying a little more than an hour and a half, there were, out of about twenty-one hundred (2,100) men of my brigade engaged, five hundred and eighty-four (584) killed or wounded, and twenty-four missing.

It will be a consolation to the friends of all to know that they died or were injured fighting manfully for their country, and in an engagement where the killed and wounded of the enemy were twice the number of our men.

All the commanding and field officers of regiments and detachments labored with equal zeal and courage to perform their whole duty. Colonels Matthias and Boomer made most extraordinary efforts and with measurably successful results. The former was more fortunate than the latter in being able to continue his efforts to the close of the engagement. They both deserve from the country the rewards that a grateful people are always ready to confer upon faithful servants. Lieutenant L. B. Martin, acting assistant adjutant general, on my staff, conducted himself with great gallantry, and labored incessantly and successfully in rallying the men who had left their commands, and bringing them into position to do good execution against the enemy. The line officers deserving especial mention for gallantry in the field during the action are named and referred to in the reports of the commanders of their respective regiments, which reports are by me approved and confirmed, and to which attention is directed.

Respectfully submitted.

JOHN B. SANBORN, *Colonel, Commanding.*

Captain R. M. SAWYER, A. A. G.,
1st Brigade, 3d Division, Army of the Mississippi.

RECAPITULATION.—5th Iowa infantry : killed 37, wounded 179, missing 1 ; total 217. 26th Missouri infantry : killed 21, wounded 74, missing 1 ; total 96. 48th Indiana infantry : killed 37, wounded 56, missing 7 ; total 100. 4th Minnesota infantry : killed 3, wounded 43, missing 2 ; total 48. 16th Iowa infantry : killed 14, wounded 48, missing 13 ; total 75. 11th Ohio battery : (unofficial,) killed 18, wounded 54 ; total 72. Total killed 130, wounded 454 ; missing 24 ; aggregate 608.

HEADQUARTERS TENTH REGIMENT MISSOURI INFANTRY,
Camp near Iuka, September 20, 1862.

CAPTAIN : I herewith submit a report of the part taken in the late action near Iuka by the force under my command, consisting of the 10th Missouri and Captain L. M. Rice's attached company, 24th Missouri infantry, in all numbering six hundred and fifty (650) men and officers.

My regiment took position in line of battle about four hundred yards to the right of the Iuka road, and parallel with it, with the view of preventing any flank movement of the enemy through the woods opposite me, and at the same time to furnish a support to the main line formed across the road, and to my left. Company A, 1st Lieutenant Walker commanding, was deployed as skirmishers along my whole front, in the edge of the woods.

The action soon became general with the main body. I remained in the position named for some time, exposed to an enfilading fire of the enemy's artillery, which severely wounded several of my men.

Discovering no attempt of the enemy to come through the woods on my front, and seeing that some of the regiments on the right of the main body were apparently falling back under the terrific fire to which they were exposed, I changed front forward on my left, with a view to furnish any support which might be required, leaving my skirmishers as originally placed. With the exception of having once ployed my regiment into close column by division on the road, being ordered to take position there, I remained on the last-named line to the end of the action and during the night, the men sleeping on their arms.

In that most trying situation of being exposed to a heavy fire, without being able to return it, my officers and men behaved with the greatest steadiness, executing the required manœuvres with the precision of ordinary drill.

I may here aknowledge the valuable assistance which I received during the action from Lieutenant Colonel John D. Foster, Major L. Horney, and Adjutant F. C. Deimling, Surgeon C. B. Payne, and Chaplain George R. Palmer, are also entitled to especial mention for their services on the field, attending to and removing the wounded. My loss was fourteen (14) wounded, a list of whom is appended.

I kept my men screened while in position by the nature of the ground as far as possible, and by lying down, which will account for the smallness of the list.

Very respectfully,

SAMUEL A. HOLMES, *Colonel, Commanding.*

Captain THOMAS H. HARRIS,
Assistant Adjutant General, 2d Brigade, 3d Division, Army of Mississippi.

List of wounded.—Augustus D. Peyton, company A, private, face, dangerously; Robert Staton, company C, private, face, severely; Stuart Wishard, company D, sergeant, thigh, slightly; Asbury Salters, company D, private, contusion in region of spine, severely; John Rebstock, company D, private, foot, slightly; Thomas Hibbler, company D, private, hand, severely; Robert B. Glass, company D, private, breast and leg, slightly; Reuben Tharp, company D, private, leg, very severely, amputated; Washington J. Deane, company D, leg, very severely, amputated; Peter Thoma, company D, private, leg, very severely, amputated; August Zunkle, company E, private, arm, seriously; James Young, company F, private, hand, severely; Alexander B. Webb, company H, private, arm, severely; John Liles, attached to 24th Missouri, company F, private, leg, severely.

CAMP IN FIELD, *September* 21, 1862.

SIR: Agreeably to orders from General Sullivan I advanced, September 19, at about 5 o'clock p. m., with my regiment and a section of the 12th Wisconsin battery, under Lieutenant Immel. After a short survey of our line of battle, I took position, with seven companies, *en cheval,* on the Iuka road, about a quarter of a mile ahead of our left wing, sent three companies to the right into a dense wood; then I put my two pieces into position, and threw a few shells in an oblique direction, where I discovered the rebel lines. My three companies in the woods reported a full brigade of the rebels advancing on our left wing, on which I withdrew them, and leaving only one company for the observation of the enemy I changed front perpendicular to our line of battle on the Iuka road. I planted my two pieces anew, and thus obtained a dominating flanking position. Being on a ridge I could watch the enemy's movements, who had to cross a broken open field in order to attack our forces; they soon emerged from the woods, opened a heavy fire, and advanced on our lines; their fire was returned, and I, too, opened with musketry and canister; the rebels wavered, fell back a little, but were soon rallied by an officer on a gray horse, and advanced again, nothing daunted by our fire, which made great havoc in their ranks; they followed our left wing into the woods, and for a short while there was no enemy in our sight, but at a sudden a full regiment marched out from the woods on their side, offering their right flank to my fire, with the evident intention to advance for the support of their forces already engaged. I opened instantly with canister and musketry, on which they fell back to the woods, formed there parallel to my regiment, advanced to the edge of the wood, and commenced a brisk fire; we replied vividly; they attempted twice to advance, but were driven back each time; we had the advantage of the ground; our fire told fearfully upon them, while we suffered next to nothing; their fire up a steep hill has been altogether too high.

In the mean time the battle wavering to and fro, and apparently approaching the Iuka road, which was our only road of retreat, I got a little alarmed lest the pieces under my charge should be cut off in case we should be compelled to fall back. At this time one of General Hamilton's aides-de-camp rode up, inquiring how matters stood on our side; he told me that the road, although raked by the enemy's fire, was still in our possession, on which I ordered the pieces back, and they were withdrawn safely. Night coming on I drew a little closer to our main body, but on the report of company I, which

I left to observe the enemy's movements, that a new body of rebels were advancing I advanced again with three companies. Advised by the noise of our steps the enemy opened and gave us several tremendous volleys. Owing to the darkness and, again, to their up-hill firing not a man was hurt. We returned their fire, and made great execution, as we found, on the morning of the 20th, all the ground strewn with dead rebels. They left part of their wounded, having carried away a great number even during the action. We may safely assert having killed between sixty or seventy, and wounded in proportion, while our loss was seven wounded, and one of my orderlies' horse killed.

Thus ended our part in this memorable fight. I have but to add that officers and men behaved with the greatest bravery. All movements have been executed promptly in spite of the shower of bullets, and I dare to say that the tenth Iowa are good soldiers.

I have yet to mention the efficient services and assistance of our brave Major N. McCalla, and of my adjutant, Wm. Manning, and also the able and brave manner in which Lieutenant M. E. Immel handled his two pieces.

Yours, respectfully,

N. PEREZEL,
Colonel, Commanding 10th Iowa Volunteers.

Captain T. H. Harris,
Assistant Adjutant General, 2d Brigade, 3d Division.

Headquarters Iowa Seventeenth Infantry,
Jacinto, Mississippi, September 22, 1862.

General: In compliance with your request, I make the following brief statement concerning the battle near Iuka on the 19th instant.

When you ordered the 17th Iowa to form line of battle across the ridge at right angles with the road leading up from the hospital building, we were filed off to the right by Colonel Rankin (then commanding) until a little more than the right wing of the regiment had filed to the right, when the regiment was halted and brought to a front, and the remainder of the left wing formed on the left of the road.

We were then ordered forward. We advanced a few paces and were ordered to give way to the right, which the right wing of the regiment obeyed, and which, I think, the left wing failed to hear. The right wing passed, I should think, thirty or forty yards to the right, ordered by Colonel Rankin to halt and come to a front.

By this movement of the right wing to the right, the regiment was divided near the centre. About this time the firing from the enemy became quite brisk, and there seemed to be a strong inclination to fall back. I communicated this fact to Colonel Rankin, and he told me to do the best I could for them, and keep them together if possible.

After this I saw no more of him during the engagement. I learned afterwards from him that his horse was shot from under him, and that he plunged him against a tree, which rendered him unable to longer command the regiment.

Lieutenant Colonel Hillis being absent, and Major Wise being under arrest, I was the next officer in rank, and I took command of the right wing of the regiment, that being all that was in sight or hearing of me. About the time I mention as having lost sight of Colonel Rankin, our men retreated without any command, which caused great confusion. They had not proceeded far to the rear, however, until I succeeded in rallying them, and got them back to about where our line was first formed, and succeeded in quieting them for a time.

About this time I saw you and told you I had assumed command, and was told to take command of the battalion and do the best I could.

I then went to near the right of the right wing and urged the men forward; we had proceeded but a short distance when a tremendous volley from the enemy caused a panic in the entire battalion, and with all my efforts, and assisted by Captain D. A. Craig, who was the only captain I saw after Colonel Rankin left the field, could not rally them until they had retreated almost to the road near the old log church. I here succeeded in stopping them, got a line partly formed and marched them forward. By the time I had got them to our former line I had, I should think, about three hundred (300) men, consisting of the right wing of our regiment and stragglers from Iowa 5th, Missouri 11th, Minnesota 4th, Ohio 39th, and some others. I now held tbem near where our first line was formed for about three-fourths ($\frac{3}{4}$) of an hour waiting orders. Not having been told by Colonel Rankin what the design was in placing us there, or whether any of our own forces were between us and the enemy, and when some of my men fired I ordered them to cease firing until ordered. About this time a soldier from the 5th Iowa, I think, came near us and told me that my men were firing upon our own men. I then ordered my men forward with the intention of taking a better position to support our men in case they should fall back. We had not proceeded far when some of my men again commenced firing, which was *apparently* answered by a tremendous volley from the direction of the enemy, but a soldier, who was some distance in advance, came rushing back and said that our own men were firing upon us. I then ordered my men to fall back in good order, so as not to come in contact with them. I fell back, I should think, about 25 or 30 yards, and to near where our original line had been, halted them, about-faced them, and ordered them to kneel. They remained in this position for some time, and until quite a number of men in front of us came back on double quick, which, together with increased firing from the front, caused another panic among the men, and in spite of all exertions ran back about one hundred yards, where I succeeded in forming another line, and having advanced a few yards I ordered the men to stand and wait for orders. We had stood here but a short time when a tremendous volley was fired by the enemy and was answered immediately by some regiment still in our rear ; we were now between two heavy fires from front and rear. This caused a dreadful stampede among the men, and all commenced firing in all directions without regard to where their guns were aimed. This, however, continued but a short time, for as soon as the guns were all discharged I had no difficulty in preventing a repetition of the fire. I again rallied the men and kept them in pretty good line until the *retreat* was sounded, when I brought the men off and formed them on the right of the 39th Ohio. I brought off, I should think, about 350 men belonging to the regiments above named.

It may be said that the foregoing would not add much to the reputation of a regiment, but this I cannot avoid. I give you a simple *statement* of the *facts* that came under my own observation, hoping to be able to give a better account of the 17th Iowa in the next engagement.

It is due to Captain Craig, company H, Lieutenants Garret and Johnson of company A, Lieutenants Rice and Snodgrass, of company I, Lieutenant Hull, company E, Lieutenant Morris, company F, Lieutenant Stapleton, company C, and one or two others, probably, who were with me during the entire engagement, to say that they acted in a very brave and unflinching manner, and deserve great credit

I do not wish to be understood as casting any insinuation upon any officer in the regiment, but I only mention those whom *I saw* in the engagement.

Respectfully submitted.

JOHN L. YOUNG,
Captain Company A, Commanding Regiment.

Brigadier General SULLIVAN,
Commanding 2d Brigade, 3d Division, Army of the Mississippi.

HEADQUARTERS TWELFTH WISCONSIN BATTERY,
Jacinto, Mississippi, September 20, 1862.

CAPTAIN : I have the honor to report the part which the 12th Wisconsin battery took in the engagement of the 19th of September, near Iuka, Mississippi. I was ordered by General Sullivan to take position, with one section of the battery, on the road leading to the left and front of line of battle, which was formed across the main road leading to Iuka. I took position five or six hundred yards to the front and left of the 11th Ohio battery, under the immediate direction of Lieutenant Colonel W. L. Lothrop, chief of artillery, and Colonel Perezel, of the 10th Iowa volunteers, whose personal bearing won the applause of myself and men. Several shells were thrown into the field and timber in front to find the position of the enemy, who soon advanced from our right through the thick timber. I then fell back a short distance and took a position, while Colonel Perezel was engaging the rebel infantry, who now came in great numbers. It was about this time the 11th Ohio battery was taken, and the enemy had cut us from the main body. At this time the enemy were driven back with great loss by the 10th Iowa, and the two guns under my charge, which were served with great dexterity by the cannoniers, most of the time using canister.

I call your attention to the great bravery of Colonel Perezel, his officers, and men, the gallant manner in which they fought, supported the artillery, and repulsed the enemy with great loss. My non-commissioned officers and men stood well to their posts. Those most meritorious I am constrained to mention are, 1st Sergeant, S. E. Jones and Sergeant Philander Cady, who nobly did their duty. At the time the enemy opened fire upon us, First Lieutenant Edward G. Harbon, chief of 1st section, left his section, and I saw no more of him till after the engagement was over.

When I returned where I had left the 2d section in command of First Lieutenant William Miles, I found the guns with the poles broken out of both pieces and caissons ; the drivers and horses all gone; the gunners and cannoniers at their posts, but their commanding officer gone, while the battle was still raging in their immediate front. I caused the pieces and caissons to be drawn off and repaired. This action lasted some time, but the battery was not under fire more than an hour or an hour and a quarter.

The loss sustained in this engagement was six (6) horses killed; one man killed, Private James C. Atherton, company D, 17th Iowa volunteers, who was on detached service in this battery, and three (3) men slightly wounded.

I am, sir, very respectfully, your obedient servant,

L. D. IMMELL,

2d Lieutenant 1st Missouri Light Artillery, Com'g 12th Wisconsin Battery.

Captain T. H. HARRIS, A. A. G.,

2d Brigade, 3d Division, Army of the Mississippi.

HEADQUARTERS 26TH REGIMENT MISSOURI VOLUNTEERS,

September 22, 1862.

COLONEL: I beg leave to submit the following report of the action of the troops under my command in the battle near Iuka, Mississippi, September 19, 1862. By order of Colonel George B. Boomer, commanding the 26th Missouri volunteers, I took command of companies A, Captain Robinson; B, Captain Welker; G, Captain Rice, and I, Lieutenant Berry, and relieved the skirmishers of the 5th Iowa. I deployed company A on the left, company B on the right of the main road, leading to Iuka, holding companies G and I as a reserve, under command of Captain Rice. I drove back the enemy's pickets without much firing, excepting on one occasion, when he had taken refuge in a house on the road, when a brisk skirmish ensued, but we soon forced him to leave his shelter, and continued to advance under a brisk fire. The enemy's cavalry attempted a charge, but seeing me prepared to receive him with the reserve, and flanking companies rallying, he promptly fell back. I again deployed and advanced, and soon came upon the main force, posted about forty yards above a ridge covered with timber and thick undergrowth; his artillery being in position in the road in front. A few shots were fired by my skirmishers, but the enemy held his fire. At this time I had advanced to the top of the ridge in the road, and discovered the position of the enemy; at this instant company B drew the fire of the whole rebel line on the right, and fell back and rejoined the regiment. Company A rallied on the right, and Captain Rice brought up the reserve, and after getting into position near the top of the ridge, these companies gave him their entire fire, and almost instantly drew the fire of their artillery and two regiments of infantry. My troops were so protected by the ridge that their fire took no effect. I gave them a few more shots, when Captain Robinson reported the enemy flanking him on the left, and Captain Rice discovered him on the right. Seeing our battery in position and line of battle formed in my rear, I gave the order to retire, and soon after received orders to rejoin the regiment and await orders. Soon after joining the regiment, Colonel Boomer went to the left, leaving Adjutant Schoenen and myself on the right. The battle soon opened with great fury. The four companies on the left, with the colors, were here detached by the Colonel, (as I afterwards learned,) and moved forward under his and Major Koniuszeski's command in support of the battery. I remained in position until the advance of the enemy had turned our left, which placed me and my right under a destructive cross-fire from the rear, left, and front. The battery had been carried, and one of the caissons came down on my left, and threw that part of my line into confusion. Seeing that I was being flanked on the left, and it being impossible to rally the left of my line, which had become disordered, I ordered my command to fall back to the field, a short distance below my first line. This movement was quickly executed and in good order, when I again formed in line of battle near the edge of timbers. I then, by order, moved back my line about 150 or 200 yards, and took position on the right of the 10th Missouri, awaiting the approach of the enemy, where I remained until the close of the engagement. I was then ordered to remain on arms, which I did until the next morning. About 7 o'clock in the evening I was here rejoined by the remnants of companies E, F, and H, bearing the colors in charge of Lieutenant Wheeler and Lieutenant Charles F. Brown, regimental quartermaster. From the opening to the end of the engagement my command was constantly under a galling and destructive fire, and my loss in killed and wounded was severe. Permit me further to report, that the officers and men under my command, with scarcely an exception, during the whole engagement, conducted themselves with rare coolness and true soldierly bearing; but Captain John Welker, T. M. Rice, Captain William M. Robinson, Lieutenant F. G. Schoenen, acting adjutant, and lieutenant C. F. Brown, regimental quartermaster, with many others, are deserving a special notice. Their conduct was truly brave, gallant, and noble; if space would permit, too much could not be said of their signal acts of daring, their coolness and skill in discharging the duties respectively assigned them on the field. The country may truly be proud of such men, for under their leadership continued success will mark the progress of our gallant army. Of those officers above named it will be doing no injustice to any for me to say that Captains Welker, Rice, and Robinson, Lieutenant C. F. Brown, regimental quartermaster, and Lieutenant Schoenen, that they have won for themselves distinguished merits, efficient in camp, brave and patriotic on the field. I can cheerfully recommend them for promotion in the army.

JOHN H. HOLMAN,

Lieutenant Colonel, Commanding 26th Regiment Missouri Volunteers.

HOSPITAL AT IUKA, MISSISSIPPI, 20TH MISSOURI,
September 21, 1862.

COLONEL: I have the honor to report that, in obedience to your orders, I marched on the morning of the 18th from camp, west of Jacinto, and camped that evening six miles east of the town, on the Iuka road. On the 19th we marched to within two miles of Inka, the 5th Iowa infantry leading the column; next 11th Ohio battery, and next 26th Missouri infantry. About 3 o'clock p. m. I relieved four companies of the 5th Iowa skirmishers with companies B, A, G, and I of my regiment, under command of Lieutenant Colonel Holman, who continued to drive back the enemy's line, till they came upon his main body, from whom they received a volley, causing considerable loss. They remained in position till the column came up, and upon my arrival I ordered them into the line, and formed the regiment according to your order, in rear of the 5th Iowa, the right down a steep ravine, the left resting near the 11th Ohio battery. You also ordered me, in case the enemy should attempt to flank on the right, to move my regiment in that direction into the open field. I reconnoitred the position on the right, and seeing no indication of a flank movement I remained in position. Shortly after the engagement opened in earnest on the front of the 5th Iowa, Colonel Matthias finding the left of his regiment next to the battery too hard pressed, called on me for assistance. I seeing that the battery was nearly disabled, and that the enemy were directing all their efforts against that point, immediately ordered Major Koniuszeski to mount and go forward with the left wing of my regiment, composed of companies F, E, H, and C, in all 162 men, exclusive of hospital details. I at the same time ordered the right wing to remain where it was and await my orders. Seeing Major Koniuszeski dismount, and that he gave no orders at all, or at least none adequate to the occasion, I took command in person, and remained until I thought the time had arrived to bring up the right wing, with which, being five large companies, I had intended to charge. In the mean time the colors, contrary to orders, had advanced with the left wing, and a short time previous to my returning to the right wing I had ordered the colors back to their former position. When I returned to where I had ordered Lieutenant Colonel Holman to remain with the right wing, I found it gone as well as the colors. I immediately returned to the left wing, where, mixed up with the disabled battery, we remained, without giving an inch, until I was severely wounded, having been slightly wounded before. I immediately after this ordered the men to retreat down the ravine, and was off the field.

We had lost seventy-nine (79) men, including five (5) commissioned officers wounded.

The fire was veiy severe, and the position in the midst of tangled horses, struggling to get away, was difficult both to take and maintain in order. I did not see Major Koniuszeski during the action; had he and Lieutenant Colonel Holman (whom I since understand ordered the right wing to retreat shortly after I left him) obeyed my orders properly, I think a charge with these fresh troops would have prevented the temporary capture of the battery. The 5th Iowa, with my four companies, fought with great desperation and effect, and we left the field at the same time. I have no means of knowing with certainty why the right wing left the field as it did, as I have not seen the command since I was carried off the field, to be able to get any accurate information, but they could not have left without orders, as they were almost completely under shelter. It will be necessary for Lieutenant Colonel Holman to explan this in his report, which should begin at the time those companies left their position.

It gives me great pleasure to mention the names of several officers engaged with me on the left wing, who behaved with distinguished gallantry and energy. Captain B. D. Dean, 2d Lieutenant J. W. Maupin, of company F; Captain Robert C. Crowell, 1st Lieutenant R. B. Denny, 2d Lieutenant J. T. Crowe, of company E; 1st Lieutenant Schirmer, commanding company H, and 1st Lieutenant J. M. Dennis, of company C. I was not present with the skirmishers in action, but understand that all exhibited great coolness and energy.

I enclose a list of killed and wounded so far as known at this time.

I am, very respectfully, your obedient servant,

GEORGE B. BOOMER.

Colonel, Commanding 26th Regiment Missouri Infantry Volunteers.

Colonel John B. Sanborn,

Commanding 1st Brigade, 3d Division, Army of the Mississippi.

Official:

L. B. MARTIN,

Lieutenant and Acting Assistant Adjutant General.

Headquarters 5th Regiment Iowa Volunteers, *September* 21, 1862.

Sir: I have the honor to submit the following report of the part taken in the engagement, near Iuka, on the 19th instant, by the 5th Iowa infantry.

We left camp, six miles from Jacinto, early on the morning of the 19th instant, leading the column of the 3d division, and soon came on to the enemy's pickets posted on the road. Three companies of my regiment, E, G, and D, were ordered forward as skirmishers, and succeeded in driving them from their positions, and continued to drive them from one position to another, which they contested for more than six miles, killing three and wounding a number, when these companies were relieved by the 26th Missouri infantry. Our loss was one sergeant, severely wounded.

The skirmishers soon came on to the main force of the enemy, placed in a strong position, and received a volley from one or more regiments. My regiment was ordered into line on the right of the 11th Ohio battery, which had just been placed in position, when I was informed that a large force was moving on my right, which compelled me to change front, and had just got into position on the crest of a hill, when the enemy in strong force—two brigades—as I learned, under Generals Green and Norton, came up in front, and poured a terrible fire of musketry into my line, which was promptly returned. The firing continued without cessation on both sides for more than a quarter of an hour, when I found the enemy was pressing my left wing near the battery, and I ordered a charge, which was executed in the most gallant manner, every officer and man moving up in almost perfect line, cheering lustily; the enemy gave way before us, when we poured a most deadly fire into their ranks, causing them to fall back down the hill; they soon returned with renewed vigor on my front and left, cheering as they came, and were received with a steady fire from the gallant boys of my regiment, holding our position under the most terrific fire possible. I then gave the command forward, and the enemy were again driven over the hill, but not until they had come so near as to boldly reach out after our colors, thus showing the United States flag, and saying "Don't fire at us, we are your friends." At this juncture the left wing of my regiment was suffering terribly from a cross-fire coming from the left of the battery; nearly every officer of the three left companies being either killed or wounded. At this moment four companies of the 26th Missouri infantry came up to the support of my left, and nobly assisted in holding the ground, until I found my ammunition was exhausted—more than an hour—when I ordered my regiment to retire to a field about one hundred yards distant, which was done in good order, where it was reformed under a galling fire. At this time the 11th Missouri infantry advanced in order of battle, and my regiment retired by the right of companies to the rear, passing the 10th Missouri infantry, which was advancing to take a position near the road, under the direction of an aide-de-camp. The regiment was here reformed in line, ammunition distributed to the men, and the firing having ceased, the men rested upon their arms for the night. The casualties in my regiment were seven (7) commissioned officers killed and eight (8) wounded, and thirty-three (33) enlisted men killed and one hundred and sixty-eight (168) wounded.

In commanding my regiment before the enemy, I was gallantly assisted on the right by Lieutenant Colonel Lampson, and on the left by Adjutant R. F. Patterson, acting major, and Lieutenant W. S. Marshall, acting adjutant, which officers, without leaving their places, repeated my commands and cheered my brave boys throughout the fierce engagement.

The long list of casualties of both officers and men is ample proof of the noble manner in which all stood at their posts. The highest praise is due to all. A grateful country will reward them for their deeds of daring.

Very respectfully,

C. L. MATTHIAS,

Colonel Commanding 5th Iowa Infantry.

Lieutenant Martin, A. A. A. G.,

1st Brigade, 3d Division, Army of the Mississippi.

HEADQUARTERS, 16*th* IOWA INFANTRY,
September 21, 1862.

SIR: I have the honor to report the part taken by the 16th Iowa infantry in your brigade, in the battle on the 19th instant, (evening,) one and a half mile south of Iuka, Mississippi. The regiment, under command of Colonel A. Chambers, was placed in position about 5½ o'clock p. m. in rear of the 11th Ohio battery, the left of the regiment extending across the road from which it had filed in position. Immediately after the regiment was formed in line, a charge of grape and shell from a battery of the enemy cut down six or seven men, including an officer, when the men were ordered to lie down ; in this position but few or none were injured by the repeated discharges of canister and ball from the rebel battery. In probably half an hour from forming in line the enemy made a charge of infantry on the battery ; our fire was reserved till the last moment in the centre of the regiment for fear of killing those manning the battery or the horses of the same, and in the two right companies, till a regiment, which were lapping them, were withdrawn. But when the enemy's lines were plainly or partially in sight, which, owing to the trees and thick underbrush, was not till they were very close, Colonel Chambers ordered the men to rise and fire, which order was instantly obeyed, for a time stopping the enemy's advance, but they again charged. The attack was evidently by a very heavy force, and with the object of capturing the battery. Our men stood their ground manfully, and I am not aware that a single officer or man failed in any part of his duty ; they were finally beaten back by the overwhelming force of the enemy. The centre, in the rear of the left section of the battery, retiring first, but warmly contending with the enemy till they were almost in our ranks ; the left, holding a comparatively safe position, did not retire till they were fired into by one of our own regiments in the rear. The entire right companies, although under a remarkably heavy fire, held their position longest, and experienced the heaviest loss. Company A, Captain Smith, was the last to leave the field, and for a time held its ground alone, the regiment on its right having, at an early hour, been compelled to retire, and the remaining companies of its own regiment the same, at a later hour.

While all the officers did so well it seems scarcely fair to particularize the conduct or bearing of one from the others, yet I deem it my official duty to notice the fact that Captain Smith exhibited in this action bravery and gallant conduct for which he cannot receive too much praise. He brought out of the battle scarcely half the men he took in it, and the same may be said of Company F, Captain Frazier.

The remaining portion of the regiment were immediately after reformed by myself, and took a position near the battle-field, it then being nearly dark, and soon after, while changing to another position, was directed to rest on the right of an Ohio regiment, formed along the Iuka road, where it remained during the night.

I regret to report the severe wounding of Colonel Chambers, by gunshot wounds, in the shoulder and neck, towards the close of the action. He was taken prisoner at the time of receiving the wounds, but was left by the enemy in the hospital at Iuka. I have the honor to enclose herewith a list of the killed, wounded and missing of the 16th Iowa infantry at the late action near Iuka, complete as it can be made at this time, summing up : Killed 14 ; wounded 48 ; missing 14. The regiment went into battle with about 350 men, exclusive of details made to take care of the wounded.

Very respectfully, your obedient servant,

ADD. H. SANDERS,
Lieutenant Colonel, Commanding 16th Iowa Infantry.

Colonel SANBORN,
Commanding 1st Brigade, 3d Division, Army of the Mississippi.

HOSPITAL NO. 2, IUKA, MISSISSIPPI, 48TH INDIANA,
September 21, 1862.

COLONEL : I respectfully report the part taken in the action by my regiment while I remained on the field, near Iuka, on the 19th instant.

In pursuance to your orders and that of General Hamilton, the regiment was formed on a line nearly with and to the left of the 11th Ohio battery, Lieutenant Sears commanding, on the crest of a hill or ridge receding to the left and semicircular in form. In rear was placed the 16th Iowa for our support, and not more than 20 yards from us, and to the left, was the 4th Minnesota, in continuation of the front.

The men were ordered to lie down and to hold their fire until they could make it effective. There was a deep gulch or ravine which it was impossible to reach with musketry as the line was then formed. To the right wing of the regiment the line of fire was much circumscribed, the range being confined to the sharp slope of the hill opposite, and to a descending plain to the front of the line on which we were formed, of not more than 25 or 30 yards in width. On the left of the regiment the descent of the ground was less rapid and abrupt, but rolling, and at many points offered a cover to an enemy's approach. The fire opened upon us by their batteries at about 5 o'clock p m., and at first seemed mainly directed at the battery on our right, but taking in its range the first and second companies of the regiment, who suffered early and severely in the engagement.

The fire from the batteries was from converging points, and therefore enfilading, under which those troops to the front and to the right and left of our battery suffered severely. After their cannonading had lasted a half an hour or more, circumstances indicated the approach of an attacking column, of which I promptly informed you.

They advanced in three lines, two deep each. As soon as they were perceived on the summit and descent of the hill on the apposite side, at about 250 yards distant, we opened our fire upon them, and continued it until they were hidden by the declivity below, resuming the fire as soon as they came within reach. Here they met us with a volley, and our support having given way, with a force in our front of at least four to one, the regigiment followed.

They fell back nearly 100 yards, where they were rallied, and although the line was irregular, they still showed a front to the enemy and continued to fire.

By your direction I advanced to the support of the battery. When within about 40 yards of it I was wounded and compelled to retire to the rear. The command of the regiment then devolved upon Lieutenant Colonel Rugg. His report, which no doubt will accompany this, will embody all the essential facts connected with the regiment after I left the field.

Considering that it was the first time the regiment had been under fire, and that it was outnumbered four to one by the veteran troops of the rebel army, and that they remained in the battle to its termination, its conduct may be deemed satisfactory, though not in all respects what I could wish it. To the officers especially much praise is due; they were prompt in the execution of every command, attentive to every duty, and remained with their men, encouraging them by word and example to the last.

To Lieutenant Colonel Rugg I am under especial obligations. He gave me every aid and assistance while I remained on the field, and contributed much to the order and good conduct of the men. His gallantry was conspicuous at every point of danger. I take pleasure in also mentioning with approbation the conduct of Adjutant Stanfield, and particularly that of Sergeant Major Ellis. Other special instances of meritorious conduct on the part of commissioned officers and enlisted men deserving notice will, doubtless, be mentioned by Colonel Rugg in his report.

I have the honor to be, very respectfully,

NORMAN EDDY, *Colonel, Commanding.*

Colonel SANBORN,

Commanding 1st Brigade, 3d Division, Army of the Mississippi.

Official:

L. B. MARTIN,

Lieutenant and Acting Assistant Adjutant General.

Report of Lieutenant Colonel Rugg.

The regiment was speedily reformed on the right of the road on which the battery was placed.

Here Major Tormans and Captains Byrkit and Wilson rendered valuable assistance. Order being restored in the regiment, I held it in waiting for the orders of a superior, not feeling authorized to move it at my own discretion; but not being called upon for further service, I moved it off the field in good order at the close of the battle. I may add that, considering the unusual fierceness of the fire of grape and musketry, to which particularly the right wing was exposed in the position assigned to it, it is not strange or discreditable to the men that they withdrew, knowing, as they certainly did, that it was impossible to withstand the murderous concentration of the enemy's fire upon it.

I take great pleasure in mentioning the name of Lieutenant White, commanding company G, for the cool courage he displayed during the battle. He deserves great credit for his gallantry.

Newton Bingham, 1st sergent company F, was also among the foremost of those who displayed remarkable bravery. There are other non-commissioned officers and privates, whose faces I remember well, but whose names I cannot now recollect, who deserve and will receive advancement for their good conduct.

The regiment went into the battle 434 strong. Our loss was 37 killed, 56 wounded, and 8 missing.

Respectfully submitted:

D W. E. RUGG,
Lieutenant Colonel, Commanding Regiment.

Official:

L. B. MARTIN,
Lieutenant and Acting Assistant Adjutant General.

HEADQUARTERS 4TH MINNESOTA VOLUNTEERS, CAMP 6 MILES SOUTH OF IUKA,
September 20, 1862.

SIR: I have the honor to make the following report of the movements of the regiment under my command during the battle of yesterday near Iuka. At 5 o'clock p. m. I moved my command at double-quick to a position on the left of the 48th Indiana, which regiment was in support of the 11th Ohio battery, commanded by Lieutenant Sears. Shortly after, the battle was opened by the battery, and raged furiously along the line for half an hour, when the 48th Indiana, being compelled to give way, fell back to the edge of the woods, leaving my regiment exposed to an oblique fire in the rear from the advancing enemy. I then ordered the right wing to fall back ten rods to the timber, which was accomplished in good order, notwithstanding the galling and incessant fire from the enemy. This change of position brought our line in the form of a semicircle, partly facing the battery; here we remained some twenty minutes, when the fire of the enemy was directed against the troops on the right of the battery.

I was then ordered to move by the right flank about forty rods up the road at nearly a right angle to my first position, then by the left flank, in order of battle, to a point near where the battery was first placed, which I did immediately. This position I occupied until a quarter past 8 o'clock, when the enemy having fallen back, I was relieved by the 80th Ohio, and ordered to the rear for a fresh supply of ammunition.

Throughout the whole, both officers and men behaved with coolness and courage, conducting themselves in a manner highly commendable.

Too much praise cannot be awarded to Surgeon J. H. Murphy and his assistants, for their unceasing attentions to the wounded through the action and during the night.

I enclose a list of the killed, wounded and missing.

I have the honor to be, with great respect, your obedient servant,

E. LEE GRO,
Captain, Commanding 4th Minnesota Volunteers.

Colonel JOHN B. SANBORN,
Commanding 1st Brigade, 3d Division, Army of the Mississippi.

HEADQUARTERS SECOND BRIGADE, THIRD DIVISION, ARMY OF THE MISSISSIPPI,
Iuka, September 20, 1862.

I have the honor to submit this report of the part the second brigade took in the battle of Iuka:

On the evening of the 18th I received orders to move the next morning, at 5 o'clock, on Tuscumbia road, towards Iuka, to join in an attack on Major General Price, who was encamped with the rebel army at that place. Leaving camp punctually at the time appointed, we arrived within one and a half mile of Iuka by 4 p. m., our advance brigade having been skirmishing with the enemy's pickets for over six miles. Halting at this point, the first brigade was formed in line of battle by General Hamilton, who was in advance, while the second was halted on the road until a reconnoissance could be made of the ground to the left, and a position obtained for the battery. Before a position could be selected the rebels opened a terrific fire along the entire front of our line, having approached us entirely unperceived, owing to the dense underbrush and broken character of the ground, at the same time attempting to turn our position by an attack on both flanks. I ordered Colonel Holmes, of the 10th Missouri, to take position guarding our right flank, while Colonel Perezel, of the 10th Iowa, with a section of the 12th Wisconsin battery, was ordered to hold a road leading to our left and rear. (Their reports are herewith enclosed.) The position occupied by Colonel Holmes was so important and so effectually checked the enemy's advance on our right, that their artillery fire was directed especially to that point. Although the enemy's fire enfiladed his line, the movements of his regiments in taking position were performed with as much precision as if on the drill ground. His officers and men are entitled to praise. Colonel Perezel, with his command, held the position assigned them, and drove back a brigade of the rebels, who were advancing to take possession of the road. He gallantly held his position, and by his determined stand led the enemy to believe we were in strong force at that point, and to desist from their attack. Before the disposition of the regiments above mentioned could be made the rebels, by bringing a vastly superior force against the left wing of the first brigade, had driven in the regiments, flanking Sands's battery, and occupied a position commanding the battery, and were moving down the road with the intention of attacking the first brigade in the rear. Forming a portion of the 80th Ohio and 17th Iowa, which had been halted in the road, two volleys, rapidly delivered, checked the enemy's advance, and drove them back to the brow of the hill. By this time portions of the 26th Missouri volunteers, 48th Indiana volunteers, and 16th Iowa volunteers, whose colonels had all been seriously wounded, with a few of the 4th Minnesota volunteers, joined my command and fought bravely through the remainder of the action. General Hamilton at this time desired me to save Sands's battery, which was entirely disabled, every officer and cannonier being either killed or wounded, and all the horses killed. At the order to advance the men gave three cheers, and with a rush drove the enemy back out of the battery, down the hill, and were yet advancing, when a murderous fire was opened on my flank by a regiment of sharpshooters, which lay concealed on my left in the woods. Ordering my men to fall back, I reformed my line, which had become somewhat disordered. The rebels, taking heart at our supposed retreat, advanced with loud cheers, but were soon undeceived by a volley, followed by an order to charge, which again drove them below the brow of the hill. Receiving re-enforcements the rebels again advanced, but were held in check, when the 39th Ohio, through a mistake and without orders, fired a volley into the rear of my line, killing and wounding more than my whole loss prior to that time. By this time it was so dark that friends could not be distinguished from foes. The enemy improved this occasion to remove the guns from their position, but were not able to take them entirely off, and were compelled to leave the caissons in their original position. At 8 o'clock the firing ceased, and the field of battle was ours. The position in which the battery was planted, and which was so hotly contested, was held by our troops. Lieutenant Colonel Bartelson, of the 80th Ohio, together with his adjutant, Joseph E. Philpot, were wounded early in the fight, when Major Lanning took command. The 17th Iowa regiment was without a field officer, and Captain Archer, the senior captain, soon fell severely wounded, when Captain Young assumed command and did his duty nobly. Our troops labored under a great disadvantage from want of knowledge of the ground, by being compelled to fight in the dense underbrush, and in a position chosen by the enemy. The enemy attacked my position in vastly superior force, a fresh brigade of the rebels having been sent to relieve the troops first repulsed. Lieutenant Immell, of the 12th Wisconsin battery, is especially mentioned by Colonel Perezel, and I desire to recommend him to the favorable notice of the general commanding. I am also indebted to Captain T. H. Harris, assistant adjutant general; Lieutenant Jacobson, assistant acting commissary of subsistence; Lieutenant Delahoyde and Lieutenant Buchanan, of my staff, for efficient service rendered on the field. They displayed a coolness under fire worthy of older soldiers. Lieutenant White, of the 48th Indiana, and the assistant adjutant general of Colonel Mower's brigade, who joined me, rendered valuable assistance. The victory gained is sufficient evidence of the bravery of the men. The number of the dead and wounded is sufficient evidence of their devotion to our glorious cause. They are justly entitled to the highest praise, for a battle against such superior numbers and on such ground has not been fought in this war. I enclose reports received from commanding officers of regiments, together with a list of the killed, wounded, and missing of my brigade.

The regiments of my brigade engaged were:

10th Iowa, Colonel Perezel.
17th Iowa, Captain Archer.
80th Ohio, Colonel Bartelson.
One section 12th Wisconsin battery, commanded by Lieutenant Immel.

I have the honor, captain, to be yours, respectfully,

GEO. C. SULLIVAN, *Brigadier General.*

Captain R. M. Sawyer, *Assistant Adjutant General.*

Carlisle, Pennsylvania, *October* 15, 1862.

General: Frequent and continued movements have hitherto prevented my reporting the operations of the left wing of the army before Iuka, between the 16th and 20th of September.

It having been reported on the 16th by Colonel Mower, commanding at Burnsville, that General Price was threatening from the direction of Iuka, with a large force at the latter place, you gave me verbal orders to prepare all my available force, consisting of Davies's, Ross's and McArthur's divisions, altogether numbering about eight thousand (8,000,) to move upon the enemy by the roads north of the Memphis and Charleston railroad. In addition to the verbal orders, the following written instructions were received from you:

HEADQUARTERS DISTRICT OF WEST TENNESSEE,
Corinth, September 16, 1862.

GENERAL: On the strength of Colonel Mower's telegram, I deem it advisable to send our forces to within supporting distance of him.

If General Ross can move, his forces had better go to Glendale, or either side of there, where water can be found, and be on the alert to give assistance if required.

Captain Reynolds can furnish any teams they may require.

Respectfully, &c.,

U. S. GRANT, *Major General.*

Major General ORD, *Commanding Post.*

HEADQUARTERS DISTRICT OF WEST TENNESSEE,
Corinth, September 17, 1862.

GENERAL: We will get off all our forces now as rapidly as practicable. I have despatched Rosecrans that all our movements now would be as rapid as compatible with prudence, informing him at the same time of where your troops now are, and that those not yet off would be at and near Glendale to-night; you, probably, with them

I directed Rosecrans to give me his routes, and will inform you of them. Take an operator with you, who has a pocket instrument, which can be attached to the wires any place desired, if there is such a place.

I will leave to-morrow for Burnsville, if to-day does not develop something to make a different plan necessary.

Respectfully, &c.,

U. S. GRANT, *Major General.*

Major General ORD, *Corinth, Mississippi.*

The latter of these two despatches was received about 5 p. m. on the 17th of September.

In obedience to these orders, the troops, which had moved up to Glendale on the 17th, were moved to Burnsville on the morning of the 18th, at which place I arrived about noon, and found you there. In the course of that evening despatches were received from General Rosecrans stating that a large portion of his command had been delayed by mistaking the route and following one of my columns, and was still about twenty miles from Iuka. Early on the morning of the 19th, by your orders, Ross's division was placed within six miles of Iuka, to hold the enemy's advanced guard and skirmishers in check. This was on the direct or town road between Burnsville and Iuka. McArthur's division was ordered to advance to within a like distance of Iuka, on the Eastport road, and intelligence having been received that the enemy were making demonstrations upon Corinth from the south and west, you directed me to retain Davies's division at Burnsville, to be ready to return to Corinth by rail at a moment's notice. I made a careful reconnoissance of the enemy's front towards Corinth, between 9 and 3 on that day. While making the reconnoissance, about 10 o'clock that morning, I received from you the following despatch:

19TH SEPTEMBER.

GENERAL: I send you despatch received from Rosecrans late in the night. You will see that he is behind where we expected him. Do not be too rapid with your advance this morning, unless it should be found the enemy are evacuating.

By order of Major General Grant.

CLARK B. LAGOW, *Colonel and Inspector General.*

After completing the reconnoissance, I returned to Burnsville about 4 p. m., and reported to you that the enemy showed a bold front towards Burnsville and the north, and that their skirmishers and ours had been engaged all day within four miles of Burnsville. You expressed the opinion that General Rosecrans was, from last accounts from him, too far from Iuka for us to attack on our front, until further information was received as to his whereabouts, which was manifestly true. At the same time you directed me to move my whole force forward to within four miles of Iuka, and there await sounds of an engagement between Rosecrans and the enemy, before engaging the latter. About 6 p. m., after you had given me these orders, and I had issued directions accordingly, the following despatch was received from General Ross, in charge of the advance division, about seven miles from Iuka:

SEPTEMBER 19, 4 *o'clock p. m.*

Major General ORD: For the last twenty minutes there has been a dense smoke arising from the direction of Iuka. I conclude that the enemy are evacuating and destroying the stores.

L. F. ROSS, *Brigadier General.*

That night, in accordance with your orders, my whole force was moved up to within four miles of Iuka, except McArthur's division, and the next morning at a. m., hearing guns in front of us, I moved rapidly into Iuka, and found it had been evacuated during the night. The guns heard that morning (the 20th, 8 a. m.) were the first heard by us, although the afternoon of the 19th the head of General Rosecrans's column had engaged the enemy two miles south of Iuka—about the time that General Ross reported a smoke in the direction of Iuka. The wind freshly blowing from us in the direction of Iuka during the whole of the 19th prevented our hearing the guns and co-operating with General Rosecrans. My loss during the approach was one man wounded. We took eleven prisoners and wounded three of the enemy during the skirmishing of the advance. Every officer and soldier of the command showed a zeal and energy highly commendable, and nothing but regret was felt and expressed when it was learned, on the 20th, that General Rosecrans's column had had a fight, and we were not by to share it, though every effort was made to do so consistent with the information possessed of General Rosecrans's movements.

Corinth still being threatened, you directed me to return with my whole force at once, leaving Crocker's brigade as a garrison in the town of Iuka, which I did.

I am, respectfully, your obedient servant,

E. O. C. ORD,
Major General Volunteers, Commanding Left Wing.

Major General U. S. GRANT, *Commanding District of West Tennessee,*
Headquarters, Jackson, Tennessee.

HEADQUARTERS 1ST BRIGADE, 4TH DIVISION,
Bolivar, September 22, 1862.

GENERAL: We left our camp, five miles north of Grand Junction, on Sunday morning, between 7 and 8 o'clock, having previously sent forward the cavalry to Grand Junction and Lagrange, and proceeded slowly until we arrived within two miles of the Junction, where I halted the column to let it close up. While resting here, Major Mudd came in from Lagrange with information that he saw there a large body of infantry and cavalry moving on the Lagrange road, towards our rear, with the evident intention of cutting off our train. Having previously received information that a large force was at Davis's Mills, I, without a momemt's delay, ordered the train to fall back, following them closely with my main column. We passed the railroad crossing, where we encamped the previous night, and where the road forks to Grand Junction and Lagrange, about twenty minutes before the rebel cavalry, closely followed, as I have since learned, by their infantry and artillery. They hung upon our rear until about 1 o'clock, when, arriving near the creek, about two miles north of Van Buren, where, finding it necessary to halt my train for rest and water, I placed my command in position so as fully to command the approaches, and sent out a small force of cavalry, to see whether the rebels were still on our track. They soon returned with the rebel cavalry at their heels. Letting them approach to within easy range, Mann's battery (Lieutenant Brotzman commanding) opened on them and sent them flying back. My train by this time having rested and watered, we continued our progress and arrived in camp at dusk.

Our casualties were few, for which I refer you to accompanying reports.

I have the honor to be, general, your most obedient servant,

J. G. LAUMAN, *Brigadier General.*

Brigadier General HURLBUT, *Commanding 4th Division, District of West Tennessee.*

List of casualties in 1st brigade, 4th division, during the march from Bolivar to Grand Junction and return, General Lauman commanding.

3d Iowa infantry, Lieutenant Colonel Trumbull commanding.—Privates M. Goss, company G, and W. A. Lister, company H, missing; total, 2.

28th Illinois infantry, Colonel Johnson commanding.—Private Samuel Sutcliff, company A, prisoner; private J. Edwards, company E, missing; privates O. P. Hurlbut, company G, and J. T. Davis, company G, deserted; total, 4.

32d Illinois infantry, Colonel Logan commanding.—Corporal Wm. Ogles, company 5; privates John Grumbaugh, company 5, and Franklin Howell, company 5, missing; private Thomas Sorrell, company D, deserted; total, 4.

53d Illinois infantry, Captain McClanahan commanding.—Acting Adjutant C. R. May, (2d Lieutenant company C,) prisoner.

15th Ohio battery, Captain Spear commanding.—Private Seth Brown, prisoner.

HEADQUARTERS 2D ILLINOIS CAVALRY,
Bolivar, Tennessee, September 22, 1862.

SIR: I have the honor to report that, in compliance with Order 200, I marched with three hundred and fifty men of my command, as the advance of the forces under command of General Lauman, and entered Grand Junction about 5 o'clock p. m. of 20th. Found everything quiet at that place, and very few inhabitants left there. From all the information I could gather, the force of the enemy near Davis's Mills was about eight thousand.

Having accomplished the reconnoissance of the place and vicinity, I returned about four miles to the camp of General Lauman and bivouacked for the night.

On the morning of the 21st, in accordance with orders from General Lauman, I went again to Grand Junction, sending two companies, under command of Major Mudd, to Lagrange, to examine that place and the country around it. At Grand Junction all was in the same condition in which I found it the evening previous. I was directed to hold this place until the arrival of General Lauman with the main force. But upon learning from Major Mudd that the enemy in large force was making a movement to pass to the rear of our army, through Lagrange, I at once retired and joined General Lauman, and with him returned to this place, the cavalry under my command being employed as flankers and reconnoitring parties.

Major Mudd was active in ascertaining the position and force of the enemy.

I have the honor to enclose his report.

I have the honor to be, very respectfully, your obedient servant,

S. NOBLE, *Colonel, Commanding 2d Illinois Cavalry.*

Captain H. BINMORE, *Assistant Adjutant General.*

BOLIVAR, *September* 22, 1862.

COLONEL: I have the honor to report the following as the part performed by the detachment of the 2d Illinois cavalry, under my command, in the recent movement on Grand Junction and Lagrange:

When, on Saturday evening, you moved forward from the main body, I took command of the advance, being company K, Captain Jones, and twenty men of company H, under Captain Higgins, and moved rapidly to Grand Junction, dispersing a squad of rebel soldiers on our way. Finding no enemy at that place, I had just pressed a guide and started Captain Jones, with his company, in direction of Davis's Mills, when you arrived and recalled him.

On Sunday morning, in accordance with your order, I, with companies H, Captain Higgins; K, Captain Jones; M, Orderly Webb commanding, and C, Captain Fullerton, moved towards Lagrange, arriving within half a mile of that place at 8 o'clock a. m. On the way we had noticed persons at distant points in several places across fields, but were not able to decide whether soldiers or citizens. We also arrested some citizens, but could gain no information from them.

My extreme advance now reported a large body of cavalry half a mile in front of the head of our column. I ordered the fences pulled down and preparations made for battle, while, with a few men, I went forward to view their movements. I soon found it to be a large body of infantry moving to the north, diagonally across the road occupied by me. They moved with celerity, and paid no attention to us, except to place pickets on the road to watch us. A citizen brought in by pickets reported that the whole rebel army had been passing through Lagrange for an hour and a half, and that their design was to fall in our rear and cut off our train. This was evident from the movement to which I was now a witness. I immediately despatched couriers to notify General Lauman and yourself of the state of affairs, called in my pickets and advance guard, and moved with haste to the main body of the army, being during the march watched, but not disturbed, by rebel cavalry on our left. Under General Lauman's direction I despatched a squad of men from company I to reconnoitre on the left. They soon reported enemies, cavalry and artillery, a little to the rear and half a mile to the left. Fearing they might be moving on our left, on parallel roads with us, I, without orders, (being without communication with yourself or General Lauman,) called out companies H and K, and with them moved north four or five miles, until satisfied that none had passed. Returning, I had just got well into the road, when I discovered the enemy in hailing distance on our last night's camp ground. I directed Captain Higgins to move forward, while with a small squad of men from companies I and K I kept the enemy at bay until my command had reached a safer position. Finding that no rear guard was following, I assumed to perform that duty, and followed at a good distance from the army, keeping the enemy at bay, picking up and urging forward stragglers, until I came up with General Lauman, with his command in order of battle, one mile this side of Van Buren. At his suggestion I despatched Captain Vieregg, with a squad of men, to watch the movements about the village. He soon returned, followed by a large body of rebel cavalry, who followed within range of our artillery, when a few rounds from Captain ———'s battery dispersed them.

When the column next moved, I occupied the ground for half an hour after the whole train had passed out of sight, during which time we could see the rebel forces slowly advancing across the field to the south and west of the point of timber on our right flank when in line. Finding they had all passed into the timber, and deeming the position no longer safe, I withdrew my little force and again took my place in rear of the column. After crossing Spring creek, in obedience to orders from General Lauman, I despatched Captain Higgins, with forty men, to reconnoitre to the left, and myself, with a small squad of men, watched the road from the edge of the timber. Captain Higgins reported all clear for two miles west. I sent my command to a suitable point to feed, and remained in the rear for an hour and a half after the column had passed, seeing no signs of enemies, when I received your orders to follow, which I did, bringing up the rear, and arriving in camp at nine o'clock p. m. without the loss of a man. To the admirable order preserved by the commanders of companies we are indebted for the safety of the men for so long a time in immediate presence of an advancing enemy. No stragglers were out. With such officers straggling would go out of fashion, and to them I am much indebted for their promptness in carrying out my orders; also to my men for the cheerful alacrity with which every command was obeyed.

I have to report the loss of two horses by company M, one killed by a fall, and the other disabled and left.

I wish to report the carbine cartridges now furnished us as being of very poor quality. They shake to pieces in riding, and at the end of each day's march many of the men find, instead of cartridges, only a mixed mass of powder, ball, and paper.

All of which is respectfully submitted, by your obedient servant,

JOHN J. MUDD, *Major 2d Illinois Cavalry.*

Colonel S. NOBLE, *Commanding 2d Illinois Cavalry.*

HEADQUARTERS ARMY OF THE MISSISSIPPI,
Office Chief of Artillery, Corinth, Mississippi, September 28, 1862.

SIR: I have the honor to submit herewith a report of the part taken by the artillery under my command at the battle near Iuka, on the 19th instant.

General Rosecran's army left Camp Clear creek, near Corinth, on the 18th instant, camped at Jacinto that night, and left the next morning for Iuka. When within about two miles of the town, the enemy was discovered in force, and Captain Sands's battery (11th Ohio volunteers, under command of First Lieutenant Sears) was ordered to the front, and near the right of the line of battle. At the same time I was ordered by General Rosecrans to take one section of the 12th Wisconsin battery, under command of Lieutenant Immell, 1st Wisconsin light artillery, together with Colonel Percell's regiment 5th Iowa volunteers, and posted them on the right of the enemy's line. This position was in an open field. The enemy was discovered in front, and I opened on them with shell; they left and disappeared in the woods; soon after this they appeared in strong force, and pressed so hard upon the section and regiment they were compelled to withdraw. At this time a general engagement occurred along the whole line, and continued until late in the evening. We remained on the battle-field during the night, and advanced the next morning on the town. When within about a half mile, the rear guard of the enemy was discovered leaving. One section of Captain Powell's battery was ordered forward, placed in position and opened upon them with case-shot, causing a hasty flight and much confusion in their ranks. I would call the attention of the commanding general to the manner in which Lieutenant Sears, his officers and men, behaved during the battle. One officer and sixteen men were killed at their pieces, several of them being bayoneted by the enemy. I cannot speak in too high terms of the bravery of the officers and men in this battery. Lieutenant Immell, 1st Missouri light artillery, and Colonel Percell's regiment 5th Iowa, also deserve particular mention. They remained until they heard the roar from the enemy in the bushes on their right, and Colonel Percell deemed it prudent to send the section back, fearing they would be cut off. Colonel Percell remained with his command on the field during the night.

CASUALTIES.

Killed.—Acting 2d lieutenant, Richard Bauer; sergeant, M. V. B. Hall; corporal, Samuel Gilmore; privates, William Crawford, John Dean, John Ettle, John J. McCowne, Charles Shifftner, J. H. Ingersoll, W. H. Bolser, J. W. Bruoer, James Casey, Jacob T. Malson, William H. Rosey, Charles P. Olson, Joseph Taylor.

Wounded.—First lieutenant commanding battery, Cyrus Sears; first lieutenant, H. M. Niel; acting second lieutenant, A. B. Alger; first sergeant, T. E. Armstrong; sergeant, H. C. Woley; corporals, George W. Bush, George W. Buckley, L. Bothwell; privates, J. B. Brooks, William Bomen, Amos B. Brewer, A. Clouse, William L. Colton, Jacob Eberhat, Isaac Dezobell, Matthew Free, Martin L. Fritz, Charles Hughlin, Benjamin Huber, John M. Ike, Noris T. Jillison, H. C. Kelton, Hiram McDonald, Henry McLaughlin, J. J. McBreight, Charles Rodes, Ira C. Swayze, Robert Swagle, Thomas Taylor, N. T. Wesinberge, Henry M. Welch, Zachariah Welch, Jerome Wolsey, Silas Wheton, S. W. Williams.

Missing—Privates, Charles Jones, William Jones, A. B. Myers.

Wounded in Captain Spoor's battery, 2d Iowa volunteers.—Corporal, A. Atkinson; privates, Robert Rose, William Eckles.

Total number killed, 16; total number wounded, 38; missing 3; total 57.

I am, sir, very respectfully, your obedient servant,

W. L. LOTHROP,
Lieutenant Colonel and Chief of Artillery.

Lieutenant Colonel H. G. KENNETT,
Chief of Staff, Army of the Mississippi.

Report of William M. Wiles, captain 22d Indiana infantry and provost marshal of army of the Mississippi, of killed, wounded, and prisoners of the enemy at the battle of Iuka, Mississippi, September 19, 1862.

Number killed, found upon the field, and buried by our men	265
Number died of mortal wounds since battle	120
Total number killed	385
Number of wounded carried off by the enemy, according to the best information, not less than	350
Number of wounded found at Iuka	342
Prisoners not wounded	361
Total loss of the enemy in killed, wounded, and prisoners	1,438

WILLIAM M. WILES,
Captain 22d Indiana Infantry, Provost Marshal, Army of the Mississippi.

List of ordnance taken on the battle-field, near Iuka, September 19, 1862.

214 rifles, Enfield.
6 rifles, Sharp's.
42 rifles.
43 rifles, Whitney.
226 waist-belts.
112 cross-belts.
29 cross-belt plates.
36 frogs for sabre bayonet.

109 Springfield muskets.	217 waist-belt plates.
111 muskets, smooth-bore.	32 sabre bayonets.
1,009 guns, mixed.	32 sabre bayonet scabbards.
75 shot-guns.	Total number of—
20 pistols, mixed.	1,629 fire-arms, guns, rifles, &c.
7 sabres.	12 sabres and scabbards.
5 sabre scabbards.	20 gun-slings.
20 gun-slings.	921 bayonets and scabbards.
572 bayonets.	718 cartridge-boxes and plates.
349 bayonet scabbards.	420 cap-boxes, cross-belts, and plates.
448 cartridge-boxes.	543 waist-belts and plates.
270 cartridge-box plates.	64 sabre bayonets and scabbards.
279 cap-boxes.	36 frogs for sabre bayonets.

W. L. LOTHROP,
Lieutenant Colonel, Chief of Artillery and Ordnance.

HEADQUARTERS 2D DIVISION, ARMY OF THE MISSISSIPPI,
Camy near Jacinto, Mississippi, September 24, 1864.

COLONEL: I have the honor to report, for the information of the major general commanding the right wing, that the 2d division, consisting of the 1st brigade, Colonel Fuller, commanding, and the 2d brigade, Colonel Mower, commanding, left our camp on Clear creek, on the 18th instant, with three days' cooked rations, and one hundred rounds of ammunition to each man, and marched the same day, by the way of Patrick's, on the Burnsville road, where we turned and marched to within one mile of Jacinto. Early the next morning we followed General Hamilton's division, on the Tuscumbia road, to Barnett's. At 2 o'clock p. m. the head of the column took the direct road to Iuka; at half past 4 o'clock p. m. the enemy opened fire, and the division was pushed rapidly to the front; arriving under fire, we found General Hamilton's entire division engaged, and hard pressed. Colonel Mower, commanding the 2d brigade, was ordered into immediate action by General Rosecrans, and by some mistake carried in only his own regiment, the 11th Missouri; they immediately became heavily engaged. The 47th Illinois, Colonel Thrush commanding, formed on the left of the 11th Missouri. The 26th Illinois was formed on the right and retired. The 8th Wisconsin and three Ohio regiments, the 27th, 43d, and 63d, were held in reserve. The 39th Ohio was carried forward and posted close to the enemy on the right-hand road. This was the disposition of the troops of my division.

The only regiment that became heavily engaged was the 11th Missouri; this regiment stood its ground under a storm of musketry, which they repaid with double interest. The other regiments of the division were more or less engaged, the officers and men all behaving with great gallantry. The attention of the general commanding is called to the gallant conduct of Colonel J. A. Mower, commanding the 2d brigade, and Major Weber, commanding the 11th Missouri.

It is a subject of regret to our officers and men that the coming on of darkness prevented their having the opportunity more fully to engage our wicked rebel enemy.

During the night Colonel J. L. Kirby Smith was very efficient in posting the artillery of the division, ready to renew the fight in the morning, but at dawn the enemy had entirely disappeared, leaving his dead and wounded. A pursuit of one mile brought us in sight of his rear guard in the village of Iuka.

Colonel Fuller's brigade led, and I immediately made dispositions to attack, but a few rounds from Powell's battery sent the enemy flying, and no further sight of them was had that day, they being in full retreat on the Fulton road.

Enclosed you will find reports of brigade, regimental, and battery commanders; also lists of killed and wounded, the latter have been duplicated by the division surgeon, Dr. Crane.

My obligations are due the members of my staff, Captain W. D. Coleman, assistant adjutant general, Lieutenants C. L. Smiedel and W. H. Sinclair, aids, for efficient and useful service on the field.

I am, very respectfully, your obedient servant,

D. S. STANLEY,
Brigadier General, Commanding.

Colonel H. G. KENNETT,
Chief of Staff, Army of Mississippi.

HEADQUARTERS 11TH MISSOURI VOLUNTEER INFANTRY,
September 22, 1862.

COLONEL: In regard to the part taken by the 11th Missouri volunteer infantry in the battle fought at Iuka, Mississippi, the 19th of September, 1862, I have to report the following:

During the day the regiment had marched as the third regiment of the 2d brigade, immediately in rear of the 3d division, army of the Mississippi, commanded by General C. S. Hamilton. The enemy was first engaged by General Hamilton, but they were in such force that General Rosecrans deemed it necessary to order forward our brigade, which he did in person. For some reason the regiments in front of us did not move forward, and by order of Colonel Mower, commanding the brigade, I immediately ordered my regiment to advance, which they did, taking the double-quick step and cheering vociferously. I advanced to General Hamilton's line of battle, and hearing heavy firing on the extreme right I hastened on in that direction. Owing to the density of the woods and briers immediately on the right of General Hamilton, I formed in the open field on the right and then moved forward in line of battle. Immediately on entering the woods we found ourselves face to face with the 4th Mississippi brigade, and not more than thirty paces from their line of battle. We fired a volley into them, which must, in consequence of our close proximity, have done great execution. At this juncture a man ran into our ranks, exclaiming, "For God's sake, stop firing into your own men; *you are firing into the 37th Mississippi.*" This information was promptly answered by a cheer and a volley more terrific than the first. The firing now became general on both sides, and the smoke of our and the enemy's guns was so dense that an object could not be seen five paces distant. We were charged upon three different times, and I am proud to report that each time the charge was equally unsuccessful. In several instances the enemy was received on the point of the bayonet and then shot off, and others were shot by officers who placed their pistols in their very faces. A number of prisoners were taken who pressed into our line—five by my color-guard alone. After about an hour's firing the enemy fell back to the top of the ridge, when I found that my ammunition was entirely gone. I reported the fact to Colonel Mower, who had just learned that an attempt was being made to turn our left flank, and he ordered us to fall back slowly, which we did in order for about eight or ten rods. The enemy did not follow. We received ammunition, and remained in our new position until morning.

During the engagement we had seven men killed, sixty-four wounded, and three missing. Our loss was thus small from the fact that our men were below the enemy, and they overshot us.

I could not speak too highly of the conduct of every officer and man of my command. I would desire to mention them by name; but brave and gallant conduct on the part of my officers was so universal that I cannot attempt it. Captain Singleton, one of our best officers, was, I regret to say, very dangerously, if not mortally, wounded while bravely doing his duty. Lieutenant W. W. Cleland, of the same company, who was acting regimental adjutant, was badly hurt by the fall of his horse, which was shot under him. Lieutenant Osgood, of company I, was badly wounded while encouraging his men. Captain Warner and Lieutenants Coperthwait and Foster were slightly wounded.

Respectfully submitted, by your obedient servant,

A. J. WEBER,
Major, Commanding 11th Missouri Volunteers.

Colonel JOSEPH P. MOWER,
Commanding 2d Brigade.

HEADQUARTERS 47TH ILLINOIS INFANTRY,
Camp near Jacinto, September 22, 1862.

COLONEL: I have the honor to submit the following report of the part taken by the 47th regiment of Illinois volunteer infantry in the battle of Iuka, fought on the evening of the 19th instant. Arriving at 4 o'clock on the afternoon of the 19th within four miles of the town of Iuka, we heard indiscriminate firing in front, and proceeded in line of march by the flank to within three miles of the town, where our column was halted. At twenty minutes past 4 o'clock heavy volleys of musketry and cannonading was heard in front, and immediately my regiment was ordered forward in double-quick time, following the 11th Missouri volunteers. Arriving near the scene of action, the 47th Illinois formed in line of battle on the left of the 11th Missouri volunteers, when, by direction of General Stanley, my regiment was ordered to the front to take position on the side of a hill and on both sides of the road leading to Iuka, and hold it, and not to attack the enemy, which position I occupied until about 2 o'clock on the morning of the 20th instant. At that time, by order of General Rosecrans, the right of my regiment was thrown to the rear, in continuation of a line formed by the 39th Ohio, and we remained on that line until about half past 5 o'clock, when we were ordered to proceed with the 1st brigade into the town of Iuka. From the town we joined in the pursuit of the rebel army, following them to Crippled Deer post office, on the Franklin road.

The position of my regiment on the field was to the left of the severe fighting, and, although we were all the time under fire, opportunity did not offer to give the enemy more than four volleys. It gives me pleasure to report the steady, cool, and soldier-like bearing of both officers and men of my command while occupying a position in which we were continually annoyed by the fire of the enemy, without being able to respond to any purpose. We captured First Lieutenant Shehan, of the 1st Missouri cavalry. I append list of casualties, and submit this report for your consideration.

Respectfully, your obedient servant,

W. A. THRUSH,
Lieutenant Colonel, Commanding 47th Illinois Volunteer Infantry.
R. W. CHAMBERS, *Adjutant.*

Colonel MOWER,
Commanding 2d Brigade, 2d Division.

List of casualties of 47th Illinois.

Hugh Galway, musician, company H, wounded slightly. Ethan A. Drake, corporal, company G, wounded in thigh. George Robinson, corporal, company A, wounded in leg. Charles Stevens, private, company A, wounded in chest. Philip Snyder, private, company F, two wounds in hips. Hiram Boardman, private, company K, killed. Major John N. Cromwell, missing.

HEADQUARTERS 26TH REGIMENT ILLINOIS VOLUNTEERS,
Camp near Jacinto, Mississippi, September 22, 1862.

LIEUTENANT: I have the honor to transmit the following report of this regiment, under command of Major R. A. Gillman, during the engagement on the 19th of September, 1862, near Iuka, Mississippi:

Were ordered forward from the road into a corn-field, there to extend the line to the right, by General Stanley in person. After holding this position for about three-quarters of an hour, Captain Temple Clark, assistant adjutant general, ordered us to move by the right flank, file left, into the woods in front of our former line; then moved, by the left flank, forward to the brow of a hill, where we remained during the night. Kept skirmishers in front of our regiment all night.

One lieutenant (J. B. Bunn, company K) wounded in hip by spent ball. George Hall, private, company K, slightly, with spent ball. Philip Hill, private, company K, wounded, ball passing through the back of the left hand and through the right wrist. Andrew Hughes and Charles J. Perkins, privates, company G, slightly, with spent balls.

I have the honor to be, lieutenant, very respectfully, your obedient servant,

R. A. GILLMAN, *Major, Commanding 26th Illinois.*
E. A. TUCKER, *Adjutant.*

HEADQUARTERS FIFTH REGIMENT MINNESOTA VOLUNTEERS,
Camp, September 22, 1862.

I have the honor to report that during the action of the 20th instant, near Iuka, Mississippi, the 5th regiment Minnesota volunteer infantry was detailed by order of Brigadier General Stanley to guard the train of transportation wagons belonging to the division, and was not brought into action. The regiment remained upon the duty assigned it as above, until the morning of the 21st instant, when it was moved to the breastworks, near Barnett's, by order of General Rosecrans.

Respectfully, your obedient servant,

L. F. HUBBARD,
Lieutenant Colonel, Commanding 5th Minnesota Volunteers.

HEADQUARTERS EIGHTH REGIMENT WISCONSIN VOLUNTEERS,
Camp near Jacinto, Mississippi, September 22, 1862.

I respectfully submit the following report of the part taken in the late engagement by the 8th regiment Wisconsin volunteers, near Iuka, Mississippi, September 19, 1862.

I was ordered with my regiment by General Stanley to take up a position in rear of the hospital, to support Captain Spoor's battery, which was posted on rising ground on my right and rear, my right resting on the road. We held this position during the engagement, exposed to a heavy fire from infantry in our front, but not very destructive, as most of the shots passed too high.

There were only two men wounded during the action, Captain J. B. Redfield and private John C. Green, both of company A. Our regimental surgeons, S. F. Thornhill and J. E. Marta, were actively engaged at hospital taking care of the wounded of other regiments.

Yours, respectfully,

G. W. ROBBINS,
Lieutenant Colonel, Commanding 8th Wisconsin Volunteers.

Colonel J. A. MOWER,
Commanding 2d Brigade, 2d Division, Army of Mississippi.

HEADQUARTERS THIRTY-NINTH OHIO REGIMENT,
Camp near Jacinto, September 23, 1862.

CAPTAIN: I have the honor to report, for the information of the colonel commanding 1st brigade, 2d division, army of the Mississippi, that, in compliance with orders, the 39th Ohio regiment marched on the 19th instant from the place of bivouac, near Jacinto, to the battle-ground of the battle of Iuka. When the regiment arrived in the immediate vicinity of the battle-ground, other troops which had the advance were already engaged, and before this regiment could be brought into action, night had closed in, and the darkness prevented further movements. The 39th Ohio was ordered to the front, and lay upon their arms during the night, upon a portion of the ground covered by the fight. The enemy retreated during the night.

I have to report six persons wounded by stray shots; no other casualties.

I am, captain, very respectfully, your obedient servant,

EDW. F. NOYES,
Lieutenant Colonel, Commanding.

Captain W. H. LATHROP,
Acting Assistant Adjutant General.

HEADQUARTERS SIXTY-THIRD REGIMENT OHIO VOLUNTEER INFANTRY,
In the Field, near Jacinto, Mississippi, September 22, 1862.

MAJOR: I have the honor to report, that in the engagement near Iuka, the evening of the 19th instant, in my command there was none killed, two wounded—Corporal Isaac Jarvis, company H, very slightly, in the breast; private George Mears, company K, in the foot, slightly; none missing.

I am, major, very respectfully, your obedient servant,

I. W. SPRAGUE, *Colonel, Commanding.*

Major W. D. COLEMAN,
Assistant Adjutant General.

HEADQUARTERS FORTY-THIRD OHIO VOLUNTEER INFANTRY,
Camp near Jacinto, Mississippi, September 22, 1862.

CAPTAIN: In accordance with general orders, dated headquarters department of the Mississippi, Barnett's, September 21, I have the honor to report, for the information of the general commanding, that my regiment, at the opening of the engagement near Iuka, was on the Jacinto and Iuka road, between one and two miles from the field of battle, being the rear regiment of the 1st brigade, 2d division. During the action it was moved forward, with the brigade, to a point near the building used during the fight as a hospital, near the headquarters of the division commander. The regiment was here halted and moved a short distance out of the road to the left; it remained in this position during the action and the night following. The regiment having taken no part in the action, I have no casualties to report.

Very respectfully, your obedient servant,

J. L. KIRBY SMITH,
Colonel 43d Ohio Volunteer Infantry.

Captain W. H. LATHROP,
Acting Assistant Adjutant General.

CAMP NEAR JACINTO, MISSISSIPPI, *September* 22, 1862.

CAPTAIN: In compliance with orders I herewith submit a report of the battery under my command at the battle near Iuka, Mississippi, on the 19th instant.

The battery marched from camp on Clear creek, September 16, 1862, attached to the 1st brigade, 2d division, Colonel J. W. Fuller, commanding. On the evening of the 19th, when near Iuka, the firing commenced about two miles in our front; the battery was ordered forward and placed in position on the right of the road, and one mile from the battle-field, remained in position during the night, and on the morning of the 20th moved up, passing the battle-ground and halting in sight of the town. The enemy having retreated during the night, the battery was ordered back on the road to Barnett's plantation and camped, moving again Sunday evening to Jacinto, having taken no active part in the engagement. No loss or casualties to report.

I am, sir, very respectfully, your obedient servant,

THOMAS D. MAURICE,
Captain 1st Missouri Light Artillery, Commanding Co. F, 2d U. S. Artillery.

Captain C. W. DUSTAN,
Assistant Adjutant General.

HEADQUARTERS TWENTY-SEVENTH OHIO INFANTRY,
In the Field, September 23, 1862.

CAPTAIN: I have the honor to report that this regiment was not called into action during the recent engagement before Iuka, and therefore met with no casualties in killed, wounded, or missing.

In accordance with orders I marched the command at double-quick time up to a point within half a mile of the scene of action, and remained under arms during the entire evening and night. On the morning of the 20th instant we marched into the town, meeting no resistance from the enemy.

I am, with respect, your obedient servant,

Z. S. SPAULDING, *Major, Commanding.*

Captain C. W. DUSTAN, A. A. G.,
1st Brigade, 2d Division, Army of the Mississippi.

HEADQUARTERS FIRST BRIGADE SECOND DIVISION,
Army of the Mississippi, September 23, 1862.

MAJOR: In obedience to orders, I have the honor to report that my command formed the rear of the column during the march upon Iuka, on the 19th instant, moving in the following order:

39th Ohio infantry, Colonel Gilbert; light company F, 2d United States artillery, Captain Maurice; 27th Ohio infantry, Major Spaulding; 63d Ohio infantry, Colonel Sprague; battery M, 1st Missouri light artillery, Captain Powell; section of battery, 8th Wisconsin, Lieutenant McLean; 43d Ohio infantry, Colonel Smith.

When within about three miles of Iuka we were halted in the road, and the batteries moved to the right of the road and placed in position near the edge of the woods and on the hill, which overlooked the open field directly south of the scene of the action.

At sunset I received orders to advance immediately to the front. As soon as the order double-quick was given, the infantry ran forward, swinging their hats and cheering lustily, but darkness brought a cessation of firing just in time to prevent our taking a part in the action. Soon after dawn it was reported that the enemy had left the field of battle, and taken a position near the town.

My command took the advance, and after passing the field, three regiments formed in line of battle, the 27th, 39th, and 43d of my brigade, and the 47th Illinois, (Colonel Mower's brigade,) and moved forward upon the town.

During the deployment Captain Powell's battery was brought forward, and threw a few shots at a body of the enemy which appeared near the Fulton road. As we neared the town a flag of truce came out, borne by a citizen, saying "the citizens desired to surrender the town, and that the soldiers (enemy) were all in the ditches dug by the federal army." We then moved forward into the town, and found that the enemy had evacuated the place, leaving by the Fulton road. My command went forward in pursuit till we reached Crippled Deer creek.

The statements of several prisoners, confirmed by a reconnoissance made by Captain Sawyer, with two companies of the Kansas 7th cavalry, proved that the enemy was several miles in advance and rapidly retreating, and in the exhausted condition of our men, and the total absence of subsistence, it was deemed impracticable to continue the pursuit further. Resting near Cripple Deer creek for the night, we commenced our return toward Jacinto about 8 o'clock on the morning of the 21st.

Herewith I send copies of reports of commanding officers, which show that six casualties occurred in the 39th Ohio, and two in the 63d Ohio.

I am, major, your obedient servant,

JOHN W. FULLER,
Colonel 27th Ohio, Commanding.

Major W. D. COLEMAN, *Assistant Adjutant General.*

CAMP NEAR JACINTO, MISSISSIPPI,
September 22, 1862.

SIR: I have the honor to report as follows of the battery under my command in the action of September 19.

On the arrival of the brigade the battery was ordered by Major Coleman to take position on the right of the road leading to Iuka, prepared to open fire if the enemy drove back our infantry in front.

The battery remained in this position until 12 p. m., when, by order of Colonel Smith, it retired six hundred yards, being replaced by Powell's battery.

Corporal A. Atkinson, privates William Eckles and Robert Rose, were slightly wounded by spent balls. Three horses received flesh wounds, but were not disabled.

The ambulance attached to the battery was engaged during the night in removing the wounded from the field, and six blankets were taken by the hospital department.

Very respectfully, your obedient servant,

N. T. SPOOR,
Captain, Commanding 2d Iowa Battery.

Lieutenant SPRAGUE,
Acting Assistant Adjutant General, 2d Brigade, 2d Division, Army of the Mississippi.

HEADQUARTERS 2D BRIGADE, 2D DIVISION, ARMY OF THE MISSISSIPPI,
Near Jacinto, Mississippi, September 22, 1862.

I have the honor to report that, in obedience to orders, I moved forward on the evening of the 19th instant, at the head of my brigade, to a position in front of the enemy. On arriving at that point I halted the head of the brigade, when I found that I had only one regiment with me, the 11th Missouri volunteers.

I opened fire on the enemy, which they briskly returned. The engagement was kept up until the men had exhausted their ammunition, and the enemy had ceased firing, when I ordered the regiment to fall back a short distance to prevent their being outflanked.

The men fell back in good order, when I halted them, and directed them to remain in that position, which they did through the night.

The 11th behaved with the greatest gallantry and determination, both officers and men standing to their posts in the midst of a most deadly fire. Where all did their duty so well, I can hardly mention any particular persons without appearing to be guilty of partiality. Major Weber encouraged the men by his presence and coolness under the fire of the enemy. I refer to his report for particulars of the engagement.

Enclosed herewith find reports of the commanders of the several regiments and the battery of the brigade, also list of the killed, wounded, and missing. I am unable to speak of what was done by the other regiments of the brigade, as they were detached from it.

I have the honor to be, very respectfully, your obedient servant,

J. A. MOWER,
Colonel, Commanding Brigade.

Major W. DEAN COLEMAN,
Assistant Adjutant General.

CAMP NEAR JACINTO, *September* 23.

Report in accordance with General Order of 21st. Was not in the recent engagement at Iuka.

Killed, none. Wounded, none. Missing, none.

Lieutenant J. D. McLEAN,
Commanding Section 8th Wisconsin Battery.

CHARLES H. DUSTAN,
Assistant Adjutant General.

CAMP NEAR JACINTO, MISSISSIPPI,
September 22, 1862.

SIR: I have the honor to submit the following report in regard to the part my battery took in the reconnoissance towards Iuka, Mississippi, under command of Colonel Mower, commanding 2d brigade, 2d division, army of the Mississippi, on the 16th day of September, 1862.

The force, consisting of three regiments of infantry, two companies of sharpshooters, several companies of cavalry, and my battery, left Burnsville early in the forenoon. About 6 miles from Iuka the command was met by the enemy's pickets, which were driven in and the force advanced. Continued reports of musketry were heard to within two miles of Iuka, where line of battle was formed on a hill commanding the ground for about a mile. In accordance with Colonel Mower's orders, I placed two of my guns (one 10-pounder Parrott, and one 12-pounder howitzer) on the brow of the hill—throwing shell to the right, left, and front, where heavy clouds of dust, moving towards Iuka, led me to suppose the enemy to be.

The other two guns of the battery were soon after brought in position, and the firing continued for about fifteen minutes.

The force now advanced through the open field below the hill, and reaching the wood on the other side, turned to the right, whereupon our infantry and cavalry advancing, opened fire on the enemy. The firing was brisk on both sides for a short time, when the colonel commanding, finding the enemy's intentions to flank us on the right, ordered a retreat, which was done in good order. I covered the retreat. The narrow road did not allow me to deploy more than one gun, the howitzer, loaded with canister and moving by a fixed prolonge. After reaching the above named hill we again halted, and I was ordered to place the howitzer and one Parrott gun in position on the hill and re-open fire. I again shelled in several directions for a short time; and everything quiet, I was ordered to cease firing, and Colonel Mower threw out sharpshooters as skirmishers in the field below the hill.

Opposite our position, on the end of the open field, a distance of about a mile, was a wood. On the advance of our skirmishers the enemy opened a brisk fire from the edge of this wood, whereupon I re-opened fire from my 10-pounder Parrott gun, shelling the enemy with such a good result that they very soon retreated from the wood, and being ordered to cease firing again, the whole force advanced in line of battle. The skirmishers on both sides continued firing for a short time, when, night approaching, the darkness prevented us continuing the fight.

It was concluded we should camp on the battle-ground for the night, but a deserter coming in from the enemy, informed the colonel commanding that General Price was in Iuka with at least 12,000 men, and that he intended to send out a force to flank us during the night, whereupon the colonel commanding ordered the whole command back to Burnsville, which place we reached about 11 o'clock p. m.

No casualties whatever occurred in the battery during the fight.

It gives me great pleasure to say that the officers and men under my command acted with great bravery and coolness.

I am, sir, very respectfully, your obedient servant,

A. W. DEES,
Captain, Commanding Dees's Battery, 3d Michigan Light Artillery.

W. DEAN COLEMAN,
Major and Assist. Adjt. Gen., 2d Division, Army of the Mississippi.

HEADQUARTERS CAVALRY DIVISION, ARMY OF THE MISSISSIPPI,
Jacinto, Mississippi, September 23, 1862.

SIR: I have the honor to submit the following report of the movements and operations of the cavalry under my command during the advance upon, and engagement with, the enemy at Iuka, Mississippi, on the 19th instant.

The 2d Iowa cavalry, under the command of Colonel Hatch, moved out early on the morning of the 19th instant, on the Tuscumbia road, with instructions to proceed to Peyton's mill, via Russelville road, and was charged with covering the movements and protecting the flanks of the advancing columns.

At Peyton's mill he fell in with and had a sharp skirmish with six hundred of the enemy's cavalry, which he drove from their position; they losing six men killed, ten wounded, and six prisoners.

The 3d Michigan cavalry, under the command of Captain Wilcox, (with the exception of four companies employed in escorting trains,) formed the advance of General Hamilton's division, which moved east on the Tuscumbia road.

At a point about nine miles east of Jacinto the enemy's pickets were met and driven in rapidly. About five miles south of Iuka the enemy's cavalry made a stand, but upon being charged by a portion of the advance guard, led by Sergeant Cutting, 3d Michigan cavalry, they were forced back. Here an officer of General Hamilton's staff was mortally wounded. Without further loss the cavalry succeeded in driving the enemy to within three miles of Iuka. This point was reached at 4 o'clock p. m. Here the infantry skirmishers were thrown in the advance. About this time the enemy's long roll was beat, and they formed in line of battle. Soon the armies became engaged, and a terrible conflict ensued. Four companies of the 3d Michigan cavalry, under Captain Wilcox, were sent to the right wing, on the right of Constable's Ohio battery. Two companies were sent to the northeast, and the remaining two to the northwest, to observe the movements of the enemy. A portion of the four companies on the right wing were dismounted, and becoming engaged with the enemy, prevented a flank movement on our right wing. At this point Captain Latimer and two men were slightly wounded.

Two companies of the 7th Kansas cavalry, under the command of Captain Swoyer, were ordered to form a junction with the 2d Iowa cavalry at Peyton's mill, which they did, and with this regiment moved to the main Fulton road; thence to Thompson's corners, where they found tents, commissary stores, and two wagons, belonging to the enemy, which they burned; then moved west to Burnett's, a point seven miles south of Iuka, where they arrived about dark.

Eight companies of the 7th Illinois cavalry, Lieutenant Colonel Prince commanding, were the advance of General Ross's division of the left wing, under General Ord, which moved on the Burnsville and Iuka road. In consequence of this division not moving forward on the night of the 19th instant, they were not engaged with the enemy except in some slight skirmishing.

Captain Dyckman, of the 3d Michigan cavalry, on the evening of the 18th instant, with his company, made a reconnoissance in the direction of Iuka, for the purpose of ascertaining the practicability of a road direct from Jacinto to Iuka, and to learn the whereabouts of the enemy. He conducted the movement in a manner very satisfactory, and worthy of high commendation.

The battle near Iuka was sanguine, the firing heavy and rapid, and the ground hotly contested. Night coming on, closed the scene of carnage.

The morning disclosed the fact that during the darkness of night the enemy had evacuated and were retreating south on the Fulton road.

Eight companies of the 2d Iowa cavalry, under command of Colonel Hatch, and eight companies of the 3d Michigan, under Captain Wilcox, were sent in pursuit of Price's retreating army, each portion of the regiments striking for different points of the enemy's column, while our infantry followed on the Fulton road. Four companies of the 2d Iowa cavalry, under command of Captain Kendrick, and two companies of the 7th Kansas cavalry, under Captain Swoyer, were directed to move on the Tuscumbia road, to check the enemy's movements at the intersection of the Tuscumbia and Fulton roads, six miles south of Iuka. The enemy's movements were greatly retarded, and his flanks attacked, and his troops harassed by frequent attacks and skirmishes, until our cavalry was forced to retire by the enemy's artillery, which was repeatedly turned upon them.

Seven miles south of Iuka the 2d Iowa cavalry came on the flank of a heavy patrol of the enemy's cavalry, which they engaged and drove nearly four miles, when his skirmishers falling back rapidly, drew the 2d Iowa upon a masked battery, heavily supported by both infantry and cavalry. The artillery and infantry opened a very sharp fire, but did not succeed in doing much damage; soon the firing ceased, and the enemy's cavalry charged, but were repulsed; 2d Iowa then fell back, fighting through the timber, until out of the range of the enemy's guns, and formed a line to receive a second charge from his cavalry in force, in which the enemy were repulsed with loss; the 2d Iowa capturing ten prisoners, from three to four hundred stand of arms, and one wagon, and losing but six men wounded.

The 3d Michigan cavalry and the two companies of the 7th Kansas continued the pursuit eleven miles, becoming several times engaged, and causing the enemy repeatedly to form a line of battle.

Our troops being much fatigued from having marched twenty miles the day previous, further pursuit was impossible.

The 3d Michigan cavalry occupied a position for the night at Peyton's mill, watching closely the movements of the enemy, and following his movements on the succeeding day until ordered to return towards Jacinto.

Taking into consideration the great exposure to which the cavalry was subjected, that our losses were so slight is most remarkable, and truly a subject of congratulation. One officer and eight men were wounded, and ten horses killed.

During the advance, engagement and pursuit, the officers and men of the cavalry division displayed great zeal, enterprise and gallantry, and are all entitled to great credit.

The conduct of all was in a high degree praiseworthy, and where all behaved so well it is difficult to particularize individual acts of bravery without a seeming neglect of the claims of others. Colonel Hatch, Major Coon, Captain Kendrick, of the 2d Iowa cavalry, Captains Wilcox, Lattimer, Dyckman, Newell, and Reise, Adjutant Buchanan, and Sergeant Cutting, of the 3d Michigan cavalry, and Captain Swoyer, of the 7th Kansas cavalry, having commands of companies and detachments, with the commands under them, performed their duty with great energy. Lieutenants McGregor and Martin, of my personal staff, conveyed with becoming spirit and ability my orders to the various parts of the field, displaying coolness and efficiency.

The usefulness and efficiency of the cavalry on this occasion cannot be too highly estimated, covering as they did so many important movements, guarding the flanks of the army, and rendering valuable service, which I feel assured will be fully appreciated, and will gain for them such confidence and respect as will fully reward them for their efforts to discharge their whole duty.

I am, sir, very respectfully, your obedient servant,

J. K. MIZNER,
Colonel, Commanding Cavalry Division.

Lieutenant C. GODDARD,
Assistant Adjutant General, Army of the Mississippi.

HEADQUARTERS SECOND IOWA CAVALRY,
Camp near Barnett's, September 19, 1862.

SIR: I have the honor to report, complying with Colonel Mizner's order to proceed to Peyton's mills, from there on the Russelville road to main Fulton road, thence *via* Thompson's house to Barnett's. Moved with my regiment at six this morning, from six miles east of Jacinto to Peyton's mills. Two miles this side of Peyton's mill began skirmishing with the pickets; drove them into the mill, and engaged a regiment of dismounted cavalry. After sharp firing of twenty minutes, routed the enemy; the enemy falling back into a swamp, escaped with nearly all their wounded, leaving three dead and two mortally wounded. Captured six prisoners, then moved forwarded to main Fulton road; from there to Thompson's Corners. Near there found tents and commissary stores, which we burned, with two wagons of the enemy's; then moved west to Barnett's to camp.

Very respectfully, yours,

EDWARD HATCH, *Colonel 2d Iowa Cavalry.*

W. A. MARTIN,
Lieutenant, Assistant Adjutant General Cavalry Division.

HEADQUARTERS SECOND IOWA CAVALRY,
Camp near Jacinto, September 22, 1862.

SIR: I have the honor to report, complying with the order of Colonel Mizner to pursue the enemy retreating southward, on the morning of the 20th, and if possible to fall upon his trains. Moved forward with my regiment from Iuka, at 9 o'clock in the morning. The enemy's trains and flankers were so heavily guarded, I could find no practicable point to attack them. Fell on the enemy's guard about seven miles south of Iuka, on the main Fulton road, attacked and drove their rear four miles, when the enemy's skirmishers falling back rapidly, my men were drawn upon a masked battery, with a support of two regiments of infantry and a strong reserve of cavalry. My men being dismounted, dropped flat upon the ground; the guns and volleys of the enemy's infantry playing over them, not hurting a man. The enemy's cavalry charged the moment the firing ceased; the charge was repulsed, our men falling back, fighting in the timber to my reserve of mounted men. Learning the enemy run two of his guns up, fell back, the enemy keeping up a fire of grape and canister down the road until out of range. I then formed four companies of my mounted rifles to receive cavalry charge in rear of fence to open fields, when the enemy charged in force over the fields, and was repulsed with loss; when the enemy again run up his guns, forcing us back to another position, where we again prepared to receive cavalry charge. Our infantry coming up rapidly, the enemy retreated. We captured ten prisoners, three to four hundred stand of arms and a wagon, when we were repulsed, destroying them. Our loss is very slight—six wounded, and three horses killed. Captain Egbert had his horse killed under him.

Very respectfully,

EDWARD HATCH, *Colonel 2d Iowa Cavalry.*

W. A. MARTIN,
Lieutenant, Assistant Adjutant General Cavalry Division.

HEADQUARTERS THIRD MICHIGAN CAVALRY,
Camp near Jacinto, Mississippi, September 23, 1862.

SIR: In relation to the movements of the 3d Michigan cavalry, from the 18th until the 22d instant, I have the honor to report as follows:

At a late hour on the 18th instant, while encamped at Davenport's mills, near Jacinto, I directed company A, Captain Dyckman, to examine the Iuka road, running northeast from the mills, and midway between the Tuscumbia and Burnsville roads, in order to determine the practicability of moving wagon or artillery trains on the road, and whether any portion of the road was occupied by the enemy.

The reconnoissance was properly and promptly made, and the road found to be impracticable for moving trains, but passable for infantry and cavalry. The road was occupied by pickets, who fired upon the reconnoitring party.

At 4 o'clock on the following morning, pursuant to instructions from Colonel Mizner, I took eight (8) companies of my command, (leaving four (4) in camp,) and proceeded in light marching order along the Tuscumbia road, east, to its intersection with the Russelville road, about six (6) miles east of Jacinto, where my command took the advance of General Hamilton's division, and moved in the direction of Barnett's Corners. I had moved about two (2) miles further, when I found indications of the presence of the rebel cavalry; the indications were more marked as we proceeded, and as we arrived at the brow of the hill, about one-half (½) mile west of Barnett's, a volley was fired into the head of the column. The rebel force seemed well supported, and I immediately dismounted twenty (20) men, and sent them, in command of Captain Latimer, into the woods to the right. Twenty more were sent into a corn-field to the left, in command of Lieutenant Mix, and companies A and F, under Captain Dyckman, were sent forward on the road. After a sharp skirmish of about fifteen minutes, the rebels were driven from the woods, leaving one man killed and one horse; also one man, horse and equipments were taken by Captain Latimer. From this point (Barnett's) a running fight was kept up, the rebels falling back to a branch of the Cripple Deer creek, distant about four (4) miles. On arriving at the branch we found that the rebel cavalry had rallied at a house situated on an elevation four hundred (400) yards distant, and commanding the road. The advance under Sergeant H. D. Cutting, company K, charged up the road at full gallop, and drove them from their position into the woods, but the enemy rallied, two squadrons strong, and forced the advance to retire. Sergeant Cutting's horse was shot, which was the only casualty occurring to my command in this instance. A number of shots were fired into the head of the column, killing a lieutenant on General Hamilton's staff. I at once wheeled the cavalry into line on the roadside, and uncovered a column of infantry, which moved to the front and deployed on either side of the road, and drove the enemy from the cover of some buildings, behind which they were sheltered.

A column of infantry then moved in advance, and position having been taken at a point about one and one-half (1½) mile from Iuka, pursuant to orders received from Colonel Mizner, I immediately moved with four (4) companies, viz: companies K, Captain Newell; company E, Captain Latimer; company F, Captain Kiese, and company A, Captain Dykman, to the front, and moved out to the right of Constable's Ohio battery, Lieutenant Adams commanding the advance guard.

After proceeding about one-half (½) mile, Lieutenant Adams perceiving a body of cavalry on a hill directly east of the battle-field, attacked and drove them away with considerable loss. I then formed my men behind the brow of the hill, dismounted a portion, and poured an irregular fire into the enemy's left flank, and, upon those who showed themselves in our front, with considerable effect—twenty-two dead having been afterwards found, who must have fallen by our hands. During the time that we were in this position the enemy occasionally gave us a heavy volley, but the nature of the ground was such that no casualties had occurred until near sundown, when the enemy seemed to manifest a disposition to gain our position. I immediately dismounted all the men that could be spared, sending the horses into the woods in our rear, and opened a destructive fire upon them. They immediately fell back, and made no further attempt to advance upon us. We took a first lieutenant, bearing the stand of colors belonging to the 3d Louisiana infantry. Captain Latimer was wounded in the shoulder, also two privates slightly. Six (6) horses were lost. After dark I moved my command to the left of the road, in rear of the infantry, where I was joined by the other four companies of my command, which had been employed in reconnoitring on either flank during the afternoon. On the morning of the 20th, pursuant to orders received from Colonel Mizner, I proceeded with my command in the direction of the Fulton road, to learn the whereabouts of Price's army. I struck the Fulton road some three or four (3 or 4) miles from Iuka, and found the rebel army still passing that point. After gaining the desired information, I immediately fell back, and proceeded down a road running nearly parallel with and about three (3) miles from the Fulton road to the Tuscumbia road, where we found that the rebels were making a stand, and the infantry were moving upon them. We encamped that night on the Tuscumbia road.

The following day I remained in the same position, prepared some rations, brought forward the four companies left at Jacinto on the 18th, and sent out Captain Reece and company on the Fulton road, with instructions to gain all possible information relative to the retreating army. He returned at night with ten (10) prisoners, having been down the Fulton road about ten miles.

The following day (22d) I moved with my entire command (12 companies) to Peyton's mill, where I remained but a short time, as orders were received soon after my arrival to proceed to Jacinto. I had, however, sent out company A, Captain Dyckman, to make a reconnoissance on the Natchez Trace road, where he took a captain belonging to the Arkansas battalion; also found two men belonging to an Iowa regiment, who had been taken by the rebel cavalry the day previous, and had succeeded in making their escape. I arrived at Jacinto on the evening of the 22d, and encamped at Davenport's Mills, where my command is now stationed. The bearing of both officers and men during the entire conflict and subsequent movements was admirable, and it gives me great pleasure to mention the valuable services of Adjutant U. Buchanan, who was always where duty called him, and who was particularly useful to me during the engagement on the 19th.

L. G. WILLCOX,
Captain, Commanding 3d Michigan Cavalry.

ADJUTANT GENERAL, *1st Brigade Cavalry Division*

HEADQUARTERS 7TH ILLINOIS VOLUNTEER CAVALRY,
Burnsville, Mississippi, September 23, 1862.

SIR: I have to report, that on the 18th day of September, 1862, the 7th regiment of Illinois cavalry was ordered forward towards Iuka, to co-operate with the infantry under the command of General Ross. The regiment was engaged in frequent skirmishes, but nothing serious resulted. On the 19th the regiment was in line, some three and a half miles from Iuka, and waiting for orders to go forward, but none was received; and, after the evacuation of Iuka was known, the regiment was ordered back by General Ross to Burnsville.

I am, very respectfully, your obedient servant,

EDWARD PRINCE,
Lieutenant Colonel 7th Illinois Cavalry Volunteers.

Lieutenant WELDEN,
Acting Assistant Adjutant General,
Cavalry Division, Army of the Mississippi.

HEADQUARTERS ARMY OF THE MISSISSIPPI, *September* 28, 1862.

GENERAL: My report of the battle of Iuka has been delayed until all the sub-reports came in. In accordance with your instructions, all the sick of your command, 900 in number, were disposed of comfortably in the general hospital at Corinth, Mississippi, and Jackson, Tennessee, by the 18th instant.

The command commenced their march from Clear creek in a rain-storm, which ceased about 9 o'clock in the morning, and left the roads a little muddy, but free from the annoyance of dust. The column reached Jacinto without much fatigue.

On the 19th the roads were in splendid order, hard, and entirely free from dust. The men marched with ease, and in fine order, none lagging and very few straggling. They reached the battle-field unwearied, and in good spirits. As soon as it became known that an engagement was impending, I established a field hospital at the only place, within two and a half miles of the field, where there was water to be obtained; as it was on the roadside, all the men saw the locality. Immediately after the firing commenced the wounded began to arrive, generally carried by two men; those whose legs were nearly shot away were carried, in some instances, on blankets, by six men. The details previously made for the purpose behaved admirably, depositing those brought off, and immediately returning for others. The surgeons did their best, and everything moved on almost like clock-work. Finding the wounded became very numerous, a second depot was established, about half a mile in the rear of the first, under the supervision of Surgeon Thrall, late medical director. Very fortunately, the night was calm, and without a breath of air stirring, so that, as the battle raged until after nightfall, we were enabled to dress the wounded by candle-light as well as if we had been inside a house.

At 11 o'clock all had been attended to, when your order came to transport the wounded to the rear. The ambulances were brought up by the aid of Captain Mott, acting commissary of subsistence, and were loaded under the energetic supervision of Surgeon Thornhill, and were received at the new depot, two miles and a half to the rear, by Surgeons Lynch and Ham. They had all reached the new depot by an hour after daylight, and the last were about to be unloaded when your order was received to move them into Iuka, the enemy having evacuated during the night. Surgeons Thrall and Ham attended to the reloading, assisted by all the surgeons present.

It was found, on reaching Iuka, that the rebel wounded occupied our old hospital, the "Iuka Springs hotel," as well as the seminary buildings. Upon consultation with Medical Director Holston, it was determined to occupy the other, "the Iuka hotel," and turn over all the rebel wounded to their own surgeons, as they had enough, and give them the seminary buildings. At this time I turned over the entire charge of the wounded to Surgeon Holston, and, in accordance with your order, reported back to your headquarters, at Barnett's, for duty.

I cannot speak too highly of the surgeons, nor discriminate between them. I doubt if the wounded of so great a carnage were ever taken care of more gently and more expeditiously. They sustained their removal with fortitude, and with but little apparent fatigue.

Appended is a list of the killed, wounded, and missing, amounting to 108 killed, 611 wounded, and 17 missing. The rebel loss was very much greater, amounting to over 520 killed, 1,300 wounded, and 181 prisoners, not including the wounded. I am satisfied that these figures are within bounds, from personal inspection and what I consider reliable information.

Very respectfully, your obedient servant,

A. B. CAMPBELL,
Medical Director, Army of the Mississippi.

Report of killed, wounded, and missing of the troops engaged in the battle at Iuka, Mississippi, September 19, 1862, Major General Rosecrans commanding.

SECOND DIVISION—GENERAL STANLEY.

Thirty-ninth Ohio volunteers.—Wounded: Hontner, sergeant, and Silas Bland, private, company C; O. P. Brown, sergeant, and Spenser Cooper, private, company D; Henry Guker, company F, and William Miller, company H, privates, and eight missing not reported.

Sixty-third Ohio volunteers.—Wounded: Isaac Jarvis, corporal, company H, and George Mars, private, company K.

Eleventh Missouri volunteers.—Killed: J. B. Robinson, corporal, and F. W. Shaybury, private, company B; John Cunningham, private, company F; Edmund Leidy, sergeant, company G; J. Bedford, sergeant, company H; William Chapman and Charles C. Easton, privates, company I; and Marshall Osburn, private, company K. *Wounded:* Samuel Brown, Alex. Brooks, J. B. Lappin, Gray H. Moore, William H. McGuire, and Ed. F. Raindan, privates, company A; Andrew Reed, Sylvester Turner, Antonio Bush, Thomas Pugh, and Elias Ross, privates, company B; M. M. Warner, captain, company C; William T. Rony, corporal, company C; John Byrd, John H. Rose, John Hines, Martin Hogue, Montgomery Sweat, James H. Hansley, Daniel Cuppis, Samuel M. Neal, and Thomas Cuppis, privates, company C; John Cowpertwaite, 1st lieutenant, company D; Jasper Shockley, John Gross, M. M. Burton, Dios C. Hagle, and James H. Davis, privates, company D; John D. Bail, color sergeant, company E, and John F. Perry, private, company E; Amos Singleton, captain, company F; W. W. Clelland, 1st lieutenant, company F; J. P. Lanson, 1st sergeant, company F; G. P. Southerland and Elias Draper, corporals, company F; J. M. Robertson, David Hamman, William Doyle, and J. McLean, privates, company F; George Quick and Patrick Morton, corporals, company G; G. Adams, John Abbee, Bedford Clark, Franklin Lewis, John Mumpower, Lewis Swagler, Thomas Wallace, Edwin Kroef, G. W. Luhr, and Jacob Cochran, privates, company G; J. Adams, sergeant, company H; John Moran, John Mills, Timothy Kinny, H. P. Kellogg, and S. B. Donnell, privates, company H; Charles H. Osgood, 1st lieutenant, company I; Cyrus Spicer, sergeant, company I; William H. Capper, corporal, company I; John Seager, Luther Vance, Cyrus Bail, Albert Bryner, and William H. Spicer, privates, company H; Charles H. Foster, 1st lieutenant, company K.

Eighth Wisconsin volunteers.—Wounded: J. B. Bedfield, captain, company A, and John Green, private, company A.

Twenty-sixth Illinois.—Wounded: Bummer, lieutenant; George Hale, Philip Hall, Andrew Hugh, and Charles Perkins, privates.

Eleventh Ohio battery.—Killed: Richard Baur, acting 2d lieutenant; M. V. B. Hall, sergeant; S. Gilmore, corporal; Joseph H. Ingersall, William H. Balser, James W. Bener, William Crawford, James Casey, John Dean, Jno. Ettle, J. J. McGowan, J. T. Malson, C. P. Olson, William H. Rosey, Charles Schifftner, and Joseph Taylor. *Wounded:* Cyrus Sears, 1st lieutenant commanding; H. M. Niel, 1st lieutenant; A. B. Elger, acting 2d lieutenant, (taken prisoner;) F. E. Armstrong, orderly sergeant; H. C. Worley, acting sergeant; G. W. Bush and L. Bothwell, corporals; G. W. Buckley, acting corporal; J. B. Brooks, W. Bowen, A. P. Brewer, O. Clonse, William L. Colton, Isaac Dezotell, Jacob Everhart, Matt. Free, M. L. Fritz, C. Haglin, B. Huber, J. M. Ike, J. F. Jellison, H. C. Kellton, H. McDonald, H. McLaughlin, J. J. McCreight, Charles Rhodes, J. C. Swayre, Robert Swegle, Thomas Taylor, M. F. Wesenberg, H. M. Welsh, Zachariah Welsh, J. Wolsey, S. Wheaton, and S. N. Williamson, privates. *Missing:* Charles Jones, William Jones, and A. B. Myers, privates.

Second Iowa battery.—Wounded: Albert Atkinson, corporal; William Eckles and Robert Rose, privates.

—

THIRD DIVISION, 1ST BRIGADE—BRIGADIER GENERAL C. S. HAMILTON.

Fifth Iowa volunteers.—Killed: Lafayette Shawl, second lieutenant; Joseph Edgar, private, company A. Elias Babcock, corporal; J. D. Bodley, M. W. Catrell, Geo. W. Lowe, Oscar B. Piper, Samuel Pitman, Henry Smeil, and Levy F. Shelby, privates, company B. Nicholas Reinehart, sergeant, company C. Jacob Oswold and David Sullivan, privates, company D. John Fowle, private, company E. A. M. Holcomb, second lieutenant; S. Fisher, acting lieutenant; Isaac Long, William J. Fulton, Isaac Green, R. B. Howell, and J. W. Seller, privates, company F. Earl Wellington and Henry Ditch, privates, company G. R. B. Hughs, sergeant; Alvin C. Ebbert, Thomas J. Nutt, Hamilton Rogers, and George Armentront, privates, company H. Samuel Hughs, P. S. O'Driscoll, N. B. Pearson, and A. B. Wright, privates, company I. Stephen W. Smith, second lieutenant; George W. Foot, corporal; Homer Ellis, S. W. T. Field, and John Shideker, privates, company K. *Wounded:* R. F. Patterson, adjutant; John Casad, first lieutenant; Luke Ingman, Parley McCracken, sergeants; Wm. C. Hawk, corporal; Joseph J. Anderson, Nelson Alexander, Wm. F. Begole, Joseph Fobes, Robert A. Fanal, Charles B. Hawass, Charles S. Hussey, Jackson Mitchell, Wm. H. Morron, (missing,) Samuel Olinger, Thomas S. Parsons, John Rumsey, John S. Smun, John C. Stone, Wm. A. Tisdale, W. E. Thurston, Freland G. A. Tubbs, Jacob F. Weaver, John F. Webb, and Hilburn Zeiter, privates, company A. Alexander Mateer, first lieutenant; James Vanata, Wm. Dangan, sergeants; James McCraskey, James B. Banks, George F. Works, David Wenor, corporals; I. T. Borden, Barnett Dewitt, J. H. M. De Long, Hiram C. Hall, I. M. Londerback, Charles M. Norris, William A. Rice, Asbury D. Romans, William Sparks, Luther K. Cary, Henry Scott, W. W. Warrell, W. C. Winslow, and J. D. Pergrine, (missing,) privates, company B. John Albaugh, captain; Albert Ellise, first lieutenant; Milton Camnel, sergeant; Wm. Gambol, R. E. Patyten, Wm. B. Wallace, corporals; John Butler, Wm. P. Brandon, Jerry Carnady, J. M. Cooper, V. Graham, E. O. Griswell, O. George, Oscar K. Haun, G. Jenkins, John F. Kellogg, Thomas F. Littleton, Robert Lynch, Willard Neal, Wm. F. Orr, Joseph S. Osborne, J. W. Palmer, Humphrey Roberts, J. F. Spafford, Isaac Schofield, James Smith, James L. Stephens, Stewart Thompson, and Clemant Zingshiem, privates, company C. Benjamin Jarvis, second lieutenant; John E. Page, Harmon Jones, sergeants; Wm. C. Hansifas, Wm. R. Brush, Wm. Mooney, James Johnson, corporals; Wm. H. Hartman, Warren B. Parrot, Amos B. Miles, Tillman H. Paton, James Reynolds, Jacob Sipe, Fred. E. Strong, Stephen Mills, and Samuel W. Williams, privates, company D. Alexander B. Lewis, first lieutenant; Wm. Bunce, sergeant; E. Cluttester, Wm. W. Baughnan, A. B. Kinsel, and Wm. H. Brown, privates, company E. James A. Renford, Abraham Long, Methel B Jones, Charles S. Miller, sergeants; Robert N. McClanahan, Henry Saunders, Ransom P. Laffer, corporals; Andrew Beard, John Cabler, Wm. Eberhardt, (missing,) D. C. Glenden, Charles W. Gross, Charles Gans, John Hall, David N. Jones, John V. Catchum, Pleasant E. Minor, Shindon G. Ross, James H. Roland, Ora Slate, Wm. L. Sweitzer, George B. Tipton, Thomas A. Shockley, (missing,) A. F. Wilson, James E. Woods, and Hardnick Vass, privates, company F. Samuel S. Sample, first lieutenant; John E. Pungborn, acting lieutenant; Basil H. Martin, sergeant; Americus Campbell, corporal; Henry V. Fisher, Pearson Mills, Byron A. Knowles, James Miskimons, John Wightman, and John Wintin, privates, company G. Joel Brown, captain; John H. Hoffman, sergeant; Jacob Oberturff, Milton W. Shaw, corporals; George W. Baldwin, Thomas P. Estail, Wm. T Hughs, Wm. Knapp, John A. Trout, Benjamin Penn, Elijah Roberts, Asbury Sutton, John Shuffleton, Simeon Muscott, John Whitton, Milton Armington, and John A. Purse, privates, company H. Wm. H. Cotton, second lieutenant, (missing;) Wm. H. Brakey, acting lieutenant; Wm. D. Thompson, Richard Barrett, sergeants; G. W. Bowsman, F. Blusch, John S. Howard, H. P. Maron, Wm. C. Morden, Charles P. Read, Wm. H. Stephens, Wm. Shuler, and S. H. Skniderlin, privates, company I. H. G. Doolittle, J. Darling, sergeants; Wm. M. Letchfield, corporal; Henry Fry, John Haley, Henry Spalding, John A. King, W. E. Little, Wm. Presho, Job K. Reinhardt, John T. Reinhardt, Semon Shryock, John W. Smith, Andrew Saul, Newton E. Terrel, R. Stutsman, T. L. Burrington, (missing,) and G. W. Bottsford, privates, company K.

Twenty sixth Missouri regiment.—Killed: Thomas Murray, private, company A; John Hommit, private, company B; Herman Brant, G. Marcel, and Joseph Smith, privates, company C; Hiram Clery, sergeant, James M. Halsey, John Horace, and George Huff, corporals, George Gamble, James Hurley, and Samuel Kee, privates, company E; Alonzo A. Bliss, sergeant, Henry Meyer, corporal, Andrew Jones and Mark Wilt, privates, company F; Silas Laughlin and August Pigunot, corporals, Bernard Bakers, James S. Laughlin and Albert Spanhaus, privates, company H. *Wounded:* George W. Boomer, colonel; A. M. Craig, E. Malone and James A. McLain, privates, company A; Thomas Jarvis, private, company B; Augustus E. Grier, sergeant, John Savage, corporal, Henry Kreumend, Vincent Morge, Herman Perick, John Selhein, Henry Schutte, Bernard Wesbeck, Frederick Weisick, Louis Langenberg, privates, and Charles Hafnagel, musician, company C; Charles Clifton, corporal, Reily D. Rice, private, company D; Robert C. Crowel, captain, Robert B. Denny, 2d lieutenant, Frederic Lenter, 1st sergeant, Michael Gress, sergeant, Jerry Casey, corporal, Adrian Combe, David Dunkeday, John K. Dixon, Isaac W. Fugit, William Grier, Eli Hiatt, George Hopkins, John Halsey, Thomas Joice, William Locke, William V. Locke, William F. Montgomery, George Oliver, James Palmer, William Verian, Isaac Yambury, and William D. Simmons, privates, company E; Benjamin Dean, captain, J. W. Mapsin, lieutenant, William M. Boan, sergeant, Thomas F. Smith, corporal, Henry Att, B. B. Bundridge, John Fletcher, Patrick Fay, William Grandiah, Carel McCalister, Henry Patric, Christian Pupple, Daniel Robertson, and Christian Voss, privates, company F; Cornelius Herrigan, John Anderson, and Anderson Colbert, privates, company G; W. B. Furgison, sergeant, B. Shaffer, corporal, Alexander Magary, John H. Allen, Henry Potting, Henry Twehouse, Anton Weitery, Joseph Marcus, G. Messerlie, and Thomas Laughlin, privates, company H; Reuben Hardin, corporal, Uriah Dodsin, Levi Renick, Frank Vardot, Andrew Roberts, Peter Leazy, and William Lewis, privates, company I. *Missing:* Earnest Bemer, private.

Forty-eighth Indiana Regiment.—Killed: Charles W. Huston, 1st sergeant, Lewis C. Haney, sergeant, Lorenzo B. Brownell and Bartlett Y. Pigg, corporals, Reuben Glottfester, Henry Huntzinger, Albert Steentsman, and Napoleon B. Upson, privates, company A; Philip Critis, Miles H. Miller, David Reddick, Benjamin H. Ross, and James Zigler, privates, company B; A. P. Bradley, Jacob Nick, Henry Taylor, and Philip F. Tutor, privates, company D; Samuel Shepley, corporal, Edward Curn, private, company E; John Saunders, sergeant, William Hiner, Thomas Kirkwood, and Wisel Manuel, privates, company F; Joseph Clemmens, Eugene Clongdon, William Nixon, and William Mack, privates, company G; William H. Alle, private, company H; Samuel L. Connell, sergeant, Noah Barnheart, Martin Cavenaugh, and Soloman Fisher, privates, company I; William Jeanes, Henry Shoup, Thomas Simmons, Louis Wilcox, and Martin Zarbomekie, privates, company K. *Wounded:* Norman Eddy, colonel; Alfred Billows, lieutenant, Henry Williams and Rudolph Ash, corporals, William Bell, George H. Bloomer, Isaiah Irwin, Jacob Raefsneider, George Shultz, Marcus Washburn, and George Byskett, privates, company A; Abraham Rhone, sergeant, Thomas H. Abshire, corporal, John Hone, Amos Heston, George Monroe, and John Sonsley, privates, company B; James H. Warner, corporal, John Hohan, Martin Hutzel, Burnett Knoff, William McCormack, George C. Rhodes, Moses H. Sanborn, and Walter Tuter, privates, company D; Thomas Simcnton, sergeant, John Martin and Abraham Bonebrake, corporals, and Edward Brisett, private, company E; William Judkins, lieutenant, James Anderson, corporal, Charles Dewy, James Lus, and Charles Lebring, privates, company F; John Gordy, Alonzo Carpenter, and John Poiser, corporals, Martin Weaver, Emanuel Hoover, and Jackson Raight, privates, company G; G. Hollingshead, sergeant, John Hemph, corporal, John Smith and T. Hilderbrand, privates, company H; Henry Lung, Joseph Heffner, Cyrus Carr, and John Blomfield, privates, company I; Albert Guthridge, captain, Samuel Rabb, William Goodin, Nathaniel Maymeyer, William Warrell, and Samuel Warren, company K.

Fourth Minnesota Regiment.—Killed: Benjamin Poole and James Casey, privates, company C; Thomas Smith, private, company F. *Wounded:* Thomas Olson, private, company A; J. W. Dunn, 1st sergeant, A Graham, sergeant, C. G. Mickel, corporal, James Neil and Edward Zebrath, privates, company B; Charles Perkins and Thomas Reeves, privates, company C; George Kimball, 1st sergeant, George Clark, J. E. Sampson, and S. M. Momeny, privates, company D; James, A. Goodwin, 2d lieutenant, Addison Phelps, sergeant, G. W. Thomas, corporal, John Bass, Enos A. Buncker, Orlando Lindersmith, Benjamin Seirs, Frederick Schaum, and Joseph Tatro, privates, company E; J. W. Burdick, corporal, Ira O. Russell, George Winchel, and Hollis E. Sergant, privates, company F; George K. Campbell, John Eike, John Fobbe, Patrick Loftes, Antone Montrail, George Reider, and Bernard Westinan, privates, company G; Charles Olson, N. S. Howland, Peter Lentz, Andrew Anderson, privates, company H; Samuel P. Isaacs, sergeant, company I; George S. Hutchison, Avon B Morse, Samuel M. Milholland, John E. McCann, and Martin Keifer, privates, company K.

Sixteenth Iowa regiment.—Killed: Jacob Shambaugh, sergeant, R. G. Kelley and Gilbert Wakefield, privates, company A; Samuel Simmons and Levy Hester, privates, company D; Alexander Britt and Franklin Woodruff, privates, company E; Harvey Whitman, corporal, Michael McGowan, George Bedford, and John Conard, privates, company F; Solomon Zook, corporal, company H; E. W. Watson, private, company, I. *Wounded:* J. V. Lawrence, sergeant, Henry Horn, Alexander Gordon, E. A. Cassidy, Frederick Osborne, Alonzo Spore, George Miller, Michael Connelly, and Humphrey Manahan, privates, company A; H. F. Heartman and J. Orpe, corporals, company B; James Correl, H. Smith, H. W. Blessing, James King, Louis Heger, John Hettinger, privates, company C; Robert Alcorn, lieutenant, David Canot, and Thomas Parr, corporals, Hawkins McNally, W. V. Goss, John Berry, H. Ellis, and H. Miers, privates, company D; George Gallespie and Franklin Forbes, privates, company E; M. K. Laird and John McGraw, sergeants, E. Wilcox, William Welsh, James Barnes, O. R. Shepard, Enoch Haworth, and John Carpenter, privates, company F; A. Peick and G. B. Scink, corporals, company G; John Mulhall and John Huntington, privates, company H; H. D. Williams, lieutenant, H. Skilling, sergeant, J. C Munger, corporal, H. Cripe, private, company I; J. H. Lucas, lieutenant, William Defore, sergeant, Harvey Harstein, corporal, David Darl and David Signer, privates, company K.

—

THIRD DIVISION, 2D BRIGADE.

Tenth regiment, Iowa volunteers.—Wounded: Peter B. Mishler, corporal, company A; Frederick A. Downs, private, company A; Henry Howard and Peter Joice, privates, company D; Philip Thoma, private, company E; Elias Deodman, private, company F.

Tenth regiment Missouri volunteers.—Wounded: A. D. Peyton and Richard Staton, privates, company C; Stuart Wishortt, sergeant, company D; Asbury Saltus, John Rolstock, Thomas Hibbler, R. B. Glass, Reuben Sharp, W. J. Deana, and Peter Thoma, privates, company D; Augustus Zungle, private, company E; Joseph Young and John Siles, privates, company F; Alex. B. Webb, private, company H.

Twelfth Wisconsin battery.—Killed: J. J. Atherton, private, company D.

Seventeenth regiment Iowa volunteers. Killed: 2d Lieutenant O. H. B. Smith, company G; Bine. S. Lee, corporal, company K; A. R. Richmore, private, company G, and William Frank, private, company K. *Wounded:* Captain S. H. Archer, company C; 1st Lieutenant William Reach, company G; 2d Lieutenant C. B. Woodrow, company K; Henry C. Willis, private, company A; John J. Zermes and Daniel S. Arnold, privates, company A; George W. Dandy, corporal, company B; Charles P. Smith and E. Y. Burns, privates, company B; T. Jackson and Thomas Stafford, corporals, company C; W. L. Godly, 1st sergeant, company E; J. S. Parkhurst, W. D. Fisher, Aaron W. Reary, A. J. Headly, R. E. Williams, and B. H. Schooler, privates, company E; W. L. Richardson, corporal, company F; W. J. Cline, private, company F; Samuel V. Duncan and Thomas Steward, sergeants, company G; John King, corporal, company G; Jesse Lee and Samuel Yard, privates, company G; A. M. Vance, 2d sergeant, company H; S. H. C. Grubb and Ezra T. Vance, privates, company H; John J. Roohbeck, sergeant, company I; Z. F. Wood, corporal, company I; Huston Smith, private, company I; Frank Orone, sergeant, company K; John Fullerton, John Anderson, and George Simmons, corporals, company K; W. McGill, Hugh White, and Jephtha Ackley, privates, company K.

Eightieth regiment, Ohio volunteers.—Wounded: Lieutenant Colonel W. H. Bartleson, commanding regiment; 1st Lieutenant Jno. E. Philpott, adjutant of regiment; H. H. Whitcraft, 1st sergeant, company A; James Andrews and J. Dentenhamer, privates, Jesse Gnomer and Andrew Hedge, corporals, company B; Simon Durst, private, company C; J. F. Huddleson, 1st sergeant, company D; Thomas Elder, Robert G. Hill, and Allen Talbott, privates, company D; H. E. Clindening, corporal, company F; Turner Drummond and Benjamin Vial, privates, company F.

I certify that the above report is correct. The report from the other brigade will be sent in as soon as received.

JOE E. LYNCH,
Division Surgeon, 3d Division, Army of the Mississippi.

CAVALRY DIVISION OF COLONEL MIZNER.

5th Missouri cavalry.—Killed: Louis Berthold, private, company C. *Wounded:* Albert Borcherdd, captain, company C; Louis Schramm, 1st lieutenant, company C; Louis Berthold, private, company C.

17th Iowa infantry.—Killed: J. J. Autherton, private, acting in 12th Wisconsin battery.

2d Iowa cavalry.—Wounded: Henry Melchert and Nelson Lovell, privates, company C; James W. Nation, private, company A; George Zeigler, 1st sergeant, company A; John Schaffer, private, company A; Allison Aurey, private, company B.

3d Michigan cavalry.—Wounded: M. M. Lattimer, captain, company E; Oliver Spooner, private, company F; —— Ayers, private, company K.

Killed, 108; wounded, 611; missing, 17.

A. B CAMPBELL,
Medical Director, Army Mississippi.

HEADQUARTERS THIRD CAVALRY BRIGADE,
Left Wing 16th Army Corps, Corinth, July 9, 1863.

GENERAL: On the morning of the 7th, having received instructions to proceed with my brigade out on the Burnsville road to make a reconnoissance in force, I left Corinth at about daylight with the 7th Kansas cavalry, Colonel T. P. Herrick, eight companies of the 10th Missouri cavalry, Major F. W. Benteen, and the detachment of the 15th Illinois cavalry, Lieutenant Colonel F. T. Gilbert, (in all about 750 men,) and moved out by the way of the North Farmington road. On reaching the corral on this road we found that the enemy, with twelve companies of mounted men, had, a short time before our arrival, surrounded and attacked the small force guarding that point, and, after overpowering and taking the most of them prisoners, had decamped with all the stock that was in the corral. After making a few inquiries from the neighborhood I started in pursuit out by the said road, when, finding that the enemy had taken a route by the way of the Hamburg road, I concluded to pursue him by that route. His traces guided us by by-roads through twamps and over hills, until we reached the main road leading from Red Sulphur Springs so Iuka, which road he had taken to that town.

Taking this last named road we came upon the enemy in force, posted in an open field on both sides of the road, with a dense woods in his front, and about a mile and a half from Iuka. He opened on us with musketry, and I immediately threw out a detachment of of the 15th Illinois (dismounted) as dismounted skirmishers, with the road as the centre of my line of battle. I ordered the 10th Missouri to deploy to the right and left of the road and dismount, which was quickly executed, with four companies on the right and three on the left-hand side. The mountain-howitzer battery was ordered into battery on the road. I then ordered some four companies of the 7th Kansas to dismount and deploy to the right and left of the road in line of skirmishers, behind the 10th Missouri cavalry, thus forming a double line of battle in the rear of my advanced skirmishers. In the mean time a very hot fire had been kept up by the enemy, the skirmishers, and the companies of the 10th Missouri on the right of the road, and I ordered Lieutenant Joyce, commanding the battery, to shell the enemy vigorously. That portion of the 7th Kansas not dismounted were held in reserve.

The order to shell the enemy was obeyed with good will, the men standing to their guns under a heavy fire of musketry without flinching and with undaunted coolness. Much of this courage must be attributed to the daring and bravery of Lieutenant Peter Joyce, who was everywhere among his men, encouraging them with his presence and assuring them by his coolness. First Sergeant W. P. Edgar, of this battery, was acting lieutenant, and deserves much praise for the efficient aid he rendered in working the guns and the unsurpassed bravery he displayed. I regret to say that he met with a serious, though not dangerous, wound, the ball passing through his hand.

Having cannonaded the enemy, as I considered, a sufficient length of time, I ordered the battery to cease firing, and advanced my whole line of battle up the hill and through the wood; and if the fire had been severe before, it now became heavier, and no sooner had my men shown themselves on the summit of the hill than the enemy discharged upon us along his whole line a tremendous and destructive volley of musketry, as severe, for the time it lasted, as any I have ever had the fortune to witness.

Here we sustained all the losses that befell us that day. Captain H. G. Bruns, of the 10th Missouri, a young and dashing and as brave a soldier as ever wielded a sword, fell at this point, pierced through the lungs by a musket ball, in advance of his men and cheering them on to victory. Two of his own men, and one of company E, 10th Missouri cavalry, were killed at this place and almost at the same time. Several men were wounded here.

From this time on, it was evident the day was ours. We continued our advance through the woods, when, after a few wavering volleys, the enemy fled in dismay, leaving us the victory and the field. As soon as the enemy began to fly, I ordered three squadrons of the 7th Kansas, under Major Jenkins, to pursue him as far as Iuka. He followed him to that place, captured a battery wagon and forge and burnt them, but saw nothing of the enemy, and returned. He had a battery of four pieces of artillery, with which he ingloriously fled to his fastnesses on Bear creek.

Having proceeded as far as my instructions directed, I made inquiries as to the enemy's numbers and position, when I learned that in front of me, towards Bear creek, his force was some twenty-five hundred strong, while there was a large force on either of my flanks. The force I had encountered numbered from fifteen to eighteen hundred.

As to the enemy's loss I have no definite means of ascertaining, but am told, on inquiry, that it was large. Four dead bodies of rebel soldiers were found by us on the field, and the traces of blood around fully corroborate the story. The total loss to my command will be found in the recapitulation at the end of this report.

After caring for my wounded and placing them in ambulances, I brought away my dead, and fell back some six miles and encamped for the night. On the morning of the eighth we took up our line of march for Corinth, and arrived here at about half past 10 o'clock.

Before closing this report, it would be neglect on my part if I did not return my thanks to the officers and men under my command for the unflinching coolness with which they met danger, and the courage with which they routed a superior force, occupying a position chosen by its own leaders. In particularizing I do not desire to be invidious, but the officers hereinafter named came more particularly under my notice Major F. W. Benteen, commanding the 10th Missouri cavalry, was where a leader should be, in the front, and by his coolness and great tact and skill did much towards gaining the day. Captain M. H. Williams, of the 10th Missouri, acting field officer, and Lieutenant I. F. Young, adjutant of the same regiment, were foremost in the line of skirmishers, rallying and urging them forward regardless of danger. Captain David Cain, acting field officer of the 10th Missouri, displayed great gallantry, and effected much in the direction of the firing of the batteries. Captains Neet, Naughton, Underwood, and McGlasson, of the same regiment, also deserve particular mention for their gallantry and daring in leading their men into the hottest of the fight.

Lieutenant Colonel F. T. Gilbert and Major E. Carmichael acted with their customary devotion to the cause, and were ever foremost in the path of danger.

Particular mention will not be undeserved in the person of Captain Ford, of that regiment, who bravely led where his men dauntlessly followed. He received a shot from the enemy in the scabbard of his sabre, deeply indenting it, thus avoiding a serious wound.

Colonel T. P. Herrick, Major Jenkins, and Captains Malone, Thornton, and Gregory, of the 7th Kansas, also came under my notice, and deserve the praise due to brave and devoted soldiers. Of the officers of the battery I have already spoken, but too much praise cannot be bestowed upon them. All honor and praise are due to the gallant dead, and it might not be amiss to mention, particularly, Captain H. G. Bruns, 10th Missouri cavalry. Reared in the lap of luxury, at the first breaking out of the war, although quite young, he enlisted in the 3d Missouri volunteer infantry, and served in that regiment through all the battles of Missouri, Booneville, Wilson's creek, and others. He was with his regiment during General Curtis's chase of the rebel Price through Missouri, and participated in every battle of that eventful campaign, including the hard-earned field of Pea Ridge.

He received a discharge from his regiment only to accept a commission in the 10th Missouri, and has served with it in every one of its engagements in this district.

Ere yet in the first dawn of manhood this polished gentleman and gallant soldier has been cut down, one among the many victims to the mad ambition of southern traitors. He has left behind him an unsullied name. Fond friends shall weep for him, comrades in arms shall mourn for him; but he died a martyr to a holy cause, sacrificed upon the altar of his country. He fell foremost in the fight, and while the victorious shouts of his comrades rent the air "all grew dark," and his fearless spirit winged its way to a brighter, happier land.

Lieutenants John W. Rice and M. McDonald, serving on my personal staff, rendered me every desirable assistance, carrying orders, regardless of flying balls, to all parts of the field.

The following is a list of the killed and wounded :

Killed.—Henry G. Bruns, captain, F. S. Burlingame, corporal, and N. Sahli, private, company G ; William Frazier, private, company E, 10th Missouri cavalry.

Wounded.—W. P. Edgar, 1st sergeant, company A ; Rogers, private, company I ; Shine, company M, 10th Missouri cavalry. Marion Cross, corporal, company D ; Charles H. Dawn, private, company E; Jacob Snyder, private, company I, 7th Kansas cavalry. Henry Shaeffer, private, company F ; John Moorly, private, company G, 15th Illinois cavalry.

Recapitulation.—Killed, 4 ; wounded, 8. Total loss, 12.

Respectfully,

F. M. CORNYN,
Colonel 10th Missouri Cavalry, Commanding Brigade.

MISSOURI CAMPAIGN.

CINCINNATI, OHIO, *February* 25, 1865.

GENERAL : I enclose, and transmit for file in your office, a copy of my official report of the late campaign against Price in Missouri ; the original, with accompanying sub-reports, was forwarded to Major General Canby, commanding the military division of west Mississippi, under whose command I was placed.

Very respectfully, your obedient servant,

W. S. ROSECRANS,
Major General.

Brigadier General L. THOMAS,
Adjutant General U. S. Army, Washington, D. C.

HEADQUARTERS DEPARTMENT OF MISSOURI,
St. Louis, December 7, 1864.

COLONEL : The commanding general of the military division is already informed, by my current official despatches, of the principal incidents of the late campaign against Price in this department, but it is proper that I should submit a more detailed and connected report of the operations for a correct understanding of their extent and the importance of the results.

From early in the spring it was known through the lodges of the "O. A. K.'s" and other rebel sources, that Price intended a great invasion of this State, in which he expected the coöperation of that "order" and of rebels generally, and by which he hoped to obtain important military and political results.

In pursuance of these plans, the lodges with rebel recruiting officers and agents sent into Missouri clandestinely, or under cover of the amnesty oath, for that purpose, began an insurrection in Platte county on the 7th of July last. From that time guerilla warfare raged in the river counties, west from Calloway in the north, and from Cooper on the south side of the Missouri.

This department having been depleted of troops, permission was obtained to raise volunteers to meet the exigencies of our situation, and under it about five complete, and as many incomplete, regiments of 12-months volunteer infantry had been organized previously to the raid.

On the 3d of September General Washburn sounded the tocsin, by information that the force under Shelby at Batesville, Arkansas, was about to be joined by Price for the invasion of our State. The ripening of the corn lent to this additional color of probability, so that, on the 6th, Major General A. J. Smith, passing Cairo, with a division of infantry, on the way to General Sherman, I telegraphed General Halleck the state of affairs, requesting orders for this division to halt at that point and wait until we could ascertain the designs of the enemy.

The division was halted, and on the 9th General Smith received orders from General Halleck to operate against Price and company ; but deeming it impracticable to penetrate between one and two hundred miles into Arkansas with a small column of infantry in pursuit of a large mounted force, the exact whereabouts as well as intentions of which were still unknown, he decided to move his command to a point near St. Louis, whence he could readily move by rail or river, and await Price's movements.

From that time information accumulated showing the imminence of the raid. On the 23d we received certain information that Price had crossed the Arkansas with two divisions of mounted men, three batteries of artillery, a large wagon train carrying several thousand stand of small-arms, and was at or near Batesville, on White river.

From this point midway between the Mississippi and the western boundary of the State there are three practicable routes of invasion: one by Pocahontas into southeastern Missouri; another, West Plains and Rolla or vicinity, north towards Jefferson City; a third by Cassville, north, either through Springfield and Sedalia or by the Kansas border to the Missouri river.

Strong military reasons favored the movement of their main force by the central route, while a detachment should go by Pocahontas, and strip southeast Missouri. Under these circumstances my first object was to secure our great depots at Springfield and Rolla. The hay cut during the summer, and our train of government wagons, required to maintain the troops in the Springfield district.

To do this and, as far as possible, save the scanty agriculture of the country from devastation, it was necessary to hold both Springfield and Rolla; indeed, to have abandoned these points would have been not only to abandon the loyal people of those districts and their property to destruction, but to invite the enemy to destroy our trains while moving them, capture our stores, and beat our troops in detail.

Generals Sanborn and McNeill were therefore informed and ordered to place the trains and public property of their districts under the protection of the fortifications at Springfield and Rolla, to put their forts in the best possible state of defence, using every foot and dismounted cavalry soldier, including citizens and local militia, to the best advantage, and with all their efficient mounted force to watch the enemy's motions and report the earliest indications of the direction of the coming storm. General Brown was ordered to concentrate all troops from the west of the central district at Sedalia, to notify the citizens, guards, and see that neither they nor their arms were exposed to capture.

On the 24th Shelby was reported south of Pilot Knob, moving toward Farmington with five thousand men and four pieces of artillery. General Ewing was ordered to concentrate the troops in the southern part of his district at Pilot Knob and Cape Girardeau, and to verify the accuracy of this report, which proved true. On the 26th General A. J. Smith, with two of his brigades, was ordered to a point on the Iron Mountain railroad, as far towards Pilot Knob as he deemed compatible with certainty that his position would not be turned and the enemy get between him and St. Louis. On the day before Sanborn had orders to move, with all his mounted force, to Rolla, it having become evident that the enemy would not probably strike west of that point. The safety of St. Louis was vital to us. I therefore telegraphed Brigadier General H. E. Paine, commanding in Illinois, who promised me assistance from some regiments of returning "hundred-day volunteers," who, though they had already served beyond their time, generously consented to come for the defence of the city. The enrolled militia of St. Louis, though but skeleton regiments, were called out, and the citizens also requested to organize and arm. General Ewing was sent to Pilot Knob, with directions to use his utmost exertions to find out whether any more than Shelby's division was in southeast Missouri, and to that end to hold Pilot Knob until he was certain. With a soldierly comprehension of the importance of his duties, while reporting the current rumors of the advance of Price with his whole force, he expressed his doubts and held his position until the 27th, when he sustained a terrific assault in Fort Davidson, a small field-work in the valley, surrounded by hills within cannon range, which he held with about 1,000 men, one-half raw troops, establishing beyond question the presence of all Price's command in that quarter. He gloriously repulsed them, killing and wounding some 1,500 of the enemy, and lost only 28 killed and 56 wounded, as appears from his report herewith.

While Ewing's fight was going on Shelby advanced to Potosi, and thence to Big River bridge, threatening General Smith's advance, which withdrew from that point to within safer supporting distance of his main position at De Soto. Previous to and pending these events the guerilla warfare in north Missouri had been waging with redoubled fury. Rebel agents, amnesty oath-takers, recruits, "sympathizers," O. A. K.'s, and traitors of every hue and stripe had warmed into life at the approach of the great invasion. Women's fingers were busy making clothes for rebel soldiers out of goods plundered by the guerillas; women's tongues were busy telling Union neighbors "*their time was now coming.*" General Fisk, with all his force, had been scouring the bush for weeks in the river counties in pursuit of hostile bands, composed largely of recruits from among that class of inhabitants who claim protection, yet decline to perform the full duties of citizens, on the ground that they "never tuck no sides." A few facts will convey some idea of this warfare carried on by confederate agents here, while the agents abroad of their bloody and hypocritical despotism—Mason, Slidell, and Mann, in Europe—have the effrontery to tell the nations of Christendom our government "carries on the war with increasing ferocity, regardless of the laws of civilized warfare." These gangs of rebels, whose families had been living in peace among their loyal neighbors, committed the most cold blooded and diabolical murders, such as riding up to a farm-house, asking for water, and while receiving it shooting down the giver, an aged, inoffensive farmer, because he was a radical "Union man." In the single sub-district of Mexico the commanding officer furnished a list of near one hundred Union men who, in the course of six weeks, had been killed, maimed, or "run off," *because* they *were* "radical Union men" or d——d abolitionists. About the 1st of September Anderson's gang attacked a railroad train on the north Missouri road, took from it twenty-two unarmed soldiers, many on sick leave, and, after robbing, placed them in a row and shot them in cold blood, some of the bodies they scalped, and put others across the track and run the engine over them. On the 27th this gang, with numbers swollen to three or four hundred men, attacked Major Johnson, with about one hundred and twenty men of the 39th Missouri volunteer infantry, raw recruits, and after stampeding their horses shot every man, most of them in cold blood. Anderson, a few days later, was recognized by General Price, at Booneville, as a confederate captain, and, with a verbal admonition to behave himself, ordered by Colonel Maclane, chief of Price's staff, to proceed to north Missouri and destroy the railroads, which orders were found on the miscreant when killed by Lieutenant Colonel Cox, about the 27th of October.

On the 28th, when information of Ewing's fight and Price's presence at Pilot Knob came to hand, General Smith, discovering the enemy on his front moving to west and north, in pursuance of his orders to hold the most advanced position compatible with the certainty of keeping between the enemy and St. Louis, determined to leave De Soto and retire behind the Meramee, a stream which, at from 10 to 15 miles south of St. Louis, offered considerable obstacles to the passage of a hostile force with wagons and artillery.

General Ewing, finding Marmaduke's and Fagen's rebel divisions before him, and his position commanded by a numerically superior artillery, acting on suggestions made when discussing with him the possibilities of the position, on the night of he 27th spiked his heavy guns, blew up the magazine, ammunition, and supplies, and with the field battery and remains of his command retreated through the hills towards the Meramee valley, hoping to reach a point on the railroad from whence he could move to St. Louis, but, as will be seen from his report, the enemy pursued him, harassed his rear on the march, which he directed along a ridge where the enemy could not flank him, and overtook him near Harrison's Station, where, seizing and extending the temporary defences constructed by the militia, he displayed such vigor that, after harassing him for 36 hours and making several attacks, on the approach of a detachment of Sanborn's cavalry the rebels left him, and he escaped with all his command to Rolla.

The enemy's strength and position thus developed, my first business was to secure the points he best would strike—St. Louis, Jefferson City, and Rolla. General Smith's 4,500 infantry and the mounted force we could raise, the 7th Kansas, just in from Memphis, part of the 13th Missouri volunteer cavalry, Colonel Cutherwood, and the recruits of Merrill's horse, hastily mounted and organized, a total of 1,500 men, were all the force we could place between St. Louis and an invading army of at least 15,000 mounted men, whose advance was within a day's march of the city. Meanwhile Brigadier General Pike, ably seconded by Generals Wolf and Miller, of the East Missouri militia, had assembled and armed skeletons of the 1st, 2d, 3d, 5th, 6th, 7th, 10th, 11th, 13th, and 52d regiments of enrolled militia. The mayor and others, under the direction of the Hon. B. Gratz Brown and Mayor Ledergerber, organized the citizens exempt from militia duty, who volunteered for the defence of the city, into companies and regiments, numbering by the 30th some four or five thousand men. The 132d, 134th, 138th, 140th, and 142d Illinois hundred-day volunteers also began to arrive on the 30th, and were all in by October 1, and formed into a brigade, under Colonel Wanglein, for the immediate defence of the city, beyond which they did not wish to serve, as all of them were out over time and many having desirable offers as substitutes.

The enemy moving up by Potosi, seemed to halt at Richwoods, about 40 miles southwest of St. Louis, in the hills between Big River and the Meramee, as if concentrating for an attack on the city. This appeared the more possible from the magnitude of his interest in it, and the fact that he did not show much force in the Meramee valley, even on the 30th. On that day Major General Smith was ordered to occupy Kirkwood, which commands the Richwood road and crossing of the Meramee to St. Louis, his cavalry to reconnoitre south and west, Colonel Merrill going as far as Franklin.

General Fisk, previously ordered to join General Brown with all his available force, reached and reported from Jefferson City to-day. At the close of it news came that a brigade of rebel cavalry had burned the Moselle bridge, and were moving north towards Franklin. General Smith was ordered to send a brigade of infantry to support the cavalry at that point, and on the 1st of October Colonel Wolfe, with his brigade, reached Franklin, and after a sharp skirmish drove the enemy from the place, but not until he had burned the depot. The rebels were now apparently at bay. With 1,500 cavalry and 4,500 infantry, General Smith was not in condition to attempt offensive movements against a force of 15,000 veteran mounted rebels, who could reach St. Louis from any point in the Meramee valley, where he might confront them in half the time it would take his infantry to reach it. Our obvious policy, under these circumstances, was to keep as close as possible to the enemy, without risking St. Louis, until General Mower's command should arrive from Arkansas, or at least we be able to join to Smith's our mounted forces at Rolla. Every hour's delay of the enemy in the Meramec valley brought Mower nearer and increased our chances of striking him, as it did the security of Jefferson City. On the 2d the enemy was reported massing in the vicinity of Union, on the road either to Jefferson City or Rolla and General Smith was ordered to Franklin; but as the enemy's movements appeared to tend westward, on the 3d General Smith was advanced to Gray's summit, and General Pike moved to Franklin. On the 4th, General Smith pushed his cavalry towards the Gasconade, advanced his infantry to Union, followed up by General Pike's militia. On the 5th Price's command took Herman, burned the Gasconade bridge, and was crossing that stream at the old State road ford. General Smith followed him. General Mower reported his arrival at Girardeau, out of supplies, his teams worn down, part of his cavalry dismounted, and many horses unshod. Transports and supply-boats were at once despatched, and on the 8th and 9th his command reached St. Louis, from whence the infantry was pushed forward by water, as rapidly as the low stage of the river would permit, to join General Smith. The cavalry under Winslow reshod and started by land from St. Louis on the 10th towards Jefferson City, which point it reached on the 16th instant, one day in advance of the infantry.

On the 6th the enemy began crossing the Osage at Castle Rock, and one or two other fords, under cover of his artillery, opposed by Colonel Phillips with the available cavalry at Jefferson City. While thus engaged, Generals McNeill and Sanborn reached Jefferson City by a forced march with all the mounted force from Rolla, and, uniting with Fisk and Brown, gave us a garrison there of 4,100 cavalry and 2,600 infantry, mostly the new and partially organized twelve-months men, with a few citizens and militia. As this force, though capable of giving a strong battle behind intrenchments, was not very formidable to act offensively against a veteran force like that of the enemy, it was decided by General Fisk, the other three generals concurring, to oppose a moderate resistance to the enemy's advance across the Moreau, a small stream with muddy banks and bad bottom, four or five miles east of the city, and then to retire and receive his attack at the defensive line, which with industry and good judgment had been prepared by the entire laboring force, civil and military, at Jefferson City. The enemy burned the Osage bridge and crossed the river on the 6th. On the 7th he advanced on the city, crossed the Moreau after sharp fighting, and developed a line of battle three or four miles long, east, south, and west of the place. But after reconnoitring its apparently formidable intrenchments, warned by his Pilot Knob experience in storming earthworks, he declined attacking, and passing his train in the rear, moved around, massing on the west, and finally retiring. On the 8th General Pleasonton, on his arrival at Jefferson, under orders to assume command, despatched General Sanborn with all the available cavalry—4,100 men—to follow and harass the enemy until General Smith's command could come up. General Smith was informed of the rebel failure at Jefferson, and directed to move by the most expeditious route to that place, where Mower's infantry were to join and the cavalry overtake him. He was to send all his cavalry under Colonel Cutherwood in advance, to report to Pleasonton, who, on its arrival, was to join Sanborn's, and assume direction of the provisional cavalry division. Thus formed, General Pike, with his militia, was charged with the control of the country and the defences of our line of communication from St. Louis to Jefferson City. Sanborn followed the rebels, attacked their rear guard at Versailles, where it was uncertain what course they would take, found they were going north towards Booneville, followed and drove them into line of battle near that place, and when he found himself nearly enveloped by their entire army, fell back out of their reach to meet Cutherwood's command and his provisions, both of which arrived at California on the 14th.

The enemy taking advantage of this, crossed the Lamine at Scott's and Dug's fords and moved north towards Arrow Rock.

Sanborn immediately followed this movement by Georgetown bridge, keeping between the Pacific railroad and the line of the enemy's march, and holding the line of the Blackwater, a western tributary of the Lamine, while Price, crossing a part of Shelby's command at Arrow Rock, on the Booneville ferry-boat, to the north side of the river, advanced on Glasgow, which he captured, after a seven hours' fight, with a part of Colonel Harding's regiment, 43d Missouri volunteer infantry, and small detachments of the 9th Missouri State militia and 17th Illinois cavalry. On the 17th our cavalry, following his westward movement, keeping south of without pressing him, until General Smith's and Mower's troops could be brought up, kept the line of the Blackwater, and on the 17th reported themselves out of supplies and the enemy between Marshall and Waverly.

On the 17th Mower's infantry, except two small regiments, arrived at Jefferson City and went at once by rail to Lamine bridge to join General Smith, who, passing Jefferson by land on the 14th, had followed the cavalry movement to that point, taking charge of the supplies, which, in consequence of the destruction of the bridge by the rebels, could go by rail no further. Winslow's cavalry marching, reached Jefferson, the advance 20 miles beyond at California, on the 16th, and was ordered to join General Pleasonton without delay.

On the 18th General Smith was ordered to move to Dunksburg, near the cavalry headquarters, taking five days' rations and leaving minimum garrisons to guard and handle stores at Sedalia and Lamine bridge. The 19th found this movement accomplished; the cavalry with its centre near Cook's store, its right behind the Blackwater, and its left near Kirkpatrick's mills, towards Warrensburg.

The enemy apparently hesitated in the vicinity of Marshall, as if uncertain whether to go west or double on his tracks between Sedalia and Jefferson, but our cavalry advance receding a few miles to meet supplies and concentrate, on the 17th and 18th, seemed to decide his movements towards Lexington, where General Curtis telegraphed me, on the 19th, the head of his column had arrived, General Blunt, after a sharp skirmish, retiring towards Independence. I informed General Curtis of our position; that our troops reported Price near Waverly; advised that Blunt check his advance at Wellington, and as soon as we were sure his main force was moving on Lexington we would endeavor by a forced march to strike him in the flank. To ascertain Price's real intentions General Pleasonton was directed to make a strong reconnoissance towards Waverly. The results of this reached me on the morning of the 20th, and Pleasonton was directed at once to push the centre of his cavalry to Lexington, and General Smith with his infantry to support the movement. At 7 p. m. Pleasonton reported the enemy had left Lexington, going west, and McNeill and Sanborn entering the town. October 21 our cavalry advance followed the enemy to Fire Creek prairie, Brown's and Winslow's brigades reaching Lexington at 2 o'clock p. m. and the infantry at 9 p. m. of the same day. General Curtis also reported a fight with the enemy's entire force at the Little Blue, from 10 a. m. to 2 p. m., and that to prevent being flanked he should retire to the Big Blue, where his militia and artillery were in strong position. Supposing the enemy could not cross the Big Blue in the face of Curtis, I despatched General Pleasonton my belief that he would move south, and that while McNeill's brigade should harass his rear, he, with the other three brigades, should move towards Lone Jack, near which would be General Smith's infantry, now marching from Lexington to Chapel Hill. At 10 o'clock p. m. a despatch from Pleasonton informed me of the receipt of these conditional orders, and that the enemy in full force was moving far to the west, followed by his cavalry. October 22 Pleasonton's cavalry reached the Little Blue at 10 a. m., found the bridge destroyed; a temporary one was constructed, the enemy's skirmishers driven, the command crossed, when the enemy opened with artillery and was steadily driven towards Independence, which place was taken by a brilliant cavalry charge, in which Cutherwood's regiment captured two guns complete, near a hundred prisoners fell into our hands, and our troops pushed the enemy's rear guard all night. At 8 p. m. Pleasonton reports: "All my brigades have been engaged. The enemy have left 40 killed and many sick and wounded in my hands. Heard nothing from Curtis. If Smith can come up in case we get a fight, it will be well. Have sent McNeill's brigade to Little Santa Fe. Price is reported intrenched this side of the Big Blue. Fighting still going on with an obstinate rear guard. Let Smith come to this place." Reluctantly General Smith was despatched to move to Independence as requested, the messenger reaching him at Chapel Hill as he was putting his column in motion to march there in response to a direct message from General Pleasonton advising him of the posture of affairs.

On the morning of the 23d Pleasonton began to move on the enemy at the crossing of the Big Blue, where the fight opened at 7 a. m. and continued until 1 p. m., when Shelby, who had been fighting General Curtis's command, finding Marmaduke and Fagan were giving way, turned on Pleasonton and "for a moment shook Sanborn's brigade," but by the skilful use of Thurben's battery, throwing double-shotted grape and canister, and the gallant charging of our troops, they were routed and fled southward, pushed by Generals Pleasonton and Curtis that night beyond Little Santa Fe.

General Smith's command, arriving at Independence at 5 p. m., was ordered to move that night by a forced march to Hickman's mills, hoping it would strike the enemy in flank while passing that point. Had he been ordered and marched for that point instead of Independence the day before, General Smith would have arrived in time to strike the enemy's compact columns and train with nine thousand infantry and five batteries, but it was too late. He did not reach the mill until long after not only the enemy's but our own columns had passed there.

News from the cavalry fronts during the night showed that nothing remained but to push the enemy with our cavalry; allowing the infantry to follow as best it could, to act as support in case of possible reverse to us, or re-enforcements which were currently reported on their way to meet the enemy.

On the 24th, with the Kansas troops in advance we pursued the enemy until within fifteen miles of the Trading Post, where, at General Curtis's request, General Pleasonton's command took the lead, and at the end of sixty miles march overtook the rebels about midnight at the Marias-des-Cygnes, began skirmishing, and on the 25th at 4 a. m. opened upon their bivouac with artillery, creating the greatest consternation, following it up by an attack which drove them promptly from the field, leaving in our hands horses, mules, wagons, arms, and some prisoners. Our troops followed them in a running fight until 2 o'clock p. m., when they came up with them at the Little Osage, crossing in position with eight pieces of artillery on their line of battle. With the instinct of a true cavalry general, Pleasonton immediately ordered an attack by Benteen and Phillips' sbrigades, which by a magnificent charge completely routed them, capturing eight guns, two stands of colors, Major General Marmaduke,

Brigadier General Cabell, five colonels, other officers, and near one thousand prisoners, besides wagons, small-arms, &c. Sanborn's brigade, which was a mile and a half behind, and the Kansas troops, still further in rear, did not arrive in time to take part in the battle, but Sanborn's brigade led in the pursuit of the routed enemy, overtook them at a small stream a few miles beyond the battle-ground, charged them in the timber, drove them across it into the open prairie, where they formed in order of battle, three lines deep. But such was the enthusiasm of the men of this brigade when they reached the edge of the wood and saw this triple line, they charged it without orders, knocked it in pieces and chased the fugitives until night closed the pursuit and the enemy fled under cover of the darkness towards the Arkansas border. Besides the wagons captured during this day at the Marias-des-Cygnes, on the way to and at the Little Osage, the enemy had destroyed many, including ammunition wagons, and for twenty-five or thirty miles beyond the Osage battle-field their route was strewn with debris of burning wagons and other property. Pleasonton's cavalry had now been in motion almost day and night for six days, during which it had marched at least 204 miles and fought four battles. It was pretty well exhausted and broken down, and went into Fort Scott that night for food and a little rest. He reported to me the results of his day's work; that the enemy was going at his utmost, and his own troops were so broken down it would be impossible without fresh horses to strike the enemy another great blow this side of the Arkansas, and recommended that Generals Sanborn and McNeill follow to support Curtis's troops in pursuit so long as there was any prospect of damaging the enemy, and then return to Springfield and Rolla.

On the receipt of the news of the enemy's rout, General Smith, whose command was out of provisions, was directed to move to Harrisonville, and thence get supplies from Warrensburg, where 100 wagons were waiting with provisions for our command, sending thirty thousand rations to the cavalry. Further reports of the enemy's condition satisfied me there would be no use of breaking down any more of our horses, since General Curtis, whose cavalry horses were fresher than ours, supported by Sanborn and McNeill, on their way down the State line, would be more than ample to deal with any resistance Price's command would offer this side of the Arkansas.

Orders were accordingly given, and General Pleasonton returned, with Phillips's brigade, the cannon and part of the prisoners, to Warrensburg. The Kansas troops and Benteen's brigade pursued the enemy's flying columns, a part of whom made their last stand at Newtonia, Missouri, where General Blunt overtook and attacked them on the 28th, but was being worsted when Sanborn, having marched 102 miles in 36 hours, arrived in time to save the day. The enemy fled, making no further stand this side of the Arkansas. In a country destitute of food for man and beast, five times defeated, pursued four or five hundred miles, with loss of nearly all their artillery, ammunition and baggage trains, demoralization and destitution and want of supplies, would the rebels recross the Arkansas—supplies at the risk of falling into the hands of Thayer's forces or Steele's cavalry, and, if allowed, would almost disintegrate and disband them on the way thither.

General Curtis thought pushing them was best, and accordingly followed, although he did not again overtake them. At his urgent instance, against my own judgment as well as that of Generals Sanborn and McNeill, I pushed their two brigades down to the Arkansas border, whence Sanborn sent an advance to Fort Smith, reaching there on the morning of the 8th, to notify General Thayer of the enemy's desperate condition, and the direction he had taken from Cane Hill, towards the Indian nation, between Fort Smith and Fort Gibson. Meanwhile, at Sherman's request, followed by orders from the general-in-chief, I directed Major General A. J. Smith to move his command by the most expeditious route to the Mississippi, in the vicinity of St. Louis, there to embark and proceed to Nashville, and report to Major General George H. Thomas. On the 3d of November I returned to St. Louis, to be there during the election, and on the receipt of the news of the enemy having crossed the Arkansas, directed the cavalry to repair to their respective districts, and Winslow's cavalry to move by the best route, and join General Thomas at Nashville.

In entering into details, I have aimed to give the general commanding a sort of military photograph of our daily condition and movements, as well for his critical judgment as for history, omitting events of whatever magnitude not having a bearing on our movements, and most of the minor ones which did enter into their determination. I trust that the precautions taken in advance of Price's movements, the preparations before we knew where he was coming, the means taken to secure our most important points, and occupy him until we could concentrate the forces to strike him with a certainty of success, outweighing any damage he could meanwhile do us; the energy and activity in concentration, vigor in pursuit, and fiery gallantry of our troops in battle, will receive the approbation of the general commanding the military division. It will appear from these details and accompanying reports that our dismounted cavalry, infantry and militia nobly performed their duty, watching, marching, and fighting, whenever and wherever opportunity offered; that by their aid, in holding our depots and supporting our mounted force, we have saved all our important posts, and most of the country from pillage, except a belt of some twenty miles wide along the route of the invasion; and with less than seven thousand effective cavalry have pursued, overtaken, beaten in several engagements, and finally routed, an invading cavalry, variously estimated at from 15,000 to 26,000 men, re-enforced by six thousand armed recruits from Missouri, taken from them *ten pieces of artillery*, two stands of colors, 1,958 prisoners of war, a large number of horses, mules, wagons, and small-arms, compelled them to destroy most of their remaining wagon trains and plunder, blasted all the political schemes of the rebels and traitors who concerted with Price to revolutionize Missouri, destroy Kansas, and turn the State and presidential elections against the Union cause; and by our triumph in the late elections have given to gallant and suffering Missouri the fairest prospect she has ever yet seen of future freedom, peace, and prosperity—all the fruit of a campaign of 48 days, in which most of our victorious troops had never before seen a great cavalry battle. Rarely during this or any war has cavalry displayed more persevering energy in pursuit, more impetuous courage and gallantry in attacking, regardless of superior numbers, or had its efforts crowned with greater fruits of success. While paying a just tribute of thanks to all the officers and soldiers of the cavalry, artillery, infantry, militia and citizen guards, who served during the raid, for their prompt and cheerful obedience to all orders, whether to labor, march, or fight, I must refer the accompanying reports of their commanders for special mentions of individual gallantry.

Major General Pleasonton deserves the thanks of the country for the able manner in which he handled and fought the cavalry, and the brilliant and fruitful victories he won over triple his own force. I hope he may receive promotion in the regular army. Major General A. J. Smith deserves thanks for promptitude, energy and perseverance in all his movements, and for the good judgment displayed in his campaign. Nor must I omit a tribute of admiration to those brave and true soldiers who, under Mower, followed Price from Arkansas, marching 300 miles in 18 days, and after going by boat from Cape Girardeau to Jefferson City, resumed the pursuit, marching another march of 462 miles before they embarked for Nashville to take part in the not doubtful contest before that city for the mastery of Middle Tennessee. The district commanders all deserve my thanks for prompt and cordial co-operation in all measures precautionary and preparatory for the raid.

General Ewing deserves special mention for military judgment, courage, and gallantry in holding Pilot Knob till he had certainty of the enemy's force, as well as for the manner in which he withdrew his troops to Rolla.

General McNeill, for promptitude and energy in putting Rolla in a state of defence, and for moving with all his force to Jefferson City in time to succor it.

General Fisk, for the prompt and cheerful discharge of very trying administrative duties, and for the energy and good sense in preparing the defence of Jefferson City, as in the subsequent repair of Lamine bridge.

General Brown displayed energy and good sense in preparing the city for a good defence; and General Sanborn, for vigilance, energy, and soldierly judgment, while commanding the cavalry advance between Jefferson City and Dunksbury, as well as throughout the campaign. Colonel J. V. Du Bois, A. D. C., chief of staff; Captain Henry, assistant quartermaster of General Steele's staff, volunteer quartermaster in the field; Captain G. Saull, chief commissary surgeon; P. V. Schenck, medical director in the field; Captain Hocke, acting aide-de-camp, engineer; Major Fisher, 5th Missouri State militia, on engineer duty; Captain J. F. Bennett, assistant adjutant general, and my personal aids, Major T. S. Bond, aide-de-camp, and Captain R. S. Thomas, aide-de-camp; Captain Hills, 12th Kansas, and provost marshal, accompanied me during the campaign, and were zealous and indefatigable in the discharge of their respective duties. Major McDermott, 1st Iowa cavalry, who, with his battalion of 1st Iowa cavalry, did such good service in northern Missouri, and behaved very gallantly in the pursuit of the rebels from Jefferson City to Booneville, commanded the escort from Sedalia, and deserves honorable mention. Brigadier General J. B. Gray, adjutant general of Missouri, and Brigadier General Pike, of the enrolled militia, are entitled to public thanks for their valuable and indefatigable service in connexion with the enrolled militia. Colonel E. J. Hains, commissary of subsistence, to whom all the armies as well as the country owe a debt of gratitude for invaluable services not likely to be overpaid, displayed his usual promptitude and foresight in providing for the wants of our troops and depots. Colonel William Myers, chief quartermaster, in supplying animals, fitting up trains, and providing for the wants of our troops, exhibited his characteristic care and skill.

I must also mention the voluntary services of those tried veterans, Colonel Waughim, of the 12th Missouri volunteer infantry, and Colonel Laibold, who did all in their power to aid in the defence of St. Louis. Senator B. Gratz Brown and Mayor Thomas, seconded by the efforts of many patriotic citizens of all classes, did much to prepare for the defence of the city, and deserve my thanks. I should be glad to call the general's attention to many military officers, such as General Craig, whose able management in the northwest in the absence of General Fisk; Colonel Gale, who so promptly organized his militia regiment (54th enrolled Missouri militia) at Franklin, and many others scattered over the State, who rendered great service to the country. But as the chief motive of these officers and the men of their commands was their country's good, the consciousness of duty manfully performed must be their chief reward until the day comes when our children, pointing to them as to others who have borne arms in this great national struggle, shall say "there go some of the men who helped to save our nation."

The accompanying reports show our total losses in this campaign were 174 killed, of whom 116 were wounded at Centralia; 336 wounded; 171 prisoners, of whom many, if not all, are illegally paroled; 601 hors-du-combat. Besides which, there were several small squads of prisoners illegally captured and paroled in southeast Missouri, and the troops at Glasgow, whose surrender was, I think, justifiable and possibly lawful.

W. S. ROSECRANS, *Major General.*

Lieut. Colonel CHRISTENSON, A. A. G.,
Military Division, West Mississippi, New Orleans, La.

MISCELLANEOUS.

OPERATIONS AGAINST CHARLESTON.

NAVY DEPARTMENT,
Washington, June 30, 1864.

SIR: At the request of Rear-Admiral John A. Dahlgren, I have the honor to forward the accompanying communication, dated the 20th instant, addressed by him to the chairman of the Committee on the Conduct of the War.

Very respectfully, &c.,

GIDEON WELLES,
Secretary of the Navy.

Hon. B. F. WADE,
Chairman of the Com. on Con. of the War, U. S. Senate.

UNITED STATES FLAG-SHIP PHILADELPHIA,
Charleston Roads, June 20, 1864.

SIR: I understand the committee to inquire whether there has been any failure in conducting operations off Charleston, To this I beg leave to reply, that in my opinion there has been no failure to accomplish all that the naval force present was capable of doing, and more, perhaps, than could properly have been expected of it.

Previous to the 10th of July, 1863, the blockade of the port was so imperfect that vessels entered and departed with so little risk that the export of cotton and import of supplies did not suffer any material interruption. I have been informed by persons who certainly have opportunities of knowing that the storehouses of the city were never more full of cotton than then. As a consequence, the rebel government and people depended chiefly on this trade for the great aid and comfort they received from foreign sympathies. Besides this, Morris island was in the hands of the rebels, and Fort Sumter continued to be a formidable fortress, which, in connexion with Moultrie, completely barred entrance to Charleston harbor.

Two attempts had been made to approach the city—one by the army, intended to operate across James island, beginning at Secessionville; the other by the navy, in a direct attack on Fort Sumter—about one year ago. Both of these failed entirely, and Charleston seemed to defy every effort on our part to disturb the prosperity that she enjoyed, and which was far greater than had ever been known under the compact of the Union. This was quickly reversed by the combined operations under General Gillmore and myself, which concluded in the capture of Morris island and the occupation of the roadstead, or main ship channel, leading into the harbor, while Sumter, though still sheltering a small rebel garrison, was reduced from its great power as a first class fortress to the condition of an outpost for Forts Johnson and Moultrie.

A perfect blockade was thus enforced, so that the illicit trade of the city was completely cut off, and the produce wrung from a degrading system of labor was compelled to find exit elsewhere. The prosperity of the city collapsed at once, and this nest of a wicked rebellion was thus made to experience some of the horrid evils which it has been so instrumental in spreading over this once happy land.

The following is a brief account of the operations of the navy and army in this quarter:

Morris island is a narrow outlying strip of sand beach about three and a half miles (statute) long and of irregular width, not exceeding three hundred or four hundred yards at the widest part, and in many places not half that.

This beach is completely insulated seaward by the main ship channel, and westward by an impassable morass, which extends landward some three thousand five hundred yards, and is there terminated by the firm land of James island. It is intersected by small streams and dotted with a few little spots of firm soil. The north end (Cummings's Point) forms the left angle of Charleston harbor in entering. From the ship channel the beach can be approached by the monitors to twelve hundred yards at low water, and at high water to one-third of that distance.

The site of Wagner is about three-fourths of a mile from the north end, stretches entirely across the island, and a battery of heavy guns occupied the extreme northern end. From Wagner to the southward the beach runs evenly for a mile and a half, when there arises a succession of sand-hills, upon which the rebels had placed cannon to command the approach from Folly island, and the narrow inlet that separated it from Morris island.

Nearly north from the north end of Morris island the heavy masonry of Sumter rises out of the water at the distance of about thirteen hundred yards.

I took command of the naval forces on the 6th of July at Port Royal, left there on the 8th, collected the scattered monitors, and on the 9th, before daylight, was off the bar of Charleston, ready to cross. The general asked for a day's postponement, and on the 10th of July, 1863, I began the attack on Morris island. The enemy were driven by the combined operation from their positions on the south end into Fort Wagner, which I cannonaded with the monitors from 9 a. m. till the evening. The next morning the general assaulted and was repulsed. Of this intention I was not informed previously, and therefore had no opportunity of assisting until all was over.

Some light batteries were thrown up, and in a week afterwards (18th July) an assault in force was made. The iron-clads battered Wagner almost out of shape, and on the afternoon of that day the flag-monitor (Montauk) lay only three hundred yards from the sea face of the work; not a gun was fired from it; not a head was visible to my glass as I stood with other officers outside watching the first symptom of renewed resistance. Our column came up, but it was too dark to discern objects from the vessels, and after a fierce and resolute effort the column fell back with a loss of fifteen hundred men.

This assault could derive no aid from the fire of our guns, because it was impossible to distinguish our troops from the enemy.

This compelled a resort to the regular approaches, and after incessant labor the rebels were finally forced to evacuate on the 7th of September.

The committee will perceive, by examining the annexed plan of the locality, that it would have been impossible for the troops to have landed on the island, or to have continued operations there, without the active assistance of the navy—the presence alone of the vessels would not suffice; the action of their cannon was required to restrain the rebels from advancing by counter approaches upon our lines, or from landing in force at the north end of the island, and marching in superior numbers upon our men, and driving them off the island.

This is evident from the very configuration of the island, and is also assumed by General Hunter as the reason for his not proceeding against Morris island, precisely as was done by General Gillmore and myself subsequently.

The letter of General Hunter is addressed to the President, and a copy of it is appended, from which it will be seen that he deemed the aid of the navy absolutely indispensable to the reduction of Morris island, and would not proceed without it.

The conviction then of General Hunter was, that he could do nothing at all on Morris island without the aid of the navy, even when the rebels were comparatively unprepared to what they were when the attack was made by General Gillmore and myself.

I will now cite the opinion of General Gillmore himself, who informed the authorities on the 20th of June that he "*could do nothing*," as the "admiral had no instructions, and did not feel at liberty to put his vessels into action," &c.

The committee will observe that the plan of General Hunter was virtually the same as that put into execution by General Gillmore.

The following will show how faithfully the aid of the vessels was rendered, being a brief exhibit of the occasions when they engaged the different rebel works:

Date, object engaged, vessels engaged.

July 10, 1863; Fort Wagner; iron-clads Kaatskill, (flag-ship,) Montauk Nahant, Weehawken.

July 11, 1863; Fort Wagner; iron-clads Kaatskill, (flag-ship,) Montauk, Nahant, Weehawken.

July 18, 1863; Fort Wagner, assault; iron-clads Montauk, (flag-ship,) Ironsides, Kaatskill, Nantucket, Weehawken, Patapsco; gunboats Paul Jones, Ottawa, Seneca, Wissahickon.

July 20, 1863; Fort Wagner; iron-clad Ironsides.

July 22, 1863; Fort Wagner; iron-clad Nantucket; gunboat Ottawa.

July 24, 1863; Fort Wagner, to cover advance of our shore batteries; iron-clads Weehawken, (flag-ship,) Ironsides, Kaatskill, Montauk, Patapsco, Nantucket; gunboats Paul Jones, Seneca, Ottawa, Dai Ching.

July 25, 1863; Fort Wagner; gunboats Ottawa, Dai Ching, Paul Jones.

July 28, 1863; Fort Wagner; iron-clads Weehawken, Kaatskill; gunboat Ottawa.

July 29, 1863; Fort Wagner; iron-clads Ironsides, Patapsco, Passaic.

July 30, 1863; Fort Wagner; iron-clads Ironsides, Kaatskill, Patapsco; gunboat Ottawa.

July 31, 1863; Fort Wagner and rebel batteries on Morris island; gunboat Ottawa.

August 1, 1863; Fort Wagner; iron-clads Montauk, Patapsco, Kaatskill, Weehawken, Passaic, Nahant; gunboat Marblehead.

August 2, 1863; Fort Wagner; gunboats Ottawa, Marblehead.

August 4, 1863; Fort Wagner; iron-clad Montauk; gunboat Marblehead.

August 6, 1863; Fort Wagner; gunboat Marblehead.

August 8, 1863; Fort Wagner; gunboats Ottawa, Marblehead, Mahaska.

August 11, 1863; Fort Wagner and vicinity; iron-clads Patapsco, Kaatskill.

August 13, 1863; Fort Wagner and rebel batteries on Morris island; gunboats Dai Ching, Ottawa, Mahaska, Wissahickon, Racer.

August 14, 1863; Fort Wagner and rebel batteries on Morris island; gunboats Wissahickon, Mahaska, Ottawa, Dai Ching; mortar boats Racer, Dan Smith.

August 15, 1863; Fort Wagner; mortar boats Racer and Dan Smith.

August 17, 1863; Fort Wagner and other rebel batteries on Morris island, in order to divert their fire from our shore batteries, which opened on Sumter; iron-clads Weehawken, (flag-ship,) Ironsides, Montauk, Nahant, Kaatskill, Passaic, Patapsco; gunboats Canandaigua, Mahaska, Ottawa, Cimarron, Wissahickon, Dai Ching, Lodona.

August 18, 1863; Fort Wagner; to prevent assault anticipated by General Gillmore; iron-clads Ironsides, Passaic, Weehawken; gunboats Wissahickon, Mahaska, Dai Ching, Ottawa, Lodona.

August 19, 1863; Fort Wagner; iron-clad Ironsides.

August 20, 1863; rebel batteries on Morris island; iron-clad Ironsides; gunboats Mahaska, Ottawa, Dai Ching, Lodona.

August 21, Forts Sumter and Wagner; iron-clads Ironsides, Patapsco; gunboats Mahaska, Dai Ching.

August 22, 1863; Fort Wagner; iron-clads Weehawken, Ironsides, Montauk.

August 23, 1863; Fort Sumper, (night attack;) iron-clads Ironsides, Weehawken, (flag-ship,) Montauk, Passaic, Patapsco, Nahant.

August 31, 1863; Fort Moultrie; iron-clads Passaic, Patapsco, Weehawken, Nahant.

September 1, 1863; Fort Sumter and obstructions in channel, (night attack;) iron-clads Weehawken, (flag-ship,) Montauk, Passaic, Patapsco, Nahant, Lehigh.

September 2, 1863; Gregg and Fort Sumter; iron-clad Ironsides.

September 5, 1863; between Sumter and battery Gregg; iron-clads Ironsides, Lehigh, Nahant.

September 6, 1863; Fort Wagner and battery Gregg; iron-clads Ironsides, Patapsco, Lehigh, Nahant, Montauk, Weehawken, Passaic.

September 7, 1863; Forts Moultrie and batteries on Sullivan's island, to cover the Weehawken, (ashore;) iron-clads Ironsides, (flag-ship,) Patapsco, Lehigh, Nahant, Montauk, Weehawken, (ashore.)

September 8, 1863; Fort Moultrie and batteries on Sullivan's island, to cover the Weehawken, (ashore;) iron-clads Ironsides, Patapsco, Lehigh, Nahant, Montauk, Weehawken, (ashore,) Passaic in a disabled condition.

The following telegrams from General Gillmore will inform the committee of the value that was attached to the power of the vessels:

Telegrams from General Gillmore.	*Replies from Rear-Admiral Dahlgren.*
JULY 30—8 a. m.	
The enemy firing musketry from Wagner, and interferes with my working. Can you not help me to subdue him?	I have just ordered a monitor and a gun-boat into action.
AUGUST 11—2.35 a. m.	
Please open as soon as possible; the enemy's fire is very heavy.	All right.
AUGUST 17.	
To save Sumter, the enemy may attempt a sortie in the morning. Can you get monitors in position as early as to-day?	A detachment of iron-clads will be in position at daybreak.
AUGUST 17.	
The enemy are mounting a heavy gun on the sea-face of Wagner.	I have sent two monitors up to keep them quiet in Wagner.
AUGUST 19.	
If you could replace them (Whitworth guns) with 8-inch guns, and 300 or 400 rounds of ammunition for each gun, it would help us greatly.	I will have them replaced immediately.

AUGUST 21.

My approaches to Wagner are suspended on account of the annoyance from the enemy's sharp-shooters. Can you not stop it?	I will try to do so.

AUGUST 21.

The fire from Wagner is very galling.	I am now going to move up with the monitors.

AUGUST 22.

Wagner has opened a heavy fire on our works. Unless the navy succeed in silencing them, there is great danger of their dismounting our guns.	I will send up two or three monitors at once.

AUGUST 22.

Colonel Turner telegraphs me from the front that, unless the navy opens speedily, two of our guns will certainly be dismounted.	Orders have been given, and the monitors are moving up.

AUGUST 23.

Can you let me have some 100-pounder Parrott shells? I am entirely out.	I can let you have 250 shell, and 100 shot; also, 100 Schenkl shells.

AUGUST 27.

Can I take another 8-inch gun and a 100-pounder Parrott from your vessels?	You can take the guns.

It will be perceived that, besides the assistance ordinarily given, it frequently happened that exigencies arose when the fire of the iron-clads was specially needed; and these at times were so pressing that the request was repeated before the iron-clads could get up their anchors and steam into position, and, by referring to the previous minutes of occasions when they were in action, it will be seen that they never failed to render what was asked.

Besides this assistance from the heavy guns of the batteries our men and boats with their light guns were often asked for and always accomplished their work satisfactorily.

At the crossing of Light-house inlet the column was conveyed in our boats, under Lieutenant Commander Bunce and Lieutenant Mackenzie, and covered by the navy howitzers.

A picket of launches was placed in the creek on the left flank of the works on Morris island, and the boats of the vessels were also frequently stationed at night on the sea-shore of the island to guard against the enterprise of the enemy.

I also landed some rifle cannon with seamen under Captain Parker, with which a battery was armed, and engaged with the other batteries in battering Sumter.

And yet efforts have been made to give the credit of the capture of Wagner and all the consequent results entirely to the general commanding the troops and to the engineering operations which he conducted on Morris island. Every mail from this locality teemed with glowing accounts of what was achieved by the army, while the co-operation of the navy received little notice and no credit, for which I need only refer you to the columns of some of the daily papers.

These partial notices finally took the forms of direct attacks on myself. It was affirmed that I was at variance with General Gillmore, thereby doing injury to pending operations, and this at the very time when those operations were proceeding most harmoniously and successfully. It was not only untrue that there had been any variance between General Gillmore from the first—and these infamous libellers knew it—but at last they went so far as to assert that General Gillmore intended to resign because of these difficulties; whereupon the general found it proper, of his own accord and without the first word from me upon the subject, to address me the following note:

"MORRIS ISLAND, S. C., *September* 23.

"ADMIRAL: I am much chagrined at the reports in the newspapers about my tendering my resignation in consequence of a disagreement between you and myself, and that we did not co-operate cordially. It is not necessary for me to assure you that I am entirely ignorant of the slightest foundation for such reports, and had no idea that they existed until they appeared in the papers. They were doubtless started by some scribbling sensationist in lieu of news. I will see that they are authoritatively contradicted.

"Sincerely yours,

"Q. A. GILLMORE.

"Rear-Admiral DAHLGREN."

I was utterly at a loss to comprehend the motion of these assaults for a long time, but have been somewhat enlightened on the subject lately.

It is with great reluctance that I now permit myself to notice them, for I felt that in a cause so great, and when the suffering country demanded every exertion from her sons, it illy became them to yield to their private griefs.

I came here prepared to give my best efforts to the flag I had served so long, and to make any sacrifice that was demanded of me; every moment of my time was given to the duties about me, and the smallest matter that could be useful was not too small for my personal attention. I could not understand that actual witnesses of what was going on could so degrade themselves by the scandal of misinterpreting and underrating my own exertions and everything that was done by the navy.

I have thus briefly, but I hope clearly, explained the nature and effect of the operations upon Morris island, and the full share which the navy had in its occupation, as well as the reduction of Fort Sumter to a heap of ruins.

The rebels had no alternative but to abandon Wagner and the smaller works north of it on the island, for if they had not it would have undoubtedly been taken by assault on the 7th of September, and the garrison would have been captured as well as the works.

But they would not evacuate what was left of Sumter, and, as the sequel proved, with good reason.

It was no longer what it had been, a first class work with a powerful armament, co-operating with Moultrie in forbidding passage to ships-of-war, and bearing with great effect on the interior anchorage; but it served as an outpost to Forts Johnson and Moultrie, and with a small garrison was capable of maintaining a fire of musketry and light artillery, which would prevent us from effectually removing the obstructions between Sumter and Moultrie, and interfere to a great degree with our scout boats in traversing the lower harbor.

Moreover, there was every reason to apprehend that by some exertion they would convert the ruins into a better defence than had been the solid walls, and even succeed in establishing cannon on the fronts inaccessible to our batteries.

If, on the contrary, the rebels were driven out they would be deprived of these advantages, and we would have access to the lower harbor on terms nearly as good as they had.

Subsequent experience has shown that I did not overestimate the importance of mastering this spot, and impressed with the advantages that seemed so plain to me, I decided to assault it while the confusion and depression caused by the loss of Morris island were still in full force.

I fully appreciated the difficulties that were to be expected in making the assault, but believed that the great advantages in view fully justified the undertaking.

Great care was taken in organizing the column of attack; there were no better men at hand, and they were led by officers whose standing fully justified their selection. A strong detachment of marines formed part of the column, in all about four hundred and fifty men, while the force of the rebel garrison was afterwards learned to be two hundred and fifty to three hundred men.

The rebels evacuated Wagner on the nights of the 6th and 7th of September, and the assault on Sumter was made about an hour after midnight of the 8th and 9th of September.

It failed, and the causes will never be well understood, as few who participated could see far in the darkness of the night.

It seems that General Gillmore had intended to make the same attempt on the same night.

Of this I knew nothing until late in the day, when I became acquainted with it on sending to borrow some of his boats. A proposal to co-operate was at once acceded to by me; but on account of the difficulty of communicating promptly and correctly by signal I sent Lieutenant Preston ashore, (the acting fleet-captain,) who returned and reported that all was arranged satisfactorily, so we proceeded. It was now past midnight; the navy column with the greatest celerity pushed straight for the work, supposing that the military column would join, and in the darkness never paused to see whether it did so or not, but resolutely went to its task. After a brief conflict the fire of the enemy was found to be too heavy, and our men fell back.

I learned afterwards that the army boats had not been able to get out of the creek in time.

The committee will perceive that the failure to co-operate was just such an occurrence as frequently mars combined operations.

I was so intent on acting together, that while waiting for Lieutenant Preston I wrote an order recalling my boats, in case he returned without being able to effect an arrangement. It was, of course, *not sent* when Lieutenant Preston reported that the co-operation was satisfactorily adjusted. And I went myself up the channel in order to insure personally the desired connexion of my column with General Gillmore's. The attack began, however, when I was within a few hundred yards of Sumter, and ended very quickly.

It should not escape notice that the intention of the general coincided exactly with my own plans, in time of attack, number of men, and belief in the practicability of the breach; so that if my judgment was at fault, General Gillmore shared the error, and I may venture to believe that our concurrent opinion was more reliable at the time than that of other parties present or absent, who could not have had the same opportunities for opinion.

Of course, judgments formed after an event have facts to proceed upon which are wanting previously.

I am by no means sure that a greater force would have improved the chances of success, while our losses would have been greater.

Had this attempt succeeded, it would have materially changed the aspect of affairs in conducting future operations.

As it was, I believe now, as I did then, that the possession of the remains of the work was all-important, and my only regret is that my attempt failed to obtain it.

As it was, Sumter remained with the rebels. General Gillmore opened the batteries from Wagner and Gregg, as soon as he had completed them late in October, and I also sent two monitors with rifles.

Together, the walls of the fort were again battered until the gorge and sea-face were one heap of ruins.

The monitors made excellent work, and cut through the nearest and furthest walls.

No attempt was made to assault it by the army, though a large force was sent one evening to feel the state of its defence.

So that if my assault failed, nothing else has succeeded to this day, for the rebel garrison still occupies Sumter.

I should have premised this account of the effort to capture Sumter, by saying that accident had also contributed to disappoint me in another respect. I had ordered the Weehawken (monitor) to take position in the only channel rearward of Sumter, where she could float; in doing so, she grounded where the batteries of Moultrie had full sweep, and I not only lost her service in covering the assault, but was obliged to order up other iron-clads to prevent her being disabled, which brought on a severe conflict, that bore with considerable severity on the vessels, and was hoped at the time had caused at least equal inconvenience to the rebels. The Ironsides hauled off with little ammunition left, and her associates were roughly handled.

I learned afterwards from a deserter, who was in battery B, that not a gun or man was hurt there, and the parapet was only pierced in a few places.

Four guns of eighteen were dismounted in Moultrie, and the only serious casualty was produced by a 15-inch shell, from the Weehawken, which landed in a large pile of loaded shells; by its explosion some twenty men were killed, and the same number wounded. So that, for all effective purposes, our fire had not impaired these works.

I now proceed to explain why the operations have been delayed in reaching Charleston itself:

1st. The landing on Morris island was a complete surprise, and its result was to afford us foothold from which we could gain possession of the entire island and the main ship channel, besides reducing the great power of Sumter as a fortress.

Had there been sufficient force, we could have overpowered Wagner by assault, and entered the harbor before the rebels were able to complete the interior defences or recover from their panic.

But there was supposed to be no greater land force than sufficed to overcome Wagner by the slow process of engineering, and the rebels contrived to keep us out of possession for nearly two months, during which time no exertion was spared to extend and perfect the works that defended the interior harbor.

The incessant battering to which the monitors had been exposed while bearing their part in reducing Wagner and Sumter, required considerable repair in order to fit them to endure the fire of works far more formidable than Wagner.

And the scanty resources of the improvised workshops at Port Royal did not permit this being effected with the promptness that would have been very easy at New York or other cities with large establishments. Material must be brought from a distance, and machinery and tools, and the workmen, who could hardly be obtained here in great numbers when they were scarce at the north at any prices.

Moreover, if they had been, all of the monitors could not have been removed from Charleston and put under repair at the same time, because a certain number was absolutely indispensable at Charleston to prevent the rebel iron-clads from coming out.

The bottoms of the monitors had also become so foul that the speed was reduced to three or four knots—a very material consideration in battle.

And besides the repair, there were certain additional pieces to be put on to strengthen the construction, which work I found in progress when I took the command, and necessarily caused to be discontinued in order to commence operations.

2d. I was in expectation of additional monitors about the 1st of October; these were postponed from month to month by the failure of the contractors, and have never reached me to this date, for, when they were finally completed, about the middle of April, they were needed in the James river, where they now are.

3d. It was not until late in October that Wagner and Gregg had been turned upon the rebels and armed, so that their assisting fire was not available before that period.

It was, therefore, impossible to have moved with seven battered monitors upon the strong works which lined the approach to the city, without certain hazard to all that had been gained, and without any certainty of positive advantage.

At the instance of the Navy Department, I convened a council of the iron-clad captains—officers well experienced in the offensive power of their vessels and the defences of the rebels; they were as follows:

Commodore S. C. Rowan, commanding Ironsides; Captain G. F. Emmons, fleet-captain; Commander Daniel Ammen, special staff duty and formerly in command of the Patapsco (monitor) during attack on Sumter, April 7, 1863.

Commander T. H. Stevens, commanding Patapsco; Commander A. Bryson, commanding Lehigh; Commander E. R. Colhoun, commanding Weehawken; Lieutenant Commander E. Simpson, commanding Passaic; Lieutenant Commander J. L. Davis, commanding Montauk; Lieutenant Commander G. Cilley, commanding Kaatskill; Lieutenant Commander J. J. Cornwell, commanding Nahant.

A full and unrestrained discussion took place, and the following propositions were voted on as follows:

Would there be "extreme risk incurred without adequate results" by entering the harbor of Charleston with the seven monitors, the object being to penetrate to Charleston?

Ayes six. Noes four.

Should the Ironsides enter with the monitors?

Ayes four. Noes four. Doubtful two.

If the present force were not sufficient to enter the harbor, would it be advisable to co-operate with the army in an attack on Sullivan's island?

Ayes nine. Noes one.

Can Forts Moultrie and Johnson be reduced by the present force of iron-clads, unsupported by the army?

Unanimously, no.

It will be understood, of course, that in thus speaking and deciding the monitors were pre-supposed to be in good fighting order. This, however, was not the case at the time, nor soon afterwards.

My own opinions were not stated to the council, and I took no further part in the deliberations than to state the question and regulate the order of business.

In viewing the question of further operations, it was to be premised that the co-operation of the army was at an end, and that whatever was to be done in attacking the interior defences was to be the work of the navy alone.

A view of the harbor showed what this was to be. On the right lay Sullivan's island, with a continuous line of batteries from Bee, at the inner end, to Moultrie. Somewhat further on, and to the left, Fort Johnson, a strong earthwork with eight or nine 8-inch and 10-inch smooth and rifled cannon, supported seaward by Battery Simkins, and to the rear by Battery Cheves. Beyond Johnson, some fifteen hundred yards, was Wampler, with two 10-inch guns;

then Glover and another earth-work—force not known. Nearly opposite Johnson was Fort Ripley, with two or three heavy guns.

These past, we confront the city batteries; Ramsay, at the lower angle of the city, with seven heavy cannon; above it, on the Ashley, at Chisholm's Mills is Battery Waring, with two heavy guns ; and opposite, the battery defending the entrance of Nappoo.

Ascending the Cooper river, on a wharf not far from White Point, is the English 13-inch 700-pounder; at the foot of Lawrence street is another battery; and further on, lying somewhat back, is the half-moon battery. Castle Pinckney enters into the system, but has no material strength.

Other batteries at Habbrell's Point, Mount Pleasant, &c., are on the right shore of the harbor, but would not be important in this connexion, though their guns are heavy.

There were also three iron-clads similar to the Atlanta, one of which (the Charleston) was new, and reported to be a better vessel.

The torpedo defences cannot be accurately estimated, but the best information left no doubt that they were largely relied on by the rebels as an important offensive element.

Under these circumstances, what could possibly result from the entrance of iron-clads alone? At the best they could only drive the rebels from the earthworks and silence their fire for the time; but they could not expect to destroy any one of the batteries. Day after day tons of shell had been expended on Wagner, and Sumter, and Moultrie, and yet cannon alone, whether in the vessels or in the trenches, had failed to give us possession of either; they were effective only to give the opportunity which the troops were to secure. If this was the case with Wagner, what must be expected of Johnson and its contiguous batteries, to which Wagner was insignificant?

We know now that on the 8th of September the incessant fire of the "ironsides" and five monitors for three hours had not hurt a man in Battery Bee, and only dismounted four guns of eighteen in Moultrie; some forty men being killed and wounded in the latter by a shell from the Weekawken plunging into a pile of loaded shells, inflicting more injury on the garrison than the direct fire of all the other vessels.

This established fact, together with what was witnessed daily at Wagner, gave no encouragement that the seven monitors could produce any permanent effect on the interior batteries, unless there were troops acting concurrently to take advantage of the effect produced by their guns; and upon this proposition the council was unanimous.

The iron-clads might steam in and make a promenade of the harbor, suffering much damage, and inflicting little, then retire. To remain in, would only be a useless expenditure of valuable vessels, which could not soon be replaced.

Some thought that if the iron-clads could occupy a position near the city, it would compel the rebels to abandon their exterior defences lying seaward. An inspection of the locality would show that this could not possibly apply to James island or Sullivan's island; and if not to them, to what?

The truth is, that the entrance of the iron-clads could only make sure of the destruction of the city, and not this without undue risk, if there were only seven monitors.

The act itself could not be objected to by the rebels, for it was understood to be their intent to destroy the place themselves rather than we should occupy it; if so, it was quite as logical that we should destroy it rather than they should occupy it.

At all events, upon the proposition to enter and penetrate to the city, the vote in council of war stood six to four, and with the majority voted all the senior officers, including my next in command, Commodore Rowan.

At one time General Gillmore agreed, if he could be re-enforced, to co-operate against James island, but he told me that additional troops were refused, and there it ended.

And thus the winter passed away, in close blockade, and in restoring the monitors to good fighting condition.

I was called to Washington upon the business of my command, and when I returned found the seven monitors at disposal.

It was the first time since taking command in July, 1863, that all the iron-clads of the squadron were in good fighting order.

It was reported that the rebels had been active improving the defences of Sumter, and mounting some heavy guns on the channel front.

It occurred to me as a fitting opportunity to bring into action the iron-clad squadron.

And I summitted the question to a council of the iron-clad captains as follows:

Commodore S. C. Rowan, commanding Ironsides; Captain J. F. Green, to command the monitor Nahant; Commander G. H. Cooper, commanding Sangamon; Commander N. B. Harrison, commanding Kaatskill; Lieutenant Commander E. Simpson, commanding Passaic; Lieutenant Commander J. M. Bradford, fleet captain; Lieutenant Commander William Gibson, commanding Lehigh; Lieutenant Commander S. B. Luce, commanding Nantucket; Lieutenant Commander J. L. Davis, commanding Montauk.

After a full discussion, it was decided by a vote of seven to two that it was not advisable "with the present force of iron-clads, viz: seven monitors and the ironsides, to attempt the reduction of the offensive and defensive powers of Sumter, as now existing, having due regard to the general interests in this quarter intrusted to this squadron; to the consequences that would ensue in the event of a serious disaster to the iron-clads, and to the views of the Navy Department, set forth in communications dated October 9 and November 2, 1863."

Among the majority were the senior officers—Commodore Rowan, Captain Green, Commanders Cooper and Harrison.

The committee will perceive, therefore, that in refraining from entering the harbor of Charleston, with a view to interior operations with such force as I could command, I was supported by the opinions of the ablest naval officers about me.

At the same time, if the judgment of those who can give the order inclines to a different view, it is only necessary to give me that order, and it shall be obeyed to the fullest extent, for nothing will so well accord with my feelings.

I have now laid before the committee the principal points that present themselves to my mind at this time, not by any means as I would wish to do, but as well as the demands of public service permit.

It may seem to the committee that sufficient time has elapsed since my statement was required to have expressed myself to the fullest extent; but since that, the affliction of losing my gallant son, Colonel Ulric Dahlgren, and the never-ceasing cares of a command like this, have not allowed me that opportunity for correcting misapprehensions which I might have properly desired.

I have the honor to be, very respectfully, your obedient servant,

JOHN A. DAHLGREN,

Rear-Admiral, Commanding Naval Forces off the coasts of South Carolina and Georgia.

Copy of a letter from Major General Hunter to his excellency the President of the United States.

DEAR SIR: It is more than six weeks since the attack by the iron-clads upon Charleston—an attack in which, from the nature of the plans of Admiral DuPont, the army had no active part.

On the day of that attack the troops under my command held Folly island up to Light-house inlet. On the morning after the attack we were in complete readiness to cross Light-house inlet to Morris island, where, once established, the fall of Sumter would have been as certain as the demonstration of a problem in mathematics. Aided by a cross-fire by the navy, the enemy would soon have been driven from Cummings's Point, and, with powerful batteries of one and two hundred-pounder rifled guns placed there, Fort Sumter would have been rendered untenable in two days' fire. Fort Pulaski was breached and taken from Goat's Point, on Tybee island—a precisely similar position—with 32-pounder Parrott guns, 42-pounder James guns, and a few 10-inch columbiads, the 13-inch mortars used in that bombardment having proved utterly valueless. I mention these things to show how certain would have been the fall of Sumter under the fire of the one and two hundred-pounders rifled now at my command.

On the afternoon after the iron-clad attack on Fort Sumter the troops on Folly island were not only ready to cross Light-house inlet, but were almost in the act, the final reconnoissance having been made, the boats ready, and the men under arms for crossing, when they were recalled, as I hoped, merely temporarily, by the announcement of Admiral DuPont that he had resolved to retire, and that consequently we could expect no assistance from the navy.

Immediately the admiral was waited upon by an officer of my staff, who represented the forwardness of our preparation for crossing, the evidently unprepared condition of the enemy to receive us, while any delay, now that our intentions were unmasked, would give the enemy time to erect upon the southern end of Morris island, commanding Light-house inlet, those works and batteries which he had heretofore neglected. To these considerations, earnestly and elaborately urged, the admiral's answer was, that "he would not fire another shot." A lodgement on Morris island was thus made impossible for us, the enemy having powerful works on the island, more especially at the northern end, out of which we could not hope to drive him unless aided by a cross-fire from the navy. I therefore determined to hold what we had got until the admiral should have had time to repair his vessels; and to this hour we hold every inch of ground on Folly and Cole's, and Seabrook's island that we held on the day of the expected crossing.

Since then I have exercised patience with the admiral, and have pushed forward my work and batteries on Folly island with unremitting diligence, the enemy, meanwhile, thoroughly aroused to their danger, throwing up works that completely command Light-house inlet, on the southern side of Morris island, so that the crossing, which could have been effected in a couple of hours and with little sacrifice six weeks ago, will now involve, whenever attempted, protracted operations and a very serious loss of life. And to what end should this sacrifice be made without the co-operation of the navy? Even when established on the southern end of Morris island, the northern end, with its powerful works, and commanded by the fire of Forts Sumter and Johnson, would still remain to be possessed. The sacrifice would be of no avail without the aid of the navy; and I have been painfully but fully convinced that from the navy no such aid is to be expected. I fear Admiral DuPont distrusts the iron-clads so much that he has resolved to do nothing with them this summer, and, therefore, I most urgently beg of you to liberate me from those orders to co-operate with the navy, which now tie me down to share the admiral's inactivity. Remaining in our present situation, we do not even detain one soldier of the enemy from service elsewhere. I am well satisfied that they have already sent away from Charleston and Savannah all the troops not absolutely needed to garrison the defences, and those will have to remain in the work whether the enemy be in sight or not.

Liberate me from this order to "co-operate with the navy in an attack on Charleston," and I will immediately place a column of ten thousand of the best drilled soldiers in the country (as unquestionably are the troops of this department) in the heart of Georgia; our landing and march being made through counties in which, as shown by the census, the slave population is seventy-five per cent. of the inhabitants.

Nothing is truer, sir, than that this rebellion has left the southern States a mere hollow shell. If we avoid their few strongholds, where they are prepared for and invite us to battle, we shall meet no opposition in a total devastation of their resources, thus compelling them to break up their large armies and garrisons at a few points, into scores of small fractions of armies for the protection of every threatened and assailable point. I will guarantee, with the troops now fruitlessly, though laboriously, occupying Folly and Seabrook islands, and such other troops as can be spared from the remaining posts of this department, to penetrate into Georgia, produce a practical dissolution of the slave system there, destroy all railroad communication along the eastern portion of the State, and lay waste all stores which can possibly be used for the sustenance of the rebellion. My troops are in splendid health and discipline, and, in my judgment, are more thoroughly in sympathy with the policy of the government than any other equal body of men in the service of the United States to-day.

* * * * * * * *

I have the honor to be, very respectfully, your obedient servant,

D. HUNTER,
Major General Commanding.

OPERATIONS IN DEPARTMENT OF THE GULF.

Testimony of Major General N. J. T. Dana.

FRIDAY, *April* 22, 1864.

Major General N. J. T. DANA sworn and examined.

By Mr. Chandler:

Question. What is your rank and position in the army at this time?

Answer. Major general of volunteers, since the 29th of November, 1862. I am not at the present moment on duty. I have just been relieved from duty in the department of the Gulf, at my own request, by order of the major general commanding the department there.

Question. How long were you connected with the department of the Gulf?

Answer. I arrived at New Orleans and reported for duty there about the middle of September last, and I have been continuously on duty there since that time until I left New Orleans on the 9th of April, the present month.

Question. During that time where were you operating?

Answer. Immediately on reporting for duty I was assigned to duty in the 13th corps, and reported to Major General Ord, then commanding the corps. By him I was ordered to Morganzia, on the Mississippi river, to relieve General Herron, who was in command of the detachment of the 13th corps there. I relieved him, if my memory serves me aright, on the 27th day of September, in the afternoon.

Question. Will you give, in your own way, a narrative of such events as came under your observation and knowledge during your connexion with that department, such as may be important to the matters before this committee?

Answer. That will be a narrative of the history principally of current events, that might be made very extended and be of very little interest.

Question. Make it as brief as possible, giving important events, not going minutely into them, but such as may be of importance, and as brief as may be.

Answer. At the time that I relieved General Herron, the 2d division of the 13th army corps was supposed to be there. I relieved him, as I said, on the 27th of September in the afternoon. I was informed by him that he had two regiments of infantry and a section of artillery in his advance, eight miles in front of Morganzia. The reason assigned for having them at this distance was that there was no water between Morganzia and the point on Bayou Fardoche where this detachment lay. This point was pretty nearly half the distance to the Atchafalaya river by the direct road. On the other side of the Atchafalaya river lay the rebel Greene, a brigadier general in the confederate service, with his force, supposed to be very much superior to that which was at Morganzia. With the detatchment in front, General Herron stated to me that he had a small body of cavalry, a little over one hundred men I think; that this cavalry kept a daily reconnoissance to the Atchafalaya, and that Greene had not the means of crossing the Atchafalaya in force; that he was convinced that he could not cross it, and had no intention of crossing it; but if he crossed it the cavalry would give immediate notice of it.

General Herron left in the evening, and in the morning I sent out orders to this detachment and an officer to inspect its position. He never found the detachment and I never saw it. The messenger whom I sent out found the enemy between Morganzia and the detachment in force, as he stated. I immediately sent a regiment out to clear the road, supposing that some of their scouts had gotten between Morganzia and the detachment. The whole detachment was captured, with the exception of those who escaped, after being broken up by three brigades of the enemy's troops under Greene.

Question. Do you mean that the two regiments of infantry and the artillery were destroyed?

Answer. Most of the infantry and the artillery were captured. The cavalry escaped. They fought out until they were cut into little squads of four or five and took to the swamps. I reported this state of things immediately, and I found that my command there was only about 1,600 men, in most wretched condition, without a tent or shelter of any kind to cover them, ragged and dirty, lying in the mud and exposed to the rain on the river bank, without any purpose apparently in view; and what the end intended to be accomplished by sending this detachment there and leaving it on the river bank was, I was not informed. I made report immediately of its condition and the small force. I ascertained immediately afterward that General Ord was greatly surprised at the weakness of the detachment. It was not the division in fact, although it was in name. Nearly half the division, if not quite half, was left at Carrollton, near New Orleans. The force with which Greene crossed the Atchafalaya and gobbled up this advance party was acertained from the prisoners who were captured by me to be about 4,000, between 3,500 and 4,000. It was three brigades and a battery of six pieces. They attacked them on all sides simultaneously, and the five hundred men who were captured are still prisoners in Texas, two of the finest regiments we had.

I may state that nothing was ever explained to me of the plans which were had in view by the commander-in-chief at that time. He himself, with his staff and with his main column, composed of the greater part of the 13th corps and the 19th corps, were at that time on a second campaign up the Téche. From the conversation which I heard between General Ord and General Banks at the time that I received orders to go up to Morganzia, I gathered that it was the intention of the commander-in-chief to move this stong column up to Alexandria, and that the way having been cleared in my front by driving Greene away from the Atchafalaya, I was at some future time to join with my small body of troops this main column; and meanwhile I was forbidden to carry any supplies to these men, to bring up any re-enforcements of the stragglers and the troops that were left behind at Carrollton, or even to carry up the knapsacks of the men who were ragged and in such a filthy condition. They had gone up to Morganzia and left everything they had at Carrollton. They were comfortless and in a wretched condition. I disregarded the instructions received so far as to carry the men's knapsacks up to them when I went up myself, and it added no little to their comfort. The men were reported by their officers to be lousy from having no change of clothes. They were told they were to go up there for two or three days, and they were there I should think a month.

Soon after the affair of the Bayou Fardoche, probably two weeks after, General Banks being then upon the Téche with his column operating, I received a despatch sent to me by telegraph to Port Hudson, and from there by a special steamer, to report at headquarters for instructions. I went immediately to New Orleans. General Banks was not there. I had received intimations that the instructions I was to receive would be of a delicate nature; and I therefore doubted the propriety of my going down into the field to find General Banks, as inferences might be drawn from that. I then put myself in communication with the chief quartermaster of the department of the Gulf, Colonel Holabird, whom I supposed to be in General Banks's intimate confidence. I told him that I had come down to report, as soon as I saw him, and he said, "I know all about it." I found that he knew all the instructions that I was to receive, and I believe now that he was the only one that knew anything about it. He told me that General Banks did not want me to go down to the Téche, but wanted me to wait there, and had given him details of all his plans, and what he wanted me to do. I put myself in communication with General Banks, and received direct from him, through Colonel Holabird, a telegram saying that he had explained everything to Colonel Holabird, who would explain matters to me, and I received from Colonel Holabird information that I was desired not to telegraph or write to General Banks on the subject, as the telegrams and despatches might be examined by persons whom he did not care to be initiated into the plans. The orders were for me to prepare an expedition to the Texas coast. The force that I had I was ordered to bring immediately down from Morganzia, and rejoin the balance of it which was lying in camp at Carrollton, to organize it and put it in complete condition for the field, with such other forces as should report to me, and to prepare for embarcation. With the assistance of Colonel Holabird, the whole thing was carried out as near to perfection as it could be. I obtained from General Banks a *carte blanche* for drawing supplies from the different administrative members of his staff, who were directed to furnish my requisitions without question and without delay. I prepared a large fleet of steam transports, and on the 26th day of October embarked with them and about six thousand men for Brazos Santiago.

I had no communication with General Banks during all the time that I was preparing the expedition, although he was in New Orleans, except to ask him for instructions, and he told me that they were already prepared, and I would receive them before I embarked. All the communication that had been made to me up to this time was verbally by Colonel Holabird. Colonel Holabird informed me that our expenditures down on the Rio Grande would have to be entirely coin, probably; that he had sent a quartermaster to Washington to procure $100,000 in coin, from the Treasury Department. This was procured, as I heard the quartermaster state who came for the money. He said it was with great effort it was obtained, and with some opposition. I carried down arms and equipments to arm and equip a thousand infantry and a thousand cavalry, I think, in case I could raise them on the Rio Grande or in Texas, and was promised all I should call for afterwards; thirty-days' rations for my whole force, over and above the ten days, which I distributed to the command when we sailed; forage for thirty days over and above the ten days distributed to the command when we sailed. It is not necessary to go into the details. The general result I suppose is what you want.

The day before I sailed, being on board the flag-ship myself, at the wharf in New Orleans, the rest of the fleet having been despatched to its anchorage at the head of the pass of the Mississippi, I was awaiting orders, having not even then received my instructions. General Banks then sent a staff officer down on board the vessel to say that he would like half of the state-rooms reserved for himself and his staff. This was the first intimation I had of General Banks going to Texas. I expressed some surprise to Colonel Holabird about it. I asked him if he knew all the time that the general was going. I understood him he did not; that he did not think the general intended to go until the day before. He said the general wished me to conduct the affair just exactly as if he were not there; that I would be in command, and that I would give all the orders that were necessary, and he did not expect to interfere at all. I con-considered this very complimentary, and was very willing to do all the work I could do, but as to being the commanding officer when there was a superior officer present, I knew enough about soldiering to know what that meant.

A landing was made at Brazos Santiago, in Texas, and the command was pushed forward to Brownsville, some twenty-six miles up the Rio Grande, opposite Matamoras.

I ought to mention that I had not then received any instructions. On the way down, on board the flag-ship, Colonel Holabird mentioned to me something about his instructions. I then asked him if he had got them. He said he had; he had received them that day; he had them in his pocket, and he had also seen mine, and asked me if I had got mine, and appeared surprised that I had not. He said he had read them himself, and that the general had probably forgotten to hand them to me, and that I would get them within a day or so if I did not that day. I read his instructions, which he handed me to read, and I never heard anything more about mine.

A few days after we arrived at Brownsville General Banks and his staff left. He ordered me to send certain troops from Brownsville to Point Isabel for embarcation, and he left for Aranzas Pass, carrying with him four regiments of white troops, infantry, and four pieces of light artillery, and two siege guns without troops attached to them, that I heard of. A landing was made on Mustang island. The fort belonging to the rebels, which was on it, surrendered to our troops under Brigadier General Ransom, who made his report to me, without any loss, I believe, on either side.

General Banks had told me that it was his purpose to collect all of the corps which I then commanded, General Ord having gone to the north sick—all of the 13th corps in Texas; that he expected to be able to take possession of Pass Cavallo and Fort Esperanza, and that the main portion of the troops would be collected in that part of Texas, and that we should march into the interior of Texas from Indianola, or that vicinity. It was his purpose to establish himself at Indianola or Powder Horn; he made use of the latter name, I believe, and it was from there he would issue his address to the people of Texas.

The day after the surrender of the fort on Mustang island Brigadier General Ransom, with his troops, crossed over to St. Joseph's island, on the northern side of Aranzas Pass. He was joined by other troops belonging to the 13th corps, which were being then transported from Louisiana down to Texas, and two brigades, commanded by General Ransom and Colonel Washburne, moved up St. Joseph's island across Cedar bayou to Matagorda island, marched up the whole length of that island, and invested Fort Esperanza, which was evacuated in the night time, its magazines blown up by the enemy, and they retreated into the interior by crossing the bayous between the island and the mainland, over such ferries as they had constructed there.

During all this time I had been left on the Rio Grande, at Brownsville, without any specific instructions. When General Banks left he told me it was well if I could prepare an expedition to go up as high as Roma, one hundred and twenty miles up the Rio Grande, above Brownsville. There were three high-pressure steamboats on the Rio Grande, belonging to notorious rebels who had put them under the Mexican government, and by some arrangement between General Banks and the American consulate in Matamoras these boats were put into the possession of General Banks. The matter never was explained to me as to what promises had been made about them. I knew enough to know that the way in which General Banks had become possessed of them bound him in honor to make a fair settlement for them, whosoever's property they were. I received a private letter, the only one I received from Colonel Holabird after he went to New Orleans, in which he stated that some arrangement ought immediately to be entered into about those boats, and that they ought to be immediately purchased. The best of them had been carried up the coast by General Banks, and was up at Matagorda bay. The other two were river craft, and of no service outside the Rio Grande, and very little service in it at that time, we having no use for them.

In a communication which I made to General Banks or to his headquarters, I think it was personally to him, I stated the matter of these steamboats, and, if I remember aright, I urged that some settlement should immediately be made about them. I feared that some grand bills would be run up against the government for the daily service of steamboats which were not used at all, or used but very little at that time. They were afterwards used a great deal. I had an interview with the agent of the owners of the boats, the same man who was afterwards imprisoned on the question of a forced loan in Matamoras, and who required the interference of the authorities to get him out, Mr. Galvan, and he stated to me that these three boats were worth $100,000 in coin—that would make them, at the price of gold at that time, somewhere near $155,000. I jeered him a little about the even sum that had occurred to him, and told him that, though I did not suppose he was in earnest about insisting on that particular amount, still I had no doubt that there would be a fair settlement of some kind made with him, and I wrote to General Banks—I think to him personally, at all events to his headquarters—suggesting that some settlement should be made for these boats, and that the only fair settlement that could be made in justice to the government was that three steamboat men should be sent down from New Orleans, who would be conversant with making estimates of the value of boats, and that they should agree on the real value of these boats at the time they were put into our hands, and that that should be paid for them, and interest at six per cent. on that sum from the time that we had them until the time of settlement. I do not know what has been done about those boats. I am told that $100,000 in specie has been paid for them and their services.

By Mr. Odell:

Question. Do they now belong to the government?

Answer. I understand that they do. They are in our possession, and they can never go out of it, I suppose. I have heard that they have been settled for. I left there before the settlement was made, and therefore I do not know anything about it. At the time General Banks and his staff were about to leave Brownsville, I was about being left there without any funds. We had taken possession of about 130 or 140 bales of cotton there. I had thirty days' supplies, less a certain amount which General Banks would be obliged to take away up to Aranzas. I supposed that supplies would constantly follow us, and immediately. I had never had a doubt about it up to that time. Still I was ordered to purchase horses in Mexico to mount such recruits as we should raise down there, and also to remount such dismounted cavalry as I had, and for all sorts of uses, transportation, &c.; and Colonel Holabird appointed an agent down there, who showed me subsequently his authority from the colonel for acting as an agent in the purchase of horses. He was to receive a daily compensation by that agreement. I mention this merely to show that funds would be necessary. If the simple assertion that an army in the field does not require funds to subsist upon is not enough, that order to purchase horses will show that there was a necessity to have a sum of money. I requested an order from General Banks to have funds turned over to my chief quartermaster who was to be left there, and to the commissary. General Banks issued an order directing his chief quartermaster to furnish such funds to the chief quartermaster left with the forces on the Rio Grande as were required. He left with him $12,500 in gold, and a few thousand dollars in greenbacks; not so much as that, but I forget the amount; I think about $5,000. I was ordered to send all the cotton that I collected in Texas direct to New Orleans, and the chief quartermaster, Colonel Holabird, was ordered to sell it. Subsequently I was obliged to sell cotton there or starve to death. My action in that matter was sanctioned, and I was ordered to send what I did not require for the use of the troops to New Orleans. I succeeded in getting some 1,200 or 1,400 bales of cotton. The first 400 bales, or a little over that, I shipped direct to New Orleans; but there never was, from the time that I was left there until more than two months afterwards, when I was ordered up the coast of Texas, any supply of forage sent from New Orleans to the Rio Grande, except when animals were sent; the rations of those animals were put on board ship with them. Our rations ran short with the men, so that I was compelled to buy in the Matamoras market. I was compelled to buy corn in the country, on the Mexican side, and from merchants in Matamoras, and cargoes of it at the mouth of the river, at anchor, entered at the Mexican custom-house, and this corn cost from $2 to $3 a bushel in coin. I clamored considerably for money, knowing that $100,000 in coin had been sent down for the use of that force from Washington; and not getting the money, either paper or gold, I thought it was rather imprudent in me to get rid of all my cotton too, and I sold all the cotton except the first lot shipped. I think about 200 bales of cotton were released to Union men who owned it. About 200 bales were left undisposed of at the time I left Brownsville and turned the command over to General Herron. The rest of the cotton was sold for the highest price it would bring at Matamoras, from thirty-one to thirty-three cents a pound in gold, and the funds were turned over to the quartermaster's department, the commissary department, and the medical department, and expended for the subsistence of that force.

Question. How did you sell it?

Answer. Anybody that would offer the most for it got it. There was no plan about it. We only sold it as we required the money. The balance of it I intended to ship to New Orleans if they ever sent us any supplies. There was no margin on cotton there. Speculators frequently came from New Orleans expecting that they could buy cotton there the same as they did on the Mississippi river, at from ten to fifteen cents a pound in greenbacks; but there was a competition in Matamoras that kept it up at from thirty-one to thirty-three cents in gold all the time; and then their expenses were heavy to put it on board vessels at the mouth of the Rio Grande, which could only be done occasionally in a calm sea. It had to be carried out five miles from shore over a bad bar by steam lighters, and loaded on to a vessel that lay at the mouth, and then carried to its destination. I never could see that there was any margin for speculation in buying cotton down there at thirty-three cents a pound in gold. But we were paying enormous amounts for the grain we were using. We were paying there $2 a bushel for corn in gold, which made it $3 a bushel all the time.

Question. Was that the result of combination or scarcity?

Answer. Scarcity. It was all imported into Mexico; none raised there.

Question. Who were the purchasers of the cotton?

Answer. Merchants in Matamoras; sometimes foreign merchants; in fact, mostly foreign merchants, I think. Mr. Galvan, I remember, bought one lot of about one hundred bales, or, perhaps, not quite so much.

Question. Was it bought by the attachés of the government, army, or other officers?

Answer. No, sir, not at all. I do not think it was. It was all bought in by merchants. There was nobody else there who had any coin to pay for it.

A few days after General Banks left I sent an expedition up to Roma, 120 miles up the Rio Grande river. It was composed both of cavalry and infantry, with two pieces of artillery. It was gone some time, and suffered considerable privation; discovered no enemy, nor heard of any exceeding 180 in that part of the country. I sent expeditions out in the direction of the interior of Texas, towards Corpus Christi, about seventy miles or more, and discovered no enemy; nor was there any enemy between the Nueces river and the Rio Grande that could stand up before 300 of our men at any time. The objects of the expedition, further than the occupation and reclamation of Texas, were never explained to me. All the object we could accomplish on the Rio Grande had been accomplished by the occupation of Brownsville. The effect of it was to stop that grand outlet which the rebels had heretofore made use of for letting out their cotton and bringing in their military supplies. But it did not stop the trade. The starting point for the Rio Gande is San Antonio, in the centre of Texas. It is a much shorter road from San Antonio to Eagle Pass, which is 350 miles above Brownsville, on the Rio Grande, than it is from San Antonio to Brownsville. The rebel cotton could just as easily be sold on the Mexican side, opposite Eagle Pass, as it could at Matamoras. The effect was, then, only to divert the trade, and all the trade that had theretofore been carried on across the Rio Grande, at Matamoras, has since been carried on at Eagle Pass. A force to occupy the whole of the Rio Grande up to Eagle Pass would be very large, and the expense of it would be tremendous. I addressed, without being invited, more than one communication to General Banks on the subject of the disposition of the troops in that part of Texas. Having never received any explanation from him of his plans, or any detailed instructions as to what was expected of me, I felt very great hesitation in advancing any opinions whatever. I did it, however, in as delicate a manner as I could. I repeated the advice, if it may be called so; I repeated the despatches to him more than once; but I never have received an acknowledgment of them. I advised him that the force was out of position on the Rio Grande, although it was proper that it should have been at first carried there; but that its proper position, if it was to effect the object of closing up the trade on the Rio Grande by itself, without co-operation with any other force to fight the enemy, was to move it somewhere on the Nueces river, probably at Corpus Christi, with a view of occupying San Antonio, or that district of country. If that were occupied, the whole trade on the Rio Grande would be at an end.

I had at the same time sent a desperate refugee, who volunteered his services, up to Eagle Pass with authority to collect such refugees as he could, and help himself up there in any way that he wanted. His directions were to destroy anything on the road that he could not carry away; to take all the cotton and other property that he could get within reaching distance of the Rio Grande and put it in a Mexican custom-house, on the other side of the river, in the name of the United States, and then, after that, to make "Jordan a hard road to travel;" to make the road from San Antonio to Eagle Pass, over which the traitorous Jews of that district carry on their contraband trade, so perilous that they would abandon it. He was just the man to do this job; and I have received despatches from him since that he had 150 men up there, but he could not get arms for ten of them, and the enemy, getting notice of his intentions, had sent a cavalry force to Eagle Pass, which was just enough to keep him away. The country between Brownsville and Eagle Pass (350 miles) is barren. A cavalry force cannot subsist on it. From Corpus Christi to Eagle Pass, and from there to Loredo, the country is better. The roads are shorter than from Brownsville to either of those places, and a force stationed on the Nueces river would control all that part of the country, whereas any amount of force stationed at Brownsville would not. I went into detail somewhat in the despatches I wrote to headquarters, but I never was encouraged to repeat them. My proposition was to leave 700 men on the Rio Grande—500 of them at Brownsville, which I had fortified very strongly; 200 at Brazos island, to guard the depot, and to take the rest of the force around to Corpus Christi, the cavalry, artillery, and transportation by land, with a sufficient guard of infantry, and the remainder of the infantry around by water to Aranzas Pass and Corpus Christi.

At that time my information goes to satisfy me that San Antonio was not fortified. There was no garrison at Corpus Christi, and there never has been one since we have been in Texas, all the reports of a thousand prisoners there to the contrary notwithstanding; and there were no troops west of the Guadalupe river which could contest the advance of a single brigade. The main forces of the enemy had all been moved to the east of the Colorado river by orders of Magruder, and all the people of Texas who desired protection were, in proclamations, directed to move to the eastward of that river—that that should be the line of defence.

When the troops moved up the coast with General Banks, a regiment of white infantry was left at Aranzas Pass. This regiment soon after sent down to me for rations. We had then but a few days' rations on hand, and they stated that they were about out. I had received information that a large steamship with 50,000 rations on board, which had arrived at Aranzas Pass, was carried back with her whole load from there without landing a ration, and this was what shortened their supply. I never heard what was the reason of that, but the chief quartermaster, Colonel Holabird, it was reported to me, went back on her, and General Banks was there at the time.

About the 1st of January I received orders to turn over the command on the Rio Grande, of the forces there, to Major General Herron, to move myself up the coast to Pass Cavallo, and to take personal command of all the troops on the coast. I arrived at Pass Cavallo about the 12th of January, and found there Major General Washburne in command. He had with him the 1st and 3d divisions of the 13th corps, and two and a half regiments of the 4th division of the same corps, four light batteries, one siege battery, and no cavalry. He complained of considerable dissatisfaction with the way in which he had been required to conduct military affairs on the coast. He read me some despatches, which showed that he had made the same complaints to headquarters, and he was warm in his feelings against the manner in which he had been required to conduct affairs. He stated to me that when Fort Esperanza was evacuated by the enemy he could have immediately marched up with what force he had, some 4,000 or 4,500 men, to the mouth of the Brazos river, and have taken possession of the forts at that mouth, and established a base there which would have been of inestimable value to us in the reduction of Texas. He stated he had no doubt of this; and, from all I have ascertained since, I think he was right. He was prevented from doing it by orders; he was ordered to remain on Matagorda island, so he informed me. But when he received that order he was in motion across the pass to Matagorda peninsula for the purpose of moving up the peninsula, and he so far departed from his instructions as to land what troops he had already embarked on the peninsula opposite, and retain them there and the forces which subsequently joined him; and he moreover stated to me that, from the information he had from the interior, the 11,000 or 12,000 men that he had there then were not worth as much to him as the 4,000 or 4,500 which he had at the time Fort Esperanza was evacuated, owing to the preparations which the enemy had made, and their entire helplessness almost at the time Fort Esperanza was so much surprised by the appearance of our forces there. He also stated to me that he was required to act on the defensive, and was not authorized to move into the interior or to occupy the mainland; but I found that the mainland was occupied at Indianola by two brigades under Brigadier General Fitz Henry Warren.

I assumed command immediately of the forces there. I ordered all the white troops from Matagorda island over on the Matagorda peninsula, and ordered the remainder of the division, two brigades of which were at Indianola, General Washburn's division, to join it up there, and I commenced the movement with what means I had on hand, with a view of moving all my force towards Indianola and Lavacca and preparing for an advance into Texas, for I confess that I had not up to that moment realized the idea that I had gone down to Texas to act on the defensive or to remain quiet. I reported very soon after I arrived there, in some detail, to General Banks personally, the changes that I had made there, where I had moved the troops to, and proposing to him a plan of campaign, not in great detail, because I had never been consulted; but considering myself, as the senior officer in Texas, partly responsible for the idleness of the troops there, and expressing myself in my despatch that at all events I would be by public opinion held responsible for it, I volunteered some more advice. It was never responded to. I desired cavalry beyond all things. I desired the control of the force on the Rio Grande, in order that they might be made to co-operate with this force in moving into Texas. I consider that, had those forces co-operated, and a reasonable amount of cavalry been supplied, the campaign in Texas was as certain a thing as we have ever had to practice on during this war.

The stories that have been told about Unionism in Texas I am satisfied are true, and that the mountains of Texas are filled with refugees looking for the flag, who have been hidden in the bushes for eighteen months there, and that in Texas itself there are numbers of people ready to show their hands the moment our troops approach, and some of whom have been imprudent enough, on our appearing on the coast, to assert a little more independence than they had been able to assert for the last few years, and have got into difficulty on that account. I invited all the people at Indianola, and all within our lines, to take advantage of the oath prescribed in the proclamation of the President. They all took it, with the exception of one man who desired to be made a martyr of, and succeeded.

Soon after, I was directed through the headquarters of the corps. I had then been superseded in command of the corps by the arrival of General Ord, about the 20th of January, from sick leave from the north, and his headquarters were established at New Orleans. I was ordered to fortify my positions in Texas in the strongest manner, and to make requisitions for engineering materials for that purpose, and for such heavy artillery as I required to defend myself with. It was necessary perhaps to fortify Indianola, but I never comprehended the necessity for fortifying a large force on Matagorda island. I was ordered further not to occupy the mainland with a view to permanent occupation, and to be prepared to be called on for a considerable portion of the force that I had at Matagorda bay, and to prepare Matagorda island with strong defences for a garrison of six thousand men. I confess it was a damper on my feelings; but I supposed that these were mere precautionary measures, and even then did not realize that that would be carried out. But Indianola has since been evacuated, and all the troops on Matagorda bay who remained there, about five thousand five hundred men, are strongly fortified on Matagorda island; and before I left there, there were two major generals and three brigadier generals belonging to that command, without counting Major General Washburne, whose division it was; and I do not believe there were five hundred rebels within a hundred miles of them.

I felt the evacuation of Indianola more than anything that I have felt during the whole war. I had heard that in Louisiana, before towns had been occupied, the people had been compelled to take the oath of allegiance—whether this is true or not I do not know—and that within a very few days afterwards they were left to the tender mercies of the rebels, and that some of them had been hung. The people of Indianola said they would be treated in that way if we left them; but it was evacuated, although it was strongly fortified, and with us about two hundred of the population left for fear of their lives.

I take upon myself the whole responsibility of offering the oath of allegiance to the people in our lines in Texas. I will do the same thing wherever they come within my lines, unless I am prohibited from doing it; but I have been told that I was responsible for it, and that I was responsible for the occupation of the mainland. I have written records which will show the whole state of things, and I dislike to avoid any responsibility like either of these, though I had no responsibility for the occupation of the mainland.

Six thousand men, in round numbers, were drawn from Matagorda bay to Louisiana. They had been sent down at great expense for the campaign in Texas, which had never been carried on. They had suffered on the coast for want of supplies whilst they were under the command of General Washburn, as he stated to me. They were then, at the time they were called back, fully equipped, had every comfort that soldiers ought to have, and were only requiring orders to march into the interior of Texas. They were taken back at similar expense to Louisiana. Not only that, but I think there were eight steam vessels which came down for loads for them, bringing nothing down, and which went back immediately without any loads. That much surplus transportation was sent down for those troops, more than was required. I mention this to show the bad management.

Question. Who was responsible for that?

Answer. The quartermaster's department in some of its ramifications—I do not know who in particular; but a quartermaster was sent down there to take charge of the transportation of those troops, and he knew just how many there were, and how many loads there were to go, and, as I said before, eight steamboats were sent down empty and went back empty.

The campaign in Texas has, up to the present time, resulted in the occupation of the line of the Rio Grande up to Brownsville, or a little above there, and the occupation of Brazos Santiago, Aranzas Pass, and Pass Cavallo, on the coast, but the trade across the Grande is still continued; and the interior of Texas has been left intact, although the deserters, both commissioned officers and enlisted men, who came into camp, were agreed in their assertions, that a considerable portion of the army of General Magruder would join our forces if we would move into the interior of Texas. Those that did leave it, and came to our lines, ran the greatest risk of their lives in getting out.

There is something very greatly to be admired in the character of the Texas refugees. They are a very different class of men from any other refugees that I have seen during this war. As a general thing, they are a noble set of fellows, bound up in the Union, and so sincere in their feelings that they divide with each other the last dollar they have got until they get to our camps, and there, as a general rule, the first thing they want to do is to enlist in the Texas campaign.

By Mr. Loan:

Question. What time did you leave there?

Answer. I left Matagorda island, I believe, on the 6th of this month. There were then on Matagorda island in round numbers, white and black, about 5,500 men. I believe that now on Matagorda island there are one major general and three brigadiers with that force—Major General McClernand, and Brigadier Generals Benton, Warren, and Lawler.

Question. General Banks went up to Matagorda island with a force after he left you at Brownsville. How long did he remain there before he returned to New Orleans?

Answer. I can only state what I heard about that matter, because I was not present with that force; but I am satisfied that he never landed in Texas again after he embarked at Point Isabel, when he left Brownsville. I have been informed by the officers who made their statement to me, that when he left the troops at Fort Esperanza, it was not evacuated, and that he went from there to New Orleans with the expectation that that would be a slow matter, but it was, I believe, evacuated the same night of the day on which he sailed for New Orleans. I was informed by the officers who were present at that time, that General Banks left there with the expectation that that would be a siege.

Question. Who was left in command of that force on Matagorda island?

Answer. I believe General Washburn. General Washburn could give you much more information about matters in Matagorda bay, and the forces in Texas and Louisiana, because he was in the campaign up the Teche, and I was not; he was much longer in Louisiana than I was. I learned the day before yesterday from the chairman, with some surprise, that General Washburn had not delivered any testimony here. He is much better informed on these matters than I am; and some of this history, which I have given you, was received from him. He felt warmly on the subject on account of his command and his men, and the way in which he thought he had been restricted there.

By Mr. Chandler:

Question. Do you consider this Texas movement a success or a failure in its results?

Answer. I cannot answer that question without knowing what the plans of the commander-in-chief were. Now I do not see that he had any particular objective in going to Texas. He has not accomplished anything in proportion to the outlay, and the effort that has been made use of.

Question. If so, to what do you attribute that failure—to lack of energy in its execution, or lack of orders to vigorously assault?

Answer. I attribute it entirely to inaction—inaction of the troops in Texas, and a lack of cavalry to begin operations with.

Question. And do you attribute that inactivity to orders from headquarters, or to the action of the generals in command in the field?

Answer. Entirely to a want of orders from headquarters. I do not believe there was an officer or a man in Texas that was not impatient to begin to work, and that was not tired of lying still and doing nothing.

Question. Do you consider that the force which was in Texas would have been adequate, with a proper amount of cavalry, to overrun the State substantially, taking possession of the various salient points?

Answer. I think there was a fair prospect of success with the force that was in Texas if two thousand cavalry had been sent down, which they had to send. If the divisions which were being carried down had been filled up, if the convalescents had been returned to their regiments in Texas, and the portions of troops sent down which were ordered for embarcation, I consider there was sufficient force at that time to have done the work. At all events the trade on the Rio Grande would have utterly been broken up. The despatches which I received from this man McManus, whom I sent up to Eagle Pass, stated to me that there were between five and six thousand bales of cotton collected at Eagle Pass in the month of February. The trade along that road was large.

By Mr. Odell:

Question. Do you know that the cavalry which you say was required could have been furnished?

Answer. It was in New Orleans. I merely know that, however, from the public prints. The newspapers were filled with glowing accounts of the reviews of the cavalry force all the winter in New Orleans.

Question. At the time you were calling for them?

Answer. Some of that was the cavalry I was asking for. There was also cavalry down on the Rio Grande. There were eight hundred cavalry certainly on the Rio Grande, which I asked for, but it lay there. I was not permitted to touch any of that force on the Rio Grande. It certainly was not wanted at Rio Grande, in my opinion.

Question. You spoke of being authorized to take equipments for a thousand cavalry and a thousand infantry.

Answer. Yes, sir; the equipments for a thousand cavalry were never landed. They were shipped on board transports which could not go over the bars of Texas. They lay at anchor till they got unseaworthy, and were carried back to New Orleans. I suppose I have written more despatches about that load of cavalry equipments than any one thing, but never succeeded in getting it back. It has been reported to me by the officers of the ordnance department in New Orleans that they had at three separate times taken those equipments down to the landing at New Orleans for shipment again to Texas, and that they had been refused transportation by the quartermaster's department because they had other things to carry down; and an ordnance officer told me they were sent down a second time and sent to the wrong place, and carried back a second time. But there was a set of cavalry equipments sent down there subsequently, composed of citizens' saddles, which are unfit for military operations, and I was obliged to use those. General Washburn made a great complaint about the refusal to bring his supplies down by the quartermaster's department, and he made official reports to General Banks on the subject, and in his report, which he read to me, he stated that when his men were out of rations a steamship came down there almost loaded with sutler's goods, and that he had information that public supplies had been taken off some vessels to make room for sutler's goods. His indignation was very great about it.

Question. You spoke of paying your own expenses. How did that come out? Did you get cotton enough to pay the expenses of the expedition?

Answer. Yes, sir. When I left the Rio Grande I left about two hundred bales of cotton in the hands of General Herron, as I stated, and I turned over to him all the coin that the quartermaster's department had in possession, which was eight or ten thousand dollars—I have forgotten how much—and a good lot of supplies, besides forage for two or three weeks.

Question. What became of the $100,000 in coin?

Answer. That I never heard of since. We got $12,500 of it; but I do not know what was done with the balance. Perhaps it is on hand still in New Orleans.

By Mr. Chandler:

Question. Do you know anything of the loyalty of the people of Louisiana at this time?

Answer. Not of my own knowledge, but only from conversation with people in New Orleans, and from common report.

Question. Give us that, then.

Answer. My impression, made up from those conversations and from common report, was, that the people of Louisiana are not as well disposed towards the government to-day as they were within a very short time of its occupation by our forces. I am of the impression that but few if any of the old inhabitants of Louisiana voted at the recent elections. I am of the impression that their bitterness is very great against us; and my impressions, which I have grown up with during this war, that rebels cannot be coaxed, but must be whipped, have been very much strengthened in Louisiana. The only way to rule this people is by authority, and by letting the civil machine, which has now been organized and initiated, run on with just as little friction as can be applied to it; to punish all offenders, and not undertake to govern as much as they are being governed now; let the thing run on as in any other State.

By Mr. Odell:

Question. Without military interference?

Answer. Without military interference. Now we are deceiving ourselves, and nobody else. We are not deceiving the rebels down there by the recent method of introducing Louisiana into the Union. We are not deceiving the people of Louisiana, nor the army down there; but we are deceiving our friends in the north wonderfully.

Question. Have you ever met any who were rebels in the beginning that have become friends to Unionism?

Answer. I have never seen any. I do not believe there are any. I think the rebels down there are more bitter now than they were when Louisiana was first occupied.

Question. I do not confine my question to Louisiana, but to Texas and all over?

Answer. It is my opinion, that if a column of troops were marched into Texas sufficient to sustain itself now, Texas would require no management to bring her back into the Union. She would come back into the Union; she would revolutionize herself, and the rebels would be whipped out of her, so that she would want no assistance after one or two battles. Let the rebel army be beaten in Texas, and the people of Texas will take care of all the rest without any fostering or nursing at all; but they want to be tenderly treated; they want to understand that we are going to do the fair thing when we take hold; that we have come there to win their liberties, and not to divide their subsistence.

By Mr. Chandler:

Question. By that you refer to Union men?

Answer. Certainly. There are a great many rebels in the State of Texas, I have no doubt, who are rebels by compulsion, (they cannot help themselves,) who would come in and take advantage of the President's proclamation of amnesty, and remain true after that.

By Mr. Odell:

Question. You said that the people wanted to understand that we meant to deal fairly with them?

Answer. Yes, sir.

Question. Do you mean to say by that, that our military policy has been that of spoliation?

Answer. I cannot say that our military policy has been that of spoliation; but although no instances have ever come under my knowledge of the rebel population beng plundered after they had given in adhesion to the Union, still stories are rife about those things, and about abuses that have existed in different parts of the country, and about encouragement given to speculators from the north, under whatever name they go.

Question. What do you know about them?

Answer. I know nothing; I say nothing of that kind has ever come under my personal observation.

TRADE REGULATIONS, &c.

MOUND CITY, ILLINOIS, *April* 23, 1864.

Captain ALEXANDER M. PENNOCK sworn and examined.

By the chairman:

Question. What is your opinion in regard to the effect of the late treasury regulations in relation to trade up and down the river?

Answer. The abuse of those regulations is so great that I think the trade should be stopped. From all the information I can obtain, smuggling is carried on to a very great extent to the aid and comfort of the rebels.

Question. Cannot that smuggling be prevented under this general order for trade?

Answer. In my opinion it cannot.

Question. Will you state how that general order operates?

Answer. I will give you an example: A short time since, on the Tennessee river, in Captain Shirk's command, a boat went up with supplies, and with regular permits all correct and in accordance with the regulations. She was convoyed by a gunboat, and landed her goods and left. She had left but a short time when Captain Shirk received information that a part of those very goods had fallen into the hands of the rebels. He then returned, ascertained that that information was correct, and destroyed the remainder of the goods to prevent them from falling into the enemy's hands.

Question. Is that your constant experience of the operation of this rule?

Answer. It is. From the best information I can receive, when the trade was first opened, after the capture of Memphis, several steamers trading from St. Louis were captured by the gunboat stationed at Island No. 10, and sent up to Cairo. They had pistols, quinine, cloth for rebel uniforms, buttons, and other articles.

Question. Had they the regular permits, according to the regulations of the department?

Answer. They had, in many instances, permits for "cases of goods," without specifying the contents; when these cases were opened, the goods which I have mentioned were found in them.

Question. Can this contraband trade be prevented except by a total prohibition of this kind of trade?

Answer. I think not. The passengers on board these boats had large quantities of quinine in their valises; and quinine was often secreted in the clothes of the women; long bags were found tied around the waists of women containing from forty to fifty little jars of quinine. A man by the name of Tatem was captured on the Mississippi by one of the gunboats; he had embarked on board the steamboat at St. Louis; had gone down to New Orleans and landed there, and was on his return up the river. There was found with him trunks containing rebel uniforms, pistols, buttons, a gold watch, a rebel flag, and other articles marked "St. Louis, February 24, 1864," for the first Missouri battery, that is, the flag was so marked. There was a government aid on this boat, which took this man down the river, whose duty it was to examine all persons and articles on board the boat. The man said he hired an Irishman to take his trunk on board, and that nobody knew of its being on board the boat except the Irishman, whom he believed was shipped as a hand on board the boat, and went down the river at the same time he did; that after he landed the trunks were thrown overboard from the steamer, and he and another man received them; he said that this Irishman threw these trunks overboard for him.

One of the gunboats captured a man in a skiff who had about 300,000 percussion caps with him, taking them across the river. The owner of the caps had gone down on one of the steamers from Cairo or St. Louis.

And a large rebel mail was captured on one of these steamers. I considered it of so much importance to General Curtis, who was then in command at St. Louis, that I sent it up to him with a special despatch boat.

Question. Have you reason to suppose that these practices were connived at, if not openly encouraged, by these government aids?

Answer. I suspect it is so. In conclusion, I would say that all the available force here has been constantly on the move night and day. I have ample instructions from Admiral Porter how to act during his absence; and also with instructions to act in his name in an emergency in accordance with my judgment.

(See testimony about Fort Pillow for Captain Pennock's opinion about requisite force at Cairo and Mound City.)

Captain JAMES W. SHIRK (commanding 7th division of Mississippi squadron) sworn and examined.

By the chairman:

Question. What do you say in regard to the operations of the treasury general trade regulations permitting trade up and down the river?

Answer. I think it merely supplies the rebels with provisions, medicines, and clothing.

Question. Is it possible for you naval officers to be so vigilant as to prevent successful frauds and smuggling under that order?

Answer. I think not.

Question. Have you heard the testimony of Captain Pennock upon that subject?

Answer. I heard a part of it.

Question. Do you agree with him as to the impolicy of this trading order, and the difficulty of so executing it as to prevent fraud under it?

Answer. Yes, sir, I do agree with him.

Question. Can you state any instances illustrating the impolicy of such regulations?

Answer. Yes, sir. About the middle of last month (March) I went up the Tennessee river with the gunboat Peosta, bearing the divisional flag. A trading boat convoyed by a gunboat was already up the river with supplies and regular permits from the Treasury Department.

Question. Did the papers appear to be regular?

Answer. Everything was just according to the regulations. The captain of the gunboat convoying the trading boat had particular orders from me not to allow a single thing to go on shore unless it was all right according to the regular forms of the Treasury Department. When I came in sight of Saltillo, about two hundred miles from the mouth of the Tennessee, I saw quite a quantity of salt, sugar, molasses, coffee, clothing, and medicines on the bank of the river, just landed from this boat. The trading boat and her convoy were still in sight going up the river. I went on about ten miles, and was then overtaken by a man on horseback, who had ridden up from Saltillo, who told me that the rebels were at Saltillo taking possession of these goods. I immediately returned, and there found the gunboat Tamak, which I had directed to follow me up the river, shelling the rebels, who were about fifty in number. These rebels had already broken into those packages, and taken salt in bags, and coffee, and dry goods, and made way with them. They also shot two men in federal uniform who were there, calling themselves "home guards;" one of them was killed, and the other was wounded, and the rebels were about to kill him, when a woman asked them for God's sake not to kill him in her yard. Whereupon they threw him across a horse, wounded as he was, and took him out into the road and fired a pistol ball into his head. They also shot a negro, who was not in uniform, through the back. Feeling assured that if I left those goods remaining on the bank they would fall into the hands of the rebels, I ordered Captain Smith, of the Peosta, to destroy them, which he did, excepting the dry goods, which I took down to ———, Tennessee, and delivered to the commander there; and a large box of medicines which I kept on board the gunboat for the use of those on the gunboat. I have been told over and over again that articles which were permitted to go up the Tennessee from Paducah, some of them, went directly into the hands of rebels in arms. I will state another instance. There were some goods sent up directed to a man who persons up there told me was actually a lieutenant at that time in Wisdom's regiment of Forrest's cavalry.

Question. Do these treasury agents interpose any effective impediment in the way of this course of proceeding?

Answer. No, sir; no impediment that I ever saw. They give a permit to every person who comes to them. Certain men on these boats are appointed as storekeepers. Their goods are cleared from the custom-house, and they go up in these boats, and a treasury agent goes with them. Wherever the boat stops, a man or a woman, no matter which it is, comes on board, takes the oath before the treasury agent, and the storekeeper then sells them what they want. There are generally two persons; one gives the permit, and the other takes them down to the storekeeper, and they are allowed to buy any articles he has. My experience is, that any man in Tennessee or Kentucky will swear to any oath so as to get what goods he wants, no matter whether they are for himself or for his rebel friends. They have no idea of an oath except to break it.

Question. What is your opinion of the extent of this trade?

Answer. When I discovered how the thing was working I wrote a note to the collector of customs at Paducah on the 24th or 25th of March, informing him that I should not allow anything more to go up the Tennessee river, to be landed on the west side of the river, even if it had a permit; and the thing is stopped now. I knew perfectly well that it would go into the hands of the rebels.

Question. Are not the faithful navy officers here compelled to encroach upon that order of the Treasury Department, in order to protect ourselves from the danger of this trade with the rebels?

Answer. Yes, sir; although there is a general order from the Navy Department directing us not to interfere in any manner with trade carried on under the regulations of the Treasury Department, except for important military necessity.

Question. The object of these orders of the department is, that the trade shall be carried on with Union citizens?

Answer. Yes, sir; and if it was so carried on it would be all right.

Question. Is the oath prescribed by the department really any impediment to cheating and fraud?

Answer. No, sir; because the rebels will swear to a lie as readily as the truth.

(See testimony of witness upon Fort Pillow as to necessary force at Cairo and Mound City.)

CAIRO, ILLINOIS, *April* 24, 1864.

Major General STEPHEN A. HURLBUT sworn and examined.

By the chairman:

Question. Has your attention been turned to the operation of trade along the Mississippi river? How does it operate in regard to favoring the enemy?

Answer. My attention has been turned to it very seriously. As it is conducted on the Mississippi river it is disastrous to the Union cause for many reasons. As the system is now carried on the commercial ports on the river are, intentionally or unintentionally, but points of supply for the enemy. Even when the trade restrictions are complied with, it is done by false oaths taken by parties who desire to obtain supplies. The people who trade at those points do not consider an oath of any binding efficacy at all, and will take it at any time in order to obtain anything they want. I refer now to the legitimate trade. The illegitimate trade is carried on at all points, and no amount of watchfulness on the part of the officers of the customs, or of the army, or the navy, can suppress it. For example, there must be wood-yards on the river, and each and every one of them, as long as this trade is permitted, is converted into a place for the fraudulent landing of goods. The ultimate virtue of an army is always in its pickets and outposts. For example, the pickets on the roads leading out from Memphis are the last points where there is an opportunity for catching contraband goods, yet while this trade continues these pickets and outposts can be purchased and corrupted, and it is done, and it cannot be prevented. I have been informed by the treasury officer at Memphis that $11,000,000 of goods, custom-house valuation, have been brought to that place since trade was opened in 1862. The mere statement of that fact is enough to show what that trade must have been.

Question. In what does this trade consist principally?

Answer. It should consist in nothing but family supplies. It does consist in about everything that anybody can find the means of buying.

Question. Have you reason to suppose that articles contraband of war go through to the rebels in this way?

Answer. I know they do, because occasionally we find them. I have one man in Memphis now, under sentence of death, to be hung next Friday, for endeavoring to carry out a very large amount of percussion caps and powder; and I had another man under sentence of death for a similar offence, who has been pardoned by the President.

Question. How was that done, under a treasury order or not?

Answer. By smuggling. There is another very serious difficulty that arises from this trade on the Mississippi, in the corruption that the gambling operations in cotton bring upon everybody—citizens, officers, and soldiers. Mr. Mellen, the treasury agent, has stated publicly that parties were authorized, under the treasury regulations, to buy cotton from anybody that has it to sell, and licenses are so given. No cotton, of course, is allowed to pass the confederate lines, unless with their permission; and the business is therefore a business of exchange between the cotton operators of the confederate authorities, either for their private benefit or for the benefit of their government, I do not know which, for I believe they have as great rascals as we have. To a certain extent, military operations are, of necessity, subordinate to the claims of what is called trade.

Question. Have you any reason to suppose that any officers of the government and of the army are concerned in those speculations?

Answer. I have made my report on that subject to the military authorities, and would refer to that.

Question. You can state whether you have reason to believe so or not?

Answer. I have reason to believe that officers of the army are connected with cotton purchasers and cotton speculations for profit.

Question. Is there any opportunity down there for these treasury agents to enter into these speculations?

Answer. Certainly; more than for anybody else. These treasury agents grant the licenses; they can determine who shall and who shall not go to a particular place. Licenses are sometimes issued at Washington granting special, extraordinary privileges; I have seen them.

Question. Does not that place those treasury agents under strong temptations to commit or permit frauds?

Answer. It places everybody who is connected in any way with it, either civil or military, under the strongest temptations to defraud, of course.

Question. What amount of percussion caps, medicines, and other contraband articles, do you suppose, reach the rebels through this river trade—any considerable quantity?

Answer. I should think, judging from the arrests which have been made, that a very considerable quantity of such things did reach them, for I take it that very few seizures are made in proportion to the amount that gets through. For example, a man can put in a carpet bag or a small trunk a very considerable amount of percussion caps and take them through the lines, or he can carry quinine, although there is not so much of that taken through to them now as there was when I first went to Memphis. I have closed up drug stores in Memphis and sold their goods for selling medicines to agents of the enemy since I have been there. Cavalry boots and cavalry equipments have been the articles in most demand there of late and all along.

Question. Can this trade possibly be regulated so as to prevent these frauds?

Answer. I think not.

Question. Can it be carried on under such regulations that it will be safe?

Answer. I think not.

Question. What remedy would you then propose?

Answer. The remedy I would apply would be this: I would have nothing go below but army and navy supplies, and the necessary supplies for the people within such ports as we actually hold, simply provisions, &c., necessary to keep them from starving and suffering. I am satisfied, and I know I express the feelings of the other officers who have been on the river, that if, upon our occupation of Memphis, in June, 1862, all trade with the Mississippi country had been cut off, except to supply the necessities of the army and the people within the ports that we actually held with garrisons, the States of Mississippi, Arkansas, and Louisiana would have been clear of the enemy before this time.

By Mr. Gooch:

Question. What has been the effect of opening these ports in Kentucky, &c.?

Answer. The effect has been to accumulate large amounts of goods at such points, for example, as Paducah, to obtain which was one great inducement for Forrest's raid. From Paducah and Columbus large amounts of supplies have been sent out which have gone down directly into the hands of the confederate officers.

By the chairman:

Question. Your intercourse along the river has been extensive and of long continuance, I believe?

Answer. Yes, sir.

Question. I will inquire of you, what is your opinion as to the loyalty of any considerable portion of the people along through Arkansas, and western Kentucky, and Tennessee?

Answer. Arkansas, I think, is an exception; I believe there is a sentiment of loyalty in Arkansas, but not immediately on the river. There is no loyalty where there is a plantation. Wherever you find a poor man on a small piece of ground on which he works himself, there you find loyalty. Wherever you find a plantation on which there is a master and negroes, there you find disloyalty.

By Mr. Gooch:

Question. Is it your understanding that, in the exchanges for cotton, we take their cotton and pay for it in contraband articles?

Answer. Not precisely in contraband articles, or rather not necessarily so, although a large proportion of it is. They will not sell their cotton for money—only for "supplies," as they call it, which they require. But if you sell them negro blankets they will make very good blankets for soldiers. If Kentucky jeans are sold for negro clothing, they make very good confederate uniforms. If they are allowed to take mules and horses to work their plantations, they are either allowed to be held there by toleration of the confederate authorities, or taken into the confederate armies, and that is the result of cultivating plantations on the Mississippi—merely furnishing the rebels with mules and horses whenever they choose to come and take them. Propositions have been repeatedly made, professing to come from high authorities in the confederate armies, to sell the cotton of the confederate government, and to allow all their private cotton to go out without any hindrance. The proposition has been made to me, and forwarded by me to Washington, and refused; and the proposition was made to General McPherson.

Question. What were the terms of the proposition?

Answer. The terms were that the cotton on the Red river, and on the Wachita, which is among the objects of this present expedition up there under General Banks, should be sold to General McPherson at these rates; the confederate cotton at either twenty or twenty-five cents per pound, when they would allow private cotton to come through without molestation, to be sold at whatever price could be obtained for it. That proposition was sent on to Washington and refused. I have understood that the same proposition was made and allowed to a private individual by the authorities at Washington.

Question. Who is that private individual?

Answer. It is reported to have been Mr. Casey, at one time a member of Congress from Kentucky.

(See also the testimony of General Mason Brayman, commanding the district of Cairo, in relation to the Fort Pillow massacre, where he expresses the opinion that one of the principal objects of the rebel Forrest's raid was to secure the large amount of goods which had been allowed to go into Kentucky and Tennessee under the regulations of the Treasury Department.)

Captain JAMES H. ODLIN sworn and examined.

By the chairman:

Question. What is your position in the service?

Answer. I am a captain and assistant adjutant general, and chief of staff for General Brayman, for the district of Cairo, where I have been stationed since the 23d of January, 1864.

Question. Will you state what you know about the operations of the system of trade established upon the river, whether it is beneficial or detrimental to the service, in your opinion, and your reasons for the opinion you have?

Answer. In my opinion it is very detrimental indeed to the service. My attention was first called to it after being assigned to the position of assistant adjutant general for the district of Cairo. General Sherman's order was received notifying us to not interfere with the trade permits; that free trade was opened with Missouri and Kentucky, and that we had nothing to do with the permit business, but was to allow trade to go on.

As soon as this order came out everybody rushed goods right into the little towns, whose citizens, as is well known to military commanders, embraced rebel sympathizers to the extent of a majority of their number. In the town of Hickman, Kentucky, we had the most persistent trouble. From all the information I can gain, there has never been but about one or two men from that town in the Union army; and there are, or were, not more than ten truly loyal men there. The first day after they received the news through the papers that trade was opened, 240 barrels of salt and a large invoice of whiskey were shipped to Hickman. On the second day about a thousand bushels of salt, a proportionate amount of whiskey, besides all sorts of groceries and coffee, in sacks, were shipped there. General Reid, commanding the district of Cairo at that time, assumed the responsibility of stopping that salt, on the second day, at Columbus, Kentucky, until he could ascertain the facts. As soon as possible he sent a provost marshal and some troops from Columbus to Hickman—one company of the 34th New Jersey, and one piece of artillery, with the proper complement of men. The provost marshal took an invoice of the number of stores there, and the amount of goods on hand, and also ascertained about the number of inhabitants and business men there. There were 12 stores, about a thousand bushels of salt, and about an equal number of barrels of whiskey, to a population of about 1,200 inhabitants; making about one bushel of salt to each person before this large amount was sent down under the new treasury regulations. The rebels come in there every few weeks, rob the stores and carry off the goods, and the citizens come up here and say their goods have been taken, and want a new supply.

From the best information we have, goods are taken to all the points in this district—to Paducah, Columbus, Hickman, and other places—under those regulations, and from those places they go out into the country to supply the rebels; and it can be proved that the storekeepers of Hickman sold their saltat the rate of a barrel of salt for a bale of cotton. That is what the trade amounts to there. We suppressed this to a great extent by placing troops there; but it was impossible to prevent it altogether, as we had positive orders not to interfere with the trade regulations.

Question. Does this still continue?

Answer. Yes, sir.

Question. Is it not easy for the rebels to receive large amounts of military stores, of all kinds, under this free trade regulation?

Answer. It is; and in my opinion they do every day receive stores through Missouri and Kentucky in this way, those being the two States opened to free trade. We found out that they were receiving goods, and we have now under arrest an officer of our army, a former district provost marshal of this place, charged with passing goods through to the rebels.

Question. Do these treasury agents, who have charge of this matter, prove to be any serious check upon this contraband trade?

Answer. I cannot say anything in regard to their duties; but we have seized contraband goods on boats which had government agents on board, who had made their inspection of the goods and passed them; and in a number of cases the goods were seized after they were landed. In one instance there was an officer of the rebel army got on board a steamboat at St. Louis, travelled on that same boat all the way to New Orleans, and returned on the same boat to an island in the Mississippi, where he got off, taking off a trunk, which was afterwards seized, and found to contain a number of rebel officers' uniforms, a large number of buttons, and other articles for the rebels. The buttons were stamped "Waterford, Connecticut," as the place of manufacture. There was also found a rebel flag inscribed "Missouri Battery." I forget the number, but I think it was the "First," with the date, "February 24, 1864; from the ladies of St. Louis;" Captain Pennock, of the navy, I believe, now has the flag in his possession.

At another time a man came down on a steamboat and got off on the Missouri shore. In undertaking to get across the river in a skiff he was seen by one of the gunboats and taken prisoner. He had with him a carpet sack, which he had brought down on the steamboat, which contained 300,000 percussion caps, which he was endeavoring to convey through to the enemy. This carpet sack had been passed by a government aid, and allowed to be taken down on the boat.

Question. Do you know who that government aid was?

Answer. No, sir; I do not. There was also a government aid on the boat on which the man went down to New Orleans and back, whose trunk, containing rebel uniforms, &c., was captured. There are government aids, I believe, on all the passenger boats running on the river.

Question. They do not seem to furnish much protection to the government.

Answer. No, sir. Like other classes, that class has among its number a great many rascals. At Paducah the same trouble existed in regard to trade regulations. Immense supplies were run in there; and Colonel Hicks, commanding there, had information from different sources that at some time or other, he could not tell when, there would be an attack upon the place. The report was that the rebels would come and try to take the place, but to that we gave no credence. There is now lying in that town over a thousand barrels of salt in one place, which the rebels tried to roll out and carry off, but our fire from the fort and the gunboats prevented their doing it. That is but one lot in the large amount there is there. Some of the barrels are now lying near the gutter where they tried to get them out. Paducah, Columbus, and Hickman have been considered by the military authorities here as points from which the rebels are supplied under these treasury regulations, the military having positive orders not to interfere. But the abuse was so great that General Reid felt it to be his duty—and I think justly—to stop it and inquire into the matter, and try to prevent it.

Question. Is the oath they are required to take when they trade any protection at all to the government?

Answer. Our experience is that they disregard the oath entirely; that they have no respect for an oath at all. In these places there are Union men whom the authorities know, but they have to suffer in consequence of there being so many traitors and disloyal men there who will come forward and take the oath for the sake of obtaining goods, which they try to get through to the rebels for the high prices which they get for all they can get through.

Question. In your opinion, what remedy can be applied for this? Can trade be carried on so as to secure the government from these frauds, or must it cease altogether?

Answer. My judgment is, that if the government ever expects to put down this rebellion they must stop this trade to the rebel States, unless it is carried on under very stringent regulations, agreed upon by the military commanders and the Treasury Department; and it will then require very stringent orders and careful watching to prevent these frauds. In my opinion, if any trade is allowed, none but certain kinds of goods should be allowed to go down the river or through our lines to any of the people of the country. The people through the country can live by obtaining provisions from us; as a general thing, they make their own clothing. But if free trade is allowed, they will, of course, buy clothing, which is taken away from them by the rebels; if not with their consent, then by force. In the towns of Hickman and Paducah, at the time of their capture by the rebels, there was an immense amount of supplies belonging to the citizens there, and taken there for sale, which the rebels carried off. The military authorities, under existing orders, could not interfere with the goods being taken there, and they had no time to take them away when the rebels were coming.

Question. Does your experience and opinion upon that subject correspond with that of all the other officers along the river with whom you are acquainted?

Answer. Yes, sir; I think it does. I would further state that, after this attempt of Forrest to take different posts in the district, General Bragman issued an order at first to prohibit all boats landing on the Kentucky shore; to seize and confiscate for the time being, until properly examined into, all boats, skiffs, barges, or anything of the kind landing on the Kentucky shore between Paducah and Columbus. He also issued another order, in obedience to instructions from Major General Hurlbut, commanding 16th army corps, prohibiting all boats from landing any goods at any point between and including Paducah and Columbus; and since Forrest's raid, and up to this time, we have not permitted goods, except a few supplies for officers and families which are absolutely in need, to be landed at any of these points, for fear of their being captured by the rebels.

Question. Is not that order in opposition to the trade regulations of the Treasury Department?

Answer. Yes, sir; but it was issued as a military necessity, to prevent Forrest from obtaining supplies, he having control of the whole country outside of our lines, and his troops pressing our troops at the different posts very hard.

COLUMBUS, KY., *April* 24, 1864.

Colonel WILLIAM H. LAWRENCE (34th New Jersey, commanding at Columbus, Ky.) sworn and examined.

By the chairman:

Question. Have you had opportunities to observe the course of trade upon the river, and how it affects the interests of the government?

Answer. I have.

Question. Please give us the result of your observation, and your opinion of the practical effect of this trade?

Answer. I find that large amounts of goods, both those contraband of war and those not contraband, have been shipped down the river to this place and to Hickman. Those goods have come particularly under my notice. During the first two weeks after free trade was opened on the river I noticed over $100,000 worth of goods that were shipped to Hickman. At that time there was no military force at Hickman. I seized, on my own responsibility, some five hundred barrels of salt at this port on its way down to Hickman; but it was afterwards allowed to go on by the general then commanding this district. I found that goods were passed out of the picket lines here to the surrounding towns in large quantities, which goods found their way into the rebel lines; and I furthermore found that all articles wanted by the rebels have been supplied to them in this way. I know that Forrest's forces have completely cleaned out Hickman, Clinton, Moscow, and other places. The goods go to unguarded points near the Tennessee State line, and people come over and make purchases without being questioned as to where they are going to take the goods they buy.

Question. Have you found that these aids of the Treasury Department do much to restrain this trade and keep it in proper channels?

Answer. In my own judgment, I do not think they have; it has struck me several times that they have not. I have understood from several persons that permits could be obtained for powder and shot, and everything of that kind.

Question. They are instructed, I believe, to sell to Union men, and those men take an oath prescribed by the Treasury Department as a test of their loyalty. So far as you know, is that oath regarded or disregarded by the people of these places who take it?

Answer. I would not give a sixpence for any of their oaths.

Question. How can this contraband trade be prevented? Can this free trade be so regulated, short of absolute prohibition, as to prevent the rebels from obtaining these supplies?

Answer. I think not. I do not think any goods should be allowed to go down the river except military supplies for our forces.

Question. Have you conversed on this subject with other commandants of posts along the river?

Answer. Yes, sir.

Question. What is their experience and their opinion upon this subject?

Answer. Exactly the same as mine. It is the universal opinion of military officers, so far as I have heard it expressed, that these trade regulations have inflicted the most serious injury upon our cause.

FORT PILLOW, TENN., *April* 25, 1864.

Captain JAMES MARSHALL, United States navy, commanding gunboat New Era, sworn and examined.

By the chairman:

Question. Has your attention been called to the effect of trade under the late treasury regulations on this river?

Answer. Yes, sir, it has.

Question. Do you consider the system of free trade, as shown by the results, to be the most beneficial to the United States government or to the rebels?

Answer. I think it is a great drawback to our cause to allow any goods to go down this river except what goes to the army and navy.

Question. In your opinion, can free trade be so regulated here as to prevent contraband articles getting through into the hands of the rebels?

Answer. It cannot be in any way that I can see, unless, perhaps, in one of two ways. One is, to secure agents in whom you have confidence—those who cannot be bought; or, let everything on board be inspected by guards and officers, and then allow no traffic except at points where gunboats are stationed, and keep the whole matter in government hands. That is the only way I can see.

Question. Have you reason to believe that the rebels have received large supplies of contraband articles through the medium of this free trade?

Answer. Yes, sir. I have seen the order taken from the person of a rebel woman, directing her to get a lot of stuff, caps, ammunition, opium, and quinine, and land it at Haynes's Point, in care of Mr. Godwin. It was an order from a rebel colonel who was killed here at Fort Pillow, and she has given me the names of two persons who are engaged in this business.

Question. Are these oaths of allegiance of any avail to prevent frauds?

Answer. Not a particle. Some of the worst rebels have been captured here with oaths of allegiance in their pockets. Major Bradford captured some whom he knew personally to be the worst of rebels.

MEMPHIS, TENN., *April* 26, 1864.

Captain THOMAS PATTISON sworn and examined.

By the chairman:

Question. What is your position in the navy?

Answer. I am a lieutenant commander in the navy, and the commandant of the navy yard in this place.

Question. Have you observed the operation and effect of the late treasury regulations permitting trade, and whether the enemy through them are enabled to obtain supplies of contraband goods?

Answer. Yes, sir; I feel certain that they do obtain such supplies.

Question. Can that be prevented while this trade is permitted?

Answer. No, sir; I do not think it can.

Question. State whether, in your opinion, large supplies of contraband articles find their way to the rebel army in this way.

Answer. I think they do; I feel most certain that they do.

Question. What remedy would you propose to stop that?

Answer. I know of no remedy but to stop the trade altogether. The want of honor and honesty among a very large portion of the people who come here and get these permits prevent us from forming any opinion as to the truth of their statements. They swear that they have such and such families, so many negroes, and that each of them needs a suit of clothes, when they may not own a single negro.

Question. Then the oath that is prescribed is of little avail to prevent these frauds?

Answer. I think it has very little force with these people.

Reuel Hough sworn and examined.

By the chairman:

Question. Are you in the service of the government in any capacity?

Answer. I am the collector of internal revenue for this district, the first district of Tennessee.

Question. How long have you been acting in that capacity?

Answer. Since I left the custom-house on the 5th of November last. Previous to that I was acting surveyor of customs.

Question. How long have you been in Memphis?

Answer. I came here in 1859.

Question. Has your occupation been such as to call your attention to the course of trade here, and how it affects the interest of our government; whether, in the way it is conducted, it ministers to the advantage of the enemy?

Answer. I have been intimately connected with it, and I should say it did.

Question. In your own way give us your views upon that subject?

Answer. I have no doubt that the enemy get contraband goods, not under the trade regulations, but in violation of them.

Question. In spite of the regulations?

Answer. Yes, sir; they get them in various ways.

Question. What is the extent of the trade here now, say, daily or weekly?

Answer. I could not give an estimate of it, not having the proper data upon which to make it.

Question. When people come here to trade, what guarantee do they give that the goods they purchase will not find their way immediately into the rebel lines?

Answer. They are bound by the prescribed oath.

Question. Is there any other assurance than the oath?

Answer. Much is left to the discretion of the officer, who is bound to know something of the character of the man purchasing the goods.

Question. Do not all kinds of persons come here to trade—men, women, &c.?

Answer. They do.

Question. How is the officer supposed to know much about them?

Answer. The intention is, and the effort is, to get down to their own immediate wants in such a manner that they cannot assist the enemy with what they get. I think there is very little actually permitted from the officers here that finds its way to the enemy; it is that which is smuggled through in various ways.

Question. What opportunities are there to smuggle under the present regulations?

Answer. The opportunities that have always existed for taking goods out clandestinely. They, of course, run the risk of being caught by the pickets, and no doubt they sometimes bribe the pickets. I have no question in my own mind that they bribe pickets and bribe officers. There have been larger quantities of goods permitted to go out by military permits than even by treasury permits—goods that never should have been permitted to go out; that is my opinion about it, and done in violation of the treasury regulations. The files of the inspector will show that.

Question. Will they show what officers have interposed their military authority to get goods through which were not authorized by law?

Answer. I think they will, if the same files are there that I left there.

Question. I want to know of you, as a person of experience in this matter, whether you suppose it is possible to carry on trade with a people situated as these are here in this part of the country; as I understand, some few Union men, a great many violent secessionists, and not a great way from the rebel lines. Is it possible that trade can be carried on here to any considerable extent without those articles, which the rebels stand so much in need of, finding their way to them?

Answer. I have no doubt a great many of these articles do find their way to them; more by being seized by rebel scouts than by being carried to them.

Question. What is there to prevent a rebel sympathizer coming here to-day, taking the oath, getting a considerable amount of goods, and immediately taking them to the rebel lines?

Answer. There would be nothing to hinder him from carrying them to the rebel lines after he got them. The object is to ascertain his own wants so fully as not to allow him to take more than would be necessary to supply those wants.

Question. How would the treasury agent be expected to do that in this this community? By what means could he ascertain the character and wants of each individual who comes to trade with him?

Answer. When I was in that department I had an extensive acquaintance in Mississippi and Tennessee. I had charge of this railroad south, running almost the whole length of Tennessee and Mississippi, and I know something about almost all the prominent people who come here, and I endeavored to restrict the matter as far as possible.

Question. I have no doubt about that; but with all your endeavors, what chance was there to really know what these people were, and what they actually needed?

Answer. Of course, there is no chance to know.

Question. Then it comes to this, that all the security the government has is the oath prescribed to be taken by the person purchasing the goods?

Answer. And the restrictions thrown around the purchase by the officer; restricting the man to such goods as his own family may require, and endeavoring, as far as possible, to keep from him those goods which would naturally be used in the confederate army.

Question. Suppose a man should send his daughter up here to-day to purchase a hundred dollars' worth of goods, and next week should send up another daughter, under another name, to purchase a similar quantity of goods; how would you know that you were supplying the same family?

Answer. When I was in the Treasury Department, I confined women to women's wear, and what they wanted for themselves. I did not allow women to take out general plantation supplies, unless it was proved she was a widow, and had charge of a family.

Question. Is it your opinion, with the experience you have had, that the government has any reliable assurance against frauds where this trade is permitted, or that there is any other safe way for the government but to restrict this trade?

Answer. Or to prohibit it. I do not see any other way.

By Mr. Gooch :

Question. Have permits been granted here to take out any considerable quantity of goods, except by treasury agents ?

Answer. They have.

Answer. By whom have those permits been granted ?

Answer. By General Hurlbut and General Veatch.

Question. Did General Veatch precede General Hurlbut in the command here ?

Answer. General Veatch was under General Hurlbut. General Hurlbut was commander of the 16th army corps. General Veatch really had command of the post at the time.

Question. Did those permits cover goods to any considerable extent ?

Answer. Yes, sir, I think they did.

Question. Can you give us any idea of the extent ?

Answer. On some boats I think they amounted to $15,000 or $20,000 at a time.

Question. Where did those goods go ?

Answer. To different landings on the Mississippi river—on both sides of the river.

Question. Were those goods restrained to any further extent after the permits were granted ?

Answer. There was a government aid appointed. They would pick up a man and appoint him government agent on a boat to see that the goods went to the persons to whom they were directed.

Question. Who selected that government aid ?

Answer. At first he was appointed by the surveyor; afterwards it was taken out of the surveyor's hands, and put into the hands of the assistant supervising agents.

Question. The government aid was only to deliver the goods to the parties named in the permits ?

Answer. Yes, sir.

Question. Do you know the general character of the goods thus permitted by the military authorities ?

Answer. General plantation and family supplies, prohibiting entirely cavalry boots and all kinds of heavy boots, and such kinds of brogans as it was supposed would be used by the enemy's army.

Question. How was it in fact ? Were the goods thus sent out such as could be made useful to the enemy for military purposes ?

Answer. Yes, sir; for instance, calico prints are supposed to be women's wear solely. But, in the absence of blankets, the confederates use quilts. And, of course, with calico and cotton they could make very comfortable camp bedding without blankets.

Question. Have you any knowledge whether, in fact, that was done ?

Answer. No instance occurs to me now, though I have no doubt it was done to a considerable extent.

Question. Have the officers to whom you have referred continued to grant those permits as long as they remained at the post here ?

Answer. I do not know what they have done since I left the custom-house.

Question. Did they continue to do it as long as you remained in the custom-house ?

Answer. Their practice in that matter would change; sometimes the lines would be entirely closed, and no goods allowed to go out; then they would allow goods to go—sometimes freely.

Question. Were there any particular persons who seemed to enjoy special favor in regard to permits ?

Answer. I can hardly say that, though I sometimes thought so. Still I would not like to swear that I was positive it was so. There was a man here—I think his name was Dr. Walker—who was said to have got a large amount of permits through General Veatch's office, for which Dr. Walker was paid. Some of the merchants—one in particular—came to my office and said: "There are parties who get goods through here, and I cannot get any through General Veatch's office; it is done, and I am going to find out how it is done." Afterwards I learned that he had got permits through General Veatch's office, and I asked him how he did it. He told me confidentially that he paid a third party for doing it, and the third party got them through.

Question. Did these military officers give permits for goods to go into the country around here?

Answer. Yes, sir. They were not supposed to give permits within the trade limits, but their permits generally went beyond the limits that were fixed by the Treasury Department. For instance, the commanding general is communicated with, and is asked to define his lines within which trade can be carried on. The lines were for a long time confined to the Mississippi on the south. I got up a regulation myself that no goods should be permitted beyond Nonconnah creek, from the fact that when they once got beyond that they would go into Mississippi. General Hurlbut said he did not know of any regulation that stopped goods at Nonconnah, and they were permitted to go to any point south in Tennessee. I felt the responsibility resting upon me to that extent that I did not like to have goods going beyond Nonconnah getting into Mississippi; therefore I would not allow goods to go beyond there without military permits.

Question. Did these generals continue to give permits as long as you remained in the custom-house?

Answer. Yes, sir, at times.

Question. What would you say about the amount of goods that went out under military permits, and under permits of the special agents of the treasury?

Answer. The permits given by the military covered a very much larger amount than those given by the treasury agents—that is, one man would be allowed to take out more under a military permit than under a treasury permit. Of course the military did not interfere in all cases; they only permitted goods to go to certain locations to which the treasury did not feel authorized to permit.

Question. Then, in order to remedy the evil, it would be best to restrict the military permits as well as the treasury permits?

Answer. I think if the military had not had anything to do with it, it would have been better; that less goods would have gone out.

CAIRO, ILLINOIS, *April* 28, 1864.

J. C. SLOO sworn and examined.

By the chairman:

Question. What is your position under the government?

Answer. I am the postmaster at this place.

Question. Will you tell us what, if any, communication can be kept up with the rebels by reason of the present mail arrangements?

Answer. The mails on the Kentucky shore from this point and Evansville, Indiana, are delivered all down the river, including Paducah, Henderson, Uniontown, &c. I suppose there are fifteen or twenty places at which mails are delivered four times a week up, and four times down.

Question. What is the character of the inhabitants, the postmasters, &c., into whose hands these mails go?

Answer. I do not know personally a single postmaster on the whole line. But we understand here that the inhabitants are as disloyal as they are in

Paducah—I mean from Green river to the Tennessee line; and I think Paducah is one of the most disloyal towns in the whole country.

Question. Is any portion of the county in which these mails circulate now in possession of the enemy?

Answer. So far as Forrest and his raid are concerned, it has been in their possession. I do not know this from personal observation, but from general report. I understand that they have been conscripting over in Bellair county, within fifteen or twenty miles of this place.

Question. The consequence is, that if the rebels have any agents here or anywhere in the north, and want to send letters to their sympathizers, they can do so.

Answer. Yes, sir.

Question. Is it your opinion that it is unsafe to the interests of the government to keep up those post offices now?

Answer. I think it is unsafe to send the mails there; I have thought for some time that it was against the interest of the country to do so.

Question. Does it furnish an easy means of communication with the rebels?

Answer. Most unquestionably it does, so far as sending intelligence from Paducah, Henderson, and other points on the river.

DANIEL ARTER sworn and examined.

By the chairman:

Question. What position do you occupy under the government?

Answer. Surveyor of the port of Cairo.

Question. How do the late treasury regulations concerning trade operate? Are they most beneficial to us or to the rebels?

Answer. Until the abrogation of the restrictions in regard to Missouri, Kentucky, and Western Virginia, I think very few goods were carried over that it was possible to put to any improper use. My instructions were, that rebels within our lines must be fed, but sparingly. But since the abrogation of those restrictions there have been a great many goods passed through this district into Kentucky—how many I am not able to tell—because boats that run on the Ohio do not exhibit their manifests unless they go below. Boats running exclusively on the Ohio or up the Mississippi do not exhibit their manifests as they used to do. Along before they became aware of the privileges they possessed, almost all the boats would fill, as usual, through manifests. If I recollect aright, some 600 packages of ammunition were distributed along the Kentucky shore from Evansville to this point in one week. But I have no knowledge of or any way of ascertaining the amount of goods since then. According to the order of the treasury department they can take anything they please. The instructions are, that trade is free, the same as in time of peace.

Question. Is there any doubt that the rebel authorities receive vast amounts of military stores and contraband goods through this source?

Answer. I am just as well satisfied that they do as I am of anything on earth that I do not actually see.

Question. What security is there now that the rebels will not receive any amount of contraband articles they please?

Answer. None at all whatever, except so far as the military interfere.

Question. If the military interfere to prevent it, are they not compelled to do so against the treasury regulations as a matter of military necessity?

Answer. I think so.

Question. Has it not seemed to you most singular that while we take so much pains to guard the Atlantic coast against the admission of contraband articles, we leave the way open for their admission here?

Answer. I think it is one of the most extraordinary circumstances that has occurred since the commencement of the war. I have expressed my opinion to Mr. Turnbull in regard to this matter. I stated, in short, that hundreds of thousands of dollars' worth of goods had gone and were then going through this district to Kentucky, some of which I had no doubt were then in Richmond. It opened a sluice-way that there was nothing to guard. There was a paper blockade, it is true, for it was provided that none of the goods should be passed out of these states into an insurrectionary State; but there was nothing to prevent it.

Question. There was no security against that?

Answer. None whatever.

Question. Is the oath which is prescribed any security to the government?

Answer. There is no oath to take.

Question. Where they take an oath to trade with what are called loyal people, does it furnish any security?

Answer. I never had much confidence in their oaths. I think there are a great many men who have sworn falsely. I have refused to receive their oaths, for I knew they would swear falsely.

Question. Can you give any instances of contraband goods finding their way to the rebels?

Answer. I only have reports, but I have them in abundance; for instance, when General Smith came up here he told me that he had come across large quantities of those goods on their way to the enemy that had passed through here, and he was very much put out about it. Before these restrictions were removed, family supplies were allowed to persons who made oath that they had only so much on hand; that the goods they asked for were for their own use; that no part of them was to be disposed in any way to give aid to persons in insurrection against the United States; and then they took the oath of allegiance also. With a great many of those men I was personally acquainted. If any one applied with whom I was not personally acquainted, I would question him as to the number of his family, the amount of his stock, the size of farm he had; and then I would cut him down to such a quantity as I thought he should have. But those restrictions are now removed, and they can take any quantity without limit.

Question. What is your opinion in regard to the quantity of supplies that Forrest's forces found here prepared for them in consequence of this open trade?

Answer. That the amount was large I have no doubt in the world. A great many goods were shipped to Hickman, and, as I always did believe, a great many goods have been carried there from time to time under an arrangement for the rebels, who paid the parties for them, and then under pretence of a raid came and took the goods away.

Question. What is there to prevent such an arrangement being made all over Kentucky?

Answer. Nothing in the world.

Question. Is there any reason to suppose that Forrest's raid was in consequence of the vast amount of goods prepared here for the rebels?

Answer. In one of my official letters to the department I stated in advance that these goods there would be an incentive to these guerillas, robbers and murderers to overrun the country, and I have no doubt that was the case. This country was perfectly bare of goods before the restrictions were removed, and all the goods going in there since were just so much in favor of the rebels.

Major General C. C. WASHBURN sworn and examined.

Question. What is your rank and position in the service?

Answer. I am major general of volunteers, and am now commanding the district of West Tennessee.

Question. What information have you in relation to the late attack on Fort Pillow and the massacre there?

Answer. I have seen and conversed with a number of white and colored soldiers who were there at the time of capture. Their statements more than confirm all that has been published in regard to that affair; but as the committee have already the sworn statements of most of the parties that I have seen who were present, I refer to their testimony for further answer.

Question. Do you know whether or not Fort Pillow could have been re-enforced from Memphis after notice of its threatened attack; and what notice had the commander of this district that such an attacked was threatened?

Answer. I do not know at what time notice was received by the commander of the district that an attack was threatened. I am informed that the last letter received from Major Booth was dated April 3, in which he expressed confidence that he should not be attacked, and that he could hold out if he was. It could easily have been re-enforced within eight hours after notice was received at Memphis. Forrest was known to be in the interior, with a force of seven or eight thousand men, for several days before Fort Pillow was attacked.

Question. What, in your opinion, has been the effect of the treasury regulations permitting trade with citizens in this district?

Answer. In my opinion, the effect has been most disastrous to the cause and interests of the general government. From the day I reached the Mississippi river, after the campaign in Arkansas in 1862, to the present moment, my opinion has remained unchanged. I believe that permitting trade has been of vast assistance to the rebel armies; that it has had a most demoralizing influence upon our army. I intend these remarks to be general, and to apply to every department in which I have served. I know of many disasters to our arms, which, in my judgment, would never have taken place, had not cotton, sugar, and trade in general, invited our arms to places where they should not have gone. Permitting trade invites a horde of hungry unprincipled camp followers. It leaves us to the mercy of the spies of the enemy, who, under the system, come and go at pleasure. It brings little money into the treasury, but fills the pockets of the class of people before named—a class who, being from home, escape conscription and their just liabilities to the government, and who, of all others, are least entitled to favor. The extent of the trade daily passing outside of our lines here, into the enemy's country, is estimated, by Brigadier General Buckland, commanding the district of Memphis, at from $40,000 to $50,000 daily. Articles contraband of war, such as arms, percussion caps, and ammunition, are often captured in attempting to smuggle them through the lines; and so long as the lines are kept open, it is not possible to prevent large quantities of such articles from reaching the enemy.

The hope of obtaining large supplies by capture at Paducah, Columbus, and Fort Pillow, and through the trade regulations at Memphis, I have no doubt, was one great inducement for Forrest's late raid.

The only opportunity I have had since I have been in the service to exercise authority over this question was for a short time at Helena, Ark. On the 3d of April, 1863, I was placed in command of the United States forces there. On the 4th day of April I issued the following order, viz:

"SPECIAL ORDERS No. 9.

"HEADQUARTERS UNITED STATES FORCES,
"*Helena, Ark., April* 4, 1863.

"I. The lines of this army will be closed from this date.

"II. Passes will only be granted on the most urgent cases, and then only to persons of *known* loyalty.

"III. War and commerce with rebels being utterly inconsistent, all supplies to go beyond the federal lines are prohibited.

"By order of— C. C. WASHBURN,
"*Major General.*
"W. H. MORGAN,
"*A. A. General.*"

Under that order the lines were closed and trade suspended outside the lines, while I remained. I was soon after ordered into another department, and I think that trade was immediately thereafter resumed.

I have the most positive and reliable testimony that thousands of bales of cotton, belonging to the confederate government, have been sold in Memphis, and paid for in gold, greenbacks, and supplies, which have gone to replenish the confederate treasury, and feed, clothe, and arm confederate officers and soldiers.

Question. What, in your judgment, is the remedy for the evils you have mentioned?

Answer. The remedy is to close the lines and suspend all commercial intercourse with the districts that are in a state of rebellion.

C. C. WASHBURN,
Major General.

This deponent states: That the provost marshal of Vicksburg, Wardell, is a thorough secesh friend; that the said Wardell sells passes to the rebels to get through the lines; that he speculates in cotton, and has abused his influence with the government to let confiscated plantations to such individuals who are friends of the previous owners, and who divide the proceeds with the said Wardell; that the provost marshal, Wardell, is actually smuggling large stocks of goods through the lines, and that his brother keeps a very large store in Vicksburg, supplying the enemy with goods; that said Wardell has made over one hundred thousand dollars in a very short space of time, and that he was worth nothing when he left Chicago, his place of residence.

And this deponent further says: That every storekeeper in Vicksburg has to bribe said Wardell by sums from $500 to $2,000 to carry goods through the lines; that one merchant, A. Genella, is Wardell's especial protege; that said Genella is a rank secesh, and that before the attack on Vicksburg, by General Grant, said Genella offered $5,000 to the battery that may sink the first Yankee cannon-boat; that other prominent secessionists and merchants at Vicksburg, who conspire with said Wardell against the United States government, are Joseph Botta and J. Baum; that one Kirshky (a Jew) is Wardell's especial accomplice in supplying the rebels with contraband goods, said Kirshky having, at the siege of Vicksburg, supplied the rebels with barrels full of brandy free of charge to fight the more fierce against the "damned Yankees," as he expressed himself; that Lewis Hoffman and Frederick Boni (two other prominent secessionists in Vicksburg) are Wardell's intimates, and were among the first who received permits to keep stores; that all these persons publicly brag they could have for *money* everything done by those miserable Yankees; that all the true Union people under such sway have left and are leaving Vicksburg on account of not being able to get permits to trade unless they are willing or able to bribe the provost marshal with heavy amounts of money.

And deponent further says: That almost all the members of the corps of officers, from General McPherson, Generals Hurlbut, McCarter, down to captains and quartermasters, are interested in trade and administration of plantations so as to form a perfectly linked chain of thieves; that the depot quartermaster, Finker, a German Jew from Milwaukie, who has been already under court-martial in the Potomac army, is one of the chief thieves, and the right arm of Provost Marshal Wardell; that the depot of Vicksburg was put on fire by these united thieves and secesh friends after the grain stored there had been removed over the river to the enemy, so as to make it appear the fire had consumed the immense quantities of provisions stored at the depot aforesaid; that the surrender of Fort Pillow was known two weeks before at Vicksburg, and was publicly spoken of as being agreed between the officers of both the United States and the enemy.

And deponent further says: That many millions worth of goods and luxuries—intentionally for the rebels—are stored yet in Vicksburg, and that they can easy be seized *by closing at once all the stores of the secesh sympathizers* there who received their permits from or through Provost Marshal Wardell; that any and all the members of the loyal Union League, in Vicksburg, can and will furnish witnesses any moment who will prove the assertions made by this deponent; that the chief of the permit office in Vicksburg, whose name this deponent does not know, is linked in with the provost marshal, and that the aforesaid officer only grants permits for trading to such secesh sympathizers as are pointed out by the said Wardell; that the clerks in the provost marshal's office, and those in the permit office, can give sufficient evidence in the case, and that the books and papers of both offices, when seized, will develop a mass of swindles on the government unheard of before.

A. GUDATH.

STATE OF NEW YORK,
City and county of New York, ss:

On this twenty-ninth day of April, A. D. eighteen hundred and sixty-four, personally appeared before me A. Gudath, personally known to me to be the person described in and who made and signed before me the above statement.

EDMUND J. KOCH,
Notary Public in and for the city and county of New York.

BATTLE OF CEDAR MOUNTAIN.

Testimony of Major General N. P. Banks.

WASHINGTON, D. C., *December* 14, 1864.

Major General N. P. BANKS sworn and examined.

Having testified in relation to the Red River expedition, the witness said:

There is another subject upon which I wish to make a statement. I am sorry to say that I have made very few reports; and, as so many people report things that do not happen, it is perhaps excusable if there is one man who does not report things that do happen. I had an engagement at Cedar mountain on the 9th of August, 1862, which was a part of General Pope's campaign. I desire to call the attention of the committee to that for a moment, for this single reason, it has never been explained, and I have never had a chance to put it on record before, except in a report to the War Department, from whence no information comes to the public at all; and it leaves me under a wrong impression in the public mind, as you will see when I have made my statement. I was in command of a corps in August, 1862, in the Shenandoah valley. I was ordered to General John Pope's command, in the Rappahannock valley. Under his orders I moved to Culpeper on the 9th day of August, arriving there about seven o'clock in the morning. His headquarters were in the town, and my command was in the outskirts of the town. Immediately on my arrival at Culpeper, I received orders from General Pope to move to the front, which was six miles in advance of Culpeper, where a brigade of my command had been stationed for a week, occupying the outposts under General Crawford. That order was received at eight o'clock, and in thirty minutes was countermanded. At 9.45 on the same day I received another order from General Pope to move immediately to the front. The order was in these words—I will read from the original paper, in the handwriting of my adjutant general, Colonel Pelouze:

"CULPEPER, 9.45 A. M., *August* 9, 1862.

"From Colonel Lewis Marshall: General Banks will move to the front immediately, assume command of all the forces in the front, deploy his skirmishers if the enemy approaches, and attack him immediately as soon as he approaches, and be re-enforced from here."

This order was given to me verbally by the officer who brought it. He delivered it in the presence of five of my staff officers. I immediately said to him, "You will please give this order to my adjutant general, that he may reduce it to writing." Colonel Pelouze was sitting at a table at the moment, and the officer who bore the order stepped up and repeated it to him, and it was written from his lips as he pronounced it. Colonel Pelouze then read the order to him in order to see if it was correct, and he approved it. This took place in the presence of five of my staff officers and some other officers who did not belong to my command. Within an hour from 9.45 my troops were on the march. We reached the point indicated, five miles to the front, between one and two o'clock. On their way out I left the head of my column and went to General Pope's headquarters, he occupying then a house belonging to Mr. Wallach, the editor of the "Evening Star" in this city. I told General Pope that my troops were on their way, and asked him if he had any other orders. He said, "I have sent an officer acquainted with the country who will designate the ground you are to hold, and will give you any instructions he may deem necessary." I continued my march, and reached the ground occupied by General Crawford, who occupied a line in front of the enemy. On my arrival there I met Brigadier General Roberts, chief of staff to General Pope. I said to him that General Pope had told me that he would indicate the line I was to occupy. Said he, "I have been over this ground thoroughly, and I believe this line"—meaning the one which General Crawford's brigade then held—"is the best that can be taken." I concurred with him in that opinion, and placed my command there. I had about six thousand men.

The enemy had all the morning been moving his forces, with a view to action, as I learned from General Crawford. Slaughter's mountain, or, as we call it, Cedar mountain, was in the vicinity of our position. There were dense woods in front, occupied by the enemy. General Crawford occupied a line a little to the rear and centre of an open plain between us and the enemy. My force took up the position which was indicated by General Roberts, who had looked over the ground. It was the best position for attack, which was the object indicated by my orders. If I had been instructed simply to act upon the defensive, we should have taken a line in the woods behind Cedar creek, because it would have concealed our forces and given us the benefit of the creek—where, by the way, when we retired at nightfall, we lost one piece of artillery—but our object being different, I was instructed to take this line. The enemy had been moving troops down to the rear of the mountain during the day. It was supposed that they would occupy a hill, and move upon us from the left. We made a reconnoissance from the front. I went down to the front with some officers, and we were impressed with the idea that, while they were openly moving on the other side, they were coming down upon the right; and if they got possession of those woods and attacked us, we would be obliged to fall back. Being impressed with the feeling that they were coming down on our right, I directed Brigadier General Crawford to send one regiment to feel them. They in the mean time had sent a line of skirmishers from the woods out to the front, and were gradually creeping up. General Crawford went up with a regiment to the right, and said, "The enemy begins to appear here; I must have more force." I sent him a brigade. The enemy by that time had massed his forces on our right—his left—and was moving forward, and began an attack upon us, when my force encountered him. The battle had been going on with artillery from two until four o'clock. About five o'clock, which is the usual time for them to make an attack, they made a desperate attack upon our right. Of course, we had to strengthen that with all our force. It is certain that General Jackson was there with twenty-three thousand men, for he was in that neighborhood. Our troops never fought better in the world than there. They had been retreating up to that time, and panted for a fight. The battle raged for two hours, and until the combatants were separated by the darkness, with as much stubbornness as ever men fought in the world. Alexander's troops never fought better. They held their position until dark; but the enemy was so much stronger that it was impossible for us to advance. In the evening, after dark, they fell back to the line they had occupied in the day-time, General Pope coming up after dark with his command. I say it was after dark, because, after my troops were in line, understanding that General Pope was coming up, I rode to the rear to meet him, and passed him, because it was so dark that I could not distinguish him. I sent to General Pope every hour, from one or two o'clock, information of what was transpiring. I did not say the enemy was in force, because I did not know it; and I was a little desperate, because we supposed that General Pope thought we did not want to fight. General Roberts, when he indicated the position, said to me, in a tone which it was hardly proper for one officer to use to another, "There must be no backing out this day." He said this to me from six to twelve times. I made no reply to him at all, but I felt it keenly, because I knew that my command did not want to back out; we had backed out enough. He repeated this declaration a great many times, "There must be no backing out this day." At the crisis of the battle he left. It was really and honestly a drawn battle. We held our line, but we had suffered very severely. The enemy was stronger than we were, and we knew that we could not overcome him. Late at night General Pope came up with his forces. In the morning the enemy retreated, recrossed the Rappahannock, and did not advance again for ten days after the battle at Cedar mountain, when the same troops came forward on the other side of the river and made a detour up towards Washington with the whole of that army. By that time General McClellan had been able to get his forces in the neighborhood of Washington, and we were enabled to meet them after a fashion. I regard that that battle prevented the advance of the enemy's forces for some days.

What I want to say is that this battle was fought under positive orders in the presence of the chief of staff of General Pope; but I am sorry to hear that he represents in his report that it was a battle fought honestly by me, but against orders and without being expected by him. Here is the original order, which I will read again:

"From Colonel Lewis Marshall: General Banks will move to the front immediately, assume command of all the forces in the front, deploy his skirmishers if the enemy approaches, and attack him immediately as soon as he approaches."

We were obliged to fight or retreat, and no battle has ever been fought in better faith or in a better manner. We were five thousand men against twenty-five thousand in those woods and on that hill. It was a well-fought battle.

Letter of Major General Pope to Hon. B. F. Wade, chairman of the Joint Committee on the Conduct of the War, with accompanying papers and testimony concerning the battle of Cedar mountain, August 9, 1862.

HEADQUARTERS DEPARTMENT OF THE NORTHWEST,
Milwaukie, Wisconsin, January 12, 1865.

SIR: It has come to my knowledge that Major General Banks, while in Washington city recently on leave of absence with one or two of his staff officers, gave some testimony before your honorable committee concerning a portion of the battle of Cedar mountain.

Of course your honorable committee would not permit an *ex parte* statement on so important a subject to be recorded in their proceedings without notifying and examining other officers concerned, and without giving the whole subject that careful and full investigation which justice and fair dealing demand, and which has characterized the proceedings of your committee hitherto.

In this view, and upon one point concerning which General Banks has given some testimony, I desire to invite your attention to the following facts, which I submit as my own testimony on the subject. Whilst it would not be consistent, probably, with the interests of the public service that I should, for the present, be called away from my official duties in this department, I would respectfully request that the officers hereinafter mentioned be summoned to give their testimony in the case.

I understand that General Banks seeks, by his testimony and that of one or two of his staff, to rid himself of the responsibility of the battle of Cedar mountain by attempting to show that he acted under my orders in making the attack.

The facts herein stated, and which the testimony of the officers hereinafter mentioned will fully establish, will plainly exhibit to your committee the value of General Banks's plea, and of the testimony he brings forward to justify it.

General Banks alleges that he received a verbal message from me from the lips of Colonel L. H. Marshall, an officer on my staff, in the following words, viz: "General Pope directs that you move to the front with your corps, and take up a strong position at or near the point occupied by Crawford's brigade of your corps. If the enemy advances against you, you will push your skirmishers well out and attack. Re-enforcements will be sent forward from Culpeper."

Upon this order, which I never gave, but which General Banks says he received, he bases his justification in leaving the strong position he was ordered to take up, and in advancing two miles (nearly) to attack an enemy well posted and in superior force.

It is not necessary to point out to your honorable committee that even if the message had been precisely in the words alleged by General Banks, yet it nowhere contains any order for him to leave his strong position, nor is there the slightest intimation in it that he was expected to do so. The interpretation put upon it by General Banks, no doubt the result of afterthought, does more credit to his ingenuity than his judgment. As interpreted by General Banks, the order bears absurdity and contradiction on its face so plainly that I venture to say that no man, except under the pressure of very strong personal motives, could have ever understood it as General Banks says he did.

What possible object could there be in ordering General Banks to take up a strong position against the advancing enemy, when the moment that enemy advanced he was to leave it and march forward to attack? In this case, too, it was not the enemy that advanced against Banks's strong position, but Banks who advanced against the enemy's chosen position.

The movements of the army for concentration to fight Jackson were perfectly well known to everybody in the army, and of necessity to General Banks. His corps was pushed forward to occupy and hold a strong position, behind which the concentration of McDowell and Sigel was to be made.

I venture to point out the absurdity of General Banks's interpretation of the verbal order which he says he received, but which in no manner authorizes his forward movement against Jackson, because it is manifest that much dependence is placed upon the superficial reading often given to such papers. I submit also an official letter from Colonel Marshall on the subject, from which it is manifest that I neither gave any order through him which authorized General Banks to leave his strong position and attack the enemy, nor did Colonel Marshall intend to convey any such idea to General Banks.

Whatever, however, may have been the facts in reference to Colonel Marshall's delivery of the verbal order referred to, and whatever that order may have been as delivered, I do not perceive that it has the slightest bearing upon the question. It was delivered to General Banks, according to his own statement, at 8 o'clock on the morning of the 9th of August, whilst his corps was still encamped two miles northwest of Culpeper. It was, in fact, his first order to move to the front. From the fact that neither General Banks nor his witnesses refer to any subsequent orders or instructions, they purposely leave the inference that he received no subsequent orders on the subject; and that from 8 o'clock in the morning until 6 o'clock in the afternoon of the 9th of August he received no orders from me concerning his operations. This omission on the part of General Banks is the more singular, because, aside from subsequent orders sent him on several occasions whilst he was on the field, in order to make sure that there would be no mistake about my orders and intentions, I subsequently (at 9½ o'clock in the morning) sent Brigadier General Roberts, senior officer of my staff and an old army officer, to the field with full and precise orders to General Banks that he should take up a strong position near where Crawford's brigade of his corps was posted, and if the enemy advanced upon him that he should push his skirmishers well to the front and attack the enemy with them, explaining fully that the object was to keep back the enemy until Sigel's corps and Rickett's division of McDowell's corps could be concentrated and brought forward to his support. General Roberts was directed to remain with General Banks until further orders, and he accordingly did remain with him until I reached the field in person, just before dark, when Banks had been driven back to the position he took up in the morning.

General Roberts was authorized by me to give such orders to General Banks, or any other officer on the field, as were necessary to secure the execution of the plans and purposes above stated. I presume there was not an officer at my headquarters who did not know what my purpose was. In fact, the object was so plain that no military man could fail to see it. I conferred freely with General McDowell about it, and to his official report, published by the House of Representatives, I refer for a corroboration of my statement that that was the understanding of my purpose.

General Roberts, in obedience to the orders above specified, reported to General Banks early in the day on the 9th of August; gave him my orders, as above stated, and, in conjunction with him, selected the strong position he was to take and hold.

General Banks posted his corps accordingly, but during General Roberts's absence, reconnoitring the extreme right of the position, General Banks began to move his corps forward; and when General Roberts returned he found General Banks moving forward with his whole corps to attack the enemy.

He immediately remonstrated against the movement, and some conversation between himself and General Banks ensued, Roberts protesting against the movement, and saying that the enemy was in heavy force—Banks replying that they were not in strong force, and that he could beat them and take their batteries; but at no time pretending even that he had orders from me to attack.

The above statement is a quotation almost verbatim from the testimony of General Roberts on the subject of the battle of Cedar mountain, delivered before the McDowell court of inquiry at Washington city in January, 1863. I transmit enclosed a certified copy of his testimony from the original record. The testimony taken by the McDowell court of inquiry has never been published, but it is on file in the War Department, and easily accessible to your committee, if it be necessary to verify the copy herewith enclosed.

Colonel L. H. Marshall, who is the officer said to have given General Banks the verbal order which he presents, is at present on duty as mustering and disbursing officer at Milwaukie, Wisconsin, and can readily appear before your committee. Brigadier General B. S. Roberts is still in service, and his station can be ascertained at the War Department. Captain J. McC. Bell, assistant adjutant general on General Roberts's staff during the battle, is now on duty with me, and I wish him to be examined concerning the orders and despatches from me received by General Banks on the field during the 9th of August. Captain Bell was present when General Banks read these orders aloud to General Roberts. All my copies of these orders and despatches have been lost, but General Banks, doubtless, has the originals, the substance of which can be given by Captain Bell. They are all subsequent to the alleged verbal order given by Colonel Marshall in the morning.

The object in sending Banks's corps to the front to take and hold a strong position against the advancing enemy, until Sigel's corps and Ricketts's division of McDowell's corps could be united in his rear, was so plain, and so clearly understood by every man of ordinary intelligence, that I find it impossible to believe that General Banks did not understand it.

It is clear to me, from his own reports at the time, that he *did* understand it. Although in easy communication with me all day, and although I received, at regular intervals, reports from him, he, on every occasion, expressed the belief that the enemy did not intend to attack him, and at no time intimated to me that *he* intended to attack the enemy. He neither asked for re-enforcements nor intimated that he needed them. His last report was dated at 4.50 p. m., and is as follows:

"AUGUST 9, 1862—4.50 p. m.

"To Colonel RUGGLES, *Chief of Staff:*

"About 4 o'clock shots were exchanged by the skirmishers. Artillery opened fire on both sides in a few minutes. One regiment of rebel infantry advancing now deployed as skirmishers. I have ordered a regiment from the right (Williams's division) and one from the left (Augur's) to advance on the left and in front."

"5 p. m.—They are now approaching each other."

This is the last despatch of General Banks, but before I received it I was half-way to the field with Ricketts's division, the rapid firing inducing me to believe that an engagement was going on. For General Banks's despatches and my reasons for going to the front with Ricketts's division, see my official report and General McDowell's in the volume printed by resolution of the House of Representatives.

I had not the slightest idea when I went forward that General Banks had moved from his position. He at no time stated to me his purpose to do so, and I supposed, of course, when I went forward, that the enemy had attacked him in the strong position he had been ordered to take up, and that he was still holding it. I presumed he would need help in defending that position, though he did not at any time say so, but constantly reported his belief that the enemy was not in force and would not attack.

I accordingly went to the front with Ricketts's division as a precaution, but when I arrived on the field I found to my surprise that General Banks had not only left the position in which he was posted in the morning, but had actually advanced two miles nearly in the belief that he could beat the enemy, as they were not in large force.

When near the field even I received word from Banks that he was "driving the enemy," which information I at once communicated to Ricketts's division.

As I have stated in my official report, I never designed that Banks should attack the enemy before McDowell and Sigel joined him, and gave no order whatever to that effect. The whole weight of the facts and circumstances, the general understanding of everybody, and Banks's own despatches, are against the fact that he himself, *at the time*, thought of understanding otherwise than that he was to hold his position against the enemy.

It is proper to state to your committee that on the 13th of August, three days after the battle of Cedar mountain, I sent a long telegraphic report of the battle to Major General Halleck, which was published in all the papers immediately, and which, as it was seen a day or two after its publication by most if not all the officers belonging to the army, must necessarily have been known to General Banks.

In fact, I am positive it was known to him, since I sent him a copy of General Halleck's despatch acknowledging its receipt, and containing some remarks complimentary to the *gallantry* of General Banks and his corps. In that telegraphic report I stated precisely what is stated in my detailed official report, viz: that General Banks departed from his order by leaving the position he was ordered to take up and advancing to attack the enemy. I several times called upon General Banks, while he remained under my command, for a report of the battle of Cedar mountain, and when I was relieved from command of the army of Virginia, in September, 1862, the general-in-chief of the army, (Major General Halleck,) at my request, issued positive orders to General Banks, and one or two other corps commanders, to make reports to me immediately of the operations of their respective corps during the campaign of the army of Virginia, to be used in making up my own official report.

Yet up to this time not one word has been received from General Banks on the subject by me or by any other military official of the government. Now, at the end of more than two years, General Banks, being on leave of absence in Washington, procures the testimony of himself and one or two of his staff officers to be taken by your committee in relation to a verbal order, which he says he received from Colonel L. H. Marshall early in the morning of the battle of Cedar mountain, before his corps had even gone to the front. He seems to have interpreted this alleged order in the light of afterthought, without alluding to subsequent orders he received, and without notifying me or any other officer concerned in that battle that he intended to give or had given any testimony before your committee on the subject. Pure accident alone brought to my knowledge the fact that he had given such testimony, and enabled me, I trust in time, to present this paper and these facts as the basis of further examination of the subject, which I hereby respectfully solicit in the cause of justice and fair dealing.

I leave your committee to characterize such a transaction as it merits.

As General Banks, however, has chosen to pursue so questionable a course in this matter, it is but justice to the officers and men concerned, whether of his own or other corps of the army, that your committee examine thoroughly into the battle of Cedar mountain, and that for this purpose you procure the testimony of such of the division and brigade commanders of his corps and of other officers as are within reach.

I present the names of Major General Augur, Brigadier General A. S. Williams, Brigadier General George H. Gordon, Brigadier General Henry Prince, Brigadier General Geary, Brigadier General B. S. Roberts, Colonel L. H. Marshall, Captain J. McC. Bell, and such others as the official records show were with General Banks or under his command at that battle. I am much deceived and misinformed if their testimony does not exhibit the fact that, if even General Banks had received positive orders to attack, and had had every advantage on his side, his remarkable arrangements for that battle and his singular manner of making the attack did not render it next to certain that the result must necessarily have been defeat and disaster to his corps.

In my official reports I endeavored, as far as I possibly could, to avoid the censure justly chargeable upon General Banks for his management of that battle, though I was warned at the time by officers of high rank that it was misplaced generosity, and that my forbearance would assuredly be used against me thereafter. I did not then believe it possible, and felt disposed to deal with General Banks with the utmost tenderness, as I knew and sympathized with him in his mortification at the result of his previous encounter with Jackson, and perfectly understood his natural anxiety to avail himself of the first opportunity to retrieve his reputation. I was very unwilling under such circumstances to criticise his operations at Cedar mountain with any sort of harshness; but as he himself has chosen at this late day to reopen the question of the battle of Cedar mountain, by endeavoring to place on your records an ex parte statement of only one incident connected with it, it seems but proper that your honorable committee now examine thoroughly into it, in order that the whole subject may be fully and fairly presented to the country, and the measure of praise or censure be correctly fixed upon the parties concerned.

I am, sir, respectfully, your obedient servant,

JOHN POPE,
Major General U. S. V.

Testimony of Brigadier General B. S. Roberts, U. S. V., concerning the battle of Cedar mountain, given before the McDowell court of inquiry.

WASHINGTON, D. C., *January*, 1863.

Brigadier General BENJAMIN S. ROBERTS, United States volunteers, a witness, was duly sworn.

By General McDowell:

Question. What was your position on General Pope's staff in the late campaign in Virginia?

Answer. In the early part of the campaign I was chief of cavalry of that army; the latter part of it I was inspector general.

Question. What do you know of the orders of General Pope to General Banks relative to the battle of Cedar mountain, 9th day of August, 1862?

Answer. Early in the morning of the 9th day of August I was sent by General Pope to the front of the army with directions, when General Banks should reach a position where the night before I had posted General Crawford's brigade, that I should show to General Banks positions for him to take, to hold the enemy in check, if he attempted to advance towards Culpeper. Two days previous, the 7th and 8th, I had been to the point; knew the country, and had reported to General Pope my impression that a large force of General Jackson would be at Cedar mountain, or near there, on the 9th, re-enforcing Ewell's troops, who were already there. General Pope authorized me, before going to the point, to give any orders in his name to any of the officers that might be in the field senior to me. I understood his object was to hold the enemy in check there that day, and not to attack until the other troops of his command should arrive and join General Banks.

Question. Was the battle of the 9th day of August at Cedar mountain brought on by the enemy or by General Banks?

Answer. In the early part of the day the battle was brought on (artillery battle) by the enemy's batteries opening from new positions on General Crawford's artillery. I had been directed by General Pope to send information to him hourly of what was going on, and I had expressed to General Banks my opinion, about three o'clock in the afternoon, that Jackson had arrived; the forces were very large. General Banks expressed a different opinion, saying that he thought he should attack the batteries before night. I stated to General Banks then my reasons for believing that an attack would be dangerous; that I was convinced that the batteries both on Cedar and Slaughter's mountains were supported by heavy forces of infantry massed in the woods. He expressed a different opinion. He told me he believed he could carry the field. His men were in the best fighting condition, and that he should undertake it. I immediately sent a despatch to General Pope—I think my despatch was dated half past four—telling him that a general battle would be fought before night, and that it was of the utmost importance, in my opinion, that General McDowell's corps, or that portion of it which was between Culpeper and the battle-field, should be at once sent to the field. Ricketts's division of General McDowell's corps was in the immediate vicinity of the crossing of the road leading from Stephensburg with the road leading from Culpeper to the battle-field, or about two miles from Culpeper, and about five from the battle field.

The court adjourned to meet to-morrow morning, January 9, 1863, at 11 o'clock a. m.

THIRTY-NINTH DAY.

Court-room, corner of 14th street and Penn. Av.

WASHINGTON, D. C., *January* 9, 1863.

The court met pursuant to adjournment. Present: Major General George Cadwalader, United States volunteers; Brigadier General John H. Martindale, United States volunteers; Brigadier General James H. Van Alen, United States volunteers; Lieutenant Colonel Louis H. Pelouze, assistant adjutant general, recorder of the court, and Major General McDowell, United States volunteers, and Brigadier General Benjamin S. Roberts, United States volunteers, the witness under examination.

The proceedings of the preceding day were read by the recorder, and approved by the court.

* * * * * *

Brigadier General Benjamin S. Roberts, witness under examination, desired to state that, with reference to his testimony of the previous day, such portion of it as reads (page 472) "General Pope authorized me, before going to the front, to give any orders in his name to any of the officers that might be in the field senior to me," needs to be so qualified as to read that I was authorized to give any orders, so far as to carry out General Pope's views, as had been expressed to me, (General Roberts,) in relation to holding the enemy there until his (General Pope's) forces could come up.

By General McDowell:

Question. If General Banks had not attacked General Jackson in force on the 9th, do you think Jackson would have attacked Banks?

Answer. I do not think Jackson would have attacked Banks in a position where he was first posted on coming on to the field. The position was exceedingly strong, and one which a small force like General Banks's could have held against a larger one of the enemy. General Jackson's troops had made a long march that day, and I do not think they were in a condition to attack General Banks.

Question. Is the witness to be understood that General Banks fought the battle on his own responsibility, and against witness's advice, and the known expectation of General Pope?

Answer. When General Banks first came on to the field I met him, and went to the front with him, showing him positions where the enemy had batteries already posted, and where I had discovered they were posting new batteries, and showed General Banks the positions where his own corps could take position to advantage, and hold those positions, as I thought, if attacked. I then told him that General Pope wanted him to hold the enemy in check there until Sigel's forces could be brought up, which were expected that day, and all his other forces united to fight Jackson's forces. I mean to be understood to say that it is my impression that General Banks fought that battle entirely upon his own responsibility, and against the expectations of General Pope, and those expectations had been expressed to General Banks as I have already stated, perhaps more strongly.

Question. Do you know why General Banks advanced to make a division movement upon the enemy on the 9th of August without the aid of General McDowell's troops? If so, state why.

Answer. I can only state impressions from facts which I can relate. General Banks had seen nothing of the enemy on that day, or not much of the enemy, as the country was such (and well known to them) as to enable them to conceal their movements from General Banks. After he first came on to the field, and I had suggested positions to the left of Crawford's brigade, where his main force should take position, he proceeded to put those forces in position in support of Crawford, and on his left. I went to the extreme right with one of his brigades (Gordon's) to put it into position, and was gone an hour or more, I should think, as I went some distance to the right, under the belief that a part of the enemy's forces were endeavoring to turn that flank. On returning back to the field I found General Banks had advanced his lines in order of battle, considerably toward the enemy, so that very sharp musketry firing had already commenced. I then expressed to General Banks my convictions—and I think this was about three and a half o'clock—that the enemy was in very large force, and massed in the woods on his right.

General Banks replied that he did not believe the enemy was in any considerable force yet, and said he had resolved to attack their batteries, or to attack their main force. It was either one or the other. From this state of facts I am convinced that General Banks made the attack in the belief that the enemy was not in large force, and that he would succeed in his attack without the aid of other troops.

Another reason for this belief is that General Banks supposed that his own force was between twelve and thirteen thousand, whereas it was three thousand sand less than that number. He was led to this belief by some mistake in returns, which he did not discover until after the battle was fought.

The court adjourned to meet to-morrow, January 10, 1863, at 11 o'clock a. m.

L. H. PELOUZE,
Lieutenant Colonel and Recorder.

A true copy of the record.

W. H. W. KREBS,
Captain and A. D. C.

A true copy.

JAMES McC. BELL,
Captain and A. A. General.

MILWAUKIE, WISCONSIN, *December* 26, 1864.

GENERAL: I have the honor to acknowledge the receipt of your note calling my attention to an order which General Banks states that I delivered to him verbally.

General Banks states that I ordered him to leave the strong position he was ordered to take up, and advance and attack the enemy.

The order received from you and delivered by me to General Banks, about eight o'clock on the morning of the 9th of August, before he moved from Culpeper to the front, was, to the best of my recollection, as follows:

"GENERAL: The general commanding directs that you move to the front and take up a strong position near the position held by General Crawford's brigade; that you will not attack the enemy unless it becomes evident the enemy will attack you; then, in order to hold the advantage of being the attacking party, you will attack with your skirmishers thrown well to the front."

The above is the exact language used by me to General Banks as near as I can remember; my understanding of your intention was, that you wished to hold the enemy in check, and put off a general engagement until Sigel's and McDowell's corps could be got up, and I think that such was the understanding of every one in the army.

My understanding of your order was, that General Banks was to attack with his skirmishers, and my intention was for him so to understand the order.

I am, general, very respectfully, your obedient servant,

L. H. MARSHALL,
Colonel and A. A. D. C.

TREATMENT OF PRISONERS.

WASHINGTON, *May* 27, 1864.

A. J. PALMER, being duly sworn, was examined as follows:

By Mr. Gooch:

Question. State your position, company, and regiment?

Answer. I am a private in company D, 49th New York volunteers.

Question. How long have you been in the service?

Answer. Since July, 1861.

Question. Have you, at any time, been captured by the rebels; and if so, when?

Answer. I was captured on the 18th of July, 1863, in the assault on Fort Wagner, before Charleston, South Carolina.

Question. Where were you taken after you were captured?

Answer. I was taken to the Charleston jail and kept three days, then to Columbia, South Carolina, and kept about two months. About the 24th of September, I think, I was taken to Richmond and put in the Libby prison, and about the last of September was sent to Belle Island. I was at Belle Island about a month when I went into the hospital.

Question. What was your treatment while you were at Belle Island?

Answer. The treatment was very poor. When I went there, in September, they gave wheat bread, I should judge about half a pound a day, and sometimes a little black bean soup.

Question. Was the quantity of food which they gave you sufficient?

Answer. No, sir; nothing like sufficient.

Question. Why did you go to the hospital?

Answer. I was sick. On the 27th of October I was taken sick with typhoid fever.

Question. Did you have any tents while you were at Belle island?

Answer. Yes, sir. I was in a tent. I would not have had one but for the fact that 700 men went north the day I reached there, and I went into one of their tents. The men did not all have tents.

Question. How long did you remain in that hospital?

Answer. From the 27th of October until the 16th of April.

Question. Were you employed in any capacity while at the hospital; and if so, what?

Answer. Yes, sir; for the last month or two I was employed as clerk to the surgeon in charge of the hospital.

Question. How were you treated while in the hospital?

Answer. While in the hospital as a patient, the treatment, as far as kindness would go, was very well, because our men were the attendants there; some of them were very mean, though, and were very little better than their men.

Question. How was it in respect to the food furnished?

Answer. I do not think they had as much, in quantity, as the men on Belle island got. Sick men did not need as much. They meant to issue about the same quantity, but there were six or eight nurses who received what they wanted, and of course the patients did not get as much.

Question. State whether or not you made any copy of the records of diseases and deaths in that hospital during the quarter ending March 30, 1864?

Answer. Yes, sir. I had made a report for the surgeon in charge to the Surgeon General or medical director, I am not certain which.

Question. Have you a copy of that report with you?

Answer. I have.

The witness produced the following copy of the report referred to:

Diseases and deaths of federal prisoners at Richmond, Va., for the quarter ending March 31, 1864.

Diseases.	January.		February.		March.	
	Cases.	Deaths.	Cases.	Deaths.	Cases.	Deaths.
Febris, cosit. cons.	5	....	3	1	10	2
Febris, int. quah.	6	....	23	....	20	5
Febris, int. test.	4	....	20	....	....	....
Febris, rem.	10	....	20	....	11	4
Febris, typhoides	18	12	35	28	35	29
Erysipelas.	11	1	3	1	1	1
Rubeola.	14	1	15	7	6	4
Variola and Varioloid, convalescents	....	....	....	....	77	....
Diarrhœa, acuta	31	18	100	13	27	13
Diarrhœa, chronic	229	193	337	265	283	250
Dysentery, acuta	6	4	23	6	9	3
Dysentery, chronic	18	12	34	24	27	20
Dyspepsia	1	1	1	....	2	1
Enteritis	....	....	1	....	....	....
Gastritis	1	....	....	....	1	....
Heppetetis, chronic	4	....	2	1	4	3
Peterris	4	....	1	....	4	3
Parotetis	....	....	3	....	3	....
Tonsellitis	....	....	7	3	....	....
Asthma	1	1	1	1	....	....
Bronchitis, acuta	21	....	46	7	12	3
Bronchitis, chronic	20	6	45	16	50	39

Diseases and deaths of federal prisoners at Richmond, Va.—Continued.

Diseases.	January.		February.		March.	
	Cases.	Deaths.	Cases.	Deaths.	Cases.	Deaths.
Catarrhus, epidemic	....	....	1	....	....	....
Catarrhus	10	1	35	4	17	9
Laryngetis	....	....	2	....	1	1
Phthisis, pul	6	2	8	5	1	1
Pluritis	9	1	10	5	12	9
Pneumonia	63	38	207	97	126	109
Anæmia	....	....	1	....	....	....
Caritretes	....	....	1	....	....	....
Epilepsia	1	....	1	....	....	....
Nemnegitis	1	1	1	....	....	....
Neuralgia	1	....	3	....	1	....
Paralysis	1	....	....	....	1	1
Tetenus	4	2	....	....	....	....
Bubo, syph	1	....	....	....	....	....
Cystetis	....	....	1	....	....	....
Gonorrhœa	5	1	....	....	1	....
Nephretis	1	....	11	....	6	....
Orchitis	1	....	1	....	....	....
Syphilis, prim	2	....	....	....	1	....
Syphilis, consect	2	....	2	....	....	....
Annacarete	6	4	7	2	8	7
Ascetis	....	....	....	....	1	....
Lumbago	1	....	....	....	....	....
Rheumatism, act	11	....	23	....	12	1
Rheumatism, chronic	40	4	42	12	14	3
Absessis	2	....	2	....	....	....
Anthrox	....	....	....	....	1	....
Ulcus	....	....	4	....	1	....
Contusio	....	....	....	....	1	1
Gelatis	....	....	....	....	15	6
Vulnis, inuim	....	....	1	....	....	....
Vulnis, scropt	20	1	27	....	20	3
Otitis	1	....	....	....	....	....
Debilitas	15	4	107	17	33	21
Hemorrhoix	....	....	2	1	6	2
Merbe, cutis	....	....	6	....	9	....
Scorbutis	7	....	7	3	17	7
Tumores	....	....	1	....	....	....
Dry gangrene, and frozen feet	27	3	23	4	....	....

Total cases 2,781
Total deaths.. 1,396

The above report is a true copy of the official report made by the surgeon in charge of the Confederate States military prison hospital to Surgeon General Moore, C. S. A., of the diseases and deaths of federal prisoners under his charge, for the quarter ending March 31, 1864.

Question. Is that a true copy of the report which you drew for the medical officer?

Answer. It is.

Question. Have you anything which you wish to add in relation to the treatment of our men while in hospital?

Answer. Yes, sir. After our men were dead and put in the dead-house, nearly every morning, the eyes and cheeks were eaten out of them by the rats, before they were put in their coffins. It was complained of several times, and the rebel surgeon in charge slightly reprimanded the undertaker, but he took scarcely any notice of it, and it had not been stopped when I came away.

Question. What was the condition of the hospital as to cleanliness?

Answer. Every bed was very thickly covered with vermin. A man would be taken with the small-pox, and after he was sent to the small-pox hospital sometimes the clothes would not be changed, and a man would be put into the same bed. The vermin were very thick. They would wash a little, but not enough to have a change of clothes once in two months.

Question. Was the hospital to which they sent our patients very much crowded?

Answer. Yes, sir. As soon as a man was able to have his clothes on he was put on to the floor. In a ward where there were 70 beds there were a hundred and eight, nine, or ten men; and then there were 10 nurses who would sometimes take the beds. Sometimes they did not have ten, and sometimes more than that.

WASHINGTON, *January* 27, 1865.

Sergeant C. W. THURSTON sworn and examined.

By Mr. Loan:

Question. Will you state to what company and regiment you belong?

Answer. I am a sergeant of company K, 6th New Hampshire volunteers.

Question. About what time and where were you taken prisoner by the rebels?

Answer. I was captured on the 30th of September last, at what I think is known by the name of Jones's farm. It was the time the attempt was made to cut the Southside railroad near Petersburg.

Question. To what place were you taken and confined?

Answer. I was first taken with others to Petersburg, and kept over night, then to Richmond and put into what is called the Pemberton building, and than to Salisbury, North Carolina.

Question. How long were you kept in Richmond?

Answer. Only over one night.

Question. How long were you at Salisbury?

Answer. Until the 18th of last month, when I made my escape.

Question. What number of prisoners were at Salisbury, and how were they treated?

Answer. When I was first taken there, there were comparatively few prisoners there, but within three or four days there were upwards of 10,000. I know that when I had charge of the bakery for the prisoners, I made out requisitions for more than 10,600 men.

Question. What kind of a place were you kept in?

Answer. At the time I went there, there was a building that was made to hold probably 2,000 men. The rest had no cover or shelter at all. The enemy had taken away from us our blankets and knapsacks and a great deal of our clothing. About the 6th of November the quartermaster gave us some tents, in the proportion of one Sibley tent and one small wall tent to each 100 men, but not more than 50 of the 100 could get in and lie down in the tents; the rest had no covering, and used to dig holes in the ground with their pocket knives and plates, because they could get no shovels or picks, and they would crawl in those holes and lie down.

In regard to the rations for the men, what was called the regular ration was a pound of bread made of corn and cobs ground together, to each man for 24 hours; they usually got only about 12 ounces even of that bread; then, for meat, the men usually received 22 pounds of beeves' heads, tripes, and gullets to each 100 men; but that was not received every day, only about once in four days on an average, and then there was usually given about half a pint of soup to each man a day; the soup was made of rice and water; that is, a large bucketful of rice would be put into a large kettle of water, holding, say, 20 gallons; sometimes a little salt, sometimes no salt at all. They would dip out the water and but little of the rice, and then fill up again and again until 1,000 men had been served from the one bucketful of rice. Upon the slightest provocation the rations would be cut off entirely for a day or two. I have lost the principal diary I kept while there; but I find, in a memorandum book which I have here, that on Friday the 28th of October the men received no rations; on Saturday they received nothing but soup; on Sunday they received bread and meat, so that there were two days when they received nothing but a little soup. In regard to the treatment of our men in other respects, I can illustrate it by an incident I saw myself: I was standing one day by the hospital, (I had been to see Mr. Davis, one of the prisoners who had been appointed superintendent of the hospital,) and one of our negro soldiers, captured at the time of the explosion of the mine near Petersburg, was standing near by engaged in "skirmishing," as we prisoners call it, examining his clothes for vermin. A sentinel there, at whom I happened to be looking at the time, drew up his musket, took deliberate aim and fired, killing the negro on the spot One of our boys asked him "What he did that for?" And he replied that he did it "to see the damned black son of a bitch drop." That I saw done myself.

Question. What notice was taken of that by the rebel authorities there?

Answer. None that I know. The report is that they get 30 days' furlough for shooting a Yankee: that it is encouraged. Mr. Davis, the superintendent of the hospital, assured me that he has, at the present time, the names of 1,800 of our men who died there between the 1st day of October and the 15th day of December, 1864.

Question. Who is this Mr. Davis?

Answer. He was the chief clerk of the Ohio senate, so I understand, and a correspondent of the Cincinnati Gazette. He escaped when I did, and I understand he is now in this city.

Question. He was a prisoner at Salisbury?

Answer. Yes, sir; and Mr. Richardson of the New York Times, and Mr. Browne of the New York Tribune.

Question. What means had Mr. Davis to know the number of deaths?

Answer. He was the superintendent of the hospital, and Mr. Richardson was clerk of the hospital.

Question. Appointed by the rebel authorities?

Answer. Yes, sir; we made an attempt to break out of the prison one day, in which we killed four of the guards and wounded quite a number of them. They killed fifteen of our men, and wounded fifty-seven. They fired upon the boys for twenty-two minutes after they had given up and gone into their tents. They fired right through the tents—they could see no one—riddling them completely, and they discharged cannon several times, loaded with canister, or rather with little plugs of iron punched out of boilers where they made them. We have kept an account of upwards of 900 federal soldiers who have enlisted in the rebel service merely to avoid starvation. Generally, for a day or two before they were enlisted they would be deprived of everything to eat but a little soup.

Question. What rations do the rebels furnish their own soldiers?

Answer. They told me that they got a pound of flour and a half a pound of bacon or other meat to a man. They were put on short rations there, or "half rations," as they called it.

Question. What else was furnished them?

Answer. Very little of anything else than a little tobacco; at least that is what they told me. They said they had to have provisions sent them from home, for they could not live on their rations there.

Question. What became of the beeves, the heads and tripes of which, you say, were given to the prisoners?

Answer. I cannot tell; sometimes we would get a little of the beef, but very seldom; we got very little beef in proportion to the heads and tripes. I had twelve men of my own regiment who enlisted in the rebel service.

Question. Did much sickness result from this diet?

Answer. The diarrhœa was the prevalent sickness, caused principally by the water, I think. The boys did not have what water they wanted. They had to go a quarter of a mile to a little creek, twenty at a time, with a guard, but they did not get all they wanted. There was water in the yard, but so thick with mud that they could not drink it. The only well that had good water in it was closely guarded and kept for the hospital. The morning I escaped, there were 7,603 prisoners there. We never received any of the clothing or supplies of the Sanitary Commission which we understood had been sent to us. Before our soldiers would be enlisted in the rebel service, they would usually get nothing to eat for two or three days. Then an officer would come in with a guard, and when the prisoners were collected around him, he would tell them that they would not be exchanged before the end of the war; but if they would enlist in their service, they would have plenty of food and clothing, and be placed on garrison duty, and not be called upon to fight. I have seen men brought up for that purpose, who were so weak that they could not walk without staggering.

Question. Were any threats made as to what would be the consequences if they did not enlist?

Answer. No, sir; there was no need of threats; the boys knew they would die if they stayed there. The rations kept growing poorer and poorer all the time. God only knows what they are by this time, or how the poor fellows get along.

Question. State more fully about your being deprived of clothing, &c., when you were captured.

Answer. When we are first taken, they generally take from us all our money, watches, and other valuables. When we were taken to Petersburg, an officer came in with a guard, where we were, and took a great many of our rubber and woollen blankets. The guard kept coming in and stealing our clothing, the men resisting; but, of course, resistance was useless. They took our shelter tents and overcoats from us while we were in Petersburg. When we got to Richmond and were put in the Pemberton building, we were formed into line on each side of the building, and made to take off our knapsacks, haversacks, and canteens, and pile them up in the middle of the room, and they were carried off by them. They said they were going to search us for money, and we were invited to give up what money we had voluntarily, and told that if we did so we should have a receipt for it, and it would be given back to us when we were exchanged; but we were told that if we did not do that, and any money was afterwards found on us, it would be confiscated. Then they took us on to Salisbury, many of our boys having nothing but what they had on; when their clothes wore out they had to do without. When I left not one-half of them had more than a blowse and a pair of pantaloons, some nothing but a shirt and pantaloons, still others nothing but pantaloons and a piece of old cloth about their shoulders; hundreds were barefooted and without hats or caps, without clothing to keep them any way comfortable.

Question. Then they must have suffered much from the inclemency of the weather?

Answer. Yes, sir; I understood that some of them froze to death; I have no doubt that many perished in that way. I have had men come to the bakery, where I was, shivering and shaking with cold, as if they had the ague, and beg to be allowed to come in and warm themselves. I would let a few in at a time, and then, after a short time, make them go out and let others come in. When prisoners died they used to strip them of their clothing, which they would sometimes give to the most needy of the living. The dead were put in a dead-house, and then pitched into a cart any way, just as many as it would hold, and, as I understood, carried off and tumbled into a ditch and covered up. This I was told by some of our men who were detailed as grave-diggers, and given double rations for that duty.

Question. You have no personal knowledge that any of the prisoners froze to death?

Answer. No, sir; I saw none when they were freezing, but I was told so, and I have no doubt of it. The men would get very weak, and would crawl into their holes, and I have no doubt they froze to death there. One man was taken out from under the hospital who had been there so long that he had begun to decay, and was all covered with vermin; we supposed he had crawled under there to get out of the cold and there died. I was told by a rebel doctor there, I forget his name, that not one in ten of the men who died there would have died if they had had proper food and shelter.

Question. From all that you have seen, are you satisfied in your own mind that our soldiers have died there in consequence of not having proper food and clothing?

Answer. I know so, as well as I can know anything of that nature. There was a snow-storm there, which changed to a cold rain, and lasted for two days, and the morning after I saw six men taken out of one hole, into which they had crawled, and had there died.

Question. How long were you in effecting your escape?

Answer. We left on the 18th of December, and reached Knoxville on the 13th of January. From there I went to Chattanooga, and was ordered by General Thomas to report here in Washington, and I came right on here.

Question. You are here for the purpose of joining your regiment?

Answer. Yes, sir; I want to join it immediately.

WASHINGTON, *January* 30, 1865.

Mr. ALBERT D. RICHARDSON sworn and examined.

By the chairman:

Question. I understand that you are one of the newspaper correspondents who lately escaped from Salisbury, North Carolina. Will you give the committee a statement of such matters as you may deem important in relation to your experience as a prisoner, and what you have observed in reference to the treatment of our prisoners by the rebel authorities?

Answer. I am a Tribune correspondent, and was captured by the rebels May 3, 1863, at midnight, on a hay bale in the Mississippi river, opposite Vicksburg. After confinement in six different prisons I was sent to Salisbury, N. C., February 3, 1864, and kept there until December 18, when I escaped. For several months Salisbury was the most endurable rebel prison I had seen. The six hundred inmates exercised in the open air, were comparatively well fed and kindly treated. But early in October 10,000 regular prisoners of war arrived there, and it immediately changed into a scene of cruelty and horrors. It was densely crowded; rations were cut down and issued very irregularly; friends outside could not even send in a plate of food. The prisoners suffered constantly and often intensely for want of water, bread, and shelter. The rebel authorities placed all the prison hospitals under charge of my two journalistic comrades (Messrs. Brown and Davis) and myself. Our positions enabled us to obtain exact and minute information. Those who had to live or die on the prison rations always suffered from hunger. Very frequently one or more divisions of a thousand men would receive no rations for twenty-four hours; sometimes they were without a morsel of food for forty-eight hours. The few who had money would pay from five to twenty dollars, rebel currency, for a little loaf of bread. Most of the prisoners traded the buttons from their blowses for food. Many, though the weather was very inclement and snows frequent, sold coats from their backs and shoes from their feet. Yet I was assured, on authority entirely trustworthy, that the great commissary warehouse near the prison was filled with provisions; that the commissary found it difficult to obtain storage for his flour and meal; that when a subordinate asked the post commandant, Major John H. Gee, "Shall I give the prisoners full rations," he replied, "No, God damn them, give them quarter rations." I know, from personal observation, that corn and pork are very abundant in the region about Salisbury. For several weeks the prisoners had no shelter whatever. They were all thinly clad; thousands were barefooted; not one in twenty had either overcoat or blanket; many hundreds were without shirts, and hundreds were without blowses. At last one Sibley tent and one "A" tent were furnished to each squad of one hundred. With the closest crowding these sheltered about one-half the prisoners. The rest burrowed in the ground, crept under buildings, or shivered through the nights in the open air upon the frozen, muddy, or snowy soil. If the rebels, at the time of their capture, had not stolen their shelter tents, blankets, clothing, and money, they would have suffered little from cold. If the prison authorities had permitted a few hundred of them, either upon parole or under guard, to cut logs within two miles of the garrison, the prisoners would gladly have built comfortable and ample barracks in one week. But the commandant would never, in a densely wooded region, with the cars which brought it passing by the wall of the prison, even furnish half the fuel which was needed.

The hospitals were in a horrible condition. By crowding the patients thick as they could lie upon the floor they would contain six hundred inmates. They were always full to overflowing, with thousands seeking admission in vain. In the two largest wards, containing jointly about two hundred and fifty patients, there was no fire whatever. The others had small fireplaces, but were always cold. One ward, which held forty patients, was comparatively well furnished. In the other eight the sick and dying men lay upon the cold and usually naked floor, for the scanty straw furnished us soon became too filthy and full of vermin for use. The authorities never supplied a single blanket, or quilt, or pillow, or bed, for those eight wards. We could not procure even brooms to keep them clean, or cold water to wash the faces of the inmates. Pneumonia, catarrh, and diarrhœa were the prevailing diseases, but they were directly the result of hunger and exposure. More than half who entered the hospitals died in a very few days. The deceased, always without coffins, were loaded in a dead-cart, piled upon each other like logs of wood, and so driven out to be thrown into a trench and covered with earth.

The rebel surgeons were generally humane and attentive. They endeavored to improve the shocking condition of the hospitals, but the Salisbury and Richmond authorities both disregarded their complaints and protests.

On November 25 many of the prisoners had been without food for forty-eight hours. Desperate from hunger, without any matured plan, a few of them said, "We may as well die in one way as another; let us break out of this horrible place." Some of them wrested the guns from a relief of fifteen rebel soldiers just entering the yard, killing two who resisted and wounding five or six. Others attempted to open the fence, but they had neither adequate tools nor concert of action. Before they could effect a breach every gun in the garrison was turned upon them, two field-pieces operated with grape and canister, and they dispersed to their quarters. Five minutes from the beginning the attempt was quelled and hardly a prisoner was to be seen in the yard. My own quarters were a hundred and fifty yards from the scene of the insurrection. In our vicinity there had been no participation at all in it, and yet for twenty minutes after it was ended the guards upon the fence on each side of us, with deliberate aim, fired into the tents upon helpless and innocent men. They killed, in all, fifteen and wounded about sixty, not one-tenth of whom had taken part in the attempt, many of whom were ignorant of it until they heard the guns.

Deliberate cold-blooded murders of peaceable men, where there was no pretence that they were breaking any prison regulation, were very frequent. On October 16, Lieutenant Davis, of the 155th New York infantry, was thus shot dead by a guard, who the day before had been openly swearing that he would "kill some damned Yankee yet." November 6, Luther Conrod, of the 45th Pennsylvania infantry, a delirious patient from one of the hospitals, was similarly murdered. November 30, a chimney in one of the hospitals fell down, crushing several men under it. Orders were immediately given to the guard to let no one approach the building, on the pretext that there might be another insurrection. Two patients from that hospital had not heard the order, and were returning to their quarters, when I saw a sentinel on the fence, within twenty feet of them, without challenging them, raise his piece and fire, killing one and wounding the other. Major Gee, at the time, was standing immediately beside the sentinel, who must have acted under his direct orders. December 16, Moses Smith, of 7th Maryland (colored) infantry, while standing beside my quarters, searching for scraps of food from the sweepings of the cook-house, was shot through the head. There were very many similar murders. I never knew any pretence, even, made of investigation or punishing them. Our lives were never safe for one moment; any sentinel, at any hour of the day or night, could deliberately shoot down any prisoner, or into any group of prisoners, black or white, and he would not even be taken off his post for it.

Nearly every week an officer came into the prison to recruit for the rebel army. Sometimes he offered bounties; always he promised good clothing and abundant food. Between 1,200 and 1,800 of our men enlisted in two months. I was repeatedly asked by prisoners, sometimes with tears in their eyes, "What shall I do? I don't want to starve to death. I am growing weaker daily; if I stay here I shall follow my comrades to the hospital and dead-house; if I enlist I may live until I can escape."

I had charge of the clothing left by the dead, and reissued it to the living. I distributed articles of clothing to more than 2,000 prisoners; but when I escaped there were fully 500 without a shoe or a stocking, and more yet with no garment above the waist except one blouse or one shirt. Men came to me frequently upon whom the rebels, when they captured them, had left nothing whatever except a light cotton shirt and a pair of light ragged cotton pantaloons.

The books of all the hospitals were kept, and the daily consolidated reports made up, under my supervision. During the two months, between, October 18 and December 18, the average number of prisoners was about 7,500. The deaths for that period were fully 1,500, or twenty per cent. of the whole. I brought away the names of more than 1,200 of the dead; some of the remainder were never reported; the others I could not procure on the day of my escape without exciting suspicion. As the men grew more and more debilitated, the percentage of deaths increased. I left about 6,500 remaining in the garrison, December 18, and they were dying then at the average rate of 28 a day, or thirteen per cent. a month.

The simple truth is, that the rebel authorities are murdering our soldiers at Salisbury by cold and hunger, while they might easily supply them with ample food and fuel. They are doing this systematically and, I believe, intentionally, for the purpose of either forcing our government to an exchange or forcing our prisoners into the rebel army.

I will also, with the consent of the committee, lay before them a sworn affidavit I obtained in Louisville, Kentucky, from one of the prisoners at Salisbury, North Carolina, who escaped at the time I did. It is as follows:

I am a mariner by profession, and reside at Mystic River, Connecticut; was master of the bark Texana, captured and burned by the rebels near the mouth of the Mississippi river June 10, 1863; was confined in Richmond, Virginia, until the 20th of July, 1864, when I was sent to the military prison at Salisbury, North Carolina, and kept there until my escape on the 18th of December last. After the transfer of prisoners of war to Salisbury in October last, I mingled with them constantly, and was familiar with their treatment in all respects. For a month before my escape I was ward-master of one of the largest hospitals in the prison. The prisoners were in a most pitiable condition. They all, without exception, and at all times suffered greatly for want of food, the most of them for the want of clothing, and a large portion of them for want of shelter. Very few out of the whole number were in good health, and the deaths were very numerous. Mine was called a ward for convalescents; it usually contained from one hundred to one hundred and twenty inmates; the deaths averaged fully six per day, and sometimes reached ten and twelve. The sickness and mortality were directly traceable to hunger, exposure, and cold. I can give no just idea in this brief statement of the horrors of the prison and hospitals, and the general treatment of the prisoners. It is barbarous beyond anything I ever before saw or heard of. I believe it is the deliberate intention of the rebel authorities to leave the prisoners no alternative between freezing and starvation or enlistment in the rebel army.

THOMAS E. WOLFE.

Subscribed and sworn to before me this 17th day of January, 1865.

JOSEPH CLEMENT,
Justice of the Peace.

WASHINGTON, *January* 30, 1865.

Mr. JUNIUS HENRI BROWNE sworn and examined.

By the chairman:

Question. I understand that you were a prisoner at Salisbury, North Carolina, and escaped at the same time Mr. Richardson, who has just testified, made his escape. You have heard his testimony; will you state whether you concur with him in what he has stated, and also give such additional statements as you may deem necessary?

Answer. I concur with Mr. Richardson in all his statements, so far as the facts to which they relate came to my knowledge. In addition to what he has said, I would further state that I am a journalist by profession; have been since the breaking out of the war an army correspondent of the New York Tribune; was captured in that capacity in the middle of the Mississippi river, while running the batteries of Vicksburg, on the night of May 3d, 1863, our expedition having been destroyed by the rebel siege guns. I was held prisoner some twenty months, having in that time been an occupant of seven southern prisons, the last being the Salisbury, North Carolina, penitentiary, where I was kept, with my co-laborer, Albert D. Richardson, for almost eleven months, making my escape therefrom in his company on the night of December 18, 1864.

The treatment of our prisoners was bad enough everywhere, but it was so barbarous and inhuman at Salisbury for two months previous to my escape that I regard the exposure thereof a duty I owe to the thousands who still remain there. Early in October from nine to ten thousand of our enlisted men were sent to Salisbury from Richmond and other points; and as they had been robbed of their clothing and blankets, and received very little food or shelter, the mortality among them became almost immediately widespread and alarming.

Every tenement within the prison limits was converted into a hospital, and I offered my services as medical dispenser and assistant to the rebel surgeons. I soon made daily visits to the sick—who could not obtain admission to the overcrowded hospitals—lying in tents on the ground, without covering, and with very scant raiment, and living in holes they had dug in the earth, or under buildings where they had crept for protection from the cold rains, the snow, and the biting winds, and performed such poor service as lay in my limited power. Their condition was distressing in the extreme. They had no means of keeping warm except by fires of very green wood that filled the rude shelters with bitter smoke; and which, added to the carbonic acidized atmosphere from so many breaths, and the emanations from unwholesome and unwashed bodies, packed together like figs, entirely poisoned the air, and destroyed the health of almost all who inhaled it.

The sickness and mortality in those outside quarters, as well as elsewhere, continually increased, and the marvel was that any one survived. Starved and freezing, with hardly water enough to drink, much less to wash their persons, or the scant clothes they wore, the poor fellows naturally and necessarily despaired, and not a few of them were anxious to die, to escape from the slow torture of their situation.

I had the best means of knowing, and it is my firmest belief that, out of eight or nine thousand prisoners at Salisbury, there were not at any time five hundred of them in sound health—an opinion in which all the rebel surgeons to whom I expressed it fully coincided.

The deaths during the last two months I passed at Salisbury ranged from twenty-five to forty-five per day; diarrhœa, dysentery, catarrh, pneumonia, and typhoid fever, all engendered by scarcity of food, shelter, and raiment, being the principal diseases. I have no doubt, if the prisoners had been properly treated—as prisoners of war in the north are, to the best of my knowledge and information, treated—the mortality in Salisbury would not have been more than one-eighth of what it was—a view in which the rebel surgeons with whom I talked fully concurred.

The capacity of the so-called hospitals, nine in number, which were without any of the comforts or concomitants of those institutions, was not to the fullest over five or six hundred patients; and the number of prisoners who ought to have been inmates thereof was at least as many thousands. The hospitals merely afforded some protection from the cold and rain, and furnished rather better rations than were given to the men who were supposed by a transparent fiction to be in good health. Hardly any one would go to the hospitals so long as he could help himself, or induce any one to help him; the daily spectacle of ghastly and hideous corpses going therefrom to the dead-house filling all beholders with horror, and inducing the soldiers to believe that all who entered those filthy and pestiferous tenements were doomed.

The prison limits at Salisbury revealed a scene of wretchedness, squalor, despair, and suffering such as I, accustomed as I am to army life and the horrors of military hospitals and battle-fields, had never before witnessed. The prison authorities—especially after the massacre attending the attempted outbreak of November 25th—appeared not only indifferent to the miserable condition of the men, but to be actuated by a brutality and malignity towards them that I could not reconcile with my ideas of human nature. They permitted the guards to shoot prisoners whenever they pleased, without the least pretext or explanation, and no man's life was safe for a day or an hour. The air was full of pain and pestilence, and all the horrors of imagined hells seemed realized in that most wretched place, of which I shall never think without a shudder and an augmented faith in the naturally abhorrent doctrine of total depravity.

TREATMENT OF REBEL PRISONERS.

POINT LOOKOUT, MARYLAND, *April* 14, 1865.

Brigadier General JAMES BARNES sworn and examined.

By Mr. Gooch:

Question. What is your rank and position in the army?

Answer. Brigadier general United States volunteers.

Question. What is your present command, and how long have you held the same?

Answer. I am in command of the district of St. Mary's, which embraces the county of St. Mary's, Maryland, within which is situated the military prison at Point Lookout, at the entrance of the Potomac river into the Chesapeake bay. I have been in command of the district since the 6th of July, 1864.

Question. How many prisoners are there now in the camp of the prisoners of war at Point Lookout, Maryland?

Answer. There are at this time twenty-one thousand two hundred and fifty-five, (21,255.)

Question. What has been the greatest number of prisoners in the camp, and how many have they averaged during your command?

Answer. The present number is the largest that has been here at any one time. The table appended, from the provost marshal, (marked A,) exhibits the average number each month since the establishment of this post as a depot for the prisoners of war, in July, 1863.

Question. Give a detailed account of your mode of subsisting the prisoners, including their daily ration, the manner in which they are sheltered, their medical treatment, the average mortality, and all other facts pertaining thereto.

Answer. The annexed statement of Lieutenant C. H. Whittemore, (marked B,) acting as commissary of subsistence for the prisoners of war, presents, in detail, a correct account of the mode of subsistence of the prisoners of war, and the daily rations issued to them.

The accompanying statement of Dr. J. H. Thompson, surgeon-in-chief of this district, (marked C,) exhibits full details of the hospital arrangements provided for the prisoners and their medical treatment, the average mortality, and other facts connected with the subject.

The statement marked D, presents an exhibit by the provost marshal, Major Brady, of the veteran reserve corps, of the manner in which the prisoners are sheltered, the means provided for cleanliness both of the prisoners and camp, the weekly inspection, and the general arrangements for preserving order and the necessary discipline required for their government, the amount of clothing issued to the prisoners by the government, and a monthly statement of the number of prisoners in the camp, and all essential particulars relating thereto.

It will be seen that the government has made a liberal provision for the health and necessary protection of the prisoners.

I would further state that a library has been formed, containing about eight hundred (800) volumes, for their use by contribution. A school has been held daily by some of the prisoners qualified to teach, and there may be seen grown men, some learning their letters and studying their spelling-book; some studying the elements of arithmetic and geography; some, more advanced, studying Latin, Greek, and French. Through the camp may be seen ingenious manufacturing of fans from pine wood, chains from horse-hair, gutta-percha rings inlaid neatly with gold and silver ornaments, and all these things are permitted to be sold, and the proceeds received by the provost marshal for the benefit of the prisoners who make them. Money and other valuables, as watches, &c., in possession of the prisoners on their arrival at the post, are placed in the hands of the provost marshal, and recorded in his books, all of which are returned to them when they leave the post, paroled for exchange; or if transferred to another post, a schedule of their private property is made out and the property transferred with the prisoner.

The general conduct of the prisoners has been very good; in a few instances, perhaps half a dozen, the punishment of a ball and chain, not unusual in armies, has been awarded for a brief period for attempting to escape, but these have been very rare.

A good deal of labor in the quartermaster's and commissary department at this post has been performed by the prisoners, and also work on the forts. But this labor is always voluntary on the part of the prisoner, and for which he is invariably compensated, either in money or in extra rations of tobacco, &c., as he may choose. This labor is sought eagerly by the prisoners.

Very rarely has any complaint of any ill treatment on the part of our soldiers towards the prisoners been made. I cannot at this time recall a single instance, if I may except a few cases which arose between them and some of the colored troops, but even with them nothing of any moment.

I believe I have answered as fully as necessary the questions submitted to me.

JAMES BARNES,

Brigadier General, Commanding District of St. Mary's, Maryland.

A.

Consolidated report of prisoners of war at Point Lookout, Md., from the date of first arrival of prisoners, July 31, 1863, *to April* 18, 1865, *inclusive.*

Date.	Received.	Transferred.	Exchanged.	Died.	Released.	Escaped.	Total present end of month.	Avera'e No. prisoners per month.
July 31, 1863.*	....	....	....	....	....	....	136	......
August	1,691	....	....	....	3	5	1,819	1,018
September	2,123	7	....	14	1	11	3,909	2,441
October	3,676	439	....	33	1	2	7,110	5,012
November	2,261	380	....	119	2	3	8,867	8,564
December	286	93	502	158	4	12	8,384	8,697
January, 1864	237	57	....	138	687	....	7,739	8,179
February	939	22	....	128	381	....	8,147	7,994
March	333	65	1,969	82	218	....	6,146	7,010
April	122	21	246	43	217	....	5,741	5,998
May	6,876	2	362	24	196	6	12,027	8,534
June	3,473	651	4	105	250	1	14,489	13,320
July	258	4,528	....	204	20	2	9,993	12,376
August	1,426	4,111	....	211	7	2	7,088	7,530
September	1,603	51	696	110	5	1	7,828	7,118
October	5,983	....	2,878	111	431	3	10,388	9,465
November	717	62	603	52	11	....	10,376	10,070
December	325	1	....	86	27	....	10,588	10,516
January, 1865	1,272	414	556	161	25	....	10,704	10,722
February	1,527	232	4,145	223	36	....	7,595	9,271
March	3,737	24	3,230	175	76	2	7,825	7,025
To April 18	12,276	83	....	97	9	....	19,912	14,328
Total	51,277	11,243	15,191	2,274	2,607	50	....	......
Total in prisoners' camp	....	....	....	....	....	....	19,912	......
Total in U. S. gen'l hospital	....	....	....	....	....	....	130	......
Paroled prisoners from other stations	....	....	....	....	....	....	1,213	......
Grand total at Pt. Lookout, Md	....	....	....	....	....	....	21,255	......
Total average of prisoners of war, from July 31, 1863, to April 18, 1865, inclu'e—equivalent number for the whole period	....	....	....	....	....	....	....	8,252

* Date of first arrival of prisoners.

N. B.—The average in the last column is obtained by taking the number of prisoners each day and adding the whole together, and dividing the number thus obtained by the number of days in the month: the number of prisoners in camp is therefore equivalent to this number through the whole month.

HEADQUARTERS DIST. ST. MARY'S,
PROVOST MARSHAL'S OFFICE,
Point Lookout, Md., April 19, 1865.

A. G. BRADY,
Major V. R. C. and Provost Marshal.

HEADQUARTERS ST. MARY'S DISTRICT,
Office A. A. General, April 19, 1865.

Sworn to before me.

C. C. DREW,
Capt. V. R. C., A. A. A. General, Judge Advocate.

SPECIAL ORDER, No. —. HEADQUARTERS ST. MARY'S DISTRICT, *Point Lookout, Md., Sept.* 1, 1864.

The following regulations heretofore established for the government of the camp of the prisoners of war are republished for the information of all concerned:

I. Hereafter at reveille the bugle will sound in front of the sergeant major's quarters, when the several details for general and company police will be formed under their respective non-commissioned officers, and a thorough police of the entire camp will be made.

II. The acting first sergeant, detailed from the prisoners of war, will be under the direction of the corporal of police for their respective divisions, and will give special attention to their company streets and quarters, causing all filth and waste water to be thrown into a barrel kept for that purpose, and emptied every morning, and oftener if necessary.

III. Breakfast hour will be at 6½ o'clock a. m., dinner at 1½ p. m., which will be announced by the sound of the bugle.

IV. There will be two stated roll-calls each day; that of the enlisted men will take place at reveille and retreat. Each company will fall into line at the sound of the bugle, and the first sergeants will make their reports to the sergeant major promptly. Sergeant E. Young will call roll in the officers' camp at 7 a. m. and 5 p. m., and will make his report to the A. P. M. immediately.

V. No prisoners will be permitted to pass above the lower ends of the kitchens unless employed in cook and mess room, except to their meals.

VI. Every company and division, commencing with the first in number, will be kept at their maximum number of one hundred and one thousand men each, and in all cases when any company or division is reduced below the standard by sickness, exchange or otherwise, they shall be immediately filled by men from the last division, or those discharged from hospital, and all fractional companies shall be provisioned at a designated cook-house, from which all extra meals, coffee, and rations issued to other than prisoners will be supplied.

VII. Mess and cook rooms will be provided for one thousand and fifteen hundred men each, in which stoves, cauldrons, and all other necessary cooking utensils will be placed.

VIII. A sufficient number of men will be provided from the prisoners to perform the various duties required. The arrangement for the present will be as follows: Four men will be assigned to the duty of cooking the victuals, ten to drawing the rations, two to providing the cooks with wood and water, and four to attend to the duties in the mess-room. This will include the setting of the tables, cleaning floor, tables, and all other articles used in mess-room.

IX. Each room will be under the superintendence of a sergeant from among the prisoners, who will be held responsible for the faithful performance of the duties assigned to his room, and will be required to report any neglect of duty by the men under him to the lieutenant in charge of the commissary department, who will make frequent inspections of the quarters.

X. The prisoners will be marched to and from the mess-room by the sergeants in charge of squads, and no man being absent when his squad is called to meals will be allowed to fall in with another squad.

XI. Loud talking when in the mess-room will be strictly forbidden, and it will be the duty of the sergeants in charge of cook and mess rooms to see that no unnecessary waste is made, and also that a degree of cleanliness is observed. Meal calls will be made ten minutes before opening the mess-room doors, when the sergeants in charge will see that their men are ready.

XII. The sergeant major will make all details for fatigue duty from those eating at the first table on the day such detail is called for. All working parties will be formed and marched by the sergeant in charge precisely at 7½ a. m. to the main entrance, but no detail for any purpose whatever shall be allowed to leave the camp without a sufficient guard and the written authority of the provost marshal. Neither will any prisoner be permitted to visit the Point for any purpose whatever without special permission from the general commanding. All persons in charge of detachments from the camp will be held strictly responsible for their return before sunset, when the gates will be shut and no one allowed to pass or re-pass except the guards and officers having proper authority.

XIII. Prisoners will not be allowed to hold any communication whatever with the guard or any individual without special permission from the provost marshal, and no letters will pass to or from prisoners except through the proper channels. The guard and patrol will not permit any prisoner to remain outside of his tent after dark except on business of necessity.

XIV. A police sergeant will be detailed with a sufficient number of men from each company to attend to the constant and thorough cleanliness of his company street and quarters. An efficient non-commissioned officer and fifty (50) men will be permanently detailed as general police, whose duty it shall be to keep scrupulously clean the vicinity of the kitchens and parts of the camp not occupied.

XV. Fires and lights will be promptly extinguished and all loud conversation suspended in the camp of enlisted prisoners at taps; in the prison camp for officers, lights and conversation will be permitted one-half hour later.

XVI. No citizen, enlisted man, or officer, except those on guard duty or general officer from headquarters, will be permitted to walk upon the fences around the prison camps without special permission from the provost marshal.

By command of Brigadier General James Barnes:

A. G. BRADY,
Major and Provost Marshal.

(*a.*)

Copy of the weekly inspection report of the provost marshal at Point Lookout, Maryland, of the prisoners of war, April 2, 1865. *Submitted with report of the provost marshal.*

HEADQUARTERS DISTRICT OF ST. MARY'S,
Point Lookout, Md., April 2, 1865.

SIR: I have the honor to submit the following inspection report of the condition of the prisoners of war at this station for the week ending April 2, 1865:

1. Conduct—Good.
2. Cleanliness—Good.
3. Clothing—Fair.
4. Bedding—One blanket to each man.
5. State of quarters—Good.
6. State of mess-houses—Good.
7. State of kitchen—Clean and in good order.
8. Food, quality of—Good.
9. Food, quantity of—Fair, and in accordance with regulations.
10. Water—Good.
11. Sinks—Clean and in good condition.
12. Police of grounds—Good.
13. Drainage—Fair.
14. Police of hospital—Good.
15. Attendance of sick—Good; there are 358 attendants.
16. Hospital diet—Good, same as that of United States General Hospital.
17. General health of prisoners—Good.
18. Vigilance of guard—Good.

Remarks and suggestions.

There were received during the week (4,040) four thousand and forty prisoners of war at this station, as follows:

From Fort Monroe, Va., (162) one hundred and sixty-two; from City Point, Va., (3,043) three thousand and forty three; from Washington, D. C., (149) one hundred and forty-nine; from United States General Hospital at this post, (120) one hundred and twenty; from Newbern, N. C., (566) five hundred and sixty-six. Transferred to Washington, D. C., (10) ten officers. Paroled and transferred to Aikin's Landing, Va., for "exchange," (500) five hundred prisoners of war. Released upon taking the oath, (4) four prisoners. The average rate of mortality for the week was ($4\frac{1}{7}$) four and one-seventh per day.

Very respectfully, your obedient servant,

A. G. BRADY,
Major and Provost Marshal, Inspecting Officer.

Brigadier General JAMES BARNES,
Commanding District of St. Mary's.

A true copy:

M. H. CHURCH, *Captain and Asst. Pro. Marshal.*

Remarks by commanding officer.

Respectfully forwarded. I have nothing of particular importance to add to this report.

Respectfully referred to the commissary general of prisoners.

J. BARNES,
Brig. Gen'l, District of St. Mary's.

HEADQUARTERS DISTRICT OF ST. MARY'S,
Provost Marshal's Office, Point Lookout, Md., April 18, 1865.

Statement of clothing issued by the United States to prisoners of war at Point Lookout, Md., from July 1, 1864, *to February* 13, 1865, *since which time the so-called rebel government have issued supplies of clothing.*

Where issued.	Pairs of shoes.	Pairs of socks.	Pairs of pants.	Pairs of drawers.	Jackets.	Shirts.	Great-coats.	Wool blankets.	Forage caps.
Prisoners of war camp.....	4,543	3,227	1,616	823	799	6,179	1,006	5,668	9
Prisoners of war hospital...	358	505	639	1,500	158	1,553	......	200	3
Total	4,901	3,732	2,255	2,323	957	7,732	1,006	5,868	12

I hereby certify that the above is a true statement of the clothing issued to prisoners of war during the time named.

A. G. BRADY,
Major V. R. C., and Provost Marshal.

HEADQUARTERS OF ST. MARY'S DISTRICT,
Point Lookout, Md., April 20, 1865.

Sworn to before me.

C. C. DREW,
Captain V. R. C., A. A. A. G., Judge Advocate.

B.

OFFICE OF A. C. S. OF PRISONERS OF WAR,
Point Lookout, Md., April 15, 1865.

GENERAL: I have the honor most respectfully to submit the following statement of the amount of rations daily issued to prisoners of war, mode of issuing the same, and extra rations allowed prisoners employed on public works. Prisoners of war, in accordance with General Order No. 1 of Brigadier General H. W. Wessels, commissary general of prisoners, dated Washington, January 13, 1865, are now allowed the following rations, viz:

Pork or bacon, 10 ounces, (in lieu of beef;) salt or fresh beef, 14 ounces; flour or soft bread, 16 ounces; hard bread, 10 ounces, (in lieu of flour or soft bread;) corn meal, 16 ounces, (in lieu of flour or bread.)

To 100 rations: beans or peas, 12½ pounds; or rice or hominy, 8 pounds; soap, 2 pounds; vinegar, 2 quarts; salt, 2 pounds; which rations are of the same quality as those issued to the United States troops, and are drawn by the assistant commissary of subsistence of prison camp from the post commissary on requisition for the number of prisoners in camp, and re-issued to each mess-house in bulk, there to be cooked in large boilers made for the purpose, and served out to the prisoners thus. Each cook-house—of which there are seven, originally intended to feed one thousand men per diem, being able to accommodate five hundred at a time—is now made to furnish food for two thousand and upwards—is under the charge of two sergeants, one to superintend the cooking of the rations, and the other (both are prisoners) the serving of them out. The camp being laid off in divisions of a thousand men each, it is so arranged that each cook-house, as far as practicable, shall feed two divisions twice a day, and, to avoid any confusion, each division furnishes to the cook-house where it gets its food daily the number of men present, which must agree with the number stated on the morning the report is made to the provost marshal.

Bread is delivered each noon, for the twenty-four hours succeeding, to the sergeant in charge of companies of one hundred men, who issue it to the men they have in charge. Each day at dinner the prisoners receive a large cup of bean or pea soup, and in the morning receive the ration of beef or pork, as stated. They are marched up by companies to the number of five hundred at a time to each cook-house, and eat the rations prepared for them and set on long tables, out of tin ware, which is always kept clean and bright.

Rations are drawn from the post commissary by the assistant commissary of subsistence of prison camp once every ten days, and consist usually of two days' pork, two days' fresh beef, two days' salt beef, and four days' salt fish, together with beans or peas, salt, vinegar, and soap. Occasionally, by order of the general commanding, potatoes are drawn and issued to the prisoners over and above the regular ration. Rations are issued to the cook-houses by the assistant commissary of subsistence of prison camp daily, and for the exact number of men reported in the divisions that each house feeds. It requires the entire forenoon to prepare the soup issued at dinner, and as it is necessary to commence cooking the meat for the next day immediately after dinner has been served, it is impossible, for want of time, to furnish more than two meals daily.

Every care is taken to keep the cook-houses perfectly clean and the food properly cooked and served. Once each week the provost marshal inspects the houses, and the medical officer of the day inspects the food daily. The assistant commissary of subsistence of prison camp visits each house daily, and is strict in seeing that food, utensils, and houses are kept clean, and that each of the employés attends to his duty.

Sugar and coffee or tea are issued to the sick or wounded, in conformity to General Order No. 1, above referred to, in the manner therein specified.

Prisoners employed on public works are allowed the following rations, viz:

Pork or bacon, 12 ounces, (in lieu of beef;) salt or fresh beef, 16 ounces; flour or soft bread, 18 ounces; hard bread, 12 ounces, (in lieu of flour or soft bread;) corn meal, 18 ounces, (in lieu of flour or bread.)

Per 100 rations: beans or peas, 15 pounds; rice or hominy, 10 pounds, (in lieu of beans or peas;) coffee, (ground,) 5 pounds; coffee, (green,) 7 pounds, (in lieu of coffee;) tea, 16 ounces, (in lieu of coffee;) sugar, 12 pounds; vinegar, 3 quarts; soap, 4 pounds; salt, $3\frac{3}{4}$ pounds; which they receive in the following manner: These prisoners receive daily, in the same way that other prisoners do at the cook-houses, the same rations that are issued to the bulk of the prisoners, and once every ten days the assistant commissary of subsistence of the camp issues to the sergeant of each detailed squad the difference between the ration already received and the allowance as above. The sergeants in charge of details then divide this surplus equally between the men under them. There are about one thousand men employed on public works, viz: 350 on fortifications, and 650 by the post quartermaster.

Soft bread is almost invariably furnished; in fact, hard bread has never been issued except to prisoners arriving at this depot too late to have bread baked at the bakery on the Point. In all instances the rations are fresh and good, and are the same in quality as those issued to the United States troops. Every care is taken to have the rations (and they are) fairly served out, and especial care is taken to have them properly cooked and prepared. Rations are now issued to about 19,500 prisoners, exclusive of those in hospitals.

Very respectfully, your obedient servant,

C. H. WHITTEMORE,
Lieutenant and A. C. S. of Prisoners of War.

Brigadier General JAMES BARNES,
Comd'g District of St. Mary's, Point Lookout, Md.

HEADQUARTERS DISTRICT OF ST. MARY'S,
Provost Marshal's Office, Point Lookout, Md., April 20, 1865.

Sworn to before me this the 20th day of April, 1865.

A. G. BRADY,
Major and Provost Marshal.

"B[2]."

List of articles with their appropriate numbers composing the extra diet.

No.		No.	
1.	Tea.	15.	Beef tea.
2.	Coffee.	16.	Beefsteak.
3.	Milk toast.	17.	Soft-boiled eggs.
4.	Bread and butter.	18.	Steamed potatoes.
5.	Apple sauce.	19.	Custard.
6.	Farina.	20.	Soda crackers.
7.	Corn starch.	21.	Milk.
8.	Barley.	22.	Rice.
9.	Vegetable soup.	23.	Mackerel.
10.	Baked apples.	24.	Bread.
11.	Molasses.	25.	Raw Irish potatoes.
12.	White sugar.	26.	Raw onions.
13.	Cocoa.	27.	Cheese.
14.	Chicken soup.	28.	Sweet potatoes.

Gross amount of articles purchased from hospital fund for extra diet from July, 1864, to March, 1865, inclusive.

Article	Unit	Amount	Article	Unit	Amount
Butter	pounds	6,087	Corn starch	dozen	177
Cheese	pounds	5,107	Macaroni	pounds	3,000
Condensed milk	dozen	276	Vermicelli	pounds	3,000

Eggs....dozen..	2,976	Pearl barley....pounds..	2,498
Soda crackers....barrels..	189	Onions....barrels..	77
Apples....barrels..	50	Turnips, and other vegt's..barrels..	348
Farina....pounds..	1,782		

I certify that the above is a true statement, compiled from the monthly statement of hospital fund for the months included above.

J. H. THOMPSON,
Surgeon U. S. Volunteers, in charge.

C.

PRISONERS' HOSPITAL,
Point Lookout, Md., April 15, 1865.

GENERAL: In compliance with your request, I have the honor to submit the following report regarding the medical treatment of prisoners of war under your command:

The camp is divided into divisions of one thousand men each; each division is under the charge of volunteer medical officers from among the prisoners, whose duty it is to treat those slightly sick in quarters, and report all serious cases to the United States medical officers in charge of all the divisions of camp, for examination with reference to their admission into hospital.

A daily sick call is held in each company, the same as in regiments of our own troops.

The hospital proper consists of nine large wooden wards, each ward having sixty hospital beds, complete.

In addition to these wards there are sixty hospital tents, floored, and with beds.

There are separate and detached wards for measles, erysipelas, and other contagious diseases. (See accompanying plan "A².") The hospital for small-pox is located one mile from the prisoners' camp and hospital.

The medicines drawn for use of the prisoners are the same in kind and quantity as issued to our own troops at military posts.

The diet of the sick is the same as in United States general hospitals for the treatment of our own sick. The savings on the army rations constitute the hospital fund, and is expended the same as in other hospitals, in the purchase of articles of extra diet for the sick, such as butter, cheese, milk, corn starch, farina, vermicelli, macaroni, soda crackers, eggs, apples, onions, and such other vegetables as the market affords; the amount thus expended from July, 1864, to March, 1865, inclusive, being fourteen thousand four hundred and forty-eight dollars and six cents ($14,448 06.) (See accompanying list and abstract "B².")

Large issues of clothing have been made to prisoners coming to the hospital in a destitute and suffering condition.

A large percentage of the sick treated have been those received from the front in a feeble condition, or coming from other parts. Especially is this true of scurvy and diseases of scorbutic and malarial origin.

Accompanying this report (abstract "C²") is a copy of the general summary of monthly report of sick and wounded, with a tabular list of the most common diseases and deaths, by which it will be seen that, with an average of nine thousand three hundred and seventy-four (9,374) prisoners per month, from July, 1864, to March, 1865, inclusive, there were one hundred and forty-seven deaths monthly, being a ratio of fifteen and seven-hundredths per one thousand men. From September, 1863, to June, 1864, inclusive, with an average of seven thousand four hundred and ninety-one (7,491) prisoners per month, there were sixty-two deaths monthly, being a ratio of eight and four-tenths per one thousand men.

This, I think, will be regarded as a remarkably light percentage of deaths under the most favorable circumstances, and especially so when we consider the debilitated condition in which many of the prisoners are when received, and the depressing effects of long imprisonment, if rendered ever so light.

The prevailing diseases are diarrhœa, dysentery, remittent, intermittent, and typhoid fevers, pneumonia and scurvy.

I am, very respectfully, your obedient servant,

J. H. THOMPSON,
Surgeon U. S. Volunteers, in charge.

Brigadier General J. BARNES, *Commanding.*

HEADQ'RS DIST. ST. MARY'S, PROVOST MARSHAL'S OFFICE,
Point Lookout, Md., April 20, 1865.

Sworn to before me this the 20th day of April, 1865.

A. G. BRADY,
Major and Provost Marshal.

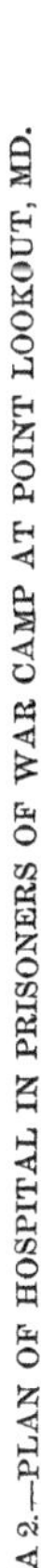

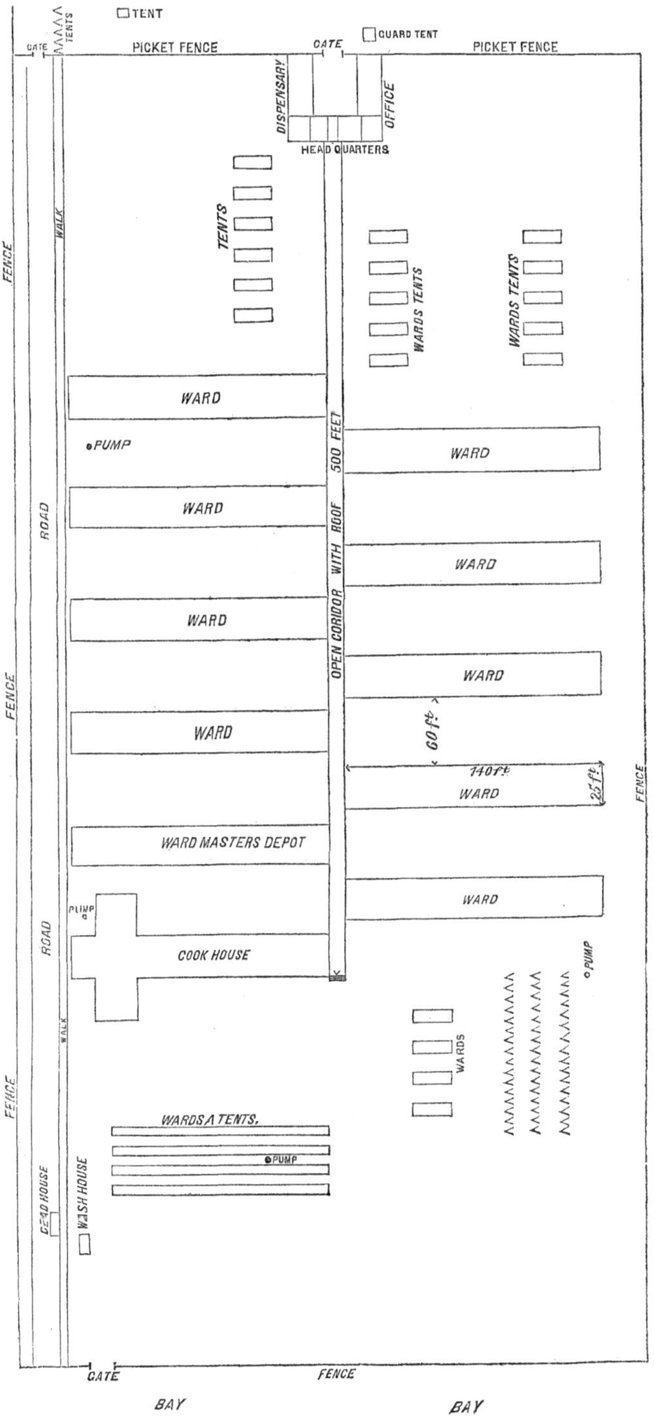

A 2.—PLAN OF HOSPITAL IN PRISONERS OF WAR CAMP AT POINT LOOKOUT, MD.

C[2].—*Copy of general summary from the monthly reports of sick and wounded, with tabular list of common diseases and cause of deaths.*

Months, 1863 and 1864.	Remaining last report.			Taken sick or wounded during the month.			Aggregate.	Returned to duty, &c.	Died.	Remaining.		
	Sick.	Wounded, &c.	Total.	Taken sick.	Wounded, &c.	Total.				Sick.	Wounded.	Total.
September, 1863	-----	-----	-----	666	5	671	671	433	14	219	5	224
October, 1863	219	5	224	2, 266	20	2, 286	2, 510	2, 062	32	396	20	416
November, 1863	396	20	416	2, 483	1	2, 484	2. 900	2, 134	35	730	1	731
December, 1863	730	1	731	2, 114	3	2, 117	2, 848	2, 219	86	543	-----	543
January, 1864	543	-----	543	1, 136	5	1, 141	1, 684	1, 104	105	471	4	475
February, 1864	471	4	475	1, 137	11	1, 148	1, 623	1, 013	108	490	12	502
March, 1864	490	12	502	1, 255	5	1, 220	1, 762	1, 117	77	567	1	568
April, 1864	567	1	568	1, 373	13	1, 386	1, 954	1, 452	43	458	1	459
May, 1864	458	1	459	3, 080	39	3, 119	3, 578	2, 610	24	906	38	944
June, 1864	906	38	944	4, 961	14	4, 975	5, 919	4, 415	105	1, 358	41	1, 399

Months, 1863 and 1864.	Taken sick or wounded during the month.								Mean strength of command.			Average No. on sick report daily.			Diseases, &c., &c.								
	Commissioned officers.				Enlisted men.																		
	Sick.		Wounded.		Sick.		Wounded.																
	Cases.	Deaths.	Cases.	Deaths.	Cases.	Deaths.	Cases.	Deaths.	Officers.	Enlisted men.	Total.	In hospital.	In quarters.	Total.	Typhoid fever.	Remittent fever.	Intermit'nt fever.	Diarrhœa.	Dysentery.	Small pox.	Scurvy.	Pneumonia.	Gunshot wounds, &c., &c.
September, 1863	-----	-----	-----	-----	666	14	5	-----	-----	2, 676	2, 676	30	173	203	7	4	96	160	79	7	97	-----	5
October, 1863	-----	-----	-----	-----	2, 266	31	20	1	8	5, 007	5, 015	76	263	339	41	-----	229	523	191	76	488	49	20
November, 1863	-----	-----	-----	-----	2, 483	35	1	-----	-----	8, 426	8, 426	76	590	666	16	10	230	450	320	167	302	58	1
December, 1863	-----	-----	-----	-----	2, 114	86	3	1	7	8, 671	8, 678	191	357	548	30	18	347	628	334	105	38	63	3
January, 1864	-----	-----	-----	-----	1, 136	104	5	1	8	8, 181	8, 189	233	282	515	-----	53	229	334	168	42	16	29	5
February, 1864	-----	-----	-----	-----	1, 137	108	11	-----	-----	7, 613	7, 613	272	239	511	12	86	176	316	116	26	29	33	11
March, 1864	38	-----	-----	-----	1. 217	76	5	1	335	6, 591	6, 926	414	128	542	3	63	140	341	62	10	47	13	5
April, 1864	99	-----	-----	-----	1, 274	43	13	-----	358	5, 613	5, 971	415	137	552	-----	47	164	296	70	1	30	8	13
May, 1864	152	-----	9	-----	2, 928	23	30	1	454	7, 647	8, 101	380	236	616	12	92	365	1, 346	100	3	96	7	39
June, 1864	240	3	-----	-----	4, 721	99	14	3	484	12, 839	13, 323	518	622	1, 140	30	69	581	2, 751	397	1	50	38	14

Mean strength, 7. 491; number of deaths, 629; average deaths per month, 62 9-10; ratio of deaths per 1,000 men, 8 4-10, or 84-100, or nearly 4-5 of 1 per centum per month.

I certify that the above is an accurate copy of the general summary from the retained copies of the monthly reports of sick and wounded on file in the office of the surgeon in charge.

J. H. THOMPSON, *Surgeon U. S. Vols., in charge.*

C[2].—Copy of general summary from the monthly reports of sick and wounded, and tabular list of common diseases and cause of deaths.

Months, 1864 and 1865.	Remaining last report.			Taken sick or wounded during the month.			Aggregate.	Returned to duty, &c.	Died.	Remaining.		
	Sick.	Wounded, &c.	Total.	Taken sick.	Wounded, &c.	Total.				Sick.	Wounded.	Total.
July, 1864	1,358	41	1,399	4,203	5	4,208	5,607	4,219	203	1,161	24	1,185
August, 1864	1,161	84	1,185	1,857	9	1,866	3,051	1,670	211	1,142	28	1,170
September, 1864	1,142	28	1,170	1,655	7	1,662	2,832	1,782	110	934	6	940
October, 1864	934	6	940	1,718	24	1,742	2,682	1,619	109	943	11	954
November, 1864	943	11	954	1,370	25	1,395	2,349	1,328	52	805	164	969
December, 1864	805	164	969	1,651	15	1,666	2,635	1,512	85	859	179	1,038
January, 1865	859	179	1,038	1,812	32	1,844	2,882	1,652	161	1,019	50	1,069
February, 1865	1,019	50	1,069	1,390	25	1,415	2,484	1,495	226	757	6	763
March, 1865	757	6	763	797	61	858	1,621	870	174	569	8	577

Months, 1864 and 1865.	Taken sick or wounded during the month.								Mean strength of command.			Average No. on sick report daily.			Diseases, &c., &c.								
	Commissioned officers.				Enlisted men.																		
	Sick.		Wounded.		Sick.		Wounded.																
	Cases.	Deaths.	Cases.	Deaths.	Cases.	Deaths.	Cases.	Deaths.	Officers.	Enlisted men.	Total.	In hospital.	In quarters.	Total.	Typhoid fever.	Remittent fever.	Intermitt'nt fever.	Diarrhœa.	Dysentery.	Measles.	Scurvy.	Pneumonia.	Gunshot wounds, &c., &c.
July, 1864		1			4,203	201	5	1	44	12,693	12,737	696	612	1,308	12	127	599	2,159	423	43	58	11	5
August, 1864		5			1,857	201	9	5	17	7,270	7,287	829	309	1,138	7	118	211	708	199	7	200	4	9
September, 1864					1,655	109	7	1	13	7,025	7,038	767	359	1,126	2	120	190	595	190	1	282		7
October, 1864					1,718	109	24			9,805	9,805	1,133	277	1,410	1	126	223	706	187		151	8	24
November, 1864					1,370	52	25			10,084	10,084	359	294	653	1	117	126	475	150		74	11	25
December, 1864					1,651	85	15			10,504	10,504	582	355	937	34	85	258	502	297		76	14	15
January, 1865					1,812	161	32			10,898	10,898	746	516	1,262	1	103	250	613	284	9	94	42	32
February, 1865					1,390	226	25			9,602	9,602	598	326	924	5	34	210	352	116	37	202	87	25
March, 1865					797	173	61	1		6,408	6,408	571	155	726	3	19	108	146	58	34	127	66	61

Mean strength, 9.374; number of deaths, 1,331; average deaths per month, 147 8-9; ratio of deaths per 1,000, 15.07, or 1½ per centum per month.

I certify that the above is an accurate copy of the general summary from the return copies of the monthly reports of sick and wounded on file in the office of surgeon in charge.

J. H. THOMPSON, *Surgeon U. S. Vols., in charge.*

N. B.—The "mean strength of command" in this report differs from the "average number of prisoners per month" in the provost marshal's report, in consequence of taking the number present every five days, and making the average from that number. It is not, therefore, so accurate as that of the provost marshal's report, which results from the actual number present each day. It is, therefore, only an approximate average.

D.

HEADQ'RS DIST. ST. MARY'S, PROVOST MARSHAL'S OFFICE,
Point Lookout, Md., April 19, 1865.

GENERAL: In accordance with your instructions, I have the honor to report the manner in which the prisoners of war camps are conducted at this post.

The prisoners are divided into divisions of one thousand each, in charge of a non-commissioned officer detailed for that purpose from regiments doing duty at this post, and again divided into companies of one hundred each, in charge of a non-commissioned officer selected from the prisoners, who are held responsible for the cleanliness and good behavior of the prisoners under their charge. On the arrival of prisoners, they are required to deliver to the provost marshal for safe-keeping all moneys and valuables in their possession. Each package is marked with the owner's name, regiment and company, and is so registered and returned to them when leaving for exchange or discharge. Of the available currency a book is furnished them, upon which they are allowed to purchase from the sutler such articles as are allowed by the commissary general of prisoners. Any money sent them during their confinement is placed to their credit in the same manner. Letters are allowed to be written and received by the prisoners, and when examined, if found unexceptionable, are immediately delivered. They are allowed to receive from their friends, "upon a permit from the provost marshal," such articles of clothing as they may require, provided they are of the proper quality and color.

The prisoners are comfortably quartered in Sibley tents, wedge tents, and wooden structures covered by shelter tents. The camps are thoroughly inspected every Sunday morning, and the prisoners paraded by divisions, each man with his blanket, and any found in a filthy condition are required to bathe and wash themselves and clothing at once. For this purpose they are allowed free access to the shore in rear of the camp on the Chesapeake bay. Report of the above inspection is made weekly, a copy of one of which (marked *a*) is herewith enclosed. The camps are thoroughly policed daily, and the sanitary condition is fully equal, if not superior, to any regiments of our own troops in the field.

I transmit herewith a tabular statement of prisoners of war at this post from its establishment, July 31, 1863, to April 18, 1865, marked A.

Very respectfully, your obedient servant,

A. G. BRADY,
Major and Provost Marshal in charge Prisoners of War.

Brigadier General JAMES BARNES,
Commanding District St. Mary's, Point Lookout, Md.

HEADQ'RS DIST. ST. MARY'S, OFFICE ASS'T ADJ'T GENERAL,
April 19, 1865.

Sworn to before me.

C. C. DREW,
Capt. V. R. C., A. A. A. G., Judge Advocate.

EXCHANGE OF PRISONERS.

Testimony of Lieutenant General U. S. Grant.

WASHINGTON, *February* 11, 1865.

Lieutenant General U. S. GRANT sworn and examined.

By the chairman:

Question. It is stated, upon what authority I do not know, that you are charged entirely with the exchange of prisoners.

Answer. That is correct; and what is more, I have effected an arrangement for the exchange of prisoners, man for man and officer for officer, or his equivalent, according to the old cartel, until one or the other party has exhausted the number they now hold. I get a great number of letters daily from friends of prisoners in the south, every one of which I cause to be answered, telling them that this arrangement has been made, and that I suppose exchanges can be made at the rate of 3,000 per week. The fact is, that I do not believe the south can deliver our prisoners to us as fast as that, on account of want of transportation on their part. But just as fast as they can deliver our prisoners to us I will receive them, and deliver their prisoners to them.

Question. There is no impediment in the way?

Answer. No, sir; I will take the prisoners as fast as they can deliver them. And I would add, that after I have caused the letters to be answered, I refer the letters to Colonel Mulford, the commissioner of exchanges, so that he may effect special exchanges in those cases wherever he can do so. The Salisbury prisoners will be coming right on. I myself saw Colonel Hatch, the assistant commissioner of exchanges on the part of the south, and he told me that the Salisbury and Danville prisoners would be coming on at once. He said that he could bring them on at the rate of 5,000 or 6,000 a week. But I do not believe he can do that. Their roads are now taxed to their utmost capacity for military purposes, and are becoming less and less efficient every day. Many of the bridges are now down. I merely fixed, as a matter of judgment, that 3,000 a week will be as fast as they can deliver them.

Question. The fact is, that there is no impediment now in the way except the lack of transportation?

Answer. That is all. There is no impediment on our side. I could deliver and receive every one of them in a very short time if they will deliver those they hold. We have lost some two weeks lately on account of ice in the river.

Question. It has been said that we refused to exchange prisoners because we found ours starved, diseased, and unserviceable when we received them, and did not like to exchange sound men for such men?

Answer. There never has been any such reason as that. That has been a reason for making exchanges. I will confess that if our men who are prisoners in the south were really well taken care of, suffering nothing except a little privation of liberty, then, in a military point of view, it would not be good policy for us to exchange, because every man they get back is forced right into the army at once, while that is not the case with our prisoners when we receive them. In fact, the half of our returned prisoners will never go into the army again, and none of them will until after they have had a furlough of thirty or sixty days. Still, the fact of their suffering as they do is a reason for making this exchange as rapidly as possible.

Question. And never has been a reason for not making the exchange?

Answer. It never has. Exchanges having been suspended by reason of disagreement on the part of agents of exchange on both sides before I came in command of the armies of the United States, and it then being near the opening of the spring campaign, I did not deem it advisable or just to the men who had to fight our battles to re-enforce the enemy with thirty or forty thousand disciplined troops at that time. An immediate resumption of exchanges would have had that effect without giving us corresponding benefits. The suffering said to exist among our prisoners south was a powerful argument against the course pursued, and I so felt it.

ADMINISTRATION OF DEPARTMENT OF ARKANSAS.

HEADQUARTERS CAVALRY DEPOT,
St. Louis, Missouri, March 3, 1864.

SIR: Your letter of the 24th ultimo, as chairman of the Committee on the Conduct of the War, has just reached me from Cairo.

I will prepare at once a statement as you desire, and forward it in two or three days. I will endeavor to furnish facts, susceptible of proof, without any deductions from them of my own; and I believe they will reveal a state of mismanagement of affairs, both civil and military, in Arkansas, detrimental to the interests of our country.

I am, sir, with high respect, your most obedient servant,

J. W. DAVIDSON,
Brigadier General.

Hon. B. F. WADE, *United States Senate.*

HEADQUARTERS CAVALRY DEPOT,
St. Louis, Mo., March 4, 1864.

SIR: In reply to your letter of the 24th February I have the honor to submit to the committee the following statement of facts in regard to the administration of the affairs of the government in Arkansas, both military and civil: Up to the 10th February, 1864, the army of Arkansas had lain at Little Rock and adjacent posts for five months, within fifty miles of one of the finest navigable rivers of the west—the White river. It is navigable all the year round up to Jacksonport. There is a railroad connexion with this river from Little Rock to Duvall's Bluff; and alongside of the railroad exists a good wagon road, which a few weeks of labor in laying corduroy in marshy places would have made passable all the winter; yet, notwithstanding this, the troops of the army have been repeatedly during the winter on reduced rations, and there was not on the 10th February more than twenty days' subsistence on hand. Twenty-five hundred horses, as the requisitions will show, have died and been lost to the service of the government for the want of hay, which could have been easily transported by steamer and rail under proper management. The railroad from Duvall's bluff to Brownsville was taken possession of, with its important bridges, on the 26th of August, 1863, and on the 10th of September the remaining portion of the road to Little Rock fell into our hands, with some considerable amount of rolling stock upon it. All the wants of the road could have been ascertained at once, a competent officer despatched north to supply them, and the road put in proper working trim in forty days after our occupancy of Little Rock.

When I left Little Rock I was informed by the generals of the infantry divisions that the horses of their artillery and field officers were in too poor condition to move. I estimate the loss of stock to the government, from neglect and mismanagement, at over half a million of dollars. This is a small estimate.

General Steele's encouragement of horse-racing, at the time when the public stock was in too poor condition to be used and needed the greatest care, was demoralizing in a high degree to the cavalry arm of the service and injurious to the public animals. My chief of cavalry, Major John W. Noble, 3d Iowa cavalry, informed me that he could scarcely get a squadron of one regiment to trot in line, so completely had the stock been spoiled for cavalry service. I issued repeated orders forbidding animals to be taken from the camp except on public service, and that horses owned by soldiers and hired to the United States (some regiments of my division mounted themselves) were public horses, but these orders did but little good where the commanding general was one of the most prominent individuals at the race. It was a frequent occurrence to see from five hundred to twenty-five hundred cavalry, officers, soldiers, teamsters, and General Steele, all mixed up together at one of these races, and men gambling upon their blankets spread on the ground near the race-track and the public road.

General Order No. 109, War Department, series of 1862, requiring commanders in the field to take in the rebellious States whatever was necessary for their armies, provided it was taken in an orderly manner, was not obeyed by General Steele. Instead, he flooded the country with safeguards or protection papers for property owned alike by loyal and disloyal persons. I have known forage parties of my division to have to travel twenty miles from Little Rock for forage to get out of the circle of these protection papers. Some of the most noted secession families had them. This system was ruinous to the cavalry service particularly. Many horses taken under this order, as had been the practice in Mississippi under Grant, and as recommended by the general-in-chief, were ordered to be returned to their owners. I myself saw an order of General Steele's to return a horse captured in battle by Lieutenant T. H. Barnes, 1st Iowa cavalry, and purchased from the government after an appraisement of its value, when its claimant was the noted rebel Danley, of Little Rock.

Private freight has been repeatedly passed over the Little Rock railroad to the exclusion of public stores, when at the time the troops were living on reduced rations. On one occasion (some time in the month of January I think) this was made the subject of serious complaint by Captain W. W. Cantine, subsistence department, chief commissary. On one occasion when Captain Carr, chief quartermaster of the army of Arkansas, thought he was to be relieved by Captain Swain, of the quartermaster's department, he passed private freight for individuals for three days in succession. This I have from Colonel J. Richmond, 126th Illinois infantry, commanding post at Duvall's Bluff. Lieutenant Wilson, 29th Iowa infantry, former quartermaster at Duvall's Bluff, now on General Samuel Rice's staff, is good evidence of this fact and other facts connected with the mismanagement of this railroad. Colonel Richmond informed me that where the return of one month showed the proceeds of the road to have been about four thousand dollars, it had really amounted to about fifteen thousand. Every bale of cotton that goes over the road pays ten dollars freight.

On one occasion a flag of truce from the confederate army, borne by a Major Rapsley, I think in the month of December, was brought into the town of Little Rock and entertained at the headquarters of the commanding general, instead of being detained outside of our lines. This Major Rapsley was permitted to walk about the town of Little Rock, was visited by his rebel friends of the city, and lionized, to the disgust of every loyal officer and soldier of the army who saw it.

In the month of January another flag of truce, borne by Majors Snead and Schomberg, adjutant generals respectively to Generals Price and Smith, of the rebel army, was brought by Colonel F. H. Manter, General Steele's chief of staff, within the camp of the 1st Missouri cavalry, a regiment camped about four miles from Little Rock, and ordered to be entertained there. This created a great feeling of dissatisfaction among the officers and men of that regiment. Colonel Manter came out to visit them and got drunk with them, and made a public and disgraceful exhibition of himself before the officers and men of the regiment. Secessionists, both male and female, were permitted to go out and visit them and hold unrestricted intercourse with them. This flag remained in that camp two days.

Major Weatherspoon, of the rebel service, who was captured by Lieutenant Colonel Caldwell, 3d Iowa cavalry, was sent up north as a prisoner of war some time in January. The day he left the military prison he was visited by the secessionists of the city and a gala day held there. When he reached Duvall's Bluff, General Steele ascertained that his wife had come up from the rebel lines to visit him. He telegraphed to Duvall's Bluff to have the major sent back to have an interview with his wife. He was brought to Little Rock and an interview had. Mrs. Weatherspoon returned south, bearing with her several letters and packages, franked at General Steele's headquarters, to go through our lines unexamined. Mrs. Judge English, of Little Rock, (whose husband was chief justice of Arkansas under the rebel rule, and then at Washington, Arkansas,) wrote a letter to the judge and sent it to him with a box of articles, the whole unexamined and franked at General Steele's headquarters to go through our lines. This was taken south by Mrs. Major Weatherspoon also. In several instances articles of clothing, blowses, high-top boots, &c., have been permitted at General Steele's headquarters to go direct to rebel officers.

In many instances letters from parties in Little Rock to parties in the rebel lines have been franked without examination at General Steele's headquarters and permitted to go through our lines.

As one instance of the general negligence attending public business, a square redoubt, which is the only defensive work at Little Rock, and about fifty yards on a side, had been four months building, and not a platform for a gun was erected in it when I left. This work could have been built in three days by the details of any division I ever saw in the army of the Potomac.

There are no defences at Duvall's Bluff, except a few useless rifle-pits. It is our great depot of supplies, and the most important point to the army it holds in Arkansas.

On the 14th of September I made the following report to General Steele:

HEADQUARTERS CAVALRY DIVISION,
Little Rock, September 14, 1863.

Colonel F. H. MANTER, *Chief of Staff:*

I have the honor to report that the night of my arrival here I organized a force out of the tired troops of my division, consisting of the 7th and 8th Missouri cavalry, Merrill's horse, the 10th and 13th Illinois, and the 1st Indiana cavalry, and Stanges and Clarkson's batteries, to pursue the enemy, and placed the whole under command of Colonel Lewis Merrill. I regret to state that the expedition returned the day after its march without accomplishing anything, and, in my opinion, did not pursue the enemy with the necessary vigor. The reports from officers of the expedition make it advisable this should be inquired into.

I am, sir, &c.,

J. W. DAVIDSON, *Brigadier General.*

Hon. B. F. WADE, *U. S. Senate,*
Chairman Committee on the Conduct of the War.

Our attack upon Little Rock was one of those cases in which we encountered the enemy, both parties having their lines of retreat free. Our object was the destruction of Price's army; the mere occupancy of Little Rock was a barren victory; therefore the pursuit should have done the principal work. To abandon the pursuit was to give up the fruits of our victory. Yet, although Colonel Merrill did this—though he allowed Price's army to escape, and the fact, as the above letter shows, was duly communicated to General Steele, he took no notice of the grave error committed.

General Orders No. 86, department of the Missouri, series of 1863, requiring returning rebels not only to take the oath of allegiance, but to give bond, with approved security, for the faithful performance of it, and to reside in such county as is designated by the provost marshal, was not carried out in Arkansas. The only requirement was the taking of the oath; in some instances that was not required. In one or two instances men who had fought our troops but a day or two before were mustered into the Arkansas regiments. I have no doubt this course of action threw many guerillas back of our lines. We were acting at this time under the general orders of the department of the Missouri.

Some time in the month of December, 1863, I think, General Steele directed me to have one Miss Sophie Crease, a noted rebel woman, paid for eighteen head of cattle which she claimed had been taken by officers of the cavalry division for the commissary department of the division. I examined the matter carefully, and found from the reports of Lieutenant William White, 1st Missouri cavalry, the officer charged with taking the cattle, and Captain Charles H. Thompson, subsistence department, that the cattle had not been taken by the one nor received by the other. I so informed General Steele. A few days afterwards he came down to my office, saying in an angry tone, "By God, sir, the cavalry division gives me more trouble than all the rest of the army; I have been trying for ten days to get Miss Sophie Crease paid for her cattle, and can't do it." After repeating to General Steele the fact that they had not been received by my commissary department, I asked him if he still ordered her paid; he replied that that was his order, and I sat down and directed Captain Thompson, my commissary of subsistence, to pay her.

The vouchers of Captain Charles H. Thompson, a bonded commissary of the subsistence department, will show that this rebel was paid in treasury notes for eighteen head of cattle that *he*, Captain Thompson, never received. This rebel lived twenty-five miles outside of Little Rock, and was in the habit of passing in and out of our lines at will almost daily. In the month of January General Steele came to my quarters one morning, and in a very excited manner said that "Miss Sophie Crease had been insulted by one of the officers of my division, Captain Mills, of the 1st Missouri cavalry; that he intended to get her statement, send it to the Secretary of War, and have him, Captain Mills, mustered out of the service." I asked him to suspend action until this officer's statement could be heard. Knowing Captain Mills to be a faithful officer, I sent for him and directed him to furnish me his statement of the matter, together with such other evidence as he might have had at hand. I never saw an officer so shocked as he was when I informed him of the summary action about to be taken against him on a rebel's word. He furnished me with his own affidavit, and those of several non-commissioned officers who were with him on the forage party ordered to Sophie Crease's house. So far from having insulted this rebel, she herself was abusive in her language towards the "Yankees." These affidavits were sworn before the judge advocate of the division, and I sent them by the hands of my adjutant general to General Steele, in order to extricate this officer from his difficulty. General Steele's reply was, "By God, sir, I had rather take Sophie Crease's word than the affidavits of all the officers and men that were there. I have known that woman just long enough to know that she won't lie." To show the criminal negligence and blindness which prevailed at headquarters, on one occasion I was visiting my outposts in company with some members of my staff, I think in the month of January, 1864, and in passing from one outpost to another, becoming lost in the woods, I found a *furloughed rebel soldier* at a house three (3) miles outside of our extreme line of videttes with a pass in his pocket from General Steele's headquarters to pass in and out of our lines *at will* for thirty days. This man was just what I state him to be, a *furloughed rebel soldier*, not a rebel who had surrendered himself and taken the oath of allegiance. The officers present with me at the time of this discovery were Captain A. S. Burrows, 1st Missouri cavalry, First Lieutenant James R. Gray, 7th Missouri cavalry, and First Lieutenant G. K. McGunnegle, jr., 1st Wisconsin cavalry.

Mr. Burgevin, of Little Rock, a rebel, formerly adjutant general of the State of Arkansas, the man who tore down the United States flag over the United States arsenal at Little Rock, was permitted to sell his property in Little Rock in the month of October, 1863, said property being by the acts of Congress confiscated to the United States, and realize the proceeds of the sale in United States currency, and having done this, allowed to go south under a pass from Major General Steele. It was ascertained by Lieutenant Colonel H. C. Caldwell, commanding the post of Benton, Arkansas, that said Burgevin had passed through our lines with a million of dollars in confederate bonds and scrip upon his person. General Steele retained upon his staff certain officers in high positions who were obnoxious to the thinking portion of his general officers, and, with few exceptions, to his colonels, for their profligacy, drunkenness, imbecility, disgraceful behavior, and neglect of duty. These officers were, his chief of staff, Colonel F. H. Manter, 32d Missouri infantry, who did not belong to any regiment of General Steele's command, and his adjutant general, Lieutenant George O. Sokalski, 2d United States cavalry, and his provost marshal general, Lieutenant Colonel J. L. Chandler, 7th Missouri cavalry. General Steele has been repeatedly advised of the injury these men were doing to him, the army, and the country.

In a conversation which I had with him on one occasion he said to me that his relations with Lieutenant Sokalski were of such a character that he could not dismiss him. I have told him often and often that his staff were a millstone around his neck, clogging the business of the army. I think Colonel Manter injured the re-enlistment of the veterans of that army. In October before I left for St. Louis Major William Thompson, 1st Iowa cavalry, inspector of division, had prepared an address to the 1st Iowa cavalry, codifying the War Department orders upon the subject of veterans, and urging them to re-enlist. It was issued in circulars and published in the Little Rock Democrat. This address had been submitted to me, and was substantially correct. On my return from St. Louis about the 12th of November I found that the editor of the Little Rock Democrat had in an editorial commented upon this address, pronouncing it erroneous in some respects; that the time had passed by for the men to be called veterans, &c. I sent for the editor, and he informed me that he got his information from Colonel Manter, who authorized him to put it in the paper. Colonel Manter told Lieutenant Colonel Marks and Dr. Davis, of the 18th Illinois infantry, that the order of the War Department concerning veterans was a ridiculous one, and they had not made up their minds yet how to act. This was in response to some inquiries of those gentlemen in regard to the terms upon which their regiments could be re-enlisted.

Some statements made to me by Colonel J. Richmond, 126th Illinois infantry, with regard to an indorsement made by Colonel Manter upon a letter of Bailey Thompson's, left the impression upon my mind, and such an impression also existed in the mind of Colonel Richmond, that the name of this Bailey Thompson had been used in certain cotton transactions without his authority, by Colonel Manter.

A rebel bearing the name of Merrick, who informed my adjutant general that he had been a colonel in the confederate service, and his last service with that army having been as a clerk in the commissary department, came into our lines and remained in the city of Little Rock, and was employed as a clerk in the Treasury Department under the eyes and with the knowledge of the military authorities. He sat daily in that office, under pay, in a rebel uniform, for two weeks, without having taken the oath of allegiance, until the storm of public opinion forced the authorities to administer it to him. On his first arrival in the city Colonel Merrick was brought into my office by the outposts on his way to General Steele's, and upon being interrogated as to his motives in returning to Little Rock, stated distinctly that he had simply returned in order to be with his family and provide for their comfort, and that he did not wish to take the oath of allegiance to the United States government.

General Steele has not only retained in office, but promoted to the positions successively of provost marshal general of the army of Arkansas, and of the department of Arkansas, Lieutenant Colonel Chandler, 7th Missouri cavalry, an officer who has been guilty of the following named acts: A form of voucher had been established by the subsistence department in the west to be used by officers of that department in the districts in rebellion. It is not always in these districts easy to distinguish friends from foes; hence this form, while it effectually, under proper care, excluded the rebel from payment, secured to the loyal man his claim upon the government. These vouchers were also issued in conformity with the design of General Orders No. 109, from the War Department, series of 1862.

In the cases of Henry Keatts, M. H. Badgett, R. Fletcher, and D. Lewis, vouchers of this character were issued by my authority as a division commander, having the words "done by order of Brigadier General Davidson," particularly used, and signed by my division commissary, Captain Charles H. Thompson, a bonded officer of the subsistence department. In all these cases Lieutenant Colonel Chandler erased himself the words "payable, upon proof of loyalty, at the end of the rebellion," thus altering the character and intent of these vouchers over Captain Thompson's signature, and certified upon the backs of the vouchers that the parties were loyal. In the case of Mr. R. Fletcher, whose voucher bore this alteration and a certificate that he was a loyal man, I ascertained in the presence of these witnesses, Judge Murphy, Colonel Fishback, and Lieutenant Montgomery of my staff, that Mr. Fletcher never had taken the oath of allegiance to the United States; that it was not required of him by Lieutenant Colonel Chandler, the provost marshal; that he was unwilling then and now to take it; that he was a "*Union as it was*" man, and was not prepared to sustain any of the acts of Congress or the proclamation of the President with reference to slaves. I hold that in this case the erasure and alterations upon the face of the voucher and the certificate of Lieutenant Colonel Chandler upon the back of it made it fraudulent, and would, if not examined by me, have secured payment from the government to one whose property was by law confiscate to that government. In the case of Andrew McAllister vouchers were issued by order of Brigadier General Kimball, commanding a division, and signed by his assistant commissary of subsistence. The same erasures were made in these vouchers by Lieutenant Colonel Chandler and his certificate of the loyalty of the parties placed upon their back. The vouchers sustaining these statements are in my hands, as also letters of Captain Cantine, subsistence department, Brigadier General Nathan Kimball, United States volunteers, and Captain Charles H. Thompson, subsistence department.

On the 19th of September, 1863, this provost marshal paroled a prisoner of war who did not take the oath of allegiance to the United States—this in violation of General Orders No. 86, department of the Missouri, series of 1863, and the practice of our armies. This man was arrested by me at the outposts of the army about the 1st of December, 1863. He had been living, between these two times, twenty miles from Little Rock, on the ground intermediate between the out posts of the United States and rebel armies. His name was Dodd, belonged to Captain Miller's independent company, never mustered into the service of nor paid by the so-called Confederate States—in short, a guerilla.

Major John W. Noble, 3d Iowa cavalry, and Captain J. Baird, 1st Missouri cavalry, were with me at the time of this arrest and cognizant of all the facts herein stated.

This provost marshal, Lieutenant Colonel Chandler, has stated to Mrs. General Fagan, now residing in Little Rock, the wife of Brigadier General Fagan, of the rebel army, that the government of the United States would be forced to pay her, at the end of the rebellion, for the property taken by the United States troops from her plantation. This information is derived from a letter written by Mrs. Fagan to the person in charge of her plantation, and which was captured in a mail, and read by Lieutenant Colonel Caldwell, 3d Iowa cavalry, and Surgeon J. E. Lynch, 1st Missouri cavalry.

The provost marshal, Lieutenant Colonel Chandler, had repeatedly franked, and permitted to be conveyed through the lines of the army, letters from rebels in the city of Little Rock to rebels within the enemy's lines. In some instances these letters have been so franked and conveyed through our lines without any examination by him of their contents, thus giving comfort to the enemy. Surgeon James C. Whitehill, medical department, United States volunteers, is a witness to the last-mentioned fact.

The provost marshal, Colonel Chandler, did, in the month of September, release from imprisonment, and permit to pass through our lines, a prisoner of war, without due exchange, or authority for the same. The evidence of this fact is furnished by the affidavit of a person who heard the agreement made between the provost marshal and the prisoner's wife, and knows the release and subsequent escape of the prisoner. I hold this affidavit in my hands. The officer to whom this statement was first made is Assistant Surgeon Lothrop, of 1st Iowa cavalry.

Complaints of the alterations of the vouchers referred to were made to General Steele by General Kimball and myself. The reply I got was that Colonel Chandler was guilty of a "misapprehension of power and propriety," yet this officer was promoted to a higher position immediately by General Steele. Many of the other facts herein stated were made known by me in conversation to General Steele. After all this, this officer was again promoted to another higher position, the provost marshal generalship of the department of Arkansas.

It was a matter of common remark in the army that a better provost marshal for the rebels than Lieutenant Colonel Chandler couldn't be gotten out of Price's army.

There was a general negligence, and inaptitude, and distaste for public business displayed at General Steele's headquarters. The file of general orders of the army of Arkansas for five months will show that there was not one mind at headquarters that grasped the command of the army, or the magnitude of the enterprise before us. The whole aim seemed to be pleasure—dogs, horses, drives, dinners, women.

I never saw a drill or an inspection of troops ordered by the general commanding the army during the five months I was with the army. I never saw him among his troops. He never visited a post or a line of communication.

After our entry into Little Rock, on the 10th of September, 1863, I was appointed by General Steele the commander of the city and its vicinity. About two days thereafter I called on General Steele, asking him to let me pubiish to the people the confiscation act of Congress and the President's emancipation proclamation, in order that these people might see the light in which they stood towards a government which they had offended. His reply was, substantially, that he did not wish it done; it would be annoying to these people. General Steele, Colonel Manter, and Captain Scammon, of General Steele's staff, have been heard by Doctor James C. Whitehill, United States volunteers, medical director, army of Arkansas, to *denounce* the President's emancipation proclamation. I myself have heard General Steele say that he did not believe the confiscation act would ever be enforced.

A copperhead newspaper, called the National Democrat, edited by one Doctor Meador, who had been a surgeon in the rebel army, was fostered at General Steele's headquarters. Doctor E. D. Ayres and Colonel William M. Fishback can give a great deal of testimony upon this subject. It is believed that Colonel Manter wrote a great many of the articles for it. Doctor Meador has been frequently heard to say, with an air that no words can describe, that his views were indorsed by headquarters; that he was the exponent of the views of headquarters. I and Doctor Kirkwood have told General Steele more than once of the injury this man was doing to him in the army, and among the truly loyal men of Arkansas, and to the future prospects of the State. The general's reply was, "Oh, this man is only a pimp for my headquarters." Yet, with all this, this man had the entrée at headquarters, and still continued to publish his pestiferous articles, and to announce his paper as the organ of the military authorities. Now in order to understand the harm done by this paper and by this man, some account of the political state of Arkansas must be given. The government of Arkansas, just before the rebellion, was an oligarchy. The Johnson clique manufactured public opinion, and controlled it. When we entered Arkansas some few of that clique were still left. Around them rallied the rich, the Bertrands, the Tuckers, cotton speculators, and those that held a remnant of pro-slavery doctrines, and Meador and his newspaper, and Steele and the before-mentioned members of his staff. These called themselves "the better class." There was another class in Arkansas, the middle class, the poor men of the State—men who were to fill the confederate ranks—men who had been hunted like game through the hills of Arkansas by conscriptors, "Mountain Feds," refugees—men in whose bosoms the fires of loyalty had burned throughout the whole rebellion—men who were willing to have the State come back into the Union upon any terms proposed by the administration, so it but came back. I will not call them radicals, nor immediate emancipationists, nor apply any party phrase to them. They were men whose views were in accord with those of their government. If the old oak at Hartford that preserved the Magna Charta is yet regarded with veneration, how much more should have been those loyal breasts which had preserved their fealty to their government! These are the men who are to fill, and are now filling, our ranks in that State, who can shoulder the musket, and who can till the soil. These men had no rallying point, no newspaper to express their views. Resolutions passed by Union meetings held by this class of men, sound in principle and in devotion to the government, were refused publication in Meador's paper. A set of resolutions introduced at a public meeting on the night of the 24th of December, under canvas, by Doctor Meador, which contained a laudatory resolution concerning General Steele, with a lot of copperhead resolutions appended, having been objected to by a member of that meeting, the reply of Dr. Meador was, "They are indorsed by Colonel Manter." I saw an order just before I left Little Rock to divide the patronage of the government in public printing between Meador's paper and the unconditional Union newspaper; all the printing having previously been given to the unconditional Union paper, except that from General Steele's headquarters, which was given to Meador. It is my firm belief that had the unconditional Union party—a party that was in accord with the views of the government—been met with open arms by our military authorities, there would have been but one party in Arkansas to-day, and the State been back in the Union more than a month ago. Instead of this the principal advisers at army headquarters were C. P. Bertrand, Dr. Meador, and Colonel F. H. Manter. No words of mine can present this matter to your committee as it actually existed. Judge Murphy, General E. W. Ganett, Dr. E. D. Ayres, Colonel W. M. Fishback, Judge Warner, Dr. John Kirkwood, Colonel J. M. Johnson, and Lieutenant Colonel H. C. Caldwell, 3d Iowa cavalry, can give you an idea of this matter as they saw it. Colonel J. M. Johnson, who is now in Washington claiming a seat in Congress from Arkansas, saw, n the very few days that he was at Little Rock, that Steele was surrounded by a set of politicians, who were endeavoring to use him for party purposes; and that he was either in accord with them, or else had not the capacity to see through their designs. So thoroughly heart-sick had I become with the conduct of affairs that about the close of November I quietly gave up the command of the city. There is a move making now in Arkansas to get the Arkansas troops sent out of the State. Those who have fattened under confederate and federal rule alike dread the future if these troops remain in the State.

I want your committee to distinctly understand that it was talked of among the army and the truly loyal men of Arkansas, and believed by them, that it was better to be a rebel than one who had been and was loyal, in order to get any favor at army headquarters. Calvin C. Bliss, named for lieutenant governor of the State of Arkansas by the convention of January last, can give a good deal of evidence upon this point. He told me distinctly, before I left Little Rock, that there was not a Union man who felt that he had any sympathy at army headquarters.

About the first of December I wrote the following letter to the Hon. S. H. Boyd, M. C. from Missouri:

"I wrote a letter of introduction to you for Mr. E. W. Gault, of Arkansas. He is a reclaimed rebel, and I hope you will do all for him you can. He desires the good of Arkansas, and is sound not only on the emancipation proclamation, but on the whole question, and desires a convention of the State to repeal the slavery clause in the constitution of Arkansas. You will find he is a man of talent, and acts with that great party which proclaims and will have universal emancipation. Gault stands high with the President, I am informed, for the course he has taken, and will tell you all about the *conciliatory policy* here which up to this hour, ninety days after we took possession of Little Rock, has not *reclaimed* one rebel, and is disheartening to the really Union men of this State, and disgusting to this whole army. All the stories you see in the Chicago Times about secessionists coming in and laying down their arms and their *prejudices* are sheer lies. Those who came in were always Union men; not made so by any conciliatory policy, but, having been hunted like game through the hills of Arkansas, are coming in because they found a rallying point—a federal army. Not one rebel in Little Rock has come forward anp renewed hs allegiance to his government, and no conciliatory policy could make them do it, but it makes them only more obstinate in their opinions. You may rely on what I write you as facts. The Union men of Arkansas are 'unconditional Union men,' and, strange as it may appear, in favor of expunging the perpetual slavery clause, or any other slavery clause, from the State constitution. You can use my name for these facts whenever you please, for they are vouched for by Gault, Judge Isaac Murphy, and other thorough men, and my own observation."

This letter was not intended for publication. It was written to Mr. Boyd in his capacity as a legislator, and, when he used the facts, to give me as authority for it. It was, nevertheless, published by him in the Missouri Democrat of the 5th of January, 1864. On the 11th of February I was relieved from duty in the department of Arkansas, on General Steele's application, as I am privately, but none the less correctly, informed, and on the same day saw in the columns of the Missouri Democrat of February 4, 1864, the following letter:

"HEADQUARTERS ARMY OF ARKANSAS,
"*Little Rock, January* 17, 1864.

"Hon. S. H. BOYD, *M. C.:*

"DEAR SIR: The Missouri Democrat, of the 5th instant, contains what purports to be a letter, or an extract from a letter, addressed to you by Brigadier General J. W. Davidson. I write to inform you that certain statements therein contained, relating to the 'conciliatory policy,' are false. If General Davidson is the author of this letter, he has proved himself an ungrateful scoundrel. 'You can use my name for these facts whenever you please.'

"I have the honor to be, very respectfully, your obedient servant,

"FRE'K STEELE, *Major General.*"

Now, I desire you to understand that I never learned from General Steele by any message, letter, or interview, that he found any fault with my letter. That the letter of his to Hon. S. H. Boyd, published above, was the first intimation I ever had from him that he found fault with my letter, (except camp reports,) and that reached me, as I said before, by way of Washington city, twenty-five days after he saw my letter in the paper. I leave it to your committee to judge the act thus committed by an army commander upon one of his general officers.

The "Articles of War" forbid the sending of a challenge; yet, while they do this, the government constitutes itself in some sense the custodian of an officer's honor. It remains for me to see whether that pledge will be kept. Par. 220, Army Regulations, is in these words: * * "And all publications relative to transactions between officers of a private or personal nature, whether newspaper or handbill, are strictly prohibited."

True to my principle, that the cause which I had espoused was above all party or personal consideration, I forbore any assault upon General Steele, because he was at that distance the representative of my government; I forbore to make any protest against my removal from a command that I had formed and that regarded me with affection; I forbore to send letters and a telegram from the provisional governor of the State, which will appear below. I complied with my orders to report at Cairo, and from that place the following telegraphic correspondence occurred:

CAIRO, *February* 26, 1864.

PRESIDENT UNITED STATES, *Washington:*

I desire to come to Washington; I have facts to lay before the Judge Advocate General; I have been relieved of a command I had formed, and no reason assigned made known to me. I have to send the following telegram from Governor Murphy; I did not send it from Little Rock, because I did not wish to add to your anxiety about the discord there:

LITTLE ROCK, ARK., *February* 15, 1864.

To A. LINCOLN, *President United States:*

Brigadier General Davidson is a true man and soldier; a patriot in whom the unconditional Union men of Arkansas trust with unlimited confidence. Any action against him will be against the Union element here and against your own policy. This an investigation will show.

ISAAC MURPHY,
Provisional Governor of Arkansas.

I cannot do duty with honor until this question of the insult put upon me by General Steele be investigated.

With high respect,

J. W. DAVIDSON,
Brigadier General.

WASHINGTON, *February* 27, 1864.

To General DAVIDSON, *Cairo:*

Whether you shall come to Washington I must submit to the general-in-chief.

A. LINCOLN.

WASHINGTON, *February* 27, 1864.

To Brigadier General DAVIDSON, *Cairo :*

Your application to the President to come to Washington, not sent through proper channels, is not granted.

H. W. HALLECK,
General-in-Chief.

On the 8th of February the President telegraphed Judge Murphy, who had been elected provisional governor of Arkansas by the convention which assembled in January, that he yielded his plan to the plan of the convention, (this changed the day of election of State officers from the 28th of March to 14th of March;) that General Steele was to aid Judge Murphy all in his power, and to show this telegram to him, (General Steele.) Yet why, after this, was General Steele's address to the people of Arkansas delayed until the 29th February, about an election that was to come off on the 14th of March? It is proper to state here that there are now two candidates for the governorship of the State of Arkansas. One Judge Murphy, the *people's* candidate, the man nominated by the convention, the type of those men who will shoulder the musket and till the soil, of those who have always been loyal, through persecution, to their government; the other, Mr. A. C. Rogers, around whom the "better class," those who have fattened alike under confederate and federal rule, will cling.

I have endeavored thus far to give your committee only facts which I can substantiate by my own testimony and that of other intelligent officers and citizens. I will now give you one or two statements, of the truth of which I am morally convinced in my own mind. I believe that the administration of the provost marshal's department and the quartermaster's department is corrupt in the army of Arkansas, and that a thorough investigation, if it can be had, will develop the fact. Colonel Richmond, 126th Illinois infantry, told me that he had a copy of a letter from one Marshall to one Price, saying that his permit from the provost marshal to ship goods was all right; but there was one more thing necessary, and that was to grease the hands of the authorities. I believe the whole move of getting boats up the Arkansas to be an arrangement gotten up by the cotton speculators. This river is not our true line of communication. It is parallel to the enemy's front, and is in reach, all along it, of the enemy's artillery. The true line of communication is the White river and its connecting railroad. But there are several thousand bales of cotton near Pine Bluff to go out of the Arkansas! Captain Grace, of the United States gunboat Fawn, of the fleet stationed at the mouth of the White river, told me that one man alone had offered him a thousand dollars to aid in getting the gunboats up the Arkansas. I think much information can be gotten from Commodore Phelps, Captain Pritchard, and Captain Grace on this subject.

I am informed by Dr. Samuel Whitehorn, former assistant surgeon of the 5th Kansas cavalry, that Colonel Clayton, General Steele's commander at Pine Bluff, and Mr. Rogers and Mr. Snow, of Pine Bluff, were in partnership in cotton speculations; that Colonel Clayton allowed Rogers and Snow to seize and sell the cotton of rebels in that vicinity, and that none of the money obtained for this cotton was paid over to the government. I am informed by several officers that about the same state of affairs existed at Pine Bluff as at Little Rock; that rebels had protection papers for their property, forage, &c., and that articles of clothing were permitted to pass through the lines south.

Captain Cantine, commissary of subsistence, is my informant of the latter fact. In addition to the witnesses specially named throughout these pages, I desire to add the following, whom it would be well for the committee to call: Brigadier General Nathan Kimball, U. S. volunteers; Brigadier General Samuel A. Rice, U. S. volunteers; Brigadier General John M. Thayer, U. S. volunteers; Brigadier General C. C. Andrews, U. S. volunteers; Lieutenant H. C. Caldwell, 3d Iowa cavalry; General E. W. Ganett, of Arkansas; Major William Thompson, 1st Iowa cavalry; Division Inspector Judge Warner, of Little Rock; Judge Youley, of Little Rock; Colonel A. Cummings, 19th Pennsylvania cavalry, superintendent of colored recruiting service for Arkansas. Major Noble, 3d Iowa cavalry, is with me in this city, and can be summoned at the same time I am.

I must not forget to mention here that Colonel J. M. Johnson, of Arkansas, informed me that at Fort Smith, and all along the road from Little Rock to Fort Smith, the policy pursued by General Steele was different from the policy pursued by the commanders at Fort Smith, under the orders of the department of the Missouri and the policy of the administration. I am constrained to say here that General Steele forgot the public good in his efforts to attain popularity.

I ask of your committee that the names of the officers that I have given above may not be published until after they shall have given their own testimony, as they are most of them now serving under General Steele's command.

It may be asked how I came to write the Boyd letter, and to have anything to do with the politics of Arkansas. I have not been able yet in this war to separate fighting the rebel armies and fighting the cause which keeps them in the field. It is forced into my mind by every forward step I have taken, yet I never attended a political meeting in Little Rock, much less made a speech at one of them, though other officers of the army have repeatedly done so there. But, as the general commanding the city, thrown in direct contact with it people, I saw the practical ill effects of the mal-administration of affairs at headquarters. I heard loyal men say it was better to have been a rebel than to have been true.

As the general commanding the cavalry of the army, and having ten times as much stock as any general of an infantry division, it was ten times more strongly brought to my mind, the injuries worked upon the special arm of the service by protection papers, and returning horses taken from rebels.

I saw a magnificent division of cavalry, by the ignorance and maltreatment of headquarters, melt away.

The loyal people of Little Rock (the unconditional Union men) finding they had no real sympathy at headquarters, came to me for comfort and counsel, and made me the repository of their hopes and fears. I would have been a moral traitor to my country had I not listened to them and comforted them. This is why I am here, and not there, to-day.

I am your committee's most obedient servant,

J. W. DAVIDSON,
Brigadier General U. S. Volunteers.

Hon. B. F. WADE,
U. S. Senate, Chairman Committee on the Conduct of the War.

I think Bishop Ames, of the Methodist Episcopal church, saw in his twenty-four hours' visit to Little Rock how affairs generally were conducted.

Captain Gideon Scull, of the subsistence department, sent by Colonel T. J. Haines, chief commissary of the west, to inspect the affairs of his department in Arkansas, can give evidence of the looseness he observed there.

General C. C. Andrews can show that the aid obtained from General Steele in furthering the plans of the convention of January last was drawn out of him instead of being promptly and cheerfully rendered.

J. W. DAVIDSON,
Brigadier General.

INDEX OF VOL. III.

SHERMAN—JOHNSTON.

LIGHT-DRAUGHT MONITORS.

MASSACRE OF CHEYENNE INDIANS.

ICE CONTRACTS.

ROSECRANS'S CAMPAIGNS.

MISCELLANEOUS.

www.ingramcontent.com/pod-product-compliance
Lightning Source LLC
LaVergne TN
LVHW021234110826
845150LV00002B/338